AF682465

RECUEIL DES COURS

437 (2024)

L'Académie de droit international de La Haye

honorée du prix Wateler de la Paix (1936, 1950), du prix Félix Houphouët-Boigny pour la recherche de la paix (1992), de l'ordre du Rio Branco, Brésil (1999), et de la médaille de l'Institut royal d'études européennes, Espagne (2000)

The Hague Academy of International Law

awarded the Wateler Peace Prize (1936, 1950), the Félix Houphouët-Boigny Peace Prize (1992), the Order of Rio Branco, Brazil (1999), and the Medal of the Royal Institute of European Studies, Spain (2000)

© Académie de droit international de La Haye, 2024
The Hague Academy of International Law, 2024

Tous droits réservés All rights reserved

ISBN 978-90-04-69913-7

Printed by/Imprimé par Triangle Bleu, 59600 Maubeuge, France

ACADÉMIE DE DROIT INTERNATIONAL

FONDÉE EN 1923 AVEC LE CONCOURS DE LA
DOTATION CARNEGIE POUR LA PAIX INTERNATIONALE

RECUEIL DES COURS

COLLECTED COURSES OF THE HAGUE ACADEMY OF INTERNATIONAL LAW

2024

Tome 437 de la collection

BRILL | NIJHOFF

Leiden/Boston

COMPOSITION DU CURATORIUM DE L'ACADÉMIE DE DROIT INTERNATIONAL DE LA HAYE

PRÉSIDENT HONORAIRE

Y. DAUDET, professeur émérite de l'Université Paris I (Panthéon-Sorbonne)

VICE-PRÉSIDENTE

Y. NISHITANI, professeure à l'Université de Kyoto

MEMBRES

M. S. ABDEL WAHAB, Professeur à l'Université du Caire; doyen de la Africa Arbitration Academy

K. BOELE-WOELKI, doyenne de la faculté de droit de Bucerius, Hambourg; présidente de l'Académie internationale de droit comparé

H. BUXBAUM, professeure à l'Université de l'Indiana

H. CHARLESWORTH, juge à la Cour internationale de Justice

G. CORDERO-MOSS, professeure à l'Université d'Oslo

D. P. FERNÁNDEZ ARROYO, professeur à l'école de droit de Sciences Po, Paris

P. GALVÃO TELES, Professeure à l'Université autonome de Lisbonne; membre de la Commission du droit international

M. T. INFANTE CAFFI, juge au Tribunal international du droit de la mer

B. B. JIA, professeur à l'Université de Tsinghua, Pékin

M. KAMTO, professeur à l'Université de Yaoundé II

M. M. MBENGUE, professeur à l'Université de Genève

N. ORAL, Directrice du Centre de droit international de l'Université nationale de Singapour; membre de la Commission du droit international

N. J. SCHRIJVER, professeur émérite de l'Université de Leiden; Conseiller d'Etat au Conseil d'Etat des Pays-Bas

L.-A. SICILIANOS, doyen de la faculté de droit de l'Université d'Athènes; ancien président de la Cour européenne des droits de l'homme

P. TOMKA, juge et ancien président de la Cour internationale de Justice

T. TREVES, professeur émérite de l'Université de Milan; ancien juge au Tribunal international du droit de la mer

SECRÉTAIRE GÉNÉRAL DE L'ACADÉMIE DE DROIT INTERNATIONAL DE LA HAYE

J.-M. THOUVENIN, professeur à l'Université Paris-Nanterre

COMPOSITION OF THE CURATORIUM OF THE HAGUE ACADEMY OF INTERNATIONAL LAW

HONORARY PRESIDENT

Y. DAUDET, Emeritus Professor at Paris I University (Panthéon-Sorbonne)

VICE-PRESIDENT

Y. NISHITANI, Professor at Kyoto University

MEMBERS

M. S. ABDEL WAHAB, Professor at Cairo University; Dean of Africa Arbitration Academy

K. BOELE-WOELKI, Dean of Bucerius Law School, Hamburg; President of the International Academy of Comparative Law

H. BUXBAUM, Professor at Indiana University

H. CHARLESWORTH, Judge at the International Court of Justice

G. CORDERO-MOSS, Professor at the University of Oslo

D. P. FERNÁNDEZ ARROYO, Professor at the Sciences Po Law School, Paris

P. GALVÃO TELES, Professor at the Autonomous University of Lisbon; Member of the International Law Commission

M. T. INFANTE CAFFI, Judge at the International Tribunal for the Law of the Sea

B. B. JIA, Professor at Tsinghua University, Beijing

M. KAMTO, Professor at the University of Yaoundé II

M. M. MBENGUE, Professor at the University of Geneva

N. ORAL, Director of the National University of Singapore Centre for International Law; Member of the International Law Commission

N. J. SCHRIJVER, Emeritus Professor at Leiden University; State Councillor at the Netherlands Council of State

L.-A. SICILIANOS, Dean of the Law Faculty of the University of Athens; former President of the European Court of Human Rights

P. TOMKA, Judge and former President of the International Court of Justice

T. TREVES, Emeritus Professor at the University of Milan; former Judge at the International Tribunal for the Law of the Sea

SECRETARY-GENERAL OF THE HAGUE ACADEMY OF INTERNATIONAL LAW

J.-M. THOUVENIN, Professor at the University Paris-Nanterre

ACADÉMIE DE DROIT INTERNATIONAL DE LA HAYE

— FONDÉE EN 1923 AVEC LE CONCOURS DE LA DOTATION CARNEGIE —

HONORÉE DU PRIX WATELER DE LA PAIX (1936, 1950), DU PRIX FÉLIX HOUPHOUËT-BOIGNY POUR LA RECHERCHE DE LA PAIX (1992), DE L'ORDRE DU RIO BRANCO, BRÉSIL (1999), ET DE LA MÉDAILLE DE L'INSTITUT ROYAL D'ÉTUDES EUROPÉENNES, ESPAGNE (2000)

L'Académie constitue un centre d'études et d'enseignement du droit international public et privé, et des sciences connexes. Son but est de faciliter l'examen approfondi et impartial des problèmes se rattachant aux rapports juridiques internationaux.

L'enseignement de l'Académie est principalement donné au Palais de la Paix, à La Haye, par des personnalités de différents États. Il porte sur le droit international, sous ses aspects théoriques et pratiques, et sur la jurisprudence internationale. La durée de ses deux principales sessions est en été de six semaines s'étendant sur les mois de juillet et d'août, et partagée en deux périodes, consacrées l'une au droit international public, l'autre aux relations privées internationales, et, en hiver, de trois semaines, consacrée en janvier au droit international. L'enseignement est dispensé en français ou en anglais, avec traduction simultanée dans l'autre langue. Les sessions de l'Académie se déroulent sous l'autorité du Secrétaire général.

L'enseignement de l'Académie est conçu dans un esprit à la fois pratique et hautement scientifique. Nettement différencié des enseignements similaires des universités et écoles nationales, il s'adresse à tous ceux qui possèdent déjà des notions de droit international et ont, par intérêt professionnel ou curiosité d'esprit, le désir de se perfectionner dans cette science.

Il n'existe pas de cadre permanent de professeurs à l'Académie. Le Curatorium, qui est le corps chargé de la direction scientifique de l'institution, et qui se compose de dix-huit membres appartenant statutairement à des nationalités différentes, adresse chaque année, en toute liberté, ses invitations aux personnes qu'il estime qualifiées pour donner un cours ou une conférence à l'Académie. Les personnes ayant donné des cours à l'Académie ne sont donc aucunement fondées à s'intituler professeur de ou à l'Académie de droit international de La Haye.

L'Académie décerne un diplôme à ceux des auditeurs qui, réunissant les qualifications spéciales exigées par le règlement en vigueur, auront subi avec succès des épreuves d'examen devant le jury de la session à laquelle ils se sont inscrits. Elle délivre en outre aux auditeurs un certificat attestant l'assiduité aux cours de l'Académie à la fin de la session suivie.

Toute personne désirant suivre l'enseignement de l'Académie doit faire parvenir par voie électronique au secrétariat de l'Académie, au Palais de la Paix, à La Haye, un formulaire d'inscription dûment rempli. L'Académie perçoit des droits d'inscription fixés par le Conseil d'administration de l'Académie.

Un programme de bourses d'études permettant d'assister aux cours d'été ou d'hiver est institué auprès de l'Académie. Le mode d'attribution de ces bourses fait l'objet d'un règlement disponible sur le site Internet de l'Académie.

Tous les cours professés à l'Académie durant les sessions d'été et d'hiver font, en principe, l'objet d'une publication dans le *Recueil des cours de l'Académie de droit international de La Haye*, ainsi que sur une plateforme Internet, dans la langue dans laquelle ils ont été professés. Certains cours sont également publiés ou réédités dans des collections spéciales.

THE HAGUE ACADEMY OF INTERNATIONAL LAW

— FOUNDED IN 1923 WITH THE SUPPORT OF THE CARNEGIE ENDOWMENT —

AWARDED THE WATELER PEACE PRIZE (1936, 1950), THE FÉLIX HOUPHOUËT-BOIGNY PEACE PRIZE (1992), THE ORDER OF RIO BRANCO, BRAZIL (1999), AND THE MEDAL OF THE ROYAL INSTITUTE OF EUROPEAN STUDIES, SPAIN (2000)

The Academy is an institution devoted to the study and teaching of Public and Private International Law and related fields. Its mission is to further the thorough and impartial examination of issues arising from international legal relations.

The courses of the Academy are dispensed principally at the Peace Palace in The Hague by personalities from different States. They deal with the theoretical and practical aspects of international law, including international jurisprudence. The duration of its two main sessions is, in Summer, of six weeks in July and August, divided into two periods of three weeks each, one devoted to Public International Law and the other to Private International Law, and, in Winter, of three weeks, in January, devoted to international law. They are taught in either English or in French, with simultaneous interpretation into the other language. The Secretary-General is responsible for managing the sessions of the Academy.

The education offered by the Academy is designed to be both practical and highly academically advanced. Clearly distinct from the teachings provided in national universities and law schools, it is intended for those who already possess some notion of international law and who, out of professional interest or intellectual curiosity, desire to deepen their knowledge in this field.

There is no permanent teaching staff at the Academy. The Curatorium, which is the body entrusted with the scientific management of the institution, and which consists of eighteen members of different nationalities, invites each year, in its unfettered discretion, whomsoever it deems best qualified to dispense a course or give a lecture at the Academy. It follows that no one who has lectured at the Academy is entitled to style himself or herself Professor of or at The Hague Academy of International Law.

The Academy awards a Diploma to those attendees who possess special qualifications as set out in the regulations, after having successfully passed examinations before the Jury of the session in which they are registered. It also delivers a certificate of attendance to registered attendees at the end of the session.

Anyone wishing to attend the courses at the Academy must send a completed electronic registration form to the Secretariat of the Academy at the Peace Palace in The Hague. The registration fee for each session of courses is fixed by the Administrative Board of the Academy.

The Academy manages a programme of scholarships to allocate at its discretion to attendees at the Summer and Winter Courses. The regulations governing scholarships are published on the website of the Academy.

All courses taught at the Academy during the Summer and Winter Courses are, in principle, published in the *Collected Courses of The Hague Academy of International Law*, which also exist in electronic format, in the language in which they were delivered. Some courses are also published or reissued in special collections.

GENERAL TABLE OF CONTENTS

THE AIMS AND METHODS OF POSTCOLONIAL INTERNATIONAL LAW

by

CHIN LENG LIM

CHIN LENG LIM

TABLE OF CONTENTS

BIOGRAPHICAL NOTE

Chin Leng Lim, born 18 October 1970 in Georgetown, Island of Penang.

Read Law (LLB; BCL; LLM) at the universities of Buckingham, Oxford and Harvard, awarded PhD by the University of Nottingham. Called to the English Bar and to the Singapore Bar. Part-time Tutor and Law Research Student at Nottingham; appointed Lecturer at the University College of Wales, Aberystwyth and at Queen Mary & Westfield College, University of London; served in the United Nations Secretariat in Geneva; then Assistant, and then Associate, Professor at the National University of Singapore; also State Counsel at the Attorney-General's Chambers of Singapore and Director, Singapore Society of International Law. Since living in Hong Kong, has worked first as Professor at the Faculty of Law and member of the Senate and Court of the University of Hong Kong; among other advisory roles, member of a Trade and Industry Department committee which advises the Commerce Secretary; returned to the National University of Singapore briefly as Lionel Astor Sheridan Visiting Professor; currently Choh-Ming Li Professor of Law at the Chinese University of Hong Kong. Member of the UNIDROIT/ICC Institute Working Group on International Investment Contracts; Delegate to UNCITRAL Working Group III; One of the editors of the *International and Comparative Law Quarterly*; Membre associè de l'Institut de droit international; Honorary Senior Fellow of the British Institute of International & Comparative Law; Visiting Professor at King's College London. In practice as a barrister at the Bar of England and Wales with chambers outside the Temple; arbitrator, counsel and expert in various international arbitrations and included in the European Commission's list of arbitration chairpersons for disputes under the European Union's bilateral free trade agreements.

PRINCIPAL PUBLICATIONS

Books

Treaty for a Lost City: The Sino-British Joint Declaration, Cambridge, Cambridge University Press, 2022.

International Investment Law and Arbitration: Commentary, Awards and Other Materials, with a foreword by E. Gaillard, Cambridge, Cambridge University Press, 1st ed. 2018; 2nd ed. 2021 [with J. Ho and M. Paparinskis].

The Cambridge Companion to International Arbitration, with a foreword by Lord Neuberger of Abbotsbury, Cambridge, Cambridge University Press, 2021 [editor].

Law of the Hong Kong Constitution, Hong Kong/Singapore, Sweet & Maxwell, 1st ed. 2011; 2nd ed. 2015; 3rd ed. 2021 [co-editor with J. M. M. Chan and specialist contributors].

Alternative Visions of the International Law on Foreign Investment: Essays in Honour of Muthucumaraswamy Sornarajah, Cambridge, Cambridge University Press, 2016 [editor].

The Trans-Pacific Partnership Agreement: A Quest for a 21st Century Agreement, Cambridge, Cambridge University Press, 2012 [co-editor with D. K. Elms and P. Low].

The Paradox of Consensualism in International Law, with a foreword by M. Koskenniemi, The Hague, Kluwer, 1998 [with O. A. Elias].

Principal chapters in books

"Investment Treaty Policies and Arbitrations in Asia", in L. E. Sachs, L. J. Johnson and J. Coleman (eds.), *Year Book on International Investment Law & Policy 2019*, Oxford, Oxford University Press, 2021, chap. 17.

"Finding a Workable Balance between Investor Protection and the Public Interest in the Trans-Pacific Partnership", in B. Kingsbury *et al.* (eds.), *Megaregulation Contested: Global Economic Ordering after TPP*, Oxford, Oxford University Press, 2019, chap. 25.

"Trade Law and the Vienna Treaty Convention's Systemic Integration Clause", in J. Chaisse and T.-Y. Lin (eds.), *Essays in Honour of Mitsuo Matsushita: A Critical Assessment of International Economic Law and Governance*, Oxford, Oxford University Press, 2016, chap. 8.

"The Strange Vitality of Custom in the International Protection of Property and Contracts", in C. A. Bradley (ed.), *Custom's Future*, Cambridge, Cambridge University Press, 2016, chap. 8.

"Fragrant Harbour and Oyster Mirror: Beijing's Treaty Policy Towards Hong Kong and Macao", in L. E. Sachs and L. J. Johnson (eds.), *2015-2016 Year Book on International Investment Law and Policy*, Oxford, Oxford University Press, 2018, chap. 11.

" 'The Law Works Itself Pure': The Fragmented Disciplines of Global Trade and Monetary Cooperation and the Chinese Currency Problem", in C. L. Lim and B. Mercurio (eds.), *International Economic Law After the Global Crisis*, Cambridge, Cambridge University Press, 2015, chap. 6.

"The Conventional Morality of Trade", in C. Carmody, F. Garcia and J. Linarelli (eds.), *Distributive Justice and International Economic Law* (American Society of International Law Studies in International Legal Theory), Cambridge, Cambridge University Press, 2011, chap. 5.

"The Question of a Generic Definition of Terrorism under General International Law", in V. V. Ramraj, M. Hor and K. Roach (eds.), *Global Anti-Terrorism Law and Policy: Regional Perspectives*, Cambridge, Cambridge University Press, 2005, chap. 3.

Principal articles and notes

"Neutral Rights and Collective Countermeasures for *Erga Omnes* Violations", *International & Comparative Law Quarterly*, Vol. 72 (2023), pp. 1-31 [with Ryan Martinez Mitchell].

"Taming Leviathan as Merchant: Lingering Questions about the Trans-Pacific Partnership's State-Owned Enterprises Rules", *World Trade Review*, Vol. 19 (2019), pp. 402-423 [with Mitsuo Matsushita].

"The Function of the Transnational Chinese Contract", *Journal of World Investment and Trade*, Vol. 20 (2019), pp. 313-334.

"Worldwide Litigation over Foreign Sovereign Assets", *Dispute Resolution International*, Vol. 10 (2016), pp. 145-160.

Quartet of notes beginning with "Britain's 'Treaty Rights' in Hong Kong", all in *Law Quarterly Review*, Vol. 131 (2015), pp. 348-354; Vol. 132 (2016), pp. 552-556; Vol. 136 (2020), pp. 19-23; Vol. 137 (2021), pp. 11-16.

"Injuncting Foreign Sovereigns in Aid of Arbitration", *Law Quarterly Review*, Vol. 130 (2014), pp. 193-197.

"Foreign Sovereign Counterparties to Hong Kong Contracts", *Capital Markets Law Journal*, Vol. 9 (2014), pp. 157-176.

"The Chief Justice and International Law", in H. T. Chao *et al.* (eds.), *The Law in His Hands: A Tribute to Chief Justice Chan Sek Keong*, Singapore, Academy of Law, 2012, pp. 181-219.

" 'You Don't Miss Your Water 'Til Your River Runs Dry': Regulating Industrial Supply Shortages after 'China Raw Materials' ", *Stanford Journal of Law, Business & Finance*, Vol. 18 (2012), pp. 72-120 [with J. H. Senduk].

"East Asia's Engagement with Cosmopolitan Ideals Under Its Trade Treaty Dispute Provisions", *McGill Law Journal*, Vol. 56 (2011), pp. 821-862.

Trilogy of notes beginning with "State Immunity in Post-Handover Hong Kong", all in *Law Quarterly Review*, Vol. 127 (2011), pp. 159-162; Vol. 127 (2011), pp. 495-499; Vol. 128 (2012), pp. 6-10.

"Cast Light and Evil Will Go Away: The Transparency Mechanism for Regional Trade Agreements Three Years After", *Journal of World Trade*, Vol. 45 (2011), pp. 375-400 [with J.-A. Crawford].

"China and the Doha Development Agenda", *Journal of World Trade*, Vol. 44 (2010), pp. 1309-1331 [with J. Wang].

"Withdrawing from Custom", *Duke Journal of Comparative & International Law*, Vol. 20 (2010), pp. 143-156 [with O. A. Elias].

"Neither Peacocks Nor Sheep: T.O. Elias and Postcolonial International Law", *Leiden Journal of International Law*, Vol. 21 (2008), pp. 295-315.

"Saving the WTO from the Risk of Irrelevance", *Journal of International Economic Law*, Vol. 11 (2008), pp. 899-925 [with H. Gao].

"From Constructive Engagement to Collective Revulsion: The Myanmar Precedent of 2007", The Twenty-First Singapore Law Review Lecture, *Singapore Law Review*, Vol. 26 (2008), pp. 204-225.

"The Uses of Pacific Settlement Techniques in Malaysia-Singapore Relations", *Melbourne Journal of International Law*, Vol. 6 (2005), pp. 313-341.

"The Constitution and the Reception of Public International Law: *Nguyen Tuong Van* v. *Public Prosecutor*", *Singapore Journal of Legal Studies* (July 2005), pp. 218-233.

"The Amicus Brief Issue at the WTO", *Chinese Journal of International Law*, Vol. 4 (2005), pp. 85-12.

"On the Law, Procedures and Politics of United Nations Gulf War Reparations", *Singapore Journal of International & Comparative Law*, Vol. 4 (2000), pp. 435-478.

"Sanctions Without Law? The Lockerbie Case (Preliminary Objections)", *Austrian Review of International & European Law*, Vol. 4 (1999), pp. 204-229 [with O. A. Elias].

"The Right of Passage Doctrine Revisited", *Leiden Journal of International Law*, Vol. 12 (1999), pp. 231-245 [with O. A. Elias].

“General Principles of Law, Soft Law and the Identification of International Law”, *Netherlands Yearbook of International Law*, Vol. 28 (1997), pp. 3-49 [with O. A. Elias].

PREFACE AND ACKNOWLEDGEMENTS

I have sought to address the questions of colonialism, postcolonialism and decoloniality from the perspective of a discipline beginning in Renaissance Spain and reaching to the present day. The effect is twofold. On the one hand, international law begins with the *ius gentium* as criticism of colonialism, rather than as colonialism itself, which some now claim. On the other, the European positivist standard of civilisation that emerged to replace the *ius gentium* is not explained away as only a European regional or special custom. Rather, nineteenth-century international law, call it the "Law of Nations" or what we will, was about the application of European rules to the whole world, even if debates about international law were European. Chapter I's survey of the classical writings seeks to keep faith with the continuity of the subject. It places "postcolonialism" – without a hyphen, that is as a scholarly approach – within the context of that continuity. Chapter II offers an interpretation of the effort of an earlier generation of post-colonial lawyers, where "post-colonial" (with a hyphen) denotes a distinct period during the United Nations decolonisation era. Theirs was not simply a failure in reformulating international law as it is now commonly described but rather a demand for colonial reparations. Reparations conceived not narrowly as restitution but more widely to include demands for the prevention of continued and future colonial wrongs. Chapter III illustrates this by discussing attempts under the General Agreement on Tariffs and Trade, for example, to modify international trade rules, and also the twentieth-century Arab oil and other nationalisations. I argue that these were not special pleading come to naught. Reformulated trade rules were claimed as rights. Nationalisations rather than being just contests over the meaning of property or sovereignty were demands for restitution. Chapter IV then goes on to discuss the development and refinement of modern international arbitration as a by-product of colonial battles fought over contractual and property rights. In terms of the law applied by tribunals there was also a retreat from European positivism, once the standard of civilisation fell into obsolescence, and the re-enactment instead of a new twentieth-century natural law intended not only to protect foreign-owned property in post-colonial territories but also to prevent the newly decolonised nations from being able to refuse their consent to pre-existing European rules. The rules of European intercourse now were presented as unalterable and entrenched, as were European acquired rights. Finally, Chapter V assesses the current state of post-colonial international law, including the postcolonial movement, its practical aim and a crisis in methods.

I am indebted to Anthony Carty in Berlin; Olufemi Elias in Washington, DC; Bing Bing Jia in Beijing; Ryan Mitchell in Hong Kong; Ambassador Mario Oyarzábal of Argentina; Thomas Skouteris in Cairo; Muthucumaraswamy Sornarajah and Kalana Senaratne in Colombo; and Joel Trachtman in Medford. They offered courage, detailed comments, more often both. I am grateful also to Xueji Su for transforming my scribblings and who compiled the list of cases and bibliography; the Chinese University of Hong Kong; not least, the Curatorium of the Academy, its remarkable Secretary-General, Jean-Marc Thouvenin, and his staff, Anna Vasilyeva, Monique Legerman and Sabine Amiel. Finally, I would like to thank Suzanne Ossewaarde at the Peace Palace Library.

All views and all faults are mine alone.

CHAPTER I

THE QUESTION OF UNIVERSALITY

A. Introduction

Today, they say that international law is institutionalised colonialism. A first major theme in these lectures is that modern international law began as criticism of Spanish colonialism, as a critique of imperialism if you will. I say this although it is already a familiar story because somehow, and suddenly, we have forgotten it. Instead, people now say that international law began as a colonial tool; that it is an apparatus of colonial domination and always will be. My second theme is that colonial redress or colonial reparations, which we now hear discussed, is not a new idea and also that it is more complex, it always was more complex, than some people might now suggest. Fifty to sixty years ago the idea of colonial redress had gone beyond reparations and extended to rule change and rule-making to prevent the recurrence of past injustice.

I am interested in all this because we think that international law or how we have thought about international law has affected, in fact shaped, the world we live in and that how we think about it now and into the future will also, somehow, shape the future. I do not know if this is true, or whether it is just one way of attempting to explain the world, but it may still be useful to think about how people – by which I also mean international law commentators and scholars themselves – have come to discuss international law's relationship with colonialism today.

Many accounts of the law's role in decolonisation begin, typically [1], with the failed attempt to include in the Covenant of the League of Nations what was then the new principle of self-determination or of nationality. That attempt failed but, in the way the story is told, there was still hope at the beginning. A concession was made for a league of "nations" rather than a league of "States" [2]. That glimmer of hope was then to sparkle and then flash when eventually there was Chapter XI of the UN Charter, which addressed colonial non-self-governing

1. P. Sands, *The Last Colony*, London, Weidenfeld & Nicolson, 2022, at chaps 1, 2 and 5.

2. A. Cassese, *Self-determination of Peoples*, Cambridge, Grotius, 1995, at p. 27.

territories [3], and following which there was UN General Assembly Resolution 1514 [4], a landmark resolution in which the impatience of colonial peoples everywhere with the Charter's scheme of a gradual development of self-government erupted into a demand for immediate self-determination and independence for colonial peoples. However, there was the shameful episode of the *South West Africa* cases. The challenge to South African apartheid [5], however, culminated in the UN General Assembly's termination of the South African Mandate over South West Africa/Namibia but only after an astonishing and dispiriting judgment by the International Court of Justice (ICJ) in 1966 [6], the facts of which are as scandalous as they are by now well known. There was what can only be described as an audacious effort before the judgment, which succeeded, to oust Judge Sir Muhammad Zafrulla Khan of Pakistan on account no doubt of his sympathies [7]. Then there was the *Namibia* advisory opinion of 1971, which declared South Africa's annexation of Namibia to have been unlawful [8]. More recently, there was the *Chagos* advisory opinion of 2019, which was the subject of Philippe Sands' Summer Lectures here two years ago [9]. Interestingly, as late as 1983, Sir Philip Haddon-Cave, then Chief Secretary of Hong Kong, had quoted Sir Ian Sinclair's opinion that the United Kingdom never had accepted "and never would accept that continuance of colonial status contravenes any existing or emerging norms of *jus*

---

3. Charter of the United Nations, signed 26 June 1945, San Francisco, entry into force 24 October 1945, see Arts. 73 *(b)* and 76, which speak of "self-government".

4. UNGA Res. 1514 (XV), "Declaration on the Granting of Independence to Colonial Countries and Peoples", adopted at the 947th plenary meeting of the 15th session of the UN General Assembly, 14 December 1960, UN Doc. A/RES/1514(XV).

5. The challenge was unsuccessful. In 1966, despite an earlier finding of jurisdiction, the Court considered by a majority vote, with Judge Jessup dissenting, that Ethiopia and Liberia had lacked the legal standing to bring a claim. See the *South West Africa* cases (*Ethiopia* v. *South Africa*; *Liberia* v. *South Africa*), Second Phase, Judgment of 18 July 1966, *ICJ Reports 1966*, p. 6. See further the note in "The South West Africa Cases", *Washington University Law Quarterly*, Vol. 2 (1967), p. 159 *et seq.*

6. UNGA Res. 2145 (XXI), "Question of South West Africa", adopted at the 1454th plenary meeting of the 21st session of the UN General Assembly, 27 October 1966, UN Doc. A/RES/2145 (XXI).

7. V. Kattan, "Decolonizing the International Court of Justice: The Experience of Judge Sir Muhammad Zafrulla Khan in the *South West Africa* Cases", *Asian Journal of International Law*, Vol. 5 (2015), pp. 310-355.

8. *Legal Consequences for States of the Continued Presence of South Africa in Namibia (South West Africa) Notwithstanding Security Council Resolution 276 (1970)*, *ICJ Reports 1971*, p. 14.

9. *Legal Consequences of the Separation of the Chagos Archipelago from Mauritius in 1965*, *ICJ Reports 2019*, p. 92. Sands' lectures were subsequently published as "Colonialism: A Short History of International Law in Five Acts", *Recueil des cours*, Vol. 431 (2023), pp. 285-410.

cogens" [10]. Yet eight years before that the application of the principle of self-determination to non-self-governing territories had already been accepted by the ICJ in the *Western Sahara* advisory opinion [11]. Thirteen years later in *East Timor (Portugal* v. *Australia)* the Court declared it to be an "irreproachable" suggestion that the principle had acquired a *jus cogens* character [12]. Thus, according to this usual telling, international law finally delivered on its promise to non-European peoples, peoples who initially had been excluded from the principle of self-determination and whose well-being had been portrayed or painted instead as a sacred trust of Western civilisation [13].

The current critical literature puts it all differently, arguing persuasively that the history of colonial domination shows that international law was used to justify territorial annexation. However, it may be relevant that the European Law of Nations itself lacked effective territorial principles at the time. Today, it still does not explain adequately how States have territory rather than generally being defined as already being in possession of it. So, when it came to non-European territories and non-European peoples, sovereignty was the idea that was used to exclude them from civilised international society because of their lack of European forms of political and economic organisation. Lacking sovereignty non-Western communities and kingdoms thereby lacked even title to their territories [14].

For other kinds of Asiatic, Far Eastern and African peoples who somehow were considered sovereign by the Europeans dealing with them, today our textbooks say that even where such non-European rulers had a full legal capacity to enter into treaties over particular

---

10. C. L. Lim, *Treaty for a Lost City*, Cambridge, Cambridge University Press, 2022, at p. 62.

11. *Western Sahara*, Advisory Opinion of 16 October 1975, *ICJ Reports 1975*, p. 12, at para. 59.

12. *East Timor (Portugal* v. *Australia)*, Judgment of 30 June 1995, *ICJ Reports 1995*, p. 90, at para. 29. See also *Arbitration Tribunal for the Delimitation of the Maritime Boundary between Guinea and Guinea-Bissau*, Award of 14 February 1985, (1986) 25 ILM 252.

13. This idea found expression in Article 22 of the Covenant of the League of Nations, at least in respect of the "native" populations of the Axis Powers' former colonial territories.

14. Meanwhile in Europe the concept of territory as property eventually came to be replaced by the notion of exclusive jurisdiction. See e.g. C. L. Lim, Book review of Carty, *The Decay of International Law*, 2nd ed. (2019), *International and Comparative Law Quarterly*, Vol. 72 (2023), pp. 269-271. Today, following that line of doctrinal evolution, we speak as often of competence as we speak of sovereignty. For the theory of "competence" in Kelsen and Verdross, see B. Conforti, "The Theory of Competence in Verdross", *European Journal of International Law*, Vol. 5 (1994), pp. 70-77.

areas, these were principally for the purpose of recognition of European sovereignty or protection over such areas as between the Europeans themselves. As De Pont-Jest put it at the time [15]:

> "[T]hese letters of submission . . . are only serious for the European powers, in the event of territorial disputes. As for the black sovereign who signs them, he does not worry for a single moment."

In this way, Europeans were free to treat each other as possessing plenary title over non-European territories and peoples [16], even in disregard of the actual, precise terms of any indigenous-European treaty. All of this would operate within the framework established by the General Act of the Berlin Conference of 1884-1885 [17], in two well-known articles contained in Chapter VI concerning the occupation of Africa's coastal areas:

> "Article 34
>
> Any Power which henceforth takes possession of a tract of land on the coasts of the African continent outside of its present possessions, or which, being hitherto without such possessions, shall acquire them, as well as the Power which assumes a Protectorate there, shall accompany the respective act with a notification thereof, addressed to the other Signatory Powers of the present Act, in order to enable them, if need be, to make good any claims of their own.
>
> Article 35
>
> The Signatory Powers of the present Act recognize the obligation to insure the establishment of authority in the regions occupied by them on the coasts of the African continent sufficient to protect existing rights, and, as the case may be, freedom of trade and of transit under the conditions agreed upon."

Thus, by the time of the Berlin Conference, the emergence of a requirement of "native" consent as evidence of a claim was already

---

15. R. de Pont-Jest, "L'expédition du Katanga d'après les notes de voyage du Marquis Christian de Bonchamps", *Le Tour du monde*, Vol. 66 (1893), pp. 257-272, at p. 260.

16. While in the case of protectorates, continued "sovereignty" on the part of the "native" ruler was maintained in theory. See e.g. *Case Concerning Rights of Nationals of the United States in Morocco (France* v. *US)*, *ICJ Reports 1952*, p. 176, at p. 188.

17. General Act of the Berlin Conference on West Africa, signed 26 February 1885, Berlin, entry into force 19 April 1886.

beginning to be at odds with title acquired through occupation. There then were two novel doctrinal developments that could only have deepened the European hold over diverse peoples.

The first development, driven by Ferdinand von Martitz (1839-1921), was that land that was not wholly unoccupied could still be colonised. Thus seen, all non-European territory could now be regarded as *terra nullius*. Even though the Institut de droit international rejected such a view, Martti Koskenniemi's reading of that debate is that its members could not agree upon the kind of government that would be needed to prevent colonial occupation [18]. My own reading is that there was not an insignificant body of opinion among members of the Institut that shared the sense of some delegates at the Berlin Conference that the rights of the indigenes ought somehow to be recognised. Even if in the end the Institut rejected the two interconnected articles, being draft articles I and II of the draft international declaration prepared by Martitz, for being delicate, unwieldy and/or falling outside the mandate of the relevant commission. Draft article I had stated: "It is considered as *territorium nullius* all areas which 'are not effectively under the sovereignty' or under the protection of one of the States which are a part of the community of the law of nations, little matter that the region is or is not occupied," whereas draft article II had stated: "All States have the right to acquire by occupation territories that are not occupied. They can be acquired (1) in sovereignty, (2) being in protectorate" [19]. In short, the draft articles' unwieldiness in their references to areas "not occupied", and the impossibility of pinning down the conditions for determining whether the area was so, a question avoided at the Berlin Conference, was only one factor. It appears that some members of the Institut were not entirely unenlightened in their sentiments. Monsieur Féraud-Giraud had said the group had done well to delete Martitz's draft article I whose interpretation could become dangerous and serves no purpose other than to legitimate acts of plunder [20].

The second development was that a protectorate treaty does not exclude annexation, and thus was born the special category of the

18. M. Koskenniemi, *The Gentle Civilizer of Nations*, Cambridge, Cambridge University Press, 2001, at pp. 146-141, citing *Annuaire de l'Institut de droit international*, Vol. 10 (1888-1889), pp. 177-184.

19. A. Rivier, "Extrait du procès-verbal de la séance plénière tenue par l'Institut, à Lausanne, le 7 septembre 1888, sous la présidence de M. Rivier", *Annuaire de l'Institut de droit international*, Vol. 10 (1888-1889), pp. 176-201, at pp. 177, 184. Unless otherwise stated, translations are my own.

20. *Ibid.*, at p. 185.

"colonial protectorate"[21]. This last, although admitting some basis too in the General Act of the Berlin Conference, was sought to be reconciled by commentators like the late James Crawford, albeit criticised by J. A. Andrews in the *Law Quarterly Review*, by simply separating the European Law of Nations, which would not generally permit such elasticity being given to the term "protectorate" from British constitutional practice, which would[22]. A casual student of the law would see the difficulty in reconciling any other position with the pronouncements of tribunals and the ICJ, and the question still creates the most enormous difficulties in practice today. Members of the Institut de droit international did not accept what today is the Crawford position when the question of occupation by protectorate arose in respect of Martitz's draft article II, which I mentioned a few moments ago. The Secretary-General had put that question to the members, causing Ernest Glasson to ask whether, notwithstanding that unoccupied territories cannot be occupied as protectorates, a State having occupied indigenous territory could go on nonetheless to hold the territory as a protectorate. Edouard Engelhardt had earlier thought the Secretary-General's question best avoided while Paul Pradier-Fodéré had argued that a protectorate always supposes the existence of some treaty. Although subsequently, in response to Glasson, Pradier-Fodéré then appeared to admit the logical possibility of an occupation that, somehow, subsequently becomes a protectorate. However, the intervention of the President, Alphonse Rivier, put an end to further debate by declaring Glasson's example to have contained an incompatibility since a State that occupies necessarily does so as a sovereign, and only another sovereign State can occupy the title of a protectorate, that is, become a protectorate[23]. Martitz's draft article II was deleted in whole.

---

21. M. Craven, "Between Law and History: the Berlin Conference of 1884-1885 and the Logic of Free Trade", *London Review of International Law*, Vol. 3 (2015), pp. 31-59, at p. 47, citing J. Westlake, *International Law*, Vol. 1, Cambridge, Cambridge University Press, 1910, at pp. 123-124. See also M. F. Lindley, *The Acquisition and Government of Backward Territory in International Law*, NY, Longmans, 1926, at p. 148, discussing Westlake and Hall.

22. See J. Crawford, *The Creation of States in International Law*, 2nd ed., Oxford, Oxford University Press, 2006, at pp. 301-302. For British constitutional practice in treating "protectorate" as colonies as distinct from the classical European practice of "protected States", see *ibid.*, at pp. 286-287. For criticism of the "ethnocentricity" of this viewpoint in England, see e.g. J. A. Andrews, "The Concept of Statehood and the Acquisition of Territory in the Nineteenth Century", *Law Quarterly Review*, Vol. 94 (1978), pp. 408-427, at p. 416.

23. Rivier, note 19, at pp. 184-186.

As to the practical problem that still arises today, however, consider the following example. A European colonial power grants sovereign authority to a chartered company in the nineteenth century to enter into territorial agreements with indigenous rulers, maintaining the fiction through a conniving benevolence that it is either included in or removed, depending upon the convenience of the situation, from the actual administration of the "native" peoples. Thus, as an example, on 4 June 1914 a letter was despatched from the offices of the British North Borneo Company on Threadneedle Street in London seeking the use of the designation of Governor, without any necessary formal conferment of that title, by the Company's Representative in British North Borneo [24]. The reply from Downing Street reads [25]:

> "We have hitherto not referred to the 'Governor' because the Company's Charter refers solely to that officer by the title of 'The Company's Principle Representative in Borneo'; but if you wish it the Secretary of State will be prepared to connive in a benevolent spirit in the use of the expression 'Governor', and to permit its use in our official correspondence, as a convenient designation."

It avoids any direct responsibility for the indigenous inhabitants. At the same time, plenary title is claimed against other European powers. Questions about such a practice of informal empire were not resolved by the Institut [26], yet subsequently the colonial power grants sovereignty and independence, albeit now with the interposition of the colonial metropolitan State. Such claims to sovereignty over territory are today questioned by others, such as those who claim to derive title from the original "native" ruler, and these problems can come before tribunals and courts.

A recent arbitration brought by the heirs of the Sultan of Sulu, in which they were awarded US$14.92 billion against Malaysia [27], involved a nineteenth-century agreement the arbitrator considered to be commercial in nature but which the Malaysian Government considers a treaty ceding North Borneo territory initially to a chartered company, in fact in this case to the North Borneo Company. The kind of legal

24. Letter from Ridgeway to Anderson, 4 June 1914, in "Title of the Territory Administered by the British North Borneo Co.", 26 June 1914, TNA/FCO141/16187.

25. Letter from Anderson to Ridgeway, 17 June 1914, in *ibid.*

26. See e.g. Koskenniemi, *Gentle Civilizer*, note 18, at pp. 150-151.

27. *Nurhima Kiram Fornan* et al. v. *Malaysia*, *Ad hoc* Arbitration, UNCITRAL Arbitration Rules 2010, Final Award of 28 February 2022. See also Cour d'appel de Paris, Pôle 5 – Chambre 16, No. RG 22/04007, 8 March 2022.

issue involved is hardly unusual. In the *Island of Palmas* arbitration, the distinguished Swiss arbitrator Max Huber, having first considered that there were questions of construction pointed out that even if a chartered company – in that case the Dutch East India Company – were to acquire "native" territory by such an instrument, some European State needed still to be internationally responsible for it, and therefore in respect of such territories the exact relationship as a matter of the Law of Nations was between that of a sovereign and its vassal[28]. Crawford has suggested further that such questions of informal empire were somehow exclusively or only a matter of regional European international law. That is a curious view that, while holding the promise of separating or sanitising modern international law from some of the most difficult issues of its colonial past, would at the same time fail to resolve entirely questions carried over from that past. Here is the passage from Crawford[29]:

> "Although in many cases an extensive system of capitulations and concessions was established, Asian States . . . were early recognized as independent States subject to international law. Treaty practice in particular reflected that position. This did not necessarily mean that the same rules were applied to or by such States as were applied by European States between themselves. But that is to be explained not by any distinction between 'civilized' and 'barbarous' States but because many of those rules were what would now be called regional or local customs rather than general international law."

This passage seems to me to be incorrect in several places. First, the Asian States were not "early recognized", although I suppose it depends what one means by "early"; however, as we will see, well into the twentieth century the Far Eastern States (except Japan) were not recognised by the writers[30], most notably Lassa Oppenheim, who rejected the idea that international law was anything other than European while rejecting the view that it should always be Christian[31]. Secondly, the British Government eventually came to the realisation that the East India Company's Indian treaties were a farce from

28. *Island of Palmas (Netherlands* v. *USA)*, (1928) 2 RIAA 829, at p. 858.
29. Crawford, *Creation of States*, note 22, at p. 261.
30. See L. Oppenheim, *International Law*, Vol. 1, 2nd ed., London, Longmans, Green & Co, 1912, at p. 34, discussing the cases of China, Persia and Siam.
31. *Ibid.*, at p. 30.

which local rulers derived their sovereignty rather than the other way around – at least, they would be farcical without the interposition of the British Government [32]. Thirdly, as we will see with Charles Henry Alexandrowicz's complaint [33], international law viewed from a European perspective comprised "European" State practice even if that practice in fact consisted of treaty relations with non-Europeans. In other words, only the European reading counted for international law. Fourthly, European States, while viewing international law as European, were not conscious of only locally or regionally or specially applicable rules but of European rules which ought to apply to the world.

Also, colonial doctrines were adopted most willingly by the newly decolonised Asian, African and Middle Eastern States themselves. We find this when we investigate the jurisprudence of the ICJ [34]. Examples of such colonial doctrines include the doctrine *of terra nullius*, prescription – that is, title through usage and acquiescence – as well as the doctrine of effective occupation/*effectivités*. In connection with the *Sulu* arbitration I mentioned above, Malaysia argued before the Paris Court of Appeal that the nature of the 1878 Agreement, on account of its "colonial character", rendered the dispute non-arbitrable and excluded any recourse to commercial arbitration [35].

What does post-colonial international law say to all of this? Here we enter an altogether different and strange world. Those who would take us there say there can never be progress if we do not now reject the idea of a universally applicable international law, which applies to Europeans and non-Europeans alike. Some proponents of the Third World Approaches to International Law (TWAIL) movement add that our view of international law as the science of peace, as a progressive device, as a solution to the universal problem of war which has also helped to achieve decolonisation, is misplaced. I should say something about the atmosphere in which TWAIL emerged by the 2000s. By the 1980s and 1990s, international law writing had taken a conceptual

---

32. M. Koskenniemi, *To the Uttermost Parts of the Earth*, Cambridge, Cambridge University Press, 2022, at p. 773.

33. C. H. Alexandrowicz, "G. F. de Martens on Asian Treaty Practice (1964)", in C. H. Alexandrowicz, *The Law of Nations in Global History*, edited by D. Armitage and J. Pitts, Oxford, Oxford University Press, 2017, pp. 180-193.

34. See further R. Lesaffer, "Argument from Roman Law in Current International Law: Occupation and Acquisitive Prescription", *European Journal of International Law*, Vol. 16 (2005), pp. 25-58.

35. Cour d'appel de Paris, Pôle 5 – Chambre 16, No. RG 21/21386, 6 June 2023, at para. 51.

turn towards uncovering or deconstructing international law's hidden structures, or the structure of international legal argument, often in criticising liberalism in international law or the idea that political differences could be resolved by impartial rules. It was in that feverish intellectual climate that TWAIL emerged, seeking to disclose the deep colonial structures of international law.

Today, postcolonial international lawyers emphasise the fact that 84 per cent of the world was in colonial times under European control [36], and where such control was achieved by war and maintained by the use of force. They adhere to the view, against the international law textbooks, that even now the former colonial territories, rather than simply to be considered sovereign independent nations, are in fact bound inextricably and persistently in relationships of neocolonialism with the Western world. A number of them go so far as to say that teaching international law is not to educate but to propagandise [37], and some, as I have mentioned, would reject international law altogether. In sum, today's international lawyers who are "postcolonial", that is those without a hyphen between "post" and "colonial", want to trigger radical legal change, but in doing so they have not presented any prospect of the continuity of international law either. For now, they say: "TWAIL has made it uncomfortable for the white supremacist version of international law to roam unhindered" [38].

The argument is misconceived. We are, as I will try to show, barely halfway through a debate about redressing colonial wrongs and barely halfway through the greatest question raised in that debate, which is this. What rights do post-colonial States have to prevent renewed plunder?

At the same time, many Third World international lawyers [39], what I call "post-colonial" lawyers with a hyphen, have not rejected international law or its universal application to all States. Instead,

36. P. T. Hoffman, *Why Did Europe Conquer the World?*, Princeton, NJ, Princeton University Press, 2015, at pp. 2-3.

37. Al Attar, below, cites B. Rajagopal, "Counter-hegemonic International Law: Rethinking Human Rights and Development as a Third World Strategy", *Third World Quarterly*, Vol. 27 (2006), pp. 767-783.

38. M. Al Attar, "The Peculiar Double-Consciousness of TWAIL", *Indonesian Journal of International Law*, Vol. 19 (2022), pp. 239-262, at pp. 250-251.

39. This term has caused the gravest difficulty but is only used here to refer to the States that emerged out of the twentieth-century United Nations decolonisation process, and the Latin American States. See F. E. Snyder and S. Sathirathai, *Third World Attitudes toward International Law*, Dordrecht/Boston, Nijhoff, 1987. For a complaint about the use of the term in this way, see F. Nozari's review of the book in *International Journal of Legal Information*, Vol. 17 (1989), pp. 69-70.

they have been working, less dramatically, on its reconstruction. In past decades they focused on (1) self-determination [40], (2) permanent sovereignty over natural resources [41], (3) the legal status and effects of General Assembly resolutions [42], (4) the emerging field of the international law on foreign investment [43], and (5) on resolving the more abstract "civilisational" debate [44]. What a previous generation sought was colonial redress but in a very different sense from that which we have become accustomed. Rather than rejecting international law as a colonial subterfuge, they understood that the claim for redress can be expressed using the conceptual tools of international law more effectively than without them.

Still, we will need to address the radical view, not because one's colleagues are in fact white supremacists, but because international law is a social construct [45]. Put simply, such talk strikes, is intended to strike, at how we generate knowledge, and a tendency towards dramatic language, perhaps for its own sake, polarises and sometimes distracts from pressing issues.

B. Treaty and territorial principles were inadequate

TWAIL risks at times oversimplifying nineteenth-century international law. Let us begin with how international law became, supposedly,

---

40. W. Ofuatey-Kodjoe, *The Principle of Self-determination in International Law*, New York, Nellen, 1977.

41. K. Hossain and S. R. Chowdhury (eds.), *Permanent Sovereignty over Natural Resources in International Law: Principle and Practice*, New York, St. Martin's Press, 1984.

42. O. Asamoah, *The Legal Significance of the Declarations of the General Assembly of the United Nations*, The Hague, Nijhoff, 1966.

43. M. Sornarajah, *The International Law on Foreign Investment*, 5th ed., Cambridge, Cambridge University Press, 2021.

44. Y. Onuma, *A Transcivilizational Perspective on International Law*, Leiden, Martinus Nijhoff, 2010.

45. N. Kirsch, "The Dynamics of International Law Redux", *Current Legal Problems*, Vol. 74 (2021), pp. 269-297, at p. 285. Perhaps the most well-known view of international law as constituted by social facts sufficiently resembling developed systems of national law is that of Herbert Lionel Adolphus Hart. See H. L. A. Hart, *The Concept of Law*, Oxford, Clarendon, 1961, p. 231. For the foundational attempt to articulate an "inductive approach", albeit by focusing simply on the facts of state practice, see G. Schwarzenberger, *The Inductive Approach to International Law*, London, Stevens, 1965, whose approach at the time stood in contrast with Lauterpacht's, for whom sovereignty, rather than a hindrance to the development of a complete legal system, was merely a bundle of competencies conferred by international law itself. See H. Lauterpacht, *Private Law Sources and Analogies*, London, Longmans, 1927; H. Lauterpacht, *The Function of Law in the International Community*, Oxford, Clarendon, 1933; also M. Koskenniemi, "Hersch Lauterpacht (1897-1960)", in J. Beatson and R. Zimmermann (eds.), *Jurists Uprooted*, Oxford, Oxford University Press, 2004, pp. 601-680, at p. 617.

an instrument of colonialism. It is said that this was accomplished through territorial and treaty principles. Both the territorial and treaty claims appear plausible. Professor Antony Anghie has written that international law [46]

> "legitimised conquest as legal, and decreed that lands inhabited by people regarded as inferior and backward were *terra nullius*. In other cases imperial powers claimed that native chiefs had entered into treaties which gave those powers sovereignty over non-European territories and peoples. The ability of natives to enter into such treaties was paradoxical, given that they were characterised as entirely lacking in legal status. What is clear from an examination of the treaties, however, is that international lawyers granted the natives such status, quasi-sovereignty, for the purposes of enabling them to transfer rights, property and sovereignty".

Such claims at least appear also to be accepted in practice by States that uphold today an "unequal treaties" doctrine, most famously China, although it is also a doctrine well known in the history of Korean and Japanese international law [47]. It is not found explicitly in the Vienna Convention on the Law of Treaties but is argued to be implicit [48].

In the first place, greater care is needed when saying that treaty law or territorial principles were colonial tools. How treaties were *used* was another matter [49]. Still, the opposite has recently been suggested, that the Final Act of the Berlin Conference, when read on its terms,

46. A. Anghie, "The Evolution of International Law: Colonial and Postcolonial Realities", *Third World Quarterly*, Vol. 27 (2006), pp. 739-753, at p. 745. See also K. A. Hermes, "Peace Treaties Between Colonial Powers and Indigenous Peoples in North America", in V. Arnke (ed.), *Handbuch Frieden im Europa der Frühen Neuzeit / Handbook of Peace in Early Modern Europe*, Berlin, De Gruyter, 2021, pp. 413-434, at p. 413.

47. See e.g. S. Han, "The Endeavour to Revise Unequal Treaties in East Asia in the Early 1880s", *International Journal of Korean History*, Vol. 23 (2018), pp. 87-115.

48. T. Wang, "International Law in China: Historical and Contemporary Perspectives', *Recueil des cours*, Vol. 221 (1990), p. 195 *et seq.*, at pp. 333-344. See also I. Detter, "The Problem of Unequal Treaties", *International and Comparative Law Quarterly*, Vol. 15 (1966), pp. 1070-1089; H. Chiu, "Comparison of the Nationalist and Communist Chinese View of Unequal Treaties", in J. A. Cohen (ed.), *China's Practice of International Law: Some Case Studies*, Cambridge, MA, Harvard University Press, 1972, pp. 239-267; P. Wesley-Smith, *Unequal Treaties 1989–1997: China, Great Britain and Hong Kong's New Territories*, Hong Kong, Oxford University Press, 1983, at pp. 184-187.

49. J. Vandersmissen, "The King's Most Eloquent Campaigner . . . Emile de Laveleye, Leopold II and the Creation of the Congo Free State", *Belgisch Tijdschrift voor Nieuwste Geschiedenis*, Vol 41 (2011), pp. 7-57, at p. 41.

stood for noble and "philanthropic" aspirations, including of neutrality and free trade, at least between the Europeans themselves, and that it was somehow just misunderstood [50]. The Anglo-Dutch Treaty of 1824, which demarcated Malaya from the Dutch East Indies, contained a most-favoured-nation clause, but there is no disguising what it was, and of course criticism of the Berlin Conference is well known and accepted. No doubt, putting neutrality and free trade aside, the Final Act of the Conference prohibited the slave trade, but it is well known too that this was important for public acceptance.

Historical treaties with "native" peoples often are controversial also because the latter had no necessary understanding of their significance. Treaties were essentially proof offered by one European sovereign to another of their title to non-European territories [51], particularly when towards the end of the nineteenth century they were needed to establish legitimacy. Their validity was often disputed in that context. Portugal disputed King Leopold II's claims to the Congo [52]. Ironically, Leopold's claims were based on the more progressive notion of the necessity of "native" consent, which John Westlake at Cambridge (1828-1913) denied could be of any worth in the first place or as a source of validity because the "native" populations had no title to give. As Professor Craven is to quote him: a "stream . . . cannot rise higher than its source" [53]. Or as the President of the Institut de droit international had put it, and if I might translate loosely, these were treaties where "a chief without importance, a little local tyrant, sells doubtful sovereign rights for pieces of cotton or bottles of rum" [54]. Likewise, the Secretary-General at that 1888 session in Lausanne had asked whether, in the case of "distant territories belonging to barbarous peoples", "if they don't have international faith", *foi internationale*, then how can one look to treaties for a justification of occupation [55]?

---

50. Craven, "Between Law and History", note 21, at p. 49, and also generally.

51. De Pont-Jest, "L'expédition du Katanga", note 15, at p. 260 ("D'ailleurs ces lettres de soumission de ces petits tyrans africains, auxquels on lit quatre longues pages, dont, le plus souvent, ils ne comprennent pas un mot, et qu'ils approuvent d'une croix, afin d'avoir la, paix et des présents, ne sont sérieuses que pour les puissances européennes, en cas de contestations de territoires. Quant au souverain noir qui les signe, il ne s'en inquiète pas un seul instant.")

52. Vandersmissen, note 49, at p. 41, quoting the Belgian professor Egide Arntz's attempt to rebut this challenge.

53. J. Westlake, *Chapters on the Principles of International Law*, Cambridge, Cambridge University Press, 1894, at p. 144; Craven, "Between Law and History", note 21, at p. 48.

54. Rivier, note 19, at p. 181.

55. *Ibid.*, at p. 182.

The Institut had rejected the idea of specific treaty doctrines for the purpose of colonisation. I am not suggesting that there were not colonial doctrines in operation, even if the Institut rejected the possibility of satisfactorily defining them, but when it came to the law of treaties, that was in its entirety in an infant state. There were no clear limits between lawful and unlawful treaty renunciations. Application of the doctrine *rebus sic stantibus* was uncertain, as was the concept of a repudiatory breach [56].

And, turning from treaty to territorial principles, acquisition of non-European territories had often to do with the perceived absence of a European-style of government [57], as well as lack of a European form of economic life on the part of non-Europeans. In the opinion of some writers, agricultural activity was sufficient to demonstrate economic organisation [58], but that was not always the view taken. For Johann Kaspar Bluntschli (1808-1881), departing from earlier opinion that property rights were natural rights, agricultural activity would not in his view have founded property rights let alone sovereignty [59]. There were no real principles then, and still none now, to explain how a new sovereign acquires its territory [60]. Lack of European "sovereignty" was what mattered. "Recognition" was then used as an evidentiary rule to establish sovereign status, but it was an arbitrary creature, a creature of expediency [61]. My point is that it was as much the absence of satisfactory law that allowed colonialism, and that we should be wary of exaggerating the instrumentality of doctrine, otherwise today's postcolonial complaint about European international law will want rigour and risk confusion and insularity, rather

56. See G. Fitzmaurice, "Second Report on the Law of Treaties", UN Doc. A/CN.4/107, at p. 19, para. 2, extracted from the full report in *Yearbook of the International Law Commission*, 1957, Vol. 2.

57. See the *Western Sahara* advisory opinion (1975), note 11.

58. At least an agricultural people could claim title to the land they improved. See R. Tuck, *The Rights of War and Peace*, Oxford, Oxford University Press, 2000.

59. See L. Nuzzo, "Territory, Sovereignty and the Construction of Colonial Space", in M. Koskenniemi *et al.* (eds.), *International Law and Empire: Historical Explorations*, Oxford, Oxford University Press, 2017, pp. 263-292, at p. 274.

60. Anthony Carty, who also argues that nineteenth-century international law did not effectively restrain States and was used instead as a tool to justify the annexation of territory because the law lacked and still lacks an adequate conception of how territorial States come into being, asserts that this allowed sovereignty, which itself is rooted in notions of political organisation and civilisation, to be used to exclude non-European peoples from civilised international society. See Lim's review of Carty's *Decay* (2nd ed.), note 14.

61. See e.g. Koskenniemi, *Gentle Civilizer*, note 18, at p. 133, discussing Travers Twiss.

than being a sophisticated, cosmopolitan rebuke of the European Law of Nations.

C. Sovereignty and civilisation

There were of course treaties between the European powers and indigenous rulers [62]. European sovereigns considered that treaties ought to be obeyed whether as between themselves or with "native" rulers, even if they kept these domains between intra-European treaties and native treaties separate. Yet during the nineteenth century we could not have stated when a treaty could lawfully be renounced or repudiated, unlike what we now have under the Vienna Convention on the Law of Treaties [63]. We now adopt a strict approach [64]. In the past, however, commitments undertaken following the Congress of Vienna were governed by what A. J. P. Taylor called that "perpetual quadrille", that is, of maintaining the European balance [65]. There was certainly debate

---

62. For a discussion of Georg Friedrich de Martens's *Cours Diplomatique ou Tableau des Relations extérieures des Puissances de l'Europe tant entre elles qu'avec d'autres, see états dans les diverses parties du globe*, see Alexandrowicz, "G. F. de Martens", note 33.

63. See VCLT, Arts. 60 and 62. Article 60, which regulates the consequences of a treaty breach, is based upon a principle of reciprocity and "aims at striking a balance between the need to uphold the stability of treaties and the need to ensure a reasonable protection for the innocent victim". See M. Fitzmaurice, "The Practical Working of the Law of Treaties", in M. D. Evans (ed.), *International Law*, 4th ed., Oxford, Oxford University Press, 2014, pp. 166-201, at p. 167. See also C. Tams, "Regulating Treaty Breaches", in M. J. Bowman and D. Kritsiotis (eds.), *Conceptual and Contextual Perspectives on the Modern Law of Treaties*, Cambridge, Cambridge University Press, 2018, pp. 440-467. As for the doctrine of *rebus sic stantibus*, James Leslie Brierly and Hersch Lauterpacht, both of whom had been involved in the ILC's work, drew analogies with contract law. On Lauterpacht, see A. G. Toth, "The Doctrine of Rebus Sic Stantibus in International Law", PhD thesis, University of Exeter, 1970, which discusses related shifts from the first to eighth editions of Oppenheim's *International Law*. For Brierly, see J. L. Brierly, "Some Considerations as to the Obsolescence of Treaties", *Transactions of the Grotius Society*, Vol. 11 (1925), pp. 11-20. Both saw the problem as one concerning what the parties had originally intended; A. Carty, *The Decay of International Law: A Re-appraisal of the Limits of Legal Imagination*, Manchester, Manchester University Press, 1986, at pp. 79-81. See further J. Kulaga, "A Renaissance of the Doctrine of Rebus Sic Stantibus?", KFG Working Paper Series No. 32, Berlin Potsdam Research Group "The International Rule of Law: Rise or Decline?", Berlin, May 2019.

64. M. Fitzmaurice, "Practical Working", note 63, at p. 167, 169. See further *Gabčikovo-Nagymaros Project (Hungary/Slovakia)*, Judgment of 25 September 1997, *ICJ Reports 1997*, p. 7. For the procedural aspects in respect of termination, see e.g. A. Ciampi, "Invalidity and Termination of Treaties and Rules of Procedure", in E. Cannizzaro (ed.), *The Law of Treaties beyond the Vienna Convention*, Oxford, Oxford University Press, 2011, pp. 360-378.

65. A. J. P. Taylor, *The Struggle for Mastery in Europe 1848-1918*, Oxford, Clarendon, 1954, at p. xix.

about which, in case of conflict, was to take priority; maintaining a balance of power or preserving the sanctity of treaties. The idea that there was a "law" of treaties prior to the twentieth century is today more often assumed than explained [66]. As Dionisio Anzilotti (1867-1950) had taught, there was no more than a moral sentiment that treaties should be kept [67]. This has implications for postcolonial thought. As far as capitulations and treaties of cession were concerned, it is true that they offered only a thin veneer of law, but still there was not much treaty law shaped by the colonial encounter beyond the fact that whatever treaties had been agreed with "native" rulers would not affect treaties between purely European States. Neither type of treaty meant necessarily what they mean today. If we adopt Crawford's approach that colonial treaty practice was simply a form of European special customary regime, the argument – which I do not accept – becomes even stronger that there was no general colonial international law.

Another question had to do with the basis of treaty obligation. At times a treaty breach, such as that which saw Italian unification under the leadership of Sardinia, held little real consequence, but in other cases, a breach went directly to a perceived need to maintain the existing European balance [68]. Here, breaches count for very much. They count for everything. It has therefore been suggested that the making and breaking of treaties was governed by the needs of *realpolitik* [69]. The Congress of Vienna's Final Act of 1815 had restored "monarchic-feudal dynastic legitimacy" in Europe, but then there emerged a new principle: nationalism [70]. In any event, the European balance came

66. F. Berman, "A 'Modern' Law of Treaties?", in M. J. Bowman and D. Kritsiotis (eds.), *Conceptual and Contextual Perspectives on the Modern Law of Treaties*, Cambridge, Cambridge University Press, 2018, pp. 22-42.

67. See A. Carty, *The Decay of International Law? A Re-appraisal of the Limits of Legal Imagination in International Affairs, With a New Introduction*, 2nd ed., Manchester, Manchester University Press, 2019, at p. 6, citing M. Donaldson, "The Survival of the Secret Treaty: Publicity, Secrecy, and Legality in the International Order", *American Journal of International Law*, Vol. 111 (2017), pp. 575-627.

68. Carty, *Decay* (1986), note 63, at pp. 69-74.

69. Notwithstanding British insistence on the sanctity of treaties. See the discussion in Carty, *Decay* (1986), note 63, at pp. 72-73, of the *Pontus* case concerning Russian repudiation of a clause in the 1856 Treaty of Paris and Earl Granville pronouncing that "the assumption is made that Russia, upon the strength of her own judgment . . . is entitled to release herself from certain other stipulations of that instrument. . . . Yet it is quite evident that the effect of such doctrine . . . is to bring the entire authority and efficacy of Treaties under the discretionary control of each one of the Powers". Despatch from Earl Granville, British Secretary of State for Foreign Affairs, to the British Ambassador at St Petersburgh, dated 10 November 1870, in A. McNair, *Law of Treaties*, Oxford, Clarendon, 1961, at pp. 495-496.

70. *Ibid*., at p. 72.

subsequently under strain, a condition which was to persist throughout the remainder of that century [71]. The London Protocol of 1871, with its assertion that treaties may not be renounced unilaterally, stated only a general principle [72]. Perhaps connected with the dismal view of treaty sanctity is criticism of Emmerich de Vattel's (1714-1767) view of States as equals. The basis of that criticism is that, with Vattel, States became their own judges of legal and treaty impropriety. This, the critics say, led to the "subjectivisation of natural law . . . at a time when the conception of Europe as a cultural and moral community was at its strongest" [73]. It might also be recalled, against the now beleaguered Vattel, that the State as a corporate body did not exist during the Middle Ages. Change came with Niccolò Machiavelli's (1469-1527) writings, in which Machiavelli considered rulers to be unbound by any rules, and later also with Jean Bodin's (1530-1596) *Six Books on the Commonwealth*, published in 1576 [74], to which the idea of sovereignty owes so much [75]. The separation of national conflict of laws rules from public international law has also been attributed to Vattel's influence, as well as to John Westlake and Albert Venn Dicey (1835-1922) in England and to Carl Georg von Wächter (1797-1880) in Germany, who is said to have initiated the forum-oriented approach in the United States [76].

Coming back, if we may, to capitulatory treaties, even if these were commonplace in colonial territories for the most part, there was little that was specific to an underdeveloped "law of treaties" that was particularly colonial [77]. Rather the complaint is that treaty law allowed, or permitted, injustice. Previous Third World lawyers had addressed this complaint. During the Vienna Conference on the Law of Treaties, some developing countries and countries from the Communist bloc,

---

71. See Taylor, note 65.

72. "The plenipotentiaries of the North-German Confederation, Austria-Hungary, Great Britain, Italy, Russia, and Turkey, assembled today in conference, recognize that it is an essential principle of the law of nations that no power can liberate itself from the engagements of a treaty, nor modify the stipulations thereof, except as the result of the consent of the contracting parties by means of an amicable understanding", quoted in J. B. Scott, "The Achievement of International Justice", *Advocate for Peace*, Vol. 79 (1917), pp. 212-215, at p. 214.

73. Carty, *Decay* (1986), note 63, at p. 71.

74. J. Bodin, *Six Books of the Commonwealth*, Oxford, Blackwell, 1967 (translation by M. J. Tooley of *Les Six livres de la République*, 1576).

75. S. C. Neff, *Justice among Nations: A History of International Law*, Cambridge, MA, Harvard University Press, at p. 144 *et seq*.

76. M. Oyarzábal, "The Influence of Public International Law upon Private International Law in History and Theory and in the Formation and Application of the Law", *Recueil des cours*, Vol. 428 (2023), p. 129 *et seq*., at p. 155.

77. Although I will mention one notable exception in Chap. II.

building upon past doctrines, sought to include considerations such as undue burden, an imbalance between the parties, and also – as we have seen with the notion of "unequal treaties" – considerations of equity [78]. In his Hague Lectures, the late Chinese scholar Wang Tieya – who had a fondness for the classical works – traced the "unequal treaties" doctrine to Hugo Grotius (1583-1645), Richard Zouche (1590-1661) and even to Vattel, but observed that the notion fell into abeyance with the rise of positivist thinking, of which more will be said in a moment. Fascinatingly, he considered that it was left therefore to the newly decolonised, newly independent Third World sovereigns to revive naturalist thought [79].

When it came to territorial principles, the 1884-1885 Berlin or West Africa Conference was precisely a response to such undeveloped or missing principles [80]. Of course, there was conquest and prescription borrowed from Roman law [81]. However, while territorial transfers were effected by analogy with Roman private law and by reference to principles of property and contract [82], and also territorial change between existing sovereign States could be achieved by treaties of cession [83], political questions concerning the legitimacy of a new sovereign's territorial claim lay outside the law and were – they still are – resolved through diplomatic recognition. This was unlike questions of boundary delimitation occurring between existing sovereigns. The critical historical view therefore is that in Europe jurists struggled for an answer to such political and territorial issues only to conclude that the law of territory was nothing more than the recognition of states

78. Carty, *Decay* (1986), note 63, at p. 86.

79. Wang, "International Law in China", note 48, at p. 334.

80. At issue were competition between rival European powers, which manifested itself in a call for proof of effective occupation, as well as in calls for "neutralisation", "internationalisation" and freedom of navigation, as well as the question of whether a private body such as Leopold II's Association internationale du Congo could enter upon agreements to acquire title over "native" territories. See e.g. Vandersmissen, note 49.

81. B. Kingsbury and B. Straumann, "Introduction: The Roman Foundations of the Law of Nations", in B. Kingsbury and B. Straumann (eds.), *The Roman Foundations of the Law of Nations*, Oxford, Oxford University Press, 2010, pp. 1-18, at p. 6.

82. A. Carty, "The Deformation of the Law of Territory between 1880 and 1930: With Implications for Selected Present Day Controversies", undated, m/s on file, at pp. 6-7. By the mid- to late twentieth century, post-colonial States were vested with *imperium* but – in a crucial development of the law – not *dominium* over territory such that even newly acquired sovereignty did not free them from foreign property and contractual rights.

83. R. Y. Jennings, *The Acquisition of Territory in International Law*, Manchester, Manchester University Press, 1963, at pp. 7-9.

of affairs that had stood the test of time[84]. There was little law about territorial acquisition and the fact that some at the Berlin Conference sought to enact such principles as "effective occupation" does not make the international law of territorial titles culpable for colonialism. In fact the argument has been made forcefully, whether or not one is persuaded, and I am not, that the Berlin Conference was somehow anti-colonial[85], rather than being the narrow instrument for the management of competing colonial claims which it was. Any serious student of this matter should turn to the discussions at the Institut de droit international of 7 September 1888, in which the members of the Institut engaged in a comprehensive debate on the question of the occupation of territories. Draft article 1 of a draft prepared by Martitz that *territorium nullius* was territory "not effectively under the sovereignty or protection of one of the States which are part of the law of the community of nations, little matter that the region is or is not occupied" (pas effectivement sous la souveraineté ou sous le protectorat d'un Etats qui forment la communauté du droit des gens, peu importe que cette région soit ou non habittée) caused such controversy among the members that in the end the article was abandoned in its entirety. In other words, the formulation of a doctrine of colonial occupation was considered frankly impossible by the members of the Institut[86].

Ultimately, the abstract doctrine that presented itself seemingly obviously for blame was the positivist notion of a European standard of civilisation[87]. It is not altogether correct to pin blame there since, as we will go on to discuss, natural law thought was equally adaptable to colonial acts from the time of Juan Ginés de Sepúlveda (1494-1573). Grotius's ideas about occupation were not far different from the classical notion that if you occupy a seat then it is yours. In any case, this phantasm, the European civilisational standard, has since been scrubbed from the

84. Carty cites that pioneer of air law, Paul Fauchille's *Traité de droit international public*, 2 vols, Paris, Rousseau, 1922, in Carty, "Deformation", note 82, at p. 6.

85. See Craven, "Between Law and History", note 21, generally. There are disturbing parallels between Craven's argument and Félicien Cattier's defence of Leopold's Free Congo State as not amounting to the imposition of rule over the indigenous population, even if Craven couches his argument carefully as the overall failure of an ideal project of global capitalism that went against formal colonialism. See further, on Cattier, Koskenniemi, *Gentle Civilizer*, note 18, at p. 159 *et seq*. Even so, Professor Craven's account is formalistic. A more contextual reading would suggest, as he does acknowledge, in all fairness to him, that new doctrines for the imposition of colonial rule were devised contemporaneously, indeed in the context of the Berlin Conference.

86. Rivier, note 19, at pp. 177-186.

87. G. Gong, *The Standard of "Civilization" in International Society*, New York, Oxford University Press, 1984.

textbooks, which makes learning international law for the new student similar to reading a heavily redacted document and an arid exercise. The reason, or excuse, given is that it is an anachronism but that it is simply an embarrassment may be closer to the truth. The important issue, which the standard of civilisation sought to address, was – who had sovereignty?

An idea evolved, firstly, from scholastic notions of common humanity to the divine right of Christian rulers in Bodin's writings [88], then to Thomas Hobbes's (1588-1679) fictionalised social contract [89], before leading to other ideas, for example that of having a recognisably European form of government as the basis of a legitimate claim to sovereignty.

Before the crystallisation of the Montevideo criteria of Statehood – of governmental authority, independence in the conduct of one's foreign relations, a stable population and relatively well-defined territory [90] – a God-given right and subsequently equally abstract notion of social contract had emerged. By the nineteenth century a people civilised in the European sense, who had a European form of government, were permitted to call themselves sovereign and possess international legal rights. We might compare it with when scholasticism had prevailed, when what mattered was having a common humanity and the capacity to apprehend the principles of natural law [91].

88. Bodin, note 74. Bodin, incidentally, wrote also of non-Christian sovereignty.

89. T. Hobbes, *Leviathan*, edited by E. Curley, Indianapolis, Hackett, 1994.

90. This is not also to suggest unreserved agreement with the view that the origins of the idea of international law lie in the Peace of Westphalia of 1648 and which solely was a product of Western Christendom. There is the argument that such modern origins lie earlier in the commencement of a Mediterranean international community comprising the Franks, the Byzantine Empire and the Arabs. See R. Ago, "Pluralism in the Origin of the International Community", *Italian Yearbook of International Law*, Vol. 3 (1997), pp. 3-30; O. Elias, "Regionalism in International Law-Making", in C. Harding and C. L. Lim (eds.), *Renegotiating Westphalia: Essays and Commentary on the European and Conceptual Foundations of International Law*, The Hague, Nijhoff, 1999, pp. 25-44, at p. 28. Or the argument that "historical types" of international law had existed in Africa, Ancient China, India, or indeed elsewhere. See G. Abi-Saab, "International Law and the International Community: The Long Road to Universality", in R. St. J. Macdonald (ed.), *Essays in Honour of Wang Tieya*, The Hague, Nijhoff, 1993, p. 31 *et seq*., also the sources quoted in Elias, "Regionalism", p. 26, and also p. 31, citing Abi-Saab, above. For a similar line of argument about Ancient China's "Warring States Period" (476-221 BC) preceding the formation of a unified China being similar to the Greek City States during the Mediterranean Age, see Wang, "International Law in China", note 48, at p. 205 *et seq*.

91. Anghie, "Evolution of International Law", note 46, at p. 745, who cites C. H. Alexandrowicz, *An Introduction to the History of the Law of Nations in the East Indies (16th, 17th and 18th Centuries)*, Oxford, Clarendon, 1967. It is Alexandrowicz's body of work which, in a real sense, constituted the groundwork for TWAIL's historical turn.

Thus, according to this explanation of colonialism through law [92]:

> "Positivist jurists . . . devised a series of formal doctrines that used explicitly racial and cultural criteria to decree certain states civilised, and therefore sovereign, and other states uncivilised and non-sovereign. Thus non-European societies were expelled from the realm of international law. Lacking legal personality, these societies were incapable of advancing any legally cognisable objection to their dispossession, and were thus reduced to objects of conquest and exploitation."

Another kind of expulsion, as the father of post-colonial international law, C. H. Alexandrowicz showed, was by treating even European-Asian treaties "which could hardly support the idea of a European-centred positive law of nations" as simply "European" State practice [93]. The complaint of the postcolonial movement today is that such "argumentative patterns" remain notwithstanding whatever efforts had been made to scrub any mention of a standard of "civilisation" from the classroom textbooks [94]. That, because the textbooks have been sanitised we do not see these patterns, but yet they exist.

D. Law-giver to colonial adventurers

Returning to nineteenth-century sovereignty, the question was whether colonial peoples were politically and economically organised. Where one was thought to have lacked in civilisational attributes either wholly or partially, occupation, treaties of capitulation, of protection and cession were the instruments imposed by the Western world. Which lands were already occupied and which unoccupied became a key question which, as we shall see, never was fully resolved. Grotius, however, distinguished between the West Indies, which he considered to have been unoccupied, from the East Indies [95]. This contrasted with Francisco de Vitoria (1483-1546) who had much earlier in his 1539 lecture treated the Amerindians nonetheless as being in full possession

92. Anghie, "Evolution of International Law", note 46, at p. 745.
93. Alexandrowicz, "G. F. de Martens", note 33.
94. See Fofana's review of Tzouvala, in I. P. Fofana, "Buchbesprechungen", *Zeitschrift für ausländisches öffentliches Recht und Völkerrecht*, Vol. 81 (2021), pp. 1059-1064, at p. 1059.
95. C. H. Alexandrowicz, "Treaty and Diplomatic Relations between European and South Asian Powers in the Seventeenth and Eighteenth Centuries", *Recueil des cours*, Vol. 100 (1960), p. 203 *et seq.*, at p. 221.

of both public and private *dominium* [96], leading Salamanca and Coimbra to follow. As had Thomas Aquinas (1227-1274), who so influenced Vitoria, and who had taught that the *ius humanum* upon which *dominium* was based applied to both Christians and non-Christians and could not be overridden by the *ius divinium* [97]. We need to be clear: Vitoria had viewed humanity as one which, though it had become divided, could once again be reunited [98].

He was critical of the Spanish colonial enterprise. Such that if he were treated as the father of our subject, then modern international law began as criticism of colonialism. Not as some academic quarters would have us believe today. Vitoria, his student Domingo de Soto (1494-1560), Soto's correspondent Bartolomé las Casas (1484-1566) and whose famous debate with the wicked Sepúlveda, convened by Charles V in 1550, had been summarised by Soto for posterity [99]. These early modern theologians are distinguishable from the writers of later modernity. In our field we cannot dismiss the whole of Western modernity, as in some fields in which the decolonial movement is imbued with a radical fervour. Whatever the academic controversies over Vitoria, in that he did conceive of instances in which the Spanish were within their rights, international law as we understand it today began with an attack on colonialism. It is something we know but now many cannot hear.

It was only after the *ius gentium* was seen as a voluntary law, beginning with Grotius [100], then in Christian Wolff's (1679-1754) and Vattel's writings [101], that the notion of a united humanity eventually fell away. A European Law of Nations that applied purely among those who shared Western civilisation was to emerge. This intra-European law was especially prominent in the English writings at the height of the British Empire [102], and a significant amount of blame has since been laid there – but the idea was hardly exclusive to the English writers that all

96. See also for a contemporary account, F. Pirie, *The Rule of Laws*, London, Profile Books, 2021, at p. 340 *et seq*. See F. de Vitoria, *Political Writings*, A. Pagden and J. Lawrence (eds.), Cambridge, Cambridge University Press, 1991, at pp. 231, 240-241.

97. Alexandrowicz, "Treaty and Diplomatic Relations", note 95, at p. 223.

98. R. Hernández, "The Internationalization of Francisco de Vitoria and Domingo de Soto", *Fordham International Law Journal*, Vol. 15 (1991), pp. 1031-1059, at p. 1044.

99. *Ibid.*, at pp. 1044-1059.

100. Neff, *Justice among Nations*, note 75, at pp. 151-160.

101. M. Koskenniemi, *From Apology to Utopia: The Structure of International Legal Argumentation*, Helsinki, Finnish Lawyers' Publishing Company, 1989, at p. 85 *et seq*.

102. Otherwise bereft of an intellectual framework, see Koskenniemi, *Uttermost Parts*, note 32, at p. 687 *et seq*.

"Europeans" share common values [103]. The notion of an international society of shared values is something we see put very forcefully again under today's global circumstances.

E. The savage and the wild and barbarous

In short, the dominant explanation is that the acquisition of colonial territory was informed, in European nineteenth-century thought [104], by a general standard of European civilisation. Colonial territories were deemed savage in the absence of organisation into a sovereign princely kingdom, in the absence in other words of political organisation in the European sense, and thus characterised or depicted, the "native" peoples concerned had no sovereignty over the lands that they occupied. The land itself was in other words *territorium nullius*, and could be occupied provided that did not harm the rights of another State [105]. Perhaps nineteenth-century Italians chafing under what they considered unlawful French and Austrian occupation would have identified with it, as with Poles, Romanians or Hungarians. Yet this was hardly a complete story as we saw with the so-called "treaties" with the princely kingdoms of India, and indeed with others elsewhere, not just in the East Indies but also in the Middle East.

In any case, by the latter half of the nineteenth century, the existence of government in a European sense had become the "internationally"

103. See e.g. W. E. Hall, *International Law*, 1st ed., Oxford, Clarendon, 1880, at pp. 34-35.

104. Earlier nineteenth-century North American history was similar, for example in attempts to "civilise" Native Americans through land allotments under the Dawes Act and a broader policy of assimilation and the "Americanising" of Native Americans. See C. G. Calloway, *First Peoples: A Documentary Survey of American Indian History*, Boston, Bedford/St. Martin's, 2016. Elsewhere, the story did not involve a civilisational mission, and for the annexations of Puerto Rico and the Philippines following the Spanish-American War of 1898, the establishment of a Cuban protectorate, and in Panama the grant under the Hay-Bunau-Varilla Treaty of rights in respect of the construction of the Panama Canal "as if it were a sovereign" over "use of the land said canal be built, the surrounding land for construction purposes, and all islands within the limits of the zone" (Arts. II and III). See B. A. Coates, *Legalist Empire: International Law and American Foreign Relations in the Early Twentieth Century*, New York, Oxford University Press, 2016; also the book review of *Legalist Empire* by J. F. Murphy in the *American Journal of International Law*, Vol. 113 (2019), pp. 210-212, at p. 210.

105. See e.g. Hall, *International Law* (1st ed. 1880), note 103, at p. 36 adding that proviso in respect of unoccupied territory, which when transposed to the context of colonial territories meant, as Westlake had also stressed, that what would matter are the rights of other Western European States in these circumstances. See also Chap. II.A below for a discussion of the Berlin Conference of 1884-1885.

accepted test of civilisation, just as Aryan superiority had become coterminous in Bluntschli's – co-founder of the Institut de droit international – writings with the expansion of international law [106]. The following is from Westlake, exemplifying a late Victorian sensibility [107]:

> "When people of European race come into contact with American or African tribes, the prime necessity is a government under the protection of which the former may carry on the complex life to which they have been accustomed in their homes, which may prevent that life from being disturbed by contests between different European powers for supremacy on the same soil, and which may protect the natives in the enjoyment of a security and well-being not less than they enjoyed before the arrival of the strangers. Can the natives furnish such a government, or can it be looked for from the Europeans alone? In the answer to that question lies, for international law, the difference between civilisation and the want of it."

There was, as I have mentioned, a second category of colonial territories, not territory occupied by "savages", and therefore unoccupied in the legal sense, but rather "barbarous" regions such as the Ottoman Empire, the Chinese Kingdom or the Kingdoms of Japan or of Siam [108], and Persia, and princely kingdoms elsewhere in the East Indies and Middle East, which were considered sufficiently like a European sovereign as they sometimes possessed what recognisably was a form of organised government, as well as, we might add, a legal capacity to enter into capitulatory treaties granting extraterritorial rights. These kingdoms were not "politically deprived" [109], so means other than occupation were required for their subjugation. Enter, therefore, capitulatory or extraterritorial treaties [110]. Put more recently,

---

106. See G. Gozzi, *Rights and Civilizations: A History and Philosophy of International Law*, Cambridge, Cambridge University Press, 2019, at p. 109 *et seq.*

107. Westlake, *Chapters*, note 53, at p. 141.

108. For Siam, see S. M. Hell, "Siam and the League of Nations: Modernization, Sovereignty, and Multilateral Diplomacy, 1920-1940", PhD thesis, Leiden University, 2007, available at https://scholarlypublications.universiteitleiden.nl/handle/1887/12395.

109. Carty, *Decay* (1986), note 63, at p. 55, albeit discussing the Italian viewpoint within the nineteenth-century European Law of Nations, as exemplified by the views of Pasquale Fiore (1837-1914).

110. For the argument that they were viewed originally to have been mutually beneficial, see T. Kayaoğlu, *Legal Imperialism: Sovereignty and Extraterritoriality in Japan, the Ottoman Empire, and China*, Cambridge, Cambridge University Press, 2010. For the debate on the significance of Article 6 of the 1856 Treaty of Paris for

there was, there is still the viewpoint, which grows, of a necessary linkage between legal personality and having a certain form of "internal governance structure" [111].

It has been said that there were no criteria for applying the standard of civilisation [112]. To William Edward Hall (1835-1894), Johann Kaspar Bluntschli or, later, Lassa Oppenheim – Hall and Oppenheim writing at the full height of the British Empire – what mattered was recognition by the family of European nations [113]. According to Hall, an entity fulfilling the conditions of Statehood would have a right to be recognised as a sovereign State but because its fulfilment of those criteria would need to be verified by other States, recognition became necessary as proof of satisfaction of those conditions [114]. In any event, recognition became an additional requirement, on top of organised government, independence in international relations, a defined territory and a defined population. This perhaps also explains why, or how, one might have at the same time treaty relations with European nations but not possess recognition as a civilised State. I mean that a capacity to enter into international relations was only one of the many subsequent Montevideo criteria and was divisible in colonial practice.

By the early part of the twentieth century, even the Far Eastern kingdoms, China and Japan, would find themselves in possession of, at least formal, sovereign equality with the European States [115]. The same recognition was granted to, or gained eventually, by other Asiatic and African States during the course of the twentieth century, albeit less through recognition of "civilisational" attributes than by way of a demand for independence as of right. In either case it was to mark a radical break from nineteenth-century international legal thought, rather than the gradual evolution that, as we will see, Lassa Oppenheim had anticipated. Self-determination for non-European peoples, what

---

Ottoman recognition, see M. S. Palabiyik, "The Emergence of the Idea of 'International Law' in the Ottoman Empire before the Treaty of Paris 1856", *Middle Eastern Studies*, Vol. 50 (2014), pp. 233-251.

111. N. Tzouvala, *Capitalism as Civilisation: A History of International Law*, Cambridge, Cambridge University Press, 2020, p. 2; Fofana, "Buchbesprechungen", note 94, at p. 1059.

112. Since "European behavior never followed a criterion", Koskenniemi, *Gentle Civilizer*, note 18, at p. 134.

113. See Hall, *International Law* (1st ed. 1880), note 103, at p. 35, giving the example of Turkey; Oppenheim, *International Law* (2nd ed. 1912), note 30, at p. 30.

114. Hall, *International Law* (1st ed. 1880), note 103, at p. 73.

115. Albeit not until after the Russo-Japanese War in the case of Japan, and not until after the First World War for China, even if extraterritorial treaties were to remain until 1945.

we might term "colonial" self-determination, had also emerged as an important if uncertain organising principle [116].

F. Illegitimate conquest

Saying that modern international law was, up to that point, produced by colonialism is an exaggeration, although sometimes there can be truth in exaggeration. The concept of *terra nullius* found renewed expression during the colonial experience. Some international law was the product of the colonial encounter, which is hardly surprising if we are talking about the last 500 years, beginning with Columbus in 1493 [117]. Theological debate in Spain had marked the beginnings of classical international law, one ruled by a question of Christian conscience. By what precepts should interaction with the "native" population of America be conducted? A mid-sixteenth-century debate between Sepúlveda and Las Casas, in the context of the Spanish conquest of the Indies, is well known. Sepúlveda had considered that the Amerindians lacked human reason or understanding and therefore were natural slaves in the Aristotelian sense [118], and that they could not apprehend the laws of nature from which the *ius gentium* derives. Las Casas took the contrary view which coincided with Francisco de Vitoria's expressed a few years earlier, in which Vitoria had explained that what the Amerindians lacked was a European upbringing [119]. This passage is perhaps already very familiar to the student of international law, or perhaps not:

116. Carty, *Decay* (1986), note 63, at p. 55.

117. But it was as much the Roman *ius gentium*. Thus Isidore of Sevilla was to say: "*Ius gentium* is occupation, construction, fortification, wars, captivity, the right of regaining citizenship after captivity, slavery, treaties, peace, armistice, the inviolability of ambassadors, the prohibition of mixed marriages; and it is the *ius gentium* because nearly every nation uses it." See L. Winkel, "The Peace Treaties of Westphalia", in R. Lesaffer (ed.), *Peace Treaties and International Law in European History*, Cambridge, Cambridge University Press, 2004, pp. 222-237, at p. 226, quoting Isidore of Seville's *Etymologiae*.

118. Aristotle, *Aristotle's Politics*, translated by B. Jowett, Oxford, Clarendon, 1908, I.5.8, I.5.9, I.5.10, and I.5.11, at pp. 33-34.

119. V. M. Salas, Jr, "Francisco de Vitoria on the *Ius Gentium* and the American *Indios*", *Ave Maria Law Review*, Vol. 10 (2012), p. 331 *et seq.* Under Vitoria's teachings, the notion of a universal international law, and indeed of universal human rights, were to find their origins. Vitoria, however, was not uncontroversial from a postcolonial viewpoint as he had also asserted the Spanish rights to travel and trade with the Amerindians. See further G. Cavallar, "Vitoria, Grotius, Pufendorf, Wolff and Vattel: Accomplices of European Colonialism and Exploitation or True Cosmopolitans?", *Journal of the History of International Law*, Vol. 10 (2008), pp. 182-209, at pp. 186-192; N. M. Seuffert, "Vitoria's *On the Indians*, Legal Subjectivity and the Right to Travel", *Social & Legal Studies*, Vol. 30 (2021), pp. 14-31.

> "[T]he aborigines undoubtedly had true dominion in both public and private matters, just like Christians, and that neither their princes nor private persons could be despoiled of their property on the ground of their not being true owners."

"In both public and private matters", meaning title to property as well as jurisdictional authority [120], or both *dominium proprietatis* or *dominium rerum* and *dominium iurisdictionis*. Thus, non-Christian rulers possessed a degree of legitimacy. In our language now, they were "sovereign" for want of a better equivalent term, although we rush to add that international law was not viewed as a law between sovereigns at the time [121]. Still, Vitoria had argued that the Amerindians possessed their own government, laws and religion [122].

The point of Renaissance Salamanca as represented by Vitoria was that conquest was illegitimate in the eyes of God [123]; it was also illegitimate under a naturalist and universalist view of international law [124]. The *ius gentium* was a universal law applying both to Christians and pagans alike, so long as the latter were capable of human reason and thus of apprehending natural law. These were the principal themes in *Readings on the Indians and on the Law of War* [125].

However, the decline of the *ius gentium* had already begun by the mid-sixteenth century. The Christian humanist view had begun to falter, between the time of Francisco de Vitoria (1483-1546) and Alberico Gentili (1552-1608). The Chicago classicist Daragh Grant, attributing it to Jean Bodin (1530-1596), writes that by the Renaissance, a reinterpretation of the *ius gentium* had emerged, with a new notion of the supreme authority of princes at its heart [126]. In Professor

120. D. Grant, "Francisco de Vitoria and Alberico Gentili on the Judicial Status of Native American Politics", *Renaissance Quarterly*, Vol. 72 (2019), pp. 910-952, at p. 911.

121. Neff, *Justice among Nations*, note 75, at pp. 151-160.

122. Alexandrowicz, "Treaty and Diplomatic Relations", note 95, at pp. 220-221. For Alexandrowicz's work, see further C. H. Alexandrowicz, "The Afro-Asian World and the Law of Nations", *Recueil des cours*, Vol. 123 (1968), pp. 117-214, at p. 121. See also Alexandrowicz, *History of the Law of Nations*, note 91.

123. That Native Americans were pagans offered no excuse; conversion by coercive means was impermissible.

124. M. C. Ortega, "Vitoria and the Universalist Conception of International Relations", in I. Clark and I. B. Neumann (eds.), *Classical Theories of International Relations*, London, Macmillan, 1999, pp. 99-119, at p. 113.

125. J. B. Scott, *The Spanish Origin of International Law: Francisco de Vitoria and His Law of Nations*, Oxford, Clarendon, 1934. See also de Vitoria, *Political Writings*, note 96, at pp. 240-251.

126. Grant, "Francisco de Vitoria and Alberico Gentili", note 120, at p. 927.

Stephen Neff's magnificent work, he discusses natural law and its "less regarded junior partner", the *ius gentium*, being pulled apart, such that by the time of Grotius's *ius gentium voluntarium*, the task had been completed of distinguishing and separating international law from the medieval scholastic natural law [127]. By the time of the Peace of Westphalia, Protestant and Catholic kingdoms were on an equal footing, while the princes and cities within the Holy Roman Empire had now also the power to engage in international relations on their own, both between themselves and with those outside the Holy Roman Empire. Westlake concluded that with this "[t]here was now a society" and "[i]nternational law was born" [128], born from the demise of natural law. Sovereign authority as did emerge from the Westphalian Peace was such that it knew no secular bounds, and princes were answerable only to God. With this there emerged also in Gentili's view a notion that order between them was to be maintained through a balance of power [129].

It is to Gentili, writing a half-century before this great Christian European settlement, that we would attribute to uncivilised tribes an "abominable lewdness" that rendered them "savage and barbarous violators of the law of nature" [130]. Let us observe Gentili, whom in nineteenth-century England, Thomas Erskine Holland (1835-1926) had tried to get us to accept as international law's true father [131]:

> "I approve the more decidedly of the opinion of those who say that the cause of the Spaniards is just when they make war upon the Indians, who practised abominable lewdness even with beasts, and who ate human flesh, slaying men for that purpose. For such sins are contrary to human nature, and the same is true of other sins recognized as such by all as such except haply by brutes and

127. Neff, *Justice among Nations*, note 75, at pp. 151-160.
128. Westlake, *Chapters*, note 53, at pp. 55-59.
129. Grant, "Francisco de Vitoria and Alberico Gentili", note 120, at pp. 911-912; P. Schröder, "Vitoria, Gentili, Bodin: Sovereignty and the Law of Nations", in B. Kingsbury and B. Straumann (eds.), *The Roman Foundations of the Law of Nations*, Oxford, Oxford University Press, 2010, pp. 163-186, at p. 164. See also A. Clapham, *Brierly's Law of Nations*, 7th ed., Oxford, Oxford University Press, 2012, at p. 44.
130. Grant, "Francisco de Vitoria and Alberico Gentili", note 120, at pp. 911-912.
131. A. Gentili, *De Jure Belli Libri Tres*, Vol. 2, translated by J. C. Rolfe, Oxford, Clarendon, 1933, I.25, at p. 122. See T. E. Holland, *Studies in International Law*, Oxford, Oxford University Press, 1898, at pp. 1-39, discussed also in I. De la Rasilla, "Grotian Revivals in the Theory and History of International Law", in R. Lesaffer, *The Cambridge Companion to Hugo Grotius*, Cambridge, Cambridge University Press, 2021, pp. 578-596, at p. 580.

brutish men. And against such men . . . war is made as against brutes."

By Holland's time a universalist conception of the *ius gentium* had become eroded and replaced by positivism and the standard of civilisation. Just as in the East nearly a century before, the global potential of Islamic and Hindu political and legal thought had been extinguished by the decline of the Asian State [132]. All roads were leading to European positivism [133]. According to Henry Wheaton (1785-1848), nothing of Cicero's law of right reason remained [134]. By "international law" one meant only the positive European Law of Nations, rather than the Asian practice even in the European-Asian capitulatory treaties [135]. The shift had been completed from Francisco de Vitoria's Christian Humanist view to a voluntary law of nations, first through Francisco Suárez (1548-1617) and eventually through Hugo Grotius [136]. A standard of civilisation was sustained until the early twentieth-century plebiscites and mandates [137]. Here we also trace the beginning of the oil concessions entered into between the Seven Sisters oil companies, such as the Anglo-Iranian Oil Company and Texaco, and the local rulers. And so the subsequent arbitration of Third World disputes with the big oil companies, but this is to rush the story [138]. Let me again quote Westlake [139]:

> "The inflow of the white race cannot be stopped where there is land to cultivate, ore to be mined, commerce to be developed, sport to enjoy, curiosity to be satisfied. If any fanatical admirer of savage life argued that the whites ought to be kept out, he would only be driven to the same conclusion by another route,

132. Alexandrowicz, "Treaty and Diplomatic Relations", note 95, at pp. 310-313.

133. See further L. Nuzzo, *Origini di una scienza. Diritto internazionale e colonialismo nel XIX secolo*, Frankfurt am Main, Klostermann, 2012.

134. H. Wheaton, *Elements of International Law with a Sketch of the History of the Science*, Vol. 1, London, B. Fellowes, 1836, at pp. 50-51.

135. *Ibid.*, p. 54.

136. Neff, *Justice among Nations*, note 75, at pp. 151-160.

137. Incidents such as the brutal treatment of African people in Leopold's Congo Free State, which had also scandalised European society, later the manoeuvrings of Sir Percy Spender and Sir Gerald Fitzmaurice in the context of the *South West Africa* cases before the ICJ, and later still, the pronouncement in the advisory opinion of the ICJ in respect of the Chagos Islands, all cast doubt on the credibility of the closely held belief that the interests of "native" peoples mattered.

138. See B. Garth, "Dealing in Virtue: A Perspective from Almost 25 Years Later", in C. L. Lim (ed.), *The Cambridge Companion to International Arbitration*, Cambridge, Cambridge University Press, 2021, p. 38 *et seq.*, at p. 43.

139. Westlake, *Chapters*, note 53, at pp. 142-143.

> for a government on the spot would be necessary to keep them out. Accordingly international law has to treat such natives as uncivilized. It regulates for the mutual benefit of civilised states, the claims which they make to sovereignty over the region, and leaves the treatment of the natives to the conscience of the state to which the sovereignty is awarded."

Still, to dwell on this aspect unduly, no doubt of bigotry and injustice, risks ignoring a concomitant moral indifference to European populations, at least until events such as the American War of Independence and the French Revolution became precursors to later colonial self-determination in the twentieth century [140]. In any event, mainstream international lawyers have become understandably cautious and defensive when all trust and pride in the development, over time, of international law is denied as all a part of and being apiece with oppression [141].

G. Modern international law

There were two successive developments. First, nineteenth-century writers saw themselves applying a common standard, whether it be to nineteenth-century Bulgaria or "savages". Were a certain people sovereign in fact? They could have been intellectually dishonest in the application of that standard, of course, such as in Koskenniemi's discussion of Travers Twiss's (1809-1897) realisation that there was no difference between the ideas and faith of Cristian and Oriental nations but rather the potential for Oriental treaty renunciations [142]. Hall, in his fourth edition of *International Law* of 1895, discusses the French blockade of Formosa after China had adapted itself to international law.

---

140. By the end of the First World War "national", rather than "colonial", self-determination was dead, according to Alfred Cobban. See A. Cobban, *National Self-determination*, Chicago, University of Chicago Press, 1948. Others might disagree and choose to view colonial self-determination as an aberration.

141. The mainstream view is not without its own limitations. Koskenniemi wrote of how until the early twentieth century, international law had been an ideal, and he mourns the decline of this "gentle civiliser of nations". See Koskenniemi, *Gentle Civilizer*, note 18. Some may wipe away a tear when reading that extensive work, but it almost repeats the idea that only European history may be worth telling, a criticism voiced, if too harshly, by Priya Satia in a recent book review. See P. Satia, "Risking a Colonial Anticolonialism", *European Journal of International Law*, Vol. 32 (2021), pp. 1017-1026, at p. 1023.

142. Koskenniemi, *Gentle Civilizer*, note 18, at pp. 132-133.

The context was that China had communicated to Britain its view that the latter should deny its ports to the French, yet Hall wrote [143]:

> "Tacitly, and by inference from a series of acts, states in the position of China may in the long run be brought within the realm of law, but it would be unfair and impossible to assume, inferentially acceptance of the law as a whole from isolated acts or even from frequently repeated acts of a certain kind . . . it cannot be hoped that China, for a considerable time to come, would be able, if she tried, to secure obedience by her officers and soldiers even to the elementary European rules of law."

In truth, as Koskenniemi has explained, there is evidence of British realisation that were these Far Eastern kingdoms to be recognised, they would soon press for the renunciation of capitulatory treaties [144]. Secondly, beginning in the 1960s, certainly by the 1970s and 1980s, the newly decolonised nations had themselves participated in making so much of what today is modern international law, from the law of treaties to the law of the sea.

However, eventually what had changed was international law. Here is Oppenheim, whose second edition was written less than two decades after Hall's fourth edition, explaining – as he had in the first edition [145] – that no distinction can be drawn any longer on the basis of civilisational differences [146]:

> "The range of the dominion of the Law of Nations is controversial. Some publicists maintain that the dominion of the Law of Nations extends as far as humanity itself, that every State, whether Christian or non-Christian, civilised or uncivilised, is a subject of International Law. On the other hand, several jurists teach that the dominion of the Law of Nations extends only as far as Christian civilization, and Christian States only are subjects of International Law."

He rejected both views, the first which he attributed to Bluntschli and the second to Georg Friedrich de Martens (1756-1821), as discordant with the facts of international life and the basis of the law of nations.

143. W. E. Hall, *International Law*, 4th ed, Oxford, Clarendon, 1895, at pp. 43-44.
144. Koskenniemi, *Gentle Civilizer*, note 18, at pp. 132-133.
145. Lassa Oppenheim, *International Law: A Treatise*, Vol. 1, 1st ed., London, Longmans, Green, and Co., 1905, p. 30.
146. Oppenheim, *International Law* (2nd ed. 1912), note 30, at pp. 29-30.

To be sure, Oppenheim, unlike Travers Twiss, simply accepted the Christian origin of the law of nations and the "perpetual enmity" between Christian and Mohammedan states, as well as the absence of "constant intercourse" with Buddhist states. However, he accepted that change was coming. According to Oppenheim, past enmity as previously had existed between Christian and Muslim no longer existed, while "there is still a broad and deep gulf between Christian civilization and others, many interests, which knit Christian states together, knit likewise some non-Christian and Christian states" [147]. Thus on the basis of consent, the family of nations and the dominion of the law of nations had become enlarged [148]. This essentially was the same as what he had written in the first edition seven years before [149]. However, Oppenheim is interesting here when we get to his particular examples. In the first edition of 1905, he wrote that "the present range of the dominion of International Law" comprises the "old Christian States of Europe", the body of Christian States which grew up outside Europe, the Turkish Empire through its formal reception into the "Family of International Law" under Article 7 of the Peace Treaty of Paris of 1856, and – at least by 1905 – "[a]nother non-Christian member" – that is, Japan – "[s]ince her war with China in 1895" [150]. However, "[t]he position of such States as Persia, Siam, China, Korea, Abyssinia, and the like, is doubtful" [151]. In his second edition, Oppenheim then inserted an additional reference to "China, Persia and Siam", which had made "efforts . . . to raise their civilisation . . . as yet they have not accomplished this task, and [so] they are not yet able to be received into the Family of Nations as full members". He then adds that they will succeed in the near future [152]. As with the first edition, all of this was subject to his statement, a few pages earlier, that [153]

> "Persia, Siam, China, Morocco, Abyssinia, and the like . . . are certainly civilised States . . . however, it must be emphasised that not particularly Christian civilisation, but civilisation of such kind only is conditioned as to enable the State concerned and its subjects to understand and to act in conformity with the principles of the Law of Nations".

147. *Ibid.*, at p. 30.
148. *Ibid.*
149. Oppenheim, *International Law* (1st. ed. 1905), note 145, at pp. 30-31.
150. *Ibid.*, at pp. 32-33.
151. *Ibid.*, at p. 33.
152. Oppenheim, *International Law* (2nd ed. 1912), note 30, at p. 34.
153. Oppenheim, *International Law* (1st. ed. 1905), note 145, at p. 31.

Long criticised for upholding the standard of civilisation, Oppenheim, who had also supported the Eight Nation Alliance against China as a lawful intervention short of war [154], appears now to be envisioning its obsolescence [155]. In editing the third edition, Ronald Francis Roxburgh simply repeats the second edition, saying of China, Persia and Siam that while they were "for some parts within the circle of the Family of Nations, they remained for other parts outside" [156], applying the same conclusion too notwithstanding the fact that these nations, unlike Abyssinia, had by then become members of the League of Nations [157]. George Grafton Wilson's *Handbook of International Law* was to similar effect [158].

Compare Hall, earlier, and, as late as 1933, Holland at Oxford, who was similarly motivated by what he called "facts to be proven". Holland, too, would exclude China, even though he had stated that natural law as a basis for the Law of Nations drew no distinction between Christians and non-Christians. He wrote [159]:

> "The full applicability of International Law to any other States is, I venture to suggest, not to be presumed but to be proved, as it unquestionably in some cases can be, e.g., in the case of Japan, where the extra-territorial jurisdictions, which were maintained in Turkey up to the war of 1914, were withdrawn in 1899. Her respect for International Law was abundantly proved during her war with China, and, on a larger scale, during the war with Russia (February 1904, to September 1905)."

The late Indian scholar, Ram Prakash Anand, was quick to point out, in discussing the First Sino-Japanese War (1894-1895), the Russo-Japanese War (1904-1905) and the subjection of Korea to protectorate status (1910), the incongruity of a legal order in which civilisational

154. R. Mitchell, *Recentering the World: China's Reception and Contention of International Law*, Cambridge, Cambridge University Press, 2022, at p. 92.

155. See further Anghie who views Oppenheim's invocation of a "community" of States as paving the way conceptually for the introduction of the standard of civilisation. A. Anghie, *Imperialism, Sovereignty and the Making of International Law*, Cambridge, Cambridge University Press, 2005, at p. 48, 55-56. See also Ryan Mitchell's discussion of Chinese attitudes in *Recentering the World*, note 154, at pp. 57-120.

156. Oppenheim, *International Law* (2nd ed. 1912), note 30, at p. 34.

157. Lassa Oppenheim, *International Law: A Treatise*, Vol. 1, 3rd ed., edited by R. F. Roxburgh, London, Longmans, Green, and Co., 1920, at p. 35.

158. G. G. Wilson, *Handbook of International Law*, St. Paul, MN, West Publishing Co., 1910, at pp. 22-24, 32, 35-37.

159. T. E. Holland, *Lectures on International Law*, London, Sweet & Maxwell, 1933, at p. 39.

status is earned by waging war [160]. There is a famous quotation of a Japanese diplomat, who was supposed to have said [161]:

> "We show ourselves at least your equal in scientific butchery, and at once we are admitted to the council tables as civilized men."

One of the two Japanese professors who were despatched to the battle front in the Sino-Japanese War had returned to publish a testimony of the civilised conduct of the Japanese campaign, was subsequently to be Westlake's guest and had then obtained further testimonials from him and also from Holland at Oxford concerning the contrast between a civilised Japan and China [162]. There followed an avalanche of further testimonials in Wheaton, Hall and Oppenheim, for whatever reason but which Anand criticised fearsomely as "sycophancy" [163]. The truth is likely to be that the standard of civilisation was not immune from considerations of *realpolitik* – Britain and Japan were in alliance.

Holland went on to write, some thirty years later [164]:

> "The Governments of many other Oriental races profess, no doubt, an admiration for the International Law of the West, and would be glad to be thought to have accepted it, as one claim the more to be considered fully civilised States. Several of them have sent in their adhesion to the Geneva Convention of 1864. China adhered as lately as June 20, 1904, and she subsequently signed that of 1906. . . . Some of these Governments caused translation to be made of Wheaton's *Elements* and of the *Oxford Manual of the Laws of War*. . . . They provided public instruction in the science, for example, by Dr. Martin in Pekin *[sic.]*. Several

160. R. P. Anand, *Studies in International Law and History: An Asian Perspective*, Leiden/Boston, Nijhoff, 2004, at pp. 48-54. See further S. Yamauchi, "Civilization and International Law in Japan during the Meiji Era (1868-1912)", *Hitotsubashi Journal of Law and Politics*, Vol. 24 (1996), pp. 1-25. See also J. Lai, "Sovereignty and 'Civilization': International Law and East Asia in the Nineteenth Century", *Modern China*, Vol. 40 (2014), pp. 282-314.

161. Quoted in Anand, *Studies in International Law and History*, note 160, at p. 60, taken from the Dutch jurist Bernard Victor Aloysius ("Bert") Röling.

162. Sakuyé Takahashi's *Cases on International Law During the Chino-Japanese War*, Cambridge, Cambridge University Press, 1899, was written under John Westlake's guidance, who wrote the introduction to it. Thomas Erskine Holland wrote the preface. The massacre at Port Arthur (the Battle of Lüshunkou), was not mentioned.

163. The causality here is ambiguous as the avalanche could have also been the result of the shifting geopolitics of that era, Japan having (as it is today) become a valuable new British ally, at the time against Russia and potentially against Germany.

164. Holland, *Lectures on International Law*, note 159, at p. 89.

> . . . maintained permanent legations at European courts, and . . . sent representatives to Hague Conferences. They can hardly be said not to have been admitted into at least the outer courts of the charmed circle. But this lends no authority to the view that the whole system is applicable, without scrutiny of the facts, to the relations between European and Oriental Powers."

H. The English commentators

Whether it had truly begun with Alberico Gentili, or with the celebrated Francisco de Vitoria [165], things came to a head in the nineteenth century. Skipping past Hugo Grotius, Samuel von Pufendorf (1632-1694), Christian Wolff and Emmerich de Vattel [166], there was a remarkable uniformity in the views of the English Imperial writers from John Westlake at Cambridge and the Alpine enthusiast William Edward Hall to Thomas Erskine Holland at Oxford. In Travers Twiss, too, who had played a key role in advancing Leopold II's claims to the Congo [167], we find sentiments perhaps reminiscent of Gentili's much earlier view that non-Europeans were "pirates and even cannibals" [168]. It was not until some eight years later that one notices perhaps the tone at the Institut de droit international changing, during the 1888 session in Lausanne, in the aftermath of the experience of the Berlin Conference of 1884-1885 [169].

Georg Cavallar has argued that it is to these English writers that a clear racial distinction between sovereign and non-sovereign peoples is to be attributed, and that the earlier classical writers were more

165. On the tensions in Vitoria, see Cavallar, "Vitoria, Grotius, Pufendorf, Wolff and Vattel", note 119, at pp. 186-192; Seuffert, "Vitoria's *On the Indians*", note 119. Vitoria has also been criticised for allowing non-Christians to be converted and for allowing Spanish rights of travel and trade. See Seuffert, "Vitoria's *On the Indians*", generally.

166. See Cavallar, "Vitoria, Grotius, Pufendorf, Wolff and Vattel", note 119. For a short introduction to these classical writers, as well as to Cornelius van Bynkershoek (1673-1743), who gave custom priority over natural reason on the pretext of reason being doubtful on the particular point, see e.g. Westlake, *Chapters*, note 53, at pp. 60-77. See further the new, illuminating work, F. Iurlaro, *The Invention of Custom: Natural Law and the Law of Nations, ca. 1550-1750*, Oxford, Oxford University Press, 2021.

167. A. Fitzmaurice, "The Justification of King Leopold II's Congo Enterprise by Sir Travers Twiss", in S. Dorsett and S. Hunter (eds.), *Law and Politics in British Colonial Thought*, London, Palgrave Macmillan, 2010, pp. 109-126.

168. He had excluded Turkey, Siam, China and Japan. See Koskenniemi, *Gentle Civilizer*, note 18, at p. 133, citing T. Twiss, "Rapport", *Annuaire de l'Institut de droit international*, Vols. 3-4 (1879-1880), pp. 301-304.

169. See Rivier, note 19, at pp. 184-186.

ambiguous than some postcolonial writing has come to suggest [170]. Vitoria had accepted the right of the Spaniards to travel freely under a right to hospitality, insofar as it did no harm, the right to proselytise and to intervene on humanitarian grounds against cannibalistic practices for example, both of which were considered helpful to the Amerindians themselves, and famously considered that the latter possessed human understanding and mental capacity. Grotius, who shared much with Vitoria, nevertheless dismissed the justification of a civilising mission, even if his arguments in favour of free trade foretold the later views of Locke and Vattel [171]. In Grotius's time, Portugal pressed the Christian mission while the Dutch pressed free trade [172]. There were elements – in today's hyperbole – of the "racial" and "capitalist" genes of modern international law, but they were uncertain elements lacking the firmness of nineteenth-century international law scholarship.

170. For that ambiguity in the classical writings, see Cavallar, "Vitoria, Grotius, Pufendorf, Wolff and Vattel", note 119.
171. *Ibid.*, at pp. 188-197.
172. Alexandrowicz, "Treaty and Diplomatic Relations", note 95, at p. 230.

CHAPTER II

HOW THE AIMS AND METHODS HAVE EVOLVED

A. The Berlin Conference (1884-1885)

Let us then liberate the classical writings from the stranglehold of some of the more sweeping assertions in today's "postcolonial" scholarship. We saw earlier that rather than being simply colonial, international law as we know it began with natural law thought's criticisms of colonialism. The first generation of post-colonial writers, "post-colonial" with a hyphen, understood this. Perhaps even the notorious views of nineteenth-century diplomats and scholars were more complex and nuanced than they are sometimes portrayed today. Taking John Westlake as an example, he drew a distinction between the moral rights of the non-European peoples, which he accepted, and their lack of any legal rights. He had also based this absence of rights on the facts of the Berlin Conference of 1884-1885, albeit whose chief aim was not to regulate the relationship between the European and non-European worlds but between the European nations themselves in respect of their African colonial ambitions and the Africa trade. However, its colonial context seems even today to be denied by those who argue that "apparent aspirations" simply became disconnected from the "modalities for their realisation" and that the Conference's outcomes were but a "confounding of its own expectations" [173]. There were broadly two views, the first that the Final Act was a noble attempt to achieve neutrality and open trade but failed due to other factors, and a second, opposing, conventional view that the Berlin Conference triggered African partition [174]. Virtually all of that vast continent and great parts of Asia had been colonised. There was immense rivalry between the European nations. The Spanish Empire had passed into history and it was by then the age of free trade. Great Britain was already in decline while a united Italy and a united Germany had been formed out of the tumultuous events of the nineteenth century. The challenge presented to Britain by both the United States and Germany,

173. Craven, "Between Law and History", note 21, at p. 35.
174. *Ibid.*, at p. 49.

the latter the organiser of the Berlin Conference, was perhaps foremost in Westlake's mind [175].

The American delegate in the course of approving Articles 34 and 35 of the General Act spoke, first, in the tradition of Vitoria, Pufendorf and Wolff, of a need as a matter of international law to recognise the right of the "native" tribes to alienate territory and thus a need for their voluntary consent in such acts of cession; and secondly, while the General Act of that Conference stipulated only "the minimum of the conditions which must necessarily be fulfilled in order that the recognition of an occupation may be demanded", "[i]t is always possible that an occupation may be rendered effective by acts of violence which are foreign to the principles of justice, as well as to national and even international law", and that in such case, "it is reserved to the respective signatory powers to determine all the other conditions from the point of right as well as of fact which must be fulfilled before an occupation can be recognised as valid" [176]. The German undersecretary, presiding, considered the United States plenipotentiary's first proposition to have involved a "delicate" subject "upon which the conference hesitated to express an opinion", and as to his second proposition, the Conference "did not limit the right which the powers possessed of causing the recognition of the occupations which might be notified to them to be preceded by such an examination as they might consider necessary" [177].

Were these nations then free to subjugate the "native" peoples by force? Westlake considered non-European rights to have been only of a moral kind [178]:

> "It cannot be doubted that if the aggrandisement was made at the expense of a civilised population without its consent, or was attended with proceedings of great inhumanity to an uncivilised population, this would be a good ground of objection on the part of any power that pleased to take up the cause. But it would be going much further, and to a length which the conference declined to go, if we were to say that . . . an uncivilised population has rights which makes its free consent necessary to the establishment over it of a government possessing international validity."

---

175. Westlake, *Chapters*, note 53, at p. 138.
176. *Ibid.* See also Lindley, *Acquisition*, note 21, at pp. 33-34, and 45-46 (discussing Phillimore's views).
177. Westlake, *Chapters*, note 53, at p. 138.
178. *Ibid.*

In rejecting the American suggestion of a precondition of "native" consent, he wrote [179]:

> "Any such principle, had it been adopted, would have tended to defeat one of the chief objects of the conference, namely to avoid collisions between its members by regulating more clearly their mutual positions on the African coast."

Postcolonial scholarship now rejects any claim that modern international law that grew directly out of the European Law of Nations can have any universal application. Let me quote Professor Makau Mutua [180]:

> "The regime of international law is illegitimate. It is a predatory system that legitimizes, reproduces and sustains the plunder and subordination of the Third World by the West. Neither universality nor its promise of global order and stability make international law a just, equitable, and legitimate code of global governance for the Third World."

TWAIL discourse of such kind is distinctive, one whose intellectual history lies outside the received history of international law, in the fields of sociology, literary criticism and the other great humanist subjects, but which now is on the cusp of becoming mainstream international law thought. There is the influence of Critical Race Theory in the United States [181]. The reference to "subordination" is to the literary concept of the subaltern and the subaltern standpoint, that is, to the concept of lower, displaced or marginalised peoples [182]. There is the view that one does "not feel bound by post-enlightenment social knowledge, its structures of thought, and related constructions of political subjectivity, to which international law is central" [183]. "Legitimation" in turn has connotations of Max Weber, and Jürgen Habermas of the German Marxist Frankfurt School [184]. The emphasis on "reproduction" can

179. *Ibid.*, at p. 139.

180. M. Mutua, "What is TWAIL?", *Proceedings of the Annual Meeting (American Society of International Law)*, Vol. 94 (2000), pp. 31-40.

181. See D. G. Williams and R. R. Land, "The Legitimation of Black Subordination: The Impact of Colour Blind Ideology on African American Education", *Journal of Negro Education*, Vol. 76 (2005), pp. 579-588.

182. See G. C. Spivak, "Can the Subaltern Speak?", in C. Nelson and L. Grossberg (eds.), *Marxism and the Interpretation of Culture*, Basingstoke, MacMillan, 1998, pp. 271-313.

183. Al Attar, "Peculiar Double-Consciousness", note 38, p. 256, citing Professor James Thuo Gathii.

184. J. Habermas, *Legitimation Crisis*, translated by T. McCarthy, Cambridge, Polity, 1975.

be traced to Marx's *Das Kapital*. The attack on universality, too, is distinctly postmodern, with its suspicion of claims to an unmediated view of the reality and objectivity of international law, containing in it a value system that is contingent only but which reproduces existing global hierarchies. Mutua goes on to say [185]:

> "The construction and universalization of international law were essential to the imperial expansion that subordinated non-European peoples and societies to European conquest and domination."

So there we have it, an objectified, universal international law that is no more than a social construct, a simulation, or figment of hyperreality, will need to be exposed and then rejected [186].

Of course, you could have an American view, or French or British or Chinese view of the development of some specific rule of international law. You could have some States asserting a rule to be a rule of international law and other States denying that it is a legal rule at all. Notwithstanding these routine differences one assumes that all States are referring to the same body of rules or principles that we call international law. However, many postcolonial scholars now deny this last proposition, particularly those in the decolonial movement. It is reminiscent of the wholesale rejection of "capitalist" international law, at least in Marxist theoretical thought [187], which eventually was tempered by acceptance of mutual rules, indeed, of a mutual legal framework between both the capitalist and socialist world as a part of a larger framework of peaceful coexistence [188]. That, in any event, is the true scale of postcolonial cultural revisionism.

B. *Rejecting international law's promise*

Today, postcolonial thought produces revisionist readings, while the aim of the first generation of post-colonial lawyers was to make,

---

185. *Ibid.*

186. See J. Baudrillard, *Simulacra and Simulation*, translated by S. F. Glaser, Ann Arbor, University of Michigan Press, 1994.

187. See E. Pashukanis, "General Theory of Law and Marxism", in E. Pashukanis, *Selected Writings on Marxism and Law*, edited by P. Beirne and R. Sharlet, translated by P. B. Maggs, London, Academic Press, 1980, pp. 32-131.

188. See G. I. Tunkin, *Theory of International Law*, translated by William Butler, Cambridge, MA, Harvard University Press, 1974. I am told that by the 1930s in the USSR and 1949 in China, the idea that at least some rules of international law had to be accepted was already well established.

even to remake, positive international law rules. They responded to an emerging narrative, according to which non-Western peoples had recovered or achieved their sovereignty and achieved independence after the Second World War, the United Nations Charter had recognised and implemented political self-determination and, crucially, the sovereignty and equality of the newly independent Asian and African nations with Western nations – those that had derived their civilisation and political systems from European civilisation – had become legally assured. That generation of non-Western post-colonial international lawyers [189], many of whom worked as legal advisers to the newly independent nations, sought to challenge this simple and attractive view, particularly during the 1960s and 1970s. They wanted to stop what they saw as a continuation of Western plunder as well as to reverse past plunders.

What they did not do was to reject international law's promise. Unlike that generation, a new generation of scholars, the "Twailers", now express their discontent at the first generation's attempts, and crucially, or so I would argue, key figures in this second generation have denied that international law can stop let alone reverse Western plunder of the Third World. Their voices grow louder and we now hear accusations of "racial capitalism" [190].

I would like to ask if we should reject international law's claim to universality [191], a claim that has sometimes been described as the idea of "one global order" [192]. Today, a Third World "approach" consists of diverse strands of critical scholarship. These include a turn towards historical aspects, taking methodological inspiration from the Critical Race Theory movement, and catchphrases such as talk of international

189. Less visible today are their earlier precursors, arguably the true first generation, comprising Luis Maria Drago of Argentina, known for the eponymous Drago Doctrine and the Drago-Porter Convention of 1907, the anti-Nazi Salvadoran former President of the PCIJ Jose Gustavo Guerrero, the Chinese revolutionary and scholar Zhou Gengsheng, the Hong Kong-born Wang Chonghui and others. See e.g. Mitchell's discussion of the early Chinese international lawyers, in Mitchell, *Recentering the World*, note 154, pp. 98-120, which throws much new light on the events of that era.

190. J. T. Gathii and N. Tzouvala, "Racial Capitalism and International Economic Law: Introduction", *Journal of International Economic Law*, Vol. 25 (2022), pp. 199-206.

191. By which we do not mean that there are such things as "universal treaties" but, simply, that they reject the idea of a unified or single, continuous international law order that had developed from the European Law of Nations.

192. R. Lesaffer, "Treaties in the History of International Law", in M. J. Bowman and D. Kritsiotis (eds.), *Conceptual and Contextual Perspectives on the Modern Law of Treaties*, Cambridge, Cambridge University Press, 2018, pp. 43-75, at p. 61.

law's "logic of biology" [193]. There is now a deep scepticism about international law's promise. Ignacio de la Rasilla has written that [194]

> "the corollary of the post-colonial historiographical argument is that 'colonial international law' has been transmuted into contemporary structures, institutions and legal concepts through revamped versions of colonial doctrines such as the 'standard of civilisation'".

Some have suggested not only that the contemporary structures, institutions and legal concepts should be abandoned wholesale, but that we should reject the aims of the previous generation of Third World scholars because they – it is claimed – have accepted too uncritically modern international law with its roots in slavery.

My argument, throughout these lectures, will be that an earlier generation was not only more rigorous, sophisticated and comprehensive in their reformulations of doctrine but that they also had anticipated much of contemporary scholarship and had dismissed it in preference for more serious and practical concerns.

That earlier generation sought to remake international law not piecemeal but on a grand scale. The New International Economic Order (NIEO) is the best known of these efforts [195]. Following declaration of the NIEO's demise, there was a second turn. Efforts had been devoted to "transcivilisationalism" and "co-progressiveness", for example [196], with the former being directed at the late nineteenth- and early twentieth-century standard of civilisation and the latter being more reminiscent of Bandung. Now, there is a third turn with the self-styled TWAIL movement, which – as with many critical discourses in elite academic communities – began as a graduate student movement at the Harvard Law School. It led to a loose appropriation of the first generation's work, dubbed "TWAIL I" in contrast with the now more *avant garde* "TWAIL II" [197]. I shall simply refer to the first generation as

---

193. See Tzouvala, note 111, at p. 2.

194. I. De la Rasilla, *International Law and History*, Cambridge, Cambridge University Press, 2021, at p. 119.

195. If we extend it beyond the debate on standards of compensation for expropriation to debates about succession to colonial debt, the use of the resources of the deep seabed, the search for special and differential treatment in the GATT/WTO, and so on.

196. I am merely using examples from the Asian continent. I do not speak of "Asian" international law as there is little evidence of that. There is no "Asian Charter", no "Organisation of Asian Unity", no "Asian Court".

197. B. S. Chimni, "Toward a Radical Third World Approach to Contemporary International Law", *International Centre for Comparative Law and Politics Review*,

that, the "first generation" of post-colonial lawyers, rather than today's proponents of "TWAIL".

International law now confronts more than just a new way to read the textbooks or a call to read different books written by a wider array of authors, or the toppling of statues in public places. It confronts its legitimacy as a discipline.

C. The cultural thesis

There is a cultural thesis in contemporary postcolonial scholarship, a thesis about how international law has been imagined and also why it must be rejected. The search for European legal principles at the height of the colonial experience is exemplified in the rule of effective occupation. Negotiations had commenced in earnest during the Berlin Conference that took place from 15 November 1884 to 26 February 1885. Heightened squabbling over African spoils were to be settled once and for all. Formally, Berlin was about the abolition of slavery, free trade, neutrality and the rules as between European nations when it came to the occupation of African territories, but what Berlin truly symbolised was the prestige that came with colonial possessions. There is no better example of how colonialism did shape at least a part of international law's development. What flowed from that Conference was a felt need that occupation now needed to be effective. Such need had been triggered by Portugal's vast claims regardless of the effectiveness of Portuguese occupation and Great Britain's use of protectorates as a means of disguising occupation. The new effectiveness rule illustrates how international law's turn to colonial purposes threw up distinct questions [198]. In light of this, should we then simply reject international law? Alison Renteln puts the modern perception problem this way [199]:

> "[N]on-European states may feel alienated by rules they regard as biased and possibly illegitimate. Some may even go so far as to take the view that the enforcement of international law, where it is based on European values, is a form of cultural imperialism or

Vol. 5 (2002), pp. 14-26. For the view that TWAIL is not novel, see D. P. Fidler, "Revolt Against or From Within the West? TWAIL, the Developing World and the Future Direction of International Law", *Chinese Journal of International Law*, Vol. 2 (2003), pp. 29-76, at p. 32.

198. Even though the new rule was not applied. See Koskenniemi, *Gentle Civilizer*, note 18, at pp. 121-127.

199. A. D. Renteln, "Cultural Bias in International Law", *Proceedings of the Annual Meeting (American Society of International Law)*, Vol. 92 (1998), pp. 232-243, at p. 242, footnotes omitted.

> neocolonialism. If states take this view of international law, they may be disinclined to submit disputes to international tribunals rules. Thus, the perception of cultural bias in the international system may limit the possibility of enforcement."

Suspicion has long been rife among Third World States that international law has not shaken off the colonial experience, certainly in respect of arbitration, as shown by the Arab oil arbitrations of the mid-twentieth century, and also adjudication in the early days of the ICJ because of the *South West Africa* affair. However, the general view today, as I have mentioned, is that such suspicions are now – perhaps with the exception of investment arbitration still, and to a lesser extent with discrete debates such as in respect of the International Criminal Court [200] – a thing mostly of the past. Consider that effective occupation has, after all, been applied without quarrel to the claims of post-colonial States against each other, such as in the successful resolution of territorial disputes between Indonesia and Malaysia [201], or between Malaysia and its former component territory of Singapore. Similarly, Chinese claims in the South China Sea and Indian claims at the Sino-Indian border all take the continuity of modern international law seriously, applying the old rules of the European Law of Nations.

This is not to suggest that culture does not matter at all. To quote Renteln again [202]:

> "The apparent Eurocentricism of international law gives rise to a number of concerns. Even though international law is presented as neutral, it is widely viewed as based on European norms."

In turn this matters, as has been mentioned, to how post-colonial States might behave. For example, the States of Northeast Asia do not yet resolve their territorial disputes through international adjudication. They present a contrast to the behaviour of the South Asian and Southeast Asian nations. Might this be because of the colonial influence in the case of the latter group, indeed the Europeanised character, of

---

200. See e.g. S. Singh, "A TWAIL Critique of International Criminal Justice", *Berkeley Journal of International Law*, online post, 26 April 2022, https://www.berkeleyjournalofinternationallaw.com/post/a-twail-critique-of-international-criminal-justice.

201. *Sovereignty over Pulau Ligitan and Pulau Sipadan (Indonesia/Malaysia)*, Judgment of 17 December 2002, *ICJ Reports 2002*, p. 625; *Sovereignty over Pedra Branca/Pulau Batu Puteh, Middle Rocks and South Ledge (Malaysia/Singapore)*, Judgment of 23 May 2008, *ICJ Reports 2008*, p. 12.

202. Renteln, note 199, at pp. 241-242, footnotes omitted.

the South and Southeast Asian states – India, Cambodia, Indonesia, Malaysia, Singapore? As opposed to Japan, China and Korea. I have already mentioned the example of those fairly "newly independent" post-colonial States speaking not just of the legitimacy but sometimes the near sacrosanct nature of colonial acts for they constitute the very basis of these new States' claims to ownership of territory. Japan, China and Korea, while facing a multitude of territorial disputes between themselves, do not however rely on colonial constitutive acts for their existence.

Viewed against just this example of one region of the world, we might wonder if contemporary postcolonial scholarship strives to make too large a claim in saying that international law in its entirety is an organised colonial enterprise, rather than that some of colonialism's effects in some places may be lasting. Still, such a claim is readily accepted by those who already are inclined to accept it, is largely rejected by international lawyers [203], and seeks to gain ground in university law schools.

Yet there once was a movement whose battles became folklore in the African and Asiatic universities. These battles were fought by Mohammed Bedjaoui, Taslim O. Elias, Wang Tieya and others [204] whose views coincided also with the positions of their nations during the height of developing country unity in international lawmaking. They were probably not taught elsewhere, or are no longer taught now. Today, the TWAIL Movement is widely known; it is at the same time a radical movement with all the seductions of being so. In the previous section, we saw Mutua proclaim the "regime of international law" to be "illegitimate" [205]. But then he draws back suddenly [206]:

> "While it is certainly true that a certain degree of universality is inevitable, and even desirable, TWAIL frowns on attempts to confer universality on norms and practices that are European in origin, thought and experience."

There is a curious ambivalence in TWAIL's rejection of the present structures, institutions and concepts of international law. So which

---

203. *Ibid.*, at p. 236.

204. Along with these three, Ignacio de la Rasilla cites Ram Prakash Anand, Nagendra Singh, Surya Prakash Sinha, J. J. G. Syatauw, Georges Abi-Saab, Christopher Gregory Weeramantry, and Anand's great teacher Charles Henry Alexandrowicz. See De la Rasilla, *International Law and History*, note 194, at p. 121.

205. Mutua, note 180.

206. *Ibid.*, at p. 37.

parts should we abandon, and what necessary and desirable aspects should be preserved? The passage itself is frustrating. Mutua singles out "human rights and particular economic values, such as the protection of intellectual property" through the Agreement on Trade-Related Aspects of Intellectual Property Rights ("TRIPS Agreement") but says "TWAIL does not believe that free-market, private property, or trade values are superior to, or automatically trump, other human values" [207]. What we might draw from this, albeit single, example of second-generation writing is that a basis of international obligation is accepted but certain doctrines are rejected. However, unless one at least rejects the organising principles of the international legal order – for example, sovereignty, and sovereign lawmaking – it becomes harder to see how the radical rejection of the "legitimacy" of the "international legal order" is sustained. Disagreement over particular rules is hardly radical, and if anything, TWAIL's self-image is of a radical, politically charged movement.

Almost any international law student is aware of the developing countries' efforts to reshape the theory of sources and to reformulate the international law on expropriation in the following series of UN General Assembly resolutions:

1. Resolution 3171 (XXVII), "Permanent Sovereignty over Natural Resources", 17 December 1973, adopted by a vote of 108 to 1, with 16 abstentions [208]
2. Resolution 3201 (S-VI), "Declaration on the Establishment of a New International Economic Order", 1 May 1974, adopted without a vote [209]
3. Resolution 3281 (XXIX), "Charter of Economic Rights and Duties of States", 12 December 1974, adopted by 120 votes to 6, with 10 abstentions, with a separate vote for its controversial paragraph 2 (2) *(c)* [210]

207. Mutua, note 180, at p. 37.

208. UNGA Res. 3171 (XXVII), "Permanent Sovereignty over Natural Resources", adopted at the 2203rd meeting of the 28th session of the UN General Assembly, 17 December 1973, UN Doc. A/RES/3171(XXVIII).

209. UNGA Res. 3201 (S-VI), "Declaration on the Establishment of a New International Economic Order", adopted at the 2229th plenary meeting of 6th special session of the UN General Assembly, 1 May 1974, UN Doc. A/RES/3201(S-VI). Also UNGA Res. 3202 (S-VI), "Programme of Action on the Establishment of a New International Economic Order", adopted at the same, UN Doc. A/RES/3202(S-VI).

210. UNGA Res. 3281 (XXIX), "Charter of Economic Rights and Duties of States", adopted at the 2315th plenary meeting of the 29th session of the UN General Assembly,

First-generation post-colonial international law scholarship concentrated not just on remaking rules, even entire bodies of rules of international economic law, but also the reform of methods of international lawmaking and the reformulation of the theory of sources. Their views went to the basis of obligation, the legitimacy of the international legal order, indeed to the necessity of international law.

D. Did they go far enough?

Fresh anthropological work has shown that certain suppositions about the views of the first generation of post-colonial international lawyers may have been too hasty. Whether it was Elias, Bedjaoui, Anand or Wang, the suggestion that these members of the first generation did not go far enough lacks nuance. A more granular view is needed.

E. Revolutionary

Let us begin with Grégoire Mallard's study [211]. Briefly, in 1962 the Evian Accords had established cooperation between France and the future Algerian Republic in exchange for assurances of respect for acquired French rights and compensation for expropriation [212]. Bedjaoui was legal adviser to the provisional government and had perceived the Accords – or so Mallard argues – through the prism of a Maussian exchange, that what in fact was portrayed as a gift was a ritualised enactment of obligations accepted by the future Republic of Algeria. Algeria had adopted a new set of obligations for the post-colonial era.

All of this was to play out subsequently in Bedjaoui's role in drafting the rules of State succession to colonial debts [213]. In 1962, in the same year as the Evian Accords, the International Law Commission (ILC) had taken up the issue of succession of States and governments while the UN decolonisation process was underway. Bedjaoui was appointed Special Rapporteur in 1967 of one of the three components, namely "Succession in respect of Rights and Duties resulting from Sources other than Treaties". In other words, it fell to Bedjaoui to state the customary

12 December 1974, UN Doc. A/RES/3281(XXIX). The results of the separate vote on para. 2 (2) *(c)* were 104 votes to 16, with 6 abstentions.

211. G. Mallard, *Gift Exchange: The Transnational History of a Political Idea*, Cambridge, Cambridge University Press, 2019.

212. *Ibid.*, at pp. 158-159.

213. *Official Records of the United Nations Conference on Succession of States in Respect of State Property, Archives and Debts, Vol. 2*, United Nations, Sales No. E.94.V.6.

law position. Following thirteen reports, the ILC finalised in 1981 the draft convention which became the Vienna Convention on Succession of States in respect of State Property, Archives and Debts [214]. In a key provision [215], Article 38 (1), the Convention states that

> "no state debt of the predecessor state shall pass to the newly independent state, unless an agreement between them provides otherwise".

This controversial clause had been hard won. It applies to State debts, which are defined further in Article 33 [216]. In effect, Article 38 (1) applies to situations involving a newly independent State and upholds the clean slate theory as the general rule, but at the same time it allows exceptions that are agreed between the predecessor and successor States. Such agreement is subject to additional words of limitation in Article 38 (1) itself [217], and Article 38 (2) also states:

> "The agreement referred to in paragraph 1 shall not infringe the principle of the permanent sovereignty of every people over its wealth and natural resources, nor shall its implementation endanger the fundamental economic equilibria of the newly independent State."

State practice and the opinion of writers were divided. India had assumed British India's public debts while at the same time Pakistan's portion was owed directly to India. However, while Indonesia had assumed the Dutch colonial administration's debt, it was later to renounce it by decree. In contrast, the General Assembly resolved in Resolution 388 (V) A to exempt Libya from paying any portion at all of Italy's public debt [218].

214. Vienna, 8 April 1983, not yet in force. See further J. Oesterhelt, "Vienna Convention on Succession of States in respect of State Property, Archives and Debts", in R. Bernhardt (ed.), *Encyclopedia of Public International Law*, Instalment 10: *States, Responsibility of States, International Law and Municipal Law*, North-Holland, Elsevier, 1987, pp. 521-523.

215. See P. K. Menon, "The Succession of States and the Problem of State Debts", *Boston College Third World Law Journal*, Vol. 6 (1986), pp. 111-141, at pp. 132-136.

216. To mean: "any financial obligation of a predecessor State arising in conformity with international law towards another State, an international organization or any other subject of international law".

217. These are, in Article 38 (1), the words "in view of the link between the State debt of the predecessor State connected with its activity in the territory to which the succession of States relates and the property, rights and interests which pass to the newly independent State".

218. UNGA Res. 388 (V), "Economic and Financial Provisions relating to Libya", adopted at the 326th plenary meeting of the 5th session of the UN General Assembly, 15 December 1950, UN Doc. A/RES/388(V)A-B. See also Menon, note 215, at p. 132.

Bedjaoui, however, did not confine himself to the codification of existing custom or even its progressive development. In the first place, as Mallard points out, his mandate was to take special account of the views of the newly independent nations. Secondly, since the task was to produce a draft convention, it mattered not if the output was not confined merely to codification and progressive development. It would be for States to decide whether or not to adopt the treaty ultimately [219], and this view, as we shall see, is in concord with T. O. Elias's approach to post-colonial international law reform. Thirdly, as the Indonesian-Dutch scholar Ko Swan-sik pointed out, in referring to the commotion caused by the submission of Bedjaoui's second report to the ILC, there was as well the nature of the subject matter.

From the viewpoint of Western creditor nations, at its heart were Western acquired rights. Such rights feature both under the law on the protection of aliens and their property as well as in connection with State succession [220]. The Permanent Court of International Justice (PCIJ) had previously considered, in 1924, a German claim concerning the liquidation of a factory at Chorzów and an allegation of Polish expropriation of certain rural estates in *German Interests in Polish Upper Silesia* [221]. That dispute was related to the subsequent *Chorzów Factory* case of 1928 [222]. In the former, the PCIJ considered the liquidation to have violated the Geneva Convention of 15 May 1922 concerning Upper Silesia and acquired rights protected under customary international law [223]. Bedjaoui, however, declined to take account of this case because, as he reasoned, it had in truth involved a point of treaty construction rather than general international law. In criticising Bedjaoui, Ko reproduced a number of passages from the Court's judgment concerning the protection of vested rights under customary international law [224]. Also, at the same time that the related *Chorzów Factory* case was being addressed at the preliminary objections stage,

---

219. G. Mallard, "We Owe You Nothing: Decolonization and Sovereign Debt Obligations in International Public Law", in P. Pénet and J. F. Zendejas (eds.), *Sovereign Debt Diplomacies*, Oxford, Oxford University Press, 2021, pp. 189-212, at pp. 193-194.

220. See e.g. S. Ko, "The Concept of Acquired Rights in International Law: A Survey", *Netherlands International Law Review*, Vol. 24 (1974), pp. 120-142.

221. *Certain German Interests in Polish Upper Silesia*, Merits, PCIJ, Series A, No. 2 (1924).

222. *Case Concerning the Factory at Chorzów (Claim for Indemnity)*, Merits, PCIJ, Series A, No. 17 (1928).

223. See further Ko, note 220, at p. 130.

224. *Ibid.*

another earlier case, the *Mavrommatis Concessions* case, was to come again before the Court [225]. It concerned a Greek national who held three Ottoman concessions [226]. However, Great Britain, having acquired the Mandate for Palestine, chose to grant overlapping concessions to another. In the *Mavrommatis* case [227], the Court considered Britain bound by the Turkish concessions on the basis that subrogation was a "general principle of international law", that is, on the basis of Turkey's obligation to Mavrommatis [228].

Bedjaoui's view was therefore an outlier, but it was supported by that distinguished iconoclast, the late Ian Brownlie, who distinguished between judicial pronouncements that succession does not in itself extinguish vested rights and a requirement that the successor State should maintain such rights [229]. That treaty is yet to be ratified, but the point of this illustration is that Bedjaoui saw the aims of post-colonial international law to be the remaking of international law. Not its complete remaking. But insofar as the interests of the newly decolonised countries required it, new international rules that took account of those interests should be made. We have a further clue to Bedjaoui's thinking where in his second report he had alluded to colonial reparations. Without rushing the story, "reparation" is a word that is sometimes used loosely. It need not always mean restitution or corrective justice but was also used by international lawyers in the post-colonial period to refer to the remedy of preventing a continuing wrong or even a future wrong. It required attention to remaking international law rather than simply full restitution, which is the narrower sense in which the term "reparations" is typically used today.

We should understand the multiplicity of meanings attached to the idea of addressing colonial wrongs.

F. Democrat

As for T. O. Elias, he had been Nigerian Attorney-General and Chief Justice, and subsequently President of the ICJ [230]. He had said much

225. See further O. Spiermann, *International Legal Argument in the Permanent Court of International Justice: The Rise of the International Judiciary*, Cambridge, Cambridge University Press, 2005, at pp. 191-226.

226. These were in respect of the provision of an electric tramway service, electricity services and water services.

227. *Mavrommatis Concessions*, PCIJ, Series A, No. 2 (1924).

228. Ko, note 220, at p. 130.

229. See his final edition, I. Brownlie, *Principles of Public International Law*, 7th ed., Oxford, Oxford University Press, 2008, at pp. 654-655.

230. This section draws on some of my earlier views outlined in C. L. Lim, "Neither Sheep nor Peacocks: T. O. Elias and Post-colonial International Law", *Leiden Journal of International Law*, Vol. 21 (2008), pp. 295-315.

about the approach that the first generation of post-colonial international lawyers should take towards the idea of a universal international legal order. Persistent inequalities existed between the Third World and the First World. Thus, the first generation sought to construct a new international economic order. The conclusion, expressed by scholars such as Antony Anghie, is that they failed [231]. Dan Danielsen has argued that it may be time to reject "universal" legal solutions to the problems of the developing nations. Another strand of criticism by the thoughtful and distinguished critic James Thuo Gathii is that by failing to recognise the fundamentally imperialist and capitalist roots of international law, the first generation managed only to mount a "weak" effort [232]. These criticisms are apiece and would lead us to the history of the development of the European Law of Nations, the emergence of the standard of civilisation, its linkage with commercial needs, and so on, and a claim that the idea of a universal international legal order is as false today as in Henry Wheaton's time [233].

It can hardly be supposed, let alone said, that Bedjaoui, Elias and others were unaware of the role that the standard of civilisation had played in preventing the recognition of non-European sovereign Statehood. Why did they not adopt the radical option of rejecting the possibility of a universal and inclusive international legal order? Instead they sought not just to reform substantive rules but also our view of the sources of law and the basis of obligation.

Elias, despite his conservative reputation [234], sought a new method of lawmaking that while accepting sovereignty would curtail that notion further than Western States would allow. He rejected the notion that a rule is opposable to a State which, and only if it has, consented to that rule. The idea of consent was something that the Western States had held on to in the face of the overwhelming number of new States that had emerged and were emerging. So far as Elias was concerned, a majoritarian form of international lawmaking was beginning to emerge.

231. See Anghie, *Imperialism*, note 155, generally; also Danielsen's review of Anghie's *Imperialism* in the *American Journal of International Law*, Vol. 100 (2006), pp. 757-765. For a study of failure caused by local political conflict in Egypt, see S. Salem, "'Stretching Marxism' in the Postcolonial World: Egyptian Decolonisation and the Contradictions of National Sovereignty", *Historical Materialism*, Vol. 27 (2019), pp. 3-28.

232. J. Gathii, "International Law and Eurocentricity", *European Journal of International Law*, Vol. 9 (1998), pp. 184-211, at p. 189.

233. H. Wheaton, *Elements of International Law*, 3rd ed., Philadelphia, Lea and Blanchard, 1846, at p. 40.

234. See Lim, "Neither Sheep", note 230, at pp. 302-303.

It would become key to achieving inclusiveness and a universal international legal order. As he put it [235]:

> "The new world order necessarily envisages clearer and bolder definitions of the rights and duties of States as between developed and developing ones than have hitherto been attempted or accepted in customary international law. The Declaration [on the New International Economic Order] and the Charter [of Economic Rights and Duties of States] reflect the new spirit that has been abroad underlying the Universal Declaration of Human Rights and the related covenants, the Declaration on Peaceful Coexistence and Friendly Relations, and that section of Part V of the Vienna Convention on the Law of Treaties which declares certain treaties invalid on certain vitiating grounds – especially those treaties that conflict with a peremptory norm of general international law *(jus cogens)*. A new world order seems truly to be in the making."

And, that [236]:

> "The whole problem . . . seems to hinge ultimately upon the setting up of a device or mechanism which must ensure, and be seen to ensure, the holding of the scales fairly between the understandable fears and apparently excessive precautions of the industrialized nations on the one hand and the equally understandable fears and apparently groundless scepticism of the developing nations. The former are afraid of numbers, as their experience of the United Nations and its agencies has shown that they cannot, except in the Security Council, always have their own way. . . . Most of the latter have too recent experiences of colonization. . . . And, yet, representation on the central Council of the proposed International Sea-Bed Authority has to reflect the preponderance of numbers of developing States if the Authority is to have the chance of being acceptable to the majority of the world."

In his *Africa and the Development of International Law*, Elias had written about newly emergent ideas among Soviet international lawyers,

---

235. T. O. Elias, *New Horizons in International Law*, 2nd ed., Dordrecht, Nijhoff, 1992, at p. 27.

236. T. O. Elias, *Africa and the Development of International Law*, Leiden, A. W. Sijthoff, 1972, at p. 75.

what Edward McWhinney described as a "tangled web of Soviet theories"[237] about "consensus international law-making"[238]. What Elias detected was that while some Soviet jurists would reject General Assembly resolutions and General Assembly voting as a lawmaking device, such as Grigorii Tunkin, or that some such as M. V. Yanovskii might yet insist upon unanimity in lawmaking, or like G. I. Morozov require still that the communist and capitalist blocs should agree[239], there were those like Vratislav Pechota, of then Czechoslovakia, who would speak of "the developing juridical conscience of people" in the form of General Assembly resolutions[240]. Elias cited Professor Richard Falk for the idea that opposition by one or more States should not prevent the General Assembly from having a lawmaking capacity, and Manfred Lachs for the notion of the emergence of a limited form of legislative authority on the international plane[241]. Later, he was to criticise Clarence Wilfred Jenks and Gerald Fitzmaurice for their blanket dismissal of the legal status of General Assembly resolutions, preferring the more flexible views of Philip Jessup, Wolfgang Friedman and Robert Jennings[242].

Notice that in its "diplomatic sense" consensus would mean that disagreement by one State would prevent its achievement. In Elias's use of the term "consensus", however, the views of any one State or group of States should not be permitted to prevent "consensus law-making"; sometimes he referred to a "two-thirds majority", other times to a "unanimous vote", and on yet other occasions to resolutions and declarations of a "reasonably universal import"[243], by which he generally meant lawmaking by majority will[244]. Elias expressed his majoritarianism in the following way[245]:

237. E. McWhinney, "The Changing United Nations Constitutionalism: New Areas and New Techniques for International Law-Making", *Canadian Yearbook of International Law*, Vol. 5 (1967), pp. 68-83, at p. 83.

238. Discussed also in Lim, "Neither Sheep", note 230, at p. 304.

239. In fact, G. I. Morozov was criticised by Tunkin for considering General Assembly resolutions to be binding. See Tunkin, *Theory of International Law*, note 188, at p. 164.

240. See E. McWhinney, "Changing International Law Method and Objectives in the Era of the Soviet-Western Détente", *American Journal of International Law*, Vol. 59 (1965), pp. 1-15, at pp. 3-14.

241. Elias, *Africa*, note 236, at 70-71; discussed also in Lim, "Neither Sheep", note 230, at p. 304.

242. Elias, *New Horizons*, note 235, at p. 391.

243. *Ibid*,

244. Elias, *Africa*, note 236, at pp. 70-73; Lim, "Neither Sheep", note 230, at p. 304.

245. Elias, *Africa*, note 236, at p. 72.

> "[A]dvocates of consent . . . are also the first to insist that the three-quarters of the world that took no part in its formation must be regarded as bound by it, consent or no consent."

In Elias, therefore, we find an example of a first-generation post-colonial international lawyer who, while not rejecting a universal international legal order, in fact proposed to curtail a foundational organising principle of international law as it had developed out of the positivist European Law of Nations – namely, individual sovereign consent. Recall that in the history of the European Law of Nations, there first had emerged the idea of the will or command of the European sovereign with Jean Bodin in the sixteenth century, above which there was no higher earthly authority. Sovereignty was absolute, but "[e]ventually, when it became impossible to fix the location of such power in any definite person or organ within the state, sovereignty was seen as an attribute of the personified state itself" [246]. Thus conceived an international rule is opposable to a State only if the personified State has consented to that rule. We see this reflected too in our earlier discussion of succession to colonial debts. Does not sovereignty mean a clean slate, or an ability to pick and choose one's obligations as sovereign? This is not the place to go deeply into the matter [247], but such a picture of sovereign lawmaking has raised questions, for example in James Leslie Brierly, because [248]

> "this assumption, that international law consists of nothing save what states have consented to, is an inadequate account of the system we see in actual operation; and even if it were a complete account of the contents of the law, it would fail to explain why the law is binding".

Moreover [249]:

> "A customary rule is observed, not because it has been consented to, but because it is believed to be binding; and whatever may be the explanation or the justification for that belief, its binding force does not depend, and is not felt by those who follow it, to depend on the approval of the individual or the state to which it is addressed."

246. Clapham, note 129, at p. 44.
247. See O. A. Elias and C. L. Lim, *The Paradox of Consensualism in International Law*, The Hague, Kluwer, 1998.
248. Clapham, note 129, at p. 50.
249. *Ibid.*

Consent is, shall we say, paradoxical in that way as an explanation of the basis of legal obligation [250]. In his review of Brierly's *Basis of Obligation in International Law*, Charles Anthony Woodward Manning [251] had observed, astutely, that what had exercised Brierly was "the obligatory character of, rather than 'the basis of obligation in', international law" [252]. Brierly himself considered that no juridical explanation can be provided, but that this question must fall to legal philosophy to answer [253]. One influential legal philosophical view is that statements about the law (in this case, about legal sources or lawmaking) contain as well assertions about the law's justification [254]. Lawyers do question obedience to wicked legal systems, where the question of wickedness then falls into the realm of legal philosophy rather than that of what Brierly called the "juridical" realm. If we adopt this sort of view then what Elias did by questioning the Western view of sovereign consent was to advance a view not just about how international law is made but also about its justification. If consent reflects the liberty of European States then majoritarianism would express the view of the new States. In other words, he argued that the developing countries had their own political philosophy about the basis of a new kind of universal legal order, one which depended upon majoritarianism rather than sovereignty. In any event, the developing countries could hardly be expected to accept Western notions of consent when they had not consented to the law that the Western nations had imposed on them.

Elias attributed to democratic majority voting in a plenary, following consideration of reports by study groups or a subcommittee of the General Assembly, the following achievements and successes: the 1948 Universal Declaration of Human Rights [255], the aforementioned

---

250. See generally Elias and Lim, note 247.

251. Also a notable representative of the English School of international relations and an apologist for apartheid.

252. C. A. W. Manning, Book review of Brierly, Lauterpacht and Waldock, *The Basis of Obligation in International Law and Other Papers* (2019), *International Affairs*, Vol. 35 (1959), p. 82.

253. For a contemporary attempt to ground international legal obligation in the fulfilment in practice of criteria of legitimacy inherent in the concept of law, see J. Brunnée and S. J. Toope, *Legitimacy and Legality in International Law*, Cambridge, Cambridge University Press, 2010.

254. See R. Dworkin, "Legal Theory and the Problem of Sense", in R. Gavison (ed.), *Issues in Contemporary Legal Philosophy*, Oxford, Oxford University Press, 1987, pp. 9-20. Also R. Dworkin, *Law's Empire*, Cambridge, MA, Belknap Press of Harvard University Press, 1986, at pp. 108-113.

255. UNGA Res. 217 (III), "International Bill of Human Rights", A: "Universal Declaration of Human Rights", adopted at the 183rd plenary meeting of the 3rd session of the UN General Assembly, 10 December 1948, UN Doc. A/RES/217(III).

Declaration on the Granting of Independence to Colonial Countries and Peoples (1960) [256] and Charter of Economic Rights and Duties of States (1974) [257], the 1970 Declaration on Friendly Relations [258] and the 1966 Resolution on Apartheid as a Crime Against Humanity [259]; as well as the two human rights covenants of 1966 [260], the 1973 Apartheid Convention [261] and the 1948 Genocide Convention [262]. It hardly amounts to a meek acceptance of the idea of a universal legal order that compels non-European acceptance of the European Law of Nations [263]. Elias's was instead a frontal attack [264]. He wrote at a time when there was a gulf still between "Marxist" and "bourgeois" conceptions. His "democratic justification" for international law – the idea that numbers can outvote power – was certainly not as radical as a Marxist conception, but by rejecting individual sovereign consent, Elias had rejected the positivist European view. It was a more radical view than Bedjaoui's that the progressive development of international law understood only as a "gap-filling" exercise would still fail to accommodate the views of developing countries. As Bedjaoui had viewed it, any draft convention could still be rejected, properly speaking, by the Western States. In other words, Bedjaoui still accepted the doctrine of individual consent.

---

256. UNGA Res. 1514 (XV), note 4.

257. UNGA Res. 3281 (12 December 1974), note 210; UNGA Res. 39/163, 103rd plenary meeting, 39th session, 17 December 1984, UN Doc. A/RES/39/163.

258. UNGA Res. 2625 (XXV), "The Declaration on Principles of International Law concerning Friendly Relations and Co-operation among States", adopted at the 1883rd plenary meeting of the 25th session of the UN General Assembly, 24 October 1970, UN Doc. A/RES/2625(XXV).

259. UNGA Res. 2202 (XXI), "The Policies of Apartheid of the Government of the Republic of South Africa", adopted at the 1496th plenary meeting of the 21st session of the UN General Assembly, 16 December 1966, UN Doc. A/RES/2202(XXI).

260. UNGA Res. 2200 (XXI) A, "International Covenant on Economic, Social and Cultural Rights, International Covenant on Civil and Political Rights and Optional Protocol to the International Covenant on Civil and Political Rights", adopted at the 1496th plenary meeting of the 21st session of the UN General Assembly, 16 December 1966, UN Doc. A/RES/2200(XXI). The ICESCR came into force on 3 January 1976, the ICCPR on 23 March 1976.

261. UNGA Res. 3068 (XXVIII), "International Convention on the Suppression and Punishment of the Crime of *Apartheid*", adopted at the 2185th plenary meeting of the 28th session of the UN General Assembly, 30 November 1973, entry into force 18 July 1976, UN Doc. A/RES/3068(XXVIII).

262. UNGA Res. 260 (III), "Prevention and Punishment of the Crime of Genocide", adopted at the 179th plenary meeting of the 3rd session of the UN General Assembly, 9 December 1948, entry into force 12 January 1951, UN Doc. A/RES/260(III).

263. Wheaton, *Elements of International Law* (3rd. ed. 1846), note 233, at p. 40.

264. For a defence of consent, arguing for a sociological view of its binding force that pays heed to what States and others claim to be the basis of international legal obligation but which accepts consensualism as dominant presently, see Elias and Lim, note 247, at pp. 255-277.

How can such a view about the sources of international law fail? For that was what was involved, not just a reformulation of the substantive rules of international economic law.

We will return later to how different present-day postcolonial views – involving the rejection of "racial capitalism", "decoloniality", and the rejection of Western modernity – are from such earlier views, but the idea that by the mid- to late 1990s a group of graduate students at Harvard, who now are distinguished professors and distinguished colleagues, might ask "whether it was feasible to have a third world approach to international law and what the main concerns of such an approach might be" was in a sense strange [265].

G. Optimist

Where Bedjaoui had tested the limits of "progressive development", citing the futility of filling in the gaps left in codifying colonial practice, and Elias had, similarly, sought to reshape sources doctrine, R. P. Anand considered that a "complete rejection of the rules of international law" would have been infeasible [266]. In this, Anand saw the existing order as having already been transformed by the emergence of the new Asian and African States.

Recall Anand's account of how Japan's efforts to gain the recognition of the European society of nations had led to acceptance of colonial conquest as an "international" ideal and how its conduct in the First Sino-Japanese War (1894-1895) was celebrated by Westlake at Cambridge and Holland at Oxford. The historical record shows how this ran against opinion in the British Government where unease had set in, against the backdrop of an Anglo-Japanese Alliance concluded in 1902. In any event, Japan won recognition as a civilised power. Within that nation it proved the Meiji Restoration a success and had considerable consequences for Korea, the rise of Japan as the pre-eminent Asian power, the conditions which led to the Russo-Japanese

265. J. T. Gathii, "TWAIL: A Brief History of Its Origins, Its Decentralized Network, and a Tentative Bibliography", *Trade, Law and Development*, Vol. 3 (2011), pp. 26-64, at p. 28.

266. P. Singh, "Reading RP Anand in the Post-Colony: Between Resistance and Appropriation", in J. Von Bernstorff and P. Dann (eds.), *The Battle for International Law: South-North Perspectives on the Decolonization Era*, Oxford, Oxford University Press, 2019, pp. 297-318, at p. 301, citing B. S. Chimni, "The World of TWAIL: Introduction to the Special Issue", *Trade Law and Development*, Vol. 3 (2011), pp. 14-25, at p. 18.

War (1904-1905) and, finally, to Japan's role in the First and Second World Wars.

Following the end of the Second World War, during the Tokyo Trials, Judge Radhabinod Pal of India uttered his famous dissent as a member of the International Military Tribunal for the Far East [267]. Citing Hans Kelsen, he considered the trials, notwithstanding atrocities such as the Rape of Nanjing, to have been no more than victors' justice, applying retrospectively the crime of aggression and crimes against humanity [268]. Pal considered that the United States had forced Japan into the war and that the absence of representatives from the defeated powers was an injustice [269]. Allied personnel, he said, were free from prosecution [270]. The Indian Government distanced itself [271], and, as Singh has described it, so did R. P. Anand as a consistently strong advocate of international adjudication. Yet notwithstanding his belief in the promise of international law, his support for international adjudication and enthusiasm for the UN Conference on the Law of the Sea [272], and his reputation as perhaps the most cosmopolitan scholar in Asia, Anand was acutely aware of the uneven history of the European Law of Nations [273].

His corpus puts the lie to the proposition today that a "turn to history" owes its impetus to recent scholarship. He was decades ahead of today's re-readings of the prehistory of modern international law. In an article in the *American Journal of International Law* Anand drew a sharp distinction between the tradition of "Vitoria, Suarez, Gentili, Grotius, Pufendorf, Bynkershoek, Wolff and Vattel" who had conceived of a universal system, and "Wheaton, Phillimore, Hall, Oppenheim,

267. The *United States of America* et al. v. *Araki, Sadao* et al., Pal J. dissenting; see "Judgment of the Member from India", in B. V. A. Röling and C. F. Rüter (eds.), *The Tokyo Judgment: The International Military Tribunal for the Far East (IMTFE), 29 April 1946-12 November 1948*, Vol. 2, Amsterdam, APA-University Press Amsterdam, 1977, reprinted in *International Military Tribunal for the Far East: Dissentient Judgment of Justice Pal*, Tokyo, Kokusho-Kankokai, 1999.

268. *Ibid.*, at p. 10.

269. *Ibid.*

270. *Ibid.*

271. Singh, "Reading RP Anand", note 266, at p. 308.

272. R. P. Anand, *Compulsory Jurisdiction of the International Court of Justice*, London, Asia Publishing, 1961; R. P. Anand, *Studies in International Adjudication*, Dobbs Ferry, NY, Oceana Publications, 1969; R. P. Anand, *International Courts and Contemporary Conflicts*, New York, Asia House, 1974; R. P. Anand, *Legal Regime of the Sea-Bed and the Developing Countries*, Leiden, A. W. Sijthoff, 1976; R. P. Anand, *Origin and Development of the Law of the Sea*, The Hague, Nijhoff, 1983.

273. See also B. V. A. Röling, *International Law in an Expanded World*, Amsterdam, Djambatan, 1960.

Fauchille, Westlake and others" as promoters of a standard of civilisation in international law that had put paid to a universal legal order [274]. To the "others" we might add Travers Twiss, who thought non-Western peoples lacked the capacity for reciprocity, although as Professor Koskenniemi has argued, this was due to fears that the Far Eastern kingdoms would reject treaties which they considered unequal [275], and also Henri Bonfils, who shared views very similar to Wheaton's [276]. Anand had been inspired by the natural lawyer, universalist and pioneer of the history of international law C. H. Alexandrowicz [277], and while today we might redraw the lines differently, blame Gentili [278], re-read Vitoria [279], or ask if we treat Oppenheim unjustly, non-Western international legal historians owe an inestimable debt to the late Polish scholar.

Anand himself had, wrongly I believe, considered that there was no Asian-African view [280], and in any case, that a (truly) universal order should be preferred instead [281]. It was a different time. A time before the claim which we hear today that the efforts of the first generation had "failed", attributing the reason for such alleged failure to the earlier post-colonial generation's refusal to reject a "Western-led" international

274. R. P. Anand, "Role of the 'New' Asian-African Countries in the Present International Legal Order', *American Journal of International Law*, Vol. 56 (1962), pp. 383-406. See also R. P. Anand, "Attitude of the Asian-African States Toward Certain Problems of International Law", *International and Comparative Law Quarterly*, Vol. 15 (1966), pp. 55-75.

275. See Koskenniemi, *Gentle Civilizer*, note 18, at p. 133.

276. See further A. Heraclides and A. Dialla, *Humanitarian Intervention in the Long Nineteenth Century*, Manchester, Manchester University Press, 2015, at chap. 3.

277. See C. H. Alexandrowicz, "Doctrinal Aspects of the Universality of the Law of Nations", *British Yearbook of International Law*, Vol. 37 (1967), p. 507 *et seq*.

278. Grant, "Francisco de Vitoria and Alberico Gentili", note 120.

279. R. Lesaffer, "International Law and its History: The Story of an Unrequited Love", in M. Craven, M. Fitzmaurice and M. Vogiatzi (eds.), *Time, History and International Law*, Leiden, Martinus Nijhoff, 2006, pp. 27-41; A. Anghie, "Francisco de Vitoria and the Colonial Origins of International Law", *Social and Legal Studies*, Vol. 5 (1996), pp. 321-336.

280. Anand wrote that this was "due to geographical, political, social, cultural and other factors, these countries exhibit great differences, not only in their ways of life, but even in their thinking and practice"; Anand, "Attitude", note 274, at p. 56.

281. Anand, as we have seen, wanted solidarity among the developing countries, and particularly on the Asian continent. In 2004, as his guest in New Delhi to speak on the creation of an Asian Society of International Law, he said he had waited too long to see its creation but doubted that he would do so in his lifetime. See also M. Sornarajah, "Special Panel in Honour of Professor R. P. Anand", 28 August 2021, UN Audiovisual Library, https://legal.un.org/avl/ls/anandpanel.html.

legal order[282]. Anand was also an optimist, and I have tried in this lecture to capture the optimism of his age. He wrote that[283]:

> "With the threat of a limited use of force reduced, because of the danger of its developing into a devastating nuclear war, they [the developing nations] can maintain their positions even against the might of the big Powers. This would not have been possible before the Second World War. The existence of an international forum, such as the United Nations, where they can make their voices heard and where they have some scope for concerted action, enhances their power and helps them in pursuing their purposes. They are further helped by the rivalry between the big Powers, since it has incapacitated the 'potential directorate of the five permanent members of the Security Council' and has shifted the power to the General Assembly, the stronghold of the small countries, where they enjoy complete formal equality with the big Powers and, of course, numerical superiority."

He was deeply interested in questions of power, specifically in shifts in power[284], but in this too he shared something with Elias. There was what he termed the "horizontal extension of international society", and he thought that a "true world society" was emerging[285]. This was also, not merely coincidentally, the New Haven language of the Yale School of International Law[286]. Whether or not he was embraced by that school[287], it was for him not that the international legal order had

---

282. Lim, "Neither Sheep", note 230, at p. 301; Danielsen, Book review of Anghie's *Imperialism*, note 231, at p. 763.

283. Anand, "Attitude", note 274, at p. 55.

284. Sornarajah, "Special Panel", note 281.

285. Anand, "Attitude", note 274, at p. 55.

286. The sociological method of the Yale School focuses on "participants", "perspectives", "situations", "base values", "strategies" and "outcomes". In this regard, there had been, in Anand's view, a shift in participants, perspectives, the arena, situations and base values, raising questions about strategies and possible outcomes. See e.g. Michael Reisman, "McDougal's Jurisprudence: Utility, Influence, Controversy", *Proceedings of the Annual Meeting (American Society of International Law)*, Vol. 79 (1985), pp. 266-285, p. 273; L. Chen, *An Introduction to Contemporary International Law: A Policy-Oriented Perspective*, New Haven, CT, Yale University Press, 1989, at p. 16; R. Higgins, *Problems and Process: International Law and How We Use It*, Oxford, Oxford University Press, 1994; R. Higgins, "International Law and the Avoidance, Containment and Resolution of Disputes: General Course on Public International Law", *Recueil des cours*, Vol. 230 (1991), pp. 9-342; M. S. McDougal, "International Law, Power and Policy: A Contemporary Conception", *Recueil des cours*, Vol. 82 (1953), pp. 137-258.

287. There is the suggestion that he was not embraced by the Yale School, unlike V. S. N. Murty.

to be rejected in order to effect its change, but that the social structure of that legal order had already been transformed [288]:

> "The alteration in the sociological structure of the international society must, of course, be accompanied by an alteration in law. Law, it has been well said, is not a constant in a society, but is a function. In order that it may be effective, it ought to change with changes in views, powers and interests in the community. The conditions under which the classical, traditional law of nations developed, the views which it contained and the interests which it protected, have all greatly changed."

H. Rejectionism today

For Anghie of the TWAIL movement, imposing loan conditions requiring trade and investment liberalisation, improvements in the rule of law, particularly in the legal protection of property and contracts, and encouragement of international arbitration, all hold developing countries to a new standard of civilisation [289]. Aside from the emphasis on the continued role of the civilisational standard, his views do not differ that markedly from the previous generation, while there were always those who had advocated a more radical path towards the transformation of the international legal order. Socialist internationalism, for example, was seen as a force productive of "disorder and anarchy", not least in advocating the self-determination of colonial peoples [290]. Its influence and effect on the global order and the international legal order in the twentieth century cannot be denied or ignored. For many non-Western nations, however, the preferred path may have been non-alignment, but still, as Antonio Cassese once wrote, notwithstanding the USSR's rejection of "bourgeois treaties" [291]:

> "In fact, the Soviet Government did not reject international law wholesale – indeed, it could not have done so without becoming

288. Anand, "Attitude", note 274, at p. 63.

289. See e.g. Anghie, "Evolution of International Law", note 46, at p. 749; A. A. Shalakany, "Arbitration in the Third World: A Plea for Reassessing Bias under the Specter of Neoliberalism", *Harvard International Law Journal*, Vol. 41 (2000), pp. 419-468.

290. A. Cassese, *International Law in a Divided World*, Oxford, Oxford University Press, 1986, at p. 58, citing R. Lansing, *Papers Relating to the Foreign Relations of the United States, 1917-1919*, Vol. 2, Washington, US Government Printing Office, 1932, at pp. 247-248, 253.

291. Cassese, *Divided World*, note 290, at p. 59.

> an outcast in the world community: one cannot be a member of a social group and at the same time dismiss all its rules, at least some of them must be complied with since otherwise international relations become impossible with the group as a whole ostracizing the recalcitrant member by condemning it to complete isolation."

Yet this now, as we shall see, is what some of today's postcolonial scholars would urge, while those like Makau Mutua caution that "a certain degree of universality is inevitable" [292], as does Anghie, as will also be evident when we come back to this discussion later.

There is at the same time nothing new about criticism of sovereignty as an organising principle, as an explanation of legal personality and the sources of international law. It is something already familiar following the emergence of a new stream of international law scholarship by the 1980s. To take just the example of Anthony John Carty's *Decay of International Law*, first published in 1986, we find there the strongest criticism of the idea of a system of equal sovereigns [293].

The latest development today, however, is a decolonial approach. While redressing "racial capitalism" is linked, it is not what distinguishes decoloniality. Many Twailers view themselves as a part of an intellectual and political movement that aims not only to deconstruct international law, like Carty and other critical international lawyers, but also to present the subject from a postcolonial viewpoint [294]. They criticise the idea of an imagined impartial or universal perspective as Elias's generation had sought to articulate in their pursuit of universalism. Decolonial international lawyers now go further and argue that even postcolonial scholars, even when they are located in the Global South, will be unable to critique international law effectively since they continue to operate within a framework of coloniality. Decoloniality identifies that framework as Western modernity itself [295]. According to this latest turn, which one might characterise as epistemological, "the fact that one is socially located in the oppressed side of power relations

292. Mutua, note 180, at p. 37.

293. Carty, *Decay* (1986), note 63, at pp. 1-2 (only an incomplete system), 27 (a rudimentary law of treaties), 69-74 (difficulties with discovering legal consciousness); Carty, *Decay* (2nd ed. 2019), note 67, at pp. 29-30, 60, 87-90.

294. Mutua, note 180, at p. 36; J. T. Gathii, "Twenty-Second Annual Grotius Lecture: The Promise of International Law – A Third World View", *Proceedings of the Annual Meeting (American Society of International Law)*, Vol. 114 (2020), pp. 165-187, at p. 178.

295. See W. D. Mignolo, *The Darker Side of Western Modernity: Global Futures, Decolonial Options*, Durham, NC, Duke University Press, 2011.

does not automatically mean that he/she is epistemically thinking from a subaltern epistemic location" [296].

Where the first generation had included prominent government legal advisers, diplomats and practitioners, perhaps because of the TWAIL movement's oft-unspoken antipathy today towards mainstream international legal practice, they often huddle at a distance. And I mean not just at a distance from barristers' chambers or law firms or the doors of foreign ministries but, with a few exceptions, also in the routine activities of international lawmaking. This last includes efforts today to develop such things as model investment contracts or a reformed system for the settlement of investment disputes. The decolonial movement, which in effect is, as I have said, largely a turn to philosophy, lies at an even greater remove than the TWAIL movement. Decoloniality sees knowledge as colonialism, it rejects any possibility of erasing the vestiges of the latter, including from international law, without an accompanying rejection of Western modernity. Decoloniality rejects not just capitalism but also our Enlightenment notions of technological advancement, scientific progress and modern industrial life [297]. Emerging from "postcoloniality" in the 1980s [298], decoloniality imagines a world "before the West", as it were [299], and rejects universal conceptions of progress within which we might include our present ideas about international law.

I. The quest for colonial redress

Finally, there is the issue of colonial redress and how we might understand it.

When the Dutch international lawyer B. V. A. Röling asked the Indian Prime Minister Jawaharlal Nehru who the most distinguished

296. D. G. Sánchez, "Transforming Human Rights through Decolonial Lens", *The Age of Human Rights Journal*, Vol. 15 (2020), pp. 276-303, at p. 279, quoting Ramón Grosfoguel.

297. "The master's tools will not dismantle the master's house"; Audre Lorde, *Sister Outsider*, Berkeley, CA, Crossing Press, 2007, at p. 112, quoted in C. D. Walsh and W. Mignolo, *On Decoloniality: Concepts, Analytics, Praxis*, Durham, NC, Duke University Press, 2018, at p. 7.

298. J.-F. Lyotard, *The Postmodern Condition*, Manchester, Manchester University Press, 1986 (translation by G. Bennington and B. Massumi of *La Condition postmoderne*, Paris, Les Editions de Minuit, 1979); W. Mignolo, "Modernity and Decoloniality", in *Oxford Bibliographies (Latin American Studies)*, last modified 28 October 2011, last reviewed 5 May 2017, https://doi.org/10.1093/OBO/9780199766581-0017.

299. With apologies to A. Zarakol, *Before the West: The Rise and Fall of Eastern World Orders*, Cambridge, Cambridge University Press, 2022.

international lawyers in India were, Nehru replied that they had not yet emerged since currently the international lawyers were educated in England [300]. In postcolonial lawyering's late forms, by which I mean TWAIL, whose roots lie in American Critical Race Theory and American constitutional jurisprudence [301], there is now the opposite problem, a discernible thinness in engagement with the old colonial metropolitan centres. Yet it is in the old colonial centres where the debate over reparations is sometimes at its most acute. In postcolonial international law's latest guise, characterised by a growing interest in the current decolonial movement, the view taken is for example that [302]

> "decolonising states were born into law. Yet, these foundations are historically contingent and culturally prejudicial, with a single worldview continuing to occupy the centre-ground. Those who apply a decolonial critique thus take aim at epistemology, treating everything else – including the decolonisation era – as symptoms of epistemic authoritarianism".

Tell that to those who fought for UNGA Resolution 1514. Now, three-quarters of humanity is no longer a battle cry in multilateral diplomacy but an intellectual stance inheriting Michel Foucault's more pessimistic notions about the historical contingency of (all) knowledge, absence of any absolute knowledge, the role that power plays in shaping knowledge and its directions, and about the role that knowledge plays in the perpetuation of power [303]. "Pessimism" is the word that Bedjaoui uses of today's latest form of postcolonial international law scholar-

300. Singh, "Reading RP Anand", note 266, at p. 306.

301. See e.g. A. Freeman, "Legitimizing Racial Discrimination through Antidiscrimination Law: A Critical Review of Supreme Court Doctrine", *Minnesota Law Review*, Vol. 62 (1978), pp. 1049-1119; D. Bell, *And We Are Not Saved: The Elusive Quest for Racial Justice*, Basic Books, New York, 1987; R. Delgado, "Derrick Bell and the Ideology of Racial Reform", *Yale Law Journal*, Vol. 97 (1988), pp. 923-948; D. Bell, *Afrolantica Legacies*, Chicago, Third World Press, 1998; K. Crenshaw, "Race, Reform, and Retrenchment: Transformation and Legitimation in Antidiscrimination Law", *Harvard Law Review*, Vol. 101 (1988), pp. 1331-1387. For a short student introduction, see C. L. Lim, "Critical Race Theory", in T. Murphy (ed.), *Western Jurisprudence*, Dublin, Thomson Round Hall, 2004, p. 383 *et seq*.

302. M. al Attar and S. Abdelkarim, "Decolonising the Curriculum in International Law: Entrapments in Praxis and Critical Thought", *Law & Critique*, Vol. 34 (2021), pp. 41-62, at p. 42.

303. M. Foucault, *The Archaeology of Knowledge*, London, Vintage, 1982; *Madness and Civilisation*, London, Vintage, 1988; *The Order of Things*, London, Vintage, 1994.

ship [304]. In more recent writings, it is now argued that it is impossible merely to "decolonise the curriculum" in the universities. Accounting for diverse voices in the curriculum only reinforces Eurocentric international law's legitimacy [305]. There is no way of achieving a decolonised international legal consciousness by only tinkering with lists of what is to be read [306].

We will see in the next two lectures that redressing colonial injustice is what the different generations of post-colonial international lawyers share in common. However, there are significant generational differences. The earlier post-colonial scholars did not struggle with questions about restitution, for example in respect of looted art, and compensation for colonial-era slavery. Colonialism was not viewed as something in the distant past. Stopping the plunder was important, so was preventing its recurrence. The developing countries were to take this approach to another front, towards the creation of new rules at the frontiers of twentieth-century international law and economic life. Seventy per cent of the world is covered by the oceans and this was to capture the imagination of early post-colonial international law thought. The culmination of the UN Conference on the Law of the Sea, which had lasted a long decade, quite apart from affirming the general principle of the freedom of the high seas, and establishing a new 12-mile territorial sea limit which in fact only amounted to recognition of the new customary reality in respect of fisheries limits [307], created new regimes in the form of an exclusive economic zone and continental shelf, and a new deep seabed regime [308]. As Daniel Patrick O'Connell had put it: "It was not, however, the question of fishery limits that initiated the Third Law of the Sea Convention, but the question of access to the mineral resources of the deep sea" [309]. The developing

304. M. Bedjaoui, "Observations sur le texte d'Antony Anghie", in M. Toufayan, E. Jouannet and H. Ruiz-Fabri (eds.), *Droit international et nouvelles approches sur le Tiers-monde : entre répétition et renouveau*, Paris, Société de législation comparée, 2013, p. 81-92, at p. 83.

305. Decolonising the curriculum is "neurotic" since our "enchantment" with the "grandeur of international legal expertise", as they term it, "represents a continuous song, one that changes its sound from time to time to immortalise its spell". See al Attar and Abdelkarim, "Decolonising the Curriculum", note 302, at p. 20.

306. *Ibid.*, at p. 17.

307. *Fisheries Jurisdiction (United Kingdom* v. *Iceland)*, Merits, *ICJ Reports 1974*, p. 1.

308. It was a forum in which postcolonial concerns were aired, including on the subject of a new institution for third-party dispute settlement. See Sands, *Last Colony*, note 1, at chap. 3.

309. D. P. O'Connell, *The International Law of the Sea*, Vol. 1, edited by I. A. Shearer, Oxford, Clarendon, 1982, at p. 25.

countries had sought to enact the rules for an imagined future world [310]. Their inspiration was the Maltese Ambassador Arvid Pardo [311]. It is not difficult to discern the scheme of collectivist production introduced by the Latin American States [312]. It was broadly supported as a kind of ministry of production of a collective State [313], while delegations like the United States had objected [314].

Third World concerns were not always expressed as a demand for reparations but an attempt to define the rights and duties of post-colonial states. Yet, as we shall see, they fit today within the structure and content of our contemporary Articles on the Responsibility of States for Internationally Wrongful Acts (ARSIWA). Assume that a colonial wrong can be shown to be an international wrong [315]. Attempts to stop the plunder or prevent its recurrence would fall not within Chapter II ("Reparation for Injury") of Part II of ARSIWA but within Chapter I ("General Principles") of the same part concerning cessation and non-repetition [316]. Such attempts to prevent colonialism and its recurrence were forward-looking and, unlike in Chapter II, leave a broader choice

310. C. C. Joyner, "Legal Implications of the Concept of the Common Heritage of Mankind", *International and Comparative Law Quarterly*, Vol. 35 (1986), pp. 190-199. See further S. Ranganathan, "Decolonization and International Law: Putting the Ocean on the Map", *Journal of the History of International Law*, Vol. 23 (2021), pp. 161-183.

311. Quoted in H. S. Rana, "The 'Common Heritage of Mankind' and the Final Frontier: A Revaluation of Values Constituting the International Legal Regime for Outer Space Activities", *Rutgers Law Journal*, Vol. 26 (1994), p. 225 *et seq.*, at p. 236.

312. Working Paper on the Regime for the Sea Bed and Ocean Floor and Its Subsoil Beyond the Limits of National Jurisdiction, UN Doc. A/AC.138/49, 4 August 1971; Ranganathan, "Decolonization and International Law", note 310, at p. 172.

313. See also Elias, *New Horizons*, note 235, at p. 65 *et seq*.

314. In the same vein, it was also to reserve any claims to sovereignty in Antarctica, notwithstanding the Antarctic Treaty. Though it was not alone in this. See e.g. C. R. Buxton, "Property in Outer Space: The Common Heritage of Mankind Principle v. the 'First in Time, First in Right' Rule of Property Law", *Journal of Air Law and Commerce*, Vol. 69 (2004), pp. 689-707, at p. 696.

315. As presently is the subject of an ongoing Belgian national debate but where so far an apology has been rejected by the commission established by the Belgian Federal Parliament. See further S. El Amouri and S. Smis, "Inter-State Apologies for Colonial Injustices from a State Responsibility Perspective: A Commentary on the Belgian Controversy", *ASIL Insights*, Vol. 27 (2023), https://www.asil.org/insights/volume/27/issue/4.

316. Specifically, Art. 30 concerning "cessation and non-repetition", and not Art. 31 concerning "Reparation". See Articles on the Responsibility of States for Internationally Wrongful Acts (ARSIWA), adopted by the ILC at its 53rd session, 2001, *Yearbook of the International Law Commission, 2001*, Vol. 2, Part 2.

of means of redress rather than being confined to the standard of "full reparation"[317].

This was how the first generation of post-colonial international lawyers saw colonial redress.

317. See Art. 43 (2) *(b)* in Chap. I, Part III, ARSIWA, under which an injured State can – in other words, is free to – specify "what form reparation should take in accordance with the provisions of part two".

CHAPTER III

RIGHTS OF THE POST-COLONIAL STATE

A. To prevent injustice recurring

We have seen how lawmaking is linked to the obtainment of redress through rules that would prevent future injustice. In turn, redress was linked to the articulation of the rights of the newly decolonised State. The whole effort, however, has been misrepresented, also in current misreadings in the TWAIL literature, as some form of anti-capitalist project.

Third World approaches are identified today with criticism of free trade and of investors' rights that developed from the classical right to hospitality [318]. It creates a risk of misimpression. The idea that the developing countries and Third World lawyers were opposed to global trade and ownership rights is false. In the wake of decolonisation, they reformulated rules of commerce and views about ownership rights that had been previously justified on civilisational and colonial grounds. These included the legitimacy of colonial acquisition of private ownership and the promotion of trade as part of the civilising mission. The developing countries, having become independent, now sought access to world markets on their own terms as well as freedom from unjust debt burdens, and they sought to reclaim their extractive and other industries. What rights and duties the new States should possess had by now become a central question. In this regard [319]:

> "There are two ways to understand historic wrongdoing, prospectively or retrospectively. To focus retrospectively is to focus on redress and rectification. . . . To focus prospectively is to focus on the relationship of historic wrongdoing to international law today and to seek to change the law."

318. As Christopher Dietrich puts it, "[a]nticolonial lawyers" forming an invisible college have now "inhabited and employed the structural process of decolonization to create a school of legal thought about the international distribution of wealth and power". See C. Dietrich, "Erasing the Marks of Domination: Economic Sovereignty, Decolonization, and International Lawmaking in the 1950s and 1960s", *Journal of the History of International Law*, Vol. 23 (2021), pp. 113-136, at p. 118.

319. J. Linarelli, M. Salomon and M. Sornarajah, *The Misery of International Law*, Oxford, Oxford University Press, 2018, at p. 66.

The first post-colonial generation were as aware of "reparations" as today's postcolonial international lawyers and while they appeared to be concerned with an equitable redistribution of access to the deep seabed's resources, or "non-reciprocal" trade concessions from the industrialised West, or a clean slate in connection with colonial debt, none of these were pleas but demands. They were formulating the rights, the entitlements, of the post-colonial State and rather than merely seek "full reparation" for the past, they also sought to prevent the perpetuation of injustice. They looked forwards not just backwards, but without sacrificing a sense of right.

B. Tariffs and reprisals

In nineteenth-century Northeast Asia, resistance to European international law took the form of assertions of tariff autonomy and, as with nineteenth-century Latin America, there was fear of armed reprisals by foreign nations. The Boxer Intervention had been cited by Lassa Oppenheim as a key example of legitimate armed reprisals, Franz von Liszt having earlier considered occupation to be a legitimate act of reprisal unregulated by the laws of war rather than by Christianity and humane considerations. But by the preparations for the 1927 session of the Institut de droit international in Lausanne, Zhou Wei (Tchéou Wei), China's first Francophone international lawyer, had proposed the rejection of armed reprisals, saying that we would surely be doing an inestimable service for all of humanity by removing from it that constant scarecrow perspective that the great powers' military often used, and that the facts in the past are too numerous for him to need to quote them [320]. Here was a Chinese embrace of the Latin American Calvo doctrine [321]; after all, we might observe, Calvo's great work had been published in Paris.

Turning to India, a century earlier the East India Company too had claimed the sovereign right of reprisal [322]. While Vitoria, Pufendorf and Wolff had deliberated upon the status of unknown lands inhabited by non-Europeans, Grotius considered the East Indies to have been organised, and during the sixteenth and seventeenth centuries some of these indeed were, as with Mughal India, treated as sovereign, independent

320. W. Tchéou, "Observations de M. Tchéou-Wei. Genève, le 21 mars 1926", *Annuaire de l'Institut de droit international*, Vol. 33 (1927), p. 515 *et seq.*, at p. 517.

321. See further Mitchell, *Recentering the World*, note 154, pp. 92, 156.

322. Koskenniemi, *Uttermost Parts*, note 32, at p. 768.

entities possessing a capacity to enter into treaty relations. Or at least they were nominally treated as such. Thus was the kaleidoscopic terrain of international relations at the time, and it was Alexandrowicz who famously quoted Grotius's words, which later were crossed out of the *De Jure Praedae*: "Alia enim India, alia Americana ratio est" [323]. Franciscus Seraphim de Freitas (1570-1633) also considered these to be occupied territories, and Alexandrowicz said that Freitas had used the word "discovery" only in a geographical rather than juridical sense [324]. It was only later that the same territories and peoples were considered to be vassals, dependencies and protectorates.

Yet wherever there was colonialism, in East or West, there appeared also a common commercial thread. A seventeenth-century Grotius-Freitas debate, perhaps less well known than the Grotius-Selden debate [325], took place over whether sovereignty could constrain freedom of commerce in the form of the seaborne trade. The story of the seizure near Singapore by the Dutch East India Company of the Portuguese carrack, the Santa Catarina, containing a massive bounty taken as prize continues to find a place in popular accounts today [326]. The 21-year old Grotius had written what perhaps became the best known international law opinion given for a fee, one still cited after more than 400 years. *Mare Liberum*, which Freitas referred to as "The Incognito", was published anonymously in 1609 and three years later was included in the Spanish Inquisition's index of forbidden works [327]. Grotius answered "no", citing in his defence Vitoria and the radical Catholic jurist and humanist Fernando Vázquez de Menchacha (1512-1569) [328], for whom people and things in their natural state were unbounded, thus laying an early foundation for the consent of the governed to become the basis of sovereignty. Ten years later, during negotiations between the Dutch and English, Grotius went on to reply somewhat inconsistently to being shown his own writing that freedom of commerce could nonetheless be limited by treaty and that Dutch treaties in particular had granted

323. Alexandrowicz, "Treaty and Diplomatic Relations", note 95, at p. 221.
324. *Ibid.*, at pp. 228-229.
325. M. Brito Vieira, "*Mare Liberum* v. *Mare Clausum*: Grotius, Freitas, and Selden's Debate on Dominion over the Seas", *Journal of the History of Ideas*, Vol. 64 (2003), pp. 361-377.
326. R. G. Almond, "Lords of Navigation: Grotius, Freitas and the South China Sea", *The Diplomat*, 22 May 2016, https://thediplomat.com/2016/05/lords-of-navigation-grotius-freitas-and-the-south-china-sea/.
327. Brito Vieira, note 325, at p. 362.
328. See further David Armitage's introduction in H. Grotius, *The Free Sea*, Indianapolis, Liberty Fund, 2014, at p. xv.

monopoly rights to exclude England from the East Indies trade. War between the two countries resulted [329]. This, perhaps the relatively lesser discussed aspect of Grotius's views on the freedom of the seas and of commerce, has an obvious significance for a colonial reading of the history of international law.

The centrality of an economic justification for colonialism was also notable in Adam Smith's (1723-1790) *Wealth of Nations*, in which we find Smith saying [330]:

> "China seems to have been long stationary, and had probably long ago acquired that full complement of riches which is consistent with the nature of its laws and institutions. But this complement may be much inferior to what, with other laws and institutions, the nature of its soil, climate, and situation might admit of. A country which neglects or despises foreign commerce, and which admits the vessels of foreign nations into one or two of its ports only, cannot transact the same quantity of business which it might do with different laws and institutions."

Clearly, the Chinese knew not what to do with that which providence had bestowed upon them. Smith adds [331]:

> "The policy of China favours agriculture more than all other employments. . . . The Chinese have little respect for foreign trade. Your beggarly commerce! was the language in which the Mandarins of Pekin used to talk to Mr. de Lange, the Russian envoy, concerning it. Except with Japan, the Chinese carry on, themselves, and in their own bottoms, little or no foreign trade; and it is only into one or two ports of their kingdom that they even admit the ships of foreign nations. Foreign trade therefore is, in China, every way confined within a much narrower circle than that to which it would naturally extend itself, if more freedom was allowed to it, either in their own ships, or in those of foreign nations."

Still, exclusive European rights were rejected by Gentili, Pufendorf, and Wolff. In Wolff's case, this was because he considered the

---

329. B. Arneil, "John Locke, Natural Law and Colonialism", *History of Political Thought*, Vol. 13 (1992), pp. 587-603, at p. 590. See further Alexandrowicz, "Treaty and Diplomatic Relations", note 95, at pp. 226-229.

330. See A. Smith, *An Inquiry into the Nature and Causes of Wealth of Nations*, London, T. Nelson and Sons, 1852 (orig. 1776), I.11.

331. *Ibid.*, IV.9.

Chinese, however imprudent, had nonetheless a right to restrict foreign commerce [332].

C. Commerce

This idea of global free trade is arguably as old as Vitoria as a component of the right to hospitality under natural law, which in turn formed the basis of the *ius gentium*. Vitoria balanced on the one side aboriginal title and jurisdiction while on the other side were Spanish rights to communication and hospitality – based upon the human good of sociability or friendship [333]. Grotius later wrote in the context of the Dutch East India Company's competition with Portugal for the East Asian trade that: "The wealth of our state is chiefly if not entirely sustained" by "commerce with Asia" [334]. While Vattel did go on later to accept that non-Western societies may exclude others from their domain, he however criticised such exclusions as a violation of the duty of humanity [335].

Coming back to Grotius, it was he who advanced greatly an incipient version of the Lockean, and later Vattelian, agricultural thesis [336], according to which those who worked the land owned it. Grotius considered that as such, Europeans had the right to use and effective occupation [337]. It is in Samuel von Pufendorf, about whom I shall say a little more later, that we find the existence rather of a perfect right of non-European peoples to ownership as against only an imperfect right of hospitality, and the right of non-Europeans to reject European trade [338].

---

332. Cavallar, "Vitoria, Grotius, Pufendorf, Wolff and Vattel", note 119, at p. 201.

333. Anghie, "Evolution of International Law", note 46, at p. 743; A. Fitzmaurice, "Property, Trade, and Empire", in R. Lesaffer, *The Cambridge Companion to Hugo Grotius*, Cambridge, Cambridge University Press, 2021, pp. 275-290, at p. 281, commenting on Vitoria.

334. In his *De jure praedae commentarius*, as quoted in A. Fitzmaurice, "Property", note 333, at p. 280. See also, commenting on *De jure praedae*, De la Rasilla, "Grotian Revivals", note 131, at p. 580. See further P. Borschberg, "Grotius and the East Indies", in R. Lesaffer (ed.), *The Cambridge Companion to Hugo Grotius*, Cambridge, Cambridge University Press, 2021, pp. 65-88, at p. 70, on Grotius having written his *Mare Liberum* in defence of Dutch interests.

335. G. Baker, "Right of Entry or Right of Refusal? Hospitality in the Law of Nature and Nations", *Review of International Studies*, Vol. 37 (2011), pp. 1423-1445, at p. 1430.

336. G. Cavallar, *Imperfect Cosmopolis: Studies in the History of International Legal Theory and Cosmopolitan Ideas*, Cardiff, University of Wales Press, 2011, at p. 27.

337. *Ibid.*

338. *Ibid.*, at p. 28.

But ultimately it is Vitoria whom Professor Antony Anghie today condemns for asserting such a right to hospitality in the first place; whose argument boils down to saying that while Vitoria treated the Amerindians as formally equal he, Vitoria, well knew that the Indians could not travel to Spain. Therefore, there could never have been any violation of aboriginal rights, unlike with the Spaniards who travelled to the West Indies and whose right of self-defence was triggered by the several confrontations which followed and which in turn expanded the Spanish conquest [339]. Anghie then takes a further, and I think very controversial, step where he then argues that Vitoria's treatment of the aborigines as people was somehow strategic, that it was a ruse. In other words, the allegation is that Vitoria was deceitful [340]. According to this criticism, by replacing the *ius divinium* with a universal *ius gentium*, Vitoria had also removed papal authority, which facilitated untrammelled Spanish conquest.

Others suggest an altogether different reading; that allowing the removal of indigenous rulers would have paved the way even for the removal of Catholic kings and that Vitoria would have been well aware of that danger. It is interesting that, unlike saying for example that international law began with criticism of colonialism, Vitoria has instead to be destroyed to preserve the coherence of Anghie's argument.

What does it matter, however, what writers like Vitoria and countless others thought privately unless we can show that bigotry shaped their writings? Do we now go in search of bigotry, finding it everywhere? Professor Koskenniemi has said that James Lorimer (1818-1890) was a racist and he probably was, but this begs the question [341] as to whether no one else was too, or whether sometimes we judge historical events by our own standards of present-day morality. And, even if we read Vitoria in the elaborate way Anghie would have us do, it is another thing to say that Vitoria initiated an "overarching design from the 1500s to today" [342], or that he devised an imperial international law whose uncontested and unchanging rules and doctrines were then applied

339. Anghie, "Evolution of International Law", note 46, at pp. 743-744.

340. See Anghie, *Imperialism*, note 155, at p. 20.

341. M. Koskenniemi, "Race, Hierarchy and International Law: Lorimer's Legal Science", *European Journal of International Law*, Vol. 27 (2016), pp. 415-429, at p. 416.

342. A. Gurmendi, "Borderline History at Borderline Jurisprudence: Some Thoughts on Anne Orford's *International Law & the Politics of History (Part II)*", *Opinio Juris*, 21 October 2021, https://opiniojuris.org/2021/10/21/borderline-history-at-borderline-jurisprudence-some-thoughts-on-anne-orfords-international-law-the-politics-of-history-part-ii/.

continually, uniformly and unquestioningly, throughout the course of a half millennium. Vitoria as a story of conniving deceit now transforms into an epic tale. Rather, as Alonso Gurmendi suggests, the appropriation of international law to colonial uses was primarily a nineteenth-century enterprise [343], and by the nineteenth century the Latin American and other nations had made serious efforts to put an end to gunboat diplomacy, even if postcolonial scholars today argue that it was all simply the culmination of Vitoria's ideas about Spanish rights to hospitality [344]. In fact, that right had been transformed completely from a right of communication in Vitoria to a right to free trade in Grotius's writings [345]. Pufendorf and Kant were later to develop the right to hospitality further but after that the term "largely disappears" [346].

I mean to say it matters very much when pinning the blame for colonialism on international law whether you look to Vitoria or Grotius, and if we look to Vitoria there is the fact of his defence of the indigenes, and if that is true, then international law began with criticism of colonialism. It was only later that free trade became colonialism's logic, and it was only later, when the constraints laid originally by Vitoria had compelled engagement with non-Europeans to be characterised as trade concessions and capitulations, that frustration finally broke out in the nineteenth century among the European nations. This frustration culminated in the Berlin Conference and proposed restrictions upon what can or cannot be occupied. Even if the General Act of the Conference did skirt the issue, there was subsequently the turn to civilisational arguments instead and the increasing use of treaties and agreements as licence for usurpation. I do not wish to seem unappreciative or, worse, dismissive of the occasional richness of Twailian re-readings. It is only that while as a form of literary criticism these may succeed very beautifully, that is not always adequate for understanding doctrinal disputes and differences.

D. From Berlin to Bretton Woods

It was then during the Berlin Conference that the fig leaf of free trade also had begun to yield to more overt policies. By then Britain ruled

343. *Ibid.* See also Cavallar, *Imperfect Cosmopolis*, note 336, at p. 19, citing Dr Paul Keal.

344. See further Baker, note 335, generally.

345. Baker, note 335, at p. 1433.

346. *Ibid.*, at p. 1424.

so much of the world. In time, the shift to overt, direct colonialism became bound up with debate about Britain's place in the trading world, where it could rely on preferential trade with the colonies and impose import tariffs on food. At stake was an unconditional most-favoured-nation (MFN) clause developed from the age of British free trade and which, unlike the American clause – at least until 1928 when the United States finally adopted the unconditional British clause – would accord "immediately and unconditionally" any more favourable treatment accorded to any third country [347]. A familiar account given is that of beggar-thy-neighbour policies then being adopted widely during the later interwar period, of attempts to export as much to your neighbour while simultaneously raising tariffs, as well as of the practice of widespread currency manipulation during that same period. These events in the 1930s particularly were seen as contributory to the Second World War, in the midst of which Cordell Hull, as Secretary of State, sought to dismantle the many tariff walls, doing so by employing MFN clauses in what were initially bilateral US treaties. This device eventually became "multilateralised" in the form of the unconditional and general MFN clause in Article 1 of the General Agreement on Tariffs and Trade (GATT) [348].

Following the conclusion of the Second World War, John Maynard Keynes (1883-1946) and Harry Dexter White (1892-1948) went on to develop the architecture for a post-war international economic order. In its essence, current account liberalisation would not be accompanied by capital account liberalisation. Rather, capital accounts would remain closed. Capital was not intended to flow freely across international borders but rather payments for international trade will. The aim was to rebuild a world devastated by war by rebuilding international trade through a new International Trade Organisation (ITO). Trade would not, however, be facilitated without the existence of currency stability. Thus, to stabilise currencies, the International Monetary Fund's Articles of Agreement had initially required national currencies to be pegged either to gold or to the US dollar in an attempt to reintroduce a semblance of the Gold Standard and a stability that had previously existed from the 1870s to the 1920s, then briefly again from the late 1920s to 1932. The collapse of the Gold Standard, too, was seen to have

347. McNair, *Law of Treaties*, note 69, at pp. 274-276.

348. K. Dam, "Cordell Hull, the Reciprocal Trade Agreement Act and the WTO", John M. Olin Law and Economics Working Paper No. 228, Chicago Working Paper Series, October 2004.

been a contributory cause of the Second World War. The International Bank for Reconstruction and Development (IBRD, which very soon after its creation joined with the International Development Association to form the World Bank) would in turn be tasked with post-war European reconstruction [349]. Although the IBRD was technically a specialised agency of the United Nations, and thus should have featured in the twentieth-century struggle by the new States of Asia and Africa for a new international economic order, in reality the international financial institutions – both the International Monetary Fund and the World Bank – had operated independently of the UN and the politics of decolonisation [350]. The ITO, for its part, was stillborn and it was the GATT, which had been concluded in preparation for the ITO, that the world turned to in order to regulate international trade. At its heart was a great "tariff accelerator" – Article I, an unconditional, multilateral MFN clause that required any trade liberalisation to be granted immediately and unconditionally to all other GATT members.

However, the par value system collapsed when the United States declined to peg the dollar to gold. Since currencies were required to be pegged either to the dollar or to gold, the US dollar could claim to be pegged to itself. In the words of US Secretary for the Treasury John Connally, the dollar is "our currency, but your problem" [351]. As for the World Bank, it was superseded by the US Marshall Plan.

Thus the whole Bretton Woods design never worked, but the institutions remained, as did, in the case of the ITO, its rump, the GATT. In respect of the international financial institutions, there were subsequent criticisms of policy proliferation, opaqueness, lack of accountability, and of the these institutions killing the patient with its bad medicine [352]. I have already written elsewhere about some of these aspects, and of the "turn" in the 2000s to the World Trade Organization (WTO), the GATT's successor, as another form of developmental organisation. At the WTO,

349. Cassese, *Divided World*, note 290, at pp. 325 *et seq.*; C. L. Lim and B. Mercurio, "The Fragmented Disciplines of International Economic Law after the Global Financial and Economic Crisis: An Introduction", in C. L. Lim and B. Mercurio (eds.), *International Economic Law after the Global Crisis*, Cambridge, Cambridge University Press, 2015, pp. 1-30, at pp. 8-13; A. Lowenfeld, *International Economic Law*, 2nd ed., Oxford, Oxford University Press, 2007, at pp. 595-753.

350. See e.g. D. Van Den Meerssche, "International Law as Insulation: The Case of the World Bank in the Decolonization Era", *Journal of the History of International Law*, Vol. 21 (2019), pp. 459-484.

351. Lim and Mercurio, note 349, at p. 10.

352. See e.g. J. Einhorn, "The World Bank's Mission Creep", *Foreign Affairs*, Vol. 80 (2001), pp. 22-35.

the developing countries would have a direct hand in creating market opportunities through negotiating such opportunities and shaping the rules [353], even if some might say the developing countries were not the ones asking for a "Development Round". But by the 2010s, the WTO had brought average industrial tariffs down to around 4 per cent, and it contained a system that came close to one of compulsory adjudication. It became in many ways the centrepiece of international economic law. In the absence elsewhere in the international economic law field of multilateral institutions with hard rules and, as with the WTO, a near-compulsory adjudicatory system [354], international lawyers pointed to WTO dispute settlement as the fulfilment of the nineteenth-century aim to "close the gap" in international law by subjecting international disputes to adjudication as a means of peaceful settlement [355].

However, outside the mainstream, postcolonial scholars were swift to criticise the role and functioning of the WTO [356].

E. Rewriting trade rules

Today's post-GATT era, despite the prominence given to the ill-fated Doha Development Round, operates within a WTO established partly by the post-colonial States. It is probably true to say that it was not the developing countries that had sought a "Development Round" in 2001 in the first place, but rather went along with it. Although varied, developing countries' negotiating concerns in the Doha Round, shaped by leading members such as India and Brazil, focused upon agricultural

353. See C. L. Lim, "The Turn to Trade", in "Do International Financial Institutions Repress Development" section, *Proceedings of the Annual Meeting (American Society of International Law)*, Vol. 102 (2008), pp. 231-237, at pp. 231-237.

354. Wherein absence of a consensus against the formation of a panel and, unless appealed, a consensus against the adoption of a panel report, the WTO dispute settlement system is virtually a compulsory system of adjudication even if, technically, panel and appellate reports require adoption by a supervisory political organ, the Dispute Settlement Body, and even if the argument can be made that adopted reports are not "binding" in the sense that there are options open to the losing WTO Member other than compliance with the recommendations therein such as compensation and, failing that, being subject to authorised retaliation. See further J. H. Bello, "The WTO Dispute Settlement Understanding: Less is More", *American Journal of International Law*, Vol. 90 (1996), pp. 416-418.

355. J. B. Moore, *International Adjudications: Ancient and Modern*, Oxford, Oxford University Press, 1929, at pp. xxxvi–xci.

356. As well as the international financial institutions. See e.g. B. S. Chimni, "The WTO, Democracy and Development: A View from the South", in C. D. Birkbeck (ed.), *Making Global Trade Governance Work for Development: Perspectives and Priorities from Developing Countries*, Cambridge, Cambridge University Press, 2011, pp. 261-300, at p. 267.

subsidies in the United States, EU agricultural tariffs and market access demands. Of course, there was also interest in maintaining special and differential treatment. China was to emerge during this time to become the world's second largest economy with major export interests [357].

Rather than challenging neoliberalism in the West, the largest of these developing countries supported trade liberalisation. China is keenly aware that a shift in the WTO power balance lies in their favour precisely because of their integration into global markets. If anything, the crisis now facing the WTO is probably the result not of developing countries rejecting but rather embracing the institution [358]. It does not mean that there has not been criticism of the WTO [359], but such criticisms today have largely only a rhetorical impact [360].

In contrast, criticism of trade rules during the twentieth century was an altogether different matter. It puts into question the idea today, suggested by TWAIL scholars, that the NIEO had failed. An account of how the developing countries advanced their trading interests should begin with the 1958 report by Gottfried Haberler, the Austrian-American economist. The Haberler Report showed a decline in the terms of trade of commodity-producing countries. Commodity prices had fallen by 5 per cent from 1955. Industrial prices had risen by 6 per cent. The findings were similar to those in the earlier 1949 report by Raúl Prebisch, President of Argentina's Central Bank. Prebisch is known for the Prebisch-Singer thesis (with Hans Singer) that "peripheral" developing countries' terms of trade deteriorate over time due to a decline in the price of primary commodities relative to that of manufactured goods produced by the "centre". A second Prebisch Report followed in 1964, which then triggered demands from developing countries for preferences at the newly established United Nations Conference on Trade and Development (UNCTAD). Prebisch had blamed the developed countries for not opening their markets to the poor countries. Spurred on, the developing countries in the GATT rejected the idea that when obtaining trade concessions they ought to reciprocate. They proclaimed a principle of "non-reciprocity", sought

357. C. L. Lim and J. Wang, "China and the Doha Development Agenda", *Journal of World Trade*, Vol. 44 (2010), pp. 1309-1332.

358. See K. Hopewell, *Breaking the WTO*, Stanford, CT, Stanford University Press, 2016.

359. B. S. Chimni, "Third World Approaches to International Law: A Manifesto", *International Community Law Review*, Vol. 8 (2006), pp. 3-28, at p. 10.

360. See e.g. the racial capitalist critique in M. Fakhri, "Markets, Sovereignty, and Racialization", *Journal of International Economic Law*, Vol. 25 (2022), pp. 242-258.

"preferential" market access and "special and differential treatment" [361]. These principles became a part of the struggle for a NIEO [362], with the developing countries arguing for positive discrimination [363], or substantive rather than formal equality.

The most visible symbol of the success of such demands was a Generalised System of Preferences facilitated by the so-called "Enabling Clause" [364], which allowed concessions to be given to developing countries without requiring them to be made to other GATT Contracting States [365].

There were other developing country provisions. GATT Article XVIII allows trade restrictions by the developing countries when experiencing balance-of-payment problems [366]. In other words, it

361. See R. E. Hudec, *Developing Countries in the GATT Legal System*, reprint ed., Cambridge, Cambridge University Press, 2010 (orig. 1987).

362. Thus the issue of unfavourable terms of trade was also to find its way into the 1974 Declaration on the Establishment of a New International Economic Order. See UNGA Res. 3201 (S-VI), note 209.

363. See further, for all the above, Martin Wolff, "Differential and More Favorable Treatment of Developing Countries and the International Trading System", *World Bank Economic Review*, Vol. 1 (1987), pp. 647-668, at pp. 653-655.

364. Reversing the MFN rule that requires any more favourable tariff concession made to any GATT-WTO or non-GATT-WTO Contracting State or member to be granted immediately and unconditionally, that is without any accompanying demand for a reciprocal concession, to all Contracting States or members.

365. In relaxing GATT's MFN rule, GATT Art. XXIV had permitted regional trade agreements to be formed if trade barriers towards other Contracting States were not raised, and such members of unions and free trade also committed to eliminating duties and other restrictive regulations on substantially all the trade between themselves. See GATT Art. XXIV:5 (in subparagraphs *(a)* and *(b)*, the "shall not be higher or more restrictive" standard or "external" requirement) and Art. XXIV:8 (in subparagraphs *(a)* and *(b)*, the "substantially all trade" or "internal" requirement). See further H. Gao and C. L. Lim, "Saving the WTO from the Risk of Irrelevance: The WTO Dispute Settlement Mechanism as a 'Common Good' for RTA Disputes", *Journal of International Economic Law*, Vol. 11 (2008), pp. 899-925; J.-A, Crawford and C. L. Lim, "Cast Light and Evil Will Go Away: The Transparency Mechanism for Regulating Regional Trade Agreements Three Years After", *Journal of World Trade*, Vol. 45 (2011), pp. 375-400, at p. 394 *et seq*. The developing countries wanted these stringent requirements relaxed in order that they may be granted non-reciprocal preferences which, at the same time, would not require the grantor to relax its trade barriers to other countries. The solution was to obtain a waiver from the application of Art. XXIV's requirements and eventually that waiver became permanent in the form of the "Enabling Clause".

366. "Governmental Assistance to Economic Development", which in Section B (GATT Art. XVIII:B) allows poor countries to impose tariffs, quotas and other trade restrictions where a GATT Contracting State or Party "in rapid process of development" – i.e. a developing country Contracting State – experiences "balance of payments difficulties arising mainly from efforts to expand their internal markets as well as from the instability in their terms of trade". See further the *India – Balance of Payments Measures* case: *India – Quantitative Restrictions on Imports of Agricultural, Textile and Industrial Products*, adopted 22 September 1999, WT/DS90/AB/R.

allows emergency protectionist measures [367]. However, in response to the Haberler Report the developing countries now also sought market access on a preferential basis in order to improve their terms of trade. The GATT's 1963 Programme of Action led to what is now Part IV of the GATT [368]. The new Part IV provisions conceded that "[t]here is need for a rapid and sustained expansion of the export earnings of the less-developed contracting parties" [369], that "[t]here is need for positive efforts designed to ensure that less-developed contracting parties secure a share in the growth in international trade commensurate with the needs of their economic development" [370], and that "[g]iven the continued dependence of many less-developed contracting parties on the exportation of a limited range of primary products, there is need to provide in the largest possible measure more favourable and acceptable conditions of access to world markets". The Enabling Clause, mentioned above, also refers to these provisions of Article XXXVI [371], but it is paragraph 8 of that article that states an important principle, that of non-reciprocity [372]:

> "The developed contracting parties do not expect reciprocity for commitments made by them in trade negotiations to reduce or remove tariffs and other barriers to the trade of less-developed contracting parties."

Article XXXVII then goes on to state corresponding developed country commitments: "The contracting parties shall collaborate jointly, within the framework of this Agreement and elsewhere, as appropriate, to further the objectives set forth in Article XXXVI" [373].

---

367. See e.g. J. H. Jackson, *World Trade and the Law of GATT*, Charlottesville, VA, Michie, 1969, at chap. 25; also Decision on Safeguard Action for Development Purposes, Decision of 28 November 1979, GATT Doc. L/4897; Declaration on Trade Measures Taken for Balance-of-Payment Purposes, adopted on 28 November 1979, GATT Doc. L/4904; Understanding on the Balance-of-Payment Provisions of the General Agreement on Tariffs and Trade 1994, see Annex 1A.

368. See Protocol Amending the General Agreement on Tariffs and Trade to Introduce a Part IV on Trade and Development, 8 February 1965, entry into force 27 June 1966, GATT Doc. 13S/2; GATT Secretariat, *Guide to GATT Law and Practice*, 6th ed., 2 vols., Geneva, WTO, 1994, at p. 964.

369. GATT Art. XXXVI:2.

370. GATT Art. XXXVI:3

371. Enabling Clause, at para. 7.

372. GATT Art. XXXVI:8.

373. GATT Art. XXXVIII:1. See GATT Panel Report, EC – Refunds on Exports of Sugar, BISD (27th Supp.) 69-98, March 1981, adopted on 10 November 1980, where the panel found the European Communities to have violated Art. XXXVIII.

Such demands for flexibility – which also appeared, subsequently, in the Uruguay Round's agreements [374] – are often taken to be special pleading, or based upon a claim about distributive justice, but arguably what the post-colonial States wanted was to prevent the continued effects of colonialism and to correct historical distributions so as to prevent continuing and future injustice [375]. To achieve this, the rights of the new States had to be defined. It was to become more urgent and important than restitution or monetary damages, which is what today's "postcolonialists" speak of [376].

F. Foreign ownership

At the same time, developing countries did seek restitution through nationalisations, particularly in the oil and other extractive industries. For Pufendorf, unlike Grotius, necessity cannot cause private property to revert back into common use and be acquired through use of common dominion [377]. Pufendorf had defended indigenous property ownership [378]. But American property rights in Latin America and the ancient hospitality rights of European charter companies stretching from the Congo to China had also to be defended vigorously, typically by a doctrine of armed reprisals. Subsequently, twentieth-century international law was to develop the law of responsibility for injury to aliens into a law for the protection of foreign investments, leading also to successful claims brought by the multinational oil companies.

374. Thus, for example, the preamble to the Marrakesh Agreement refers to sustainable development as one of the WTO's objectives, the General Agreement on Trade in Services of the World Trade Organization (GATS) contains a balance-of-payment difficulties provision in GATS Article XII, while least developed country WTO members were granted a longer time frame under Article 66 of the TRIPS Agreement to implement that agreement's commitments. There are 183 special and differential treatment provisions across the whole range of WTO agreements and decisions, many requiring account to be taken of developing country interests and many others granting flexibilities. See further "Special and Differential Treatment Provisions in WTO Agreements and Decisions", Note by the Secretariat, 2 March 2021, WT/COMTD/W/258.

375. See Linarelli *et al.*, note 319, at p. 66.

376. Cf. M. L. Bush, "US Must Fight the Right Fight over Special Treatment at the World Trade Organization", *The Hill*, 5 January 2023, https://thehill.com/opinion/international/3800991-us-must-fight-the-right-fight-over-special-treatment-at-the-world-trade-organization/.

377. Baker, note 335, at p. 1424.

378. *Ibid.*, at pp. 1435-1436.

The Don Pacifico affair remains a well-known illustration of the use of reprisals for injury to a national or their property [379], in which Lord Palmerston had despatched a naval squadron to blockade the Port of Piraeus and impose an embargo on Greek shipping. In the longest speech in British Parliamentary history he had declared, famously:

> "[W]hether, as the Roman, in days of old, held himself free from indignity, when he could say civis Romanus sum; so also a British subject, in whatever land he may be, shall feel confident that the watchful eye and the strong arm of England, will protect him against injustice and wrong."

The analogue in the Far East, when Palmerston again played a leading role, was the "Second Opium War", which had begun on a pretext. Chinese maritime officials had seized a Chinese-manned ship, which although its registration in Hong Kong had expired, nonetheless continued to fly the British flag. As a consequence of the eventual Chinese defeat, the 1858 Treaty of Tientsin opened ten further Chinese ports and granted Britain, Russia, France and the United States a right of legation. It granted foreign rights to navigate the Yangtze freely and rights to foreigners to travel inland. Subsequently, the Peking Convention of 1860 ceded the Kowloon Peninsula to Great Britain, established the freedom of religion, allowed British ships to carry indentured labourers to America, provided for war reparations and legalised the opium trade. Reparations were so punitive that in Article 37 (3) ARSIWA today, we find the late Gaetano Arangio-Ruiz's view that satisfaction should never amount to humiliation:

> "1. The State responsible for an internationally wrongful act is under an obligation to give satisfaction for the injury caused by that act insofar as it cannot be made good by restitution or compensation.
>
> 2. Satisfaction may consist in an acknowledgement of the breach, an expression of regret, a formal apology or another appropriate modality.
>
> 3. Satisfaction shall not be out of proportion to the injury and may not take a form humiliating to the responsible State."

379. A. McNair, *International Law Opinions*, Vol. 2, Oxford, Oxford University Press, 1956, at pp. 238-241; O. T. Johnson and J. Gimblett, "From Gunboats to BITs", in K. P. Sauvant (ed.), *Yearbook on International Investment Law & Policy 2010-2011*, Oxford, Oxford University Press, 2012, pp. 649-692, at p. 652.

Eight years after this 1860 treaty, the Argentinian jurist Carlos Calvo published his great work, *Derecho internacional teórico y práctico de Europa y América* [380]. It is sometimes thought that the Calvo doctrine was principally about an American controversy; if so, its ideas nonetheless made their way into the main General Assembly resolutions with which the new Asian and African States attempted to establish (writers in the Western hemisphere might say "change") the rules of international economic law as they applied to the newly independent States. There was a period in between, during the pre-war and interwar periods, which had produced some notable arbitrations, including the *de Sabla* and *Norwegian Shipowners' Claims* cases [381], which had upheld responsibility for injury caused to aliens and their property. Notwithstanding that the Russian Revolution and the Mexican Agrarian Revolution, and the famous exchange between Cordell Hull and his Mexican counterpart [382], had already signalled the changing winds. The Mexican Minister invoked Calvo [383]:

> "Mexico admits, in obedience to her own laws, that she is indeed under obligation to indemnify in an adequate manner; but the doctrine which she maintains on the subject, which is based on the most authoritative opinions of writers of treatises on international law, is that the time and manner of such payment must be determined by her own laws."

So far as the authoritative opinions of writers were concerned, Calvo was the most authoritative of them all.

Latin American and, later, Asian, African, and Middle Eastern scholars had not simply sat and watched, uncomprehending. In various places it was the beginning of great activity to learn the new devastating science. Among China's first international lawyers, the best known was

380. C. Calvo, *Le droit international théorique et pratique*, 4th ed., Paris, A. Rousseau, 1888 (translation of *Derecho internacional teórico y práctico de Europa y América*, Paris, D'Amyot, 1868).

381. *Marguerite de Joly de Sabla (United States)* v. *Panama*, 6 RIAA 357 (1933); *Norwegian Shipowners' Claims (Norway* v. *US)*, 1 RIAA 307 (1922).

382. US Secretary of State (Hull) to Mexican Ambassador (Castillo Nájera), 21 July 1938; Mexican Minister for Foreign Affairs (Hay) to American Ambassador (Daniels), 3 August 1938; US Secretary of State (Hull) to Mexican Ambassador (Castillo Nájera), 22 August 1938. All can be located in *Foreign Relations of the United States Diplomatic Papers 1938*, Vol. 5: *The American Republics*, Washington, DC, US Government Printing Office, 1956.

383. See G. H. Hackworth, *Digest of International Law*, Vol. 3, Washington, DC, US Government Printing Office, 1942, at pp. 655-661; also Lowenfeld, note 349, at pp. 475-481.

probably Wellington Koo [384]. China had been admitted to the League of Nations, together with Japan and Turkey, which had, it is said, achieved parity with the European States even earlier by the Treaty of Paris of 1856. Koo and others, whose efforts are described in Mitchell's new book, engaged in a concerted effort to abolish the law of reprisals and have Calvo's doctrine adopted as a universal principle [385]. By 1907 there was the Drago-Porter Convention, which prohibited force for the recovery of debt, and in 1928 the award in the *Naulilaa* arbitration between Portugal and Germany had defined the conditions for a lawful reprisal [386]. Also, by 1928, or at any rate by 1945, there had emerged the general prohibition on the use of force in international relations. Finally, the emergent global legal order had moved on from the use of armed reprisals [387].

The battle over armed reprisals having faded, the post-war newly independent nations as well as others then argued for a doctrine of "permanent sovereignty" over natural resources. Together with UNGA Resolution 1803 of 1962 [388], there were the 1973 Declaration on Permanent Sovereignty over Natural Resources [389], the 1974 Declaration on the Establishment of a New International Economic Order [390] and the 1974 Charter of Economic Rights and Duties of States, adopted by 120 votes to 6, with 10 abstentions, with a separate vote for its controversial paragraph 2 (2) *(c)*, with 104 votes to 16, with 6 abstentions [391]. Whereas Resolution 1803 of 1962 was an attempt to reaffirm the Hull standard, the 1974 Charter's Article 2 (2) *(c)* presented the Calvo doctrine as a universal doctrine, more than a hundred years after publication of Calvo's book and more than three decades after the Mexican rejection

384. Koo was President of the Council of the League of Nations, a judge at the PCIJ and, at the time, the only Chinese leader, during his brief tenure as Acting President, to have adopted a Christian name.

385. Mitchell, *Recentering the World*, note 154, at pp. 98-120.

386. Preceding wrongful act under international law, an unsatisfied demand for reparations, and proportionality. See *Portugal* v. *Germany* [the *Naulilaa* arbitration], (1928) 2 RIAA 1011-33. See also J. Zollmann, *Naulila 1914: World War I in Angola and International Law. A Study in (Post-)Colonial Border Regimes and Interstate Arbitration*, Baden-Baden, Nomos, 2016.

387. See further J. Paulsson, *Denial of Justice in International Law*, Cambridge, Cambridge University Press, 2005, at p. 13 *et seq.*

388. UNGA Res. 1803 (XVII), "Permanent Sovereignty over Natural Resources", adopted at the 1194th meeting of the 17th session of the UN General Assembly, 17 December 1962, UN Doc. A/RES/1803(XVII).

389. See Chap. II.C; UNGA Res. 3171 (XXVII), note 208.

390. UNGA Res. 3201 (S-VI), note 209, adopted without a vote; see also draft UN Doc. A/9556.

391. See Chap. II.C; UNGA Res. 3281 (XXIX), note 210.

of Cordell Hull's claim of a universal rule concerning the protection of foreign-owned property.

However, by the 1950s, there was to be another major shift. It was a doctrinal shift from saying that the Hull standard was a general customary rule towards saying that the protection of foreign-owned property and contracts was based upon "general principles of law". Its earlier beginnings lay in the *Lena Goldfields* case [392] concerning a gold mining concession in which the tribunal recognised that the application of Soviet law could be excluded by contract [393]. Later, Lord Asquith in the *Abu Dhabi* arbitration was to admit that while the concession contract was connected most closely with Abu Dhabi, it could hardly be supposed that such a primitive region would have modern commercial law and therefore the general principles of law recognised by civilised nations should apply [394]. Importantly, Lord Asquith viewed such general principles, as he put it, as a "sort of 'modern law of nature'" [395]. Now that independence from colonialism had been won there was a remarkable resurgence of naturalist thinking and scholars like Lauterpacht led the way [396].

In the *Qatar* arbitration the new naturalist view was repeated [397], where the arbitrator had applied "the principles of justice, equity and good conscience", bolstered by the tribunal's view that the ruler of Qatar, who would have profited handsomely, could hardly have intended to choose Islamic law as that would risk the contract, or parts of it, being declared void. In the *Aramco* arbitration [398], there was an impressive treatment of the ability of a sovereign State to bind itself by contract, and of the view that this created acquired rights on the part of the investor whose violation would also violate the rule against non-retroactivity. If there is doubt about the content or the meaning

392. *Lena Goldfields* v. *USSR*, *The Times*, 3 September 1930, at para. 22.

393. But see e.g. V. V. Veeder, "The Lena Goldfields Arbitration: The Historical Roots of Three Ideas", *International and Comparative Law Quarterly*, Vol. 47 (1998), pp. 747-792; A. Nussbaum, "Arbitration between the Lena Goldfields Ltd. and the Soviet Government", *Cornell Law Review*, Vol. 36 (1950), pp. 31-53.

394. *Petroleum Development (Trucial Coast) Ltd.* v. *Sheikh of Abu Dhabi*, Award of September 1951, (1951) 18 ILR 144, at p. 149.

395. *Ibid.*

396. J. Paulsson, *The Unruly Notion of Abuse of Rights*, Cambridge, Cambridge University Press, 2020, at p. 80 *et seq.*, esp. pp. 83-84, discussing Hersch Lauterpacht's naturalism in the latter's *The Function of Law in the International Community*, note 45.

397. *Ruler of Qatar* v. *International Marine Oil Co.*, Award of June 1953, (1953) 20 ILR 534, at pp. 544-545.

398. *Saudi Arabia* v. *Arabian American Oil Co. (Aramco)*, Award of 23 August 1958, (1958) 27 ILR 117, at p. 168 .

of the agreement itself, then, according to the *Aramco* tribunal, resort must also be had to general principles of law not only to interpret but also if necessary to supplement such agreements. The tribunal cited dutifully Lord Asquith's "modern law of nature". Likewise, in *Sapphire Petroleum* [399], the former Swiss federal judge Pierre Cavin considered that a reference to the rules of good faith meant that [400]:

> "It is therefore perfectly legitimate to find in such a clause evidence of the intention of the parties not to apply the strict rules of a particular system but, rather, to rely upon the rules of law, based upon reason, which are common to civilized nations. These rules are enshrined in Article 38 of the Statute of the International Court of Justice."

It was a naturalist interpretation of the Statute of the ICJ that arguably had been rejected during its drafting.

Then, in the best known of the oil arbitrations, *Texaco* v. *Libya* [401], this award was notable, first, for asserting an international order of contracts and, second, for rejecting claims to permanent sovereignty and ultimately the Calvo doctrine [402]. Admittedly, General Assembly resolutions are not in themselves binding upon States and require acceptance. In that regard Resolution 1803 had stated, in effect, that agreements entered into between the oil companies and States were binding and that arbitration agreements were also binding [403]. According to René-Jean Dupuy, that resolution was "supported by a majority of Member States representing all of the various groups", and one needed to distinguish between General Assembly resolution provisions "stating the existence of a right on which the generality of the States has expressed agreement, and those provisions introducing new principles which were rejected by certain representative groups of States and having nothing more than a *de lege ferenda* value" [404]. In this regard, the international standard for the protection of foreign-owned

399. *Sapphire International Petroleums Ltd.* v. *National Iranian Oil Co.*, Award of 15 March 1963, (1963) 35 ILR 136, at pp. 172-176.

400. *Ibid.*

401. *Texaco Overseas Petroleum Co./California Asiatic Oil Co.* v. *Government of Libya*, Award on the Merits, 19 January 1977, (1977) 17 ILM 1.

402. *Ibid.*, at para. 85. Libya had argued on the basis of UNGA Res. 3171 (see note 208) that compensation for expropriation should be determined by Libyan courts under the host State's laws (i.e. that the Calvo doctrine represents customary international law).

403. UNGA Res. 1803 (XVII), note 388, at paras. 4 and 8.

404. *Texaco*, note 401, at paras. 86-87.

property and contractual claims [405], as shown in Resolution 1803, had remained unchanged notwithstanding Resolutions 3171, 3201 and 3281 [406]. Dupuy bolstered this conclusion further by citing Michel Virally's observation that while the draft of Resolution 3281 had been presented by the Group of 77 as a "first measure of codification and progressive development", even that description had subsequently been deleted due to "the opposition of several States" [407]. Dupuy had applied a doctrine that arguably has never been international law, which is that a practice is "general" only if it represented all the major groupings [408].

The reaction of developing countries to international arbitration was less than receptive, as international arbitration illustrated how possessing *imperium* or *dominium iurisdictionis* as the newly independent States no doubt did was nonetheless distinct from *dominium proprietatis* or *dominium rerum*. Newly reclaimed sovereignty would not affect foreign property and contractual rights.

G. Occupation, protectorates and the penetration of civilisation

Westlake had rejected the suggestion that "uncivilised natives" and "savages" could cede or transfer sovereignty in the first place since they did not possess it [409]. In the classical teachings there were roughly two views. Gentili had rejected Vitoria's view of indigenous title to territory [410], albeit not in respect of private property [411], and while Grotius objected to the European civilising mission [412], nonetheless he considered that *dominium* could be acquired by occupation [413].

405. In other words, by treating contractual claims as property, or what common lawyers call a "chose in action".

406. See J. Cantegreil, "The Audacity of the *Texaco/Calasiatic* Award: René-Jean Dupuy and the Internationalization of Foreign Investment Law", *European Journal of International Law*, Vol. 22 (2011), pp. 441-458.

407. *Texaco*, note 401, at para. 88.

408. *Ibid.*, at paras. 85-86.

409. Westlake, *Chapters*, note 53, at pp. 142-143.

410. On Gentili, see also Schröder, note 129, at pp. 176-179, for his argument that rather than to rely upon a standard of civilisation, Gentili was concerned with their ability to uphold and abide by the law of nations, a criterion which subsequently the late Victorian international lawyers Westlake, Holland and Hall were to employ in distinguishing between the civilised Japanese and the Chinese.

411. See Nuzzo, "Territory", note 59, at p. 273, discussing Gentili.

412. See Cavallar, "Vitoria, Grotius, Pufendorf, Wolff and Vattel", note 119, at p. 194.

413. Except that, in his view, the Portuguese Empire, rivals to the Dutch, could not occupy the oceans.

On the other side, the good Pufendorf challenged the idea of acquisition by occupation, arguing that dominion can only be acquired with the consent and agreement of the indigenous inhabitants [414]. I am not suggesting that the classical writers can be read simply as being "colonial" or "anti-colonial" today but that essentially was Pufendorf's view even if in his writings on "sociality" or human "sociability", and notwithstanding his invaluable contribution to our modern thought on equality and human dignity, the contemporary reader will find discomfiting passages from the great secular natural lawyer [415]. Similarly, Christian Wolff considered that "unknown lands inhabited by a nation" cannot be occupied [416]. The English scholar Vaughan Lowe has similarly criticised the view that colonisation was through occupation [417]:

> "It is sometimes supposed that the European States marched into Africa, Asia and the Americas and announced that they were acquiring uninhabited lands. . . . That is not so. Lands occupied by communities which stood their ground and dealt with the colonizers, were generally not regarded as unoccupied. Much of the process of colonization was dealt with through agreements."

Was the shift to treaties and agreements with "native" rulers a rejection of the view that "savages" had no *dominium* [418]? Clearly, the minor princes of India were not Westlake's "savages". A second possible explanation could be that he, Westlake, wrote at a time when the East India Company's treaties in India had come to be called into question in Britain, which made it easier to reject such treaties. A third explanation, by Crawford [419], is that Westlake was referring to the European Law of Nations rather than British constitutional practice where the latter did consider such Indian treaties, for example, to be binding. The truth probably was, fourthly, that while there was by then widespread scepticism about native sovereignty and native treaties, it

---

414. Arneil, note 329, discusses this at p. 598. For divided opinions, see Lindley, *Acquisition*, note 21, at pp. 18 *et seq.*
415. For example, in Pufendorf's Aristotelian defence of slavery in *De jure naturae*, but let us not snatch at isolated passages rather than read things whole. See K. Saastamoinen, "Pufendorf on Natural Equality, Human Dignity, and Self-Esteem", *Journal of the History of Ideas*, Vol. 71 (2010), pp. 39-62, at p. 43.
416. B. Mueser, "The Nation and Property in Vattel's Theory of Territory", *Global Intellectual History*, Vol. 3 (2018), pp. 137-155, at pp. 141-144.
417. V. Lowe, *International Law*, Oxford, Clarendon, 2007, at p. 143.
418. Westlake, *Chapters*, note 53, at pp. 142-143.
419. Crawford, *Creation of States*, note 22, at pp. 301-302.

had also become increasingly difficult to consider African territories *territorium nullius* in the manner of the classical writers. Alphonse Rivier considered that once there was the appearance of some organisation then there no longer is room for occupation pure and simple but only room for having a protectorate, that this is what Germany had in fact done in Southern Africa, and that there was also a tendency to recognise States and to treat rudimentary or insignificant political bodies as such, and in fact this tendency is so strong that in the Congo European States simply hid their occupation under the fiction of treaties entered into with indigenous chiefs.[420] Edouard Engelhardt, too, had observed, similarly, that the majority of the takings in Africa after a certain period had been based on arrangements with local chiefs, and that the British had been careful to use this system before seizing vast regions in Southern Africa over which they made themselves protectors [421].

In short, new methods therefore were required to advance the colonial enterprise, and it probably was at this juncture that civilisational ideas as well as ideas of economic progress began to take centre stage instead, including the idea of colonial territories forming a sacred trust of Western civilisation [422]. By the later part of the nineteenth century, the Institut de droit international had before it the draft article proposed by Martitz, referred to in Chap. I.C above, stating that it mattered not whether a region was or was not "occupied" but that what was crucial was whether it was under the sovereignty or protection of a European sovereign [423]. During that debate, Pradier-Fodéré considered Martitz to have intended to designate a territory as unoccupied wheresoever "civilisation had not penetrated" [424].

It is also the Crawford view that if such treaties disguised the existence of colonies, in which European States sought the maximum of the pleasure of colonialism and the minimum of responsibility [425], that was only a European practice rather than what we might today call "international law" [426]. His care in distinguishing different types of protectorates – what he called protected States, international

420. Rivier, note 19, at p. 181.

421. *Ibid.*, at pp. 181-182. See further Lindley, Acquisition, note 21, at pp. 34, 43 (Africa was not *territorium nullius*) and p. 46 (not all territorial claims outside Europe could be justified by occupation).

422. Nuzzo, "Territory", note 59, at pp. 274-275.

423. Rivier, note 19, at p. 177.

424. *Ibid.*, at pp. 184-185.

425. Crawford, *Creation of States*, note 22, at pp. 286-303.

426. *Ibid.*

protectorates and colonial protectorates – stands in stark contrast with Judge Huber's view that the relationship created by agreements of the period "is more generally that of suzerain and vassal" [427]. How did these treaties arise? Chartered companies such as the East India Company had held sovereign rights from the seventeenth century. The East India Company enjoyed, for example in respect of Bengal, "all the Rights, Profits, Territories and Appurtenances . . . as We Ourselves now have and enjoy" [428], that is, derived from Charles II. In the *Sandys* case in England this was justified by the "common law" and "such other laws also as to be common to other nations" [429]. However, treaties of protection were entered into in India with the "native" princes under the fiction that sovereignty nonetheless remained with the Mughal Emperor [430]. Following from the diminution of Mughal sovereignty through intrigue and armed reprisals, the company itself became sovereign by the mid-eighteenth century [431]. By this time Bengal had

427. *Palmas*, note 28, at p. 858, discussing agreements of the Dutch East India Company. See also Alexandrowicz, "G. F. de Martens", note 33, at p. 184; Crawford, *Creation of States*, note 22, at p. 286.

428. Charter Granted to the East India Company relating to the Island of Bombay, 26 March 1669, in J. Shaw (ed.), *Charters relating to the East India Company from 1600 to 1761; reprinted from a former collection with some additions and a preface for the Government of Madras*, Madras, Hill, 1887, p. 48, quoted in Koskenniemi, *Uttermost Parts*, note 32, at p. 766.

429. According to Jeffreys C. J., for whom also sovereignty could be acquired over things belonging to no one; see Koskenniemi, *Uttermost Parts*, note 32, at pp. 599-603, discussing and quoting from *East India Company* v. *Sandys*, (1684) 10 St Tr 371.

430. Koskenniemi, *Uttermost Parts*, note 32, at p. 768. For a study of the preceding period, see D. Veevers, *The Origins of the British Empire in Asia, 1600-1750*, Cambridge, Cambridge University Press, 2020; also P. J. Stern, *The Company-State: Corporate Sovereignty and the Early Modern Foundations of the British Empire in India*, Oxford, Oxford University Press, 2011.

431. See V. A. Smith, *The Oxford History of India*, 3rd ed., edited by P. Spear, Oxford, Oxford University Press, 1958, providing the standard account of Bombay as a Presidency in 1662 and Surman's embassy to Delhi from 1714 and 1717, which governed the status of Madras and Calcutta (at p. 455 *et seq.*), through the War of the Austrian Succession (at p. 459 *et seq.*) whereupon Madras was restored to Britain under the Treaty of Aix-la-Chapelle which ended the war in exchange for Cape Breton Island in America which went to the French, to the acquisition of Bengal which went from Company factory to Presidency, being the last of the three main centres of British trade to be established (at p. 465 *et seq.*). By 1765 the Company had chosen the *diwani* of Bengal rather than directly replace the weak Mughal Emperor Shah Alam II as regent, and as Smith asserts: "This treaty provided a model for the system which Wellesley later developed by which Indian princes saved themselves from their enemies at the price of enmeshing themselves in the threads of the Company's spider web." Indeed, events in the Presidency of Penang, later in the Presidency of the Straits Settlements, which included Malacca and Singapore, and in the Northern and Southern Malay States, were to follow a similar pattern. See e.g. K. G. Tregonning, *A History of Modern Malaya*, Singapore, Eastern Universities Press for University of London Press, 1964, at pp. 71-161, which begins with frustration in 1767 in London at the balance of the

been reduced to penury, slavery and famine, with things coming to a head eventually only later in that century when the legal distinction between territorial conquest for the Crown and treaty territories held privately began to collapse with the Regulating Act of 1773 upholding the Crown's view [432]. Notwithstanding the East India Company Act of 1784 there was to be more misrule and plunder [433]. Formal British sovereignty was only established by the Charter Act of 1813.

By then, Crawford wrote, there were no longer protectorates as such under international law [434]. The method of keeping troops in the "native" State at its expense with a British resident or adviser in the conduct of foreign relations had been initiated, not only in India [435] but in places like the Malay Peninsula, in Perak and Selangor in 1874, and in Negri Sembilan and Pahang in 1888.

The reality of it was that colonial acquisition of territory did not yield any general pattern, which is what makes a general discussion of the topic difficult [436]. In India, there were the Maratha Wars, which resulted in treaties, the first war being won by the Marathas. In Sri Lanka, the Kandyan Kingdom held out against the British and was conquered eventually without a treaty. The aborigines in Tasmania did fight and the new view in Australia is that they were conquered. There is also the Treaty of Waitangi in New Zealand. Middle Eastern states were treated too variously. A one-size-fits-all theory would find it difficult to accommodate all the various situations.

China trade and the search by Madras officials for a new trading base in Southeast Asia. Tregonning's account encompassing a story of Indian-style presidencies as mentioned, treaties with Siam in the form of the 1826 Burney Treaty and the unsanctioned Low Treaty of the same year, and the eventual establishment, starting with Perak before extending to the other "Southern" Malay States of Selangor, Pahang and Negri Sembilan, of British advisers styled "residents" when Britain turned to a more assertive interventionist policy from the 1870s and the treatment of these Malay possessions as protected States, through to (what was seen as) the North Borneo protectorate treaty of 1888. See also J. Kennedy, *A History of Malaya, AD 1400-1959*, London, MacMillan, 1962, at pp. 67-186. There were as well the Anglo-Siamese Secret Convention of 1897 and the Bangkok Treaty of 1909, which was a protectorate treaty concluded in respect of the Northern Malay States. For the latter, see e.g. D. G. E. Hall, *A History of Southeast Asia*, London, MacMillan, 1955, at p. 612.

432. Koskenniemi, *Uttermost Parts*, note 32, at pp. 769-772.

433. For Warren Hasting's impeachment trial, see A. Carty, "The Illegality of Empire: Moral Evasion and Confusion of Historians and Literary Critics in Their Reflections on the Impeachment Trial of Warren Hastings", in M. Wan (ed.), *Reading the Legal Case: Cross-Currents between Law and the Humanities*, London, Routledge, 2013, pp. 90-107.

434. Crawford, *Creation of States*, note 22, at p. 286.

435. Koskenniemi, *Uttermost Parts*, note 32, at p. 775.

436. Private correspondence, Muthucumaraswamy Sornarajah, 5 December 2022.

Rather than the rules on treaties or on territory, or the concept of sovereignty, some scholars say that it was capitalism that played a key role. Adam Smith in his 1776 *Wealth of Nations* merely repeated John Locke's (1632-1704) agricultural thesis in the latter's *Second Treatise of Government*. Namely, that those who had made productive use of land and enclosed it, by mixing "[t]he labour of his body and the work of his hands" with "the common storehouse of the world", earned therefore a natural right to it [437]. Smith adapted the agricultural thesis to the China trade, that by despising trade the Chinese had forsaken industry and were engaging in waste. International lawyers were already widely aware of this adaptation. Vattel, in his 1758 *Le droit de gens*, had argued the same against those who "avoid labour" and "choose to live only by hunting and their flocks", and wrote that [438]:

> "Those who still pursue this idle mode of life usurp more extensive territories than, with a reasonable share of labour, they would have occasion for, and have, therefore, no reason to complain, if other nations, more industrious and closely confined, come to take possession of a part of those lands."

It is no coincidence that current postcolonial international law scholarship has focused on the role of capitalism in the history of international law [439].

It was Travers Twiss who was most explicit among the nineteenth-century writers. Twiss distinguished primitive acquisition by occupation from derivative acquisition by treaty [440]. Twiss, who was Leopold II's agent, explained precisely how a merchant adventurer could in fact enter into an international agreement with a foreign State [441]. As to whether "the agent of an association which had not the political character of a

---

437. J. Locke, *Second Treatise of Government*, edited by C. B. McPherson (ed.), Indianapolis and Cambridge, Hackett, 1980 (orig. 1690), at chap. V, sec. 27. See further J. Whitehead, "John Locke, Accumulation by Dispossession and the Governance of Colonial India", *Journal of Contemporary Asia*, Vol. 42 (2012), pp. 1-21, at p. 4; T. Flanagan, "The Agricultural Argument and Original Appropriation: Indian Lands and Political Philosophy", *Canadian Journal of Political Science*, Vol. 22 (1989), pp. 589-602, at pp. 592-595.

438. E. de Vattel, *The Law of Nations or Principles of the Law of Nature Applied to the Conduct of Nations and Sovereigns*, translated by C. G. Fenwick, Washington, DC, Carnegie Institution of Washington, 1916, I.7, at para. 81, pp. 37-38.

439. See Tzouvala, note 111, generally.

440. T. Twiss, *The Law of Nations Considered as Independent Political Communities*, Vol. 1, Oxford, Oxford University Press, 1861, at p. 160, 189-192.

441. Others who considered that agreement or consent was required for the transfer of non-European territory include Lindley, Merignhac and Descamps. See Koskenniemi, *Gentle Civilizer*, note 18, at pp. 140-141. Meanwhile, Westlake appeared

State, could, by a cession of the actual Sovereign of the country, acquire and exercise the sovereignty of a territory situated outside Europe", Twiss answered [442]:

> "Why should it be forbidden to a native chief to cede his territory to an international European company, which according to the law of nations, is perfectly capable of accepting and exercising such a sovereignty?"

The new States of Asia and Africa now had sovereignty over their petroleum resources, their gold, copper and other mineral deposits. That may be, says the European Law of Nations, but the oil wells, gold mines and copper mines, the coffee or tea plantations and the rubber plantations belonged nonetheless to their rightful owners. Injury to those rights would incur international responsibility. Property was always distinct from sovereignty [443]. The argument is that the developing countries may have recovered *imperium*, sovereignty and national authority, but that what oil companies, for example, had acquired was private *dominium*, be it through use and occupation, as was debated at the Berlin Conference, or by way of consent, contract or treaty [444].

---

to have considered treaties with non-Europeans to have been absurd. See *ibid.*, at p. 127.

442. T. Twiss, "La libre navigation du Congo" (II), translated and reprinted as "The Free Navigation of the Congo" in H. W. Wack, *The Story of the Congo Free State*, New York, Putnam, 1905, p. 502 *et seq.*, at pp. 504, 509, quoted in C. Sylvest, " 'Our Passion for Legality': International Law and Imperialism in Late Nineteenth-century Britain", *Review of International Studies*, Vol. 34 (2008), pp. 403-423, at pp. 412-413.

443. See L. B. Ederington, "Property as a Natural Institution: The Separation of Property from Sovereignty in International Law", *American University International Law Review*, Vol. 13 (1997), pp. 263-331. For a comparison with the Soviet notion of interrelationship between sovereignty and property, see V. Bílková, "Sovereignty, Property and the Russian Revolution", *Journal of the History of International Law*, Vol. 19 (2017), pp. 147-177.

444. The distinction between private *dominium* and *imperium* came to the fore in the late nineteenth century in connection with Leopold II's efforts to establish the Congo Free State, in discussions on whether private entities should engage in informal empire. There the distinction was drawn by Rolin-Jaequemyns, for example. See further Koskenniemi, *Gentle Civilizer*, note 18, at p. 144, citing G. Rolin-Jaequemyns, "L'année 1888 au point de vue de la paix et du droit international", *Revue de droit international et de législation compare*, Vol. 21 (1889), pp. 167-208, at p. 192 *et seq.* Alexandrowicz, relying on Ernest Nys's *De Indis* published by the Carnegie Institution, discussed the distinction drawn by Vitoria between private and public *dominium*, although he goes on to refer to "dominion" and "sovereignty" interchangeably; see Alexandrowicz, "Treaty and Diplomatic Relations", note 95, at pp. 221, 226. Also see Anghie who relies on the same quoted distinction in Vitoria between "ownership" in "both private law and public law"; Anghie, "Francisco de Vitoria", note 279, at p. 324; F. F. de Vitoria, *De Indis et de Iure Belli Relectiones*, edited by E. Nys, Washington, DC, Carnegie Institution of Washington, 1917, at p. 120 ("I ask first whether the aborigines in question were true owners in both private and public law before the arrival of the

Yet by far the most controversial aspect was the notion that European States were "bound to honor the lives and possessions of Europeans moving beyond the reach of European legal principles" [445]. What once was the subject of armed reprisals, later of capitulation and extraterritorial treaties, which also established the mixed courts in the Middle East (1875-1949) and Far East, from Cairo, Mansoura and Alexandria to Shanghai (1864-1927) [446], is now the subject of some 3,000 bilateral investment treaties (BITs), a chief characteristic of which is their provision for investment treaty arbitration [447].

H. Legislative agenda for colonial redress

What mattered to Third World lawyers was colonial redress, including changing the rules of the game and reclaiming the newly decolonised nation's extractive industries. At times, they created exceptions to general rules such as with the GATT/WTO. At others, they sought new rules either by changing the existing rules on foreign investment protection or by legislating for entirely new possibilities in respect of the deep seabed. Their overarching concepts were permanent sovereignty over natural resources, a notion credited to Chile and the other Latin American States [448], a shift from import substitution to securing better terms of trade, and a philosophy of collectivism and distributive justice when it came to new frontiers of resources and riches, be it on the

---

Spaniards"). Whereas David Armitage, reviewing Koskenniemi, discusses the latter's treatment of "sovereignty" and "property" while quoting Koskenniemi's attribution of "*dominium iurisdictionis* and *dominium proprietatis*" to the School of Salamanca; D. Armitage, "Home and the World: The Legal Imagination of Koskenniemi", *International Relations*, Vol. 37 (2023), pp. 1-19, advanced published online 25 October 2022, p. 9; Koskenniemi, *Uttermost Parts*, note 32, at p. 118. For a discussion of the "mystery" of how, conversely, indigenous title could exist while the (British) Crown retains sovereignty, see D. Sanderson, "The Residue of Imperium: Property and Sovereignty on Indigenous Lands", *University of Toronto Law Journal*, Vol. 68 (2018), pp. 319-357.

445. Koskenniemi, *Gentle Civilizer*, note 18, at p. 115.

446. The former had jurisdiction over foreign nationals generally, while the latter only possessed jurisdiction over unrepresented foreign nationals with jurisdiction over British nationals coming under the British Supreme Court in China, i.e. extraterritoriality properly called. In a sense this too was true of the criminal jurisdiction of the Egyptian mixed courts, which was restricted in favour of the jurisdiction of the Consular Courts.

447. See further e.g. C. L. Lim, J. Ho and M. Paparinskis, *International Investment Law and Arbitration*, 2nd ed., Cambridge, Cambridge University Press, 2021 (orig. 2018), generally.

448. N. Schrijver, *Sovereignty over Natural Resources: Balancing Rights and Duties*, Cambridge, Cambridge University Press, 1997, at p. 36.

deep seabed or the moon[449]. Anti-colonial international law thought was no doubt a political and economic project[450]. It was also a legal project for colonial redress[451]. Then there was another, second aspect that is less explored in current explanations. The post-colonial States of the twentieth century were not advancing economic and political ideologies so much as they wanted to replace the plethora and layers of often confusing chartered company agreements, oil concessions, varieties of protectorate treaties which may include clauses regulating concessions[452], and so on, with a single manageable legal concept that all could understand. Sovereign ownership.

449. Agreement Governing the Activities of States on the Moon and Other Celestial Bodies, signed 5 December 1979, New York, entry into force 11 July 1984, 1363 UNTS 3, at Article 11.

450. Dietrich, note 318, at p. 116.

451. In this way self-determination could become economic independence; see K. Senaratne, *Internal Self-determination in International Law*, Cambridge, Cambridge University Press, 2021, at p. 134, 140, also citing A. Getachew, *Worldmaking After Empire: The Rise and Fall of Self-determination*, Princeton, NJ, Princeton University Press, 2019. There was also the right to development; see P. Alston, "The Right to Development at the International Level", in R.-J. Dupuy (ed.), *The Right to Development at the International Level*, The Hague, Sijthoff & Noordhoff, 1989, pp. 99-114, at pp. 110-111; UNGA Res. 41/128, "Declaration on the Right to Development", adopted at the 97th plenary meeting of the 41st session of the UN General Assembly, 4 December 1986, UN Doc. A/RES/41/128. There was, importantly, also the Declaration on Friendly Relations, UNGA Res. 2625 (XXV), note 258. Gaetano Arangio-Ruiz considered that it condemns "forms of pressure and coercion other than armed force"; see G. Arangio-Ruiz, *The United Nations Declaration on Friendly Relations and the System of the Sources of International Law*, Alphen aan den Rijn, Sijthoff & Noordhoff, 1979, at p. 75. This was a revision of his Hague Lectures. There is now the Draft Convention on the Right to Development, showing again how human rights from a postcolonial viewpoint derive from economic concerns and have an economic frame. See further M. G. Reza, "Realization of the Right to Development: Prospects for Drafting a Convention on the Right to Development", *Journal of Human Rights*, Vol. 14 (2015), p. 548 *et seq.*; N. Schrijver, "A New Convention on the Human Right to Development: Putting the Cart Before the Horse?", *Netherlands Quarterly of Human Rights*, Vol. 38 (2020), pp. 84-93.

452. Examples being the British agreement of 22 December 1880 with the Chief of Bahrain, and also the Treaty of Fez of 1912. See Crawford, *Creation of States*, note 22, at pp. 291, 294-295.

CHAPTER IV

ARBITRATION'S GILDED AGE

A. Foreign commercial interests

During the twentieth century, arbitration came to symbolise the defeat of the Third World. It was through developing international commercial arbitration that post-colonial foreign ownership rights were enforced, and these foreign ownership disputes were a large part of the story of the development of arbitration in the twentieth century [453]. The result was also a confirmation of the idea of ownership rights being antecedent or prior to the creation of modern States [454]. Pierre Lalive had written that Third World scepticism of international arbitration was "too well-known to warrant much comment", and that [455]:

> "The history of international arbitration provides a long list of cases in which a State opposed arbitration on the basis of a wide range of arguments and devices, some of which at least are bound to raise doubts as regards the professional qualifications of the government's advisers or their good faith."

Third World nations rejected well-accepted European notions of the authority of the tribunal to determine its own jurisdiction [456], on the basis of an arbitration agreement that was treated as being separate from, for example, an oil concession in which it was contained, such that an attempt to nullify a concession would not affect the jurisdictional authority of an international tribunal. Attempts to exercise national

---

453. Supplementing the view that it was the "Merchants of Peace" who had emerged in the US Chambers of Commerce, particular in the NY Chamber of Commerce, and subsequently in the form of the International Chamber of Commerce in Paris to promote the idea that the resolution of international commercial disputes is conducive to world peace in the same way that inter-State arbitration was to fill a gap in international law by bringing inter-State disputes to international adjudication. See further, Garth, note 136, at p. 40.

454. Locke, note 437, chap. 9, sec. 124: "The great and chief end, therefore, of men's uniting into commonwealths, and putting themselves under government, is the preservation of their property."

455. P. Lalive, "Some Threats to International Investment Arbitration", *ICSID Review Foreign Investment Law Journal*, Vol. 1 (1986), pp. 26-35, at p. 31.

456. Moore, note 355, at pp. xivi-xivii, who when describing Merignhac's views, says: "The arbitrator, made judge of the merits of the case; therefore, *ipso facto*, be considered as invested with the right to decide of what it consists."

supervisory authority over the tribunal would fail where tribunals could, but need not always, take the view that while they determine their competence international arbitration is delocalised.

In the immediate decades following formal independence many developing countries sought to rectify perceived past injustices. Colonial redress as we saw, however, was also viewed broadly, rather than only in the narrow sense of "full reparation" for injury under Article 30 ARSIWA[457]. Article 34 states that such reparation shall take the form of restitution[458], compensation and satisfaction[459]. These provisions reflect a vision of corrective justice[460]. There are also duties of cessation and non-repetition of an international wrong in what is now Article 30 ARSIWA. Reclaiming ownership of the means of production was not necessarily an inability to understand the proper relationship between sovereignty and property but about reparations. Probably many Third World countries saw recovering their productive resources as being restitutionary, but how was this to be achieved if colonialism was not acknowledged to have been an international wrong?

The notion that emerged was that sovereignty meant having the national authority to abrogate solemn oil concession contracts, that is, applying "sovereignty to oil"[461]. The central figures in this Arab legal movement had included the Syrian-born Lebanese lawyer and economist Dr Nicolas Sarkis whose doctoral thesis at the University of Paris had criticised the old oil concessions, and the former Legal Director of the Organization of the Petroleum Exporting Countries (OPEC), UN secretariat staff member, and Harvard educated Iraqi lawyer, Dr Hasan Zakariya who wrote on curtailing the duration stipulated in these concessions or nationalisation as a legal remedy[462]. From the

---

457. Art. 30 in Chap. I, Part II, also Chap. II, Part II, ARSIWA, note 317.

458. Art. 34 in Chap. II, Part II, ARSIWA; *Chorzów*, note 222, at p. 48.

459. Art. 31 in Chap. I, Part II, also Chap. II, Part II, ARSIWA.

460. Aristotle, *The Nicomachean Ethics*, translated by F. H. Peters, London, Kegan Paul, 1884, V.4, at p. 147 *et seq.*, and the idea of restoring the parties concerned to a position of equality in "arithmetical proportion". On proportionality and debate in the ILC on crippling compensation, see J. Crawford, *State Responsibility: The General Part*, Cambridge, Cambridge University Press, 2013, at p. 482, and also the commentary to Article 34, Comment No. 5, in J. Crawford, *The International Law Commissions Articles on State Responsibility*, Cambridge, Cambridge University Press, 2002, at pp. 211-212. See further E. Weinrib, *The Idea of Private Law*, Cambridge, MA, Harvard University Press, 1995, for the ideas of "correlativity" between the parties and the exclusion of consideration of "external" social policies.

461. Dietrich, note 318, at p. 117.

462. H. S. Zakariya, "Sovereignty, State Participation and the Need to Restructure the Existing Petroleum Concession Regime", *Alberta Law Review*, Vol. 10 (1972), pp. 218-231; see further Dietrich, note 318.

UN General Assembly's Second Committee and Third Committee to the Permanent Sovereignty Commission [463], and to the Economic and Social Council (ECOSOC) itself, anti-colonial lawyers sought to establish the permanent sovereignty principle. Djalal Abdoh of Iran, likewise educated at the University of Paris, and whom Christopher Dietrich also credits with UNGA Resolution 626 (VII) [464], was to defend the Iranian oil nationalisations [465], the Afghani diplomat Abdel Rahman Pazhwak called for what became Resolution 2158 (XXI) [466], while the Palestinian Anas Qasem had explained Libya's 1955 nationalisation law at the 1959 Arab Petroleum Congress [467]. Most notably, Djalal Abdoh argued that a private contract could not restrict the exercise of Iran's national authority through legislation to affect it. How wrong he was to be. They were all, as we shall see, to be defeated by a species of legal technology designed to avoid sovereign interference: an international contractual order.

The economic debate over natural resources was also linked to other debates. First, the attempt to link the permanent sovereignty doctrine to self-determination and human rights, beginning in the 1950s, spilled over into the drafting of the two 1966 Covenants on Human Rights – the International Covenant on Civil and Political Rights and the International Covenant on Economic, Social and Cultural Rights [468]. Chile had proposed inclusion of the following paragraph in the Human Rights Covenant, which was widely endorsed by the socialist and Third World States [469]:

> "The right of the peoples to self-determination shall also include permanent sovereignty over their natural wealth and resources. In no case may a people be deprived of its own means of sub-

463. Which had been established following a recommendation by the Human Rights Commission to the General Assembly through ECOSOC.

464. UNGA Res. 626 (VII), "Right to Exploit Freely Natural Wealth and Resources", adopted at the 411th plenary meeting of the 77th session of the UN General Assembly, 21 December 1952, UN Doc. A/RES/626(VII), UN Doc. A/PV.411 (VII). See also Schrijver, *Sovereignty*, note 448, at pp. 42-49.

465. For the 1951 nationalisation of Anglo-Iranian Oil, see Schrijver, *Sovereignty*, note 448, at pp. 41-42.

466. UNGA Res. 2158 (XXI), "Permanent Sovereignty over Natural Resources", adopted at the 1478th plenary meeting of the 21st session of the UN General Assembly, 25 November 1966, UN Doc. A/RES/2158(XXI).

467. Dietrich, note 318, at pp. 118-129.

468. Especially common Article 1; see Schrijver, *Sovereignty*, note 448, at p. 49 *et seq*. See note 260 for full details of the Covenants.

469. The draft resolution of Chile can be found in UN Doc. E/CN.4/L.24, 16 April 1952; see also Schrijver, *Sovereignty*, note 448, at p. 49.

> sistence on the grounds of any rights that may be claimed by other States."

The United States, aligned with the Western States, which opposed any mention of self-determination [470], responded by stating, in reference to Resolution 626 (dubbed the "nationalisation resolution") [471] that

> "the resolution had been a serious error, and had had important economic repercussions among sources of capital available for international investment. The same idea was now being linked to the concept of self-determination . . . the attempt to combine the two ideas would surely hamper the efforts of those who supported the progressive realization of the right of peoples freely to determine their own political future and of those who wished to promote international co-operation in world economic development".

The questions raised were to emerge in several arbitrations, concerning both points of substantive law and arbitration procedure [472]. Often the poor countries were seen to make excuses. I have already mentioned what Lalive thought.

The industrialised, Western viewpoint is that the original, colonial acquisition of such vast commercial interests was entirely legitimate. While in the past "native" inhabitants were sometimes seen to possess private rights even if they lacked sovereignty [473], the twentieth century inverted this outlook. Non-Western peoples may now be sovereign but it did not mean that they owned the largest parts of their productive industries. Rather, Third World resources were by now foreign-owned. Furthermore, foreign contractual and private ownership rights usually existing under domestic law had become internationalised under the

---

470. See further Cassese, *Self-determination*, note 2, at p. 49.

471. UNGA, 3rd Committee, 646th meeting of the 10th session of the UN General Assembly, 27 October 1955, New York, UN Doc. A/C.3/SR.646, at p. 110, para. 34; see also Schrijver, *Sovereignty*, note 448, at pp. 51-52.

472. M. Sornarajah, *The Pursuit of Nationalized Property*, Dordrecht/Boston, Nijhoff, 1986; Sornarajah, *International Law on Foreign Investment* (5th ed. 2021), note 43; Shalakany, note 291, generally.

473. Koskenniemi, *Gentle Civilizer*, note 18, at pp. 113, 115, 127, discussing this aspect of the natural law legacy, for example in Martens; see also J. Westlake, "Le conflit Anglo-Portugais", *Revue de droit international et de legislation comparee*, Vol. 18 (1891), pp. 243-265, at pp. 247-249. In contrast, note Vitoria's treatment of "native" peoples as having both title and jurisdiction over their land. See e.g. Grant, "Francisco de Vitoria and Alberico Gentili", note 120, at p. 911. As to whether nomadic "native" peoples held title, see further the discussion of Grotius and Pufendorf in Cavallar, "Vitoria, Grotius, Pufendorf, Wolff and Vattel", note 119, at p. 199.

newly emergent international order of contracts [474]. Third World lawyers underestimated the malleability of doctrine and the speed with which new doctrines were emerging under a new twentieth-century "natural law".

B. An open delocalised system and internationalised contracts

As for arbitration itself, today we have what has been called an "open system" [475], one in which multinationals enjoy a direct legal standing to bring investment arbitration claims. States also created a delocalised system through instruments like the New York Convention [476]. I say States in the plural, suggesting that they have done so collectively and as a whole. At the time of the *Texaco* arbitration, however, countries like Libya did not envisage TOPCO's or Calasiatic's standing before a tribunal at all, indeed the jurisdiction of any tribunal, once they had passed legislation nullifying all the oil concessions including any arbitration agreements contained within the concession contracts. For Libya, as for many others, sovereignty meant the legislative power to enact a new international economic order, it meant applying the Calvo doctrine, and it meant the application of paragraph 2 (2) *(c)* of UNGA Resolution 3281, the Charter of Economic Rights and Duties of States:

> "Each State has the right . . . *(c)* To nationalize, expropriate or transfer ownership of foreign property, in which case appropriate compensation should be paid by the State adopting such measures, taking into account its relevant laws and regulations and all circumstances that the State considers pertinent. In any case where the question of compensation gives rise to a controversy, it shall be settled under the domestic law of the nationalizing State and by its tribunals, unless it is freely and mutually agreed by all States concerned that other peaceful means be sought on the basis of the sovereign equality of States and in accordance with the principle of free choice of means."

474. M. Sornarajah, "The Myth of International Contract Law", *Journal of World Trade*, Vol. 15 (1981), pp. 187-217.

475. J. Crawford, *International Law as an Open System: Selected Essays*, London, Cameron May, 2002.

476. Convention on the Recognition and Enforcement of Foreign Arbitral Awards ("New York Convention"), adopted on 10 June 1958, New York, entry into force 7 June 1959, 330 UNTS 3. See further T. D. Grant, "The 'Open System' and its Gatekeepers: From *Complexity in International Law*, a Seminar in Honour of James Crawford", *Journal of International Dispute Settlement*, Vol. 13 (2022), pp. 41-53.

The post-colonial campaign had already begun with Djalal Abdoh, Anas Qasem and other anti-colonial international lawyers who believed that they could approach the issue of restitution simply by invoking sovereignty. Sovereignty without the national authority to nullify concessions, to affect rights of property, they argued, would become meaningless. In the end, however, it was the system of international arbitration which showed that sovereignty was now not only commonplace but sterile. Whereas to the Third World lawyers, having learned what their peoples had lacked, and for so long, so much was viewed through the lens of newly acquired sovereignty. By the time of the UN decolonisation era, there hardly existed any non-sovereign States where once there were free cities, free zones, capitulations and protectorates as there were semi-civilised States. Now, with the exception of some places like Hong Kong, whose position remained contested until 1984 [477], the variety of types of actors on the international plane had been reduced virtually to the one type – the sovereign State in a system of sovereign and equal States.

In contrast, however, there is the international arbitration lawyer's worldview wherein sovereignty does not even entail jurisdiction and where, in the arbitration lawyer's vernacular, "delocalised" or "international" arbitration excludes the supervisory national authority even of the place of the seat of the arbitration [478]. On this view, an award that has been set aside by the national courts of the place of the seat "may" be enforced under Article III of the New York Convention, read together with Article V, which only states that an award that has been annulled "may", rather than "shall", be refused enforcement. That is why some consider the delocalised view to be the mainstream view in arbitration as it finds support in the New York Convention, at least to this extent [479]. If that is the everyday meaning of delocalisation then the late Emmanuel Gaillard had a point that this is because the New York Convention's Contracting States will it to be

477. See Lim, *Treaty for a Lost City*, note 10.

478. See further C. L. Lim, "Development of the Principal Forms from Antiquity to Arbitromania", in C. L. Lim (ed.), *The Cambridge Companion to International Arbitration*, Cambridge, Cambridge University Press, 2021, pp. 3-37, at pp. 11-22.

479. However, and having said that, the New York Convention (note 476) also supports the role of the law and courts of the place of the seat of arbitration. Article V (1) *(e)* states that an award may be refused enforcement by the courts of the place of enforcement if it "has not yet become binding on the parties, or has been set aside or suspended by a competent authority of the country in which, or under the law of which, that award was made".

so [480]. According to Gaillard, the delocalised arbitral legal order is not "anational" but rather it is a part of international law [481].

The arbitration brought by the Sultan of Sulu's alleged heirs against Malaysia, which I have already mentioned, is only the most recent and, albeit constituting a narrow example, a slightly unusual illustration of the delocalisation theory. The arbitrator stated that he had felt compelled to relocate the seat of the arbitration from Madrid to Paris as a means, according to his explanation in the Award, of protecting the integrity of the proceedings. The then Attorney-General of Malaysia considered this act to have been "highly irregular" [482]. There is a well-known paper, however, by Pierre Lalive on the conditions for transferring the seat of the arbitration [483]. As it turned out, the Paris Court of Appeal has now nullified the Award [484].

At the same time, private international law yielded to public international law. The law of the place with which a contract or transaction is most closely connected gave way, in these kinds of cases involving the international protection of property and contracts, to contracts that are enforceable directly under international law [485].

I mean to say that when sovereignty was invoked by Third World countries, everything had become internationalised and delocalised. Sovereignty became irrelevant to questions of contract and property apart from the sovereign power to be bound by contract [486]. Eventually, a customary international minimum standard of treatment was reasserted anew against the African and Asian States, consisting of (1) a requirement of compensation for expropriation, and rules on (2) denial

480. E. Gaillard, "International Arbitration as a Transnational System of Justice", in A. J. van den Berg (ed.), *Arbitration: The Next Fifty Years*, Alphen aan den Rijn, Kluwer, 2012, pp. 66-73.

481. Ambassador Oyarzábal's Hague Lectures, given only two years ago, should be consulted for his discussion of a long tradition of thought that locates private international law in the public international law order, which is what Gaillard was doing. See Oyarzábal, note 76, at p. 230 *et seq*.

482. M. Vanar and S. Lee, "Tommy Thomas Slams 'Rogue Arbitrator' over Award to Sulu Heirs", *The Star*, 4 April 2022.

483. See e.g. P. Lalive, "On the Transfer of Seat in International Arbitration", in J. Nafziger and S. Symeonides (eds.), *Law and Justice in a Multistate World: Essays in Honor of Arthur T. von Mehren*, New York, Transnational Publishers, 2002, p. 515 *et seq*.

484. RG 21/21386, note 35.

485. Lim, "Development of the Principal Forms", note 478, at pp. 16-22.

486. In UNGA Res. 1803 (XVII), note 388, contracts "by or between States", i.e. between States and oil companies, "shall be observed in good faith" (para. 8) and arbitration agreements likewise should be kept (para. 4).

of justice/fair and equitable treatment/full protection and security [487]. There is no better demonstration of the malleability and moving nature of international law.

C. Libya's challenge

The Latin American States in the nineteenth century had been the first to resist assertions of a minimum standard of treatment. They had defended themselves against gunboat diplomacy. The Calvo doctrine was the culmination of that defence [488], which was invoked famously by the Mexican Minister in the well-known diplomatic correspondence with US Secretary of State Cordell Hull in 1938 [489]. It is taught in all the textbooks today. The point of contention was not that an expropriation would always be lawful. It would not be if it were discriminatory, for example, applying an older doctrine of non-discrimination [490]. Sovereignty also did not mean a right to expropriate other than for a public purpose, all of which the Mexican Minister accepted.

The *Texaco (Topco/Calasiatic)* arbitration reasserted the minimum standard by way of a contractual analysis. Evelyne Lagrange has mounted a defence of René-Jean Dupuy's role in that arbitration [491], when he was also the Secretary-General of the Hague Academy of International Law. Lagrange says that [492]:

> "René-Jean Dupuy was one of the few in France who paid serious attention to voices from the South notwithstanding a constant will not to lose sight of the whole of international law. He certainly was no historian of international law, but hinted at the europeocentric history of international law and the European past of today's international law in an unusual way. He did not negate the link between positivism and imperialism insofar as no rule prohibited colonialism for instance. In the same vein,

---

487. See e.g. Lim *et al.*, note 447, at p. 331, citing M. Sornarajah, *The International Law on Foreign Investment*, 3rd ed., Cambridge, Cambridge University Press, 2010 (orig. 1994), p. 346 who doubts that the minimum standard of treatment extends beyond these areas.

488. P. Dumberry, *The Fair and Equitable Treatment Standard: A Guide to NAFTA Case Law on Article 1105*, The Hague, Kluwer, 2013, at pp. 13-14.

489. See Chap. III.F and note 382. Reproduced in Lim *et al.*, note 447, at pp. 12-13.

490. *Ibid.*, at p. 367 *et seq.*

491. *Texaco*, note 401.

492. E. Lagrange, "The Thoughts of René-Jean Dupuy: Methodology or Poetry of International Law?", *European Journal of International Law*, Vol. 22 (2011), pp. 425-440, at pp. 427-428.

> he scrupulously equated pretentions from the industrialized and developing world in the decades of (tried if not successful) changes from 1960 to 1980. Did he take the principle of equality of states too seriously, indeed [becoming] himself the victim of illusions fatal to the Third World? His method of 'open dialectic' . . . accounts for this balanced presentation of conflicting pretentions: he adamantly refused openly to prophesy which one would win; he devoted himself to considering not only the (im)balance of objective forces but also the strength of myths and claims to justice. So, the history of international law cannot be reduced to a system of treaties and institutions used by states in their intercourse, since all of them are vested with representations rooted in civilizational patterns or calls for change or conservation."

Yet by any reading of the award it is difficult to understand Lagrange's conclusion that Dupuy simply held the scales evenly, and it is all the more difficult to do so by Dupuy's own admission later on. It is possible Dupuy himself regretted if not what he wrote then the controversy that it had engendered. He was to explain subsequently in a wonderful book by Antonio Cassese that he had simply felt it important to advise the Third World countries regarding where they went wrong [493]:

> "[W]hether you like it or not, investors are nothing like the Red Cross. They act in function of their own interests. There is therefore a minimum of safeguards they need to receive. You cannot say, for example: 'I annul the contract, and by the same token, the arbitration clause is also annulled'."

In *Texaco*, it was. Precisely, it was Libya's view that you could say that. For Libya, it was Libyan law that supplied both the *lex arbitri* as well as the *lex causae* and both were subject to Libyan legislative authority. Thus, Libya could annul the concessions and, at the same time, demand the issue be heard before the Libyan courts. Libya and the developing world saw it as a straightforward application of the Calvo doctrine in UNGA Resolution 3281's paragraph 2 (2) *(c)* that such disputes should be heard under national law – in other words, that national law governs the contract – and heard in their national courts.

---

493. René-Jean Dupuy, in Antonio Cassese, *Five Masters of International Law: Conversations with R.-J. Dupuy, E. Jiménez de Aréchaga, R. Jennings, L. Henkin and O. Schachter*, London, Bloomsbury, 2011, p. 9 *et seq*., at p. 32.

Dupuy, however, reasoned that if that was to be the rule, it would need to reflect the views of all of the different major groupings of States, and considered that Resolution 3281 did not reflect the divergent views of the two major groupings of States in this matter [494]. Perhaps this is what Lagrange means by saying that Dupuy held the scales fairly, by making it impossible for the developing countries to change the rule built on the back of armed reprisals. In short, for him, the developing countries had outvoted the industrialised West, but so what of it?

The background to Resolution 3281 is well known but worth repeating. It had been a direct result of UNCTAD Resolution 45 (111), which on 18 May 1972 had stressed [495]

> "the urgency to establish generally accepted norms to govern international economic relations systematically and recognised that it is not feasible to establish a joint order and a stable order as long as a charter to protect the rights of all countries, and in particular the developing States, is not formulated".

The vote on Resolution 3281 in December 1974 had been 120 to 6 against [496], with 10 members abstaining [497]. When compared with developed country assertions of the international law protection of contracts [498] and the international law enforcement of arbitration agreements [499], there was by now when compared to Resolution 1803 of 1962, which had been carried by a vote of 87 to 2 with 12 abstaining, an even larger number of affirmative votes due to the developing countries' enlarged numbers. Because of the Arab Oil Crisis, which had begun the year before Resolution 3281, in October 1973, there was a sense that the time was ripe for a new charter on international economic relations [500] following the Declaration on the Establishment

494. *Texaco*, note 401, at paras. 84-90.

495. The resolution can be found in *Proceedings of the UNCTAD, Third Session, Vol. 1*, United Nations, Sales No. E.73.II/D.4., and is quoted here in S. K. Chatterjee, "The Charter of Economic Rights and Duties of States: An Evaluation after 15 Years", *International and Comparative Law Quarterly*, Vol. 40 (1991), pp. 669-684, at p. 669.

496. Those voting against were Belgium, Denmark, German Federal Republic, Luxembourg, United Kingdom and United States.

497. Those who abstained were Austria, Canada, France, Ireland, Israel, Italy, Japan, the Netherlands, Norway and Spain.

498. "Foreign investment agreements freely entered into by or between sovereign States shall be observed in good faith", UNGA Res. 1803 (XVII), note 388, at para. 8.

499. "[U]pon agreement by sovereign States and other parties concerned, settlement of the dispute should be made through arbitration or international adjudication", *ibid.*, at para. 4.

500. Chatterjee, note 495, at pp. 669-672.

of a New International Economic Order of May 1974 [501]. Just to illustrate the opposition to that sense, the French delegation had put it thus: "Although, in principle, the French government expressed its support generally for the NIEO, it entered its reservation primarily in relation to taking of foreign property." The US delegation, for its part, said [502]: "[T]he present Declaration does not couple the assertion of the right to nationalise with the duty to pay compensation in accordance with international law" [503]. In terms of the development of the law, it appears that the Third World efforts had been stymied, and postcolonial international lawyers today point to such failure as a basis for more radical claims for the "rejection of international law".

A central feature of Resolution 1803 had been to shift protection of foreign-owned property from controversy over the general customary rule to contractual protection, including the international enforceability of arbitration agreements [504]. The intended effect was to shield foreign ownership rights from any change in public international law, and later on I will say something more about the twentieth-century turn to natural law principles to achieve the same effect. In any case, according to the United States, in a diplomatic note from its embassy in Tripoli to the Libyan Government [505]:

> "The concession agreements governing the operations of the oil companies specifically provide that: 'The contractual rights expressly created by this concession shall not be altered except by mutual consent of the Parties.' They further provide for arbitration of disputes not otherwise settled. Accordingly, failing further negotiations between the Parties on the basis of respect for their contractual rights, the proper remedy for the current disputes between the companies and the Libyan Government is clearly arbitration. The US Government understands that the companies in question have requested arbitration; it expects that the Government of the Libyan Arab Republic will respond positively

501. UNGA Res. 3201 (S-VI) and its related Programme of Action (UNGA Res. 3202 (S-VI)), note 209.

502. Although some Third World lawyers now also ask if this remains the US position considering its contemporary concern with carving out public welfare measures from treaty regulation of indirect expropriation.

503. Quoted in Chatterjee, note 495, at p. 672, 674.

504. UNGA Res. 1803 (XVII), note 388, at paras. 4 and 8.

505. Quoted in R. B. Von Mehren and P. N. Kourides, "International Arbitrations between States and Foreign Private Parties: The Libyan Nationalization Cases", *American Journal of International Law*, Vol. 75 (1981), pp. 476-552, at p. 487.

> to their request since failure to do so would constitute a denial of justice and an additional breach of international law. . . . In the view of the Government of the United States, the expropriation of 51 percent of the interests of these American companies operating in Libya without resort to arbitration and without the offer of adequate compensation would be inconsistent with those assurances, inconsistent with the terms of the concession contracts, and invalid under international law."

Subsequently Libya was to expropriate the remaining 49 per cent.

Following several amendments to the concessions and to the Libyan Petroleum Law, the Texaco concession contract had chosen, as the governing law, Libyan law in common with the principles of international law. In the absence of which, the general principles of law will apply instead, including such of those principles as may have been applied by international tribunals [506]. So if one had assumed that the Calvo doctrine applies then Libyan law and international law would have been one and the same. Dupuy, however, thought that [507]

> "the application of the principles of Libyan law does not have the effect of ruling out the application of the principles of international law, but quite the contrary: it simply requires us to combine the two in verifying the conformity of the first with the second".

And, that [508]

> "a sovereign state which nationalizes cannot disregard the commitments undertaken by the contracting state".

As I have mentioned, he had also derived his authority from international law – or an "anational" legal order – which supplied the procedural law of the arbitration, thus excluding not just Libyan law but also Swiss law, which could have imposed supervision of the arbitration [509]. His approach, viewed widely as an important moment in the development of contemporary international law, may have had a lasting influence also in fostering the view today that, in the absence of

506. Libyan Petroleum Law 1955, Clause 28, para. 7; Von Mehren and Kourides, note 495, at pp. 481-482.
507. *Texaco*, note 401, at para. 59.
508. *Ibid.*, at para. 68.
509. See J. Paulsson, "Arbitration Unbound: Award Detached from the Law of its Country of Origin", *International and Comparative Law Quarterly*, Vol 30 (1981), pp. 358-387, at pp. 379-380.

agreement as to choice of law, an International Centre for Settlement of Investment Disputes (ICSID) tribunal, pursuant to Article 42 of the ICSID Convention, should be free to choose to apply international law rather than municipal law [510], even if to this day it is a subject of academic and practical controversy [511].

D. Jumping the species barrier

So just when the developing countries believed they had overcome the high hurdle of sovereignty, international law doctrine was to change again. The internationalisation of oil contracts was a story about a domestic private law notion jumping across the species barriers between domestic law and international law, and between private law and public law. Dame Rosalyn Higgins puts it this way: "At one bound, therefore, the private party has escaped the need to have his claim brought by his national government, and can invoke international law" [512].

For his part, René-Jean Dupuy had construed the parties' reference to "general principles of law" in the choice of law clause in the oil concession to have been a reference to Article 38 (1) *(c)* ICJ Statute. Thus, first, there was a choice of international law by the parties. After all, we might add, party autonomy in choice of law is itself probably a general principle of international law [513]. Secondly, he had considered too that an international arbitration agreement could situate the concession contract within an anational legal order, what he called the "international order of contracts", presumably in treating a forum selection clause or arbitration agreement as evidence of a choice of law. Thirdly, he looked at long-term development contracts, particularly those which include stabilisation clauses preventing unilateral amendment, as by their "nature" internationalised [514]. Libyan law not being capable of preventing changes to Libyan law, a stabilisation clause preventing unilateral changes to the contract must owe its enforceability to international law.

---

510. ICSID Convention, Regulations and Rules, April 1966, entry into force 14 October 1966, recorded in *History of the ICSID Convention*, Vols. I-V; E. Gaillard and Y. Banifatemi, "The Meaning of 'And' in Article 42 (1), Second Sentence, of the Washington Convention: The Role of International Law in the ICSID Choice of Law Process", *ICSID Review Foreign Investment Law Journal*, Vol. 18 (2003), pp. 375-411.

511. See e.g. L. Clover Alcolea, "Arbitral Activism and Choice of Law under the ICSID Convention", *Chinese Journal of International Law*, Vol. 21 (2022), pp. 499-546.

512. Higgins, *Problems and Process*, note 286, at p. 54.

513. Oyarzábal, note 76, at p. 287.

514. *Texaco*, note 401, at paras. 40-45.

The suggestion that Libya's lawyers must have known that by referring to "general principles of law" they in effect had referred to Article 38 (1) *(c)* and chosen international law was bold, whether the Statute of the Court is interpreted to refer to positive law or to natural law principles [515].

Baron Descamps, who chaired the Advisory Committee of Jurists tasked by the Council of the League to report on the establishment of the PCIJ, had proposed that the clause should refer to "the rules of international law as recognised by the legal conscience of civilised nations" (les règles de droit international telles que les reconnaît la conscience juridique des peuples civilisès). It was Elihu Root, although without objecting, who had considered such "conscience" to have been variable, differing from nation to nation.[516] The current formulation – "the general principles of law recognised by civilised nations" – was therefore a compromise [517], and is on its face as consistent with earlier natural law views as it is with the nineteenth-century view that there was no "universal" law of nations "binding upon the whole human race" but only the law of civilised nations [518]. Bin Cheng and likewise Antonio Cassese would have confined the general principles of law recognised by civilised nations to those "indisputably common to all major Western legal systems" [519]. Yet it is not apparent whether Dupuy

515. For a contemporary discussion of the ILC's continued work on general principles of law, see M. de Andrade, "The Two Step Methodology for the Identification of International Law", *International and Comparative Law Quarterly*, Vol. 71 (2022), pp. 983-1005.

516. See B. Cheng, *General Principles of Law as Applied by International Courts and Tribunals*, Cambridge, Grotius Publications, 1987, at pp. 6-7.

517. *Ibid.*, at pp. 6-21. The late Bin Cheng would reject the word "compromise" that, following Cançado Trindade below, I have used, arguing instead that in substance the two proposals, the Descamps proposal and the Root-Lorimer counterproposal, were in fact similar in substance. They were different ways of viewing the need to account for judicial gap-filling where custom and treaty failed to supply the governing rule. Compare, however, the separate opinion of Judge Cançado Trindade in *Pulp Mills*, which also recounts this drafting history of Article 38 (1) *(c)* but considers there to have been a sharp difference between Descamps's naturalist view and Root's legal positivism. *Pulp Mills on the River Uruguay (Argentina* v. *Uruguay)*, Judgment of 20 April 2010, *ICJ Reports 2010*, p. 14, Separate Opinion of Cançado Trindade at p. 135 *et seq.*, see p. 139; O. A. Elias and C. L. Lim, "General Principles of Law, 'Soft' Law, and the Identification of International Law", *Netherlands Yearbook of International Law*, Vol. 28 (1997), pp. 3-49.

518. According to Henry Wheaton, "the obligation of the ordinary *jus gentium*... cannot exist as to those races of men who do not recognize our law of nations"; see Wheaton, *Elements of International Law* (3rd. ed. 1846), note 233, at p. 40.

519. Cited in First Report on General Principles of Law by M. Vázquez-Bermúdez (Special Rapporteur), 5 April 2019, UN Doc. A/CN.4/732, at p. 53.

himself was referring to natural law or positive law [520]. In the earlier *Abu Dhabi* arbitration, Lord Asquith had asked [521]: What is the "Proper Law" applicable in construing this contract?

And then he answered [522]:

> "This is a contract made in Abu Dhabi and wholly to be performed in that country. If any municipal system of law were applicable, it would prima facie be that of Abu Dhabi. But no such law can reasonably be said to exist. The Sheikh administers a purely discretionary justice with the assistance of the Koran; and it would be fanciful to suggest that in this very primitive region there is any settled body of legal principles applicable to the construction of modern commercial instruments. Nor can I see any basis on which the municipal Law of England could apply. On the contrary, Clause 17 of the Agreement, cited above, repels the notion that the municipal Law of any country, as such, could be appropriate. The terms of that Clause invite, indeed prescribe, the application of principles rooted in the good sense and common practice of the generality of civilised nations – a sort of 'modern law of nature'. I do not think that on this point there is any conflict between the parties."

The view of the civilised nations had become "natural law".

The Greek authority A. A. Fatouros criticised the *Texaco* Award. He considered that this theory of internationalisation was lopsided and uneven-handed, being applicable only against the developing host country [523]. Fatouros said of Dupuy's *Texaco* Award [524]:

> "To fashion an appropriate body of law, based on 'general principles of law' and on international practice, the relevant inquiry must be directed at the principles applicable in fact to state

520. Recent research has also turned attention to the connection between notions of natural law and the *ius gentium*, once seen as the application of natural law to the relations of nations, private law and Roman law beginning in around the 1930s as a reaction to positivism which was associated with Nazism, and in this perhaps future research will emphasise Dupuy's progressiveness rather than the perspective of postcolonial scholars. See e.g. Jacob Giltaij, "The Rediscovery of the Roman *Jus Gentium* and the Post 1945 International Order", *Leiden Journal of International Law*, Vol. 32 (2011), pp. 521-533.

521. *Abu Dhabi* award, note 394, at p. 149.

522. *Ibid.*

523. A. A. Fatouros, "International Law and the Internationalized Contract", *American Journal of International Law*, Vol. 74 (1980), pp. 134-141, at p. 136.

524. *Ibid.*, at p. 137.

> contracts in national law and at the abundant recent experience with nationalizations and other types of interference with state contracts. The award at hand contents itself instead . . . with a brief reference to the doctrinal notion of the contrat administratif, as elaborated in French law, concluding that such a precise notion is not found in other legal systems."

It should not surprise us for the general principles of law recognised by "civilised nations", at least at the time when Dupuy resorted to it, was naturally a reference to the recognition of principles contained in European legal systems [525], rather than, say, a reference to Islamic principles.

Neglecting arbitration's role in decolonisation practice would result in our neglecting a revolutionary transformation of public international law, from the European Law of Nations to twentieth-century public international law in the first half of the twentieth century, and thence to the emergence of what Emmanuel Gaillard dubbed a "transnational justice system" [526], or arbitral legal order [527], an order in which a new *lex mercatoria* is shaped by tribunals in the image, as we have seen Cheng and Cassese say, of Western laws [528]. When it comes to the discovery of this body of principles [529], once delocalisation is admitted, so too are such "transnational" principles to be applied by "international" tribunals rather than the application of some governing law of the place most closely connected with, say, the oil concession and which is to be identified by the choice of law rules at the uncivilised *siège* [530].

---

525. For the deliberations of the General Assembly's Sixth Committee (Legal) on treating the phrase "civilised nations" as a current anachronism, see UNGA, "Sixth Committee Begins International Law Commission Third Cluster Review, Debating General Principles of Law, Replacement Language for 'Civilized Nations'", 23rd meeting of the 76th session of the UN General Assembly, 2 November 2021, UN Doc. GA/L/3649.

526. See E. Gaillard, "Transnational Law: A Legal System or a Method of Decision-Making", *Arbitration International*, Vol. 17 (2001), pp. 59-72. For the modern debate, for example in respect of the *lex petrolea*, see T. Daintith, "Against 'Lex Petrolea' ", *Journal of World Energy Law and Business*, Vol. 10 (2017), pp. 1-13.

527. Gaillard cites Daniel Cohen who uses the term "arbitral legal order". See E. Gaillard, *Legal Theory of International Arbitration*, Boston, Nijhoff, 2010, at p. 39. See further Gaillard, "International Arbitration", note 480, at p. 66.

528. M. Mustill, "The New *Lex Mercatoria*: The First Twenty-Five Years", *Arbitration International*, (1988), pp. 86-119.

529. In respect of the *lex petrolea*, see e.g. Daintith, note 526, containing a useful survey of modern opinion; also D. Saidov, "The Standardisation of Oil and Gas Law: Transnational Layers of Governance", NUS Working Paper 2017/017, National University of Singapore, https://law.nus.edu.sg/wp-content/uploads/2020/04/017_2017_Djakhongir-Saidov.pdf.

530. Gaillard, "International Arbitration", note 480, at p. 69.

International arbitration as it had developed out of the post-colonial battles is autonomous because it is willed by the contractual parties themselves, autonomous from non-Western domestic laws of contract, and autonomous, it appears, even from positive public international law [531]. In some moments, these were positive rules derived only from some legal systems; in others, these principles were a kind of "modern natural law", as Lord Asquith was to put it. In the field of the protection of foreign-owned property, there was to be a near inevitable return to having the law placed upon a footing derived from less controversial sources.

E. Faith in treaties

What came next were modern BITs, and today many developing countries have ended up accepting a treaty minimum standard of treatment (MST) that they had originally rejected in customary international law. It is especially ironic that following the rebalancing of such treaties in recent years, many treaty clauses tend today to say that the treaty means really no more than the customary rule, thereby readmitting the idea of a customary MST they once denied.

It is a peculiar story. Contractual and treaty protection grew originally because customary protection had become unreliable for foreign investments. Today, MST comprises (1) the international standard of compensation for expropriation, (2) denial of justice claims, and (3) protection against violence and for property [532]. Denial of justice and protection against violence and property destruction had developed partly from the *Neer* case of the US-Mexican Claims Commission [533], and also from American treaty practice [534]. The *Neer* standard is said to be particularly high, requiring a wrong to "amount to an outrage, to bad

531. For a rejection of this, see the legal opinion of M. Sornarajah in *El Paso Energy International Company* v. *The Republic of Argentina*, Case No. ARB/03/15, 5 March 2007, at para. 13.

532. D. Schneiderman, "The Paranoid Style of Investment Lawyers and Arbitrators: Investment Law Norm Entrepreneurs and Their Critics", in C. L. Lim (ed.), *Alternative Visions of the International Law on Foreign Investment: Essays in Honour of Muthucumaraswamy Sornarajah*, Cambridge, Cambridge University Press, 2016, pp. 131-155, at p. 136, discussing Sornarajah's conclusion about what claims to the existence of an MST comprise.

533. *L. F. H. Neer and Pauline Neer (U.S.A.)* v. *United Mexican States*, 4 RIAA 60 (1926), 3 ILR 213.

534. Full protection and security, or FPS, clauses also emerged from the early US Friendship, Commerce and Navigation (FCN) treaties, and the FET clause probably first appeared in Article 11 (2) of the Havana Charter, before being taken up in the more modern, post-war US FCN treaties. See J. Salacuse, *The Law of Investment Treaties*, 3rd ed., Oxford, Oxford University Press, 2021, at p. 290 *et seq*.

faith, to wilful neglect of duty, or to an insufficiency of governmental action so far short of international standards" that every reasonable person would recognise it to be insufficient [535].

By 1981, however, Frederick Alexander Mann (Francis Mann) in England was urging the view that fair and equitable treatment (FET) clauses granted protection beyond protection against arbitrary, discriminatory or abusive treatment, and that they ought to be given a broader "autonomous" meaning, autonomous, that is, from customary controversies and limitations [536]. These clauses were true enough subsequently given increasingly broad application, particularly as the world shifted to privatisations. Where in the past State ownership meant direct state control, privatisation meant that States now needed to rely upon regulatory and licensing controls instead. Thus, we began to see licensing and also contractual disputes, which in a way were reminiscent of the old oil arbitrations. Initially, licensing and other new kinds of contractual disputes were shoe-horned into claims of indirect expropriation [537], but it was an awkward fit. One may have to show an interference with a property right. It would have to be that it was the claim under contract, the chose in action, giving rise to an asset, which had been deprived rather than any purported sovereign interference with the licensing contract [538]. As Thomas Wälde wrote, in a notable dissent as arbitrator, a more supple claim of violating the investor's legitimate expectations had by then emerged [539]. In the meantime, the kinds or "heads" of FET claim also grew from claims of arbitrary, discriminatory and abusive treatment to claims of violation of due process, lack of transparent regulation, and investor expectations of a stable business and legal environment based at times upon a violation of the doctrine of good faith [540].

535. Jan Paulsson has argued, interestingly, that this never was the standard. See J. Paulsson and G. Petrochilos, "Neer-ly Misled", *ICSID Review Foreign Investment Law Journal*, Vol. 22 (2007), pp. 242-257.

536. F. A. Mann, "British Treaties for the Promotion and Protection of Investments", *British Yearbook of International Law*, Vol. 52 (1981), pp. 241-254, at p. 243. See also R. Dolzer and C. Schreuer, *Principles of International Investment Law*, 2nd ed., Oxford, Oxford University Press, 2012, at p. 130 (on the US origins of the clause) and p. 134 (as an autonomous treaty standard).

537. *Metalclad Corp.* v. *Mexico*, ICSID Case No. ARB (AF)/97/1, Award of 30 August 2000.

538. See *Emmis and Another* v. *Hungary*, ICSID Case No. ARB/12/2, Award of 16 April 2014, at para. 169.

539. *International Thunderbird Gaming Corp.* v. *Mexico*, UNCITRAL (NAFTA), Award of 26 January 2006, Thomas Wälde (dissenting).

540. Lim *et al.*, note 447, at pp. 330-366, both in respect of legitimate expectations and indirect expropriation claims.

Developing countries subscribed to such BITs with autonomous FET clauses and expanded definitions of "investment". As Rudolf Dolzer, writing with Christoph Schreuer, once asked, why then use a novel concept of FET at all rather than to refer simply to the customary MST[541]? As it turned out, as early as 2001 the North American Free Trade Agreement (NAFTA) Free Trade Commission's interpretation had already stated that NAFTA's MST clause entails no more than the customary standard even if tribunals such as the one in *Mondev* asserted, when faced with an attempt to return investment protection to the *Neer* standard, that custom itself had been changed by treaty and tribunal pronouncements[542]. The risk of tribunal overreach became the subject of widespread debate[543]. Still, American-style "qualified" MST clauses that codified the NAFTA Free Trade Commission's precedent became common; stating that MST clauses were qualified by customary international law. They then also made their way into subsequent treaties such the Comprehensive and Progressive Agreement for Trans-Pacific Partnership (CPTPP), originally the Trans-Pacific Partnership (TPP). In the end, developing countries who once argued vociferously for the Calvo doctrine ended up supporting MST clauses qualified by a supposed customary standard that they themselves once said did not exist[544]. We also see a similar expansion of treaty-based protection in connection with expropriation claims, specifically in respect of the object of expropriation. Now non-property rights can be expropriated even when the treaty is silent as to their inclusion in the definition of what constitutes an investment[545].

541. Dolzer and Schreuer, note 536, at p. 134.

542. *Mondev* v. *USA*, ICSID Case No. ARB(AF)/99/2, Award of 11 October 2002, at para. 125. Cf. *Glamis Gold* v. *USA*, UNCITRAL (NAFTA) Arbitration, Award of 8 June 2009, at paras. 600-605, esp. 604-605, which also rejects arbitral jurisprudence as evidence of State practice. See further Lim *et al.*, note 447, at pp. 357-360.

543. Schneiderman cites *Merrill & Ring Forestry LP* v. *Canada*, Award of 31 March 2010, *Ad Hoc* – UNCITRAL Arbitration Rules (2010), ICSID Case No. UNCT/07/1; see Schneiderman, note 532, at pp. 136-137. However, in that case the tribunal ultimately rejected the NAFTA Article 1105 (1) legitimate expectations claim, albeit not before rejecting the *Neer* standard as the customary standard.

544. Art. 9.6 (2) TPP/CPTPP.

545. See e.g. *Saluka Investments BV* v. *Czech Republic*, Partial Award of 17 March 2006, UNCITRAL, PCA, at para. 361 *et seq.*; *Tecnicas Medioambientales Tecmed SA* v. *Mexico*, ICSID Case No. ARB(AF)/00/2, Award of 29 May 2003, at para. 154; *Vigotop Ltd.* v. *Hungary*, ICSID Case No. ARB/11/22, Award of 1 October 2014, at paras. 328-331. See further Lim *et al.*, note 447, at pp. 346, 348, 407.

From the opposite end of divergent opinion, in recent years numerous treaties have also been subjected to a "rebalancing" exercise [546]. FET clauses have been rewritten in a now typically more narrowly worded form, in Europe in the case of the Comprehensive Economic and Trade Agreement (CETA) [547], in the Asia-Pacific such as in the case of the TPP/CPTPP,[548] and in the new Indian Model BIT [549]; all with the common aim of restricting tribunal discretion and preventing tribunal overreach [550]. At the same time, the arbitration community understands well the hazards of a backlash against tribunal awards [551]. Recently, the ICJ in *Bolivia* v. *Chile* also decided that the doctrine of legitimate expectations is not a part of customary international law [552]. States have generally refused to accept FET as a customary standard [553]. Some developing countries impose an approval system for investments if only to retain some semblance of the Calvo doctrine. Another factor is that

546. See CPTPP Art. 9.4 and fn. 14 (national treatment) as well as CPTPP Drafters' Note on Interpretation of "In Like Circumstances" under Article 9.4 (National Treatment) and Article 9.5 (Most-Favoured-Nation Treatment). For claims of a violation of the investor's legitimate expectations under FET, see Art. 9.6 (4) CPTPP; Art. 8.10 (4) CETA. As for indirect expropriation today, see Annex 8-A (3) of CETA, in which indirect expropriation claims against non-discriminatory measures to protect legitimate public welfare objectives is curtailed, even prohibited generally; similarly, the 2012 US Model BIT, Annex B, at para. 4 *(b)*; the 2012 China-Canada BIT, Annex B.10, at para. 3; the 1992 China-Uzbekistan BIT, Art. 6 (3); and the 2012 China-Japan-Korea trilateral investment treaty (CJK TIT), Protocol, at para. 2 *(c)*.

547. See the FET rule in CETA, Article 8.10 (2)-(4).

548. Art. 9.6 (2)-(4) TPP/CPTPP. See further C. L. Lim, "Finding a Workable Balance between Investor Protection and the Public Interest in the Trans-Pacific Partnership", in B. Kingsbury *et al.* (eds.), *Megaregulation Contested: Global Economic Ordering After TPP*, Oxford, Oxford University Press, 2019, pp. 551-C25.N129; C. L. Lim, "Reports of TPP's Death Have Been Greatly Exaggerated", in M. Mohan and C. Brown (eds.), *The Asian Turn in Foreign Investment*, Cambridge, Cambridge University Press, 2021, p. 242 *et seq.*

549. Which in fact makes no express mention of the concept of FET but instead lists denial of justice, "unremedied and egregious" violations of due process and "manifestly abusive" treatment, among others, as treaty violations. See Art. 3 (1) India Model BIT 2016.

550. Lim *et al.*, note 447, at pp. 333-334, 356.

551. See A. Ross, "Winter is Coming: Is Arbitration's 'Long, Golden Summer' Coming to an End?", *Global Arbitration Review*, Vol. 13 (2019), p. 7 *et seq.*

552. *Obligation to Negotiate Access to the Pacific Ocean (Bolivia* v. *Chile)*, Judgment of 1 October 2018, *ICJ Reports 2018*, p. 507, at para. 162.

553. See I. Tudor, *The Fair and Equitable Treatment Standard in the International Law on Foreign Investment*, Oxford, Oxford University Press, 2008, at p. 83, explaining that: "In the 1992 World Bank Guidelines, the Bank specifically underlined the States' consensus as to the absence of customary character of the FET." This is a reference to the World Bank's 1992 "Guidelines on the Treatment of Foreign Direct Investment". See World Bank, "Report to the Development Committee and Guidelines on the Treatment of Foreign Direct Investment", *ILM*, Vol. 31 (1992), pp. 1363-1379; also discussed in Salacuse, note 534, see p. 132 *et seq.* for the background to the Guidelines.

treaties have been terminated[554], and replaced with new model BITs that are more restrictive in the protection afforded to investors. At the time of writing, Working Group III of the United Nations Conference on International Trade Law (UNCITRAL WGIII) has been working on the EU proposal for a multilateral investment court, while another of the "three sisters of private international law"[555], the International Institute for the Unification of Private Law (UNIDROIT), has just established a new working group on investment contracts, which will begin work in the autumn of 2023.

F. Arbitrators

Today, the arbitrators have also become the subject of criticism, whether or not fairly[556], and it is here that we encounter a most notable piece of postcolonial writing[557]. In the 2000s, Amr Shalakany had sought to locate the Third World allegations of arbitration's or international law's supposed "bias" against them inside the way an arbitrator's legal imagination supposedly operates.

According to Shalakany, shorn of its traditional features (speed, informality and cost-effectiveness) international arbitration by itself is not biased; it cannot be because it consists largely of only two main doctrines, namely, *kompetenz-kompetenz* and separability. While the separability doctrine, by distinguishing the arbitration agreement from the contract in which it is contained, prevented Libya's attempt to extinguish the tribunal's jurisdiction by nullifying the concession contract, and *kompetenz-kompetenz* granted the tribunal the authority to decide this very issue, both doctrines are only means to secure, they only facilitate, a neutral means of international dispute resolution. Neutrality or the search for it surely is the opposite of bias.

And, according to Shalakany, "international law", too, is not "biased". The arbitrators in the other famous Libyan oil cases – *BP* v. *Libya*[558] and *LIAMCO* v. *Libya*[559] – and in *Texaco* had all construed the same choice

554. Lim *et al.*, note 447, at p. 589.
555. The "three sisters" being UNCITRAL, UNIDROIT and the Hague Conference on Private International Law.
556. See further, for the widespread judicial practice of citing treaty as proof of custom, S. J. Choi and M. Gulati, "Customary International Law: How Do Courts Do It?", in C. A. Bradley (ed.), *Custom's Future: International Law in a Changing World*, Cambridge, Cambridge University Press, 2016, pp. 117-147.
557. Shalakany, note 289.
558. *BP Exploration Co. (Libya) Ltd.* v. *Government of Libya*, (1979) 53 ILR 297.
559. *Libyan American Oil Co.* v. *Government of Libya*, (1977) 17 ILM 3.

of law clause differently. In *BP*, the distinguished Danish international lawyer Gunnar Largergren, sitting as arbitrator, had thought that there was no such thing as the principles of the law of Libya in common with the principles of international law, and therefore fell back in his construction of the choice of law clause in the concession on the general principles of law. In *LIAMCO*, Dr Sobhi Mahmassani considered that the identical clause in the relevant concession in that dispute meant that one applied Libyan law except where it contradicted international law. In *Texaco*, Dupuy considered that the identical choice of law clause in that dispute was plain in meaning and one should exclude such Libyan law that was inconsistent with international law. International law doctrines are therefore just too open-ended, too indeterminate, to choose decisively between Third World claims about the law and the views of the Western industrialised nations. International law has no content.

Yet we can see that in all three cases Libya lost. Libya lost, according to Shalakany, because the arbitrators themselves had situated the petroleum disputes in the purely private law realm in which State authority has no legitimate business or concern. Libya's Petroleum Law and Third World concerns cannot be permitted to undermine the sanctity of contract. In short, it was, he argues, the "commercial sensibility" of the arbitration community – their elite law school-trained liberal intuitions – that saw the Libyan oil disputes in essentially private law contractual terms which had shaped the outcome in the Libyan oil arbitrations. For Shalakany, it was the arbitrators' "liberal" mindset that became decisive. This emphasis on the liberal sensibilities or intuitions of the arbitrators and Shalakany's reliance on the concept of legal indeterminacy reflect a useful critical orientation, and it is, as I have mentioned, one of the most notable pieces of writing in the postcolonial canon. Yet here lies an intergenerational difference between "post-colonial" and "postcolonial" international law scholarship. As Mohamed Salah Eddine Madiou puts it [560]:

> "Since it acquired postmodern characteristics, postcolonialism became abstract, indeed so abstract that it lost grasp of reality."

560. M. S. E. Madiou, "The Death of Postcolonialism: The Founder's Foreword", *Janus Unbound: Journal of Critical Studies*, Vol. 1 (2021), pp. 1-12, at p. 2. Others who argue for a Marxist approach suggest that too much is made of indeterminacy and contingency, for which see Tzouvala, note 111, at p. 6; Fofana, "Buchbesprechungen", note 94, at p. 1060.

That cannot, however, be said of Shalakany's piece, which had at least succeeded in casting criticism of Dupuy and *Texaco* in a different light. It also foreshadowed today's debates about the role of the arbitrator.

G. Liberalism, autonomy, delocalisation

Returning to arbitration's autonomy, to "delocalisation", that at its simplest is the detachment of the *lex arbitri* from the law, the curial supervision, the reach of the national authority, of the seat of the arbitration. Francis Mann once wrote too that England rejects delocalised arbitration [561]. England rejects the concept as it was put so memorably in *Bank Mellat* v. *Helliniki Techniki* by Kerr L. J. of "arbitral procedures floating in the transnational firmament unconnected with any municipal system of law" [562]. There was a practical reason for this English view. If we add the new centres of arbitration, Hong Kong and Singapore, we might even call this an Anglo-Commonwealth common law view [563]. In England, the growth of commercial arbitration was highly dependent upon the commercial popularity of English standard form contracts in shipping, commodities and insurance as practised and refined by a specialist group of barristers – a specialist commercial bar – appearing before London's commercial judges. Arbitration and the courts in England are symbiotic. Emmanuel Gaillard, who should have lectured here two years ago, once considered the English approach ridiculous. And so in a way, from the perspective of the French School, it is. It is the French School, sometimes called the Dijon School, which has given the notion of international arbitration as being divorced from the control of the courts its most powerful, articulate and eloquent expression. In France the liberty of private law in private, commercial relations is an intellectual heritage, rather than being, as in England, dependent upon a particular commercial need [564].

Delocalisation is a vivid illustration of a grave tension between international arbitration and post-colonial international law thought in which sovereignty is prized. If international arbitration is characterised by a tension between national authority and party autonomy, then that tension became more pronounced with decolonisation. It was

561. F. A. Mann, "England Rejects 'Delocalised' Contracts and Arbitration", *International and Comparative Law Quarterly*, Vol. 33 (1984), pp. 193-198.

562. *Bank Mellat* v. *Helliniki Techniki*, [1984] 1 QB 291.

563. For in these two places "seat thinking" is prevalent particularly in connection with attempts to promote the seat.

564. Lim, "Antiquity to Arbitromania", note 478, at pp. 11-22.

hardly assured that the newly decolonised States would accept liberal democracy, the protection of private ownership rights and freedom of contract. The Cold War setting in which the battle was fought shaped the formation of post-colonial international law thought. This was the context in which international arbitration reached for a "neutral" means of protecting property and contract. Many Asian and African States, as we have seen, had considered international arbitration to be "biased", unsurprisingly, since arbitration of disputes over pre-colonial investments supported the Lockean agricultural thesis that they who are best placed to work the land, rather than only inhabit it, own it. Here, it is property as a natural right that applies rather than self-determination – "ours is a government of laws, not of men" [565].

It was in that mix that ICSID arbitration, which is delocalised, was to emerge [566]. An ICSID arbitration, when viewed as a hybrid form between inter-Sate and international commercial arbitration, has no seat. With only limited exceptions, it is meant to be self-contained [567], not least in its annulment and enforcement regime [568]. In this it may be compared to inter-State arbitration where one does not usually imagine a domestic court nullifying an inter-State award. However, ICSID had been preceded by pro-arbitration gains already made in the 1958 New York Convention [569], even if discussions had begun a little earlier during that singular period of great global arbitration reforms during the 1950s. In any case, by the time of the New York Convention

565. As explained by a Yale undergraduate in explaining popular sovereignty; see P. Johnston, "Johnston: Liberalism, Sovereignty", *Yale Daily News*, 24 October 2008, https://yaledailynews.com/blog/2008/10/24/johnston-liberalism-sovereignty/.

566. Barring, perhaps, more exceptional situations when the submission to ICSID arbitration assumes otherwise; see the example of a stipulation of Paris as the seat of the arbitration and as the *lex arbitri* "the Islamic Republic of Mauritania as well as the rules and customs of the international law applicable to the matter" in the 2004 CNPC-Mauritanian Taoudenni Basin, Ta 13, Production Sharing Agreement and the 2004 CNPC-Mauritanian Taoudenni Basin, Ta 21, Production Sharing Agreement, in Article 29 (29.1 and 29.2). This clause is not necessarily pathological. While Article 26 of the ICSID Convention states that consent to ICSID arbitration shall be deemed consent to exclude "any other remedy", it does also contain the usual concession to party choice. See C. H. Schreuer *et al.*, *The ICSID Convention: A Commentary*, 2nd ed., Cambridge, Cambridge University Press, 2009, discussed in C. L. Lim, "The Function of the Transnational Chinese Contract", *Journal of World Investment and Trade*, Vol. 20 (2019), pp. 313-334, at p. 324.

567. See Art. 26 ICSID Convention.

568. Lim *et al.*, note 447, at pp. 542-556. But see also the UK Supreme Court's view in *Micula* et al. v. *Romania*, [2020] UKSC 5, at para. 71-75, that Article 54 of the ICSID Convention, by requiring enforcement as if the award were a final judgment of the local court, imports any limitations on enforcement that apply to the enforcement of local court judgments.

569. New York Convention, note 476.

enforcement no longer was dependent upon the affirmation of the award under the law of the seat. There was no longer any requirement of "double exequatur". This, too, is in an important way a kind of delocalisation, or the idea, as Berthold Goldman once described it, that "[t]he arbitrator 'has no forum'" [570]. It is only that recognition and enforcement "may" still be refused under the New York Convention in a number of limited circumstances, including where the award has been set aside by the courts of the place of the seat of the arbitration (Art. V). What this means is that the courts of the place of enforcement may choose to proceed to enforce an award that the courts of the place of the seat have purportedly set aside [571]. One could put it more strongly; that the use of the word "may" in Article V of the Convention states the mainstream view that an award that has been set aside is enforceable. However, this is not because delocalisation rejects any role for national authority whatsoever. It is because States have chosen or volunteered it to be so. As Gaillard had pointed out, the New York Convention was brought into existence by choice through the exercise by its Contracting States of their national authority, their capacity to enter into international relations, their sovereign power. The pro-arbitration autonomy of international arbitration and of the arbitral legal order is international law and the result of State will, consent or assent [572]. One might compare the "autonomy" of inter-State arbitration where, absent the supervision of any court, the result is not necessarily pro-arbitration and in fact, according to the learned authorities, the opposite. States, historically at least, have not shied away from assuming the right to reject on their own inter-State awards for want of jurisdiction, and writers who have not been immune from nationalist sentiment have similarly not shied away from defending their own State's right to do so [573]. It proves Gaillard's point that delocalisation and absence of State or inter-State regulation are, potentially at least, different things.

It is true, as Jan Paulsson says, that once arbitration was accepted by the Latin American States, when they accepted *en masse* the Convention for the Pacific Settlement of International Disputes at the Second Hague Conference of 1907, denial of justice could no longer become a pretext

---

570. Quoted in E. Gaillard and J. Savage (eds.), *Fouchard, Gaillard and Goldman on International Commercial Arbitration*, The Hague, Kluwer, 1999, at para. 1181.

571. Lim, "Antiquity to Arbitromania", note 478, at pp. 11-16, 20-22.

572. See *ibid.*, and also Gaillard, "International Arbitration", note 480, at pp. 66-73.

573. See Moore, note 355, at pp. lxii-lxiii, lxxxiii-lxxxiv, citing W. E. Hall, *A Treatise on International Law*, 4th ed., Oxford, Clarendon, 1895, at pp. 878-879, and Calvo, note 382 (French edition).

for gunboats. However, any suggestion that Calvo's doctrine also no longer had a basis would be questionable [574]. The African, Middle Eastern and Asian States have accepted arbitration, at least since their participation in creating the UNCITRAL Model Law. However, there always was a concomitant concern with curial supervision and the risk of bias. Arbitration's autonomy has only prompted more questions, questions about who the arbitrators are and their professional habits and sensibilities. This also explains the practical discussions that are taking place in UNCITRAL WGIII. We see in the current discussions of investor-State dispute settlement (ISDS) reform concerns that are comparable to previous efforts. The focus may have shifted to the arbitrators themselves, particularly in the context of UNCITRAL WGIII, where recently there has been discussion about whether the UN Regional Groupings – Asia-Pacific, Africa, Latin America, the Caribbean, Western Europe and others, and Eastern Europe [575] – ought to be adopted for the appointment of judges/'ISDS tribunal members', and whether *ad hoc* judges should feature [576]. At the moment, the discussion focuses on a Code of Conduct for arbitrators. Particular attention has concentrated upon the available small pool of arbitrators, which go directly to Shalakany's claim of a community with a cohesive, even an inherent, professional sensibility, and the practice of double hatting, which is the practice of arbitrators acting concurrently or sequentially as counsel or as expert or tribunal secretary. This last also includes the "revolving door" problem. It is to these aspects, rather than to the traditional Third World criticisms, that attention has now turned. This was shown vividly at the 42nd Session [577] in connection with a rule proposed to address double hatting and repeat appointments [578]. The proposed rule, now adopted, is that an investment arbitrator shall be prohibited from acting as counsel or expert for three years in a case with

574. Paulsson, *Denial of Justice*, note 387, at p. 22.

575. For the positions of delegations from Asia, see C. L. Lim, "Investment Treaty Policies and Arbitrations in Asia", in L. E. Sachs, L. J. Johnson and J. Coleman (eds.), *Yearbook on International Investment Law & Policy 2019*, Oxford, Oxford University Press, 2021, pp. 323-338.

576. UNCITRAL WGIII, "Possible Reform of Investor-State Dispute Settlement (ISDS): Standing Multilateral Mechanism – Selection and Appointment of ISDS Tribunal Members and Related Matters", Note by the Secretariat, 8 December 2021, UN Doc. A/CN.9/WG.III/WP.213.

577. Held from 14 to 18 February 2022.

578. See further e.g. C. L. Lim, "Reaching for Utopia, Geneva as Inspiration for Investment Disputes?", in M. K. Lewis *et al.* (eds.), *A Post-WTO International Legal Order: Utopian, Dystopian and Other Scenarios*, Berlin, Springer, 2020, pp. 167-186, at p. 173.

substantially similar issues. The Code applies apparently even after an arbitrator becomes *functus officio* [579]. At its 43rd Session in September 2022, attention turned to the method of nomination of the future judges of the proposed multilateral investment court, with two options on the table: nominations by States party to an eventual agreement, or to allow self-nominations [580].

Shalakany acknowledges that the only essential features of arbitration today are the doctrines of separability and *kompetenz-kompetenz*. These facilitate neutral dispute settlement, outside the courts of the Respondent State, regardless of the State's treatment of a concession as a nullity, and by having the arbitration tribunal decide the scope of its own authority. For as Merignhac had once taught, the tribunal that is empowered to decide the merits of a dispute must also decide what the dispute consists of. Even if arbitration's neutrality disempowers Libya's regulatory authority, neutrality remains the opposite of bias. So Shalakany rejects TWAIL's allegation that international law and international arbitration are biased. Our focus should rather be on the arbitrator's liberal sensitivities through the arbitrator's elite cosmopolitan legal education to which Shalakany attributes a tendency to view the Libyan oil disputes as exclusively private and contractual in nature, rather than, as Libya claimed, an exercise of sovereign public authority. We might compare this with the argument that international law is an instrument of racial or war capitalism. Is it international law doctrine, which Shalakany urges is malleable and open-ended? At bottom, doctrine is open-ended; there remains a persistent tension in international law between sovereignty and private property and between national authority and party autonomy.

None of this requires rejection of "deep structuralist" explanations of the law, such as the "commodity-form theory" in Marxist thought according to which law is simply a part of "the superstructure" [581]. Yet few accept it in practice. Take a contemporary example, where just this

579. Arbitrators will be wary of such undertakings.

580. UN Doc. A/CN.9/WG.III/WP.213, note 576, at paras. 33-39.

581. Pashukanis, note 187, also discussed in B. Bowring, "Yevgeniy Pashukanis, His *Law and Marxism: A General Theory*, and the 1922 Treaty of Rapallo between Soviet Russia and Germany", *Journal of the History of International Law*, Vol. 19 (2017), p. 274-295, who cites the application of the commodity-form theory to international law in C. Miéville, "The Commodity-Form Theory of International Law: An Introduction", *Leiden Journal of International Law*, Vol. 17 (2004), pp. 271-302. What is interesting in Bowring's discussion of Melville's resurrection of Pasukanis's views is that they would have defied any contemporary attempt to apply the commodity-form theory to international law; see Bowring, at pp. 292-294.

last spring, at the side lines of UNCITRAL WGIII, attention turned to discussion of the procedural means of bringing claims against investors beyond the narrow confines of bringing a counterclaim. Implicit in this is a view, among legal policymakers and international lawyers, that there is nothing inherently capitalist about international law or international arbitration. Turning our attention from deep structural explanations about bias in international law towards how arbitrators are trained to think is the critical arbitration scholar's contribution to postcolonial international law thought, and it is also the view I would prefer.

CHAPTER V

AIMS AND METHODS OF POSTCOLONIAL INTERNATIONAL LAW

A. Universal legal order

Let us come back, finally, to the question of universality broached at the beginning of these lectures. It is said that starting in the mid-twentieth century, international law thought turned from "transcendental reflection" – Vitoria in the sixteenth, Grotius in the seventeenth, and Kant in the eighteenth century – towards a more doctrinal attitude. Now it fails to address questions, first, about international law's universality, secondly the basis of international legal obligation, and thirdly the relationship between the law and its larger social and political context [582]. When some postcolonial scholars now call for the rejection of Western modernity, they address these old questions anew. History, or a turn to history, is now employed – deployed may be a better word – to question mainstream assumptions about the basis of international legal obligation. In doing so postcolonial international lawyers today have recovered, successfully, that old artefact, the standard of civilisation from the deep-water wreckage of the European Law of Nations.

In their diagnosis of mainstream portrayals of international law, postcolonial commentators now say the discipline is not impartial, dispassionate or even professional. How has this occurred? In part because the idea of universal law had been justified on the basis of natural law and a Christian mission by those endowed with civilisation, on which view the law is universal and applies equally to all [583]. Yet natural law was not the culprit. The true problem was that, suddenly, all such talk of universal law ceased in European thought before its revival during the twentieth century. Luigi Nuzzo takes us back to Friedrich Carl von Savigny (1779-1861) and the introduction of the idea of a

582. M. Koskenniemi, "International Legal Theory and Doctrine", last updated November 2007, *Max Planck Encyclopedia of Public International Law*, available at https://opil.ouplaw.com/home/mpil, at paras. 2-4.

583. *Ibid.*, at paras. 6-8, discussing this tripartite classification of civilised, barbarian and savage peoples as an integral part of the historical justification of universality.

European scientific view of the law that did not apply to non-European peoples unless they could reciprocate [584].

By the mid-twentieth century, the law had also become disembodied from colonial history altogether. You could teach international law without any mention of colonialism; you still can, and in fact the subject is often taught that way the world over. During the mid-twentieth-century period there was also an attempt to recapture the nineteenth-century project. Georg Schwarzenberger's inductive approach became a touchstone for a return to a more dispassionate and "scientific" understanding [585], while others sought to transform what in effect were civilisational judgments into more modern universalisable language [586]:

> "defining their terms
> as they went along
> Inventing terms, if need be ('decision-maker', for example)
> choosing their words with care
> to say exactly what they meant."

And while minding their vocabulary as well as their observational standpoint, international law was for example analysed as a problem of "who gets what" in terms of eight values all humankind pursues through institutions, using whatever resources are available [587]. At New Haven they asked who the participants were, their perspectives and situations, their strategies and preferred outcomes and the effects of those outcomes in viewing international law as a part of a social process in which the international lawyer is charged with devising options for creating a public order of human dignity, that is, a better world.

---

584. Nuzzo, *Origini*, note 133; E. F. Malaspina, Book review of Nuzzo, *Origini di una scienza* (2012), *Comparative Legal History*, Vol. 2 (2014), p. 148-151, at p. 148.

585. Schwarzenberger, note 45.

586. C. W. T. Stephenson, *Transparency Cantos: Values for Human Dignity – Lasswell and McDougal*, Washington, DC, Torquilstone Press, 2002. See further M. S. McDougal and H. D. Lasswell, "The Identification and Appraisal of Diverse System of Public Order", *American Journal of International Law*, Vol. 53 (1959), pp. 1-29. It was presented as an empirical method, although Professor Philip Allott, for example, once described the New Haven method, as exemplified in that instance by McDougal writing with William Burke, as one by which: "the authors appear to regard their task as that of constructing rather than finding the law"; see P. Allott, "Language, Method and the Nature of International Law", *British Yearbook of International Law*, Vol. 45 (1978), pp. 79-135, at p. 121.

587. (1) Power, (2) Enlightenment, (3) Wealth, (4) Well-being, (5) Skill, (6) Affection, (7) Respect, (8) Rectitude. See Stephenson, *Cantos*, note 586, at p. 8.

Today we have supposedly a "universal" civilisational order [588]. According to some critics, the values and principles of Western civilisation are also being held up again as the rallying point for global action and as criteria to judge the performance and legitimacy of "backward" countries, "[a]s in the past international law today carries the values of Western civilization forward and provides means for their imposition on other countries and cultures" [589]. Recently words such as "barbaric" have reappeared, for example, and we see such language even in statements by Josep Borrell, the High Representative of the European Union for Foreign Affairs and Security Policy, and Ursula von der Leyen, the President of the European Commission [590]. Ms Von der Leyen has spoken of an assault on "the whole international rules-based order" [591]. Having been severed from European international legal history, the civilisational standard seems to be alive and well.

B. Refashioning doctrine

Before we come to how universality is now questioned by postcolonial international lawyers, we need to be clear that specific legal rules are, after all, not universal. Ideas of special and regional custom, the *res inter alios* rule that a treaty is binding only upon those party to it, and the *pacta tertiis* rule that it does not bind others, all of which are a part of the doctrine of sources, have been built consistently upon the voluntarist idea that an international law rule is opposable only to a State that has consented to it [592]. We can debate the application of these doctrines in particular situations, such as whether a particular special or regional customary regime exists [593], or whether the *pacta tertiis* rule applies in a specific case.

The first generation had, however, theories about the sources of international law and the basis of international legal obligation for a

588. Compare L. Mälksoo, *Russian Approaches to International Law Thought*, Oxford, Oxford University Press, 2015.

589. D. P. Fidler, "The Return of the Standard of Civilization", *Chicago Journal of International Law*, Vol. 2 (2001), pp. 137-157, at p. 146.

590. "EU's Borrell Slams Putin's 'Barbaric' Invasion of Ukraine", *Guardian* (Nigeria), 14 March 2022, https://guardian.ng/news/eus-borrell-slams-putins-barbaric-invasion-of-ukraine/; "Von der Leyen Condemns 'Barbaric' Invasion of Ukraine, Vows to Cripple Russia's Economy", *Euronews*, 24 February 2022, https://www.euronews.com/my-europe/2022/02/24/von-der-leyen-condemns-barbaric-invasion-of-ukraine-vows-to-cripple-russia-s-economy.

591. "Von der Leyen", note 590.

592. See generally Elias and Lim, note 247.

593. *Ibid.*, at p. 115 *et seq.*

truly universal legal order. Dimitri van den Meerssche mentions this aspect in a fascinating account of how the World Bank successfully insulated itself from Third World delegates' efforts to construct a desirable international institutional architecture in places such as the UN General Assembly's Fourth Committee [594]. Whatever one thinks of the assertion today that capitalist modernity saw itself as the only cure for civilisational inferiority [595], and that this was "constitutive", howsoever that should be interpreted, of international law, lawyers like T. O. Elias argued instead for a different kind of "cure" in the form of majoritarian international rules whose basis of obligation would be built upon democratic ideals. Mention has been made too of Bedjaoui's argument that we would be making international law anew by treaty which industrialised countries could still quite properly reject on the basis of the *res inter alios* rule. There was a possible third approach best described as axiological. For example, resistance by the Greek and Israeli members to "progressive development" in the ILC of the rules of State responsibility [596] had led eventually to the Asian-African Legal Consultative Committee calling for alignment with the rules and principles of the "ordre public international" contained in the first two articles of the UN Charter [597]. All these different approaches of different drummers [598] were not mutually exclusive.

The short of it is that while lack of Third World consent became a basis for rejecting the pre-United Nations international legal order, various approaches were adopted towards the basis of obligation and sources of international law, moving forward. This was how the Third World nations were to make a new, universal international legal order for all of humanity. In spite of, perhaps because of, the Cold War.

However, in comparison with the first generation, TWAIL proponents have not articulated a view about the basis of obligation in international

594. The Special Political and Decolonisation Committee. According to Van Den Meersche, note 350, at p. 461, the Third Worlders had "egalitarian, universalist and counter-hegemonic" ideals. Others aimed to do more, to address as well questions of "intra-State" wealth distribution; see U. Özsu, "Hydrocarbon Humanitarianism: Ibrahim Shihata, 'Oil Aid', and Resource Sovereignty", *Journal of the History of International Law*, Vol. 22 (2021), pp. 137-160.

595. Tzouvala, note 111, at pp. 1-2.

596. As against the Indian, Polish and Brazilian members.

597. I. P. Fofana, "Afro-Asian Jurists and the Quest to Modernise the International Protection of Foreign-owned Property, 1955-1975", *Journal of the History of International Law*, Vol. 23 (2021), pp. 80-112, at pp. 90-92.

598. I borrow the phrase in homage only. See T. L. Stein, "The Approach of the Different Drummer: The Principle of the Persistent Objector in International Law", *Harvard International Law Journal*, Vol. 26 (1985), pp. 457-482.

law. We have seen, at least in the example of investments in the Third World, the shift from positivist to naturalist thinking [599]. Many TWAIL proponents reject first-generation views about having different universal rules. The first generation had closed a gap in international law thought. International law had considered that States make law without explaining how the lawmakers themselves come to be [600]. It was the law of colonial self-determination and acceptance of an ancillary doctrine, that of *uti possidetis*, which explained, generally, how many African, Asiatic and Middle Eastern States were to gain independence and their territorial entitlements [601]. There were more specific but hardly unusual arguments that would derive the existence of the post-colonial State, or a part of it, directly from the legitimacy of colonial treaties [602].

Others in the first wave of Asian-African post-colonial international lawyers also advocated, or resurrected, equitable notions of treaty renunciation. There is the argument that an unequal treaty doctrine resides, implicitly, in the 1969 Vienna Convention on the Law of Treaties, as Wang Tieya, for example, had argued in his Hague Lectures [603]. Thus seen, the first generation had a fairly comprehensive view of legal personality and the basis and sources of international law, quite apart from their views about succession to international obligations, territorial successions, global trading conditions and ownership of productive industries and natural resources. The Twailian complaint is that all of this pays insufficient heed to the persistence of international law's colonial legacy, but TWAIL proponents have not generally sought to refashion doctrine in the same way, with some notable exceptions such as Anghie's contribution to our understanding more fully the role of sovereignty in classical writings [604]. Rather, there are statements in the nature of a Twailian manifesto [605]:

> "TWAIL does not believe that free-market, private property, or trade values are superior to, or automatically trump, other human values."

599. See Koskenniemi, *Apology to Utopia*, note 101, at pp. 267, 320.
600. See Lim's review of Carty's *Decay* (2nd ed.), note 14, generally.
601. See further the second chapter of Carty, *Decay* (1986), note 63.
602. Again, see for example the Malaysian argument before the Paris Court of Appeal: RG 21/21386, note 35, at para. 51.
603. Wang, "International Law in China", note 48, at p. 337, arguing that the doctrine is recognised, albeit implicitly, in Arts. 52 and 53 of the Vienna Convention on the Law of Treaties.
604. Anghie's *Imperialism*, note 155, was a key contribution.
605. Mutua, note 180, at p. 37.

Twailers and indeed others, many others perhaps, would seek to limit the protection of foreign-owned property, but would they reject the GATT-WTO regime [606]? The trouble is that TWAIL thought rarely condescends to detail.

C. The necessity of international law

Many in TWAIL adopt what we might call a view of "the banality of evil", that our everyday, remorseless international law routines somehow serve only to promote evil [607]. They have adopted therefore a rejectionist thesis, questioning through historical inquiry not just the basis of international law but the idea that it could have any moral-political basis. As De la Rasilla puts it [608]:

> "[T]he corollary of the post-colonial historiographical argument is that 'colonial international law' has been transmuted into contemporary structures, institutions, and legal concepts through revamped versions of colonial doctrines such as the 'standard of civilization', which justified unequal treatment of some non-Western polities during the 'age of imperialism', or what Partha Chatterjee terms the operation of 'the imperial privilege (which) still exists in a world without colonies'. This politically 'presentist' orientation in TWAIL/post-colonial approaches to international legal history in their arguing for the 'decolonization' of the international order – one that is written in the language of international law but is ultimately epiphenomenally dependent on other extra-juridical and super-structural factors – works as a shortcut to project their historical analyses as political 'interventions' in contemporary debates on the unequal dynamics of globalization."

The charge is that international law is monocultural. Let us turn again to Anghie [609]:

> "My argument is that colonialism had shaped not only those doctrines of international law explicitly devised for the

606. See further C. L. Lim, "International Law, Development, Trade and Foreign Investment", in R. McCorquodale and S. McInerney (eds.), *International Law and Sustainable Development*, Oxford, Oxford University Press, forthcoming.
607. H. Arendt, *Eichmann in Jerusalem: A Report on the Banality of Evil*, New York, Viking, 1963.
608. De la Rasilla, *International Law and History*, note 194, at pp. 119-120.
609. Anghie, "Evolution of International Law", note 46, at pp. 748-749.

> very purpose of suppressing the Third World, but also had . . . profoundly shaped the very foundations of international law, including the ostensibly neutral doctrine of sovereignty."

In apparent resignation, he says [610]:

> "Third World international lawyers, immediately following the period of decolonisation, placed a special faith in international law, believing that it could achieve these results. However, this faith proved unfounded, and many international initiatives that were explicitly humanitarian and anti-colonial – such as the Mandate System – became a vehicle for imperialism. As a result, some scholars have eloquently argued that the Third World should dispense with international law altogether. But this is not a feasible option, simply because that would leave open the field of international law to the imperial processes."

The argument that colonialism shaped doctrine and that Third World attempts, for example to establish a NIEO, had failed to reshape key doctrines ignores the larger aim that was to repair the law to prevent future wrongs, primarily through treaty, rather than just to reshape more abstract doctrines. To do this the first generation of lawyers had a view of the basis of obligation in international law, whether it was based on consent or some democratic theory of international relations and so on, whereas TWAIL has no view of why international law is obligatory.

Yet today, support for rejectionism grows ever louder. Professor James Gathii, at the American Society of International Law's 2020 Annual Meeting, cites Mutua [611]:

> "[T]he international law regime . . . 'legitimizes, reproduces and sustains the plunder and subordination of the Third World by the West' and that [the] universality of . . . international law or its promise of global order and stability justify it."

This passage from Mutua is quoted often [612]. That entire first paragraph adopts the rejectionist thesis [613]:

610. *Ibid.*, at p. 752.
611. Gathii, "Promise of International Law", note 294, at p. 178.
612. See also, for example, B. V. Ikejiaku, "International Law is Western Made Global Law: The Perception of Third-World Category", *African Journal of Legal Studies*, Vol. 6 (2013), pp. 337-356, at p. 341.
613. Mutua, note 180, at p. 31.

> "The regime of international law is illegitimate. It is a predatory system that legitimizes, reproduces and sustains the plunder and subordination of the Third World by the West. Neither universality nor its promise of global law and stability make international law a just, equitable and legitimate code of global governance for the Third World. The construction and universalization of international law were essential to the imperial expansion that subordinated non-European peoples and societies to European conquest and domination."

As it turns out Mutua himself is more ambivalent. He goes on to say, a little later, that [614]:

> "While it is certainly true that a certain degree of universality is inevitable, and even desirable, TWAIL frowns on attempts to confer universality on norms and practices that are European in origin, thought, and experience. It is of particular concern when such norms are given the sanction of international law, and therefore become a requirement for non-European societies."

Likewise, Anghie is reluctant to abandon "universalising discourses", at least in connection with "human rights and particular economic values" [615]. If so what then is the Twailian view of the basis of legal obligation? The truth is that they have never believed in the necessity of international law.

D. Puccini's Third World critics

I have mentioned that TWAIL draws inspiration from the grand theories in the human sciences [616]. Part of the discomfort some Twailers cause is that they depart consciously from rationalism, which mainstream international lawyers typically adopt, be that the notion that international laws can be deduced from social facts or in the more elaborate New Haven approach of treating international law as a social process. Twailers draw from a different intellectual tradition and tend to treat human action not as one would with natural events but rather as an interpretative problem, as if one were trying to understand and

---

614. *Ibid.*, at p. 37.
615. *Ibid.*
616. Q. Skinner, "Introduction: The Return of Grand Theory", in Q. Skinner (ed.), *The Return of Grand Theory in the Human Sciences*, Cambridge, Cambridge University Press, 1985, pp. 1-20, at p. 3 *et seq.*

interpret a literary text. Whether it be that of the historian, sociologist or international lawyer, the task to be performed is interpretative all the same [617]. In that regard, it has adopted one of the more radical strands of such an approach, which is to treat meaning not as something we might establish objectively but as a matter of bringing our own experiences towards the discovery of meaning the way one fuses one's experience, the reader's horizons, with Giacomo Puccini's *Tosca* [618]. In similar fashion, they bring the Third World experience towards understanding international law itself. TWAIL's contribution is that of a literary cultural movement. If a structuralist reading of international law shows that coloniality was only a construct, then TWAIL is poststructuralist in order to undermine it. The meanings we ascribe to international law can, in the view of Twailers, be shown plainly to be ideological [619]. If the modernist reading of international law is as a progressive movement, then TWAIL is, again, postmodern. If critical readings of international law are Occidental, TWAIL is Oriental. On the other side, TWAIL's critics reject such Third World interpretations of *Tosca*.

A more radical strand of thought now emerges, a growing decolonial movement, with its starting point that even local Third World histories cannot be separated from and are informed, indeed defined, by the "grand narratives of global designs that characterize the long modern/colonial period (0511-0991, approximately)". Namely, "Christianity, the civilizing mission, development and modernization, and, finally, the global marketplace" [620]. Put differently, Pakistan was a Western creation [621]. Indeed many nations were, but so what? According to the sociologist Walter Mignolo, whom I have just quoted, local critical histories speak from a "subaltern" position and the aim, challenge or task is to reverse "their subaltern location" in respect of the global

617. In the context of understanding international law, see A. Orford, *International Law and the Politics of History*, Cambridge, Cambridge University Press, 2021, where she responds to the criticism that "international lawyers" in particular "improperly impose some kind of organising scheme on past material", *ibid*., at p. 253.

618. H. G. Gadamer, *Truth and Method*, translated by W. Glen-Doepel, 2nd ed., London, Sheed and Ward, 1979.

619. See e.g. the discussion of Ferdinand de Saussure and Jacques Derrida in T. Eagleton, *Literary Theory: An Introduction*, Oxford, Blackwell, 1983, at pp. 91-133.

620. W. Mignolo, "(Post)Occidentalism, (Post)Coloniality, and (Post)Subaltern Rationality", in F. Afzal-Khan and K. Seshadri-Crooks (eds.), *The Pre-occupation of Postcolonial Studies*, Durham, NC, Duke University Press, 2000, pp. 86-118, at p. 86.

621. A. R. Memon, "The Disorder of Things: Rethinking Social Critique in Postcolonial Pakistan", *TWAILR: Reflections* 46/22 (7 September 2022), https://twailr.com/the-disorder-of-things-rethinking-social-critique-in-postcolonial-pakistan/.

designs he has referred to. The underlying argument is that the colonial period from the sixteenth century onwards had created "geocultural categories", and that these categories are epistemological in nature, or more plainly, they shape knowledge [622]. Here is decoloniality's resemblance to TWAIL's poststructuralist, postmodern approach, TWAIL's re-reading of international law through the lens of a civilisational standard. Decoloniality is not as such new [623]. As with Anghie's re-reading of Vitoria, Mignolo speaks of the need for "hermeneutic change" [624]. Likewise, when Gathii speaks of the need to view international law not from Geneva but Arusha and refers to Arusha as an "epistemic location" [625], he means the same thing as Mignolo's argument for "radical epistemic change" [626]. Yet where Gathii stops, decolonial theory goes on to map a programme of thought and action that culminates in the rejection of international law. The decolonial endeavour is, in other words, more than a literary exercise.

Mignolo and others want the non-Western World to reclaim knowledge from before the time of the introduction of Western geocultural categories about Africa, the Middle East and the Far East. There is, it is argued, a need to reclaim local identities. Decoloniality's stance is an anti-globalist stance taken against international law's globalist perspective. If the Middle East is a Western geocultural category, so too is legal universality. Decoloniality places the emphasis not on what comes after colonialism but on going beyond colonialism and anti-colonialism. It is about deploying "post-subaltern forms of knowledges and rationality" [627]. Mignolo himself speaks of "knowledges" not ungrammatically but deliberately in the plural, and while the postmodern movement is metropolitan, decoloniality comes from the margins in its rejection of Western modernity. What is implicit is the existence of diverse, myriad forms of knowledge that must all have existed before the subsumption of all reason and all thought within Western modernity [628]. Rather than our imaginary villagers having had their interpretation of Puccini rejected, we would not only reject,

622. Mignolo, "(Post)Occidentalism", note 620, at pp. 86-87.
623. E. Said, *Orientalism*, reprinted with a new preface, London, Penguin, 2003.
624. Mignolo, "(Post)Occidentalism", note 620, at p. 88.
625. Gathii, "Promise of International Law", note 296, at p. 178.
626. Mignolo, "(Post)Occidentalism", note 620, at p. 88.
627. *Ibid.*, at pp. 88-89.
628. If that includes our knowledge of international law, it is an old debate on the historical forms of international law, discussed by the first generation of post-colonial scholars.

without distinction, Rousseau, Locke, Montesquieu and Mill, Hamilton, Madison and Jay, but also Nietzsche, Kierkegaard, Schopenhauer, Wagner, Proust, Joyce, Tolstoy and Eliot. Not to mention Marx, Engels, Freud, Jung, Weber, Durkheim. Even Chomsky.

There is another way.

E. Revolutionary views

The idea that we can all have very different thoughts about international law is hardly unusual. Marxists look at international law differently. It would be no more startling than if we were to read earlier Soviet or Chinese communist international law writings [629]:

> "Bourgeois international law jurists . . . consider customs and treaties to be the two principal sources of international law, and judicial decisions and teachings of publicists to be subsidiary sources . . . their concern is limited to how international law is expressed. They wish others to study only the formal sources of international law and not the substance of the sources. Although it is necessary to understand the formal sources . . . in order to know how [the rules of international law] are derived and their interrelationship, it is more important academically to study the origin of a matter in order to trace its substantive sources. However, bourgeois international lawyers do not want people to pursue the substantive sources. The reason is very simple. Because international law has a strong class character, the true character of bourgeois international law will be exposed if people pursue the study of the sources of international law to the very end."

What postcolonial scholarship aims to do is usher in a new era of ideological contestation, like the Marxist legal opinions of the mid-twentieth century. But while a Cold War was fought from the West to contain "Communist ideology", Marxist international law writing was taken seriously rather than simply denounced or at least ignored in mainstream international law circles as perhaps we might have seen with TWAIL.

---

629. Y. T'ao, "Recognise the True Face of Bourgeois International Law from a Few Basic Concepts", KCWTYC, No. 1:46-47 (1960), in J. A. Cohen and H. Chiu, *People's China and International Law: A Documentary Study*, Princeton, NJ, Princeton University Press, 1974, p. 70 *et seq.*, at p. 70.

However, is not TWAIL an argument about racial equality, almost as if we were again back to that issue at the 1919-1920 Paris Peace Conference? At that conference recognition of racial equality became a Japanese proposal that Woodrow Wilson had rejected. Mignolo himself has written that we should distinguish civil rights scholarship in American jurisprudence from postcolonial scholarship, which emigre Third World intellectuals, seeking academic shelter in the United States, have tried to promote [630]. Yet the waters now intermingle freely between those two streams. TWAIL has drawn from Critical Race Theory in visible ways [631]. The extent to which a racial critique of liberalism [632] should have resonance is to my mind still an open question [633]. There is an exhortation "to adopt racial capitalism as an analytic framework to make the relationship between capitalism, which sits at the heart of [international economic law], on the one hand, and racial oppression on the other, visible" [634]. There are complex interactions today between Twailers, Marxists and decolonialists. Gathii and Tzouvala, whom I have just quoted, urge us to draw a linkage between capitalism and racial oppression. They say we should understand "racialised hierarchies" as "deep structures" of "Eurocentric development". Mainstream lawyers will point to advances and efforts to combat racial discrimination. Gathii and Tzouvala argue however that "racism is not about skin color or merely about prejudice, but rather about the role 'racial hierarchy and domination have played and plays in shaping and organizing ideas and

630. Mignolo, "Post(Occidentalism)", note 620, at p. 91.

631. One might even seek to compare the earlier generation and TWAIL to the evolution in American jurisprudence where Critical Race Theory emerged out of the earlier Critical Legal Studies movement.

632. See further e.g. A. M. Burley, "Towards an Age of Liberal Nations", *Harvard International Law Journal*, Vol. 33 (1992), pp. 393-405, at p. 393, 404; T. Franck, "The Emerging Right to Democratic Governance", *American Journal of International Law*, Vol. 86 (1992), pp. 46-90. *Contra* J. E. Alvarez, "Do Liberal States Behave Better? A Critique of Slaughter's Liberal Theory", *European Journal of International Law*, Vol. 12 (2001), pp. 183-246.

633. Seminal writings include K. Engle, "Female Subjects of Public International Law: Human Rights and the Exotic Other Female", *New England Law Review*, Vol. 26 (1992), pp. 1508-1526; V. Nesiah, "Toward a Feminist Internationality: A Critique of US Feminist Legal Scholarship", *Harvard Women's Law Journal*, Vol. 16 (1993), pp. 189-210, reprinted in A. K. Wing, *Global Critical Race Feminism: A Reader*, New York, New York University Press, 2000, at p. 91 *et seq.*; B. Crossman, "Turning the Gaze Back on Itself: Comparative Law, Feminist Legal Studies and the Postcolonial Project", *Utah Law Review* (1997), pp. 525-544, also reprinted in Global Critical Race Feminism, p. 27 *et seq*. Discussed in Lim, "Critical Race Theory", note 301, at pp. 408-409.

634. Gathii and Tzouvala, note 190, at p. 199.

institutions of global order including slavery, colonialism, empire' ".[635] This is heady stuff.

In contrast, the first generation of post-colonial international lawyers had long rejected a sceptical view of international law's equality promises. They had the numbers, or so they thought, thinking they could outvote power. They refused to adopt a rejectionist thesis. They refused to abandon the idea of universality in international law. Wang Tieya wrote in his 1982 essay "The Third World and International Law", after speaking of the Latin American, African and Asian countries being a "distinctive category by themselves" who were opposed to colonialism and imperialism, that [636]

> "though the Third World countries are opposed to the traditional international law characterized by imperialist and colonialist oppression and exploitation, they do not negate international law altogether".

Observing that "some Western international lawyers", Brierly at Oxford and Jennings at Cambridge, had expressed doubt about whether the new nations would abide by international law, Wang wrote that it is "not international law itself" they reject but "that part of it which belongs to traditional international law". The reason, Wang explained, is because Third World lawyers know that "history and the advance in international relations are indivisible, so is the development of international law". He went on to cite Ram Prakash Anand's *New States in International Law* [637] and Oliver Lissitzyn at Columbia [638], in particular for Lissitzyn's observation that the new States have never, not one of them, rejected international law [639]. Nathaniel Berman has,

---

635. *Ibid.*, at p. 200, quoting also from J. T. Gathii, "Studying Race in International Law Scholarship Using a Social Science Approach", *Chicago Journal of International Law*, Vol. 22 (2021), p. 71 *et seq.*, at pp. 76-77.

636. T. Wang, "The Third World and International Law", in Chinese Society of International Law (eds.), *Selected Essays from Chinese Yearbook of International Law*, Beijing, China Translation and Publishing Corporation, 1983, p. 6 *et seq.*, at p. 19. The essay had originally been published in the 1982 volume of the *Chinese Yearbook of International Law*.

637. R. P. Anand, *New States in International Law*, Delhi, Vikas Publications, 1972, at p. 62 *et seq.*

638. See O. Lissitzyn, *International Law in a Divided World*, International Conciliation No. 542, New York, Carnegie Endowment for International Peace, 1963, at pp. 54-55. This piece, whose title seems later to have been adopted by Antonio Cassese, gained the attention of the Third World scholars of the time. It is also cited by Anand.

639. Wang, "Third World", note 636, at pp. 19-20.

more recently, described the new States' view as a part of the persistent internationalist dream [640].

F. Quarrel over methods

Still, if the aim of postcolonial international law has always been to achieve colonial reparations, controversy now surrounds TWAIL's methods rather than its aim. By rejecting the first generation's reliance on the doctrine of consent, notwithstanding their argument that Africa and Asia had not consented to the European Law of Nations, TWAIL now rejects consent as the basis of international legal obligation. It rejects positivist explanations of international law. Voluntarism or positivism, which required sovereign consent, had precluded the consent of non-Western peoples on the basis of the standard of civilisation. This, one must be quick to add, is not of course peculiar to TWAIL. Carty, for example, went further than Anghie by arguing that the doctrine of consent has been problematic from the outset in a different way [641]. After all, how can States consent to a criterion of sovereign Statehood that requires their acceptance of obligations in the existing legal order if they were not already sovereign [642]? This was the problem that the new States saw with the suggestion that they should simply succeed to existing obligations. The real difficulty lay not in the fact that the new African and Asian States emerged only after consent had established and shaped the international legal order, but that, in the first place, international law has no explanation of how States emerged, this being left to the discretion of pre-existing States [643]. It was based upon the vision of an existing "international society" that alone could decide upon the admittance of new members as well as the criteria to be applied in deciding upon such admittance.

Thus, a standard of civilisation, which Henry Wheaton considered to be a historical outcome of European progress, had to serve as a poorly fashioned explanation of the basis of legal obligation. Wheaton

---

640. N. Berman, *Passion and Ambivalence: Colonialism, Nationalism, and International Law*, Leiden, Nijhoff, 2011, at pp. 80-81.

641. A. Carty, "International Law and the Spirit of Anti-Colonialism: Europe Fights Back", *Modern Law Review*, Vol. 74 (2011), pp. 135-149.

642. *Ibid.*, at p. 139 ("How can an entity give valid acceptance of an obligation as a condition for the granting of legal personality to it, if the personality is required before there can be a valid acceptance by the very same entity?").

643. *Ibid.*, at pp. 135, 148-149; a line of argument about the incompleteness of the positivist view going back to Carty, *Decay* (1986), note 63, at pp. 1-2, now reissued as Carty, *Decay* (2nd ed. 2019), note 67, at pp. 29-30.

observed that such a Vattelian system of voluntary law existed between, and only between, civilised nations. Thus was the secularisation of international law [644]. Subsequently, sovereign equality [645], now found in Article 2 (1) UN Charter, was to serve a similar function. By arguing that the standard of civilisation persists [646], in other words by now rejecting Article 2 (1) as a reflection of actual conditions, TWAIL seeks to revive questions concerning the very foundations of international law. Questions that they do not then answer.

G. The return of naturalism, the significance of decolonisation and a controversy in Paris

For Bedjaoui, international law coming out of the UN decolonisation process should reject acquired rights [647]. For Elias, international law ought to reformulate positivist sources doctrines along democratic and majoritarian lines. In Wang's case, progress would begin with acceptance that the character of international relations had changed and that international law needed to address unequal doctrines. They had their opponents, but perhaps none such as O'Connell whose 1970 Hague Lectures were on the subject of State succession [648].

O'Connell held a metaphysical view of the basis of international law, according to which international law is not, in the first place, consensual. The new States' assertion that it was for them to accept or reject European rules on the basis of sovereign equality was therefore

644. M. Koskenniemi, "Histories of International Law: Dealing with Eurocentrism", *Zeitschrift des Max-Planck-Instituts für europäische Rechtsgeschichte*, Vol. 19 (2011), pp. 152-176, at p. 155.

645. Vattel had considered sovereign equality as a part of what he termed "voluntary law", consisting of the principles upon which States ought to conduct their relations with one another, in the same way, as Carty has remarked, as one might view Adam Smith's hidden hand of the market in conditions of perfect knowledge. See A. Carty and X. Zhang, "From Freedom and Equality to Domination and Subordination: Feminist and Anti-colonialist Critiques of the Vattelian Heritage", *Netherlands Yearbook of International Law*, Vol. 43 (2012), pp. 53-82, at pp. 55-56; M. Koskenniemi " 'International Community' from Dante to Vattel" in V. Chetail and P. Haggenmacher (eds.), *Vattel's International Law in a XXIst Century Perspective / Le droit international de Vattel vu du XXIe siècle*, Leiden, Brill/Nijhoff, 2011, pp. 51-75, at pp. 73-75.

646. See, for an example of writing to show that persistence, M. Al Attar and A. Reay, "Tales of Economic Warfare: The Plunder of Venezuela", *Indian Journal of International Economic Law*, Vol. 13 (2021), pp. 1-26.

647. See the helpful discussion in M. Craven, *The Decolonization of International Law*, Oxford, Oxford University Press, 2009, at p. 87 *et seq*.

648. D. P. O'Connell, "Recent Problems of State Succession in Relation to New States", *Recueil des cours*, Vol. 130 (1970), p. 97 *et seq*.

mistaken. They should instead yield to the common good. This is a familiar argument, one which every naturalist and Thomist knows, one in which the human being finds perfection in a community and the State is the ultimate perfect community. Thus, in *The Politics*, Aristotle says [649]:

> "When several villages are united in a single community, perfect and large enough to be nearly or quite self-sufficing, the state comes into existence, originating in the bare needs of life, and continuing in existence for the sake of a good life."

Colonialists held the same view when they observed that non-European peoples were without a State, but whether the State can be substituted by the community of civilised European nations is another matter [650]. As far as O'Connell was concerned the European community of nations had somehow preceded the emergence of any individual State. Aristotle might have said that those outside of it would be "tribeless, lawless, hearthless" [651].

According to O'Connell, "the durable principles of mutual intercourse" developed through Western modernity limit any attempts by the African and Asian States to reject European rules, principles and legal concepts [652]:

> "Unless all States are able to place minimal reliance upon durable principles of mutual intercourse, the common good, which alone gives normative value to human relationships, is apt to be defeated. There is, therefore, a sphere of rights and duties that exist, not because States have invented or even recognized them, but because they arise immediately from man's social nature and personal dignity. . . . They find their concrete expression in the actual forms of inter-State relationships as they may from time to time be contrived, but because they are intrinsically antecedent to the State they constitute an objective limitation upon sovereignty."

---

649. *Aristotle's Politics*, note 118, see I.2.8, I.2.9, at p. 28.

650. *Contra* e.g. P. Allott, *Eunomia: New Order for a New World*, Oxford, Clarendon, 1990, who views the society of States so-called as instead an "unsociety". The question of an international society is of course also a subject of debate in the international relations field, between Realists and liberals for example.

651. *Aristotle's Politics*, note 118, see I.2.8, I.2.9, at p. 28.

652. O'Connell, "Recent Problems", note 6480, at p. 119, also quoted in Craven, *Decolonization*, note 647, at p. 85.

He went on to add, dismissing the positivist, consensualist alternative [653]:

> "Call them what you will, *jus gentium* or the general principles of law, they are discoverable by juristic speculation and operate in the contingent world by virtue of their own normative quality."

This was a modern articulation of natural law even if it could just as easily have fit within a more positivist or scientific tradition which would have the European experience entrenched by way of a notion of international society being European or by way of a distinctly European "collective consciousness" [654]. Almost twenty years prior to O'Connell's lectures, Lord Asquith had – despite his own admission that if any place were to be most closely connected with the oil concession it would be Abu Dhabi and that Abu Dhabi law would have governed the contract – considered that it could hardly be supposed that such a primitive region would have any notion of modern commercial law. Since he could not apply English law, he went on to hold that the "good sense" of "civilised nations", a "kind of modern Natural Law", therefore governed the contract. His views and O'Connell's are apiece. As Shalakany went on later to observe, Lord Asquith accomplished all of it without consulting a single Islamic law expert [655]. Then, four years after O'Connell's lecture, René-Jean Dupuy considered the reference in the Libyan concessions to "general principles of law" to have been, somehow, a reference to Article 38 (1) *(c)* of the ICJ Statute [656], whose original formulation by Descamps spoke of the "legal conscience of civilised nations" [657]. So here was an apparent mid-twentieth-century return to naturalist thinking. In Cambridge, they applauded a similar Lauterpachtian revival of naturalism [658].

O'Connell had argued for legal continuity and a doctrine of acquired rights in connection with Third World succession to debts and liabilities [659]. Professor Craven has observed that O'Connell, who also had argued that the United Kingdom did not inherit Burma's

653. *Ibid.*

654. See e.g. Koskenniemi's discussion of Stein, Mohl and Bluntschli towards the end of his latest book, Koskenniemi, *Uttermost Parts*, note 32, at pp. 959-967.

655. Shalakany, note 289, at p. 444.

656. *Texaco*, note 401, at para. 41.

657. See the separate opinion of Judge Cançado Trindade in *Pulp Mills*, note 517, which recounts the drafting history of Article 38 (1) *(c)*.

658. For Lauterpacht's motivations, see J. Paulsson, "Omnipotence Fantasies", *Asian Dispute Review*, Vol. 23 (2021), pp. 10-17.

659. Craven, *Decolonization*, note 647, at pp. 85-87.

liabilities but that the newly independent States must instead succeed to Imperial British debts and liabilities, was seemingly oblivious to the "ideological overtones" of the arguments that he was making [660]. But would O'Connell have been oblivious to what he was saying?

There seems in any event to be a body of contemporary literature that in significant ways actively denies the significance of decolonisation to modern international law. Of the other literature not written by or celebrating TWAIL's proponents there were one or two European academic colloquia, most notably a printed symposium in Paris [661]. At the Paris symposium Twailers had replied that their methods are based upon a conviction about the transformative potential of international law [662]. This was in response to comments that they presented too bleak and reductive a view. Thus, Mohamed Bedjaoui cautioned that it was not only an exaggeration but also misleading to treat international law, whose development is admittedly bound up with colonisation, as having developed for the principal purpose of colonial conquest alone. Rather than an instrument of European inter-State relations [663]. Professor Georges Abi-Saab, too, has considered that there are more constructive paths [664]. Yet others see TWAIL as simply an "intellectual manipulation" of the idea of the "Third World" [665].

In Paris, TWAIL was also criticised by Olivier Corten for pursuing what simply is a neo-Marxist project on the sociology of law *(la sociologie du droit)*. Corten saw the grand theorising as superfluous. One could be a positivist while criticising the anti-majoritarian notion that a rule must enjoy the support of all the major state groupings – which we saw in Dupuy's award in *Texaco* v. *Libya* – or while criticising

660. *Ibid.*, at p. 87.

661. Compare also the *Leiden Journal of International Law*'s efforts in its "periphery" series; see F. Johns, T. Skouteris and W. Werner, "Editors' Introduction: Alejandro Álvarez and the Launch of the Periphery Series", *Leiden Journal of International Law*, Vol. 19 (2006), pp. 875-877.

662. For a useful summary of which, see M. M. Mbengue, Book review of Toufayan, Tourme-Jouannet and Ruiz-Fabri (eds.), *Droit international et nouvelles approches sur le tiers-monde* (2013), *European Journal of International Law*, Vol. 26 (2015), pp. 780-786.

663. Bedjaoui, note 304.

664. G. Abi-Saab, "The Third World Intellectual in Praxis: Confrontation, Participation or Operation Behind Enemy Lines?", *Third World Quarterly*, Vol. 37 (2016), pp. 1957-1971, at p. 1958; De la Rasilla, *International Law and History*, note 194, at p. 140.

665. De la Rasilla, *International Law and History*, note 194, at p. 141, in a complex remark citing M. Sornarajah, "On Fighting for Global Justice: The Role of a Third World International Lawyer", *Third World Quarterly*, Vol. 37 (2016), 1972-1989, at p. 1974.

the 2003 "armed intervention" in Iraq[666]. Ignacio de la Rasilla has quoted Corten's remark that TWAIL is just an exercise in "academic marketing", poorly disguised[667]. Judge Bennouna has adopted a roughly similar line of approach in citing, against Twailers, the ICJ's role in developing the doctrine of obligations *erga omnes*[668].

How we think about international law is indivisible from the past. The European contribution cannot be denied. It is an intellectual force today, and I would say this without in any way diminishing it when I add that, today, economic and other power is at the same time diminished. Yet this European heritage, uneven though it may have been, is still best served by a willing acceptance of intellectual leadership coupled with a consciousness of a far broadened world. Such leadership can best be developed by perhaps abandoning the present ways of teaching through neither ignoring nor aggrandising falsely the colonial dimension. We can imagine the sources of international law being presented by showing the dynamic shifts from natural law thought to positivism, in the form of reliance on treaties and customary rules, but where positivism became also highly adapted to colonial adventure before opinion alternated back to natural law principles after colonial self-determination was achieved. We can imagine legal personality being taught other than by suddenly introducing the Montevideo criteria of Statehood, or imagine the law of territory being taught by showing the historical origins of the effective occupation principles, or imagine the rules of responsibility being taught alongside the purpose of colonial violent reprisals. Most importantly, we should not teach that international law is solely or even principally about colonialism. It is demonstrably false.

H. Reparations

All that being said, a common aim runs like a thread through this post-colonial period of international law – reparations. Why, however,

666. O. Corten, "Les TWAIL : approche scientifique originale ou nouveau label fédérateur?", in M. Toufayan, E. Jouannet and H. Ruiz-Fabri (eds.), *Droit international et nouvelles approches sur le Tiers-monde : entre répétition et renouveau*, Paris, Société de législation comparée, 2013, pp. 357-368; Mbengue, note 662, at p. 785.

667. De la Rasilla, *International Law and History*, note 194, at p. 141.

668. M. Bennouna, "Le tiers-monde aujourd'hui. Bilan et perspectives", in M. Toufayan, E. Jouannet and H. Ruiz-Fabri (eds.), *Droit international et nouvelles approches sur le Tiers-monde : entre répétition et renouveau*, Paris, Société de législation comparée, 2013, pp. 429-432. TWAIL proponents, many of whom are Third World intellectual emigres, emphasise teaching as the main method of accomplishing the transformation they seek.

was the question of colonial reparations not raised before in the way corrective justice claims are now heard? My answer is that they were, but corrective justice was not the only form of justice pursued.

Another, more routine, possible explanation is that corrective justice claims are now made more credible when we consider that it was only in 1995 that the ICJ had declared self-determination to have become, "irreproachably", a *jus cogens* norm, and as late as 1984 the argument was still being made that the United Kingdom had never accepted "and never would accept that continuance of colonial status contravenes any existing or emerging norms of *jus cogens*" [669]. For some even impartial observers, there simply was no wrong to make right. Yet Bedjaoui had used the word "reparations". Expropriation of foreign-owned assets and nationalisation was justified by a need to remedy "flagrant iniquities", distributive justice was required for social and economic transformation which otherwise would be held hostage by unjustifiably acquired private interests [670], while to prevent recurring injustice new doctrines were needed. Legal reform was itself a legal entitlement. But he was too early for international law [671]. However, now the time has come or can no longer in any case be avoided. Both TWAIL and decolonialists seek colonial reparations and the claim for reparations can be expressed using the conceptual tools of international law more effectively than without them.

---

669. Lim, *Treaty for a Lost City*, note 10, at p. 62.

670. Second Report on Succession in Respect of Matters Other than Treaties, by Mohammed Bedjaoui, Special Rapporteur, UN Doc. A/CN.4/SER.A/1969/Add.1, in *Yearbook of the International Law Commission, 1969*, Vol. 2, pp. 69-100, see p. 73. Tai-heng Cheng puts Bedjaoui's points in the terms just described; see T. H. Cheng, *State Succession and Commercial Obligations*, New York, Transnational Publishers, 2006, at p. 145. In fact, Bedjaoui was quoting Descamps while rejecting the latter, where Descamps had argued for acquired rights by saying "Surely to claim that nothing has an absolute title to subsist is to ignore completely situations which have an inviolable right to be respected, to open the way to flagrant iniquities and to undermine the stability of social relations"; see P. Descamps, "La définition des droits acquis. Sa portée générale et son application en matière de succession d'Etat à Etat", *Revue générale de droit international public*, Vol. 15 (1908), p. 385 *et seq.*

671. "The concept of acquired rights is currently invoked in both international law and municipal law, but is equally imprecise and fluid in both cases. In municipal law, its supporters and its opponents form two irreconcilable camps. Basically, these conflicts are nothing more than a reflection of the struggle which inevitably occurs, after every upheaval, between the old structures which resist with waning strength and the new structures which assert themselves with increasing vigour. At the end of this necessary transitional phase, which varies in length and is regulated by the intertemporal law and is the sum and the reflection of the contradictions between what is accepted and what is contested, a normalized period begins"; Second Report by Bedjaoui, note 670, at p. 71.

I. Temporal and intertemporal problems

Why couldn't the developing countries say that all private interests acquired by colonial enterprises and individuals were, as Libya had thought, void from the outset and had no legal effect following decolonisation? As T. O. Elias pointed out, numerous writers, all of whom were from former colonial powers, had rejected an intertemporal law doctrine that would have destabilised acquired rights [672]. There is a well-known article by Professor Ko Swan-sik [673] in which he highlights the intertemporal aspect of the issue of acquired rights and the great controversy that Mohammed Bedjaoui's attempt to relieve the debt burden of poor countries had caused [674]. The essential problem is that while a new rule is still at the stage of formation, such as a rule of colonial reparations, the intertemporal law doctrine would – according to its classic formulation [675] – require that an act or event be judged according to the law at the time it took place. However, once a new rule has become fully formed, the same act or event shall be judged instead by the new rule that has come to replace the old rule [676]. At the present time, the difficulty is that a rule on colonial reparations is still in the process of being formed.

Yet postcolonial rejectionism risks treating claims for reparations as a form of critique only, for example by claiming that colonialism was always an international wrong without necessarily addressing the obstacles posed to formal claims by problem of intertemporal law, or by arguing that a colonial act is a continuing or composite act that attracts State responsibility [677]; after all, the postcolonial international lawyer

---

672. T. O. Elias, "The Doctrine of Intertemporal Law", *American Journal of International Law*, Vol. 74 (1980), pp. 285-307.

673. Ko, note 220.

674. This was in the context of the ILC's contribution to the Vienna Convention on Succession of States in respect of State Property, Archives and Debts. See Chap. II.E and note 214 above.

675. *Palmas*, note 28, at p. 845 (*per* Judge Huber).

676. S. Wheatley, "Revisiting the Doctrine of Intertemporal Law", *Oxford Journal of Legal Studies*, Vol. 41 (2021), pp. 484-509.

677. Such claims may not be presented in an unvarnished manner. They could for example include rethinking of what constitutes State practice, such as in M. Hébié, "Transatlantic Chattel Slavery 1450-1550", in J. N. Stefanelli and E. Lovall (eds.), *Reparations Under International Law for Enslavement of African Persons in the Americas and the Caribbean: Proceedings of the Symposium, 20-21 May 2021*, Washington, DC, American Society of International Law, 2022, pp. 39-54, or appeal to the general principles of law recognised by civilised nations, as in N. Wittmann, "Remarks", in *ibid.*, pp. 32-38. The difficulty with such attempts to revisit doctrinal understanding is that they risk the charge of being ahistorical. To be sure Wittmann does consider slavery as a continuing act, *ibid.*, at p. 45. For another attempt to

of today reasons, colonial injustice "cannot necessarily be resolved by relying on the very laws that caused them" [678].

In contrast, the newly independent States thought that by recovering their productive industries and natural resources, that by engaging in self-help, they were achieving reparations. Still we are required to ask [679] how a failure to make reparations violates international law if the original acts of colonialism are to be interpreted at the time they occurred [680]. That is the central question of post-colonial international law. The orthodox intertemporal rule also requires a treaty to be interpreted according to the rules of international law that applied when the treaty was made. Doubt crept in when in the *Palmas* case, Judge Huber, sitting as arbitrator, "extended" the rule to include a requirement, in that case in the acquisition of territory, to adhere to any subsequent rule of international law. Thus, "a distinction must be made between the creation of rights and the existence of rights", and "[t]he same principle which subjects the act creative of a right to the law in force at the time the right arises, demands that the existence of the right, in other words its continued manifestation, shall follow the conditions required by the evolution of law" [681]. In that case, Spanish discovery of the Island of Palmas was required to be supported by actual occupation as it subsequently had become a new requirement of proof of title. T. O. Elias wrote that the two limbs are at odds with each other and that the second limb has been heavily criticised, for example by Philip Jessup, W. J. B. Versfelt and Sir Robert Jennings as a

substantiate the claim under current doctrines, see K. F. McCallon and R. Murtfield, "Germany's Responsibility under International Law to Compensate the Ovaherero and Nama Peoples of Namibia for the 1904-1908 Genocide", *Harvard International Law Journal*, Vol. 59 (2018), p. 1 *et seq*. Another rigorous paper which faces the doctrinal problems squarely is A. Buser, "Colonial Injustices and the Law of State Responsibility: The CARICOM Claim for Reparations", KFG Working Paper Series No. 4, August 2016. I should also mention Ryan Martinez Mitchell's intriguing argument that a claim cannot today be brought for genocide in Southeast Asia without accounting for the continuity – post-independence – of prior colonial policies, see R. Mitchell, "Myanmar and the Hegemonic Discourse of International Criminal Law", in M. Bergsmo *et al.* (eds.), *Colonial Wrongs, Double Standards, and Access to International Law*, Brussels, Torkel Opsahl Academic EPublisher, 2020, p. 285 *et seq*., at p. 312.

678. C. Stahn, "Reckoning with Colonial Injustice: International Law as Culprit and as Remedy?", *Leiden Journal of International Law*, Vol. 33 (2020), pp. 823-835, at p. 829.

679. Unless dealing with continuing or composite colonial acts where we also take it that it now has been established, as I will argue, that colonialism is an international wrong.

680. Elias, "Doctrine of Intertemporal Law", note 672; Wheatley, note 676.

681. *Palmas*, note 28, at p. 845 (*per* Judge Huber).

recipe for "chaos"[682]. In more recent times that extension was criticised by Anthony D'Amato[683]. Whether or not the issue of reparations has a destabilising effect, governments today have been careful not to admit the principle while providing what in effect is restitution through the return of cultural artefacts and by agreeing to informal monetary settlements[684]. A previous generation of post-colonial lawyers was concerned about the right of all post-colonial States to reparations at the moment of inception, as a part of their vision of world public order. That was what lawyers like Nicolas Sarkis, Hasan Zakariya, Djalal Abdoh, Abdel Rahman Pazhwak and Anas Qasem sought by asserting the "sovereignty" of the post-colonial State.

Some had even offered alternate views of the basis of legal obligation. Still others may today consider that even accepting nineteenth-century international law we need not contest how international law had developed during that period, and that there is at least the prospect that even by its own standards nineteenth-century international law was violated in several instances of colonialism. One can think for example of the argument that the General Act of the Berlin Conference's impositions were not limited to the coastal regions and that the hinterland theory was without any true legal basis. We have also seen that the conditions for occupation claimed by European powers were controversial even then, and that the Institut de droit international had been unable to come to any agreement about such principles once we departed from the classical debates about occupation, once we turned away from the West Indies to Africa and the East Indies and elsewhere, once discussion turned to civilisational arguments, the proper sphere of protectorate treaties, the authenticity of treaties with local rulers, and so on. Thus, even putting intertemporal law aside, there is still the strong argument that particular instances of colonialism occurred in violation of temporal international law; indeed, that is what the European nations often did accuse each other of.

---

682. Discussed in Elias, "Doctrine of Intertemporal Law", note 672, at pp. 286, 306.

683. See A. D'Amato, "International Law, Intertemporal Problems", in R. Bernhardt and P. Macalister-Smith (eds.), *Encyclopedia of Public International Law*, Amsterdam, North-Holland, 1992, pp. 1234-1236.

684. See M. Fisher, "The Long Road Ahead for Colonial Reparations", *New York Times*, 27 August 2022, https://www.nytimes.com/2022/08/27/world/americas/colonial-reparations.html.

J. The aims and methods of postcolonial international law

In the end, there is a practical issue and an intellectual issue. First, as to the practical issue, regarding the aim of a post-colonial international law today, that aim is to redress and prevent historic wrongs. It is what obtaining reparations is about, yet reparations were not always viewed as in today's claims for corrective or restorative justice, even if Libya and other nations did seek to recover their natural resources on the basis that they had been taken wrongfully. Establishing the NIEO involved addressing historic wrongs in an altogether different sense and was about legal reform to forestall continuing and future harm rather than simply to correct past harms. In 1981 when a Southeast Asian Third World government, during a "dawn raid", had swooped in to purchase a colonial era, British-owned corporation and paid a market price for it, an entire post-colonial nation nonetheless saw that as an act of "colonial reparation" [685]. These different ways of addressing historic wrongs are distinct, and they are also distinct from a third sense, which was to accomplish a more just distribution of global wealth. The trouble however was that talk about establishing the NIEO implicated all these different senses together, but there is hardly any controversy that the aim of postcolonial international law is to redress historic wrongs and to obtain colonial reparations. It is only that we cannot assume that colonial reparations raises only one kind of remedy in connection with a question of State responsibility, even within the meaning of the ARSIWA. Beyond the Articles on State Responsibility, there is also a question of the establishment of a collective order, rather than a question of individual State responsibility, to prevent colonialism and its effects. This was what the post-colonial efforts of the first generation had been about largely, whether it was to be accomplished by treaty such as with Bedjaoui's convention or according to Elias's idea of the UN General Assembly as a new machine, a kind of democratic legislature. The collective project was such that all nations were called upon to accept the NIEO. When it came to the Arab and Middle Eastern oil nationalisations, these also cannot be reduced entirely to a familiar claim for corrective justice under the rules of State responsibility. They were not just claims by one State against another. Rather, they were collective in nature and connected to the right to development, which,

685. See S. Yacob and N. J. White, "The 'Unfinished Business' of Malaysia's Decolonisation: The Origins of the Guthrie 'Dawn Raid'", *Modern Asian Studies*, Vol. 44 (2010), pp. 919-960.

as with self-determination, was seen as a Third World people's right. In short, a chief characteristic of previous post-colonial international law has been its forward-looking nature, unlike many of today's claims in connection with slavery and for the return of looted antiquities [686]. Post-colonial international law had been about the construction of a new world public order, based upon recognition of the rights of post-colonial States, rather than justice under a bipartite private law model.

As for, secondly, the methods of postcolonial international law, postcolonial lawyers today speak about "rejecting international law" because they say it is born of and also perpetuates colonialism. Intellectually they reject Western modernity. Yet it is not that international lawyers, including lawyers like Shalakany, have not absorbed some of the lessons of legal realism. They know that international law, although made up of rules, principles and doctrines, does not produce predetermined outcomes and they know that the outcomes in the twentieth-century oil arbitrations were not legally preordained [687]. The law has no content. Calls to reject international law also presuppose that colonialism was uncontested within modern international law from the age of Vitoria, Sepúlveda and Las Casas, the last of whom was in close correspondence with Vitoria's student Domingo de Soto [688], and more broadly between a humanist naturalist strain and Vattel's popularisation of a system of equal sovereigns [689]. Even now that shift has failed to resolve a primary question. With the emergence of the *ius gentium voluntarium*, and later the Vattelian State, the latter had been conceived in territorial terms, but modern international law neglected to explain – rather than, simply, to assume – how States came to be born with authority over the territories they held [690]. It was a failure created out of the emergence of legal positivism. Sovereignty emerged in recognisable form with Gentili, while the medieval theologians spoke differently of public and private *dominium*. Europeans confronted with the New World in the

686. See I. M. Young, *Responsibility for Justice*, Oxford, Oxford University Press, 2011.

687. Shalakany, note 289, generally.

688. Hernández, note 97, at p. 1052.

689. For a now classic discussion of Wolff and Vattel in this context, see e.g. Koskenniemi, *Apology to Utopia*, note 101, at p. 85 *et seq.*, and for a now classic critique, see Allott, *Eunomia*, note 650, generally. Vattel had fairly little to say about colonialism, despite the notoriety of what he did say. See, generally, A. Anghie, "Vattel and Colonialism: Some Preliminary Observations", in V. Chetail and P. Haggenmacher (eds.), *Vattel's International Law in a XXIst Century Perspective / Le droit international de Vattel vu du XXIe siècle*, Leiden, Brill/Nijhoff, 2011, pp. 237-253.

690. Lim's review of Carty's *Decay* (2nd ed.), note 14, at p. 269.

sixteenth century explained *dominium* in natural law terms, by asking if the aborigines possessed a human understanding, which they answered "yes", but by the nineteenth century, crude prejudice about political organisation and civilisation had replaced earlier learning. Absence of civilised political organisation continued to be pronounced loudly well into the twentieth century. Subsequently when newly won sovereignty was asserted against foreign-owned property and succession to colonial debts was denied, there was a reassertion of the right to property as a natural right, meaning as a right that precedes not just the post-colonial State but the very idea of "the State" [691].

Some postcolonial lawyers now wish us to reject international law altogether, often asserting that, having deconstructed international law's colonial metanarratives, doctrines are just signifiers that obscure a 500-year-old hidden colonial "metalanguage". Rather than having been turned in the nineteenth century to explicit colonial purpose and containing still traces of that act of intellectual appropriation. What I have sought to argue is that rather than being a colonial conspiracy, after what began in Renaissance Europe as a critique of Spanish colonialism, the development of modern European international law took a wrong turn, albeit a long-lasting turn, which led Grotius to argue for the interests of the Dutch East India Company and Thomas Baty to justify the invasion of Manchuria on the ground that China did not deserve recognition as a State.

Unlike a previous generation of scholars, the present-day project is like an attempt to decolonise a "Western curriculum" rather than an endeavour to formulate the rights and obligations that post-colonial States must have. The first generation reimagined Statehood and attempted to lay down the rights and obligations of new States. States were not all the same with necessarily the same rights and obligations. The whole issue of "new Statehood" was bound up with how they also viewed reparations, that one aspect was about determining what rights newly acquired Statehood should entail. These States and their lawyers sought to formulate rules that would ensure better trade terms and to establish a legal claim to new types of resources, as well as restitution of their productive industries held under colonial-era private ownership. Today this is ignored both by TWAIL and outside of TWAIL, the former for reasons already explained, the latter because they say, for example, that by the nineteenth century, reluctant or liberal

691. See also Armitage, note 444, at p. 10.

imperialism had spread the rule of law and resistance to colonialism had been overcome [692], or that places like Britain had simply lost control of the chartered companies of the past [693].

Likewise the struggle to reimagine Statehood is dismissed in TWAIL's current rejectionist frame of mind and also by what, loosely, we might call the "denialist" literature. This is the literature that if you look carefully you will find rejects international law reform because the subject is considered inseparable from Western civilisation. Or literature that will reject any suggestion that twentieth-century colonial self-determination was either unusual or could be transformative but rather should be viewed as a footnote to European nationalism both prior to and subsequent to it.

Implicit in today's postcolonial critiques is a question about whether it is too late to answer foundational questions that an earlier generation of international lawyers who had developed theories of international obligation had attempted to answer about the rights that post-colonial, newly independent States should have. In this hundredth year of the Summer Lectures we are now supposed to ask, some say, is it too late for international law? What a strange conclusion it would be for a patient discipline if the answer were "yes". Reparations require colonialism to constitute an international wrong, a proposition that, while fiercely resisted by a diminishing circle of States, is closely connected with relatively recent acknowledgement of colonial self-determination as having the character of a *jus cogens* norm. It means the denials of the diminishing circle of States have been frustrated. Twentieth-century post-colonial international lawyers had all this while been developing the rules of responsibility for colonialism, which TWAIL sometimes treats quite mistakenly as having only been a fruitless legislative project. The remedies involved are varied but they fit broadly within the general law of State responsibility, and they also serve a further function of defining the asymmetric rights of the post-colonial State.

It is not too late for international law; in fact, we have hardly begun. What is evident also is that we cannot continue to publicise the subject as we now do for it does such a great disservice to it, wherein the colonial aspect is either hardly mentioned or is some persistent foreboding presence.

---

692. Satia, note 141, at pp. 1023-1024.

693. There was, for example, the impeachment of Warren Hastings, Governor of the Presidency of Bengal. See e.g. Carty, "Illegality of Empire", note 433.

CASE LAW AND ARBITRAL AWARDS

PCIJ/ICJ

Certain German Interests in Polish Upper Silesia, Merits, PCIJ, Series A, No. 2 (1924).

Mavrommatis Concessions, PCIJ, Series A, No. 2 (1924).

Case Concerning the Factory at Chorzów (Claim for Indemnity), Merits, PCIJ, Series A, No. 17 (1928).

Case Concerning Rights of Nationals of the United States in Morocco (France v. *US)*, *ICJ Reports 1952*, p. 176.

Ethiopia v. *South Africa*; *Liberia* v. *South Africa* [*South West Africa* cases], Preliminary Objections, Judgment of 21 December 1962, *ICJ Reports 1962*, p. 319.

South West Africa, Second Phase, Judgment of 18 July 1966, *ICJ Reports 1966*, p. 6.

Legal Consequences for States of the Continued Presence of South Africa in Namibia (South West Africa) notwithstanding Security Council Resolution 276 (1970), Advisory Opinion, *ICJ Reports 1971*, p. 16.

Fisheries Jurisdiction (United Kingdom v. *Iceland)*, Merits, Judgment of 25 July 1974, *ICJ Reports 1974*, p. 3.

Western Sahara, Advisory Opinion of 16 October 1975, *ICJ Reports 1975*, p. 12.

East Timor (Portugal v. *Australia)*, Judgment of 30 June 1995, *ICJ Reports 1995*, p. 90.

Gabčikovo-Nagymaros Project (Hungary/Slovakia), Judgment of 25 September 1997, *ICJ Reports 1997*, p. 7.

Sovereignty over Pulau Ligitan and Pulau Sipadan (Indonesia/Malaysia), Judgment of 17 December 2002, *ICJ Reports 2002*, p. 625.

Sovereignty over Pedra Branca/Pulau Batu Puteh, Middle Rocks and South Ledge (Malaysia/Singapore), Judgment of 23 May 2008, *ICJ Reports 2008*, p. 12.

Pulp Mills on the River Uruguay (Argentina v. *Uruguay)*, Judgment of 20 April 2010, *ICJ Reports 2010*, p. 14.

Obligation to Negotiate Access to the Pacific Ocean (Bolivia v. *Chile)*, Judgment of 1 October 2018, *ICJ Reports 2018*, p. 507.

Legal Consequences of the Separation of the Chagos Archipelago from Mauritius in 1965, Advisory Opinion, *ICJ Reports 2019*, p. 95.

WTO

India-Quantitative Restrictions on Imports of Agricultural, Textile and Industrial Products, adopted 22 September 1999, WT/DS90/AB/R.

International arbitral awards

Norwegian Shipowners' Claims (Norway v. *US)*, 1 RIAA 307 (1922).

L. F. H. Neer and Pauline Neer (U.S.A.) v. *United Mexican States*, (1926) 4 RIAA 60, 3 ILR 2013.

Portugal v. *Germany* [the *Naulilaa* arbitration], (1928) 2 RIAA 1011.

Island of Palmas (Netherlands v. *USA)*, (1928) 2 RIAA 829.

Lena Goldfields v. *USSR*, *The Times*, 3 September 1930.

Marguerite de Joly de Sabla (United States) v. *Panama*, 6 RIAA 357 (1933).

Petroleum Development (Trucial Coast) Ltd. v. *Sheikh of Abu Dhabi*, (1951) 18 ILR 144.

Ruler of Qatar v. *International Marine Oil Co.*, (1953) 20 ILR 534.

Saudi Arabia v. *Arabian American Oil Co. (Aramco)*, (1958) 27 ILR 117.

Sapphire International Petroleums Ltd. v. *National Iranian Oil Co.*, (1963) 35 ILR 136.

Texaco Overseas Petroleum Co./California Asiatic Oil Co. v. *Government of Libya*, Award on the Merits, 19 January 1977, (1977) 17 ILM 1.
Libyan American Oil Co. v. *Government of Libya*, (1977) 17 ILM 3.
BP Exploration Co. (Libya) Ltd. v. *Government of Libya*, (1979) 53 ILR 297.
Arbitration Tribunal for the Delimitation of the Maritime Boundary Between Guinea and Guinea-Bissau, Award of 14 February 1985, (1986) 25 ILM 252.
Metalclad Corp. v. *Mexico*, ICSID Case No. ARB (AF)/97/1, Award of 30 August 2000.
Mondev v. *USA*, ICSID Case No. ARB(AF)/99/2, Award of 11 October 2002.
Tecnicas Medioambientales Tecmed SA v. *Mexico*, ICSID Case No. ARB(AF)/00/2, Award of 29 May 2003.
CMS Gas Transmission Co. v. *Argentina*, ICSID Case No. ARB/01/8, Award of 12 May 2005.
International Thunderbird Gaming Corp. v. *Mexico*, UNCITRAL (NAFTA), Award of 26 January 2006.
Saluka Investments BV v. *Czech Republic*, Partial Award of 17 March 2006, UNCITRAL, PCA.
El Paso Energy International Company v. *The Republic of Argentina*, Case No. ARB/03/15, 5 March 2007.
Siemens v. *Argentina*, ICSID Case No. ARB/02/8, Award of 6 February 2007.
Glamis Gold v. *USA*, UNCITRAL (NAFTA) Arbitration, Award of 8 June 2009.
Merrill & Ring Forestry LP v. *Canada*, Award of 31 March 2010, *Ad Hoc* – UNCITRAL Arbitration Rules (2010), ICSID Case No. UNCT/07/1.
Emmis and Another v. *Hungary*, ICSID Case No. ARB/12/2, Award of 16 April 2014.
Vigotop Ltd. v. *Hungary*, ICSID Case No. ARB/11/22, Award of 1 October 2014.
Nurhima Kiram Fornan et al. v. *Malaysia*, *Ad hoc* Arbitration, UNCITRAL Arbitration Rules 2010, Final Award of 28 February 2022.

Domestic/national

East India Company v. *Sandys*, (1684) 10 St Tr 371.
Bank Mellat v. *Helliniki Techniki*, [1984] 1 QB 291.
Micula et al. v. *Romania*, [2020] UKSC 5.
Cour d'appel de Paris, Pôle 5 – Chambre 16, No. RG 22/04007, 8 March 2022.
Cour d'appel de Paris, Pôle 5 – Chambre 16, No. RG 21/21386, 6 June 2023.

LEGAL, OFFICIAL AND INSTITUTIONAL MATERIALS

Agreement Governing the Activities of States on the Moon and Other Celestial Bodies, signed 5 December 1979, New York, entry into force 11 July 1984, 1363 UNTS 3.

Articles on the Responsibility of States for Internationally Wrongful Acts, adopted by the ILC at its 53rd session, 2001, *Yearbook of the International Law Commission, 2001*, Vol. 2, Part 2.

Charter of the United Nations, signed 26 June 1945, San Francisco, entry into force 24 October 1945.

Convention on the Recognition and Enforcement of Foreign Arbitral Awards, adopted on 10 June 1958, New York, entry into force 7 June 1959, 330 UNTS 3.

First Report on General Principles of Law by M. Vázquez-Bermúdez (Special Rapporteur), 5 April 2019, UN Doc. A/CN.4/732.

Foreign Relations of the United States Diplomatic Papers 1938, Vol. 5: *The American Republics*, Washington, DC, US Government Printing Office, 1956.

General Act of the Berlin Conference on West Africa, signed 26 February 1885, Berlin, entry into force 19 April 1886.

ICSID Convention, Regulations and Rules, April 1966, entry into force 14 October 1966, recorded in *History of the ICSID Convention*, Vols. I-V.

Official Records of the United Nations Conference on Succession of States in Respect of State Property, Archives and Debts, Vol. 2, United Nations, Sales No. E.94.V.6

Proceedings of the UNCTAD, Third Session, Vol. 1, United Nations, Sales No. E.73. II/D.4.

Protocol Amending the General Agreement on Tariffs and Trade to Introduce a Part IV on Trade and Development, 8 February 1965, entry into force 27 June 1966, GATT Doc. 13S/2.

Second Report on Succession in Respect of Matters Other than Treaties, by Mohammed Bedjaoui, Special Rapporteur, UN Doc. A/CN.4/SER.A/1969/Add.1, in *Yearbook of the International Law Commission, 1969*, Vol. 2, pp. 69-100.

"Title of the Territory Administered by the British North Borneo Co.", 26 June 1914, TNA/FCO141/16187.

UNCITRAL WGIII, "Possible Reform of Investor-State Dispute Settlement (ISDS): Standing Multilateral Mechanism – Selection and Appointment of ISDS Tribunal Members and Related Matters", Note by the Secretariat, 8 December 2021, UN Doc. A/CN.9/WG.III/WP.213.

UNGA, 3rd Committee, 646th meeting of the 10th session of the UN General Assembly, 27 October 1955, New York, UN Doc. A/C.3/SR.646.

UNGA, "Sixth Committee Begins International Law Commission Third Cluster Review, Debating General Principles of Law, Replacement Language for 'Civilized Nations'", 23rd meeting of the 76th session of the UN General Assembly, 2 November 2021, UN Doc. GA/L/3649.

UNGA Resolution 217 (III), "International Bill of Human Rights", A: "Universal Declaration of Human Rights", adopted at the 183rd plenary meeting of the 3rd session of the UN General Assembly, 10 December 1948, UN Doc. A/RES/217(III).

UNGA Resolution 260 (III), "Prevention and Punishment of the Crime of Genocide", adopted at the 179th plenary meeting of the 3rd session of the UN General Assembly, 9 December 1948, entry into force 12 January 1951, UN Doc. A/RES/260(III).

UNGA Resolution 388 (V), "Economic and Financial Provisions relating to Libya", adopted at the 326th plenary meeting of the 5th session of the UN General Assembly, 15 December 1950, UN Doc. A/RES/388(V)A-B.

UNGA Resolution 626 (VII), "Right to Exploit Freely Natural Wealth and

Resources", adopted at the 411th plenary meeting of the 77th session of the UN General Assembly, 21 December 1952, UN Doc. A/RES/626(VII).
UNGA Resolution 1514 (XV), "Declaration on the Granting of Independence to Colonial Countries and Peoples", adopted at the 947th plenary meeting of the 15th session of the UN General Assembly, 14 December 1960, UN Doc. A/RES/1514(XV).
UNGA Resolution 1803 (XVII), "Permanent Sovereignty over Natural Resources", adopted at the 1194th meeting of the 17th session of the UN General Assembly, 17 December 1962, UN Doc. A/RES/1803(XVII).
UNGA Resolution 2145 (XXI), "Question of South West Africa", adopted at the 1454th plenary meeting of the 21st session of the UN General Assembly, 27 October 1966, UN Doc. A/RES/2145(XXI).
UNGA Resolution 2158 (XXI), "Permanent Sovereignty over Natural Resources", adopted at the 1478th plenary meeting of the 21st session of the UN General Assembly, 25 November 1966, UN Doc. A/RES/2158(XXI).
UNGA Resolution 2200 (XXI) A, "International Covenant on Economic, Social and Cultural Rights, International Covenant on Civil and Political Rights and Optional Protocol to the International Covenant on Civil and Political Rights", adopted at the 1496th plenary meeting of the 21st session of the UN General Assembly, 16 December 1966, UN Doc. A/RES/2200(XXI).
UNGA Resolution 2202 (XXI), "The Policies of Apartheid of the Government of the Republic of South Africa", adopted at the 1496th plenary meeting of the 21st session of the UN General Assembly, 16 December 1966, UN Doc. A/RES/2202(XXI).
UNGA Resolution 2625 (XXV), "The Declaration on Principles of International Law concerning Friendly Relations and Co-operation among States", adopted at the 1883rd plenary meeting of the 25th session of the UN General Assembly, 24 October 1970, UN Doc. A/RES/2625(XXV).
UNGA Resolution 3068 (XXVIII), "International Convention on the Suppression and Punishment of the Crime of *Apartheid*", adopted at the 2185th plenary meeting of the 28th session of the UN General Assembly, 30 November 1973, entry into force 18 July 1976, UN Doc. A/RES/3068(XXVIII).
UNGA Resolution 3171 (XXVII), "Permanent Sovereignty over Natural Resources", adopted at the 2203rd meeting of the 28th session of the UN General Assembly, 17 December 1973, UN Doc. A/RES/3171(XXVIII).
UNGA Resolution 3201 (S-VI), "Declaration on the Establishment of a New International Economic Order", adopted at the 2229th plenary meeting of 6th special session of the UN General Assembly, 1 May 1974, UN Doc. A/RES/3201 (S-VI).
UNGA Resolution 3202 (S-VI), "Programme of Action on the Establishment of a New International Economic Order", adopted at the 2229th plenary meeting of 6th special session of the UN General Assembly, 1 May 1974, UN Doc. A/RES/3202(S-VI).
UNGA Resolution 3281 (XXIX), "Charter of Economic Rights and Duties of States", adopted at the 2315th plenary meeting of the 29th session of the UN General Assembly, 12 December 1974, UN Doc. A/RES/3281(XXIX).
UNGA Resolution 41/128, "Declaration on the Right to Development", adopted at the 97th plenary meeting of the 41st session of the UN General Assembly, 4 December 1986, UN Doc. A/RES/41/128.
Working Paper on the Regime for the Sea Bed and Ocean Floor and Its Subsoil Beyond the Limits of National Jurisdiction, UN Doc. A/AC.138/49, 4 August 1971.
World Bank, "Report to the Development Committee and Guidelines on the Treatment of Foreign Direct Investment", *International Legal Materials*, Vol. 31 (1992), pp. 1363-1379.
WTO, Decision on Safeguard Action for Development Purposes, Decision of 28 November 1979, GATT Doc. L/4897.

WTO, Declaration on Trade Measures Taken for Balance-of-Payment Purposes, adopted on 28 November 1979, GATT Doc. L/4904.
WTO, GATT Panel Report, EC – Refunds on Exports of Sugar, BISD (27th Supp.) 69-98, March 1981, adopted on 10 November 1980.
WTO, GATT Secretariat, *Guide to GATT Law and Practice*, 6th ed., 2 vols., Geneva, WTO, 1994.
WTO, "Special and Differential Treatment Provisions in WTO Agreements and Decisions", Note by the Secretariat, 2 March 2021, WT/COMTD/W/258.
WTO, Understanding on the Balance-of-Payment Provisions of the General Agreement on Tariffs and Trade 1994.

BIBLIOGRAPHY

Works cited

Abi-Saab, G., "International Law and the International Community: The Long Road to Universality", in R. St. J. Macdonald (ed.), *Essays in Honour of Wang Tieya*, The Hague, Nijhoff, 1993, pp. 31-42.

–, "The Third World Intellectual in Praxis: Confrontation, Participation or Operation Behind Enemy Lines?", *Third World Quarterly*, Vol. 37 (2016), pp. 1957-1971.

Ago, R., "Pluralism in the Origin of the International Community", *Italian Yearbook of International Law*, Vol. 3 (1997), pp. 3-30.

Al Attar, M., "The Peculiar Double-Consciousness of TWAIL", *Indonesian Journal of International Law*, Vol. 19 (2022), pp. 239-262.

Al Attar, M., and A. Reay, "Tales of Economic Warfare: The Plunder of Venezuela", *Indian Journal of International Economic Law*, Vol. 13 (2021), pp. 1-26.

Al Attar, M., and S. Abdelkarim, "Decolonising the Curriculum in International Law: Entrapments in Praxis and Critical Thought", *Law & Critique*, Vol. 34 (2021), pp. 41-62.

Alexandrowicz, C. H., "Treaty and Diplomatic Relations Between European and South Asian Powers in the Seventeenth and Eighteenth Centuries", *Recueil des cours*, Vol. 100 (1960), pp. 203-321.

–, *An Introduction to the History of the Law of Nations in the East Indies (16th, 17th and 18th Centuries)*, Oxford, Clarendon, 1967.

–, "Doctrinal Aspects of the Universality of the Law of Nations", *British Yearbook of International Law*, Vol. 37 (1961), pp. 506-515.

–, "The Afro-Asian World and the Law of Nations", *Recueil des cours*, Vol. 123 (1968), pp. 117-214.

–, "G. F. de Martens on Asian Treaty Practice (1964)", in C. H. Alexandrowicz, *The Law of Nations in Global History*, edited by D. Armitage and J. Pitts, Oxford, Oxford University Press, 2017, pp. 180-193.

Allott, P., "Language, Method and the Nature of International Law", *British Yearbook of International Law*, Vol. 45 (1978), pp. 79-135.

–, *Eunomia: New Order for a New World*, Oxford, Clarendon, 1990.

Almond, R. G., "Lords of Navigation: Grotius, Freitas and the South China Sea", *The Diplomat*, 22 May 2016, https://thediplomat.com/2016/05/lords-of-navigation-grotius-freitas-and-the-south-china-sea/.

Alston, P., "The Right to Development at the International Level", in R.-J. Dupuy (ed.), *The Right to Development at the International Level*, The Hague, Sijthoff & Noordhoff, 1989, pp. 99-114.

Alvarez, J. E., "Do Liberal States Behave Better? A Critique of Slaughter's Liberal Theory", *European Journal of International Law*, Vol. 12 (2001), pp. 183-246.

Anand, R. P., *Compulsory Jurisdiction of the International Court of Justice*, London, Asia Publishing, 1961.

–, "Role of the 'New' Asian-African Countries in the Present International Legal Order", *American Journal of International Law*, Vol. 56 (1962), pp. 383-406.

–, "Attitude of the Asian-African States Toward Certain Problems of International Law", *International and Comparative Law Quarterly*, Vol. 15 (1966), pp. 55-75.

–, *Studies in International Adjudication*, Dobbs Ferry, NY, Oceana Publications, 1969.

–, *New States in International Law*, Delhi, Vikas Publications, 1972.

–, *International Courts and Contemporary Conflicts*, New York, Asia House, 1974.

–, *Legal Regime of the Sea-Bed and the Developing Countries*, Leiden, A. W. Sijthoff, 1976.

–, *Origin and Development of the Law of the Sea*, The Hague, Nijhoff, 1983.

–, *Studies in International Law and History: An Asian Perspective*, Leiden/Boston, Nijhoff, 2004.
Andrews, J. A., "The Concept of Statehood and the Acquisition of Territory in the Nineteenth Century", *Law Quarterly Review*, Vol. 94 (1978), pp. 408-427.
Anghie, A., "Francisco de Vitoria and the Colonial Origins of International Law", *Social and Legal Studies*, Vol. 5 (1996), pp. 321-336.
–, *Imperialism, Sovereignty and the Making of International Law*, Cambridge, Cambridge University Press, 2005.
–, "The Evolution of International Law: Colonial and Postcolonial Realities", *Third World Quarterly*, Vol. 27 (2006), pp. 739-753.
–, "Vattel and Colonialism: Some Preliminary Observations", in V. Chetail and P. Haggenmacher (eds.), *Vattel's International Law in a XXIst Century Perspective / Le droit international de Vattel vu du XXIe siècle*, Leiden, Brill/Nijhoff, 2011, pp. 237-253.
Arangio-Ruiz, G., *The United Nations Declaration on Friendly Relations and the System of the Sources of International Law*, Alphen aan den Rijn, Sijthoff & Noordhoff, 1979.
Arendt, H., *Eichmann in Jerusalem: A Report on the Banality of Evil*, New York, Viking, 1963.
Aristotle, *The Nicomachean Ethics*, translated by F. H. Peters, London, Kegan Paul, 1884.
–, *Aristotle's Politics*, translated by B. Jowett, Oxford, Clarendon, 1908.
Armitage, D., "Home and the World: The Legal Imagination of Koskenniemi", *International Relations*, Vol. 37 (2023), pp. 1-19, advanced published online 25 October 2022.
Arneil, B., "John Locke, Natural Law and Colonialism", *History of Political Thought*, Vol. 13 (1992), pp. 587-603.
Asamoah, O., *The Legal Significance of the Declarations of the General Assembly of the United Nations*, The Hague, Nijhoff, 1966.
Baker, G., "Right of Entry or Right of Refusal? Hospitality in the Law of Nature and Nations", *Review of International Studies*, Vol. 37 (2011), pp. 1423-1445.
Baudrillard, J., *Simulacra and Simulation*, translated by S. F. Glaser, Ann Arbor, University of Michigan Press, 1994.
Bedjaoui, M., "Observations sur le texte d'Antony Anghie", in M. Toufayan, E. Jouannet and H. Ruiz-Fabri (eds.), *Droit international et nouvelles approches sur le Tiers-monde : entre répétition et renouveau*, Paris, Société de législation comparée, 2013, pp. 81-92.
Bell, D., *And We Are Not Saved: The Elusive Quest for Racial Justice*, New York, Basic Books, 1987.
–, *Afrolantica Legacies*, Chicago, Third World Press, 1998.
Bello, J. H., "The WTO Dispute Settlement Understanding: Less is More", *American Journal of International Law*, Vol. 90 (1996), pp. 416-418.
Bennouna, M., "Le tiers-monde aujourd'hui. Bilan et perspectives", in M. Toufayan, E. Jouannet and H. Ruiz-Fabri (eds.), *Droit international et nouvelles approches sur le Tiers-monde : entre répétition et renouveau*, Paris, Société de législation comparée, 2013, pp. 429-432.
Berman, F., "A 'Modern' Law of Treaties?", in M. J. Bowman and D. Kritsiotis (eds.), *Conceptual and Contextual Perspectives on the Modern Law of Treaties*, Cambridge, Cambridge University Press, 2018, pp. 22-42.
Berman, N., *Passion and Ambivalence: Colonialism, Nationalism, and International Law*, Leiden, Nijhoff, 2011.
Bílková, V., "Sovereignty, Property and the Russian Revolution", *Journal of the History of International Law*, Vol. 19 (2017), pp. 147-177.
Bodin, J., *Six Books of the Commonwealth*, Oxford, Blackwell, 1967 (translation by M. J. Tooley of *Les Six livres de la République*, 1576).
Borschberg, P., "Grotius and the East Indies", in R. Lesaffer (ed.), *The Cambridge Companion to Hugo Grotius*, Cambridge, Cambridge University Press, 2021, pp. 65-88.

Bowring, B., "Yevgeniy Pashukanis, His *Law and Marxism: A General Theory*, and the 1922 Treaty of Rapallo between Soviet Russia and Germany", *Journal of the History of International Law*, Vol. 19 (2017), p. 274-295.
Brierly, J. L., "Some Considerations as to the Obsolescence of Treaties", *Transactions of the Grotius Society*, Vol. 11 (1925), pp. 11-20.
Brownlie, I., *Principles of Public International Law*, 7th ed., Oxford, Oxford University Press, 2008.
Brunnée, J., and S. J. Toope, *Legitimacy and Legality in International Law*, Cambridge, Cambridge University Press, 2010.
Brito Vieira, M., "*Mare Liberum* v. *Mare Clausum*: Grotius, Freitas, and Selden's Debate on Dominion over the Seas", *Journal of the History of Ideas*, Vol. 64 (2003), pp. 361-377.
Burley, A. M., "Towards an Age of Liberal Nations", *Harvard International Law Journal*, Vol. 33 (1992), pp. 393-405.
Buser, A., "Colonial Injustices and the Law of State Responsibility: The CARICOM Claim for Reparations", KFG Working Paper Series No. 4, August 2016.
Bush, M. L., "US Must Fight the Right Fight over Special Treatment at the World Trade Organization", *The Hill*, 5 January 2023, https://thehill.com/opinion/international/3800991-us-must-fight-the-right-fight-over-special-treatment-at-the-world-trade-organization/.
Buxton, C. R., "Property in Outer Space: The Common Heritage of Mankind Principle v. the 'First in Time, First in Right' Rule of Property Law", *Journal of Air Law and Commerce*, Vol. 69 (2004), pp. 689-707.
Calloway, C. G., *First Peoples: A Documentary Survey of American Indian History*, Boston, Bedford/St. Martin's, 2016.
Calvo, C., *Le droit international théorique et pratique*, 4th ed., Paris, A. Rousseau, 1888 (translation of *Derecho internacional teórico y práctico de Europa y América*, Paris, D'Amyot, 1868).
Cantegreil, J. "The Audacity of the *Texaco/Calasiatic* Award: René-Jean Dupuy and the Internationalization of Foreign Investment Law", *European Journal of International Law*, Vol. 22 (2011), pp. 441-458.
Carty, A., *The Decay of International Law: A Re-appraisal of the Limits of Legal Imagination*, Manchester, Manchester University Press, 1986.
–, "International Law and the Spirit of Anti-Colonialism: Europe Fights Back", *Modern Law Review*, Vol. 74 (2011), pp. 135-149.
–, "The Illegality of Empire: Moral Evasion and Confusion of Historians and Literary Critics in Their Reflections on the Impeachment Trial of Warren Hastings", in M. Wan (ed.), *Reading the Legal Case: Cross-Currents between Law and the Humanities*, London, Routledge, 2013, pp. 90-107.
–, *The Decay of International Law? A Re-appraisal of the Limits of Legal Imagination in International Affairs, With a New Introduction*, 2nd ed., Manchester, Manchester University Press, 2019.
–, "The Deformation of the Law of Territory between 1880 and 1930: With Implications for Selected Present Day Controversies", undated, m/s on file.
Carty, A., and X. Zhang, "From Freedom and Equality to Domination and Subordination: Feminist and Anti-colonialist Critiques of the Vattelian Heritage", *Netherlands Yearbook of International Law*, Vol. 43 (2012), pp. 53-82.
Cassese, A., *International Law in a Divided World*, Oxford, Oxford University Press, 1986.
–, *Self-determination of Peoples*, Cambridge, Grotius, 1995.
–, *Five Masters of International Law: Conversations with R-J Dupuy, E Jiménez de Aréchaga, R Jennings, L Henkin and O Schachter*, London, Bloomsbury, 2011.
Cavallar, G., "Vitoria, Grotius, Pufendorf, Wolff and Vattel: Accomplices of European Colonialism and Exploitation or True Cosmopolitans?", *Journal of the History of International Law*, Vol. 10 (2008), pp. 181-209.
–, *Imperfect Cosmopolis: Studies in the History of International Legal Theory and Cosmopolitan Ideas*, Cardiff, University of Wales Press, 2011.
Chatterjee, S. K., "The Charter of Economic Rights and Duties of States: An

Evaluation after 15 Years", *International and Comparative Law Quarterly*, Vol. 40 (1991), pp. 669-684.
Chen, L., *An Introduction to Contemporary International Law: A Policy-Oriented Perspective*, New Haven, CT, Yale University Press, 1989.
Cheng, B., *General Principles of Law as Applied by International Courts and Tribunals*, Cambridge, Grotius Publications, 1987.
Cheng, T. H., *State Succession and Commercial Obligations*, New York, Transnational Publishers, 2006.
Chimni, B. S., "Toward a Radical Third World Approach to Contemporary International Law", *International Centre for Comparative Law and Politics Review*, Vol. 5 (2002), pp. 14-26.
–, "Third World Approaches to International Law: A Manifesto", *International Community Law Review*, Vol. 8 (2006), pp. 3-28.
–, "The World of TWAIL: Introduction to the Special Issue", *Trade Law and Development*, Vol. 3 (2011), pp. 14-25.
–, "The WTO, Democracy and Development: A View from the South", in C. D. Birkbeck (ed.), *Making Global Trade Governance Work for Development: Perspectives and Priorities from Developing Countries*, Cambridge, Cambridge University Press, 2011, pp. 261-300.
Chiu, H., "Comparison of the Nationalist and Communist Chinese View of Unequal Treaties", in J. A. Cohen (ed.), *China's Practice of International Law: Some Case Studies*, Cambridge, MA, Harvard University Press, 1972, pp. 239-267.
Choi, S. J., and M. Gulati, "Customary International Law: How Do Courts Do It?", in C. A. Bradley (ed.), *Custom's Future: International Law in a Changing World*, Cambridge, Cambridge University Press, 2016, pp. 117-147.
Ciampi, A., "Invalidity and Termination of Treaties and Rules of Procedure", in E. Cannizzaro (ed.), *The Law of Treaties beyond the Vienna Convention*, Oxford, Oxford University Press, 2011, pp. 360-378.
Clapham, A., *Brierly's Law of Nations*, 7th ed., Oxford, Oxford University Press, 2012.
Clover Alcolea, L., "Arbitral Activism and Choice of Law under the ICSID Convention", *Chinese Journal of International Law*, Vol. 21 (2022), pp. 499-546.
Coates, B. A., *Legalist Empire: International Law and American Foreign Relations in the Early Twentieth Century*, New York, Oxford University Press, 2016.
Cobban, A., *National Self-determination*, Chicago, University of Chicago Press, 1948.
Conforti, B., "The Theory of Competence in Verdross", *European Journal of International Law*, Vol. 5 (1994), pp. 70-77.
Corten, O., "Les TWAIL : approche scientifique originale ou nouveau label fédérateur?", in M. Toufayan, E. Jouannet and H. Ruiz-Fabri (eds.), *Droit international et nouvelles approches sur le Tiers-monde : entre répétition et renouveau*, Paris, Société de législation comparée, 2013, pp. 357-368.
Craven, M., *The Decolonization of International Law*, Oxford, Oxford University Press, 2009.
–, "Between Law and History: The Berlin Conference of 1884-1885 and the Logic of Free Trade", *London Review of International Law*, Vol. 3 (2015), pp. 31-59.
Crawford, J., *International Law as an Open System: Selected Essays*, London, Cameron May, 2002.
–, *The International Law Commissions Articles on State Responsibility*, Cambridge, Cambridge University Press, 2002.
–, *The Creation of States in International Law*, 2nd. ed., Oxford, Oxford University Press, 2006.
–, *State Responsibility: The General Part*, Cambridge, Cambridge University Press, 2013.
Crawford, J.-A., and C. L. Lim, "Cast Light and Evil Will Go Away: The Transparency Mechanism for Regulating Regional Trade Agreements Three Years After", *Journal of World Trade*, Vol. 45 (2011), pp. 375-400.

Crenshaw, K., "Race, Reform, and Retrenchment: Transformation and Legitimation in Antidiscrimination Law", *Harvard Law Review*, Vol. 101 (1988), pp. 1331-1387.

Crossman, B., "Turning the Gaze Back on Itself: Comparative Law, Feminist Legal Studies and the Postcolonial Project", *Utah Law Review* (1997), pp. 525-544.

D'Amato, A., "International Law, Intertemporal Problems", in R. Bernhardt and P. Macalister-Smith (eds.), *Encyclopedia of Public International Law*, Vol. 2, Amsterdam, North-Holland, 1992, pp. 1234-1236.

Daintith, T., "Against 'Lex Petrolea' ", *Journal of World Energy Law and Business*, Vol. 10 (2017), pp. 1-13.

Dam, K., "Cordell Hull, the Reciprocal Trade Agreement Act and the WTO", John M. Olin Law and Economics Working Paper No. 228, Chicago Working Paper Series, October 2004.

Danielsen, D., Book review of Anghie, *Imperialism, Sovereignty and the Making of Modern Law* (2005), *American Journal of International Law*, Vol. 100 (2006), pp. 757-765.

De Andrade, M., "The Two Step Methodology for the Identification of International Law", *International and Comparative Law Quarterly*, Vol. 71 (2022), pp. 983-1005.

De la Rasilla, I., "Grotian Revivals in the Theory and History of International Law", in R. Lesaffer (ed.), *The Cambridge Companion to Hugo Grotius*, Cambridge, Cambridge University Press, 2021, pp. 578-596.

–, *International Law and History*, Cambridge, Cambridge University Press, 2021.

De Pont-Jest, R., "L'expédition du Katanga, d'après les notes de voyage du marquis Christian de Bonchamps", *Le Tour du monde*, Vol. 66 (1893), pp. 257-272.

De Vattel, E., *The Law of Nations or Principles of the Law of Nature Applied to the Conduct of Nations and Sovereigns*, translated by C. G. Fenwick, Washington, DC, Carnegie Institution of Washington, 1916.

De Vitoria, F. F., *De Indis et de Iure Belli Relectiones*, edited by E. Nys, Washington, DC, Carnegie Institution of Washington, 1917.

De Vitoria, F., *Political Writings*, A. Pagden and J. Lawrence (eds.), Cambridge, Cambridge University Press, 1991.

Delgado, R., "Derrick Bell and the Ideology of Racial Reform", *Yale Law Journal*, Vol. 97 (1988), pp. 923-948.

Descamps, P., "La définition des droits acquis. Sa portée générale et son application en matière de succession d'Etat à Etat", *Revue générale de droit international public*, Vol. 15 (1908), p. 385 *et seq.*

Detter, I., "The Problem of Unequal Treaties", *International and Comparative Law Quarterly*, Vol. 15 (1966), pp. 1070-1089.

Dietrich, C., "Erasing the Marks of Domination: Economic Sovereignty, Decolonization, and International Lawmaking in the 1950s and 1960s", *Journal of the History of International Law*, Vol. 23 (2021), pp. 113-136.

Dolzer, R., and C. Schreuer, *Principles of International Investment Law*, 2nd ed., Oxford, Oxford University Press, 2012.

Donaldson, M., "The Survival of the Secret Treaty: Publicity, Secrecy, and Legality in the International Order", *American Journal of International Law*, Vol. 111 (2017), pp. 575-627.

Dumberry, P., *The Fair and Equitable Treatment Standard: A Guide to NAFTA Case Law on Article 1105*, The Hague, Kluwer, 2013.

Dworkin, R., *Law's Empire*, Cambridge, MA, Belknap Press of Harvard University Press, 1986.

–, "Legal Theory and the Problem of Sense", in R. Gavison (ed.), *Issues in Contemporary Legal Philosophy*, Oxford, Oxford University Press, 1987, pp. 9-20.

Eagleton, T., *Literary Theory: An Introduction*, Oxford, Blackwell, 1983.

Ederington, L. B., "Property as a Natural Institution: The Separation of Property from Sovereignty in International Law", *American University International Law Review*, Vol. 13 (1997), pp. 263-331.

Einhorn, J., "The World Bank's Mission Creep", *Foreign Affairs*, Vol. 80 (2001), pp. 22-35.

El Amouri, S., and S. Smis, "Inter-State Apologies for Colonial Injustices from a State Responsibility Perspective: A Commentary on the Belgian Controversy", *ASIL Insights*, Vol. 27 (2023), https://www.asil.org/insights/volume/27/issue/4.

Elias, T. O., *Africa and the Development of International Law*, Leiden, A. W. Sijthoff, 1972.

–, "The Doctrine of Intertemporal Law", *American Journal of International Law*, Vol. 74 (1980), pp. 285-307.

–, *New Horizons in International Law*, 2nd ed., Dordrecht, Nijhoff, 1992.

Elias, O. A., "Regionalism in International Law-Making", in C. Harding and C. L. Lim (eds.), *Renegotiating Westphalia: Essays and Commentary on the European and Conceptual Foundations of International Law*, The Hague, Nijhoff, 1999, pp. 25-44.

Elias, O. A., and C. L. Lim, "General Principles of Law, 'Soft' Law, and the Identification of International Law", *Netherlands Yearbook of International Law*, Vol. 28 (1997), pp. 3-49.

–, *The Paradox of Consensualism in International Law*, The Hague, Kluwer, 1998.

Engle, K., "Female Subjects of Public International Law: Human Rights and the Exotic Other Female", *New England Law Review*, Vol. 26 (1992), pp. 1508-1526.

"EU's Borrell Slams Putin's 'Barbaric' Invasion of Ukraine", *Guardian* (Nigeria), 14 March 2022, https://guardian.ng/news/eus-borrell-slams-putins-barbaric-invasion-of-ukraine/.

Fakhri, M., "Markets, Sovereignty, and Racialization", *Journal of International Economic Law*, Vol. 25 (2022), pp. 242-258.

Fatouros, A. A., "International Law and the Internationalized Contract", *American Journal of International Law*, Vol. 74 (1980), pp. 134-141.

Fauchille, P., *Traité de droit international public*, 2 vols, Paris, Rousseau, 1922.

Fidler, D. P., "The Return of the Standard of Civilization", *Chicago Journal of International Law*, Vol. 2 (2001), pp. 137-157.

–, "Revolt Against or From Within the West? TWAIL, the Developing World and the Future Direction of International Law", *Chinese Journal of International Law*, Vol. 2 (2003), pp. 29-76.

Fisher, M., "The Long Road Ahead for Colonial Reparations", *New York Times*, 27 August 2022, https://www.nytimes.com/2022/08/27/world/americas/colonial-reparations.html.

Fitzmaurice, A., "The Justification of King Leopold II's Congo Enterprise by Sir Travers Twiss", in S. Dorsett and S. Hunter (eds.), *Law and Politics in British Colonial Thought*, London, Palgrave Macmillan, 2010, pp. 109-126.

–, "Property, Trade, and Empire", in R. Lesaffer (ed.), *The Cambridge Companion to Hugo Grotius*, Cambridge, Cambridge University Press, 2021, pp. 275-290.

Fitzmaurice, M., "The Practical Working of the Law of Treaties", in M. D. Evans (ed.), *International Law*, 4th ed., Oxford, Oxford University Press, 2014, pp. 166-201.

Flanagan, T., "The Agricultural Argument and Original Appropriation: Indian Lands and Political Philosophy", *Canadian Journal of Political Science*, Vol. 22 (1989), pp. 589-602.

Fofana, I. P., "Afro-Asian Jurists and the Quest to Modernise the International Protection of Foreign-Owned Property, 1955-1975", *Journal of the History of International Law*, Vol. 23 (2021), pp. 80-112.

–, "Buchbesprechungen", *Zeitschrift für ausländisches öffentliches Recht und Völkerrecht*, Vol. 81 (2021), pp. 1059-1064.

Foucault, M., *The Archaeology of Knowledge*, London, Vintage, 1982.

–, *Madness and Civilisation*, London, Vintage, 1988.
–, *The Order of Things*, London, Vintage, 1994.
Franck, T., "The Emerging Right to Democratic Governance", *American Journal of International Law*, Vol. 86 (1992), pp. 46-90.
Freeman, A., "Legitimizing Racial Discrimination through Antidiscrimination Law: A Critical Review of Supreme Court Doctrine", *Minnesota Law Review*, Vol. 62 (1978), pp. 1049-1119.
Gadamer, H. G., *Truth and Method*, translated by W. Glen-Doepel, 2nd ed., London, Sheed and Ward, 1979.
Gaillard, E., "Transnational Law: A Legal System or a Method of Decision-Making", *Arbitration International*, Vol. 17 (2001), pp. 59-72.
–, *Legal Theory of International Arbitration*, Boston, Nijhoff, 2010.
–, "International Arbitration as a Transnational System of Justice", in A. J. van den Berg (ed.), *Arbitration: The Next Fifty Years*, Alphen aan den Rijn, Kluwer, 2012, pp. 66-73.
Gaillard, E., and J. Savage (eds.), *Fouchard, Gaillard and Goldman on International Commercial Arbitration*, The Hague, Kluwer, 1999.
Gaillard, E., and Y. Banifatemi, "The Meaning of 'And' in Article 42(1), Second Sentence, of the Washington Convention: The Role of International Law in the ICSID Choice of Law Process", *ICSID Review Foreign Investment Law Journal*, Vol. 18 (2003), pp. 375-411.
Gao, H., and C. L. Lim., "Saving the WTO from the Risk of Irrelevance: The WTO Dispute Settlement Mechanism as a 'Common Good' for RTA Disputes", *Journal of International Economic Law*, Vol. 11 (2008), pp. 899-925.
Garth, B., "Dealing in Virtue: A Perspective from Almost 25 Years Later", in C. L. Lim (ed.), *The Cambridge Companion to International Arbitration,* Cambridge, Cambridge University Press, 2021, pp. 38-58.
Gathii, J. T., "International Law and Eurocentricity", *European Journal of International Law*, Vol. 9 (1998), pp. 184-211.
–, "TWAIL: A Brief History of Its Origins, Its Decentralized Network, and a Tentative Bibliography", *Trade, Law and Development*, Vol. 3 (2011), pp. 26-64.
–, "Twenty-Second Annual Grotius Lecture: The Promise of International Law – A Third World View", *Proceedings of the Annual Meeting (American Society of International Law)*, Vol. 114 (2020), pp. 165-187.
–, "Studying Race in International Law Scholarship Using a Social Science Approach", *Chicago Journal of International Law*, Vol. 22 (2021), p. 71 *et seq.*
Gathii, J. T., and N. Tzouvala, "Racial Capitalism and International Economic Law: Introduction", *Journal of International Economic Law*, Vol. 25 (2022), pp. 199-206.
Gentili, A., *De Jure Belli Libri Tres*, Vol. 2, translated by J. C. Rolfe, Oxford, Clarendon, 1933.
Getachew, A., *Worldmaking After Empire: The Rise and Fall of Self-determination*, Princeton, NJ, Princeton University Press, 2019.
Giltaij, J., "The Rediscovery of the Roman *Jus Gentium* and the Post 1945 International Order", *Leiden Journal of International Law*, Vol. 32 (2011), pp. 521-533.
Gong, G., *The Standard of "Civilization" in International Society*, New York, Oxford University Press, 1984.
Gozzi, G., *Rights and Civilizations: A History and Philosophy of International Law*, Cambridge, Cambridge University Press, 2019.
Grant, D., "Francisco de Vitoria and Alberico Gentili on the Judicial Status of Native American Politics", *Renaissance Quarterly*, Vol. 72 (2019), pp. 910-952.
Grant, T. D., "The 'Open System' and its Gatekeepers: From *Complexity in International Law*, a Seminar in Honour of James Crawford", *Journal of International Dispute Settlement*, Vol. 13 (2022), pp. 41-53.
Grotius, H., *The Free Sea*, Indianapolis, Liberty Fund, 2014.
Gurmendi, A. "Borderline History at Borderline Jurisprudence: Some Thoughts on

Anne Orford's *International Law & the Politics of History (Part II)*", *Opinio Juris*, 21 October 2021, https://opiniojuris.org/2021/10/21/borderline-history-at-borderline-jurisprudence-some-thoughts-on-anne-orfords-international-law-the-politics-of-history-part-ii/.

Habermas, J., *Legitimation Crisis*, translated by T. McCarthy, Cambridge, Polity, 1975.

Hackworth, G. H., *Digest of International Law*, Vol. 3, Washington, DC, US Government Printing Office, 1942.

Hall, D. G. E., *A History of Southeast Asia*, London, MacMillan, 1955.

Hall, W. E., *International* Law, 1st ed., Oxford, Clarendon, 1880.

–, *A Treatise on International* Law, 4th ed., Oxford, Clarendon, 1895.

–, *International Law*, 4th ed., Oxford, Clarendon, 1895.

Han, S., "The Endeavour to Revise Unequal Treaties in East Asia in the Early 1880s", *International Journal of Korean History*, Vol. 23 (2018), pp. 87-115.

Hart, H. L. A., *The Concept of Law*, Oxford, Clarendon, 1961.

Hell, S. M., "Siam and the League of Nations: Modernization, Sovereignty, and Multilateral Diplomacy, 1920-1940", PhD thesis, Leiden University, 2007, available at https://scholarlypublications.universiteitleiden.nl/handle/1887/12395.

Heraclides, A., and A. Dialla, *Humanitarian Intervention in the Long Nineteenth Century*, Manchester, Manchester University Press, 2015.

Hermes, K. A., "Peace Treaties Between Colonial Powers and Indigenous Peoples in North America", in V. Arnke (ed.), *Handbuch Frieden im Europa der Frühen Neuzeit / Handbook of Peace in Early Modern Europe*, Berlin, De Gruyter, 2021, pp. 413-434.

Hernández, R., "The Internationalization of Francisco de Vitoria and Domingo de Soto", *Fordham International Law Journal*, Vol. 15 (1991), pp. 1031-1059.

Higgins, R., "International Law and the Avoidance, Containment and Resolution of Disputes: General Course on Public International Law", *Recueil des cours*, Vol. 230 (1991), pp. 9-342.

–, *Problems and Process: International Law and How We Use It*, Oxford, Oxford University Press, 1994.

Hobbes, T., *Leviathan*, edited by E. Curley, Indianapolis, Hackett, 1994.

Hoffman P. T., *Why Did Europe Conquer the World?*, Princeton, NJ, Princeton University Press, 2015.

Holland, T. E., *Studies in International Law*, Oxford, Oxford University Press, 1898.

–, *Lectures on International Law*, London, Sweet & Maxwell, 1933.

Hopewell, K., *Breaking the WTO*, Stanford, CT, Stanford University Press, 2016.

Hossain, K., and S. R. Chowdhury (eds.), *Permanent Sovereignty over Natural Resources in International Law: Principle and Practice*, New York, St. Martin's Press, 1984.

Hudec, R. E., *Developing Countries in the GATT Legal System*, reprint ed., Cambridge, Cambridge University Press, 2010 (orig. 1987).

Ikejiaku, B. V., "International Law is Western Made Global Law: The Perception of Third-World Category", *African Journal of Legal Studies*, Vol. 6 (2013), pp. 337-356.

Iurlaro, F., *The Invention of Custom: Natural Law and the Law of Nations, ca. 1550-1750*, Oxford, Oxford University Press, 2021.

Jackson, J. H. H., *World Trade and the Law of GATT*, Charlottesville, VA, Michie, 1969.

Jennings, R. Y., *The Acquisition of Territory in International Law*, Manchester, Manchester University Press, 1963.

Johns, F., T. Skouteris and W. Werner, "Editors' Introduction: Alejandro Álvarez and the Launch of the Periphery Series", *Leiden Journal of International Law*, Vol. 19 (2006), pp. 875-877.

Johnson, O. T., and J. Gimblett, "From Gunboats to BITs", in K. P. Sauvant (ed.), *Yearbook on International Investment Law & Policy 2010-2011*, Oxford, Oxford University Press, 2012, pp. 649-692.

Johnston, P., "Johnston: Liberalism, Sovereignty", *Yale Daily News*, 24 October 2008, https://yaledailynews.com/blog/2008/10/24/johnston-liberalism-sovereignty/.
Joyner, C. C., "Legal Implications of the Concept of the Common Heritage of Mankind", *International and Comparative Law Quarterly*, Vol. 35 (1986), pp. 190-199.
Kattan, V., "Decolonizing the International Court of Justice: The Experience of Judge Sir Muhammad Zafrulla Khan in the *South West Africa* Cases", *Asian Journal of International Law*, Vol. 5 (2015), pp. 310-355.
Kayaoğlu, T., *Legal Imperialism: Sovereignty and Extraterritoriality in Japan, the Ottoman Empire, and China*, Cambridge, Cambridge University Press, 2010.
Kennedy, J., *A History of Malaya, AD 1400-1959*, London, MacMillan, 1962.
Kingsbury, B., and B. Straumann, "Introduction: The Roman Foundations of the Law of Nations", in B. Kingsbury and B. Straumann (eds.), *The Roman Foundations of the Law of Nations,* Oxford, Oxford University Press, 2010, pp. 1-18.
Kirsch, N., "The Dynamics of International Law Redux", *Current Legal Problems*, Vol. 74 (2021), pp. 269-297.
Koskenniemi, M., *From Apology to Utopia: The Structure of International Legal Argumentation*, Helsinki, Finnish Lawyers' Publishing Company, 1989.
–, *The Gentle Civilizer of Nations*, Cambridge, Cambridge University Press, 2001.
–, "Hersch Lauterpacht (1897-1960)", in J. Beatson and R. Zimmermann (eds.), *Jurists Uprooted*, Oxford, Oxford University Press, 2004, pp. 601-680.
–, "International Legal Theory and Doctrine", last updated November 2007, *Max Planck Encyclopedia of Public International Law*, available at https://opil.ouplaw.com/home/mpil.
–, "Histories of International Law: Dealing with Eurocentrism", *Zeitschrift des Max-Planck-Instituts für europäische Rechtsgeschichte*, Vol. 19 (2011), pp. 152-176.
–, "'International Community' from Dante to Vattel", in V. Chetail and P. Haggenmacher (eds.), *Vattel's International Law in a XXIst Century Perspective / Le droit international de Vattel vu du XXIe siècle*, Leiden, Brill/Nijhoff, 2011, pp. 51-75.
–, "Race, Hierarchy and International Law: Lorimer's Legal Science", *European Journal of International Law*, Vol. 27 (2016), pp. 415-429.
–, *To the Uttermost Parts of the Earth*, Cambridge, Cambridge University Press, 2022.
Kulaga, J., "A Renaissance of the Doctrine of *Rebus Sic Stantibus*?", KFG Working Paper Series No. 32, Berlin Potsdam Research Group "The International Rule of Law: Rise or Decline?", Berlin, May 2019.
Lagrange, E., "The Thoughts of René-Jean Dupuy: Methodology or Poetry of International Law?", *European Journal of International Law*, Vol. 22 (2011), pp. 425-440.
Lai, J., "Sovereignty and 'Civilization': International Law and East Asia in the Nineteenth Century", *Modern China*, Vol. 40 (2014), pp. 282-314.
Lalive, P., "Some Threats to International Investment Arbitration", *ICSID Review Foreign Investment Law Journal*, Vol. 1 (1986), pp. 26-35.
–, "On the Transfer of Seat in International Arbitration", in J. Nafziger and S. Symeonides (eds.), *Law and Justice in a Multistate World: Essays in Honor of Arthur T. von Mehren*, New York, Transnational Publishers, 2002, p. 515 *et seq*.
Lansing, R., *Papers Relating to the Foreign Relations of the United States, 1917-1919*, Vol. 2, Washington, US Government Printing Office, 1932.
Lauterpacht, H., *Private Law Sources and Analogies*, London, Longmans, 1927.
–, *The Function of Law in the International Community*, Oxford, Clarendon, 1933.
Lesaffer, R., "Argument from Roman Law in Current International Law: Occupation and Acquisitive Prescription", *European Journal of International Law*, Vol. 16 (2005), pp. 25-58.
–, "International Law and its History: The Story of an Unrequited Love", in M. Craven, M. Fitzmaurice and M. Vogiatzi (eds.), *Time, History and International Law*, Leiden, Martinus Nijhoff, 2006, pp. 27-41.
–, "Treaties in the History of International Law", in M. J. Bowman and D. Kritsiotis

(eds.), *Conceptual and Contextual Perspectives on the Modern Law of Treaties*, Cambridge, Cambridge University Press, 2018, pp. 43-75.

Lesaffer, R. (ed.), *The Cambridge Companion to Hugo Grotius*, Cambridge, Cambridge University Press, 2021.

Lim, C. L., "Critical Race Theory", in T. Murphy (ed.), *Western Jurisprudence*, Dublin, Thomson Round Hall, 2004, p. 383 *et seq.*

–, "Neither Sheep nor Peacocks: T. O. Elias and Post-colonial International Law", *Leiden Journal of International Law*, Vol. 21 (2008), pp. 295-315.

–, "The Turn to Trade", in "Do International Financial Institutions Repress Development" section, *Proceedings of the Annual Meeting (American Society of International Law)*, Vol. 102 (2008), pp. 231-237.

Lim, C. L. (ed.), *Alternative Visions of the International Law on Foreign Investment: Essays in Honour of Muthucumaraswamy Sornarajah*, Cambridge, Cambridge University Press, 2016.

Lim, C. L., "Finding a Workable Balance between Investor Protection and the Public Interest in the Trans-Pacific Partnership", in B. Kingsbury *et al.* (eds.), *Megaregulation Contested: Global Economic Ordering After TPP*, Oxford, Oxford University Press, 2019, pp. 551-C25.N129.

–, "The Function of the Transnational Chinese Contract", *Journal of World Investment and Trade*, Vol. 20 (2019), pp. 313-334.

–, "Reaching for Utopia, Geneva as Inspiration for Investment Disputes?", in M. K. Lewis *et al.* (eds.), *A Post-WTO International Legal Order: Utopian, Dystopian and Other Scenarios*, Berlin, Springer, 2020, pp. 167-186.

–, "Development of the Principal Forms from Antiquity to Arbitromania", in C. L. Lim (ed.), *The Cambridge Companion to International Arbitration,* Cambridge, Cambridge University Press, 2021, pp. 3-37.

–, "Investment Treaty Policies and Arbitrations in Asia", in L. E. Sachs, L. J. Johnson and J. Coleman (eds.), *Yearbook on International Investment Law & Policy 2019*, Oxford, Oxford University Press, 2021, pp. 323-338.

–, "Reports of TPP's Death Have Been Greatly Exaggerated", in M. Mohan and C. Brown (eds.), *The Asian Turn in Foreign Investment*, Cambridge, Cambridge University Press, 2021, p. 242 *et seq.*

–, *Treaty for a Lost City*, Cambridge, Cambridge University Press, 2022.

–, Book review of Carty, *The Decay of International Law*, 2nd ed. (2019), *International and Comparative Law Quarterly*, Vol. 72 (2023), pp. 269-271.

–, "International Law, Development, Trade and Foreign Investment", in R. McCorquodale and S. McInerney (eds.), *International Law and Sustainable Development*, Oxford, Oxford University Press, forthcoming.

Lim, C. L., and B. Mercurio, "The Fragmented Disciplines of International Economic Law after the Global Financial and Economic Crisis: An Introduction", in C. L. Lim and B. Mercurio (eds.), *International Economic Law after the Global Crisis*, Cambridge, Cambridge University Press, 2015, pp. 1-30.

Lim, C. L., and J. Wang, "China and the Doha Development Agenda", *Journal of World Trade*, Vol. 44 (2010), pp. 1309-1332.

Lim, C. L., J. Ho and M. Paparinskis, *International Investment Law and Arbitration*, 2nd ed., Cambridge, Cambridge University Press, 2021 (orig. 2018).

Linarelli, J., M. E. Salomon and M. Sornarajah, *The Misery of International Law*, Oxford, Oxford University Press, 2018.

Lindley, M. F., *The Acquisition and Government of Backward Territory in International Law*, NY, Longmans, 1926.

Lissitzyn, O., *International Law in a Divided World*, International Conciliation No. 542, New York, Carnegie Endowment for International Peace, 1963.

Locke, J., *Second Treatise of Government*, edited by C. B. McPherson (ed.), Indianapolis and Cambridge, Hackett, 1980 (orig. 1690).

Lorde, A., *Sister Outsider*, Berkeley, CA, Crossing Press, 2007.

Lowe, V., *International Law*, Oxford, Clarendon, 2007.

Lowenfeld, A., *International Economic Law*, 2nd ed., Oxford, Oxford University Press, 2007.

Lyotard, J.-F., *The Postmodern Condition*, Manchester, Manchester University Press, 1986 (translation by G. Bennington and B. Massumi of *La Condition postmoderne*, Paris, Les Editions de Minuit, 1979).
Madiou, M. S. E., "The Death of Postcolonialism: The Founder's Foreword", *Janus Unbound: Journal of Critical Studies*, Vol. 1 (2021), pp. 1-12.
Malaspina, E. F., Book review of Nuzzo, *Origini di una scienza* (2012), *Comparative Legal History*, Vol. 2 (2014), p. 148-151.
Mälksoo, L., *Russian Approaches to International Law Thought*, Oxford, Oxford University Press, 2015.
Mallard, G., "We Owe You Nothing: Decolonization and Sovereign Debt Obligations in International Public Law", in P. Pénet and J. F. Zendejas (eds.), *Sovereign Debt Diplomacies*, Oxford, Oxford University Press, 2021, pp. 189-212.
–, *Gift Exchange: The Transnational History of a Political Idea*, Cambridge, Cambridge University Press, 2019.
Mann, F. A., "British Treaties for the Promotion and Protection of Investments", *British Yearbook of International Law*, Vol. 52 (1981), pp. 241-254.
–, "England Rejects 'Delocalised' Contracts and Arbitration", *International and Comparative Law Quarterly*, Vol. 33 (1984), pp. 193-198.
Manning, C. A. W., Book review of Brierly, Lauterpacht and Waldock, *The Basis of Obligation in International Law and Other Papers* (2019), *International Affairs*, Vol. 35 (1959), p. 82.
Mbengue, M. M., Book review of Toufayan, Tourme-Jouannet and Ruiz-Fabri (eds.), *Droit international et nouvelles approches sur le Tiers-monde* (2013), *European Journal of International Law*, Vol. 26 (2015), pp. 780-786.
McCallon, K. F., and R. Murtfield, "Germany's Responsibility under International Law to Compensate the Ovaherero and Nama Peoples of Namibia for the 1904-1908 Genocide", *Harvard International Law Journal*, Vol. 59 (2018), p. 1 *et seq.*
McDougal, M. S., "International Law, Power and Policy: A Contemporary Conception", *Recueil des cours*, Vol. 82 (1953), pp. 137-258.
McDougal, M. S., and H. D. Lasswell, "The Identification and Appraisal of Diverse System of Public Order", *American Journal of International Law*, Vol. 53 (1959), pp. 1-29.
McNair, A., *International Law Opinions*, Vol. 2, Oxford, Oxford University Press, 1956.
–, *Law of Treaties*, Oxford, Clarendon, 1961.
McWhinney, E., "Changing International Law Method and Objectives in the Era of the Soviet-Western Détente", *American Journal of International Law*, Vol. 59 (1965), pp. 1-15.
–, "The Changing United Nations Constitutionalism: New Areas and New Techniques for International Law-Making", *Canadian Yearbook of International Law*, Vol. 5 (1967), pp. 68-83.
Memon, A. R., "The Disorder of Things: Rethinking Social Critique in Postcolonial Pakistan", *TWAILR: Reflections* 46/22 (7 September 2022), https://twailr.com/the-disorder-of-things-rethinking-social-critique-in-postcolonial-pakistan/.
Menon, P. K., "The Succession of States and the Problem of State Debts", *Boston College Third World Law Journal*, Vol. 6 (1986), pp. 111-141.
Miéville, C., "The Commodity-Form Theory of International Law: An Introduction", *Leiden Journal of International Law*, Vol. 17 (2004), pp. 271-302.
Mignolo, W., "Modernity and Decoloniality", in *Oxford Bibliographies (Latin American Studies)*, last modified 28 October 2011, last reviewed 5 May 2017, https://doi.org/10.1093/OBO/9780199766581-0017.
–, "(Post)Occidentalism, (Post)Coloniality, and (Post)Subaltern Rationality", in F. Afzal-Khan and K. Seshadri-Crooks (eds.), *The Pre-occupation of Postcolonial Studies*, Durham, NC, Duke University Press, 2000, pp. 86-118.
Mignolo, W. D., *The Darker Side of Western Modernity: Global Futures, Decolonial Options*, Durham, NC, Duke University Press, 2011.
Mitchell, R., "Myanmar and the Hegemonic Discourse of International Criminal

Law", in M. Bergsmo *et al.* (eds.), *Colonial Wrongs, Double Standards, and Access to International Law*, Brussels, Torkel Opsahl Academic EPublisher, 2020, pp. 285-316.

–, *Recentering the World: China's Reception and Contention of International Law*, Cambridge, Cambridge University Press, 2022.

Moore, J. B., *International Adjudications: Ancient and Modern*, Oxford, Oxford University Press, 1929.

Mueser, B., "The Nation and Property in Vattel's Theory of Territory", *Global Intellectual History*, Vol. 3 (2018), pp. 137-155.

Murphy, J. F., Book review of Coates, *Legalist Empire: International Law and American Foreign Relations in the Early Twentieth Century* (2016), *American Journal of International Law*, Vol. 113 (2019), pp. 210-212.

Mustill, M., "The New *Lex Mercatoria*: The First Twenty-Five Years", *Arbitration International*, (1988), pp. 86-119.

Mutua, M., "What is TWAIL?", *Proceedings of the Annual Meeting (American Society of International Law)*, Vol. 94 (2000), pp. 31-40.

Neff, S. C., *Justice among Nations: A History of International Law*, Cambridge, MA, Harvard University Press, 2014.

Nesiah, V., "Toward a Feminist Internationality: A Critique of US Feminist Legal Scholarship", *Harvard Women's Law Journal*, Vol. 16 (1993), pp. 189-210.

Nozari, F., Book review of Snyder and Sathirathai, *Third World Attitudes Toward International Law* (1987), *International Journal of Legal Information*, Vol. 17 (1989), pp. 69-70.

Nussbaum, A., "Arbitration between the Lena Goldfields Ltd. and the Soviet Government", *Cornell Law Review*, Vol. 36 (1950), pp. 31-53.

Nuzzo, L., *Origini di una scienza. Diritto internazionale e colonialismo nel XIX secolo*, Frankfurt am Main, Klostermann, 2012.

–, "Territory, Sovereignty and the Construction of Colonial Space", in M. Koskenniemi *et al.* (eds.), *International Law and Empire: Historical Explorations*, Oxford, Oxford University Press, 2017, pp. 263-292.

O'Connell, D., "Recent Problems of State Succession in Relation to New States", *Recueil des cours*, Vol. 130 (1970), pp. 95-206.

O'Connell, D. P., *The International Law of the Sea*, Vol. 1, edited by I. A. Shearer, Oxford, Clarendon, 1982.

Oesterhelt, J., "Vienna Convention on Succession of States in respect of State Property, Archives and Debts", in R. Bernhardt (ed.), *Encyclopedia of Public International Law*, Instalment 10: *States, Responsibility of States, International Law and Municipal Law*, North-Holland, Elsevier, 1987, pp. 521-523.

Ofuatey-Kodjoe, W., *The Principle of Self-determination in International Law*, New York, Nellen, 1977.

Onuma, Y., *A Transcivilizational Perspective on International Law*, Leiden, Martinus Nijhoff, 2010.

Oppenheim, L., *International Law, A Treatise*, Vol. 1, 1st ed., London, Longmans, Green, and Co., 1905.

–, *International Law*, Vol. 1, 2nd ed., London, Longmans, Green and Co, 1912.

–, *International Law, A Treatise*, Vol. 1, 3rd ed., edited by R. F. Roxburgh, London, Longmans, Green and Co., 1920.

Orford, A., *International Law and the Politics of History*, Cambridge, Cambridge University Press, 2021.

Ortega, M. C., "Vitoria and the Universalist Conception of International Relations", in I. Clark and I. B. Neumann (eds.), *Classical Theories of International Relations*, London, Macmillan, 1999, pp. 99-119.

Oyarzábal, M., "The Influence of Public International Law upon Private International Law in History and Theory and in the Formation and Application of the Law", *Recueil des cours*, Vol. 428 (2023), pp. 129-525.

Özsu, U., "Hydrocarbon Humanitarianism: Ibrahim Shihata, 'Oil Aid', and Resource

Sovereignty", *Journal of the History of International Law*, Vol. 22 (2021), pp. 137-160.
Pal, R., *et al.*, *International Military Tribunal for the Far East: Dissentient Judgment of Justice Pal*, Tokyo, Kokusho-Kankokai, 1999.
Palabiyik, M. S., "The Emergence of the Idea of 'International Law' in the Ottoman Empire before the Treaty of Paris 1856", *Middle Eastern Studies*, Vol. 50 (2014), pp. 233-251.
Pashukanis, E., "General Theory of Law and Marxism", in E. Pashukanis, *Selected Writings on Marxism and Law*, edited by P. Beirne and R. Sharlet, translated by P. B. Maggs, London, Academic Press, 1980, pp. 32-131.
Paulsson, J., "Arbitration Unbound: Award Detached from the Law of its Country of Origin", *International and Comparative Law Quarterly*, Vol. 30 (1981), pp. 358-387.
–, *Denial of Justice in International Law*, Cambridge, Cambridge University Press, 2005.
–, *The Unruly Notion of Abuse of Rights*, Cambridge, Cambridge University Press, 2020.
–, "Omnipotence Fantasies", *Asian Dispute Review*, Vol. 23 (2021), pp. 10-17.
Paulsson, J., and G. Petrochilos, "Neer-ly Misled", *ICSID Review Foreign Investment Law Journal*, Vol. 22 (2007), pp. 242-257.
Pirie, F., *The Rule of Laws*, London, Profile Books, 2021.
Rajagopal, B., "Counter-hegemonic International Law: Rethinking Human Rights and Development as a Third World Strategy", *Third World Quarterly*, Vol. 27 (2006), pp. 767-783.
Rana, H. S., "The 'Common Heritage of Mankind' and the Final Frontier: A Revaluation of Values Constituting the International Legal Regime for Outer Space Activities", *Rutgers Law Journal*, Vol. 26 (1994), pp. 225-250.
Ranganathan, S., "Decolonization and International Law: Putting the Ocean on the Map", *Journal of the History of International Law*, Vol. 23 (2021), pp. 161-183.
Reisman, M., "McDougal's Jurisprudence: Utility, Influence, Controversy", *Proceedings of the Annual Meeting (American Society of International Law)*, Vol. 79 (1985), pp. 266-285.
Renteln, A. D., "Cultural Bias in International Law", *Proceedings of the Annual Meeting (American Society of International Law)*, Vol. 92 (1998), pp. 232-243.
Reza, M. G., "Realization of the Right to Development: Prospects for Drafting a Convention on the Right to Development", *Journal of Human Rights*, Vol. 14 (2015), pp. 548-558.
Rivier, A., "Extrait du procès-verbal de la séance plénière tenue par l'Institut, à Lausanne, le 7 septembre 1888, sous la présidence de M. Rivier", *Annuaire de l'Institut de droit international*, Vol. 10 (1888-1889), pp. 176-201.
Röling, B. V. A., *International Law in an Expanded World*, Amsterdam, Djambatan, 1960.
Röling, B. V. A., and C. F. Rüter (eds.), *The Tokyo Judgment: The International Military Tribunal for the Far East (IMTFE), 29 April 1946-12 November 1948*, Vol. 2, Amsterdam, APA-University Press Amsterdam, 1977.
Rolin-Jaequemyns, G., "L'année 1888 au point de vue de la paix et du droit international", *Revue de droit international et de législation compare*, Vol. 21 (1889), pp. 167-208.
Ross, A., "Winter is Coming: Is Arbitration's 'Long, Golden Summer' Coming to an End?", *Global Arbitration Review*, Vol. 13 (2019), pp. 7-8.
Saastamoinen, K., "Pufendorf on Natural Equality, Human Dignity, and Self-Esteem", *Journal of the History of Ideas*, Vol. 71 (2010), pp. 39-62.
Said, E., *Orientalism*, reprinted with a new preface, London, Penguin, 2003.
Saidov, D., "The Standardisation of Oil and Gas Law: Transnational Layers of Governance", NUS Working Paper 2017/017, National University of Singapore, https://law.nus.edu.sg/wp-content/uploads/2020/04/017_2017_Djakhongir-Saidov.pdf.

Salacuse, J., *The Law of Investment Treaties*, 3rd ed., Oxford, Oxford University Press, 2021.

Salas, Jr, V. M., "Francisco de Vitoria on the *Ius Gentium* and the American *Indios*", *Ave Maria Law Review*, Vol. 10 (2012), pp. 331-341.

Salem, S., "'Stretching Marxism' in the Postcolonial World: Egyptian Decolonisation and the Contradictions of National Sovereignty", *Historical Materialism*, Vol. 27 (2019), pp. 3-28.

Sánchez, D. G., "Transforming Human Rights through Decolonial Lens", *The Age of Human Rights Journal*, Vol. 15 (2020), pp. 276-303.

Sanderson, D., "The Residue of Imperium: Property and Sovereignty on Indigenous Lands", *University of Toronto Law Journal*, Vol. 68 (2018), pp. 319-357.

Sands, P., *The Last Colony*, London, Weidenfeld & Nicolson, 2022.

–, "Colonialism: A Short History of International Law in Five Acts", *Recueil des cours*, Vol. 431 (2023), pp. 285-410.

Satia, P., "Risking a Colonial Anticolonialism", *European Journal of International Law*, Vol. 32 (2021), pp. 1017-1026

Schneiderman, D., "The Paranoid Style of Investment Lawyers and Arbitrators: Investment Law Norm Entrepreneurs and Their Critics", in C. L. Lim (ed.), *Alternative Visions of the International Law on Foreign Investment: Essays in Honour of Muthucumaraswamy Sornarajah*, Cambridge, Cambridge University Press, 2016, pp. 131-155.

Schreuer, C. H. *et al.*, *The ICSID Convention: A Commentary*, 2nd ed., Cambridge, Cambridge University Press, 2009.

Schrijver, N., *Sovereignty over Natural Resources: Balancing Rights and Duties*, Cambridge, Cambridge University Press, 1997.

–, "A New Convention on the Human Right to Development: Putting the Cart Before the Horse?", *Netherlands Quarterly of Human Rights*, Vol. 38 (2020), pp. 84-93.

Schröder, P., "Vitoria, Gentili, Bodin: Sovereignty and the Law of Nations", in B. Kingsbury and B. Straumann (eds.), *The Roman Foundations of the Law of Nations*, Oxford, Oxford University Press, 2010, pp. 163-186.

Schwarzenberger, G., *The Inductive Approach to International Law*, London, Stevens, 1967.

Scott, J. B., "The Achievement of International Justice", *Advocate for Peace*, Vol. 79 (1917), pp. 212-215.

–, *The Spanish Origin of International Law: Francisco de Vitoria and His Law of Nations*, Oxford, Clarendon, 1934.

Senaratne, K., *Internal Self-determination in International Law*, Cambridge, Cambridge University Press, 2021.

Seuffert, N. M. "Vitoria's *On the Indians*, Legal Subjectivity and the Right to Travel", *Social & Legal Studies*, Vol. 30 (2021), pp. 14-31.

Shalakany, A. A., "Arbitration in the Third World: A Plea for Reassessing Bias under the Specter of Neoliberalism", *Harvard International Law Journal*, Vol. 41 (2000), pp. 419-468.

Shaw J. (ed.), *Charters relating to the East India Company from 1600 to 1761; reprinted from a former collection with some additions and a preface for the Government of Madras*, Madras, Hill, 1887.

Singh, P., "Reading RP Anand in the Post-Colony: Between Resistance and Appropriation", in J. von Bernstorff and P. Dann (eds.), *The Battle for International Law: South-North Perspectives on the Decolonization Era*, Oxford, Oxford University Press, 2019, pp. 297-318.

Singh, S., "A TWAIL Critique of International Criminal Justice", *Berkeley Journal of International Law*, online post, 26 April 2022, https://www.berkeleyjournalofinternationallaw.com/post/a-twail-critique-of-international-criminal-justice.

Skinner, Q., "Introduction: The Return of Grand Theory", in Q. Skinner (ed.), *The Return of Grand Theory in the Human Sciences*, Cambridge, Cambridge University Press, 1985, pp. 1-20.

Smith, A., *An Inquiry into the Nature and Causes of Wealth of Nations*, London, T. Nelson and Sons, 1852 (orig. 1776).
Smith, V. A., *The Oxford History of India*, 3rd ed., edited by P. Spear, Oxford, Oxford University Press, 1958.
Snyder, F. E., and S. Sathirathai, *Third World Attitudes toward International Law*, Dordrecht/Boston, Nijhoff, 1987.
Sornarajah, M., "The Myth of International Contract Law", *Journal of World Trade*, Vol. 15 (1981), pp. 187-217.
–, *The Pursuit of Nationalized Property*, Dordrecht/Boston, Nijhoff, 1986.
–, *The International Law on Foreign Investment*, 3rd ed., Cambridge, Cambridge University Press, 2010 (orig. 1994).
–, "On Fighting for Global Justice: The Role of a Third World International Lawyer", *Third World Quarterly*, Vol. 37 (2016), 1972-1989.
–, "Special Panel in Honour of Professor R. P. Anand", 28 August 2021, UN Audiovisual Library, https://legal.un.org/avl/ls/anandpanel.html.
–, *The International Law on Foreign Investment*, 5th ed., Cambridge, Cambridge University Press, 2021.
Spiermann, O., *International Legal Argument in the Permanent Court of International Justice: The Rise of the International Judiciary*, Cambridge, Cambridge University Press, 2005.
Spivak, G. C., "Can the Subaltern Speak?", in C. Nelson and L. Grossberg (eds.), *Marxism and the Interpretation of Culture*, Basingstoke, MacMillan, 1998, pp. 271-313.
Stahn, C., "Reckoning with Colonial Injustice: International Law as Culprit and as Remedy?", *Leiden Journal of International Law*, Vol. 33 (2020), pp. 823-835.
Stefanelli, J. N., and E. Lovall (eds.), *Reparations Under International Law for Enslavement of African Persons in the Americas and the Caribbean: Proceedings of the Symposium, 20-21 May 2021*, Washington, DC, American Society of International Law, 2022.
Stein, T. L., "The Approach of the Different Drummer: The Principle of the Persistent Objector in International Law", *Harvard International Law Journal*, Vol. 26 (1985), pp. 457-482.
Stephenson, C. W. T., *Transparency Cantos: Values for Human Dignity – Lasswell and McDougal*, Washington, DC, Torquilstone Press, 2002.
Stern, P. J., *The Company-State: Corporate Sovereignty and the Early Modern Foundations of the British Empire in India*, Oxford, Oxford University Press, 2011.
Swan-sik, K., "The Concept of Acquired Rights in International Law: A Survey", *Netherlands International Law Review*, Vol. 24 (1974), pp. 120-142.
Sylvest, C., "'Our Passion for Legality': International Law and Imperialism in Late Nineteenth-Century Britain", *Review of International Studies*, Vol. 34 (2008), pp. 403-423.
Takahashi, S., *Cases on International Law During the Chino-Japanese War*, Cambridge, Cambridge University Press, 1899.
Tams, C., "Regulating Treaty Breaches", in M. J. Bowman and D. Kritsiotis (eds.), *Conceptual and Contextual Perspectives on the Modern Law of Treaties*, Cambridge, Cambridge University Press, 2018, pp. 440-467.
T'ao, Y., "Recognise the True Face of Bourgeois International Law from a Few Basic Concepts", KCWTYC, No. 1:46-47 (1960), in J. A. Cohen and H. Chiu, *People's China and International Law: A Documentary Study*, Princeton, NJ, Princeton University Press, 1974, pp. 70-72.
Taylor, A. J. P., *The Struggle for Mastery in Europe 1848-1918*, Oxford, Clarendon, 1954.
Tchéou, W., "Observations de M. Tchéou-Wei. Genève, le 21 mars 1926", *Annuaire de l'Institut de droit international*, Vol. 33 (1927), pp. 515-521.
Toth, A. G., "The Doctrine of Rebus Sic Stantibus in International Law", PhD thesis, University of Exeter, 1970.

Tregonning, K. G., *A History of Modern Malaya*, Singapore, Eastern Universities Press for University of London Press, 1964.

Tuck, R., *The Rights of War and Peace*, Oxford, Oxford University Press, 2000.

Tudor, I., *The Fair and Equitable Treatment Standard in the International Law on Foreign Investment*, Oxford, Oxford University Press, 2008.

Tunkin, G. I., *Theory of International Law*, translated by William Butler, Cambridge, MA, Harvard University Press, 1974.

Twiss, T., *The Law of Nations Considered as Independent Political Communities*, Vol. 1, Oxford, Oxford University Press, 1861.

–, "Rapport", *Annuaire de l'Institut de droit international*, Vols. 3-4 (1879-1880), pp. 301-304.

–, "La libre navigation du Congo" (II), translated and reprinted as "The Free Navigation of the Congo" in H. W. Wack, *The Story of the Congo Free State*, New York, Putnam, 1905, p. 502 *et seq.*

Tzouvala, N., *Capitalism as Civilisation: A History of International Law*, Cambridge, Cambridge University Press, 2020.

Vanar, M., and S. Lee, "Tommy Thomas Slams 'Rogue Arbitrator' over Award to Sulu Heirs", *The Star*, 4 April 2022.

Van den Meerssche, D., "International Law as Insulation: The Case of the World Bank in the Decolonization Era", *Journal of the History of International Law*, Vol. 21 (2019), pp. 459-484.

Vandersmissen, J., "The King's Most Eloquent Campaigner . . . Emile de Laveleye, Leopold II and the Creation of the Congo Free State", *Belgisch Tijdschrift voor Nieuwste Geschiedenis*, Vol. 41 (2011), pp. 7-57.

Veeder, V. V., "The Lena Goldfields Arbitration: The Historical Roots of Three Ideas", *International and Comparative Law Quarterly*, Vol. 47 (1998), pp. 747-792.

Veevers, D., *The Origins of the British Empire in Asia, 1600-1750*, Cambridge, Cambridge University Press, 2020.

"Von der Leyen Condemns 'Barbaric' Invasion of Ukraine, Vows to Cripple Russia's Economy", *Euronews*, 24 February 2022, https://www.euronews.com/my-europe/2022/02/24/von-der-leyen-condemns-barbaric-invasion-of-ukraine-vows-to-cripple-russia-s-economy.

Von Mehren R. B., and P. N. Kourides, "International Arbitrations between States and Foreign Private Parties: The Libyan Nationalization Cases", *American Journal of International Law*, Vol. 75 (1981), pp. 476-552.

Walsh, C. D., and W. Mignolo, *On Decoloniality: Concepts, Analytics, Praxis*, Durham, NC, Duke University Press, 2018.

Wang, T., "The Third World and International Law", in Chinese Society of International Law (eds.), *Selected Essays from Chinese Yearbook of International Law*, Beijing, China Translation and Publishing Corporation, 1983, p. 6 *et seq.*

–, "International Law in China: Historical and Contemporary Perspectives", *Recueil des cours*, Vol. 221 (1990), p. 195 *et seq.*

Weinrib, E., *The Idea of Private Law*, Cambridge, MA, Harvard University Press, 1995.

Wesley-Smith, P., *Unequal Treaties 1989–1997: China, Great Britain and Hong Kong's New Territories*, Hong Kong, Oxford University Press, 1983.

Westlake, J., "Le conflit Anglo-Portugais", *Revue de droit international et de legislation comparee*, Vol. 18 (1891), pp. 243-265.

–, *Chapters on the Principles of International Law*, Cambridge, Cambridge University Press, 1894.

–, *International Law*, Vol. 1, Cambridge, Cambridge University Press, 1910.

Wheatley, S., "Revisiting the Doctrine of Intertemporal Law", *Oxford Journal of Legal Studies*, Vol. 41 (2021), pp. 484-509.

Wheaton, H., *Elements of International Law with a Sketch of the History of the Science*, Vol. 1, London, B. Fellowes, 1836.

–, *Elements of International Law*, 3rd ed., Philadelphia, Lea and Blanchard, 1846.

Whitehead, J., "John Locke, Accumulation by Dispossession and the Governance of Colonial India", *Journal of Contemporary Asia*, Vol. 42 (2012), pp. 1-21.

Williams, D. G., and R. R. Land, "The Legitimation of Black Subordination: The Impact of Colour Blind Ideology on African American Education", *Journal of Negro Education*, Vol. 76 (2005), pp. 579-588.

Wilson, G. G., *Handbook of International Law*, St. Paul, MN, West Publishing Co., 1910.

Wing, A. K., *Global Critical Race Feminism: A Reader*, New York, New York University Press, 2000.

Winkel, L., "The Peace Treaties of Westphalia", in R. Lesaffer (ed.), *Peace Treaties and International Law in European History*, Cambridge, Cambridge University Press, 2004, pp. 222-237.

Wolff, M., "Differential and More Favorable Treatment of Developing Countries and the International Trading System", *World Bank Economic Review*, Vol. 1 (1987), pp. 647-668.

Yacob, S., and N. J. White, "The 'Unfinished Business' of Malaysia's Decolonisation: The Origins of the Guthrie 'Dawn Raid'", *Modern Asian Studies*, Vol. 44 (2010), pp. 919-960.

Yamauchi, S., "Civilization and International Law in Japan during the Meiji Era (1868-1912)", *Hitotsubashi Journal of Law and Politics*, Vol. 24 (1996), pp. 1-25.

Young, I. M. *Responsibility for Justice*, Oxford, Oxford University Press, 2011.

Zakariya, H. S., "Sovereignty, State Participation and the Need to Restructure the Existing Petroleum Concession Regime", *Alberta Law Review*, Vol. 10 (1972), pp. 218-231.

Zarakol, A., *Before the West: The Rise and Fall of Eastern World Orders*, Cambridge, Cambridge University Press, 2022.

Zollmann, J., *Naulila 1914: World War I in Angola and International Law. A Study in (Post-)Colonial Border Regimes and Interstate Arbitration*, Baden-Baden, Nomos, 2016.

Further reading

Alatas, S. H., *The Myth of the Lazy Native*, London, Frank Cass, 1977.

Alexandrowicz, C. H., *The European-African Confrontation: A Study in Treaty Making*, Leiden, A. W. Sijthoff, 1973.

Alschner, W., *Investment Arbitration and State-Driven Reform*, Oxford, Oxford University Press, 2022.

Ashworth-Hayes, S., "Russia Has Never Been a Part of the West", *The Spectator*, 19 March 2022, https://www.spectator.co.uk/article/russia-has-never-been-a-part-of-the-west/ (subscription required).

Beckert, S., *Empire of Cotton, A Global History*, London, Vintage, 2015.

Carty, A., "General Customary Law", in *Oxford Bibliographies (International Law)*, last modified 23 March 2012, last reviewed 15 October 2014, https://doi.org/10.1093/OBO/9780199796953-0066.

Dolzer, R., and A. von Walter, "Fair and Equitable Treatment and Customary Law – Lines of Jurisprudence", in F. Ortino *et al.* (eds.), *Investment Treaty Law: Current Issues*, London, British Institute of International Comparative Law, 2007, p. 99 *et seq.*

Dumberry, P., *The Formation and Identification of Rules of Customary International Law in International Investment Law*, Cambridge, Cambridge University Press, 2016.

Fanon, F., *The Wretched of the Earth*, London, Macgibbon & Kee, 1965.

Foxcroft, L., *The Making of Addiction: The "Use and Abuse" of Opium in Nineteenth-Century Britain*, London, Ashgate, 2007.

Hannan, D., "Vladimir Putin's Monstrous Invasion is an Attack on Civilisation Itself", *Daily Telegraph*, 26 February 2022, https://www.telegraph.co.uk/news/2022/02/26/vladimir-putins-monstrous-invasion-attack-civilisation/.

Jackson, J. H. H., "The WTO DSU: Misunderstandings on the Nature of Legal

Obligation", *American Journal of International Law*, Vol. 91 (1997), pp. 60-64.

Lim, C. L., "The Conventional Morality of Trade", in C. Carmody, F. Garcia and J. Linarelli (eds.), *Global Justice and International Economic Law: Opportunities and Prospects*, Cambridge, Cambridge University Press, 2012, pp. 129-152.

Lynn, H.-G., "Globalization and the Cold War", in R. H. Immermann and P. Goedde (eds.), *The Oxford Handbook of the Cold War*, Oxford, Oxford University Press, 2013, pp. 584-602.

Seville, I., *The Etymologies of Isidore of Seville*, edited and translated by S. A. Barney *et al.*, Cambridge, Cambridge University Press, 2016.

Slaughter, A. M., "Towards an Age of Liberal Nations", *Harvard International Law Journal*, Vol. 33 (1992), pp. 393-405.

Zollmann, J., "Nationality, Property, and the Mixed Arbitration Tribunals, 1914 to c1930", in H. Ruiz-Fabri and M. Erpelding (eds.), *The Mixed Arbitral tribunals, 1919-1939*, Baden-Baden, Nomos, 2023, pp. 113-158.

THE PRINCIPLE *JURA NOVIT CURIA* IN INTERNATIONAL JUDICIAL AND ARBITRAL PROCEEDINGS

A Window on International Adjudication

by

ATTILA M. TANZI

A. M. TANZI

TABLE OF CONTENTS

BIOGRAPHICAL NOTE

Attila Massimiliano Tanzi, born in Sorengo-Lugano, Switzerland, on 10 August 1957.

Bachelor's degree in Political Sciences, University of Florence, *summa cum laude* (1981); MA in International Political Studies, University of Florence, *summa cum laude* (1984); PhD in International Law, University "La Sapienza" Roma, Faculty of Law (1987).

Lecturer in Public International Law, Faculty of Law, University of Perugia (1990-1999); Associate Professor of International Law, Faculty of Law, University of Verona (1999-2006); Chair of International Law at the University of Bologna (2006-ongoing); Visiting Professor at Queen Mary University of London (2014-2016); Visiting Professor at Université Paris II-Panthéon Assas (2018); Visiting Professor at University of Vienna (2018-2019); External Scientific Fellow at Max Planck Institute Luxembourg for International, European and Regulatory Procedural Law (2020); Visiting Professor at Université Paris Nanterre (2021).

Many times Member of the Italian delegation during UNGA sessions and to the MOP of the 1992 UNECE Transboundary Water Convention.

Chairman of the Legal Board of the 1992 UNECE Transboundary Water Convention (2004-2012); Chairman of the Compliance Committee of the 1999 UNECE Protocol on Water and Health (2007-2010); Chairman of the Implementation Committee of the 1992 UNECE Transboundary Water Convention (2013-ongoing).

Member of the Supervisory Board of the Tashkent International Arbitration Centre (TIAC), Uzbekistan (2018-ongoing); Permanent Arbitrator of the Asociación Europea de Arbitraje (Madrid, Spain). Member of the International Supervisory Board of the Organization of Islamic Cooperation – Arbitration Centre (OIC-AC) (2023-ongoing).

Conciliator at the OSCE Court of Conciliation and Arbitration (2013-ongoing); Member of the Permanent Court of Arbitration (2014-ongoing); Member of the list of the ICSID Panel of Arbitrators (2023-ongoing).

He is regularly instructed by governments, international organisations and corporations on matters of international law and acts as Counsel and Advocate in inter-State litigation before international courts and tribunals and as arbitrator in investor-State disputes.

Counsel and Advocate in inter-State litigation before international courts and tribunals

Full Professor of International Law, University of Bologna Alma Mater; Associate Member 3VB Chambers, London; President, Italian Branch of the International Law Association.

PRINCIPAL PUBLICATIONS

A. Books

Introduzione al diritto internazionale contemporaneo (*An Introduction to Contemporary International Law*), 7th ed., Padova, Cedam-Wolters Kluwer, 2023 (1st ed. 2003).

A Concise Introduction to International Law, 2nd ed., The Hague, Torino, Eleven-Giappichelli, 2022 (1st ed. 2019).

Una introducción concisa al derecho internacional, Buenos Aires, Astrea-Giappichelli, 2019.

The Economic Commission for Europe Water Convention and the United Nations Watercourses Convention: An Analysis of Their Harmonized Contribution to International Water Law, New York-Geneva, United Nations, 2015, reprinted with annexes in *The Consolidation of International Water Law: A Comparative Analysis of the UN and UNECE Water Conventions*, Napoli, Editoriale Scientifica, 2017.

L'immunità dalla giurisdizione degli agenti diplomatici (Jurisdictional Immunities of Diplomats), 2nd ed., Padova, Cedam, 2003 (1st ed. 1990).

The United Nations Convention on International Watercouses. A Framework for Sharing, Kluwer, London-The Hague-Boston, 2001 (co-authored with M. Arcari).

Edited books

La transizione ecologica nel commercio internazionale. Tra aspetti di riforma procedurali, istituzionali e diritto sostanziale, AlmaDL, 2022, with L. Chiussi Curzi, G. M. Farnelli and A. Mensi (eds.).

L'arbitrato amministrato, Editoriale Scientifica, 2021, with A. Sardu (ed.).

General Principle and the Coherence of International Law, Brill-Nijhoff, 2019, with M. Andenas, M. Fitzmaurice, J. Wouters and L. Chiussi (eds.).

General Principles of Law and International Investment Arbitration, Brill-Nijhoff, 2018, with A. Gattini and Filippo Fontanelli (eds.).

Multilateral Environmental Treaties, Edward Elgar, 2017, with M. Fitzmaurice and A. Papantoniou (eds.).

International Investment Law in Latin America: Problems and Prospects - Derecho internacional de inversiones extranjeras en América Latina: Problemas y Perspectivas, Brill-Martinus Nijhoff, 2016, with A. Asteriti, R. Polanco Lazo and P. Turrini (eds.).

The UNECE Convention on the Protection and Use of Transboundary Watercourses and International Lakes, Brill-Nijhoff, 2015, with O. McIntyre, A. Kolliopoulos, A. Rieu-Clarke and R. Kinna (eds.).

International Investment Law and Arbitration. An Introductory Casebook. Cedam-Wolters Kluwer, Padova, 2013, with F. Cristani (ed.).

Uso della forza e legittima difesa nel diritto internazionale contemporaneo (The Use of Force and Self-defence in Contemporary International Law, Jovene, Napoli, 2012, with A. Lanciotti (ed.).

La Convenzione di Aarhus e l'accesso alla giustizia in materia ambientale (*The Aarhus Convention and Access to Justice in Environmental Matters*), Cedam, Padova, 2011, with E. Fasoli and L. Iapichino (eds.).

Non-Compliance Procedures and Mechanisms and the Effectiveness of International Environmental Agreements, TMC Asser Press, The Hague, 2009, with T. Treves *et al.* (eds.).

Le immunità nel diritto internazionale (Immunities in International Law), Giappichelli, Torino, 2007, with A. Lanciotti (ed.).

Civil Society, International Courts and Compliance Bodies, TMC Asser Press, The Hague, 2005, with T. Treves *et al.* (eds.).

Peer reviewed articles and chapters

"The Potential of the Singapore Convention on Mediation for Art and Cultural Property Disputes", in *Journal of International Dispute Settlement*, 2022, with P. E. Mason.

"Adjudication at the Service of Diplomacy: The *Enrica Lexie* Case", in *Journal of International Dispute Settlement*, 2021, pp. 448-461.

"Arbitrato internazionale degli investimenti: una prospettiva italiana (*International Investment Arbitration: An Italian Perspective*)", in A. Tanzi and A. Sardu (eds.), *L'arbitrato amministrato*, Editoriale Scientifica, 2021, pp. 161-196, with G. M. Farnelli.

"Substantialising the Procedural Obligations of International Water Law Between Compensatory and Distributive Justice", in H. Ruiz Fabri, E. Franckx, M. Benatar and T. Meshel (eds.), *A Bridge over Troubled Waters Dispute Resolution in the Law of International Watercourses and the Law of the Sea*, Brill-Nijhoof, 2021, pp. 351-374.

"Ne Ultra Petita", in D. Mantucci (ed.), *Trattato di diritto dell'arbitrato. Volume XIII: l'arbitrato negli investimenti internazionali*, Edizioni Scientifiche Italiane, 2020, pp. 687-718.

"The Inter-relationship Between No Harm, Equitable and Reasonable Utilisation and Cooperation under International Water Law", in *International Environmental Agreements*, 2020, pp. 619-629?

"The Legacy of a Landmark Case in Times of Transition", in S. Forlati and M. M. Mbenge (eds.), *The Gabčíkovo-Nagymaros Judgment and Its Contribution to the Development of International Law*, OUP, 2020, pp. 229-243.

"On Judicial Autonomy and the Autonomy of the Parties in International Adjudication", with Special Regard to Investment Arbitration, in *Leiden Journal of International Law*, 2020, pp. 57-75.

"The Means for the Settlement of International Cultural Property Disputes: An Introduction", available at https://docs.pca-cpa.org/2019/12/A.-Tanzi-Lecture-of-25-October-2019.pdf.

"Il principio *ne ultra petita* nel processo internazionale" ("The *Ne Ultra Petita* Principle in International Adjudication"), in Aa.Vv. (ed.), *La vita giuridica internazionale nell'età della globalizzazione*, Editoriale Scientifica, 2019, pp. 2095-2125.

"Conclusions: Testing General Principles of Law in International Investment Law: Between Principles and Rules of International Law", in M. Andenas, M. Fitzmaurice, A. Tanzi and J. Wouters (eds.), *General Principles and the Coherence of International Law*, Brill-Nijhoof, 2019, pp. 297-306.

"The Settlement of Disputes Through Non-Judicial Means (Art. 33.1-33.9)", in L. Boisson de Chazournes, M. Mbengue, M. Tignino and K. Sangbana (eds.), *The United Nations Convention on the Law of the Non-Navigational Uses of International Watercourses. A Commentary*, OUP, 2019, pp. 349-363, with G. M. Farnelli.

"The Global Water Treaties and Their Relationship", in S. McCaffrey, C. Leb and R. T. Denoon (eds.), *Research Handbook on International Water Law*, Edward Elgar, 2019, pp. 44-58.

"The UNECE Protocol on Water and Health for the Implementation of the Right to Drinking Water and Sanitation, in S. McCaffrey, C. Leb and R. T. Denoon (eds.), *Research Handbook on International Water Law*, Edward Elgar, 2019, pp. 273-283, with G. M. Farnelli.

"Diplomacy, Responsibility and Accountability in Transboundary Water Disputes", in M. Tignino and C. Bréthaut (eds.), *Research Handbook on Freshwater Law and International Relations*, Edward Elgar, 2019, pp. 197-214.

"Under the Hood of Investment Arbitration: General Principles of Law", in A. Gattini, A. Tanzi and F. Fontanelli (eds.), *General Principles of Law and International Investment Arbitration*, Brill-Nijhoff, 2018, pp. 1-20, with A. Gattini and F. Fontanelli.

"The Relevance of the Foreign Investor's Good Faith', in A. Gattini, A. Tanzi and

F. Fontanelli (eds.), *General Principles of Law and International Investment Arbitration*, Brill-Nijhoff, 2018, pp. 193-220.

"Convention on the Prevention of Marine Pollution by Dumping of Wastes and Other Matter 1972 and 1996 Protocol", in A. Tanzi and M. Fitzmaurice (eds.), *Multilateral Environmental Treaties*, 2017, pp. 175-183, with G. M. Farnelli.

"Jurisdiction and Admissibility in Investment Arbitration. A View from the Bridge at the Practice", in *The Law and Practice of International Courts and Tribunals*, 2017, pp. 3-20, with F. Fontanelli.

"Remarks on Breaches of State Contracts for the Purposes of Jurisdiction and Admissibility in International Investment Arbitration", in E. Triggiani *et al.* (eds.), *Dialoghi con Ugo Villani*, Cacucci Editore, 2017, pp. 919-928.

"International Law and Foreign Investment in Hydroelectric Industry: A Multi-dimensional Analysis", in *International Community Law Review*, 2016, pp. 183-222.

"Breaches of State Contracts in the Interpretation and Application of International Investment Law in the Arbitration Case Law Involving Latin American Countries", in A. Tanzi, A. Asteriti, R. Polanco Lazo and P. Turrini (eds.) *International Investment Law in Latin America: Problems and Prospects – Derecho internacional de inversiones extranjeras en América Latina: Problemas y Perspectivas*, Brill-Martinus Nijhoff, 2016, pp. 303-340, with L. Mola.

"Bridging the Gap Between International Investment Law and the Right of Access to Water", in E. Levashova, T. Lambooy and E. J. Overwater (eds.), *Bridging the Gap Between International Investment Law and the Environment*, Eleven, 2016, pp. 187-214.

"Le forme della codificazione e sviluppo progressivo del diritto internazionale (Forms of Codification and Progressive Development of International Law)", in G. Nesi and P. Gargiulo (eds.), *Luigi Ferrari Bravo. Il diritto internazionale come professione*, Editoriale Scientifica, 2015, pp. 151-168.

"Introduction: The Contribution of Courts and Tribunals to the Development of International Law", in *The Law and Practice of International Courts and Tribunals (Guest Editor – Special Issue)*, 2015, pp. 7-15, with M. Arcari and E. Milano.

"Un difficile dialogo tra Corte internazionale di giustizia e Corte costituzione" ("A Difficult Dialogue Between the International Court of Justice and the Constitutional Court"), in *La comunità internazionale*, 2015, pp. 13-36.

"Controversie in materia di investimenti stranieri e soluzione arbitrale in Nord Africa (Foreign Investors' Disputes and Arbitral Settlement in Africa)", in A. Rizzo (ed.), *Investment Security in Nord Africa*, Editoriale Scientifica, 2015, pp. 15-47, with L. Mola.

"The International Water Law Process and Transboundary Groundwater: Supplementing the Water Convention with the 2012 UNECE Model Provisions", in A. Tanzi *et al.*, *The UNECE Convention on the Protection and Use of Transboundary Watercourses and International Lakes*, Brill-Nijhoff, 2015, pp. 408-420, with A. Kolliopoulos.

"Dispute Prevention, Dispute Settlements and Implementation Facilitation in International Water Law: The Added Value of the Establishment of an Implementation Mechanism under the Water Convention", in A. Tanzi *et al.*, *The UNECE Convention on the Protection and Use of Transboundary Watercourses and International Lakes*, Brill-Martinus Nijhoff, 2015, pp. 319-329, with C. Contartese.

"The No-Harm Rule", in A. Tanzi *et al.*, *The UNECE Convention on the Protection and Use of Transboundary Watercourses and International Lakes*, Brill-Martinus Nijhoff, 2015, pp. 133-145, with A. Kolliopoulos.

"Normative Feature of the UNECE Water Convention", in A. Tanzi *et al.*, *The UNECE Convention on the Protection and Use of Transboundary Watercourses and International Lakes*, Brill-Nijhoff, 2015, pp. 116-129, with A. Kolliopoulos and N. Nikiforova.

"Sulla sentenza Cost. 238/2014: *cui prodest?*" (*"On the Constitutional Court Judgment 238/2014: cui prodest?"*), in *Forum di Quaderni Costituzionali*, available at http://www.forumcostituzionale.it/wordpress/wp-content/uploads/2014/12/nota_238_2014_tanzi.pdf.

"Comparing the 1992 UNECE Helsinki Water Convention with the 1997 UN New York Convention on International Water-course: Harmonization over Conflict", in *Questions of International Law – Questions de Droit International*, available at http://www.qil-qdi.org/?p=845.

"International Law and Foreign Investment and the Hydroelectric Industry: A Multidimensional Analysis", in E. De Brabandere and T. Gazzini (eds.), *Foreign Investment in the Energy Sector: Balancing Private and Public Interests*, Martinus Nijhoff, The Hague, pp. 61-102.

"¿Se reduce la distancia entre el Derecho internacional de inversión y los derechos humanos en el Arbitraje Internacional de Inversión?" ("Reducing the Gap Between International Investment Law and Human Rights Law in International Investment Arbitration"), in *Revista Latinoamericana de Derecho Comercial Internacional/ Latin American Journal of International Trade Law*, 2013, pp. 143-156, English: pp. 299-311.

"Handle with Care: Umbrella Clauses and MFN Treatment in Investment Arbitration", in *Journal of World Investment & Trade*, 2013, pp. 978-994, with T. Gazzini.

"The United Nations Economic Commission for Europe Water Convention", in F. R. Loures and A. Rieu-Clarke (eds.), *The UN Watercourses Convention in Force. Strengthening International Law for Transbourdary Water Management*, Routledge, London, 2013, pp. 231-242.

"Public Interest Concerns in International Investment Arbitration in the Water Services Sector: Problems and Prospects for an Integrated Approach", in T. Treves *et al.* (eds.), *Foreign Investment, International Law and Common Concerns*, Routledge, Oxford, 2013, pp. 308-324.

"Recent Trends in International Investment Arbitration and the Protection of Human Rights in the Public Services Sector", in N. Boschiero *et al.* (eds.), *International Courts and the Development of International Law. Essays in Honour of Tullio Treves*, Springer, The Hague, 2013, pp. 587-598.

"Article 33 of the UN Watercourse Convention: A Step Forward for Dispute Settlement", in *Water International*, Vol. 38, 2013, pp. 166-179, with E. Milano.

"Regional Contributions to International Water Cooperation: The UNECE Contribution, in L. Boisson de Chazournes *et al.* (eds.)", *International Law and Freshwater: The Multiple Challenges*, Edward Elgar, Cheltenham, 2013, pp. 155-178.

"Il tortuoso cammino del diritto internazionale delle acque tra interessi economici e ambientali (The Winding Road of International Water Law Between Economic and Environmental Interests)", in *Diritto pubblico comparato ed europeo*, 2012, pp. 516-536.

"Riflessioni introduttive per un dibattito sull'uso della forza armata e la legittima difesa nel diritto internazionale contemporaneo *(Introductory Reflections for a Debate on the Use of Force and Self-defence in Contemporary International Law)*", in A. Lanciotti and A. Tanzi (eds.), *Uso della forza e legittima difesa nel diritto internazionale contemporaneo*, Jovene, Napoli, 2012, pp. 1-35.

"Sull'insolvenza degli Stati nel diritto internazionale *(On State Insolvency in International Law)*", in *Rivista di diritto internazionale*, 2012, pp. 66-88.

"On Balancing Foreign Investment Interests with Public Interests in Recent Arbitration Case Law in the Public Utilities Sector", in *Law and Practice of International Courts and Tribunals*, 2012, pp. 47-76.

"Liability for Lawful Acts", *Encyclopedia of Public International Law*, Oxford, 2012, online edition http://www.mpepil.com.

"State of Necessity", *Encyclopedia of Public International Law*, Oxford, 2012, online edition http://www.mpepil.com.

"Restitution", *Encyclopedia of Public International Law*, Oxford, 2011, online edition, http://www.mpepil.com.

"The Added Value of the UNECE Protocol on Water and Health for the Implementation of the Right to Drinking Water and Sanitation", in H. Smets (ed.), *Le droit à l'eau potable et à l'assainissement, sa mise en œuvre en Europe/The Implementation of the Right to Safe Drinking Water and Sanitation in Europe*, Editorial Johanet, Paris, online edition http://www.academie-eau.org/index.php, 2011, pp. 115-124, with L. Iapichino.

"Furthering International Water Law or Making a New Body of Law on Transboundary Aquifers? An Introduction", in *International Community Law Review*, 2011, pp. 193-208.

"La Palestina alle Nazioni Unite tra diritto e politica" *("Palestine at the UN Between Law and Policy")*, in *Aspenia Online*, Roma, 2011, online edition http://www.aspeninstitute.it/aspenia-online/.

"Remarks on Sovereignty in the Evolving Constitutional Features of the International Community", in M. Arsanjani *et al.* (eds.), *Looking to the Future: Essays on International Law in Honor of W. M. Reisman*, Martinus Nijhoff, Leiden – Boston, 2010, pp. 299-322.

"The Interplay Between Community Law and International Law Procedures in Controlling Compliance with the Aarhus Convention by Member States", in M. Pallemaerts (ed.), *The Aarhus Convention at Ten: Interactions and Tensions Between Conventional International Law and EU Environmental Law*, Europa Law Publishing, Groeningen, 2011, pp. 369-381, with C. Pitea.

"Reducing the Gap Between International Water Law and Human Rights Law: The UNECE Protocol on Water and Health", in *International Community Law Review*, 2010, pp. 267-285.

"Remarks on Sovereignty in the Evolving Constitutional Features of the International Community", in *International Community Law Review*, 2010, pp. 145-169.

"La gestione delle risorse d'acqua dolce internazionali di superficie", (*The Management of Transboundary Surface Waters*), in A. Fodella and L. Pineschi (eds.), *La protezione dell'ambiente nel Diritto internazionale*, Giappichelli, Torino, 2009, pp. 347-359.

"Non-Compliance Mechanisms: Lessons Learned and the Way Forward", in T. Treves *et al.* (eds.), *Non-Compliance Procedures and Mechanisms and the Effectiveness of International Environmental Agreements*, TMC Asser Press, The Hague, 2009, pp. 567-578, with C. Pitea.

"Controversial Developments in the Field of Public Participation in the International Environmental Law Process", in P.-M. Dupuy and L. Vierucci (eds.), *NGOs in International Law: Efficiency in Flexibility?*, Edward Elgar, Cheltenham – Northampton, 2008, pp. 135-152.

"Divergenze transatlantiche e diritto internazionale" *("US-Europe Differences and International Law")*, in G. Gozzi and P. Manzini (eds.), *Europa e ordine internationale*, Il Mulino, Bologna, Torino, 2008, pp. 9-28.

"La sécurité collective entre légalité et légitimité", in M. Arcari and L. Balmond (eds.), *La sécurité collective entre légalité et défis à la légalité*, Giuffré, Milano, 2008, pp. 3-14.

"Remarques sur le droit international dans une perspective constitutionnelle", in U. Leanza (ed.), *Studi in onore di Umberto Leanza*, Editoriale Scientifica, Napoli, 2008, pp. 761-784.

"Diritto comunitario: una *lex specialis* molto speciale" ("European Community Law: A Very Special *Lex Specialis*"), in L. S. Rossi and G. Di Federico (eds.), *L'incidenza del diritto dell'Unione europea sullo studio delle discipline giuridiche nel Cinquantenario della firma del Trattato di Roma*, Editoriale Scientifica, Napoli, 2008, pp. 37-70, with L. Gradoni.

"Su immunità ed evoluzione della società internazionale" *("On Jurisdictional Immunities and the Evolution of the International Society")*, in A. Lanciotti and A. Tanzi (eds.), *Le immunità nel diritto internazionale*, Giappichelli, Torino, 2007, pp. 1-22.

"Evoluzioni e involuzioni di un diritto internazionale poco cosmopolita" *("Evolutions and Set-backs of a Non-cosmopolitan International law")*, in *Cosmopolis*, 2006, pp. 107-121.

"Remarks on Democracy in Contemporary International Law", in *La Comunità Internazionale*, 2006, pp. 289-309.

"L'Organizzazione per la Cooperazione e la Sicurezza in Europa (The Organization for Co-operation and Security in Europe)", in L. S. Rossi (ed.), *Le organizzazioni internazionali come strumenti di governo multilaterale*, Giuffré, Milano, 2006, pp. 95-121.

"Biotecnologie e ambiente: tendenze evolutive nel diritto internazionale contemporaneo" ("Biotechnologies and the Environment: Evolving Trends in Contemporary International Law"), in N. Boschiero (ed.), *Bioetica e biotecnologie nel diritto internazionale e comunitario*, Giappichelli, Torino, 2006, pp. 155-185.

"Il ruolo delle organizzazioni regionali nel dibattito alle Nazioni Unite" ("The Role of Regional Organizations in the UN Debate"), in F. Lattanzi and M. Spinedi (eds.), *Le Organizzazioni regionali e il mantenimento della pace nella prassi di fine XX secolo*, Editoriale Scientifica, Napoli, 2004, pp. 1-31.

"Il consenso tiene: risposta a Glennon", in *Aspenia*, No. 25, 2004, pp. 72-80 (English version: *The Consensus Endures*, in *ibidem*, No. 25/26, 2004, pp. 70-77.

"Dike versus Ares. Etica, diritto e uso della forza nelle relazioni internazionali" ("Dike vs. Ares. Ethics, Law and the Use of Force in International Relations"), in N. Boschiero (ed.), *Ordine internazionale e valori etici, VIII Convegno della Società Italiana di Diritto Internazionale*, Verona, 26-27 giugno 2003, Editoriale Scientifica, Napoli, 2004, pp. 131-158.

"Riformare le Nazioni Unite: Mission Impossible" *("Reforming the United Nations: Mission Impossible")*, in *Aspenia*, 2003, pp. 235-243.

"The Role of Non-State Actors in International Water Disputes", in The International Bureau of the Permanent Court of Arbitration (ed.), *Resolution of International Water Disputes*, Kluwer Law International, The Hague, 2003, pp. 259-297 (with C. Pitea).

"Achievements and Prospects of the Water Law Process in the UNECE Region", in F. Bernardini *et al.* (eds.), *Sustainable Management of Transboundary Water in Europe*, ComGraph, Szczecin (Polonia), 2003, pp. 263-278.

"The Resumed Codification of the Law of Reservations to Treaties", in *Comunicazioni e Studi*, 2002, pp. 9-34.

"Evoluzione della tutela dei diritti dell'uomo nel processo di integrazione europea" ("Evolution of Human Rights' Protection in the European Integration's Process"), in *Gioventù Federalista Europea (eds.), Carta dei Diritti e Costituzione Europea*, Atti del Convegno di Verona del 7 dicembre 2001, 2002, pp. 15-19.

"Recent Trends in International Water Law Dispute Settlement", in The International Bureau of the Permanent Court of Arbitration (ed.), *International Investments and Protection of the Environment: The Role of Dispute Resolution Mechanisms*, Kluwer Law International, The Hague-London, 2001, pp. 133-174.

"Su alcuni aspetti dell'uso della norma giuridica nello studio del diritto internazionale" *("On the Use of Legal Rules in the Study of International Law")*, in N. Picardi *et al.* (eds.), *Diritto e processo. Studi in memoria di Alessandro Giuliani*, 3. voll., Edizioni Scientifiche Italiane, Napoli, 2001, pp. 449-471.

"The Relationship Between the 1992 UN/ECE Convention on the Protection and Use of Transboundary Watercourses and International Lakes and the 1997 UN Convention on the Law of the Non-Navigational Uses of International Watercourses", Geneva, 2000, UN Doc. ECE/ENHS/NONE/00/2, GE.00-30528, addendum to UN/ECE doc. MP.WAT/2000/3.

"Regional Integration and the Protection of the Environment: The UN/ECE Process on Water Law as a Model for the Global Dimension", in *Italian Yearbook of International Law*, 2000, pp. 71-112.

"The UN Convention on International Watercourse as a Framework for the Avoidance and Settlement of Water Law Disputes", in *Leiden Journal of International Law*, 1998, pp. 441-472.

"La Convenzione di New York sui corsi d'acqua internazionali" *(The New York Convention on International Watercourses)*, in *Rivista di diritto internazionale*, 1997, pp. 956-1002

"The Completion of the Preparatory Works for the UN Convention on the Law of International Watercourses", in *Natural Resources Forum*, 1997, pp. 239-245.

"La Libia tra rivoluzione e giustizia internazionale" *("Libya between revolution and international justice")*, in *Aspenia Online*, Roma, online edition, http://www.aspeninstitute.it/aspenia-online/.

"Codifying the Minimum Standards of the Law of International Watercourses: Part One and a Half", in *Natural Resources Forum*, 1997, pp. 109-117.

"Relazioni diplomatiche *(Diplomatic Relations)*", in *Digesto* IV, *Discipline pubblicistiche*, Vol. XIII, UTET, Milano, 1996, pp. 122-147.

"Notes on the 'Permanent Conference of Revision' of the United Nations Charter at the 50th Anniversary of the Organization", in *Rivista di diritto internazionale*, 1995, pp. 723-737.

"Problems of Enforcement of Decisions of the International Court of Justice and the Law of the United Nations", in *European Journal of International Law*, 1995, pp. 539-572.

"Sul progetto ONU di Codice dei Crimini Contro la Pace e la Sicurezza dell'Umanità" ("On the UN Draft-Code of Crimes Against Peace and Security and on the Prospects for an International Criminal Court"), in *Critica Penale*, 1993, III-IV, pp. 3-20.

"The Extinction of International Organisations: The IBI Case", in *La Comunità Internazionale*, 1993, pp. 731-756.

"Prospects of Revision of the United Nations Charter", in SIOI, *Prospects for Reform of the United Nations System*, CEDAM, Padova, 1993, pp. 455-479.

"International State Responsibility", in M. Bedjaoui (ed.), *International Law: Achievements and Prospects*, Unesco-Martinus Nijhoff, Paris-Dordrecht-Norwell, 1991, pp. 347-308 (co-written with E. Jiménez de Aréchaga).

"Diritto di Veto ed esecuzione della sentenza della Corte internazionale di giustizia tra Nicaragua e Stati Uniti" *("The Right of Veto and the Enforcement of the ICJ Decision in the Nicaragua Case")*, in *Rivista di diritto internazionale*, 1987, pp. 293-308.

"Is Damage a Distinct Condition for the Existence of an Internationally Wrongful Act?", in M. Spinedi and B. Simma (eds.), *United Nations of Codification of State Responsibility*, Oceana Publications, Dobbs Ferry-New York-Roma, 1987, pp. 1-33.

"Responsabilità degli Stati stranieri per incidenti stradali causati da agenti diplomatici negli Stati Uniti" ("Liability of Foreign States for Traffic Accidents Caused by Diplomatic Agents in the United States"), in *Rivista di diritto internazionale*, 1985, pp. 563-579.

"L'ambigua natura delle dichiarazioni congiunte del Canton Ticino e del Comune di Campione d'Italia" ("The Ambiguous Nature of the Joint Declarations by the Ticino Canton and the Municipality of Campione"), in *Rivista di diritto internazionale*, 1985, pp. 347-350

"La legislazione sugli indennizzi per danni arrecati a cittadini italiani all'estero" *("Legislation Compensating Italian Nationals for Damage Suffered Abroad")*, in *Rivista di diritto internazionale*, 1983, pp. 102-119.

LIST OF ABBREVIATIONS

European Court of Human Rights	ECtHR
International Centre for the Settlement of Investment Disputes	ICSID
International Court of Justice	ICJ
International Criminal Court	ICC
International Criminal Tribunal for Rwanda	ICTR
International Criminal Tribunal for the Former Yugoslavia	ICTY
International Tribunal for the Law of the Sea	ITLOS
Permanent Court of International Justice	PCIJ
Permanent Court of Arbitration	PCA
Reports of International Arbitral Awards	RIAA
United Nations Convention on the Law of the Sea	UNCLOS

ACKNOWLEDGMENTS

Creating and delivering this course was a journey made possible through the collective efforts of many dedicated individuals. Among these, I am profoundly grateful for the invaluable contributions of Gian Maria Farnelli, Ludovica Chiussi Curzi and Niccolò Ridi. Their support with dedication and expertise has been key to the successful completion of this course.

I extend my sincere gratitude to the Director of The Hague Academy, Jean-Marc Thouvenin. His leadership, support and guidance provided the foundation for this course, aiding in navigating the difficulties and ensuring its smooth execution. I am also thankful to the members of the Curatorium for their confidence.

Lastly, the incredible work of the administrative and technical department of The Hague Academy, under the leadership of Monique Legermann, cannot go unacknowledged. Their proficiency in ensuring the course's seamless delivery, despite the technical challenges posed by the pandemic, has been highly commendable. They facilitated the transition to a virtual environment, allowing for an uninterrupted and engaging learning experience. For the production of the current written version of the course, I am indebted to Ms Simone Cartier.

CHAPTER I

INTRODUCTION

A. The choice of the topic and outline

Notwithstanding its difficulties, starting from its Latin definition and the esoterism that goes with it, several reasons – both scholarly and eminently practical – militate in favour of addressing the topic of *jura novit curia*. The first reason is linked to the impressive proliferation of international courts and tribunals over the last few decades [1] and to the ever-increasing resort to international litigation, with special regard to investment arbitration [2]. It thus appears increasingly important for the wider community of legal scholars and practitioners to familiarise themselves with the law of international adjudication. International litigation before human rights and international criminal law courts and tribunals, as well as before investor-State international arbitral tribunals, are naturally open to a large portion of domestic attorneys [3].

1. T. Treves, "Le Tribunal International du Droit de la Mer et la multiplication des jurisdictions internationals", *Rivista di diritto internazionale*, Vol. 83 (2000), p. 726 *et seq*; K. Oellers-Frahm, "Multiplication of International Courts and Tribunals and Conflicting Jurisdiction – Problems and Possible Solutions", *Max Planck Yearbook of United Nations Law*, Vol. 5 (2001), p. 67 *et seq.*; B. Kingsbury, "Foreword: Is the Proliferation of International Courts and Tribunals a Systemic Problem?", *New York University Journal of Internatioal Law and Politics*, Vol. 31 (1998), p. 679 *et seq.*; P.-M. Dupuy, "The Danger of Fragmentation or Unification of the International Legal System and the International Court of Justice", *ibid.*, p. 791 *et seq.*; J. I. Charney, "Is International Law Threatened by Multiple International Tribunals?", *Recueil des cours*, Vol. 271 (1998), p. 101 *et seq.*; C. P. R. Romano, "The Proliferation of International Judicial Bodies: The Piece of the Puzzle", *New York University Journal of International Law and Politics*, Vol. 32 (1999), p. 709 *et seq.*; G, Guillaume, "Advantages and Risks of Proliferation: A Blueprint for Action", *Journal of International Dispute Settlement*, Vol. 2 (2004), p. 300 *et seq.*; B. Simma and D. Pulkowski, "Of Planets and the Universe: Self-Contained Regimes in International Law", *European Journal of International Law*, Vol. 17 (2006), p. 483 *et seq.*; P. Webb, *International Judicial Integration and Fragmentation*, Oxford, Oxford University Press, 2013; *id.*, "Factors Influencing Fragmentation and Convergence in International Courts", in M. Andenas and E. Bjorge, *A Farewell to Fragmentation: Reassertion and Convergence in International Law*, Cambridge, Cambridge University Press, 2015, p. 146 *et seq*.

2. See M. Kinnear, "The Growth, Challenges and Future Prospects for Investment Dispute Settlement", *Recueil des cours*, Vol. 423 (2022), p. 17 *et seq*.

3. As stressed by Shabtai Rosenne in his speech of acceptance of The Hague Prize on 18 June 2004, "[a]ny individual, and any attorney, can suddenly find himself or herself confronted with international law and international justice, whether that is known or not". See S. Rosenne, *Essays on International Law and Practice*, Leiden-Boston, Brill-Nijhoff, 2007, p. 1 *et seq.*, p. 8.

Moreover, when considering inter-State adjudication, we should account for the participation of lawyers from the Office of the Attorney, or Solicitor, General, or legal officers and diplomats in foreign services and ministries of justice, but also from other ministries, be they devoted to energy, water, agriculture or infrastructure. Those legal officials may find themselves involved, on different levels, with their governmental legal teams in proceedings before international courts and tribunals [4].

Be that as it may, as emphasised by Professor Samantha Besson, "current international law can no longer be understood without its judicial dimension" [5]. Indeed, and unsurprisingly, research and editorial initiatives focussing on international procedural law and adjudication have been blossoming over the last twenty years [6]. Remarkably, the topic of *jura novit curia*, at least in its public international law configuration, has not been the subject of much research, let alone teaching [7].

The second reason for choosing this topic is that it provides a powerful lens to look at international adjudication focussing on the entanglement between key adjudicative and procedural law principles and the core dynamics of the judicial application of international substantive law. In so doing, the principle at hand engages us in an overview of all the phases of litigation proceedings, from the establishment of the competence of the adjudicatory body, including a finding of whether it has jurisdiction and whether the claim is admissible, to the merits phase, and, eventually, the assessment of the forms of relief.

---

4. For further consideration on how the same dispute could attract different fields of international law, see A. Tanzi, "International Law and Foreign Investment in Hydroelectric Industry: A Multidimensional Analysis", *International Community Law Review*, Vol. 18 (2016), p. 183 *et seq*.

5. S. Besson, "Legal Philosophical Issues of International Adjudication", in C. P. R. Romano *et al.* (eds.), *The Oxford Handbook of International Adjudication*, Oxford, Oxford University Press, 2014, p. 413 *et seq*., p. 415.

6. One could mention to this effect editorial initiatives like *The Law and Practice of International Courts and Tribunals*, which started in 2002, or the *Journal of International Dispute Settlement*, whose publication began in 2010. Reference may also be had to the Andreas Zimmermann's commentary to the Statute of the International Court of Justice, which has reached three editions between 2006 and 2019.

7. See on *jura novit curia* from a domestic comparative law perspective F. Ferrari and G. Cordero-Moss, Jura Novit Curia *in International Arbitration*, Huntington, Juris, 2018, with the exception of the contribution by F. Rosenfeld devoted to international adjudication. As we shall see in due course, the domestic law perspective, even if looked at in comparative terms, appears to be of minor relevance, if at all, to the study of the contemporary configuration of *jura novit curia* in international adjudication. See, specifically on the principle under consideration, F. Rosenfeld, "*Iura Novit Curia* in International Law", *European International Arbitration Review*, Vol. 61 (2017), p. 131 *et seq*.; T. Sugihara, "The Principle of *Jura Novit Curia* in the International Court of Justice: With Reference to Recent Decisions", *Japanese Yearbook of International Law*, Vol. 55 (2012), p. 77 *et seq*.

The third and central reason flows from the unsettled complexity and the uncertainty, even a sense of mystery, which is generally attached to the principle of *jura novit curia*. Indeed, nowhere in the statute of permanent adjudicatory bodies or their rules of procedure can we find an express codification of the principle, nor do the rules of *ad hoc* inter-State, or investor-State, tribunals help us much in that respect. For its unsettled source alone, the principle deserves further study.

The present study is organised in six parts. This introductory chapter will introduce a number of working definitions of *jura novit curia*, the research questions and the methodological and structural framework of the analysis. In particular, the world of international adjudication, which serves as the field of investigation for our study, will be broken down into three main areas according to the specificities characterising the way in which the rationale of the judicial function is interpreted and applied in each such cluster. These three streams are: inter-State adjudication and investment arbitration; human rights litigation; and international criminal adjudication.

Chapter II addresses the complexity of the international legal basis of the principle under consideration in combination with its cognate principles, with special regard to *ne ultra petita* and *ne infra petita*.

In Chapter III, the relevance of *jura novit curia* will be illustrated with respect to the jurisdictional phase of proceedings, taking into special consideration its relevance in the merits phase. Here, the partition of the field of international adjudication in three areas suggested above will be followed in light of the significant differences in the operation of the principle in each of them.

Chapter IV tackles few traditional issues pertaining to the reach of the "law to be known" and applied by the judge to the merits of the case. Namely, the enabling role of *non liquet*; the blurred line between facts – particularly those of a scientific or technical relevance, including domestic law for the purposes of international law – and the law; the also blurred line between interpretation and application of the law, with special regard to the admissibility for the judge to resort to rules and principles which, even though in force between the parties, fall outside the immediate scope of the applicable law; and the relevance of the time element.

Chapter V considers the relevance of *jura novit curia* for the purposes of assessing the forms of relief, and the quantum of compensation, when any is due.

Chapter VI offers concluding observations on the different configurations of *jura novit curia* with respect to each of the above anticipated three areas of international adjudication, together with final observations.

B. A working definition of jura novit curia

Looking for an initial direction to give to our journey in search for the distinguishing features of *jura novit curia* through international practice, case law and literature, a *prima facie* working definition of the principle at hand may provide a useful reference point. One can, in fact, suggest three such definitions.

The first can be taken from a pragmatic consideration made by the renowned international practitioner, arbitrator and scholar, Jan Paulsson, which captures the taste of the issue in question, whereby "a tribunal . . . cannot content itself with inept pleadings, and simply apply the least implausible of the two" [8].

Secondly, and more generally, the maxim *jura novit curia* can be taken to express a form of adjudicative autonomy, or even discretion. In this sense, one may recall how the ICJ has rather consistently asserted "its freedom to select the ground upon which it will base its judgment" [9]. However, a qualification and a *caveat* are called for in framing *jura novit curia* as a form of discretion by adjudicators, in the sense that *jura novit curia* may only give effect to one among different forms of judicial discretion [10].

---

8. J. Paulsson, "International Arbitration and the Generation of Legal Norms: Treaty Arbitration and International Law", in A. J. van den Berg (ed.), *International Arbitration 2006: Back to Basics?*, Alphen aan den Rijn, Kluwer, 2007, p. 879 *et seq.*, p. 888.

9. *Case Concerning the Application of the Convention of 1902 Governing the Guardianship of Infants (Netherlands* v. *Sweden)*, Judgment of 28 November 1958: *ICJ Reports 1958*, p. 55, p. 62; *Application for Revision and Interpretation of the Judgment of 24 February 1982 in the Case Concerning the Continental Shelf (Tunisia/Libyan Arab Jamahiriya) (Tunisia* v. *Libyan Arab Jamahiriya)*, Judgment, *ICJ Reports 1985*, p. 192, p. 207, para. 29; *Oil Platforms (Islamic Republic of Iran* v. *United States of America)*, Judgment, *ICJ Reports 2003*, p. 161, p. 180, para. 37. See also A. Orakhelashvili, "The International Court and Its Freedom to Select the Ground Upon Which It Will Base Its Judgment", *International and Comparative Law Quarterly*, Vol. 56 (2007), p. 171 *et seq*.

10. On discretion in international adjudication, see P. Kooijmans, "The ICJ and the 21st Century: Judicial Restraint, Judicial Activism, or Proactive Judicial Policy", *International and Comparative Law Quarterly*, Vol. 56 (2007), p. 741 *et seq.*; A. K. Bjorklund, "Are Arbitrators (Judicial) Activists?", *The Law and Practice of International Courts and Tribunals*, Vol. 17 (2018) p. 49 *et seq.*; B. McGarry, "Inherent or Implied Powers in International Justice: The Distinction in Theory and Practice" (forthcoming).

As to the qualification, *jura novit curia* may at first appear as a form of discretion which is confined to the application of the law at the merits stage. Given the entanglement between the merits and the jurisdictional phases, as it will be illustrated in due course, *jura novit curia* may also apply to a decision on issues of jurisdiction and admissibility, in terms bearing on the legal characterisation of the disputed facts. Since the principle under consideration comes into play where there is a matter of judicial application of legal rules, its scope of application may also be considered in relation to incidental proceedings concerning the indication of provisional measures and also on the assessment of the forms and contents of reparation and of the quantum of compensation, when awarded [11].

As to the *caveat*, it suggests that a framing of *jura novit curia* as a form of discretion can only be preliminary and presumptive. In other words, this is only a working hypothesis, which can be disproved. In fact, in the course of the study, practice and case law may show specific circumstances and adjudicative contexts in which international adjudicators are under a duty to exercise the powers entrusted to them under *jura novit curia*.

Coming to the third preliminary definition of *jura novit curia*, one may rely on the literal meaning of the maxim in point, namely "the judge knows the law". The cognate Latin adage *narra mihi factum, dabo tibi jus* – "give me the facts, I will give you the law" – can help give a better understanding of the historical rationale of the principle *jura novit curia*. Since the early days of adjudication, these maxims expressed the basic allocation of responsibilities between the actors involved in the adjudicative process, that is to say that, while the parties are to submit and prove the disputed facts, it is for the adjudicators to settle the dispute submitted to it by applying the law to such facts [12]. Along these lines, Judge De Castro, in his Separate Opinion in the ICJ *Western Sahara* Advisory Opinion, observed that:

> "In litigation, the parties are masters of the evidence: the court has a passive role. In the words of the traditional axiom of procedure, the [C]ourt says to the Party: *da mihi factum, dabo tibi jus*. The parties put forward facts and submit the evidence that

11. To the effect that *jura novit curia* would apply only on the merits, to the exclusion of incidental proceedings, see B. McGarry, *op cit*.

12. See for all, Rosenfeld, *op. cit*. For further elaboration on the point at issue for purposes of jura novit curia, see *infra* pp. 99 and 125.

> they consider favourable to their claims, and the court takes them into consideration when making its decision *(secundum allegata et probata)*." [13]

Such "division of labour" has been repeatedly corroborated by the ICJ as a matter of consistent judicial practice. In particular, in its 1986 *Nicaragua* v. *US* Judgment on the merits case, the Court observed that

> "[f]or the purpose of deciding whether the claim is well founded in law, the principle *jura novit curia* signifies that the Court is not solely dependent on the argument of the parties before it with respect to the applicable law" [14].

Against the above preliminary background, one can approach the study of the principle at hand by following Sir Gerald Fitzmaurice's observation whereby "the maxim *jura novit curia* implies that the tribunal both knows and will apply the law, whatever the parties say, or omit to say" [15]. To which extent and how it does so, and in which stages of the proceedings, or according to which adjudicative context, is precisely for the present study to consider. Indeed, it may appear self-evident that the adjudicator is supposed to "know the law" to apply in the resolution of a given dispute. However, irrespective of whether *jura novit curia* is qualified as a form of discretion, a power or a duty, its extent and contents are far from obvious. As observed by Takane Sugihara, "[i]t is true that 'the court knows the law', but it is not clear to what extent the court must know the law" [16].

Given the problematic character of the assessment of the scope of the principle at hand, it bears noting that the Black's Law Dictionary translates *jura novit curia* as "the court knows the law; the court recognizes rights" [17]. The expression "the court recognizes rights" lends itself to ambiguity. Namely, as to whether the rights to be recognized are those which are to be found within the scope of the existing law – which the court is supposed to know – or whether the rights in question are recognised beyond the realm of positive law.

---

13. *Western Sahara*, Advisory Opinion, *ICJ Reports 1975*, Separate Opinion of Judge de Castro, p. 127 *et seq.*, at 138.
14. *Military and Paramilitary Activities in and Against Nicaragua (Nicaragua* v. *United States of America)*, Merits, Judgment, *ICJ Reports 1986*, p. 14, para. 29.
15. G. Fitzmaurice, *The Law and Procedure of the International Court of Justice*, Vol. II, Cambridge, Grotius Publication, 1986, p. 531.
16. Sugihara, *op. cit.*, p 95.
17. *Black's Law Dictionary*, 10th ed., St. Paul, Thomson Reuters, 2014, p. 1925.

The translation in Black's Law Dictionary of the principle at hand in two separate sentences ("the court knows the law" and "the court recognizes rights") militates in favour of the latter interpretation. Leaving aside the question of what authority should be bestowed to the choice of language employed by a law dictionary, this translation has stirred relevant doctrinal interest [18]. Namely, as to whether the function of *jura novit curia* would be that of grounding the power of adjudicators to award remedies not only in law, but also in equity [19]. I will revert to this particular aspect in Chapter IV in relation to the relevance of *jura novit curia* for the scope of the applicable law that an adjudicative body has the power – or duty – to apply in a given dispute [20].

To conclude this preliminary reflection, *jura novit curia* can be provisionally defined as a generally recognised legal concept which denotes the adjudicative discretion – possibly the duty, as the case may be – to apply the law in terms other than those advanced by the parties. In the following pages, the conceptual and functional contexts which the principle in hand operates are illustrated, the research questions are presented, and the methodological and structural aspects of the research are addressed. The following chapters will address the issue of the existence and configuration of an international legal rule or principle behind such a concept, which regulates the contents and boundaries of the adjudicative discretion in question will be tackled in the following chapters.

C. Applying and developing the law

From a more general perspective, the study of the principle under consideration raises the much-vexed issue of the relationship between international adjudication and the development of the law in the international society [21].

As the discussion of preliminary definitions of *jura novit curia* in the foregoing paragraph makes clear, the principle in hand concerns the adjudicator's knowledge and application of the law, understood as the existing law. A different configuration of *jura novit curia* would amount

18. See D. Shelton, "*Jura Novit Curia* in International Human Rights", in N. Boschiero *et al.* (eds.), *International Courts and the Development of International Law: Essays in Honour of Tullio Treves*, The Hague, TMC Asser, 2013, p. 189 *et seq.*, p. 190.

19. *Ibid.*

20. See Chapter IV, Sec. D.3.

21. For an overview of the debate, see A. Boyle and C. Chinkin, *The Making of International Law*, Oxford, Oxford University Press, 2007, p. 263 *et seq.*

to rendering it a rule of recognition which would afford lawmaking powers to international adjudicators [22]. According to the ordinary meaning of the wording of Article 38 (1) of the ICJ Statute, in deciding a dispute, the Court, "whose function is to decide in accordance with international law such disputes as are submitted to it, shall apply" the law as it flows from the sources of international law – though the provision does not label them as such. In other words, the provision in point can only be intended to refer to the application of existing law, or positive law, or *lex lata,* as opposed to *lex ferenda*. That is a far cry from mandating the Court to decide disputes by *creating* rights and duties for the parties, as well as from deciding *ex aequo et bono*, which is only possible based on the agreement of the parties under Article 38 (2) [23].

As we shall see in Chapter IV, there are inevitable elements of interpretive creativity in most, if not any, cases of interpretation and application of an existing rule – which is general by definition – to the specific facts under dispute. This is no less true when the existence, or interpretation, of a rule is disputed. This is particularly frequent in international law, due to the often indeterminate treaty rules which are, linguistically, the result of a difficult compromise [24], as well as in the context of the ascertainment of customary international law, due to the inherent indeterminacy of the unwritten source [25].

Allowing – and even requiring, as the case may be – a court to apply legal arguments, and possibly even rules, other than those pleaded by the parties when necessary for it to decide the dispute according to the law, does not mean that *jura novit curia* allows adjudicators to develop new rules. If and when adjudicators apply standards which have not attained legal status in international law, their conduct cannot

22. The notion of a "rule of recognition" is obviously borrowed from analytical jurisprudence and, more specifically, from the work of H. L. A. Hart. See H. L. A. Hart, L. Green, *The Concept of Law*, Oxford, Oxford University Press, 2012, p. 94.

23. For comments, see A. Pellet and D. Müller, "Article 38", in A. Zimmermann, C. Tomuschat and K. Oellers-Frahm (eds.), *The Statute of the International Court of Justice: A Commentary*, Oxford, Oxford University Press, 2019 (3rd ed.), p. 819 *et seq*., in particular pp. 881-887. See also J. E. Donoghue, "International Adjudication: Peaks, Valleys, and Rolling Hills", *Proceedings of the ASIL Annual Meeting*, Vol. 112, 2018, pp. 15-22.

24. On the "linguistic" nature of international law, see P. Allot, "Language, Method and Nature of International Law", *British Yearbook of International Law*, Vol. 45 (1971), p. 79 *et seq*.

25. D. Dyzenhaus, "Formalism, Realism and the Politics of Indeterminacy", in W. Werner, M. de Hoon and A. Galán (eds.), *The Law of International Lawyers: Reading Martti Koskenniemi*, Cambridge, Cambridge University Press, p. 39 *et seq*. See on the indeterminacy of law more generally, H. Asgeirsson, *The Nature and Value of Vagueness in the Law*, Oxford, Hart Publishing, 2020.

be justified on the basis of *jura novit curia*. Either the adjudicators are mandated by the parties to decide the dispute *ex aequo et bono* [26], or they would be incurring excess of power.

Two qualifications are called for, which corroborate by implication the point whereby *jura novit curia* applies only in relation to existing law. First, a non-legally binding international instrument, which has not been pleaded, may be referred to by an international court or tribunal under *jura novit curia* for purposes of identifying a customary rule which is part of the applicable law. This is particularly the case when the instrument in question represents the missing link of the chain crystallising the customary lawmaking process in a particular field, or when occasions State conduct as a reaction, as well as *opinio juris*, in conformity with the contents of the instrument in question. This was clearly illustrated by the ICJ in the well-known *North Sea Continental Shelf* case between the Federal Republic of Germany, on one side, and the Netherlands and Denmark, on the other [27]. There are plenty of cases in which the Court decided the dispute by relying on codification conventions which had not been ratified by one, or both, of the disputing parties, following reasoning which may well apply to any non-binding instrument. Among others, one may recall how, in the *Pulp Mills* case, the Court relied on the United Nations Economic Commission for Europe (UNECE) Espoo Convention on environmental impact assessment in a transboundary context – to which neither Argentina nor Uruguay were parties – as evidence of customary law [28].

Second, resort to a treaty non-ratified by the disputing parties, or to an otherwise non-legally-binding instrument, or to a corresponding customary rule – which falls outside the applicable law, while reference to it may have been omitted by the parties – can be taken into account in order to interpret an applicable treaty rule under Article 31 (3) *(c)* VCLT. This was the case in *Gabčíkovo-Nagymaros*, where the ICJ referred to the provisions of "a great number of instruments" in order to identify the "norms and standards" giving effect to the principle of "sustainable development", which was key to the interpretation and application of the disputed 1977 Treaty [29]. Such environmental "norms

---

26. See C. Titi, *The Function of Equity in International Law*, New York-Oxford, Oxford University Press, 2021.

27. *North Sea Continental Shelf*, Judgment, *ICJ Reports 1969*, p. 3, p. 38 *et seq*.

28. *Pulp Mills on the River Uruguay (Argentina* v. *Uruguay)*, Judgment, *ICJ Reports 2010*, p. 14, p. 82, para. 203.

29. *Gabčíkovo-Nagymaros Project (Hungary/Slovakia)*, Judgment, *ICJ Reports 1997*, p. 7, p. 78, para. 140.

and standards" had been invoked by Hungary, by way of justification of its conduct purporting to unilaterally terminate the Treaty at hand under some kind of supervened environmental necessity [30]. This argument was rejected by the Court, which instead upheld the validity of the bilateral Treaty [31]. It is arguable that in this case a modicum of *jura novit curia* may have been exercised in the interpretation of the disputed treaty in terms different from those set forward by either party. The question strikes at the problematic distinction between the interpretation and the application of the law, to which I shall revert in Chapter IV.

1. Exclusive relevance of ratio decidendi *reasoning*

When addressing the relevance of *jura novit curia* in the context of the deliberation phases within an adjudicative process, it is necessary to look at the language of the adjudicative decision in question in order to identify the legal arguments or rules which have not been put forward by the parties in any given case. For the purposes of the present study, the analysis must be confined to the legal reasoning and language which bear directly on the actual decision of the case. This is the so-called *ratio decidendi* reasoning of an adjudicative decision. Conversely, arguments that represent digressions with respect to the reasoning grounding the decision are, in principle, of no direct relevance to *jura novit curia*, since they need no legal justification, and are qualified as *obiter dicta*.

The famous statement by the ICJ concerning *erga omnes* obligations in paras. 33 and 34 of the Barcelona Traction Judgment of 1970 is the epitome of an *obiter dictum* [32]:

> "33. When a State admits into its territory foreign investments or foreign nationals, whether natural or juristic persons, it is bound to extend to them the protection of the law and assumes obligations concerning the treatment to be afforded them. These obligations, however, are neither absolute nor unqualified. In particular, an essential distinction should be drawn between the obligations of a State towards the international community as

30. *Ibid.*, p. 34, para. 40 *et seq.*
31. *Ibid.*, p. 39, para. 48 *et seq.*
32. On the concept of *obiter dictum* in international adjudication, see J. Dahlquist, "Beside the Point – on *Obiter Dicta* in Investment Treaty Arbitration", *Arbitration International*, Vol. 32 (2016), p. 629 *et seq.*; H. Gao, "*Dictum* on *Dicta: Obiter Dicta* in WTO Disputes", *World Trade Review*, Vol. 17 (2018), p. 1 *et seq.*; N. Ridi, "'Mirages of an Intellectual Dreamland'? *Ratio, Obiter* and the Textualization of International Precedent", *Journal of International Dispute Settlement*, Vol. 10 (2019), p. 361 *et seq.*

a whole, and those arising *vis-à-vis* another State in the field of diplomatic protection. By their very nature the former are the concern of all States. In view of the importance of the rights involved, all States can be held to have a legal interest in their protection; they are obligations *erga omnes*.

34. Such obligations derive, for example, in contemporary international law, from the outlawing of acts of aggression, and of genocide, as also from the principles and rules concerning the basic rights of the human person, including protection from slavery and racial discrimination. Some of the corresponding rights of protection have entered into the body of general international law (Reservations to the Convention on the Prevention and Punishment of the Crime of Genocide, Advisory Opinion, *ICJ Reports 1951*, p. 23); others are conferred by international instruments of a universal or quasi-universal character." [33]

This passage, however important for the clarification and development of the law at the time and complementing the abstract wording of Article 53 VCLT on *jus cogens*, did not affect in any way the outcome of the Judgment. The latter focussed on whether international customary law recognises the right to exercise diplomatic protection only for companies registered under the law of the applicant State, or also for the protection of national shareholders [34]. Even if international rules providing for *erga omnes* obligations were obviously never argued by the parties, the Court did not need to justify the quoted statement on *jura novit curia* grounds.

Along the same lines, when Judge Simma, in his Separate Opinion in the *Oil Platforms* Judgment in 2003, argued that the Court should have made "strong unequivocal *obiter dicta*" reasserting the principles of the

---

33. *Barcelona Traction, Light and Power Company, Limited*, Judgment, ICJ Reports 1970, p. 3, p. 32, paras. 33-34.

34. *Ibid*. For comments to the decision, see P. N. Okowa, "The International Court and the Legacy of the Barcelona Traction Case", in C. C. Jalloh and O. Elias (eds.), *Shielding Humanity: Essays in International Law in Honour of Judge Abdul G. Koroma*, Leiden-Boston, Brill-Nijhoof, 2015, p. 104 *et seq*.; D. Müller, *La protection de l'actionnaire en droit international: l'héritage de la Barcelona Traction*, Paris, ed. Pedone, 2015; G. Gaja, "Barcelona Traction, Light and Power Company (*Belgium* v. *Spain*) (1970)", in E. Bjorge and C. Miles (eds.), *Landmark Cases in Public International Law*, Oxford, Hart Publishing, 2017, p. 307 *et seq*. See also Articles 11 and 12 of the International Law Commission (ILC) "Draft Articles on Diplomatic Protection" (2006 *YB Int'l L. Comm'n*, Vol. 2, Part. 2, pp. 39-43) and commentaries thereto.

Charter on the use of force [35], he did not argue that doing so would have required any exercise of *jura novit curia* [36].

In sum, *jura novit curia* applies to *ratio decidendi* reasoning only, whereas *obiter dicta* statements simply pertain to the unfettered discretion of international courts and tribunals to make incidental remarks elucidating the existing law or to contributing to its development as they deem appropriate.

D. Research questions

The analysis will address five basic research questions, which are both discrete in and of themselves, while addressing overarching issues, which will therefore be tackled throughout the whole study.

The first question pertains to the identification of the legal source, or sources, that contemplate the principle in hand and determine its contents and scope. In its formal dimension, the issue will be addressed separately in Chapter II, but its functional relevance will be illustrated by reference to the analysis of *jura novit curia* in relation to different phases of proceedings throughout the remainder of the study.

The second question concerns the assessment of the reach of the *"novit"* part of the maxim *jura novit curia*, i.e. the kind of knowledge that the principle at hand refers to. This is necessary to answer to the already mentioned fundamental question advanced by Takane Sugihara asking "to what extent the court must know the law" [37]. The point boils down to the question of whether *jura novit curia* is confined to providing the adjudicator with the power to reach its decision only by relying on legal arguments and interpretations of the law beyond those of the parties, or whether it extends to allowing the application of legal rules that have not been invoked by the parties. And it is inextricably linked to the blurred distinction between interpretation and application of the law [38], as well as the entanglement between the jurisdictional and merits phases, insofar as *jura novit curia* would extend the adjudicative power to the recharacterisation of the parties' claims – or, in a criminal law adjudicative model, of the charges formulated by the prosecutor [39].

35. *Oil Platforms (Islamic Republic of Iran* v. *United States of America)*, Judgment, Separate Opinion of Judge Simma, *ICJ Reports 2003*, p. 324 *et seq*., p. 327.

36. For a comment on the case in point, see J. Kammerhofer, "Oil's Well That Ends Well?: Critical Comments on the Merits Judgement in the Oil Platform", *Leiden Journal of International Law*, Vol. 17 (2004), p. 695 *et seq*.

37. See *supra* footnote 14.

38. See Chapter IV, Sec. B.2.

39. See Chapter III, Sec. C.1, 2, 3, 4.

The second question, also related to the power of applying legal rules or principles other than those invoked to the disputed facts, asks whether resort may be had only to rules falling strictly within the reach of the applicable law, or also beyond, and, if so, under which requirements. Here, again, the point is closely connected with the thorny issue of the very fine line separating the interpretation and application of the law [40].

The third research question represents a natural an extension of the second one, as it concerns problematic aspects of the determination of the *"jura"* component of the maxim, i.e. the scope of the law which is to be known and applied by the adjudicator. The issue arises, again, in the context of the relationship between interpretation and application of the law. This is particularly relevant to the question of whether an adjudicator's reference to rules or principles beyond the specified applicable law pertains to the adjudicative process of interpretation, or rather of application, of the law.

Another problematic aspect, ancillary to the above, pertains to the distinction, and interactions, between law and the disputed facts, and between law and equity. The point is linked with the question of the sharing between the parties and the adjudicator of the burden to prove the facts and argue the law. Namely as to whether *jura novit curia* also concerns the power of adjudicators to consider, or even acquire, elements of fact, or only legal arguments and rules which have not been pleaded or claimed by the parties. Those issues will be shown to be equally important with regard to the declaratory part of adjudication, assessment of responsibility, forms of reparation and the quantum of compensation, when found to be due. In this regard, a first sub-question concerns the vexed issue whether and to what extent domestic law and domestic judgments represents facts or law for purposes of international law and adjudication. The second relates to the difficult characterisation of facts subject to "scientific evidence". The third pertains to inter-temporal law, that is to say, the powers *jura novit curia* may confer in determining the law to apply which was in force at a time other than that at which the facts to which it applies occurred. In that respect, we will address the distinction and interactions, for the purposes of the application of *jura novit curia* – with special regard to the so-called equity *infra legem* – as well as between law and facts, considering contentious issues such as whether and to what extent domestic law

40. See Chapter IV, Sec. B.2.

represents a matter of fact, or of law, for the purposes of international law and adjudication.

The fourth question is whether one can confirm the provisional definition of *jura novit curia* as a form of adjudicative discretion, or whether we should add an element of duty, and, if so, under which circumstances and to what extent.

The fifth and last question is whether – once *jura novit curia* is generally recognised in international adjudication – its regulation is, or ought to be, the same in all forms of international litigation, from inter-State to criminal. The point will be taken up shortly in conjunction with the methodology and structure of the analysis.

E. On methodology and structure

The methodology adopted in these lectures is legally pragmatic, or empirical. In other words, the definitions and research questions discussed in the foregoing section will be tested against the practice and case law. The answers to the research questions will be drawn from the judicial attitudes and statements taken throughout all the phases of proceedings, from the jurisdictional phase to that on reparation. The circumstance in which one of the parties fails to appear before the adjudicative body concerned will be considered as a prominent source of information in the development and consolidation of *jura novit curia*.

The analysis will be carried out looking for the positive and observable elements which define jura novit curia, on the one hand, while defining it also by testing its contents and boundaries against its cognate principles, which partly enhance it and partly constrain it, on the other. The cognate principles in question are *non liquet*, *ne infra petita* and *ne ultra petita*. *Non liquet* expresses the principle whereby the adjudicator should not avoid deciding a case submitted to it, and with respect to which it would have jurisdictional competence, on the basis of the lack of substantive rules governing the matter. In the abstract, the prohibition of *non liquet* should enhance the tribunal's power to look for rules and principles even where none appear to be directly on point, thus enabling it to decide the dispute according to the law, irrespective of the shortcomings of counsel for the parties [41].

Ne infra petita consists of the adjudicator's duty not to fall short of addressing all the claims which have been submitted by the parties

41. For further considerations on *non liquet*, see D. Bodansky, *"Non Liquet"*, *Max Planck Encyclopedias of Public International Law*, online edition (2006).

and fall within the adjudicator's jurisdictional power and the applicable law. *Ne infra petita*, too, should enhance *jura novit curia* where the parties fail to plead their case comprehensively.

Ne ultra petita expresses the duty not to address claims and causes of action which have not been advanced by the parties. Thus, *ne ultra petita* would provide, in principle, a containment of *jura novit curia* [42].

As anticipated, the principles at hand operate throughout all the phases of adjudicative proceedings. However, the primary focus of the foregoing sections will be the assessment of jurisdiction, as it may impact decisively on the merits by determining the legal characterisation of the disputed facts, thus, curtailing the scope of the dispute.

F. Different international adjudication contexts: three areas

Over the last two decades, the rules governing the functioning of international courts and tribunals have been increasingly portrayed in the legal literature within the framework of some kind of a common law of international adjudication. Professor Chester Brown has been a pioneer in this exercise in the systematisation of international procedural law [43]. This approach is ultimately consistent with the idea, as convincingly put by Professor Yuval Shany, that "international adjudication has developed through a process of replication and adaptation" [44].

One would entirely concur with this approach insofar as it concerns the body of procedural law *stricto sensu*, which governs the adjudicators' powers concerning the institution and conduct of proceedings. To that end, one would refer to the rules which address the terms, modalities and admissibility of the submission of the application, or the notice of arbitration, as the case may be, written and oral pleadings, production of evidence, intervention by non-parties or the more systemic procedural principle of the *equality of arms*, to mention a few. However, one would believe that different considerations may apply to those rules, or principles, that govern the adjudicative decision-making process. It

42. For further elements on the *ne ultra petita* principle, see A. Tanzi, *"Ultra Petita"*, *Max Planck Encyclopedias of Public International Law*, online edition (2019).

43. C. Brown, *A Common Law of International Adjudication*, Oxford, Oxford University Press, 2008.

44. Y. Shany, *Assessing the Effectiveness of International Courts*, Oxford, Oxford University Press, 2014, p. 37, referring to E. M. Heffner-Burton, D. G. Victor and Y. Lupu, "Political Science Research on International Law: The State of the Field", *American Journal of International Law*, Vol. 106 (2012), p. 47 *et seq.*, pp. 87-88.

is in that sense that one would distinguish between procedural law and the law of adjudication [45].

Jura novit curia and its above mentioned cognate principles can be said to go well beyond procedural law, but to pertain to the category of rules and principles that govern the adjudicative decision-making process. Such rules and principles are only partially to be found in the constituent instruments or rules of procedure of international courts and tribunals. Therefore, in a functional perspective, it is essential to look for the specific rationale of the adjudicative function in different kinds of litigation, based on the different nature of their mandate [46].

It is possible to anticipate that there are significantly different rationales for international adjudication in different adjudicative contexts. On the basis of such rationales, it is possible to partition the field of international adjudication into three discrete areas: first, inter-State and investor-State litigation [47]; second, human rights litigation; third, international criminal litigation.

Before addressing them, two overarching remarks are called for on the two-pronged nature of the international adjudicative function in general. These remarks may follow a reading of Article 38 (1) ICJ Statute as the generally recognised matrix for international adjudication, which allows for two components to emerge: the first one consists of the actual deciding of the dispute; the second factor of adjudication, which is generally instrumental to the first one, consists of the application of the law to the disputed facts. As stressed by Professor Chester Brown, there is a private aspect in deciding the dispute and a public aspect in the proper administration of justice, with special regard to the application of the law [48]. However conceptually separate, these aspects are functionally inseparable.

An analysis of the case law of international adjudicative bodies shows that the balance between the two aspects in question is

45. For a different distinction between procedural rules *stricto sensu* and "substantive principles relating to the proceedings", see R. Kolb, "General Principles of Procedural Law", in Zimmermann, Tomuschat and Oellers-Frahm (eds.), *op. cit.*, p. 963 *et seq.*, p. 969.

46. Shany, *op. cit.*, p. 13 *et seq*.

47. We regard investor-State arbitration "as a judicial formation governed by public international law" (*Hrvatska Elektroprivreda* case (*Hrvatska Elektroprivreda d.d.* v. *Republic of Slovenia*, ICSID Case No. ARB/05/24, Order Concerning the Participation of Counsel, 6 May 2008, para. 33). See E. De Brabandere, *Investment Treaty Arbitration as Public International Law: Procedural Aspects and Implications*, Cambridge, Cambridge University Press, 2014.

48. C. Brown, "Inherent Powers in International Adjudication", in C. P. R. Romano *et al.* (eds.), *op. cit.*, p. 827 *et seq.*, p. 843.

differently calibrated in each of the three areas under consideration. Such differences have a significant impact on the way *jura novit curia* operates in each such contexts.

The differences in calibration between deciding the dispute and the application of the law flow from the differences in the mandate conferred on the adjudicators in each of the three adjudicative contexts in point. Such differences are reflected in the different relationship between autonomy of the parties and judicial autonomy in each of the adjudicative contexts under consideration.

1. Inter-State litigation

Jura novit curia will be researched primarily in relation to inter-State litigation, given the still prevailing State-centred focus of the legal system of the international society [49]. It may be apposite to also specify that only international litigation characterised by the application of public international law will be examined, for the possibility may be envisaged of inter-State litigation being governed by domestic law. By way of a small digression, this may occur when the agreement of the parties to submit a dispute to international arbitration is governed by a domestic law and when a domestic law governs the arbitration. This was the case, for example, of the Italy-Brazil arbitration decided in 2003 [50]. There, the arbitration clause was contained in a sub-licence

49. A. M. Tanzi, "Remarks on Sovereignty in the Evolving Constitutional Features of the International Community", in M. Arsanjani *et al.* (eds.), *Looking to the Future: Essays on International Law in Honor of W. M. Reisman*, Leiden-Boston, Martinus Nijhoff, 2010, p. 299 *et seq.*. The terminological choice of the concept "society" follows the realistic approach adopted by Vaughan Lowe who thoughtfully recalls the distinction, taken from the German legal tradition, of "a community, Gemeinschaft, from a society, *Geselischaft*, on the basis that an ideal community is built around a commonality of values and purposes, whereas an ideal society is a looser, less homogenous, more structured group of people drawn together by the perception that their individual self-interests can all benefit from doing certain things together", V. Lowe, "The Function of Litigation in International Society", *International and Comparative Law Quarterly*, Vol. 61 (2012), p. 209 *et seq.*, p. 209.

50. *Italy* v. *Brazil* (ICC Case No. 12988/FM). In the *Serbian Loans* case, the PCIJ stated that "Article 38 of the Statute cannot be regarded as excluding the possibility of the Court's dealing with disputes which do not require the application of international law"(*Case Concerning the Payment of Various Serbian Loans Issued in France (France* v. *Kingdom of the Serbs, Croats and Slovenes)*, 1929 PCIJ (ser. A) No. 20 (12 July), p. 20). The point has not been taken up in the following case law, where domestic law has been referred to, either as an element of practice and *opinio juris* for purposes of determining custom, or as elements of fact subject to judicial evaluation under international law standards, usually in relation to the assessment of the existence of an internationally wrongful act in relation to a domestic legislative, judicial or administrative act at variance with an international obligation.

contract governed by English law, with the result of English law being applied as the substantive law governing the matter.

We will look at inter-State litigation – before either permanent adjudicative bodies, such as the ICJ and the ITLOS, or *ad hoc* arbitral tribunals. Adjudication by World Trade Organization (WTO) panels and the Appellate Body will be referred to only in passing and basically with a view to stressing the peculiarities of that system. Investor-State arbitration will be addressed under the same adjudicative framework insofar as, there, the relationship between the autonomy of the parties and judicial autonomy follows very much the same calibration which we find in inter-State litigation, with the exception of cases where *erga omnes* obligations are litigated in inter-State cases.

Having regard to the law applicable to traditional inter-State disputes, it bears recalling how it prevailingly consists of rules governing relations between States having a bilateral, synallagmatic nature. Such would be, for example, the rules on the treatment of foreign individuals and companies, goods and services, or the treatment of foreign officials, i.e. jurisdictional immunities or those concerning the delimitation of territorial or marine sovereignty between neighbouring or adjacent States. As alluded, international rules that afford legal protection to collective, or even universal, interests may also be disputed in international litigation, even though much less frequently. Let me mention, most recently, the *Genocide* cases against Serbia [51], Myanmar [52] and Russia [53].

We shall consider primarily *jura novit curia* in traditional bilateral disputes. First of all, because they represent the overwhelming majority of inter-State litigation; secondly, because inter-State law of adjudication was originally crafted in view of governing but disputes having a bilateral dimension, i.e. the matrix of the law of international adjudication.

Here, the autonomy of the parties emerges as a characterising factor of international adjudication. In inter-State litigation, it derives from the consensual nature of the mandate conferred on the adjudicative

51. *Application of the Convention on the Prevention and Punishment of the Crime of Genocide (Bosnia and Herzegovina* v. *Serbia and Montenegro)*; *Application of the Convention on the Prevention and Punishment of the Crime of Genocide (Croatia* v. *Serbia)*.

52. *Application of the Convention on the Prevention and Punishment of the Crime of Genocide (The Gambia* v. *Myanmar)*.

53. *Allegations of Genocide under the Convention on the Prevention and Punishment of the Crime of Genocide (Ukraine* v. *Russian Federation)*.

body, both concerning the scope of its jurisdictional competence and of the law applicable by it. As emphasised by Judge Fitzmaurice,

> "[A]n international tribunal's powers are limited to what is conferred upon it by the parties. This is equally true of such a tribunal as the International Court, as regards any powers not resulting directly from the Statute or . . . the Rules of the Court; and even the powers conferred by the Statute and the Rules of the Court derive equally from the (antecedent general) consent of the parties." [54]

The claims of the parties complement the mandate of the adjudicate body by delineating the scope of the dispute. Having regard to permanent adjudicative bodies, their jurisdictional competence and the applicable law are delineated by the parties' consent, which is expressed by their participation in the constituent treaty, but also through the unilateral declaration of acceptance of the ICJ jurisdiction, through the disputed treaty containing the compromissory clause, through the *compromis* or by way of *forum prorogatum* [55].

As to arbitral tribunals, the consent making up their mandate flows from the participation in the treaty which contains the compromissory clause, and is complemented by the acceptance of the rules of procedure, which are adopted by the tribunal in the first procedural order upon consultation with the parties.

The highly consensual nature of the mandate of inter-State adjudicators, as emphasised in the above quoted passage by Sir Gerald Fitzmaurice, may be taken to confer a large degree of arbitral nature also to permanent international judicial bodies, such as the ICJ and ITLOS [56]. This is corroborated by the binding force of their judgments being

54. Fitzmaurice, *op. cit.*, p. 524.

55. On the recent jurisdiction of the ICJ on *forum prorogatum*, see L. Ayoub, "The Death Knell of Forum Prorogatum or: How the ICJ Missed its Opportunity to Generate its Own Jurisdiction", *Hague Yearbook of International Law*, Vol. 33 (2022), p. 1 *et seq*.

56. *G. Morelli*, "La théorie générale du procès international", (1937) 61 *RCADI* 253, at 311 *et seq.* See also H. Thirlway, *The International Court of Justice (2016)*, at 38 *et seq.* See, on the other hand, Serena Forlati, on the nuanced differences between international adjudication and arbitration, though, focussing on the procedural rules on the conduct of proceedings, rather than on principles of adjudication (S. Forlati, *The International Court of Justice. An Arbitral Tribunal or a Judicial Body*?, Cham, Springer, 2014, p. 23 *et seq.*). Robert Kolb, while considering their different features also emphasises the existence of principles common to the ICJ, international arbitrations (inter-State and possibly also commercial), standing international tribunals (e.g. the ITLOS, the ECHR, etc.). See Kolb, *op. cit.*, p. 963 *et seq.*

limited to the disputing parties under Article 36. As will be argued below, different considerations apply to international human rights and criminal courts and tribunals.

As noted, in any given international jurisdiction, the balance within the two-tier adjudicative function between the settlement of the dispute, on the one hand, and the interpretation, application and development of the law, on the other hand, is very difficult to find. Within international law, this operation is rendered all the more difficult due to a number of features self-evidently placed in a tense relationship with one another.

In principle, taking the ICJ Statute as the regulatory matrix for inter-State adjudication, as is generally recognised, the two components of the adjudicative function appear naturally integrated, as indeed, in principle it should be. As anticipated, Article 38 (1) provides in simple terms that "[t]he Court['s] function is to decide in accordance with international law such disputes as are submitted to it".

The consensual nature and the enhanced autonomy of the parties in inter-State litigation suggest a reading of this provision whereby deciding the dispute is the key component of the adjudicative function in this context, obviously within the framework of the applicable law. By the same token, Article 59 of the ICJ Statute provides that "[t]he the decision of the Court has no binding force except between the parties and in respect of that particular case" [57]. Indeed, the preponderance of the Court's dispute settlement function over its role in the elucidation and development of international law cannot be easily questioned [58]. As we shall see, the basic rationale of the adjudicative function is different in HR and criminal law adjudication, and, possibly, in inter-State cases where the disputed facts fall within rules providing for *erga omnes* obligations and rights, i.e. obligations protecting international collective interests.

Going back to traditional inter-State litigation, as observed by Dina Shelton,

> "The first function assigned to international courts is akin to the resolution of private disputes by civil litigation within domestic legal systems. The purpose of such jurisdiction is to resolve the issues between the parties and end the dispute." [59]

---

57. C. Brown, "Article 59", in Zimmermann, Tomuschat and Oellers-Frahm (eds.), *op. cit.*, p. 1561 *et seq.*

58. For similar views, see Donoghue, *op. cit.*

59. D. Shelton, "Form, Function, and the Power of International Courts", *Chicago Journal of International Law*, Vol. 9 (2009), p. 537 *et seq.*, p. 558.

Against this background, *jura novit curia* may provide a tool for the adjudicator to find the legal way it deems best fit for the parties to settle the specific dispute they have submitted to it, obviously, within the boundaries of the applicable law. This does not mean that inter-State courts and tribunals may neglect their role and responsibility in the application and clarification of the law in its *ratio decidendi* reasoning. This would run counter to the plain textual and contextual interpretation of Article 38 (1) of the ICJ Statute, as opposed to para. 2, which provides the power to decide *ex aequo et bono* only upon request by parties.

Jura novit curia is no less instrumental to the more general function to apply and elucidate the law than it is to its dispute settlement role. The PCIJ, in its 1932 Judgment in the *Free Zones of Upper Savoy and the District of Gex* case, provided a pragmatic enunciation of *jura novit curia*, precisely in relation to the law declaration function, as follows:

> "[I]t cannot lightly be admitted that the Court, *whose function is to declare the law*, can be called upon to choose between two or more constructions determined beforehand by the parties, none of which may correspond to the opinion at which may arrive. Unless otherwise expressly provided, it must be presumed that the Court enjoys the freedom . . . not only to accept one or other of the two propositions, but also to reject them both." [60]

Moreover, the boundaries of the autonomy of the parties may not just end there. Limitations to the autonomy of the parties related to the justiciability of a given claim have been stated by the ICJ in the *Northern Cameroons* case in 1963. There, contrary to the usual effect of *jura novit curia*, the autonomy of the parties was contained in relation to the judicial function, not for purposes of expanding the exercise of the latter, but deciding the non-justiciability of the case. To that end, the Court referred to some kind of international public order, *ordre public*, or judicial propriety principle which it enounced as follows:

> "There are inherent limitations on the exercise of the judicial function which the Court, as a court of justice, can never ignore. There may thus be an incompatibility between the desires of an applicant, or, indeed, of both parties to a case, on the one hand, and on the other hand the duty of the Court to maintain its judicial

---

60. *Free Zones of Upper Savoy and District of Gex (France* v. *Switzerland)*, PCIJ Series A/B No. 46, p. 138.

> character. The Court itself, and not the parties, must be the guardian of the Court's judicial integrity." [61]

I wish to make two additional considerations of a general character which acknowledge the importance of the law application and elucidation function of inter-State courts and tribunals.

First, the international legal system presents features such as the lack of an international centralised legislator, associated with the lack of hierarchy between the sources of the law, with the recently emerged exception of *jus cogens*. This aspect often requires international judges and arbitrators to navigate through the troubled waters of overlapping regulation produced at different points in time, stemming from different sources, addressed to different recipients but governing the same subject matter [62]. That requires a difficult calibration between the principle whereby the later law prevails over the earlier *(lex posterior derogat priori)* and the one whereby the specific regulation prevails over the more general one *(lex specialis derogat generali)*. The second reason for the expanded importance of the judicial application and clarification of the law is the high degree of indeterminacy of international rules. We have already referred to the structural causes of such indeterminacy [63].

The above general considerations are corroborated by the pragmatic exigency of jurisprudential consistency in international adjudication, despite the inexistence of the *stare decisis* principle, or rule of precedent. Given the relatively small number of States which act as members of the international society, Professor Vaughan Lowe rightly observed as follows:

> "[P]arties who are repeat players – as game theorists say – are likely to have considerable interest not only in whether they win or lose a particular case, but also in how they win or lose it, in the rule that emerges from the decision in the case. In the context of international disputes, Governments or States are always likely to be repeat players . . . A decision in one court denying a claim to

---

61. *Case Concerning the Northern Cameroons (Cameroon* v. *United Kingdom)*, Preliminary Objections, Judgment of 2 December 1963, *ICJ Reports 1963*, p. 15, p. 29.

62. This is the well-known issue of the fragmentation of international law, amply studied by the ILC (ILC, "Fragmentation of International Law: Difficulties Arising from the Diversification and Expansion of International Law, Report of the Study Group of the International Law Commission Finalized by Martti Koskenniemi", UN Doc. A/CN.4/L.682, 13 April 2006). On the point at issue, see also O. K. Fauchald and A. Nollkaemper, *The Practice of International and National Courts and the (De-) fragmentation of International Law*, Oxford-Portland, Hart, 2012; M. Prost, *The Concept of Unity in Public International Law*, Oxford-Portland, Hart, 2012.

63. *Supra* text at footnote 26.

immunity, or an award to compensate a foreign investor for losses upon withdrawal of a government subsidy, will be likely to have repercussions in many other cases." [64]

The situation just described is epitomised by the *Norstar* case brought by Panama against Italy before ITLOS in December 2015 [65], while Italy had started an Annex VII arbitration six months before with India, in the *Enrica Lexie* case [66]. Both cases revolved around the interpretation of Articles 87, 92 and 97 UNCLOS, among other rules. Those provisions, in mutual combination, govern the balance between freedom of navigation and the exclusive jurisdiction of flag States over ships on the high seas, on one hand, and the exercise of jurisdiction by coastal States, on the other.

It soon became clear that the *Enrica Lexie* case would be decided after the Judgment on the merits in *Norstar*. Thus, the latter case was not only important for Italy as *qua* dispute, but also as providing clues as to how the provisions at issues in it could be interpreted and applied in the future and, in particular, in the context of the dispute with India.

Furthermore, the judicial interpretation and application of the law in any given international case is generally of interest also to third States, despite the principle whereby an international judgment is legally binding only on the disputing parties. The above-mentioned cases provide good examples of the problem. On the one hand, you find those States, especially landlocked States, who rely mostly on freedom of navigation. On the other hand, coastal States are interested in freedom of navigation to be interpreted in terms that may not be of hindrance to their sovereign rights as coastal State. That the issue would be of some importance has since been demonstrated by the fact that two other cases revolving around the same provisions and similar factual matrices have now been brought before an UNCLOS Annex VII Tribunal, both ending up before the ITLOS for the request of provisional measures. The first one is the case between Ukraine and Russia for the arrest and detention of vessels and servicemen of Ukrainian nationality [67]; the second relevant

64. Lowe, *op. cit.*, p. 213.

65. *The M/V "Norstar" Case (Panama* v. *Italy)*, ITLOS Case No. 25. For a summary of the case, see C. Miles, "The MV 'Norstar' Case *(Panama* v. *Italy)*", *American Journal of International Law*, Vol. 114 (2020), p. 116 *et seq*.

66. *The "Enrica Lexie" Incident (Italy* v. *India)*, PCA Case 2015-28.

67. *Case Concerning the Detention of Three Ukrainian Naval Vessels (Ukraine* v. *Russian Federation), Provisional Measures*, ITLOS Case No. 26; *Dispute Concerning the Detention of Ukrainian Naval Vessels and Servicemen (Ukraine* v. *the Russian Federation)*, PCA Case No. 2019-28.

case has been brought by Switzerland against Nigeria for the seizure of a commercial ship flying the Swiss flag *(San Padre Pio)* [68].

Consistency in the case law is thus of value both for adjudicative bodies and for potential disputing parties. As put by Dame Higgins when President of the ICJ:

> "States which have no dispute before the Court follow the judgments of the Court with the greatest interest, because they know that every judgment is at once an authoritative pronouncement on the law, and also that, should they become involved in a dispute in which the same legal issues arise, the Court, which will always seek to act consistently and build on its own jurisprudence, will reach the same conclusions." [69]

Indeed, as stressed by the International Law Commission (ILC) SR on the *identification of customary law*, Sir Michael Wood, referring himself to the ICJ, "it seems very reluctant to depart from its previous Decisions" [70]. Also Article 21 of the ICC Statute provides that

---

68. *The M/T "San Padre Pio" Case (Switzerland* v. *Nigeria)*, Provisional Measures, ITLOS Case No. 27; *The M/T "San Padre Pio" (No. 2) Case (Switzerland/Nigeria)*, ITLOS Case No. 29.

69. R. Higgins, *Problems and Process: International Law and How We Use It*, Oxford, Oxford University Press, 1995, pp. 202-203.

70. ILC, "Third Report on Identification of Customary International Law by Michael Wood, Special Rapporteur", UN Doc. A/CN.4/682, p. 44, para. 61. See also *Land and Maritime Boundary Between Cameroon and Nigeria*, Preliminary Objections, Judgment, *ICJ Reports 1998*, p. 275, at 292, para. 28 ("It is true that, in accordance with Article 59, the Court's judgments bind only the parties to and in respect of a particular case. There can be no question of holding Nigeria to decisions reached by the Court in previous cases. The real question is whether, in this case, there is cause not to follow the reasoning and conclusions of earlier cases"); see also *Application of the Convention on the Prevention and Punishment of the Crime of Genocide (Croatia* v. *Serbia)*, Preliminary Objections, Judgment, *ICJ Reports 2008*, p. 412, at 428, para. 53, "To the extent that the decisions contain findings of law, the Court will treat them as it treats all previous decisions: that is to say that, while those decisions are in no way binding on the Court, it will not depart from its settled jurisprudence unless it finds very particular reasons to do so"). On precedent in international adjudication in general, see M. Shahabuddeen, *Precedent in the World Court*, Cambridge, Cambridge University Press, 1996; R. Bhala, "The Myth About *Stare Decisis* and International Trade Law (Part One of a Trilogy)", *American University International Law Review*, Vol. 14 (1998), p. 845 *et seq.*; M. Balcerzak, "The Doctrine of Precedent in the International Court of Justice and the European Court of Human Rights", *Polish Yearbook of International Law*, Vol. 17 (2004), p. 131 *et seq.*; W. Alschner and D. Charlotin, "The Growing Complexity of the International Court of Justice's Self-Citation Network", *European Journal of International Law*, Vol. 29 (2018), p. 83 *et seq.*; N. Ridi, "The Shape and Structure of the 'Usable Past': An Empirical Analysis of the Use of Precedent in International Adjudication", *Journal of International Dispute Settlement*, Vol. 10 (2019), p. 200 *et seq.*; *id.*, "Rule of Precedent and Rules on Precedent", in E. De Brabandere (ed.), *International Procedure in Interstate Litigation and Arbitration: A Comparative Approach*, Cambridge, Cambridge University Press, 2021, p. 354 *et seq.*

"[t]he Court may apply principles and rules of law as interpreted in its previous decisions" [71].

I shall revert shortly to the point of judicial consistency in relation to the identification of the legal source of *jura novit curia*. For the present purposes, suffice it to stress how jurisprudential consistency strengthens the function of law application, or declaration, by international adjudicators. And it bears noting how, in its turn, compliance with this aspect of the judicial function provided the basis for one of the earliest applications of *jura novit curia* in international adjudication. In the case of the *Free Zones of Upper Savoy and the District of Gex* case the PCIJ observed, referring to *jura novit curia* implicitly, that

> "[I]t cannot likely be admitted that the Court, *whose function it is to declare the law*, can be called upon to choose between two or more constructions determined beforehand by the parties, none of which may correspond to the opinion at which may arrive. Unless otherwise expressly provided, it must be presumed that the Court enjoys the freedom which normally appertains to it, and that it is able, if such is its opinion, not only to accept one or other of the two propositions, but also to reject them both." [72]

The function of law application, declaration and even clarification of inter-State adjudicative bodies is significantly more important at the international level than in municipal jurisdictions for the two reasons we have already mentioned: the lack of hierarchy between legal sources of different provenance and the higher degree of indeterminacy of international rules with respect to municipal law. That being said, the application of the law remains, in the domain of inter-State litigation, entirely at the service of the task of deciding the dispute submitted to it. As recently emphasised by the former President of the ICJ, Judge Yusuf, "[t]he primary function of the Court is to settle disputes through law" [73].

---

71. According to one commentator, "the paragraph uses the noun 'may', which emphasises that the use of precedent is discretionary. It has been noted that this provision seems to state the obvious, as it seems evident that the application of the same legal provisions in different cases should result in similar outcomes . . . The function of Article 21 (2) is primarily to reject the doctrine of binding precedent or *stare decisis* that can be found in some domestic legal systems", M. Klamberg (ed.), *Commentary on the Law of the International Criminal Court*, Bruxelles, Torkel Opsahl, 2017, p. 249.

72. Case of the *Free Zones of Upper Savoy and the District of Gex*, Permanent Court of International Justice, Series A/B, judgment of 7 June 1932, p. 138.

73. *Obligation to Negotiate Access to the Pacific Ocean (Bolivia* v. *Chile)*, Judgment, Declaration of President Yusuf, *ICJ Reports 2018*, p. 566, para. 6.

(i) *Remarks on investment arbitration*

Most of the considerations made so far in relation to inter-State litigation also apply to investor-State arbitration. This flows from the fact that the importance of the autonomy of the parties is in this context equally paramount. This emerges from the circumstance that the mandate generally conferred to investment tribunals is the same as inter-State adjudication: namely, the offer to arbitrate in the disputed treaty. The choice of the rules of procedure, be it ICSID, UNCITRAL or others, together with that of the applicable law, made by the State of nationality and the host State, is obviously complemented by that of the investor triggering arbitration proceedings.

Such a consensual approach suggests a degree of priority of the dispute settlement function along the lines just described for inter-State litigation. However, in spite of few egregious exceptions, legal reasoning aimed at clarifying the applicable law in relation to the disputed case is usually extensive in investment arbitral awards – no less extensive, in fact, than in inter-State litigation [74]. References to precedents in investment case law are also worth noting. When departing from the line of reasoning of previous cases, investment tribunals usually go to great lengths to justify it in relation to the specific circumstances of the case [75]. Besides, under the ICSID system, "failure to state reasons" represents one of the causes for annulment under Article 52 of the

74. F. Ortino, "Legal Reasoning of International Investment Tribunals: A Typology of Egregious Failures", *Journal of International Dispute Settlement*, Vol. 3 (2012), p. 31 *et seq*.

75. On the use of precedent in investment arbitration, see T.-H. Cheng, "Precedent and Control in Investment Treaty Arbitration", *Fordham International Law Journal*, Vol. 30 (2007), p. 1014 *et seq*.; G. Kaufmann-Kohler, "Arbitral Precedent Dream, Necessity or Excuse?", *Arbitration International*, Vol. 23 (2007), p. 357 *et seq*.; S. W. Schill, *The Multilateralization of International Investment Law*, Cambridge, Cambridge University Press, 2009; J. Paulsson, "The Role of Precedent in Investment Arbitration", in K. Yannaca-Small (ed.), *Arbitration under International Investment Agreements: A Guide to the Key Issues*, 1st ed., Oxford, Oxford University Press, 2010, p. 699 *et seq*.; Z. Douglas, "Can a Doctrine of Precedent Be Justified in Investment Treaty Arbitration?", *ICSID Review*, Vol. 25 (2010), p. 104 *et seq*.; I. M. Ten Cate, "The Costs of Consistency: Precedent in Investment Treaty Arbitration", *Columbia Journal of Transnational Law*, Vol. 51 (2012), p. 418 *et seq*.; D. Charlotin, "The Place of Investment Awards and WTO Decisions in International Law: A Citation Analysis", *Journal of International Economic Law*, Vol. 20 (2017), p. 279 *et seq*.; N. Ridi, "Approaches to External Precedent: Invocation of International Decisions in Investment Arbitration and WTO Dispute Settlement", in S. Gáspár-Szilágyi, D. Behn and M. Langford (eds.), *Adjudicating International Trade and Investment Disputes: Between Isolation and Interaction*, Cambridge, Cambridge University Press, 2018, p. 121 *et seq*.

Convention [76], though a recent study demonstrated that applications relying on that ground have a very low success rate [77]. Even outside the ICSID system, great attention is paid to the legal reasoning underlying the decision, which is typically supported by extensive references to previous case law [78]. When apparently departing from the line of reasoning of previous case law, efforts are usually made at justifying it in relation to the specific circumstances of the case.

This appears as a spontaneous attempt at jurisprudential consistency within the investment law and arbitration system, thus enhancing its authority [79]. That is particularly relevant at a time when that system is under crossfire from a number of States driven by ideological sovereignist shifts, on the one hand, and from anti-globalisation groups of civil society, on the other [80]. Importantly, this jurisprudential process towards consistency is not only inward oriented within the system, but extends outward, reaching out to inter-State case law, enhancing the legitimacy of this body of law within the wider context of PIL.

(ii) *Remarks on the WTO dispute settlement system*

A clarification on the WTO inter-State dispute settlement mechanism is called for. It derives from the intense systemic specificities of that

---

76. On annulment in the ICSID context, see R. Doak Bishop and S. M. Marchili, *Annulment under the ICSID Convention*, Oxford, Oxford University Press, 2012.

77. It bears noting, however, that the threshold for annulment remains high: a 2021 study based on the review of 156 annulment proceedings found that while failure to state reasons was invoked as a ground for annulment in 80 per cent of the cases under investigation, its success rate did not exceed 15 per cent. See Y, Kryvoi, J. Koepp and J, Biggs, "Empirical Study: Annulment in ICSID Arbitration", BIICL & Baker Botts (2021). This contributes to reinforcing the perceived legitimacy of investment arbitration. Note, however, that some scholars have observed that annulled decisions may retain some persuasive value. See M. Csernus, "Is There Life After Death?: The Persuasive Value of Annulled Investment Awards", *Journal of International Dispute Settlement*, Vol. 13 (2022), p. 393 *et seq.*; W. Alschner, "Correctness of Investment Awards: Why Wrong Decisions Don't Die", *The Law and Practice of International Courts and Tribunals*, Vol. 18 (2020), p. 345 *et seq.*

78. See on this point De Brabandere, *op. cit.*, p. 84 *et seq.*; A. Reinisch, "The Role of Precedent in ICSID Arbitration", in C. Klausegger *et al.* (eds.), *Austrian Yearbook on International Arbitration 2008*, Wien, Manz'sche Verlags und Universitäts-buchhandlung, 2008, p. 498 *et seq.*; P. Janig, A. Reinisch, "General Principles and the Coherence of International Investment Law: of *Res Judicata, Lis Pendens* and the Value of Precedents", in M. Andenas *et al.* (eds.), *General Principles and the Coherence of International Law*, Leiden-Boston, Brill-Nijhoff, 2019, p. 247 *et seq.*, particularly p. 270 *et seq.*

79. On consistency in the case law as an element enhancing its legitimacy, see A. Stone Sweet and F. Grisel, *The Evolution of International Arbitration: Judicialization, Governance, Legitimacy*, Oxford, Oxford University Press, 2017, p. 218 *et seq.*

80. On the issue, see J. Pauwelyn, "The Rule of Law Without the Rule of Lawyers? Why Investment Arbitrators Are from Mars, Trade Adjudicators from Venus", *American Journal of International Law*, Vol. 109 (2015), p. 761 *et seq.*

body (or sub-system) of international law. The preservation of the integrity and consistency of that normative system has historically featured very highly in the priorities of WTO dispute settlement bodies. Article 3 (2) of Dispute Settlement Understanding (DSU) provides that the WTO Dispute Settlement System

> "[S]erves to preserve the rights and obligations of Members under the covered agreements and to clarify the existing provisions of those agreements in accordance with customary rules of interpretation of public international law." [81]

In other words, a "central" function of the WTO dispute settlement system is to "provide security and predictability to the multilateral trading regime" [82]. To that end, clarification of the applicable WTO law is of the essence in combination with compliance facilitation [83] and jurisprudential consistency [84].

At the same time, precisely in order to safeguard such jurisprudential consistency, the constituent instrument of the Dispute Settlement System (DSS) expressly prevents the Dispute Settlement Body (DSB)

---

81. See "Understanding on Rules and Procedures Governing the Settlement of Disputes", Marrakesh, 14 April 1994 (in force, 1 January 1995), 1869 UNTS 401 (DSU), Annex 2 to the Marrakesh Agreement establishing the World Trade Organization: see Marrakesh Agreement establishing the World Trade Organization, Marrakesh, 15 April 1994 (in force, 1 January 1995), 1867 UNTS 3, Article. II (3) .

82. WTO, *Introduction to the WTO Dispute Settlement System*, https://www.wto.org/english/tratop_e/dispu_e/disp_settlement_cbt_e/c1s3p1_e.htm.

83. R. Palmeter and S. A. Alexandrov, "Inducing Compliance in WTO Dispute Settlement", in D. L. M. Kennedy and J. D. Southwick (eds.), *The Political Economy of International Trade Law: Essays in Honour of Robert Hudec*, Cambridge, Cambridge University Press, 2002, p. 646 *et seq*., particularly at p. 654 *et seq*.; J. H. Jackson, *Sovereignty, the WTO, and Changing Fundamentals of International Law*, Cambridge, Cambridge University Press, 2006, p. 148.

84. The Appellate Body of the WTO made the point several times over, fully clarifying its position in United States – Final Anti-Dumping Measures on Stainless Steel from Mexico, WT/DS344/AB/R, adopted 20 May 2008, paras. 158-161 ("Ensuring 'security and predictability' in the dispute settlement system, as contemplated in Article 3.2 of the DSU, implies that, absent cogent reasons, an adjudicatory body will resolve the same legal question in the same way in a subsequent case"). On this point, see R. Bhala, "The Precedent Setters: *De Facto Stare Decisis* in WTO Adjudication (Part Two of a Trilogy)", *Journal of Transantional Law and Policy*, Vol. 91 (1999), p. 1 *et seq*.; *id*., "Power of the Past: Towards *De Jure Stare Decisis* in WTO Adjudication (Part Three of a Trilogy)", *George Washington International Law Review*, Vol. 33 (2000), p. 873 *et seq*.; J. Pauwelyn, "Minority Rules: Precedent and Participation before the WTO Appellate Body", in J. Jemielniak (ed.), *Establishing Judicial Authority in International Economic Law*, Cambridge, Cambridge University Press, 2016, p. 141 *et seq*.; G. Sacerdoti, "A Comment on Henry Gao, '*Dictum on Dicta: Obiter Dicta* in WTO Disputes'", *World Trade Review*, Vol. 17 (2018), p. 535 *et seq*.; N. Ridi, "United States – Anti-Dumping Measures Applying Differential Pricing Methodology to Softwood Lumber from Canada", *American Journal of International Law*, Vol. 114 (2020), p. 735 *et seq*.

to develop WTO through interpretation [85]. A degree of interpretive creativity by DSB has nonetheless been exercised for the purpose of clarifying those rules of covered agreements whose literal meaning was unclear [86].

Despite this special systemic attention to the objective and consistent adjudicative application of WTO by the DSS, as underlined in 1997 by the WTO panel in the *EC-Bananas I*, "[f]irst and foremost, that system is designed to settle disputes" [87]. Indeed, sight should not be lost of the fact that, behind the disputing States, more often than not, it is the economic operators, as the ultimate beneficiaries of the system, that trigger the WTO inter-State DSS through some form of diplomatic protection. The rulings by DSB are compulsory and exclusive under Article 23 (1) of the Dispute Settlement Understanding (DSU), apparently, on a par with other inter-State litigation.

In sum, on the one hand, as stressed under Article 21 (1) DSU, the "effective resolution of disputes" is portrayed as "essential . . . to the benefit of all Members"; on the other, under Article 3 (3) DSU, the dispute settlement function of DSB merges with that of preserving the collective legal values enshrined in the covered Agreements as if they would make up some kind of a constitutional legal framework.

As to the WTO DSS, more generally, suffice it here to flag that such DSS is geared towards the preservation of multilateral collective interests of Member States to an extent that finds no equal in traditional bilateral inter-State adjudication. This is without prejudice to the specific features of inter-State adjudication in the context of disputes bearing on *erga omnes*, let alone those stemming for *jus cogens* rules.

2. *Human rights litigation*

As to the adjudicative function of human rights courts, the importance of their role in affording an effective remedy to applicants, when legally grounded, cannot be downplayed. As emphasised by the ECtHR, in *Karner* v. *Austria* in 2003, "the primary purpose of the Convention system is to provide individual relief" [88].

---

85. Specifically, Article 3 (2) of the DSU states that "recommendations and rulings of the DSB cannot add to or diminish the rights and obligations provided in the covered agreement". See DSU, *supra* note 78.

86. Shelton, *op. cit.*, p. 563.

87. WTO, *European Communities – Regime for the Importation, Sale and Distribution of Bananas – Complaint by Ecuador – Report of the Panel*, WT/DS27/R/ECU (22 May 1997), para. 7.32.

88. European Court of Human Rights, *Case of Karner* v. *Austria*, Application No. 40016/98, Judgment, 24 July 2003, para. 26.

However, the special aspect of the judicial function of human rights courts in safeguarding the indivisible public interest in the pursuit of the fundamental human rights shared by all States Parties to the relevant Convention [89] must be highlighted. This is a public interest aspect that finds no equal in degree of importance in inter-State jurisdictions. Obviously, with the notable exception of litigation relating to *erga omnes* obligations repeatedly mentioned above.

It is fair to say that a human rights court, next to dispute settlement, pursues the function of the guardian of its constitutive Convention, much like a supreme court does in a municipal setting with the relevant constitution. Indeed, Article 19 of the European Court of Human Rights (ECHR) provides that the Court's function is "[t]o ensure the observance of the engagements undertaken by the High Contracting Parties [in the Convention and the Protocols thereto]". There, the emphasis is on State compliance, generally, as opposed to the remedial side. Differently from inter-State adjudication, or arbitration, where the mandate stems from the consent of the disputing parties, human rights conventions provide the jurisdictional competence of their courts, as well as the law applicable by them, without reservations, or derogatory consent by the parties.

The subservience of the dispute settlement function to the application of the law of human rights Courts is epitomised by the extreme fact that a human rights case may be allowed to continue even after the applicant has passed away and no heir is available. This is what happened in *Karner* v. *Austria* decided in 2003. Paradoxically, in the same case the ECtHR observed that "the primary purpose of the Convention system is to provide individual relief" [90], while no relief was provided for lack of beneficiaries [91].

Indeed, as emphasised by the very ECtHR since its early days, its function is "not only to decide those cases brought before it, but more

89. Convention for the Protection of Human Rights and Fundamental Freedoms, Rome, 4 November 1950 (in force, 3 September 1953), 213 UNTS 221 (ECHR).

90. *Case of Karner* v. *Austria*, Application No. 40016/98, Judgment, 24 July 2003, para. 26.

91. With regard to the relevance of remedies in this context, see V. Fikfak, "Changing State Behaviour: Damages before the European Court of Human Rights", *European Journal of International Law*, Vol. 29 (2018), p. 1091 *et seq*.; *id*., "Non-Pecuniary Damages before the European Court of Human Rights: Forget the Victim; It's All About the State", *Leiden Journal of International Law*, Vol. 33 (2020), p. 335 *et seq*.

generally, to elucidate, *safeguard* and develop the rules instituted by the Convention" [92].

The same function of compliance monitoring is shared by the Inter-American Court of Human Rights (IACtHR). Article 33 of the American Convention does not focus so much on the dispute settlement function as much as on the "competence with respect to matters relating to the fulfilment of the commitments made by the States Parties to th[e] Convention" [93].

As we shall see in due course, those features involve a significant expansion in the scope of *jura novit curia* in this particular adjudicative cluster.

3. *International criminal proceedings*

International criminal tribunals and the ICC obviously present features unknown to the administration of justice by traditional inter-State and investor-State litigation, but also by human rights courts.

The application of international criminal law is governed by the criminal law configuration of the principle of legality in most rigorous terms [94]. Such principle is given effect by the freedom of the accused from *ex post facto* law – i.e. the non-retroactivity principle – and by restrictive interpretation of the definition of crimes in favour of the accused. It would seem that, accordingly, there should be no room for the criminal judge to exercise any form of discretion to apply law in *jura novit curia*. As we shall see based on the case law, things are more complex than what they appear.

---

92. European Court of Human Rights, "Guide on Article 15 of the European Convention on Human Rights", available at https://www.echr.coe.int/documents/Guide_Art_15_ENG.pdf, p. 4, referring to *Case of Ireland* v. *the United Kingdom*, Application No. 5310/71, Judgment, 18 January 1978, para. 154.

93. American Convention on Human Rights, San José, 21 November 1969 (in force, 18 July 1978), 114 UNTS 213

94. On the principle of legality in international criminal law, see Rome Statute of the International Criminal Court, Rome, 17 July 1998 (in force, 1 July 2002), 2187 UNTS 3 (Rome Statute), Articles 22 and 23. See also W. Schabas (ed.) *The International Criminal Court: A Commentary on the Rome Statute*, 2nd edition, Oxford, Oxford University Press, p. 539 *et seq*; S. Lamb, "*Nullum Crimen, Nulla Poena Sine Lege* in International Criminal Law", in A. Cassese *et al.* (eds.), *The Rome Statute of the International Criminal Court: A Commentary*, Vol. 1, Oxford, Oxford University Press, p. 733 *et seq.*; F. von Liszt, "The Rationale for the *Nullum Crimen* Principle", *Journal of International Criminal Justice*, Vol. 5 (2007), p. 1009 *et seq.*; T. de Souza Dias, "Accessibility and Foreseeability in the Application of the Principle of Legality under General International Law: A Time for Revision?", *Human Rights Law Review*, Vol. 19 (2019), p. 649 *et seq.*

G. Concluding remarks

The foregoing sections constitute the backdrop against which the analysis will unfold. In sum, I anticipated a high degree of autonomy of the parties in inter-State and investor-State litigation, where the principal function is that of deciding the dispute, according to the law. Here, the commanding principle is the consensual nature of the mandate of courts and tribunals. The reverse seems to apply in international criminal justice. Human rights litigation appears to place itself in the intermediate space in the pursuit of a balanced calibration between remedying individual grievances and compliance monitoring. In the following chapters, the inquiry concerning *jura novit curia* as outlined above extend to these areas the different exercises of the judicial function by different categories of international judicial bodies.

CHAPTER II

THE LEGAL SOURCE OF *JURA NOVIT CURIA*

A. Introduction

This chapter addresses the legal source of *jura novit curia* in international adjudication. Even though we are addressing a principle of adjudication which is generally assumed to apply to the functioning of international courts and tribunals, as anticipated in Chapter I, its contents and contours are far from certain, if only due to the lack of its express codification in constitutive instruments of international courts and tribunals, let alone in their rules of procedure [95]. This indeterminacy calls for a preliminary search for some kind of legal source where to look for the contents and scope of the principle at hand.

B. The legal basis, or source, of jura novit curia

The issue of the legal basis of *jura novit curia* in international law will be addressed keeping in mind the three areas of international adjudication which have been identified in Chapter I: first, inter-State and investor-State adjudication; second, human rights adjudication; third, international criminal law adjudication.

We shall be guided – primarily, but not exclusively – by Article 38 (1) of the ICJ Statute, which is generally recognised as the matrix of the sources of international law applicable by any given international court or tribunal, subject to the consent of the parties [96]. It reads as follows:

> "The Court, whose function is to decide in accordance with international law such disputes as are submitted to it, shall apply:

95. See Chapter I, Section D.

96. A. Pellet and D. Müller, "Article 38", in A. Zimmermann, C. Tomuschat and K. Oellers-Frahm (eds), *The Statute of the International Court of Justice: A Commentary*, Oxford, Oxford University Press, 2019 (3rd ed.), p. 819 *et seq.*, in particular pp. 834-835. On the history and broader relevance of Article 38, see T. Skouteris, "The Force of a Doctrine Article 38 of the PCIJ Statute and the Sources of International Law", in F. Johns, R. Joyce and S. Pahuja (eds.), *Events: The Force of International Law*, Abingdon, Oxon; New York: Routledge-Cavendish, 2010, p. 69; J. d'Aspremont, "The Idea of 'Rules' in the Sources of International Law", *British Yearbook of International Law*, Vol. 84 (1), 2014, 103-130; M. Fitzmaurice, "The History of Article 38 of the Statute of the International Court of Justice: The Journey from the Past to the Present", in S. Besson and J. d'Aspremont (eds.), *The Oxford Handbook of the Sources of International Law*, Oxford University Press, 2017, p. 0.

a. international conventions, whether general or particular, establishing rules expressly recognized by the contesting states;
b. international custom, as evidence of a general practice accepted as law;
c. the general principles of law recognized by civilized nations;
d. subject to the provisions of Article 59, judicial decisions and the teachings of the most highly qualified publicists of the various nations, as subsidiary means for the determination of rules of law . . ."

As stressed by Sir Elihu Lauterpacht in his 1996 Hague Academy lectures on *Principles of Procedures in International Litigation*, "[i]t is . . . clear that [Article 38 ICJ Statute] serve[s] not only for the substantive rules of international law, but also for international procedural law" [97].

It seems helpful also to refer to Article 21 of the Statute of the International Criminal Court (ICC) [98], not just as a matter of referring to the specific powers of the ICC, but with a view to identifying principles that find application in international adjudication in general – indeed, much like international criminal tribunals themselves have relied on Article 38 of the ICJ Statute to identify the international sources external to their Statutes [99]. By way of alternative, Article 21 of the ICC Statute

97. E. Lauterpacht, "Principles of Procedure in International Litigation", *Recueil des cours*, Vol. 345 (2010), p. 387 *et seq*., in particular pp. 405-406. The point is also supported by Shabtai Rosenne, as edited by Malcolm Shaw, as follows "[s]ince there is no essential difference between substantive and adjectival law in the broad sense, it follows that they have similar, if not identical, origins, whether customary or conventional" (M. N. Shaw, *Rosenne's Law and Practice of the International Court: 1920-2015*, online edition, Vol. 3, para. 254). More in general, it is now undisputed that the category of general principles of law is not limited to substantive principles, but to procedural principles as well. Support for this proposition may be found in the work of the Advisory Committee of Jurists. Consider, for example, Lord Phillimore's statement to the effect that general principles ". . . were these which were accepted by all nations *in foro domestico*, such as certain principles of procedure, the principle of good faith, and the principle of *res judicata*, etc.". See League of Nations, Advisory Committee of Jurists, *Procès-verbaux of the Proceedings of the Committee, 16 June-24 July 1920, with Annexes*, The Hague, Van Langenhuysen, 1920, p. 335. As to scholars, some have been sceptical as to the existence of general principles applicable to international adjudication in general: see A. P. Sereni, *Principi generali di diritto e processo internazionale*, A. Giuffrè, 1955. However, this view was probably never mainstream, as demonstrated by one of the leading works on the topics: see B. Cheng, *General Principles of Law: As Applied by International Courts and Tribunals*, Stevens, 1953. Today, it is undisputed that rules of procedures may be sourced from general principles of law: see, *ex multis*, C. Brown, *A Common Law of International Adjudication*, OUP, 2007, pp. 53-54.

98. Rome Statute of the International Criminal Court, Rome, 17 July 1998 (in force, 1 July 2002), 2187 UNTS 3 (Rome Statute).

99. *E.g.* International Criminal Tribunal for Former Yugoslavia, *Prosecutor* v. *Kupreškić* et al., ICTY Case No. IT-95-16, Judgment, 14 January 2000, para. 540.

– particularly, where it refers to sources external to the Statute (para. 1 (1) *(b)-(c)*) – may be considered highly relevant for the purposes of a systemic interpretation of Article 38 of the ICJ Statute.

The relevant sections of Article 21 of the ICC Statute provide that:

> "1. The Court shall apply:
>
> . . .
>
> *b)* . . . where appropriate, applicable treaties and the principles and rules of international law, including the established principles of the international law of armed conflict;
>
> *c)* Failing that, general principles of law derived by the Court from national laws of legal systems of the world including, as appropriate, the national laws of States that would normally exercise jurisdiction over the crime, provided that those principles are not inconsistent with this Statute and with international law and internationally recognized norms and standards.
>
> 2. The Court may apply principles and rules of law as interpreted in its previous decisions." [100]

It is apparent that Article 21 ICC Statute goes a step forward with respect to Article 38 of the ICJ Statute, on at least two counts. First, reference is made here to "principles of international law" as opposed to just principles of law generally recognised by domestic legal systems [101]. Second, it enhances the relevance of case law as a form of guidance to judicial decision-making, even though falling short of the rule of precedent [102].

100. Rome Statute, Article 21.

101. See *supra* note 3. For further consideration on the differences between Article 21 ICC Statute and Article 38 ICJ Statute, see Mark Klamberg (ed.), *Commentary on the Law of the International Criminal Court*, Brussels, Torkel Opsahl Academic EPublisher, 2017, p. 246. See also G. Bitti, "Article 21 of the Statute of the International Criminal Court and the Treatment of Sources of Law in the Jurisprudence of the ICC", *The Emerging Practice of the International Criminal Court*, 2008, pp. 281-304, 21; N. Ridi, "Rule of Precedent and Rules on Precedent", in E. De Brabandere (ed.), *International Procedure in Interstate Litigation and Arbitration: A Comparative Approach*, Cambridge: Cambridge University Press, 2021, pp. 354-400.

102. Even on this point, there are more sceptical voices. For example, according to Professor Pellet, the provision "deviates little from the principle laid down in Article 38 (1) *(d)* of the ICJ Statute according to which the case law is a 'subsidiary means for the determination of rules of law'". See A. Pellet, "Revisiting the Sources of Applicable Law before the ICC", in M. M. deGuzman and D. M. Amann (eds.), *Arcs of Global Justice: Essays in Honour of William A. Schabas*, Oxford University Press, 2018, p. 0, 236. On the role of precedents in international litigation, with special regard to investment arbitration, see Philipp Janig and August Reinisch, "General Principles

Based on the combined consideration of the two statutory provisions in question [103], the international regulation of *jura novit curia* will be looked for in treaty law, customary law, general principles of law stemming from domestic jurisdictions – but also in general principles of international law – the practice of international courts and tribunals, or in a combination of all such sources and factors.

1. *Treaty law*

As to treaty law, one is to look at the statutes and rules of procedure of permanent inter-State courts and tribunals, such as the ICJ and ITLOS, human rights courts and the ICC. Reference is also to be made to those international agreements – bilateral or multilateral – on which the disputing parties may ground the jurisdiction of inter-State adjudicative bodies, as well as to the rules of procedure laid down by arbitration tribunals upon consultation with the parties.

From a cursory analysis of those instruments, it clearly appears that they do not expressly regulate *jura novit curia*. Where adjudicative powers, or even duties, are to be found that are germane to *jura novit curia*, they fall short from exhaustively regulating such powers and duties. By way of example, one may refer to three provisions of the ICJ Statute: first, to Article 36 (6) on the so-called *Kompetenz-Kompetenz* principle; second, and again, to Article 38 (1) on the ascertainment of the applicable law; and, third, to Article 53, on proceedings *in absentia*.

First, as to Article 36 (6), it only provides that "[i]n the event of a dispute as to whether the Court has jurisdiction, the matter shall be settled by the decision of the Court". Its minimalistic wording falls short of providing any normative parameters by which a decision over jurisdictional competence is to be made [104]. Second, as to Article 38

---

and the Coherence of International Investment Law: of *Res Judicata, Lis Pendens* and the Value of Precedents", in Mads Andenas *et al.* (eds.), *General Principles and the Coherence of International Law*, Leiden-Boston, Brill-Nijhoff, 2019, p. 247 *et seq*.

103. It is important to acknowledge that these are but two models for the regulation of the law to be applied by an international adjudicatory body, and it may be worth anticipating that Article 38 (1) is often considered a byword for "international law" in several other instruments. Notably, this is the case of the ICSID Convention, where the reference to "international law" in Article 42 of the Convention has been acknowledged as one to be read by reference to Article 38 (1) of the ICJ Statute. See Report of the Executive Directors of the International Bank for Reconstruction and Development on the Convention on the Settlement of Investment Disputes Between States and Nationals of Other States, 18 March, 1965.

104. For further comments, see Christian Tomuschat, "Article 36", in Zimmermann, Tomuschat and Oellers-Frahm, *op. cit.*, p. 712 *et seq*. On the strict connection between

(1) it has been argued – among others, by Professor Alain Pellet and Dr Daniel Mueller [105] – that, by vesting the Court with the function of deciding disputes through the application of international law, this provision affords the Court the power and duty to apply the applicable law beyond the legal arguments advanced by the parties when this necessary to decide the dispute submitted to it [106]. According to this reasoning, Article 38 (1) ICJ would represent the legal source of *jura novit curia*. Yet, even so, the provision would fall short of regulating in any way the contents and boundaries of the power or duty in question.

Third, Article 53 refers to the case of non-appearance by one of the parties – clearly the respondent [107]. Paragraph 1 vests the Court with the power to entertain the dispute submitted to it even under such circumstances, if the applicant so requires. Paragraph 2 provides that the Court is to assess its jurisdiction under Articles 36 and 37, thus, on a par with the generality of cases, in which all disputing parties participate in the proceedings [108].

---

jura novit curia and *Kompetenz-Kompetenz*, which will be further elaborated in Chapter III, see T. Sugihara, "The Principle of *Jura Novit Curia* in the International Court of Justice: With Reference to Recent Decisions", in *Japanese Yearbook of International Law*, Vol. 55 (2012), p. 77 *et seq*., at 85-86.

105. Pellet and Müller, *op. cit*., pp. 841-842. Also, Takane Sugihara, *op. cit*., at 83.

106. It is important to note that the original wording of the provision in the Statute of the Permanent Court of International Justice did not incorporate the reference to "international law", which was inserted on suggestion of the Chilean delegation at the San Francisco Conference. See Pellet, Müller, *op. cit*., at para. 47. The Permanent Court did on occasion clarify that the provision could not, in any event, be read as "excluding the possibility of the Court's dealing with disputes which do not require the application of international law". See *Case Concerning the Payment of Various Serbian Loans Issued in France*, Judgment, PCIJ, Series A, No. 20, pp. 6, 20.

107. Hans von Mangoldt and Andreas Zimmermann, "Article 53", Zimmermann, Tomuschat and Oellers-Frahm, *op. cit*., p. 1467 *et seq*. See also Gaetano Arangio-Ruiz, "Preliminary Report on Non-appearance before the International Court of Justice", in *Annuaire de l'Institut de Droit International*, Vol. 64 (I) (1991), p. 193 *et seq*., at 210-212; Robert Kolb, *The International Court of Justic*e, Oxford, Hart Publishing, 2013, p. 672. The literature deems that this provision is reflected in Article 28 of the ITLOS Statute (von Mangoldt, Zimmermann, *op. cit*., 1470; *Contra South China Sea Arbitration (The Republic of Philippines* v. *The People's Republic of China)*, PCA 2013-19, Jurisdiction and Admissibility, Award of 29 October 2015, para. 112 *et seq*.). On recent developments and practices on non-appearance, see Otto Spijkers, "Non-Participation in Arbitral Proceedings under Annex VII United Nations Convention on the Law of the Sea: Arctic Sunrise and South China Sea Compared", in Angela Del Vecchio and Roberto Virzo (eds.), *Interpretations of the United Nations Convention on the Law of the Sea by International Courts and Tribunals*, Cham, Springer, 2019, p. 171 *et seq*.; Peter Tzen, "A Strategy of Non-Participation before International Courts and Tribunals", in *The Law and Practice of International Courts and Tribunals*, Vol. 19 (2020), p. 5 *et seq*.

108. However, it bears noting that the Court cannot substitute itself to the parties as to the choice of the title of jurisdiction relied on. Thus, "a principle such as *jura novit curia* cannot appropriately be applied by the Court *proprio motu* to substitute a title

The same paragraph provides that "the Court is to satisfy itself also that the claim is well founded in fact and law". This language affords the Court the power and duty to rely on its own independent assessment of the facts and the law applicable to the merits of the case, that is to say, not only independently from the arguments that have obviously not been advanced by the absent party, but also from those put forward by the applicant [109].

There is thus no doubt that this language prescribes that *jura novit curia* may be exercised, and indeed that it requires its exercise as a duty, with regard to proceedings *in absentia*. However, the provision does not indicate whether such a duty applies in contrast to, or just like in, the case where all the disputing parties participate in the proceedings.

It appears that the *ex officio* power and the duty to assert the legal grounds of the case on the merits, independently from the positions of the parties, are provided for explicitly only in relation to proceedings *in absentia* under Article 53 (2). This is different from the obligation for the Court to assert its jurisdiction, which is provided for on an equal footing with cases enjoying regular participation. This may lead to the conclusion that, at the merits stage, the existence of such powers and duty to exercise them could only operate in those proceedings where the respondent is absent. As we shall see in due course, the jurisprudence of international adjudicative bodies disproves the proposition, in the sense that international adjudicators have always the duty to assert that the case made by the applicant is grounded in law [110]. Be that as it may,

---

of jurisdiction which has not been invoked for another which, upon investigation, is found to be inadequate": see S. Rosenne and M. N. Shaw, *Rosenne's Law and Practice of the International Court*, pp. 1920-2015, 5th ed., Leiden; Boston, Brill, 2016, at 238 *et seq.*

109. See in particular *Fisheries Jurisdiction*, *ICJ Reports 1974*, p. 3, at 9 (para. 17) and at 175, 181 (para. 18) ("The Court however, as an international judicial organ, is deemed to take judicial notice of international law, and is therefore required in a case falling under Article 53 . . . as in any other case, to consider on its own initiative all rules of international law which may be relevant to the settlement of the dispute. It being the duty of the Court itself to ascertain and apply the relevant law in the given circumstances of the case, the burden of establishing or proving rules of international law cannot be imposed upon any of the parties, for the law lies within the judicial knowledge of the Court").

110. In this sense, the ICJ, commenting Article 53, has held that "The use of the term 'satisfy itself' in the English text of the Statute (and in the French text the term *'s'assurer'*) implies that the Court must attain the same degree of certainty as in any other case that the claim of the party appearing is sound in law, and, so far as the nature of the case permits, that the facts on which it is based are supported by convincing evidence" (*Military and Paramilitary Activities in and Against Nicaragua (Nicaragua* v. *United States of America)*, Merits, Judgment, *ICJ Reports 1986*, p. 14, p. 24, para. 29.).

the fact remains that Article 53, just like Articles 36 (2) and 38 (1), falls short of regulating the contents and contours of *jura novit curia*.

These considerations apply to the constituent instruments of adjudicative bodies belonging to all three areas of adjudication under consideration. However, such instruments, despite lacking an exhaustive regulation of *jura novit curia*, are relevant to our analysis for three main reasons. First, significant case law relies on such instruments in order to fit *jura novit curia* within the so-called inherent power doctrine. Second, some constituent instruments provide indications over principles cognate to *jura novit curia*, which may be relevant to the identification of its contents and scope. I am referring to the principles of *Kompetenz-Kompetenz*, *non liquet*, *ne ultra petita* or *ne infra petita* [111], even if it may be readily admitted that no statutory provision which refers to such principles provides sufficient written indications from which to draw a comprehensive appreciation of the contents of *jura novit curia*. Third, constitutive instruments of international courts and tribunals may provide useful incorporation by reference of relevant sources external to the instrument itself. As we have just seen with regard to the ICJ and ICC Statutes, they may refer to general principles and rules, or even to judicial practice of the bodies in question.

2. *Customary law*

As to customary law, the preliminary question arises as to whether it is a suitable source for regulation of adjudicative bodies, if only because it is debatable whether there is *enough* customary international law on the matter to begin with [112].

---

111. Statutory provisions referring to *Kompetenz-Kompetenz* may be found at Article 36 (6) ICJ Statute, Article 288 (4) UNCLOS, Article 49 ECHR, Article 62 (3) IACHR, Article 41 ICSID Convention. As to *ne ultra petita*, it is directly referred to at Article 60 ICJ Statute ("[i]n the event of a dispute as to the meaning or scope of the judgment, the Court shall construe it upon the request of any party"). Similar wording may also be found at Article 33 ITLOS Statute. As to *non liquet*, such principle is spelled out in so many words exclusively at Article 42 (2) ICSID Convention ("[t]he Tribunal may not bring in a finding of *non liquet* on the ground of silence or obscurity of the law"). On the principles referenced here, see S. Forlati, *"Infra Petita"*, in *Max Planck Encyclopedia of International Procedural Law*; A. M. Tanzi, *"Ultra Petita"*, in *Max Planck Encyclopedia of International Procedural Law*; A. M. Tanzi, "On Judicial Autonomy and the Autonomy of the Parties in International Adjudication, with Special Regard to Investment Arbitration and ICSID Annulment Proceedings", *Leiden Journal of International Law*, Vol. 33 (1), 2020, 57-75.

112. On the irrelevance of the issue, see M. Forteau, "General Principles of International Procedural Law", in *Max Planck Encyclopedia of International Procedural Law*, January 2018, para. 13; Shaw, *op. cit.*, para. 254.

According to Durward Sandifer, "a pattern of agreement on the basic character and purpose of international proceedings [creates] what is tantamount to a customary law of evidence" [113]. On the contrary, according to Sergey Punzhin, "international custom and 'subsidiary means for the determination of rules of law' do not play the same role with regard to procedural law as they do *vis-à-vis* substantive international law" [114]. On the other hand, Chester Brown has observed that

> "It may appear somewhat incongruous to suggest that customary international law can represent a source of procedural law. Customary international law is usually thought to be generated by the practice of states and their expressions of *opinio juris*, and not the practice of international courts and tribunals. Yet writers have nonetheless emphasized the relevance of custom." [115]

In this sense, authors such as Chittharanjan Amerasinghe have relied on customary law, for example, to discuss the independent power of international adjudicatory bodies to order interim measures, arguing that "definite parameters . . . have been established in customary international law as reflected in the tribunal's own past practice and precedents" [116].

The issue of the suitability of customary law as a source of international procedural law may be broken down into two questions. First, whether international courts and tribunals may, in any form or shape, take part in the customary lawmaking process [117]. Second, whether

113. Durward V. Sandifer, *Evidence Before International Tribunals*, Charlottesville, University Press of Virginia, 1975, p. 458. Though the author exclusively refers to evidentiary issues, it is clear that his reasoning may well apply to any issues of procedure.

114. S. M. Punzhin, "Procedural Normative System of the International Court of Justice", in *Leiden Journal of International Law*, Vol. 30 (2017), p. 661 *et seq*., p. 682.

115. C. Brown, "The Inherent Powers of International Courts and Tribunals", in *British Yearbook of International Law*, Vol. 76 (2006), p.195 *et seq*., pp. 203-204.

116. C. F. Amerasinghe, *International Arbitral Jurisdiction*, Leiden-Boston, Brill-Nijhoff, 2011, p. 243. To the same effect, Lauterpacht, *op. cit*., pp. 405-406 ("[i]t is also clear that [the sources listed in Article 38 ICJ Statute] serve not only for the substantive rules of international law, but also for international procedural law. Thus, principles of international procedural law can be found in international conventions (such as the statutes, rules of procedure, and other constitutive instruments of international courts and tribunals); rules developed in the customary practice of international tribunals; general principles of law; and, as a subsidiary means for the determination of procedural rules, judicial decisions and the writings of high qualified publicists").

117. As a practical matter, it is undisputed that international courts and tribunals have contributed to the development of international law. See S. H. Lauterpacht, *The Development of International Law by the International Court*, Praeger, 1958; J. I. Charney, "Is International Law Threatened by Multiple International Tribunals?", *Recueil des cours*, tome 271 (1998), 101-382; T. Ginsburg, "Bounded Discretion

States can contribute to customary lawmaking concerning adjudication. Those are two aspects of the same problem. On the face of it, the answer to both questions may appear to be in the negative.

As to the first issue, one of the main tenets of the orthodoxy in international law is that only States and – possibly – intergovernmental organisations may produce custom through their conduct in matters pertaining to the exercise of their sovereignty, or statutory aims [118]. However, Sir Gerald Fitzmaurice noted that a greater role of law-making for the international judiciary may be permissible or even desirable, but with no prejudice to the predictability of the law to be applied by an adjudicatory body [119]. In terms most germane to this study, Sir Hugh Thirlway has stated that

> "[t]urning to customary law, there can be no doubt that the practice of an international tribunal may in general, if sufficiently consistent, generate a procedural rule which that particular tribunal, at least, may not lightly depart from, and which possibly also has some degree of general validity as a component of the general corpus of procedural law of international tribunals. It is difficult to equate this phenomenon with the concrete element in the formation of international custom: apart from questions of

in International Judicial Lawmaking", *Va. J. Int'l L.*, Vol. 45, 2004, 631; P. Webb, *International Judicial Integration and Fragmentation*, 1st ed., Oxford, United Kingdom, OUP, 2013; C. J. Tams and J. Sloan (eds.), *The Development of International Law by the International Court of Justice*, Also available as: eBook, 2013; see in particular S. F. Berman, *The International Court of Justice as an "Agent" of Legal Development?**, Oxford University Press, 2013. At the theoretical level, things are more complicated: when dealing with the issue, the ILC has often downplayed the importance of judicial decisions. Thus, for example, the Draft Conclusions on the Identification of Customary International Law restrict themselves to stating that "[d]ecisions of international courts and tribunals, in particular of the International Court of Justice, concerning the existence and content of rules of customary international law are a subsidiary means for the determination of such rules".

118. A sharp discussion of the traditional account is provided in H. Thirlway, *The Sources of International Law*, OUP, Oxford, 2014. On the contribution of international organisations to lawmaking in general, see J. Klabbers, "International Organizations in the Formation of Customary International Law", *Customary International Law on the Use of Force*, Brill Nijhoff, 2005, pp. 179-195; J. E. Alvarez, *International Organizations as Law-makers*, Oxford University Press, 2006; K. Daugirdas, "International Organizations and the Creation of Customary International Law", *European Journal of International Law*, Vol. 31(1), 2020, 201-233; L. Gasbarri, "The Notion of Institutional Practice in United Nations Law", *Max Planck Yearbook of United Nations Law Online*, Vol. 24 (1), 2021, 1–35.

119. G. Fitzmaurice, "The Future of Public International Law and of the International Legal System in the Circumstances of Today: Second and Final Part of an Abstract (Prepared by the Author) of a Special Report", in *International Relations*, Vol. 5 (1976), p. 949 *et seq.*, p. 964.

> *opinio juris* in the sense of recognition of the binding nature of the practice, it differs from normal state practice in that, while it may ultimately have a restrictive or coercitive effect on states as subjects of international law, it is developed rather by the actions and decisions of international arbitrators and members of international tribunals, who are not themselves subjects of international law" [120].

One might consider international courts and tribunals in their configuration as organs of an international organisation, or as international bodies in and by themselves comparable to international organisations. However, under Article 38 (1) *(d)* of the ICJ Statute, their adjudicative activity may only be considered as a "subsidiary means for the determination of a rule of law", rather than constituent elements of a rule of law, either of a substantive or procedural nature. The issue may be further elaborated along the line of reasoning of the ILC Special Rapporteur on *identification of customary international law,* Sir Michael Wood, according to whom "[t]here is no doctrine of *stare decisis* in international law", thus concluding that "[t]he decisions of international courts and tribunals cannot be said to be conclusive for the identification of rules of customary international law" [121]. According to this reasoning, the decisions of international courts and tribunals could not be constitutive elements of international customs.

However, Sir Michael acknowledged that "[e]xamples of reliance upon judicial decisions for the identification of rules of customary international law are legion" [122]. And he went so far as to mention that

> "[J]udicial pronouncements, especially of the International Court of Justice and of specialist tribunals, such as the International Tribunal for the Law of the Sea, are often seen as authoritative. The same is true of certain arbitral awards." [123]

120. H. Thirlway, "Dilemma or Chimera? Admissibility of Illegally Obtained Evidence in International Adjudication", in *American Journal of International Law*, Vol. 78 (1984), p. 622 *et seq*., pp. 623-624.

121. Third Report on Identification of Customary International Law by Michael Wood, Special Rapporteur, UN Doc. A/CN.4/682, pp. 42-44 and 46.

122. *Ibidem*, p. 44.

123. *Ibidem*, p. 43. See also F. Berman, *Authority in International Law*, (2018). "The maxim *jura novit curia* does not mean that an international court has discretionary freedom to base its decision on whatever legal analysis it chooses, whether or not that has been debated before it between the parties. That constraint can be seen to operate particularly strongly in arbitration, and an arbitral award could indeed find itself being formally challenged if the tribunal were to do so. But it applies before standing courts as well. And – quite naturally – parties arguing before the ICJ are very prone to cite

Along the same lines, the ICTY in *Kupreškić*, while affirming that in international law "judicial precedent is not a distinct source of law", acknowledged that "precedents may bear persuasive authority concerning the existence of a rule or principle" [124]. Particularly in the domain of the international criminal process, reference should be made to the above-mentioned Article 21 of the ICC Statute, whose paragraph 2 affords authoritative relevance to the Court's judicial precedents.

It would seem difficult to argue that consistent judicial practice may not bear on the law of adjudication on a par with substantive law, if not more so [125]. Recently, Hélène Ruiz Fabri and Joshua Paine came down to the point at issue as follows:

> "[I]t is quite common to find international courts and tribunals refer to the 'practice' of international tribunals to justify a particular procedural decision. In short, this may be best characterised as an instance of judicial decisions operating as a source of law." [126]

As to the second issue, namely the role of States in the development of international procedural law, there is no denying that the "practice" and reasoning of international tribunals cannot be attributed to States and that the rules governing the adjudicative function does pertain to the exercise of State jurisdiction. Rather, elements of both State

---

back to it its own previous judgments". It bears noting, however, that not all judicial decisions and arbitral awards are necessarily equally authoritative. The question is currently being investigated by the ILC. See First Report on Subsidiary Means for the Determination of Rules of International Law, by Charles Chernor Jalloh, Special Rapporteur, UN Doc. A/CN.4/760, 13 February 2023. On "ranking" subsidiary means, see N. Ridi, "The Shape and Structure of the 'Usable Past': An Empirical Analysis of the Use of Precedent in International Adjudication", *Journal of International Dispute Settlement*, Vol. 10(2), 2019, 200-247; S. T. Helmersen, "Finding 'the Most Highly Qualified Publicists': Lessons from the International Court of Justice", *European Journal of International Law*, Vol. 30 (2), 2019, 509-535.

124. *Prosecutor* v. *Kupreškić* et al., *cit.*, para. 540. On the authority of judicial decisions in international criminal law see in general L. L. Giacco, *Judicial Decisions in International Law Argumentation: Between Entrapment and Creativity*, Bloomsbury Academic, 2022.

125. This appears sensible, given the inherent power of international adjudicative bodies to conduct proceedings as they deem fit. On inherent powers, see below, subsection 4.

126. H. Ruiz Fabri and J. Paine, "The Procedural Cross-Fertilization Pull", in *MPILux Research Paper Series* No. 6, 2019, pp. 13-14. See also G. G. Fitzmaurice, "Some Problems Regarding the Formal Sources of International Law", *Symbolae Verzijl: Présentées au professeur J. H. W. Verzijl à l'occasion de son LXX-ième anniversaire*, Nijhoff, 1958, pp. 58-79, 154 ("[I]t will be suggested that the decisions of international tribunals, while not operating directly as judicial precedents, and while not therefore technically a formal source of law, have a status different from that of a merely material source, and could be characterized as quasi-formal in character").

practice and *opinio juris* concerning the rules in question can be drawn from a number of factors. Suffice it to recall the following conventional and non-conventional State practice: constitutive treaties of permanent judicial bodies [127]; special agreements setting up inter-State arbitral tribunals; the acceptance of the rules of procedure further corroborated by participation in the proceedings governed by such rules; the acceptance and compliance with the ensuing judgments; the fact that, when objections to such judgments are raised, they are seldom based on procedural grounds.

Where this is the case, it is the conduct of a given adjudicative body which is contested with respect to a given procedural rule, rather than the rule itself [128]. And this may only corroborate the rule in question, precisely through State practice and *opinio juris* [129].

In sum, there is a way to look at international judicial practice through the prism of a generalised State practice and *opinio juris* which validates the role of international courts and tribunals. Namely, by confirming, specifying and producing the development and crystallisation of international procedural rules. This process of validation flows from a combination of interrelated elements of State practice and *opinio juris* on the one hand, and jurisprudential self-reliance on the other. To that end, one may note that, not only the large majority of international judicial decisions are complied with by the disputing parties [130], but also third States rely on decisions that are not binding on them [131].

---

127. Article 30 of the ICJ Statute is particularly illustrative to this effect, as it vests the Court with the inherent powers to "frame rules for carrying out its functions". Thus, the end product of the exercise of such powers, including its rules of procedure, would be binding upon the States parties to proceedings, based on their consent as expressed in the adoption and ratification of the Statute, as an integral part of the Charter, and reiterated by the participation in the proceedings.

128. E.g. in the *Military and Paramilitary Activities* case, the United States held that the Court had applied international law in an "incorrect" manner, rather than challenging its power to assess its jurisdiction under the *Kompetenz-Kompetenz* principle, James P. Rowles, "Nicaragua Versus the United States: Issues of Law and Policy", in *International Lawyer*, Vol. 20 (1986), p. 1245 *et seq*., p. 1248.

129. Of course, there may be exceptions. A good example is provided by James Crawford with reference to the *Nicaragua* case and the apparent conflation of the notions of jurisdiction and applicable law. See J. Crawford, *Brownlie's Principles of Public International Law*, 8th ed., Oxford, United Kingdom, OUP, 2012, 33.

130. For statistics, see C. Schulte, *Compliance with Decisions of the International Court of Justice*, Oxford, Oxford University Press, 2004.

131. Reference can be made to the *Norstar* case, whereby Italy referred to the ICJ Judgment in the *Military and Paramilitary* case to corroborate its argument concerning the burden of proof (*The M/V "Norstar" Case (Panama* v. *Italy)*, ITLOS Case No. 25, Counter-Memorial of the Italian Republic, 11 October 2017, para. 284.).

It is arguable that such a generalised State attitude validates the participation of international courts and tribunals in the international lawmaking process concerning substantive law [132]. And that such reasoning applies, all the more, with regard to the rules which courts and tribunals are to apply in the exercise of their function.

When international courts and tribunals conform to international rules of adjudication, they do so with a sense of abidance by the intergovernmental process just described, as well as by their own judicial practice, as it is corroborated by that of other international adjudicative bodies. Thus, as the foregoing paragraphs show, customary international law has the potential to shape the operation of *jura novit curia*. This is also the case of general principles of law and general principles of international law, to which this study now turns.

3. *General principles of law and general principles of international law*

The maxim *jura novit curia* clearly evokes a principle, namely a "general principle recognized by civilized nations" according to the language of Article 38 (1) *(c)* ICJ Statute.

Particularly in discussing a principle of procedural law, it is imperative not to forget that this provision reproduces that of the Statute of the PCIJ, adopted in 1920, still well in the infancy of international adjudication. Even if some members of the Committee of Jurists that drafted the text at hand wished to refer to general principles of international law, the view prevailed to the effect that the "principles" in question were those that could be imported from national jurisdictions [133]. The primary

The same occurs in investment arbitration: e.g. in the *Azurix* arbitration, Argentina relied upon the *ELSI* case between the United States and Italy for the definition of arbitrary treatment (*Azurix Corp* v. *Argentina*, ICSID Case No. ARB/01/12, Award, 23 June 2006, para. 387. Similarly, see *Noble Ventures, Inc.* v. *Romania*, ICSID Case No. ARB/01/11, Award, 5 October 2005, paras. 175-176. For other examples, see Alain Pellet, "The Case Law of the ICJ in Investment Arbitration", in *ICSID Review*, Vol. 28 (2013), p. 223 *et seq*.

132. Elihu Lauterpacht stressed, also in a Hague Academy course, that "[i]t is also clear thaAs already recalled, Elihu Lauterpacht argued in his Hague lectures precisely that the sources listed in Article 38 ICJ Statute concern both substantive and procedural law. Lauterpacht, *op. cit.*, pp. 405-406 (emphasis added). One may note the double relevance of the contribution by international adjudication to the formation and identification of international customary law. See also Shaw, *op. cit.*, para. 254; Alan Boyle and Christine Chinkin, *The Making of International Law*, Oxford, Oxford University Press, 2007, p. 263 *et seq*.

133. See League of Nations, Advisory Committee of Jurists, *Procès-verbaux of the Proceedings of the Committee, 16 June-24 July 1920, with Annexes*. "M. de Lapradelle thought it superfluous, because law implies civilisation. Apart from this

requirement for such importation as a source of international law was that the domestic principles in question would be generally recognised in domestic legal systems [134].

One of the main reasons for providing for domestic principles of law as a separate source of the law applicable by the PCIJ, first, and the ICJ, later, derived from the concern that the Court might not decide a dispute due to the lack of pertinent rules discernible from any applicable international treaty or custom [135]. This situation is defined by the concept of *non liquet* [136].

General Principles of Law were clearly envisaged primarily as a gap-filler with regard to substantive law applicable in the relations between the disputing parties. However, general principles permeate the law of adjudication [137]. It is no wonder that the ILC Special Rapporteur on general principles of law listed by exemplary reference in his first report those of *res judicata*, *Kompetenz-Kompetenz* and burden of proof. And it is of immediate evidence that all general principles of procedural law are particularly useful in filling gaps in the statutes and rules of

---

special point, M. de Lapradelle remarked that custom was mentioned as a source in all the drafts proposed. He thought that a mention of this was necessary, but on the other hand wondered, how were general principles obtained, unless it was from custom? Points 2 and 3 ought to change place. If customary law had already been dealt with, from whence could general principles be derived, unless it were from the reading of judicial decisions and writers? Lord Phillimore pointed out that the general principles referred to in point 3 were these which were accepted by all nations in *foro domestico*, such as certain principles. *A Concise Introduction to International Law*, 2nd ed., The Hague, Torino, Eleven-Giappichelli, 2022, 110 *et seq*.

134. Sir Hersch Lauterpacht referred to "those principles of law, private and public, which contemplation of the legal experience of civilized nations leads one to regard as obvious maxims of jurisprudence of a general and fundamental character . . . a comparison, generalization and synthesis of rules of law in its various branches – private and public, constitutional, administrative, and procedural – common to various systems of national law", H. Lauterpacht, *International Law: Being the Collected Papers of Hersch Lauterpacht*, Vol. 1, Cambridge, Cambridge University Press, 1970, p. 74.

135. Pellet, Müller, *op. cit*., pp. 829-830.

136. D. Bodansky, *"Non Liquet"*, in *Max Planck Encyclopedia of Public International Law*, May 2006; G. Fitzmaurice, "The Problem of *Non-Liquet*: *Prolegomena* to a Restatement", in S. Bastid, C. Rousseau, *Mélanges offerts à Charles Rousseau : la communauté internationale*, Paris, Pedone, 1974, p. 89 *et seq*.; H. Lauterpacht, "Some Observations on the Prohibition of *'Non Liquet'* and the Completeness of the Law", in F. M. van Asbeck (ed.), *Symbolae Verzijl : Présentées au professeur J. H. W. Verzijl, à l'occasion de son LXX-ième anniversaire*, The Hague, Nijhoff, 1958, p. 196 *et seq*.

137. "First Report on General Principles of Law by Marcelo Vázquez-Bermúdez, Special Rapporteur", UN Doc. A/CN.4/732 (5 April 2019) para. 134. See, L. Chiussi and M. Andenaes, "Cohesion, Convergence and Coherence of International Law", in M. Andenaes *et al.* (eds.), *General Principles and the Coherence of International Law*, Brill Nijhoff, 2019, p. 10.

procedure of international courts and tribunals when a particular issue arises in the course of proceedings.

To be sure, the idea that *jura novit curia* might be considered as a principle generally recognised in domestic jurisdictions is anything but obvious. In the common law, its very existence has been questioned, while its scope varies significantly in different civil law jurisdictions [138]. Civil law judges exercise a latitude of autonomy in the deliberation process which is unknown to common law courts. Here, conversely, judges rely on counsel to an extent which is unknown in civil law countries.

Such differences have been singled out in rather emphatic terms from a common law perspective by Francis Mann, a great domestic and international legal practitioner and scholar of the last century. He was particularly well-placed to address the point, since he received an initial civil law education in Germany and later practised common law in the United Kingdom. In an article published in 1977, he observed that

> "the most spectacular feature of English procedure is that the rule *curia novit legem* has never been and is not part of English law, or, to put it affirmatively, in England there prevails what one may call the principle of judicial unpreparedness. Most English lawyers are unaware of the specific effects of this principle . . . In England counsel submits the law to the court which is assumed to know next to nothing about it" [139].

It would definitely sit uncomfortably with the above statement to ground the principle under consideration in international law in some common denominator between different municipal legal systems. However, still relying on Mann's words, one finds reference to aspects of the common law judicial attitude to *jura novit curia* which plainly coincide with what will emerge in due course as the configuration of the principle at hand in international adjudication:

> "The court may raise questions, suggest new lines of argument or amendments of the pleadings, draw attention to authorities

138. On the different configurations of the principle in hand in domestic and international adjudication, see J. Verhoeven, "*Jura Novit Curia* et le juge international", in P.-M. Dupuy *et al.* (eds.), *Völkerrecht als Wertordnung: Festschrift für Christian Tomuschat – Common Values in International Law: Essays in Honour of Christian Tomuschat*, Kehl, Engel, 2006, p. 635 *et seq.*, p. 637 *et seq.* See, more recently, F. Ferrari and G. Corder-Moss (eds.), Iura Novit Curia *in International Arbitration*, New York, Huntington, 2018.

139. F. A. Mann, "Fusion of the Legal Professions?", in *Law Quarterly Review*, Vol. 93 (1977), p. 367 *et seq.*, p. 369.

overlooked by counsel. But it is not its duty to do so. In any event points or authorities that occur to the judge ought (and are expected) to be put to counsel to prevent surprise." [140]

This passage confirms the increasingly shared view that "[t]he conflict between civil and common law is overstated" [141]. This certainly applies to principles such as that of equality of arms and its corollary, the right of the parties to be heard [142]. And the latter, as we shall see, is a procedural right which consistently emerges in association with the exercise of *jura novit curia* throughout the analysis of all three areas of international litigation [143].

Be that as it may, in the identification of a general principle of law under Article 38 (1) *(c)*, legal institutions may be found which are common to a significant number of domestic jurisdictions. However, their international configuration could not by definition reproduce any specific, individual domestic model.

As observed by Judge McNair in his separate opinion in the 1950 Advisory Opinion on the *International Status of South-West Africa*.

"[T]he duty of international tribunals . . . is to regard any features or terminology which are reminiscent of the rules and

---

140. *Ibidem*. On Mann's construction of the issue, see D. Shelton, "*Jura Novit Curia* in International Human Rights Tribunals", *supra* n. 18, at p. 190.

141. Daniel Terris and Cesare P. R. Romano, Leigh Swigart, *The International Judge: An Introduction to the Men and Women Who Decide the World's Cases*, Oxford, Oxford University Press, 2007, p. 111. On the differences between civil law and common law in general, see J. H. Merryman, "On the Convergence (and Divergence) of the Civil Law and the Common Law", *Stanford Journal of International Law*, Vol. 17 (2), 1981, 357-388; M. Taruffo, "Il processo civile di 'civil law' e di 'common law': aspetti fondamentali", *Il Foro Italiano*, Vol. 124 (11), 2001, 345, 346-359, 360. For a discussion of the influence of the civil law and common law traditions on international adjudication, see H. Lauterpacht, "The So-Called Anglo-American and Continental Schools of Thought in International Law", *British Yearbook of International Law*, Vol. 12, 1931, 31-62; J. Crawford, A. Pellet and C. Redgwell, "Anglo-American and Continental Traditions in Advocacy before International Courts and Tribunals Legal Tradition in a Diverse World: Keynote Contributions", *Cambridge Journal of International and Comparative Law*, Vol. 2, 2013, 715-737.

142. On the right to be heard and equality of arms, see E. G. Baldwin, "The Right To Be Heard: The Messy Business of Due Process", in I. A. Laird *et al.* (eds.), *Investment Treaty Arbitration and International Law*, Vol. 7, Huntington, JurisNet, 2014, p. 233 *et seq.*; R. T. Treves, "Equality of Arms and Inequality of Resources", in A. Sarvarian *et al.* (eds.), *Procedural Fairness in International Courts and Tribunals*, London, British Institute of International and Comparative Law, 2015, p. 153 *et seq.*

143. An interesting aspect relates to potential of an application of *jura novit curia* to result in a violation of the right to a fair trial (*lato sensu*) of the parties: see *Gouvernement de la République arabe d'Egypte* v. *Société Malicorp Ltd*, Cour d'appel de Paris, 19 juin 2008, 06/17901 2008. The problem has also been found to apply in the context of arbitration. See e.g. *Swiss Federal Tribunal, A.* v. *B.*, 4A_554/2014.

institutions of private law as an indication of policy and principles rather than as directly importing these rules and institutions." [144]

He paraphrased his statement by observing that "[t]he way in which international law borrows from this source is not by means of importing private law institutions 'lock, stock and barrel', ready-made and fully equipped with a set of rules" [145].

Fully subscribing to this approach in light of the case law and practice of international courts and tribunals, one would argue that it would serve little purpose to engage in some kind of comparative analysis of *jura novit curia* in domestic jurisdictions for purposes of establishing its nature as a general principle of law.

It may sound paradoxical that one of the most well-known cases in which *jura novit curia* has been invoked before the ICJ was precisely by the UK, in *Fisheries Jurisdiction* against Iceland, even though in the context of non-appearance by the defendant, which in principle does not involve, as such, the exercise of *jura novit curia*. In its Memorial on the Merits, after stating that ". . . both parties are under a basic obligation to assist the Court by assuming the burden of proving those contentions upon which their case depends" [146], Counsel for the United Kingdom argued that "[h]owever, the Court is entitled, perhaps even bound, to take note of the established statements of the law" [147]. The adversative adverb "however" suggests the view whereby the Court should "take note of the established statements of the law" irrespective of the contentions made by the parties during the proceedings. In the next section, it will be illustrated further how this was the way the Court took it.

If, once repeatedly applied at the international level, general principles of law in domestic jurisdictions transmigrate into international law, as one would be inclined to believe, at that point, it is fair to say that they become "general principles of international law" [148]. It would, therefore, serve little purpose to keep looking at domestic legal systems for principles that have already made their entry into international law and operate in that configuration, independently from their domestic origin.

---

144. *International Status of South-West Africa*, Separate Opinion by Sir Arnold McNair to the Advisory Opinion of 11 July 1950, [1950] *ICJ Reports 146*, at 148.

145. *Ibidem*.

146. "Memorial on the Merits submitted by the Government of the United Kingdom of Great Britain and Northern Ireland", in *Fisheries Jurisdiction (United Kingdom* v. *Iceland), Pleading Oral Arguments and Documents*, Vol. I, pp. 346-347, para. 228.

147. *Ibidem*, p. 347, para. 229.

148. *A Concise Introduction to International Law*, *cit.*, p. 115. See also *First Report on General Principles*, cit., para. 235.

Accordingly, it should not surprise that the expression "general principles of international law" – which finds no place in Article 38 ICJ Statute – is recurrently to be found in modern international practice and case law. Such principles not only pertain to international substantive law, but also to the law of international adjudication, just as mentioned in Article 21 (1) *(b)* ICC [149]. The expression "general principles of international law" would therefore be not so much indicative of the municipal provenance of the principles in question, but rather of their general character and of the flexibility of their content.

Qualifying a general principle as international evokes *a)* its consistent application and *b)* its widespread recognition on the international level. Both features are obviously analogous to those characterising the customary lawmaking process. The particular process in question commenced with the parsing of these principles from those recognised *in foro domestico* and developed through international jurisprudential consistency generally accepted by the international society of States.

As just indicated, there are no systemic obstacles to principles of adjudication evolving into customary law. As clearly put by Robert Kolb in his encyclopaedia entry on general principles of procedural law,

> "[T]here is no clear-cut distinction between principles and rules, but at least a grey area: a rule can be quite general and thus eventually qualify as a principle; a principle can be narrow, but qualify on account of its importance." [150]

Having regard to inter-State adjudication, one could well be satisfied with fitting *jura novit curia* into the framework of a general principle of international law as understood in the customary law sense of the

149. See *supra* n. 99. A textual reading of ICC Article 21 (1) *(b)* and *(c)*, corroborates the existence of "principles of international law" as separate from "general principles of law derived by the Court from national laws of legal systems of the world" and irrespective of the process of their formation. It bears noting, in any event, that the expression is used in a number of different ways. Consider, for example, the Declaration on Principles of International Law concerning Friendly Relations and Co-operation among States, GA Res. 2625 (XXV), 24 October 1970. Consider further James Crawford's view that the notion demonstrates that "a rigid categorization of sources is inappropriate", for "[t]he rubric 'general principles of international law' may alternately refer to rules of customary international law, to general principles of law as in Article 38 (1) *(c)*, or to certain logical propositions underlying judicial reasoning on the basis of existing international law", see Crawford, *Brownlie's Principles of Public International Law*, 37.

150. R Kolb, "General Principles of Procedural Law", in Zimmermann, Tomuschat and Oellers-Frahm, *op. cit.*, p. 963 *et seq.*, p. 963.

expression [151]. At the same time, it is fair to acknowledge that some case law and legal literature – especially in the domain of human rights and international criminal adjudication – suggest that powers such as the ones underpinning the exercise of *jura novit curia* derive implicitly from the constitutive instruments of international adjudicators or are, more generally, inherent in the very adjudicative function or administration of justice.

It is to this latter question, namely, that of the significance of implied or inherent powers as a basis for the exercise of *jura novit curia*, that this study now turns. I will then place the findings emerging from this analysis in the wider context of the considerations made with regard to other possible sources of *jura novit curia*.

4. An implied, or inherent, power

In one of the first cases decided by the PCIJ – the *Mavrommatis* case between Greece and the United Kingdom on certain concessions in Palestine – in 1924, the Court found itself confronted with a procedural issue which was not regulated by either the Statute or the Rules of Court. Namely, it had to address an objection to the Court's jurisdiction raised *in limine litis*. The Court found that

> "[I]t is entitled to adopt the principle which it considers best calculated to ensure the administration of justice, most suited to procedure before an international tribunal and most in conformity with the *fundamental principles of international law.*" [152]

Almost fifty years later, in its 1973 Judgment in the *Fisheries Jurisdiction* case between the United Kingdom and Iceland referred to above, the ICJ seemed to rely on its inherent powers precisely in order to ground *jura novit curia* powers, thus embracing the position set out by the United Kingdom, which we mentioned above [153]. As the Court put it,

> "The Court . . ., *as an international judicial organ*, is deemed to take judicial notice of international law, and is therefore required *in a case falling under Article 53 of the Statute, as in any other*

151. See Crawford, *Brownlie's Principles of Public International Law*, 37.
152. PCIJ, *Mavrommatis Palestine Concessions (Greece* v. *United Kingdom)*, PCIJ Series B No. 3, 30 August 1924, p. 16. See also J. Cazala, "Good Administration of Justice", *Max Planck Encyclopedia of International Procedural Law*, Oxford University Press, 2020, *Max Planck Encyclopedia of International Procedural Law*, 2020.
153. *Supra* text at footnotes 52 and 53.

> *case*, to consider on its own initiative all rules of international law which may be relevant to the settlement of the dispute. It being the duty of the Court itself to ascertain and apply the relevant law in the given circumstances of the case, the burden of establishing or proving rules of international law cannot be imposed upon any of the parties, for the law lies within the judicial knowledge of the Court." [154]

The following year, in the *Nuclear Tests* case, the Court elaborated on its powers to assert its jurisdictional competence, which, as it will be illustrated in the next chapter, is akin to *jura novit curia*. It stated that:

> "Such inherent jurisdiction . . . derives from the mere existence of the Court as a judicial organ established by the consent of states, and is conferred upon it in order that its basic judicial functions may be safeguarded." [155]

The same rationale plainly applies to investment arbitration. In its award on jurisdiction in 2008, the *Libananco* Tribunal observed that "[it does not] doubt for a moment that, like any other international tribunal, it must be regarded as endowed with the inherent powers required to preserve the integrity of its own process" [156].

No minor reliance on the inherent, or implicit, powers doctrine is to be found in international human rights and criminal adjudication. Jurisprudential *dicta* confirming the point abound [157].

---

154. *Fisheries Jurisdiction (United Kingdom* v. *Iceland)*, Jurisdiction, Judgment, *ICJ Reports 1973*, p. 3, p. 9, para. 17.

155. *Nuclear Tests (New Zealand* v. *France)*, Judgment, *ICJ Reports 1974*, p. 457, p. 463, para. 23.

156. *Libananco Holdings Co. Ltd.* v. *Turkey*, ICSID Case No. ARB/06/8, Decision on Preliminary Issues (23 June 2008) para. 78. The wording appears indebted to Judge Higgins' Separate Opinion in *Legality of Use of Force (Serbia and Montenegro* v. *Belgium*), Preliminary Objections, Judgment, *ICJ Reports 2004*, p. 279, at 339, para. 12; "Thus the real question is not whether the Applicant has or has not 'discontinued' the case, nor whether the present circumstances are exactly identical to the few examples where the Court itself has removed a case from the List (examples which will, in their turn, have been 'new' at the relevant time and not falling into any previously established category). The question is whether the circumstances are such that it is reasonable, necessary and appropriate for the Court to strike the case off the List as an exercise of inherent power to protect the integrity of the judicial process".

157. E.g. in the human rights context European Court of Human Rights, *Case of Guzzardi* v. *Italy*, Application No. 7367/76, Judgment, 6 November 1980, para. 62; as to the international criminal adjudication context, see, *inter alia*, International Criminal Tribunal for Yugoslavia, *Prosecutor* v. *T. Blaskić*, Decision on the Objection of the Republic of Croatia to the Issuance of *Subpoenae Duces Tecum*, 18 July 1997, paras. 24-41. For further examples, see, respectively, Dinah Shelton, "Form, Function, and the Powers of International Courts", in *Chicago Journal of International Law*,

One may gather the impression that the "inherent powers" doctrine is a silver bullet that provides legal justification to exercise all kinds of powers that an adjudicative body may find necessary to exercise its functions. However, two considerations may stand in the way of this view. First, when this doctrine is invoked by international adjudicative bodies, they often look for additional grounds that may further justify the inherent or implied character of a particular power in any given case. Second, the "inherent powers" doctrine is seldom relied upon generally, but rather with reference to a specific adjudicative power, usually of a strictly procedural nature, i.e. relating to the conduct of proceedings, thus falling short of *jura novit curia* power, which rather pertains to the core of the adjudicative decision-making process. For our purposes, the two considerations at hand, if confirmed, would bring us back to the point of having to prove whether there is a specific source of international law that contemplates *jura novit curia* as an inherent judicial power.

As to the first consideration, it is telling that Paola Gaeta, when referring to the inherent powers of international courts and tribunals, would lament that "[t]he possible source of these powers has not always been spelt out" [158]. In a similar vein, Chester Brown has expressed his objection to the self-standing character of the inherent powers doctrine in international adjudication in most logical terms, as follows:

> "[I]t is a circular argument to maintain that courts and tribunals can exercise certain powers, simply because such powers are the type of powers that 'courts' or 'tribunals' usually have." [159]

After some thorough comparative analysis of the case law of different international courts and tribunals, Brown came down to the following generous, cautious and far from clear-cut conclusion:

> "[A] significant body of practice . . . demonstrates that international courts are not restricted to exercising the procedural

Vol. 9 (2009), p. 537 et *seq.*; Gaeta, *op. cit.*; and J. Liang, "The Inherent Jurisdiction and Inherent Powers of International Criminal Courts and Tribunals: An Appraisal of Their Application", in *New Criminal Law Review*, Vol. 15 (2012), p. 375 *et seq*.

158. P. Gaeta, "Inherent Powers of International Courts and Tribunals", in L. C. Vohrah *et al.* (eds.), *Man's Inhumanity to Man: Essays on International Law in Honour of Antonio Cassese*, The Hague, Kluwer Law International, 2003, p. 353 *et seq*., p. 358.

159. C. Brown, "Inherent Powers in International Adjudication", in C. P. R. Romano, K. J. Alter and Y. Shany, *The Oxford Handbook of International Adjudication*, Oxford, Oxford University Press, 2013, p. 829 *et seq*., p. 841.

> powers which are conferred by their constitutive instruments [– whether express or implied –] but can also exercise inherent powers, *so long as applicable restrictions on their use are respected.*" [160]

For our purposes, as we shall see, such restrictions may derive precisely from the contents and scope of the very principle, or rule, of *jura novit curia*, as shaped in combination with the ancillary principle *ne ultra petita*, and the right of the parties to be heard.

I will now address the second consideration, whereby the inherent power doctrine applies to strictly procedural issues, i.e. to the conduct of proceedings, but not to the deliberation process. Again, Professor Brown observes that his support for the inherent power doctrine is conditional on the understanding that "the exercise of such powers usually relates *to procedural issues*, rather than the *endgame of international proceedings*" [161]. Now, the exercise of *jura novit curia* definitely pertains to the core of the deliberative process, which represents precisely the *endgame of international proceedings*.

In his study on inherent powers in ICSID arbitration, conceived as modelled on inter-State adjudication, Martins Paparinskis concluded that "the general trend – and rightly so – is in favour of broader inherent powers" [162]. However, in the same vein as Chester Brown, the reach of Paparinskis' conclusion was confined to clearly specific powers, which may only marginally involve the exercise of *jura novit curia*, i.e.

> "the power to grant binding provisional measures, power to deal with abuse of process, power to accept submissions of non-parties, power to deal with evidence, power to order remedies and powers at the annulment stage" [163].

In fact, very seldom has inter-State or investor-State case law relied on the inherent powers doctrine to justify the exercise of *jura novit curia* [164]. In this regard, the idea that the "inherent powers" doctrine does not regulate *jura novit curia* is subject to three crucial qualifications.

---

160. *Ibidem*, p. 846.

161. *Ibidem*, p. 846 (emphasis added).

162. M. Paparinskis, "Inherent Powers of ICSID Tribunals: Broad and Rightly So", in T. J. Weiler and I. A. Laird, *Investment Treaty Arbitration and International Law*, Vol. 5, Huntington, JurisNet, 2012, p. 11 *et seq.*, p. 42.

163. *Ibidem.*

164. E.g. in *Application of the Convention of 1902 Governing the Guardianship of Infants,* the Court implicitly referred to *jura novit curia* in expressing that it "retain[ed] its freedom to select the ground upon which it will base its judgment" without reference to any rule of the Statute (*Case Concerning the Application of the Convention of

First and more generally, *jura novit curia* appears to be inherent in the adjudicative function insofar as adjudication consists of deciding a dispute, on its merit, by applying the applicable substantive law, irrespective of the arguments advanced by the parties. That said, however, one cannot possibly find normative indications about the contents and boundaries of *jura novit curia* by resorting to the "inherent powers doctrine".

Second, even before addressing the merits of the case, the very jurisdictional competence of any given court or tribunal may be challenged. Here, the adjudicator's power and duty to decide over its jurisdiction and the admissibility of the claims – so-called *compétence de la compétence*, or *Kompetenz-Kompetenz*, which will be addressed more in depth in relation to *jura novit curia* in Chapter III – is generally exercised irrespective of the arguments put forward by the parties, and it is equally generally considered to be inherent in the adjudicative function [165]. That is so to the extent that such adjudicative prerogative may be exercised by the tribunal *ex officio*, or *sua sponte*, i.e. even where the parties do not raise preliminary objections.

The power in question is usually expressly laid down in the governing instruments of adjudicative bodies, but in very general terms. Precisely due to the little normative guidance provided by such instruments on the boundaries of the power under consideration, international adjudicators have frequently relied, more or less overtly, on the inherent powers doctrine when handling problematic jurisdictional issues and have benefited from the ample degree of flexibility flowing from the unwritten nature of the doctrine. An example of this may be seen in the *Nottebhom* case, which will be discussed in the next chapter in relation to the relationship between *jura novit curia* and the *Kompetenz-Kompetenz* principle [166].

The third qualification pertains to human rightscourts, Dispute Settlement in the World Trade Organization, as well as to international criminal tribunals and the ICC. Here, the "inherent powers" doctrine operates through the "implied powers" modulation, that is, through the powers that stem implicitly from the mandate of these bodies enshrined in their specific constituent instruments.

1902 Governing the Guardianship of Infants (Netherlands v. *Sweden)*, Judgment of 28 November 1958, *ICJ Reports 1958*, p. 55, p. 62).

165. In this sense, see *Legality of Use of Force (Serbia and Montenegro* v. *Belgium)*, Preliminary Objections, Judgment, *ICJ Reports 2004*, p. 279, p. 295, para. 36.

166. See *infra* Chapter III, Section A.

As observed by the Iran-US Tribunal in its *Decision Ruling on Request for Revision by Iran of 1 July 2011*:

> "[I]n order to determine which powers international courts and tribunals may exercise as inherent powers one must take into account the particular features of each specific court or tribunal, including the circumstances surrounding its establishment, the object and purpose of its constitutive instrument, and the consent of the parties as expressed in that and related instruments." [167]

As already alluded to in the first chapter, in traditional bilateral inter-State adjudication and investor-State arbitration, as presently shaped, the constituent instruments of adjudicative bodies, including arbitration agreements, reflect the consensual nature of the jurisdictional competence and determination of the applicable law [168]. For example, while Article 38 (1) of the ICJ Statute provides generally for the sources of the applicable law, the substantive law applicable to any given dispute depends on the choice of the parties. The ensuing decoupling between the constituent instrument and the applicable law chosen by the parties reduces the potential of the inherent powers doctrine, especially in connection with the implicit powers doctrine [169].

The WTO system offers a hybrid model between a self-contained body of international law characterised by constitutional features and one whose adjudicative system is based on the autonomy of the parties [170]. This flows from the dual "private" and "public" nature of the WTO Dispute Settlement System [171]. Such System, as expressed by the Dispute Settlement Understanding (DSU), at Article 3 (2), not only

167. IUSCT, *Decision Ruling on Request for Revision by Iran of 1 July 2011*, Decision No. DEC 134-A3/A8/A9/A14/B61-FT, para. 61.

168. See *supra* Chapter I, *passim*.

169. A different approach may seem to be found under UNCLOS, which provides for a residually compulsory adjudicative system at Article 287 (5) (see, among others, A. Proelss, *The United Nations Convention on the Law of the Sea*, Oxford-Baden-Baden, Hart-Nomos, 2017, p. 1849 *et seq.*). Article 293 UNCLOS itself constitutes the primary applicable law and Article 309 rules out reservations and exceptions to the Convention. However, the optional exceptions *ratione materiae* allowed under Article 298 to the compulsory adjudicative dispute settlement, and the limitations thereto under Article 297 (2) and (3), introduce a significant degree of consensualism into the UNCLOS system. See Proelss, *op. cit.*, p. 1907 *et seq.*

170. For an overview of the WTO DSB practice concerning inherent powers, see F. Weiss, "Inherent Powers of National and International Courts", in F. Ortino and E. U. Petersmann (eds.), *The WTO Dispute Settlement System*, 1995-2003, The Hague, Kluwer Law International, 2004.

171. On the "enforcement" nature of the WTO Dispute Settlement System, see K. J. Alter, "The Multiple Roles of International Courts and Tribunals: Enforcement, Dispute Settlement, Constitutional and Administrative Review", in J. L. Dunoff

"serves to preserve the rights and obligations of Members under the covered agreements [but also] to clarify the existing provisions of those agreements in accordance with customary rules of interpretation of public international law".

Such hybridity explains the generous and general references to inherent powers by the WTO dispute settlement bodies [172]. Having specific regard to *jura novit curia*, the WTO case law seems to partake of the common ground in international adjudication to the effect that the principle in question is encompassed by the inherent powers of an adjudicative body to assess *ex officio* its jurisdictional competence in any given case [173].

As to international human rights and criminal courts and tribunals, their mandates are characterised by the highly public order-oriented applicable law [174]. This explains how they fulfil their judicial function as guardians of their constituent instruments, next to assessing whether remedies are due to the applicant, or determining the criminal responsibility, or innocence, of the accused. And this accounts for the special reliance by the adjudicative bodies in question on the inherent powers doctrine, often in conjunction with treaty interpretations of the instrument from which implicit powers are derived [175].

To mention but one example, the Preamble of the ECHR (para. 5) refers to the "common heritage" of the contracting parties, including values such as "freedom and the rule of law", as well as to their "resolve"

---

and M. A. Pollack (eds.), *Interdisciplinary Perspectives on International Law and International Relations: The State of the Art*, Cambridge University Press, 2013; R. Brewster, "Pricing Compliance: When Formal Remedies Displace Reputational Sanctions", *Harvard International Law Journal*, Vol. 54 (2), 2013, 259–314.

172. E.g. *Mexico - Tax Measures on Soft Drinks and Other Beverages*, Report of the Appellate Body (6 March 2006), para. 45; *Mexico – Anti-Dumping Investigation of High Fructose Corn Syrup (HFCS) from the United States – Recourse to Article 21.5 of the DSU by the United States*, Report of the Appellate Body (22 October 2001), para. 36.

173. On the *ex officio Kompetenz-Kompetenz* power, see, most recently, *Russia – Measures Concerning Traffic in Transit*, Report of the Panel (5 April 2019), para. 7.53: "[t]he Panel recalls that international adjudicative tribunals, including WTO dispute settlement panels, possess inherent jurisdiction which derives from the exercise of their adjudicative function. One aspect of this inherent jurisdiction is the power to determine all matters arising in relation to the exercise of their own substantive jurisdiction". In the footnote at the end of the sentence it is specified that "[t]his is known as the principle of *Kompetenz-Kompetenz* in German, or *compétence de la compétence* in French. The Appellate Body has held that panels have the power to determine the extent of their jurisdiction".

174. See Alter, *op. cit.*; K. Dzehtsiarou, *Can the European Court of Human Rights Shape European Public Order?*, Cambridge University Press, 2021.

175. Gaeta, *op. cit.*, p. 355.

to undertake the "collective enforcement" of civil and political rights. Based on such premise, under Article 19 ECHR, the European Court of Human Rights (ECtHR) was established "[t]o ensure the observance of the engagements undertaken by the High Contracting Parties in the Convention and the Protocols thereto". This is the core mandate of the ECtHR, which appears to be more important than the settlement of disputes, as such.

As to international criminal law, in the *Blaškić* case the ICTY effectively argued that it could draw from some kind of inherent jurisdiction any kind of powers it found necessary for it to fulfil its function [176]. Such principle has been consistently reiterated in following decisions [177].

The public order approach to the judicial function of international criminal law also accounts for the special reliance by international criminal law jurisdictional bodies on the inherent and implicit powers doctrine, with specific regard to *jura novit curia*, and for its extensive application. The point will be further illustrated in due course.

Nonetheless, at the end of a thorough study on the specific application of *jura novit curia* by human rights courts as an inherent power, Professor Dinah Shelton concludes recommending constraints on the application of the principle at hand [178]. Such an attitude may seem to conform to the restrictive approach followed by traditional bilateral inter-State adjudication, but this parallel should not be taken to affect the differences in the application of the governing principles of decision-making by international adjudicators in radically different areas of adjudication, since it pertains to procedural guarantees in the conduct of proceedings having overarching relevance throughout different adjudicative contexts. In fact, professor Shelton refers in particular to the right of the parties to be heard and not to be surprised by the reasoning of adjudicators. As we shall see, such restraints generally apply to symmetric – or private law – adjudication in keeping with the consensual mandate of the parties. The same guarantees turn out to enhance the legitimacy and impartiality of human rights litigation, especially avoiding the perception that reformulation of the claims may alter the right to access to justice and fair trial [179].

---

176. *Prosecutor* v. *T. Blaškić*, *cit.*, paras. 24-41.

177. E.g. *Prosecutor* v. *Tadić*, Judgment, 15 July 1999, para. 322.

178. See D. Shelton, "*Jura Novit Curia* in International Human Rights Tribunals", *supra* n. 18, at p. 190.

179. On the issue of reformulation of claims in human rights litigation, see Shelton, *Jura Novit Curia*, cit.

In sum, on the inherent power doctrine, one may anticipate from the practice and case law the following indications: *a)* the inherent powers doctrine, given its indeterminacy, is often considered to require some further specific legal justification in order to provide the basis for the existence and exercise of a given specific judicial power. Sometimes, such justification is found in the teleological interpretation of the constitutive instrument of the jurisdictional body in question, thereby allowing recourse to the implied powers doctrine [180]; *b)* more prominent reliance on the doctrine in question for purposes of establishing a basis for *jura novit curia* may be found in international human rights and criminal case law, with respect to inter-State adjudication; *c)* and consequently, it may be inappropriate to draw from human rights and criminal adjudication general conclusions with respect to inter-State adjudication, except for disputes arising out of alleged breaches of *erga omnes* obligations [181].

There is a further consideration which may diminish the relevance of the inherent powers doctrine as the legal basis for the application of *jura novit curia*. Namely, that *jura novit curia* is associated to the inherent powers of adjudicators in terms of inherent jurisdiction in relation to the principle *Kompetenz-Kompetenz* [182]. As already alluded to, the latter affords courts and tribunals the power and duty to decide over their jurisdiction and the admissibility of claims *ex officio*, i.e. even if the parties do not raise the issue. As we shall see in due course, on the point at issue *jura novit curia* applies in most extensive terms, to the exclusion of *ne ultra petita*.

No doubt, deciding about its jurisdiction is a key aspect of the adjudicator's function, since such a decision bears on whether the adjudicator in point is going to entertain a case submitted before it, or only parts of it or not at all. In principle, this power operates at a preliminary stage of the proceedings leaving unprejudiced the merits

180. See Brown, *The Inherent Powers* (2006) *cit.*, pp. 225-227; Paparinskis, *op. cit.*, literature quoted at footnotes 11, 13 and 14.

181. Here, one is to assess whether a more extensive interpretation and application of *jura novit curia* emerges from the case law, or whether, in the absence of sufficiently established case law on the point at issue, such an extensive approach is called for.

182. This is traditionally generally recognised as an inherent power in the adjudicative function. In an oft-quoted passage of the British-US Tribunal decision in the *Rio Grande* case on 1923, "there is in this and every legal Tribunal a power, and indeed a duty, to entertain, and in proper cases, to raise for themselves, preliminary points going to the jurisdiction to entertain the claim" (*Rio Grande Irrigation and Land Company, Ltd. (Great Britain)* v. *United States*, Decision of 28 November 1923, *Reports of International Arbitral Awards*, Vol. 6, p. 131 *et seq.*, pp. 135-136). See *infra* Chap III.

phase [183], namely that of the actual decision of the case. Therefore, the scope of the inherent power grounds that justify *jura novit curia* in the jurisdictional phase does not necessarily extend to the merits phase. Thus, the legal basis of *jura novit curia* with respect to the principal phase of adjudicatory proceedings will require separate analysis.

C. A composite unwritten rule of adjudication stemming from multiple sources

Against the background of the analysis carried out so far, one may well conceive that, at the beginning of international adjudication as we know it today, given the scarce development of international procedural law until recently, *jura novit curia* might have found its way into international adjudication through some form of adjudicative constructive ambiguity. It is arguable that the principle in question may have emerged in international adjudication on the basis of the presumption of the existence of a general principle of law recognised *in foro domestico*, even though the conceptions of *jura novit curia* in different domestic legal systems might have had little in common.

183. When preliminary issues of jurisdiction and admissibility are bifurcated, decisions at the end of such incidental proceedings are endowed with *res judicata* value only with regard to the assessment of the preliminary issues in question. Once a decision has been taken in the sense of the entertainment of the jurisdictional competence in any given case, every consideration pertaining to the merits falling within the jurisdictional framework, as curtailed by the adjudicator, will not be considered with the scope of *res judicata*. See *German Interests in Polish Upper Silesia (Germany* v. *Poland)*, PCIJ Series A No. 6, 25 August 1925, p. 15 ("it is, however, to be clearly understood that nothing which the Court says in the present judgement can be regarded as restricting its entire freedom to estimate the value of any arguments advanced by either side on the same subjects during the proceedings on the merits"); *Fisheries Jurisdiction (United Kingdom* v. *Iceland)*, Jurisdiction of the Court, Judgment, *ICJ Reports 1973*, p. 3, p. 7, para. 11 ("In the present phase it concerns the competence of the Court to hear and pronounce upon this dispute. The issue being thus limited, the Court will avoid not only all expressions of opinion on matters of substance, but also any pronouncement which might prejudge or appear to prejudge any eventual decision on the merits"); and *Certain Phosphate Lands in Nauru (Nauru* v. *Australia)*, Preliminary Objections, Judgment, *ICJ Reports 1992*, p. 240, p. 262, para. 56 ("The Court must however emphasize that its ruling in the present Judgment on this objection of Australia does not in any way prejudge the merits. The present Judgment does not settle the question whether reparation would be due from Australia, if found responsible, for the whole or only for part of the damage Nauru alleges it has suffered, regard being had to the characteristics of the Mandate and Trusteeship Systems outlined above and, in particular, the special role played by Australia in the administration of the Territory. These questions are to be dealt with at the merits stage"). See also H. Thirlway, "The Law and Procedure of the International Court of Justice 1960-1989", in *British Yearbook of International Law*, Vol. 71 (2001), p. 38 *et seq*., p. 140.

In reality, such abstract legal concepts, even when little defined, operate in pragmatic terms for very concrete purposes. Namely, they are handled by adjudicators to justify the way they exercise their adjudicative function [184].

It is not difficult to imagine how, at the dawn of modern international adjudication, civil law members of an adjudicative body might have proposed to apply *jura novit curia* in their deliberation process. Such a proposal would probably have been intended differently by other civil lawyers sitting in the same forum, and even more so by their common law colleagues. And we can imagine the forum in question to finally apply the principle in point as the minimum common denominator of the various conceptions espoused by those in the room. Yet, even though in such a light configuration, the principle in point would serve as a useful tool in the exercise the adjudicative function when no explicit and comprehensive regulation of *jura novit curia* is to be found in the relevant statute or rules of procedure, when the legal arguments advanced by both parties would fall short of addressing the dispute appropriately.

Accordingly, *jura novit curia* would emerge in international adjudication through constructive ambiguity as to its source: partly as an implicit power through a teleological interpretation of the constituent instrument; partly, more extensively, as inherent in the adjudicative function; partly, as the common denominator among the judicial practice in various domestic jurisdictions; partly, as a general principle, or rule, of international law. The fact of the matter is that, based on different combinations of these sources, *jura novit curia* has been relied upon in the case law of international courts and tribunals all along.

As already alluded to, the repeated application of *jura novit curia* is inevitably associated to international court judgments and arbitral awards that are usually complied with by the States involved. As observed elsewhere, in the large majority of cases in which the losing party was found to fall short of complying with the decision of an international adjudicative body, the debate – including before international organisations – would not concern the legal reasoning

184. On the adjudicative function, see A. Paulus, "International Adjudication", in S. Besson and J. Tasioulas (eds.), *The Philosophy of International Law*, Oxford, Oxford University Press, 2010, p. 207 *et seq.*; D. Regan, "International Adjudication: A Response to Paulus: Courts, Custom, Treatis, Regimes and the WTO", in *ibid.*, p. 225 *et seq.*

underpinning the decision itself[185]. Rather, it would focus on the political dimension of the dispute submitted to adjudication, as well as on the dispute concerning the non-implementation as separate from the former[186]. Besides, when problems of compliance with international judicial decisions have been raised, hardly ever have they been based on alleged excesses of powers because of exercises of *jura novit curia*.

Despite the lack of the *stare decisis* rule in international law, it has been shown how international case law is referred to also by third States in different diplomatic and litigation contexts. This corroborates the argument of the existence of a customary rule of adjudication, largely developed by international courts and tribunals and acknowledged by States. Its general character accounts for the fact that it is frequently expressed through the label "general principle of international law", or "general principle of international adjudication".

The composite approach proposed above conforms to the language of Article 38(1)(d), whereby the Court, and international adjudicative bodies in general, "shall apply . . . judicial decisions . . . as subsidiary means for the determination of rules of law". And, as we have seen, it is also corroborated by Article 21 (2) ICC Statute, according to which "[t]he Court *may* apply principles and rules of law as interpreted in its previous decisions". The term "may" excludes that a judicial law-making function would be exercised through the rule of precedent, but does vest the Court with the discretionary power to rely on its precedents[187]. This attitude is one which is generally followed by international adjudicative bodies at large, together with the widespread expectation by States of jurisprudential consistency.

This suggests that expressions of *jura novit curia* may be found in the international case law, also in combination with the relevant statutes and rules of procedure, where available. Indeed, as finely put by Vaughan Lowe,

> "Cases make law. However one might finesse the technically nonbinding, non-precedential force of judgments and awards in international law, the principles that are laid down, refined and

---

185. A. Tanzi, "Problems of Enforcement of Decisions of the International Court of Justice and the Law of the United Nations", in *European Journal of International Law*, Vol. 6 (1993), p. 539 *et seq*., p. 543.

186. *Ibidem*.

187. Lauterpacht, *The Development of International Law by the International Court*, 22; Lauterpacht, *op. cit.*, 127; see also Ridi, *op. cit.*

> applied in particular cases are a part of the architecture of the legal system." [188]

This statement may well be deemed to apply also to the making of the rules governing the conduct of international courts and tribunals. In fact, adjudication is a key pillar of said "architecture of the legal system". Already in the early 1960s, the late Judge Sir Hersch Lauterpacht observed that "the practice of referring to its previous decisions has become one of the most conspicuous features of the Judgments and Opinions of the Court" [189].

Cross-fertilisation between different adjudicative bodies only enhances the point at issue. As stressed by Terris, Romano and Swigart in their book "The International Judge",

> "When neither the constituent instruments nor the rules of procedure nor practice directions address a particular procedural matter, it is only natural for international judges, as well as the parties, to refer to the practice of other international courts to find inspiration to resolve the question." [190]

Recently, Professor Forteau observed:

> "[I]t is not entirely clear whether or not the principles that are referred to as part of the rules applicable to an international body are general principles of law as such. They rather constitute general principles that are framed by the international body itself, on the basis of other rules and principles, or even mere standards or best practices . . . In that kind of situation, the legal basis of the principle results from the decision of the relevant body, bearing in mind that its power to decide on the rules of procedure may be qualified by a number of rules and principles." [191]

These considerations refer to procedural rules governing international institutional bodies in general. And they appear to apply all the more to the principles governing adjudicative bodies and especially *jura novit curia*.

---

188. V. Lowe, "The Function of Litigation in International Society", in *International and Comparative Law Quarterly*, Vol. 61 (2012), p. 209 *et seq*., p. 215.

189. Lauterpacht, *The Development of International Law by the International Court*, 9.

190. Terris, Romano, Swigart, *op. cit*., p. 110.

191. Forteau, *op. cit*., para. 7.

D. Concluding remarks

Pulling the threads of the analysis carried out so far in the present chapter in the search for the legal source of the principle in question in international adjudication, one may conclude that the regulation of *jura novit curia* is to be looked for in an unwritten rule, or principle, which stems from multiple sources referenced throughout the foregoing sections, and that such rule, or principle, applies in different forms to each of the three litigation areas under consideration. In that sense, one can speak of a rule which represents the "common terminus" within which different normative elements stemming from different sources flow [192].

According to this view, *jura novit curia* would be a customary rule of adjudication, which represents the normative confluence of a combination of different streams: i.e., international unilateral, bilateral and multilateral diplomatic practice; international conventional practice; domestic judicial practice; as well as international case law.

In sum, it appears that the contents and scope of *jura novit curia* in international adjudication are best looked for in a combination of legal sources which are, at one and the same time, catalysed, promoted and applied by international courts and tribunals.

One would conclude by showing how the view of the composite or multiple sources of *jura novit curia* flowing into a common terminus is epitomised by the reasoning of the ICJ in the *Nottebohm* case between

192. As observed by Elihu Lauterpacht, "[p]rinciples of international procedural law can be found in international conventions (such as the statutes, rules of procedure, and other constitutive instruments of international courts and tribunals); *rules developed in the customary practice of international tribunals*; general principles of law; and, as a subsidiary means for the determination of procedural rules, *judicial decisions and the writings of high qualified publicists*" (E. Lauterpacht, "Principles of Procedure in International Litigation", (2010) 345 *RCADI* 387, 405-406 (emphasis added)). One may note the double relevance of the contribution by international adjudication to the formation and identification of international unwritten law in international procedural law. Such "multi-source" origin is not a specific feature of *jura novit curia*. Most international rules are the common terminus of different source. Just to make one example, the rule on freedom of navigation is at the same time a rule of customary law and a rule codified at Article 87 UNCLOS. For further consideration on the point at issue, see J. R. Crawford (ed.), *Brownlie's Principles of Public International Law*, Oxford, Oxford University Press, 2012 (8th ed.), p. 37; T. Treves, "The Expansion of International Law", *Recueil des cours*, Vol. 398 (2019), p. 9 *et seq*., p. 178. On multiplicity of sources for the same norms, see T. Broude and Y. Shany, *Multi-sourced Equivalent Norms in International Law*, Hart Publishing, 2011.

Lichtenstein and Guatemala on *jura novit curia* and the *Kompetenz-Kompetenz* principle [193]. It reads as follows:

> "Since the *Alabama* case, it has been generally recognized, following the earlier precedents, that, in the absence of any agreement to the contrary, an international tribunal has the right to decide as to its own jurisdiction and has the power to interpret for this purpose the instruments which govern that jurisdiction. This principle was expressly recognized in Articles 48 and 73 of The Hague Conventions of 29 July 1899, and 18 October 1907, for the Pacific Settlement of International Disputes, to which Guatemala became a Party. The Rapporteur of the Convention of 1899 had emphasized the necessity of this principle, presented by him as being 'of the very essence of the arbitral function and one of the inherent requirements for the exercise of this function'. This principle has been frequently applied and at times expressly stated." [194]

Interestingly, the Court concluded by adding reference to a rule of customary law – the formation and contents of which it did not examine – after acknowledging that Article 36 (6) of its Statute expressly provides the power for it to decide on its jurisdiction. Yet, most interestingly for our purposes, it felt the need to stress that

> "*even if this were not the case*, the Court . . . should follow in this connection what is laid down by *general international law*. The judicial character of the Court and the rule of 'general international law' referred to above are sufficient to establish that the Court is competent to adjudicate on its own jurisdiction in the present case" [195].

This *dictum* ushers us to the next chapter, largely devoted to *jura novit curia* and decisions on jurisdiction.

---

193. On the boundaries of *Kompetenz-Kompetenz*, see C. McLachlan, "*Lis Pendens* in International Litigation (Vol. 336)", (2009), 454-455.

194. *Nottebohm case (Preliminary Objections)*, Judgment of 18 November 1953, *ICJ Reports 1953*, p. 111, p. 119.

195. *Ibidem*, p. 120.

CHAPTER III

JURA NOVIT CURIA AND THE ASSESSEMENT OF JURISDICTION OF INTERNATIONAL COURTS AND TRIBUNALS

A. Introductory remarks

The previous chapter's concluding quote from the ICJ Judgment in the *Nottebohm* Case brings us to address *jura novit curia* in relation to the jurisdictional phase of proceedings. Here, the Court ascertains its jurisdictional competence – and possibly the admissibility of the claim – in any given case submitted to it [196].

Jurisdictional issues may be – though need not be – addressed in a procedural phase separate from the merits, the so-called incidental proceedings on preliminary objections, usually when such objections are raised by the defendant. Such issues are crucial to the resolution of a case [197]: first, because they determine whether the case is going

196. On the distinction, *vel non*, between jurisdiction and admissibility with special regard to investment arbitration, see A. Tanzi and F. Fontanelli, "Jurisdiction and Admissibility in Investment Arbitration: A View from the Bridge at the Practice", *The Law and Practice of International Courts and Tribunals*, Vol. 16 (2017), p. 3 *et seq.* See also D. A. R. Williams, "Jurisdiction and Admissibility", in P. Muchlinski and F. Ortino, C. Schreuer (eds.), *The Oxford Handbook of International Investment Law*, Oxford University Press, 2008, p. 0; J. Paulsson, "Jurisdiction and Admissibility", *Global Reflections on International Law, Commerce and Dispute Resolution*, 2010, 601; Y. Shany, "Jurisdiction and Admissibility", 2013; M. Waibel, "International Arbitration: Jurisdiction and Admissibility", *University of Cambridge Faculty of Law Research Paper*, (9), 2014; J. McIntyre, "Put on Notice: The Role of the Dispute Requirement in Assessing Jurisdiction and Admissibility Before the International Court", *Melbourne Journal of International Law*, Vol. 19 (2), 2018, 546-585. It is important to note that it is possible for an adjudicator to assess its competence at a later stage: notably, before the World Court, the matter can be the object of a plea in bar which, although it may not reopen matters decided with force of *res judicata* by judgments rendered in the proceedings, may arise at any time after, and even after the Court's deliberations. See S. Rosenne and M. N. Shaw, *Rosenne's Law and Practice of the International Court, 1920-2015*, Brill Nijhoff, 2016, Vol. II, para. 229. For examples of such occurrences, see *Interpretation of the Statute of the Memel Territory*, PCIJ Series A/B 47 and 49; *Nottebohm, ICJ Reports 1955*, p. 4, at 26.

197. Naturally, even deciding *which* issues are indeed crucial for the resolution of a case may be difficult. Here, questions of decisional economy may be controlling, though it is important to heed Judge Gaja's admonition concerning the risk of incurring "false" judicial economy. See *Obligations Concerning Negotiations Relating to Cessation of the Nuclear Arms Race and to Nuclear Disarmament (Marshall Islands* v. *United Kingdom)*, Preliminary Objections, Judgment, *ICJ Reports 2016*, p. 833, Declaration of Judge Gaja, p. 1038, citing *Certain Norwegian Loans (France* v. *Norway)*, Judgment, *ICJ Reports 1957*, p. 9, Separate Opinion of Judge Lauterpacht, at 30-31, 36.

to be decided on its merit, or not; second, because where the previous question is answered in the affirmative, the adjudicatory body concerned may decide whether its jurisdiction extends to the entirety of the claim or claims submitted to it, or only to parts or some of them.

Jura novit curia is relevant to jurisdictional issues for two reasons. First, to determine whether the adjudicator has the power to assess its jurisdictional competence over the dispute, irrespective of the arguments of the parties [198]. According to the circumstances of the case, that power coincides with a duty. That is obviously the case when jurisdiction, or admissibility, are disputed by a party, usually the respondent. To that end, Article 36 (6) of the ICJ Statute provides that "[i]n the event of a dispute as to whether the Court has jurisdiction, the matter shall be settled by the decision of the Court" [199].

As discussed in the previous chapter, this provision enunciates the adjudicative power in question, whereby any court or tribunal is the master of its own competence, but falls short of determining its scope and regulating its contents. The omission was glaring enough that the ICJ in *Nottebhom* resorted to some kind of inherent power and a customary rule to that effect [200].

For the purposes of *jura novit curia*, the unregulated issue is whether the *Kompetenz-Kompetenz* power – and duty – in question applies when neither of the parties have raised a jurisdictional defence [201]. That is usually the case when the respondent does not appear. As we shall see shortly, the case law appears to answer this question in the affirmative. As we say in lawyerly Latin, the judge, or arbitrator, is supposed to act *ex officio*, *sua sponte*, or *proprio motu*. By doing so, the adjudicator

198. The connection between *jura novit curia* and non-appearance has already been made in the previous chapter.

199. Provisions to the same effect may be found at Article 288 (4) of the United Nations Convention on the Law of the Sea, Article 49 of the European Convention on Human Rights; Article 62 (3) of the Inter-American Convention on Human Rights; and Article 41 of the ICSID Convention.

200. See Chapter II, Sec. C.

201. The literature on this principle is ample. Suffice here to recall the seminal works by G. Fitzmaurice, *The Law and Procedure of the International Court of Justice*, Vol. 2, Cambridge, Grotius, pp. 530 and 755-758; M. N. Shaw, *Rosenne's Law and Practice of the International Court: 1920-2015*, online edition, Vol. 2, para. 215; H. Thirlway, *The Law and Procedure of the International Court of Justice: Fifty Years of Jurisprudence*, Vol. I, Oxford, Oxford University Press, 2013, pp. 822-823; H. Thirlway, *The Law and Procedure of the International Court of Justice: Fifty Years of Jurisprudence*, Vol. II, Oxford, Oxford University Press, 2013, pp. 1680-1611 and pp. 1716-1718.

would obviously be applying the law independently from the legal arguments invoked by the parties [202].

The second issue is whether *jura novit curia* only enables the adjudicator to curtail the confines of the dispute submitted to it or whether this power extends to the characterisation of the facts before it in terms other than those argued by the parties. This is a key issue with significant implications for the scope of the merits phase and the exercise of the jurisdictional competence in it. In this sense, it may even be argued that adjudication on jurisdiction and merits become a continuum without a definite dividing line.

In other words, the blurred character of the relationship between the jurisdictional and the merits phases does not so much lie in the fact that frequently jurisdictional issues cannot be settled separately from those of the merits; it also lies in the fact that the adjudicator's power to curtail the boundaries of the dispute on the basis of the autonomous interpretation of its mandate determines the confines within which it is going to apply the applicable law in its decision to the merits [203]. For reasons that will emerge shortly, the latter aspect will prove more easily apparent in the context of human rights and international criminal adjudication.

---

202. This may be seen as an application of the principle concerning the freedom to select the grounds on which the decision is based. See *Case Concerning the Application of the Convention of 192 Governing the Guardianship of Infants (Netherlands* v. *Sweden)*, Judgment, *ICJ Reports 1958*, p. 55. See also A. Orakhelashvili, "The International Court and 'Its Freedom to Select the Ground Upon Which It Will Base Its Judgment'", *International & Comparative Law Quarterly*, Vol. 56 (1), 2007, 171-184.

203. While the issue of the distinction between interpretation and application will be addressed in Chapter IV, some considerations are to be made here with regard to the debate over the distinction, or not, between jurisdiction and applicable law. On the one hand, the ILC has argued that "although a tribunal may only have jurisdiction in regard to a particular instrument, it must always interpret and apply that instrument in its relationship to its normative environment – that is to say 'other' international law" (International Law Commission, "Fragmentation of International Law: Difficulties Arising from the Diversification and Expansion of International Law, Report of the Study Group of the International Law Commission" UN Doc. A/CN.4/L.682, para. 423). On the other hand, the case law shows a restrictive approach according to which "it is not the proper role of [Art. 31 (3) *(c)*] to rewrite the treaty being interpreted" (*Vattenfall AB* et al. v. *Federal Republic of Germany*, ICSID Case No. ARB/12/12, Decision on the Achmea Issue, 31 August 2018, para. 154). Thus, a rule not enshrined in a convention would fall within the scope of the jurisdiction of a tribunal litigating such convention only if it poses "an incidental question that necessarily presents itself in the application of [that convention]" (*The "Enrica Lexie" Incident (Italy* v. *India)*, PCA Case 2015-28, Award, 21 May 2020, para. 811).

B. The adjudicator's power to assess its jurisdictional competence and jura novit curia

In the following sections, two key questions will be addressed. The first concerns the adjudicator's power to assess its jurisdictional competence, with special regard to *jura novit curia* powers. The second concerns the more complex issue of the existence and scope of the power of re-characterisation of the dispute submitted by the parties, thus defining the dispute falling within the adjudicator's jurisdictional competence [204].

As repeatedly recalled, based on a customary rule of adjudication – developed in the composite terms described in Chapter II – *Kompetenz-Kompetenz* affords international adjudicators the power and the duty to decide over their jurisdiction *ex officio*, i.e. even if the respondent does not raise objections. And this power is expressly provided under Article 53 ICJ Statute, relating to cases of non-appearance by the respondent. As we have seen, in the *Fisheries* case between Iceland and the United Kingdom, the Court expanded on the provision to describe the power as one of a general nature, that is to say, one that can be exercised even if it is not expressly provided for by the Statute, even beyond proceedings *in absentia*. Sir Gearld Fitzmaurice, in *The Law and Procedure of the International Court of Justice*, drew the following implication from the Court's *dictum* in that case:

> "Since the tribunal is bound to satisfy itself that it has jurisdiction in the case – this is clearly implied by Article 53 of the [Statute] – it follows inevitably that it can take jurisdictional objections, even though neither of the parties have done so." [205]

The conclusion flows from the consideration that "[t]he existence of jurisdiction of the Court in a given case is however not a question of fact, but a question of law to be resolved in the light of the relevant facts" [206]. Thus, on the one hand, issues of burden of proof do not apply

204. For an example of the exercise of powers of characterisation of a dispute by an adjudicator, see again *The "Enrica Lexie" Incident (Italy* v. *India)*, PCA Case 2015-28, Award, 21 May 2020, para. 231 *et seq*.

205. Fitzmaurice, *op. cit.*, p. 530.

206. *Border and Transborder Armed Actions (Nicaragua* v. *Honduras)*, Jurisdiction and Admissibility, Judgment, *ICJ Reports 1988*, p. 69, p. 76, para. 16.

to the jurisdiction of an adjudicative body [207]; on the other hand, a court or tribunal is entitled to consider jurisdictional issues *proprio motu* [208].

Such a conclusion implies affording *jura novit curia* a wide scope of application, as it is for the adjudicator to look at the law about the requirements for the exercise of its jurisdiction and apply them under the facts before it, irrespective of the parties arguing the point. Conversely, the applicability of the *ne ultra petita* principle would be excluded in this stage of proceedings: here, the task of an adjudicator would be that of deciding an issue which is not the object of a claim lodged by a party.

This observation warrants a further qualification. There is obviously no independent power, and no room for *jura novit curia*, for international adjudicators when the controversial nature of their jurisdiction revolves around the actual consent of the parties to jurisdiction. Furthermore, if no objection is raised by the parties – more precisely, by the respondent – the possible original lack of consent to jurisdiction could be cured by the participation of both parties in the proceedings. Under such circumstances, as observed by Professor Tomuschat, "there is no ground for the Court to step in as 'guardian' of the respondent" [209]. In procedural law jargon we speak of *forum prorogatum* [210]. That is meant to express the phenomenon by which the respondent's participation in

---

207. *Fisheries Jurisdiction (Spain* v. *Canada)*, Jurisdiction of the Court, Judgment, *ICJ Reports 1998*, p. 432, para. 38 ("there is no burden of proof to be discharged in the matter of jurisdiction. Rather, it is for the Court to determine from all the facts and taking into account all the arguments advanced by the Parties"); *contra*, *Obligations Concerning Negotiations Relating to Cessation of the Nuclear Arms Race and to Nuclear Disarmament (Marshall Islands* v. *Pakistan)*, Jurisdiction and Admissibility, Judgment, ICJ Reports 2016, p. 552, para. 41 ("[w]hile it is a legal matter for the Court to determine whether it has jurisdiction, it remains for the Applicant to demonstrate the facts underlying its case that a dispute exists"). On the matter in point, see H. Thirlway, *The Law and Procedure* (Vol. I), *cit*., pp. 700-702.

208. Appeal Relating to the Jurisdiction of the ICAO Council, Judgment, *ICJ Reports 1972*, p. 46, p. 52, para. 13 ("[i]t is certainly to be desired that objections to the jurisdiction of the Court should be put forward as preliminary objections for separate decision in advance of the proceedings on the merits. The Court must however always be satisfied that it has jurisdiction, and must if necessary go into that matter *proprio motu*"). See also Shaw, *op. cit*., para. 233.

209. C. Tomuschat, "Article 36", in A. Zimmermann, C. Tomuschat and K. Oellers-Frahm (eds.), *The Statute of the International Court of Justice: A Commentary*, Oxford, Oxford University Press, 2019 (3rd ed.), p. 712 *et seq*., p. 736.

210. On the principle in point, see in general H. Burmester, "The Basis of the Court's Jurisdiction and the Scope and Usefulness of *Forum Prorogatum*", in K. Bannelier, T. Christakis and S. Heathcote (eds.), *The ICJ and the Evolution of International Law: The Enduring Impact of the "Corfu Channel" Case*, London, Routledge, 2012, p. 87 *et seq*.; Shaw, *op. cit*., paras. 182-189; Thirlway, *The Law and Procedure* (Vol. I), *cit*., pp. 710-712.

the proceedings for reasons other than challenging the adjudicator's jurisdiction – due to vitiated consent to jurisdiction, or to a lack thereof by either party – acts as a form of acquiescence by the respondent. By participating in the proceedings, the respondent is deemed to have forgone the right to validly contest the jurisdiction of the tribunal in question at a later stage. Here, there is absolutely no room for the tribunal to reject its jurisdiction for lack of consent. The issue is expressly governed by Article 38 (5) of the ICJ Rules [211].

The tribunal's *sua sponte* exercise of the power to ascertain its own jurisdiction would therefore appear a rather academic hypothesis, given the increasingly proactive approach adopted by counsel – let alone of the legions of top-notch lawyers typically instructed by sovereign parties. In reality, it is an unlikely prospect that a defendant State, whenever it may see the opportunity to assert a jurisdictional defence, should not take advantage of it.

In empirical terms, it would accordingly seem fair to say that the *ex officio* ascertainment of an international tribunal's own jurisdiction – thus the application of *jura novit curia* to this phase of the proceedings – is confined to those cases where the defendant remains absent.

We shall revert to this point shortly. It bears briefly noting that the case law offers few, but egregious, examples where the defendant has appeared without raising preliminary objections. There, the Court has nonetheless ascertained, *sua sponte*, whether it was jurisdictionally entitled to entertain the merits of the dispute before it. Thus, there remains scope for the *proprio motu* exercise of the *Kompetenz-Kompetenz* power – in combination with *jura novit curia* – where doubts as to the existence of jurisdiction *ratione temporis* and *ratione materiae*

---

211. The provision reads: "When the applicant State proposes to found the jurisdiction of the Court upon a consent thereto yet to be given or manifested by the State against which such application is made, the application shall be transmitted to that State. It shall not however be entered in the General List, nor any action be taken in the proceedings, unless and until the State against which such application is made consents to the Court's jurisdiction for the purposes of the case". For some difficulties concerning the application of the principle of *forum prorogatum* to interpretation proceedings, see *Treaty of Neuilly (Interpretation of Judgment No. 3),* PCIJ Series A, No. 4, at 6 (basing its jurisdiction on the observation that the respondent had submitted arguments "sans exciper de l'incompétence de la Cour pour donner pareille interprétation"). Another difficulty may arise in the context of jurisdictional conflict. See *Rights of Minorities in Upper Silesia (Minority Schools)*, PCIJ Series A, No. 15, at 22-23 ("This principle only becomes inoperative in those exceptional cases in which the dispute which States might desire to refer to the Court would fall within the exclusive jurisdiction reserved to some other authority").

remain, that is to say, whether the dispute falls within the subject matter and temporal scope of the jurisdiction of the Court, irrespective of the attitude of the parties.

The point is clearly illustrated by the 2004 ICJ Judgment on jurisdiction in the *Legality of the Use of Force* case between Serbia and Montenegro and Belgium. Belgium, differently from other NATO members who also appeared as defendants, did not assert a jurisdictional defence. There, the Court observed as follows:

> "[A] distinction has to be made between a question of jurisdiction that relates to the consent of a party and the question of the right of a party to appear before the Court under the requirements of the Statute, which is not a matter of consent. The question is whether as a matter of law Serbia and Montenegro was entitled to seise the Court as a party to the Statute at the time when it instituted proceedings in these cases. Since that question is independent of the views or wishes of the Parties, even if they were now to have arrived at a shared view on the point, the Court would not have to accept that view as necessarily the correct one. [Referring to the latter question, the Court went on to say that] The function of the Court to enquire into the matter and reach its own conclusion is thus mandatory upon the Court irrespective of the consent of the parties and is in no way incompatible with the principle that the jurisdiction of the Court depends on consent."[212]

Another authoritative statement on the point at issue emerges from the *Jurisdictional Immunities* case between Germany and Italy decided by the ICJ in 2012. There, the Court, relying on its previous jurisprudence, observed that:

> "Italy has raised no objection of any kind regarding the jurisdiction of the Court or the admissibility of the Application. Nevertheless, according to well-established jurisprudence, the Court 'must . . . always be satisfied that it has jurisdiction, and must if necessary go into the matter *proprio motu*. (Appeal relating to the Jurisdiction of the ICAO Council (*India* v. *Pakistan*), Judgment, *ICJ Reports 1972*, p. 52, para. 13)'."[213]

---

212. *Legality of Use of Force (Serbia and Montenegro* v. *Belgium)*, Preliminary Objections, Judgment, *ICJ Reports 2004*, p. 279, p. 295, para. 36.

213. *Jurisdictional Immunities of the State (Germany* v. *Italy: Greece intervening)*, Judgment, *ICJ Reports 2012*, p. 99, pp. 117-118, para. 40.

By way of anticipation, one may note that the same consideration applies in human rights and international criminal adjudication, where *Kompetenz-Kompetenz* applies to the fullest extent [214].

C. The adjudicator's power to recharacterise the dispute: The blurred line dividing the jurisdictional and merits phases

1. Inter-State adjudication

In the preliminary objections phase, the significance of the old adage recalled in Chapter I *narra mihi factum, dabo tibi jus*, referring to the division of labour between the parties, who must submit and prove the disputed facts, and the adjudicator who, alone, applies the law to such facts, is considerably mitigated. In other words, the adjudicator is to confine itself to deciding a dispute within the legal framework outlined by the conflicting legal claims of the parties, so long as they fall within the boundaries of the jurisdiction of the court or tribunal.

Respect for these boundaries is crucial. In its 2013 Judgment in the *M/V "Louisa"* case between Saint Vincent and the Grenadines and Spain, the ITLOS observed that "the dispute brought before the Tribunal by an application cannot be transformed into another dispute which is different in character" [215]. The Tribunal was addressing the power of the parties, with special regard to the claimant, to submit additional claims in course of the proceedings, according to the well-established principle which prohibits a *mutatio libelli*, that is to say, the inadmissibility of new arguments during proceedings which would recharacterise the dispute as it had been submitted in the Application as of the time of its filing [216]. However, the point was made by the Tribunal in terms sufficiently general that it may also apply to its own powers to recharacterise a dispute.

214. *Infra*, Sections C.3 and C.4.

215. *M/V "Louisa" (Saint Vincent and the Grenadines* v. *Kingdom of Spain)*, Judgment, *ITLOS Reports 2013*, p. 4, p. 44, para. 143.

216. The principle is well established in international adjudication. See, *inter alia*, *Case concerning the Temple of Preah Vihear (Cambodia* v. *Thailand)*, Merits, *ICJ Reports 1962*, p. 36; *Fisheries Jurisdiction (Federal Republic of Germany* v. *Iceland)*, Merits, *ICJ Reports 1974*, p. 203, para. 72; *Certain Phosphate Lands in Nauru (Nauru* v. *Australia)*, Preliminary Objections, Judgment, *ICJ Reports 1992*, p. 240, at p. 266, para. 67). Note, however, that in *Preah Vihear*, the Court did not find Cambodia's request to be an extension of the original application, while in *Fisheries Jurisdiction* the Court found that it had jurisdiction on Germany's submission because "[t]he matter raised therein is part of the controversy between the Parties, and constitutes a dispute relating to Iceland's extension of its fisheries jurisdiction".

Here, the narrow boundaries determined by the principle *ne ultra petita*, understood as a predicate of the consensual nature of the mandate of inter-State adjudication, appear to operate at the jurisdictional level in terms preventing the adjudicator to recharacterise the dispute beyond the scope resulting from the Application and in the first response of the defendant [217]. The expression "recharacterisation" is to be understood in this context as the application to the disputed facts of rules other than those invoked in such initial context in the proceedings [218].

An additional clarification is required before further exploring the issue at hand. Specifically, it is appropriate to clarify the bearing of the issue on the blurred divide between the jurisdictional and merits phases. As already alluded to, the entanglement between the two phases lies in the fact that the court or tribunal, by delineating the dispute on the basis of the autonomous interpretation of its mandate, determines the confines within which it is going to apply the applicable law in its decision to the merits. The boundaries of such judicial power and the degree of judicial autonomy go precisely to the heart of the issue in point – as well as of *jura novit curia*, of course [219].

For our purposes, it bears noting that the reason for this entanglement is generally understood to lie in the fact that jurisdictional issues are often intertwined with the application of substantive law to the disputed facts, with the implication that such jurisdictional issues cannot be settled separately from the merits [220]. That is obviously more frequent when jurisdictional issues are not separately addressed in incidental

---

217. See A. M. Tanzi, "Il principio *ne ultra petita* nel processo internazionale", *Liber amicorum Angelo Davì. La vita giuridica internazionale nell'età della globalizzazione. Editoriale Scientifica, Naples*, Vol. 3, 2019, 2095–2127; Tanzi, *op. cit.* See also A. M. Tanzi, *"Ultra Petita"*, in *Max Planck Encyclopedia of Procedural Law*.

218. See Chapter IV, Sec. C.

219. See Marina Papadaki, "Compromissory Clauses as the Gatekeepers of the Law to Be 'Used' in the ICJ and the PCIJ", 5 JIDS (2014), 560, 560-561; for the reference to the "legal authority of Cinderella", see C. Greenwood, "Challenges of International Litigation", Lauterpacht Centre for International Law Friday Lunchtime Lecture (7 October 2011).

220. This could flow from the fact that the facts and arguments on which both the preliminary objections and the merits are based are the same (e.g. *Guyana* v. *Suriname*, PCA Case No. 2004-04, Procedural Order No. 2, 18 July 2005, para. 2), or from the risk that a decision on preliminary objections also prejudges issues in the merits (e.g. *Questions of Interpretation and Application of the 1971 Montreal Convention Arising from the Aerial Incident at Lockerbie (Libyan Arab Jamahiriya* v. *United Kingdom)*, Preliminary Objections, Judgment, *ICJ Reports 1998*, p. 9, pp. 28-29, para. 50). For a review of the case law and recent developments on the matter at hand, see S. A. G. Talmon, "Objections Not Possessing an 'Exclusively Preliminary Character' in the South China Sea Arbitration", *The Journal of Territorial and Maritime Studies*, Vol. 3 (2016), p. 88 *et seq.*

proceedings on preliminary objections by way of bifurcation, but are instead addressed in conjunction with the merits. Evidence of new elements of fact, which are relevant under the applicable law, may emerge in the course of the pleadings. It is no wonder that the general enunciation of the *jura novit curia* principle by the ICJ in the *Fisheries* case between the UK and Iceland – which was referred to in Chapter II – should be spelled out in the Judgment on jurisdiction, but in terms clearly capable of applying just as fittingly to adjudication on the merits. It is apposite to recall the *dictum*: "the burden of establishing or proving rules of international law cannot be imposed upon any of the parties, for the law lies within the judicial knowledge of the Court" [221].

Accordingly, the issue of the admissibility of the recharacterisation of the dispute by the adjudicator – and in the affirmative, of its boundaries, according to *jura novit curia* and its ancillary principles *ne ultra petita* and *ne infra petita* – may arise well beyond the jurisdictional phase in its preliminary configuration, all the more so because, together with the proven factual background, the contours and contents of the claims of both parties, too, usually become clearer in the course of proceedings on the merits.

On this note, in its Arbitral Award of 1994 in the *Boundary Dispute Between Argentina and Chile* case, the Tribunal made the following observation:

> "The competence of international judges is limited by the functions assigned to them by the parties in the case. Their powers are also limited by the extreme claims which the parties put forward in the hearings." [222]

Here, the Tribunal contemplates the delineation of the jurisdictional competence to be effected at the hearing stage where the conflicting claims feature as an integral part of the mandate [223]. It is apposite at this point to anticipate, for avoidance of doubt, that this does not

---

221. *Fisheries Jurisdiction (United Kingdom* v. *Iceland)*, Jurisdiction of the Court, Judgment, *ICJ Reports 1973*, p. 3, p. 9, para. 17.

222. *Boundary Dispute Between Argentina and Chile Concerning the Frontier Line Between Boundary Post 62 and Mount Fitzroy*, Decision of 21 October 1994, United Nations Report of International Arbitral Award, Vol. 22 (2006), p. 3 *et seq*., p. 26, para. 77.

223. It bears noting, however, that at least in proceedings before the ECtHR, the admissibility phase might be merged with the merits, which is in fact more or less the rule if application is admissible. See Council of Europe, Practical Guide on Admissibility Criteria, updated on 31 August 2022, at https://www.echr.coe.int/documents/admissibility_guide_eng.pdf (last accessed 13 May 2023).

ordinarily apply in human rights adjudication, where the issue of the characterisation of the dispute is carried out at the jurisdictional stage [224]. This is so, among other things, because in human rights litigation the mandate does not stem from the disputing parties, but from the applicable law, which is the Convention of which the Human Rights' Court is the guardian.

Getting back to inter-State adjudication, in the second *Asylum* case Judgment of 1950 between Colombia and Peru, the Court went so far as to suggest the possibility for it to legally characterise the disputed facts until after the stage of the final submissions. The Court also clarified, however, that this operation would still be strictly confined to the boundaries of the positions taken by the parties. It observed that "it is the duty of the Court not only to reply to the questions as stated in the final submissions of the parties, but also to abstain from deciding points not included in those submissions" [225].

Having determined that, procedurally, *jura novit curia* may operate in inter-State adjudication both at the preliminary jurisdictional and merits stages, we may proceed to examine its contents and contours. To this end, we will also consider the related principles *ne ultra petita* and *ne infra petita*, as they have been recalled by the ICJ in the just quoted Judgment. It is fitting to recall at this point that both principles give effect to the autonomy of the parties, whose claims in inter-State adjudication form an integral part of the adjudicative mandate. The point is corroborated by the 1994 Arbitral Award in the *Boundary Dispute* case between Argentina and Chile, which was just recalled [226].

The result is that significant constraints on the exercise of *jura novit curia* operate in inter-State adjudication as a safeguard to judicial autonomy, as well as of the principle of legality and of the proper administration of justice, or due process. It follows that even within the scope of the applicable law, the inter-State adjudicator could not apply rules other than those which ground the causes of action of the applicant and the defences raised by the defendant [227].

224. *Infra*, Section C.3.

225. *Request for Interpretation of the Judgment of November 20th, 1950, in the Asylum case*, Judgment of 27 November 1950: *ICJ Reports 1950*, p. 395, pp. 405-406.

226. See *supra* note 19 and accompanying text.

227. There is extensive literature on the interaction of the constraints imposed by jurisdiction and applicable law. Consider, *ex multis*, L. Bartels, "Jurisdiction and Applicable Law Clauses: Where Does a Tribunal Find the Principal Norms Applicable in the Case Before It", *Multi-Sourced Equivalent Norms in International Law. Oxford: Hart*, 2011, 115-141; P. Tzeng, "The Implicated Issue Problem: Indispensable Issues and Incidental Jurisdiction", *New York University Journal of International Law and*

All these indications – concerning the procedural stage in which the adjudicator's jurisdictional power is to be exercised, as well as its obligatory nature or lack thereof, and its scope – were recently confirmed by the ICJ in its 2018 decision in the *Immunities and Criminal Proceedings* case between Equatorial Guinea and France, as follows:

> "it is for the Court itself to determine on an objective basis the subject-matter of the dispute between the parties, by isolating the real issue in the case and identifying the object of the claim" [228].

The Court went on to specify that, for that purpose,

> "[i]t examines the application as well as the written and oral pleadings of the parties, while giving particular attention to the formulation of the dispute chosen by the applicant" [229].

Thus, the time limit, or phase limit, for the adjudicator to characterise the dispute goes beyond the filing of the Application and its contents, and indeed extends to the proceedings on the merits, provided that the Court does not rely on rules, and rights and duties thereto, other than those invoked by the parties.

In sum, it appears that in inter-State adjudication *ne ultra petita* has a controlling function in relation to *jura novit curia*, curtailing its scope in such a way that the adjudicator may not apply law which has not been pleaded by the parties. However, this function is also counterbalanced by the combined operation of *jura novit curia* and the *ne infra petita* principle, as the adjudicator may not fall short of deciding the *petitum*, or claims, or aspects of them, which fall within the scope of the applicable law.

Moreover, not only is *jura novit curia* boosted by *ne infra petita* as such, but it is enhanced by its combination with the *non liquet* principle, which derives from the presumption of completeness of the

---

Politics, Vol. 50 (2), 2017, 447-508; J. G. Devaney, "Introduction to the Symposium on Incidental Jurisdiction", Vol. 116, 2022, 160-163.

228. *Immunities and Criminal Proceedings (Equatorial Guinea* v. *France)*, Preliminary Objections, Judgment, *ICJ Reports 2018*, p. 292, p. 308, para. 48.

229. *Ibidem*. Problems of qualification of the claims of the Applicant also raised in the *Certain Iranian Assets* case, as highlighted in the literature (F. Paddeu, "Non-Precluded Measures Clause: Substance or Procedure? A Comment on Certain Iranian Assets", *EJIL: Talk!*, 6 March 2019). Here, the Court took "a granular approach", similar to that followed in the *Immunities and Criminal Proceedings* case (E. Methymaki and C. Tams, "Immunities and Compromissory Clauses (Part I)", *EJIL: Talk!*, 27 August 2020. Conversely, the Annex VII Tribunal in *Enrica Lexie* followed a comprehensive approach, again based on the formulation of the dispute made by the claimant in particular in its oral pleadings (*The "Enrica Lexie" Incident*, *cit.*, paras. 807-811).

international legal system and stipulates that the adjudicative body may not abstain from deciding a dispute submitted to it, or an aspect thereto, based on the alleged lack of legal rules applicable to it [230]. Where the completeness of the international legal system is assumed, the issue would not arise due to the lack of legal rules applicable to the claim or claims, but to the unlikely circumstance in which the parties would fall short of pleading the law applicable to the case.

For the sake of completeness, reference is also to be made to the possible combination between *jura novit curia* and the principle of judicial economy. The latter principle, aptly qualified as "a fundamental canon of adjudication", is aimed at the sound and efficient administration of justice [231] and allows the adjudicative body to address only those legal arguments that are strictly necessary for deciding the case [232], or to deal with them in an order different from that submitted by the parties [233]. The case may be made that these two principles may be construed together so as to allow an adjudicative body to address only jurisdictional or merits issues not raised by the parties which are strictly necessary to decide the case [234]. However, an approach of this

230. To understand the relationship between the prohibition of *non liquet* and *jura novit curia*, it is useful to recall the discussion of the matter in the context of the work of the Advisory Committee of Jurists. See League of Nations, Advisory Committee of Jurists, *Procès-verbaux of the Proceedings of the Committee, 16 June-24 July 1920, with Annexes*, 318-319 ("[Baron Descamps], in opposition to M. Ricci-Busatti, said that the various sources of law should be examined successively. The first rule was that if there were a text, a conventional rule, it must be applied. Failing a rule of this kind, international custom must be applied. If neither law nor custom existed, could the judge pronounce a *non-liquet*? The President was convinced that he could not"). On *non liquet* in general, see J. Stone, "*Non Liquet* and the Function of Law in the International Community", *Brit. YB Int'l l.*, Vol. 35, 1959, 124; T. L. H. McCormack, "A *Non Liquet* on Nuclear Weapons - The ICJ Avoids the Application of General Principles of International Humanitarian Law", *International Review of the Red Cross (1961-1997)*, Vol. 37(316), 1997, 76-91; P. Weil, "The Court Cannot Conclude Definitively . . . *Non Liquet* Revisited Chapter 1: Questions of Theory", *Columbia Journal of Transnational Law*, Vol. 36, 1998, 109-119.

231. F. Palombino, "Judicial Economy and Limitation of the Scope of the Decision in International Adjudication", *Leiden Journal of International Law*, Vol. 23 (2010), p. 909 *et seq*., p. 910.

232. WTO, *United States – Subsidies on Upland Cotton*, WT/DS267/AB/R (3 March 2005) para. 510; *NextEra Energy Global Holdings BV and NextEra Energy Spain Holdings BV* v. *Kingdom of Spain*, ICSID Case No. ARB/14/11, Decision on jurisdiction, liability and quantum principles, 12 March 2019, para. 602.

233. *Arrest Warrant of 11 April 2000 (Democratic Republic of the Congo* v. *Belgium)*, Judgment, *ICJ Reports 2002*, p. 3, p. 19, paras. 45-46. This is the so-called "absorption *strictu sensu*" (Palombino, *op. cit*., p. 913).

234. As already mentioned, this is a tenable approach so long as it does not come back to haunt the adjudicator. Such concerns were voiced by Judge Gaja in *Obligations Concerning Negotiations Relating to Cessation of the Nuclear Arms Race and to Nuclear Disarmament*. See *supra* note 2.

kind may be unlikely to be followed outside preliminary objections proceedings, since any exercise of judicial economy could ultimately be seen as a departure from the principle of *ne infra petita*. Were a judge to apply it with regard to arguments not advanced by the parties, it would also fly in the face of *ne ultra petita* and arguably impinge on the very adversarial nature of the proceedings [235]. Thus a similar situation would be easily qualified as a "misapplication [of judicial economy which] may lead to amending the decision or precluding its enforcement" [236].

2. *Investor-State arbitration*

A review of the case law supports the view that investor-State arbitration, too, adopts the same restrictive approach to adjudicative autonomy described in relation to inter-State adjudication. This is in line with the primacy which consensualism and the autonomy of the parties enjoy in the two adjudicative contexts in question.

Such restrictive approach is particularly evident in relation to the interpretation of jurisdictional clauses. For example, in *Biloune*, the claimant put forward a claim based on the alleged violation of international human rights law by the host State as an autonomous cause of action within an UNCITRAL investment arbitration proceeding. The Tribunal declined its jurisdiction to hear the case. It stated as follows:

> "This Tribunal's competence is limited to commercial disputes arising under a contract entered into in the context of Ghana's Investment Code. As noted, the Government agreed to arbitrate only disputes 'in respect of' the foreign investment. Thus, other matters – however compelling the claim or wrongful the alleged act – are outside this Tribunal's jurisdiction. Under the facts of this case it must be concluded that, while the acts alleged to violate the international human rights of Mr Biloune may be relevant in considering the investment dispute under arbitration, this Tribunal lacks jurisdiction to address, as an independent cause of action, a claim of violation of human rights." [237]

---

235. Indeed, in a similar situation, it would be the judge which would provide the conclusive argument for deciding a case, without addressing the parties' claims. See S. Forlati, *"Infra Petita"*, in *Max Planck Encyclopedia of International Procedural Law*.

236. Palombino, *op. cit.*, p. 926.

237. *Antoine Biloune and Marine Drive Complex Ltd.* v. *Ghana Investments Centre and the Government of Ghana*, UNCITRAL, Award on Jurisdiction and Liability, 27 October 1989, reproduced in *International Law Reports*, Vol. 95 (1994), p. 183 *et seq.*, pp. 202-203.

The scenario that played out in *Vattenfall* shares a number of important features with the above. The European Commission had argued in its *amicus curiae* brief that "EU law forms part of the analysis of the Tribunal's jurisdiction via Article 31 (3) *(c)* VCLT" [238] and suggested to the Tribunal that it should be taken into account in interpreting the *Energy Charter Treaty* to the effect of excluding the Tribunal's jurisdiction. The Tribunal rejected the argument, as follows:

> "To the extent that EU law may come into the interpretation analysis, as proposed by the EC, it is to be 'taken into account, together with the context' under Article 31 (3) *(c)*. It is not the proper role of Article 31 (3) *(c)* VCLT to rewrite the treaty being interpreted, or to substitute a plain reading of a treaty provision with other rules of international law, external to the treaty being interpreted, which would contradict the ordinary meaning of its terms." [239]

Thus, if a tribunal is prevented from considering rules of international law invoked by the parties but not directly referred to in the relevant treaty, it must follow, *a fortiori*, that it would not be entitled to consider such rules *proprio motu* through the *jura novit curia* principle.

The restrictive approach outlined above may also be found when considering the approaches that have been adopted in investment arbitration with regard to the characterisation of the dispute. The very first ICSID annulment, the 1985 decision of the *ad hoc* Committee in *Kloeckner* v. *Cameroon I*, provides an example. The Committee started by observing that "[i]t matters little in principle that the Tribunal's legal construction was different from that of one or the other of the parties". However, it qualified its statement by adding "so long as the right of each to be heard was respected and . . . *so long as it remains within the 'legal framework' provided by the parties*" [240].

---

238. *Vattenfall*, *cit.*, para. 151. In essence, the question was not so much whether the Tribunal could use EU law, but rather whether its interpretive use could have been such to defeat the "ordinary meaning" approach to treaty interpretation.

239. *Ibidem*, para. 154. To the same effect, *Eskosol S.p.A. in liquidazione* v. *Italian Republic*, ICSID Case No. ARB/15/50, Decision on Termination Request and Intra-EU Objection, 7 May 2019, para. 126 ("the natural result of the Commission's arguments [would be] overriding as between some ECT Contracting Parties, but not others, the 'unconditional consent' to international arbitration clearly reflected in ECT Article 26 (3). The Tribunal rejects the notion that VCLT Article 31 (3) *(c)* can be used in this way").

240. *Klöckner Industrie-Anlagen GmbH* et al. v. *United Republic of Cameroon and Société Camerounaise des Engrais*, ICSID Case No. ARB/81/2, Decision on Annulment, 3 May 1985, para. 56 (emphasis added). In this regard, an interesting

The strict requirement for tribunals to apply the law to the disputed facts within the confines of the *legal framework provided by the parties* has been consistently confirmed by subsequent case law [241]. Suffice it here to recall a few examples in which the point was clearly illustrated with an interesting emphasis on complementary procedural requirements.

Thirty years after the *Kloekner I* decision, in 2015, the *Quiborax* v. *Bolivia* Tribunal corroborated the point in particularly apposite terms. It stated as follows:

> "When applying the law (whether national or international), the Tribunal is of the view that it is not bound by the arguments and sources invoked by the Parties. The principle *iura novit curia* – or better, *iura novit arbiter* – allows the Tribunal to form its own opinion of the meaning of the law, provided that it does not surprise the Parties with a legal theory that was not subject to debate and that the Parties could not anticipate." [242]

Indeed, the year before, the *Caratube ad hoc* Committee had observed that

> "[A] tribunal (and also a committee) is only free to adopt its own solution and reasoning without obligation to submit it to the parties beforehand, if it remains within the legal framework established by the parties." [243]

---

question which has arisen at times relates to the use of authorities as "delimiters" for the claim and the law applied by the Tribunal. Considering that the parties will inevitably cite authorities to describe and characterise the dispute, is failure to engage with such authorities an annullable error? Investment jurisprudence answers this question in the negative: see *Hussein Nuaman Soufraki* v. *United Arab Emirates*, ICSID Case No. ARB/02/7, Decision of the *Ad Hoc* Committee on the Application for Annulment of Mr Soufraki, 5 June 2007, para. 128; *Duke Energy International Peru Investments No. 1 Ltd.* v. *Republic of Peru*, ICSID Case No. ARB/03/28, Decision on Annulment, 1 March 2011, para. 217; *Continental Casualty Company* v. *Argentine Republic*, ICSID Case No. ARB/03/9, Decision on the Application for Partial Annulment of Continental Casualty Company and the Application for Partial Annulment of the Argentine Republic, 16 September 2011, para. 130.

241. For a review of the ample case law on the matter in point, see A. Tanzi, "On Judicial Autonomy and the Autonomy of the Parties in International Adjudication, with Special Regard to Investment Arbitration and ICSID Annulment Proceedings", *Leiden Journal of International Law*, Vol. 33 (2020), p. 57 *et seq*.

242. *Quiborax SA, Non Metallic Minerals SA and Allan Fosk Kaplún* v. *Plurinational State of Bolivia*, ICSID Case No. ARB/06/2, Award, 16 September 2015, para. 92.

243. *Caratube International Oil Company LLP* v. *The Republic of Kazakhstan*, ICSID Case No. ARB/08/12, Decision on Annulment, 21 February 2014, para. 93.

Investment tribunals are still consistently following this approach [244], occasionally linking *jura novit curia* with *Kompetenz-Kompetenz* [245] or to the possibility of re-qualifying the respondent's objections [246]. At times, tribunals have adopted more nuanced positions with a view to stressing their freedom in selecting the applicable law. For example, the *Gavazzi and Gavazzi* Tribunal held that:

> "In international investment arbitration, where arbitrators have to apply international investment treaties and general principles of international law, because of the international law dimension and issues in which the public has a stake, the principle of *iura novit curia* has even a more substantial impact than in international commercial arbitration. *The Parties have no veto right on the international legal principles to be applied.* The Tribunal can reach its legal reasoning on the outcome of the case independently from the legal theories defended by the Parties as long as it has submitted the legal theories for comments to the Parties in a fair and appropriate manner." [247]

244. Reference may be made, by way of example, to *Vestey Group Ltd.* v. *Bolivarian Republic of Venezuela*, ICSID Case No. ARB/06/4, Award, 5 April 2016, para. 118; *Churchill Mining and Planet Mining* v. *Pty Ltd.* v. *Republic of Indonesia*, ICSID Case No. ARB/12/14, Award, 6 December 2016, para. 236; *Burlington Resources Inc* v. *Ecuador*, ICSID Case No. ARB/08/5, Decision on reconsideration and award, 7 February 2017, para. 45.

245. In *Krederi Ltd.*, the Tribunal referred to *jura novit curia* in a footnote while expressing that it "must first decide whether it has jurisdiction which requires that the conditions of Article 25 ICSID Convention are fulfilled including, most importantly, that the Parties have consented to the jurisdiction of the Centre and thus of this Tribunal" (*Krederi Limited* v. *Ukraine*, ICSID Case No. ARB/14/17, Award, 2 July 2018, para. 232, footnote 7).

246. "[T]he Tribunal notes that, in its analysis of the governing law, it is not limited to the arguments or sources invoked by the Parties, but is required, under the maxim *iura novit curia* or, better, *iura novit arbiter*, to apply the law on its own motion. This approach corresponds to the Tribunal's public function as an adjudicatory body that is part of the administration of international justice. It justifies reliance on arguments and authorities on the governing law not submitted by the Parties, provided the latter are given an opportunity to comment on arguments and legal theories that were either not addressed or could not reasonably be anticipated. It also justifies that the Tribunal treats Respondent's objections in a different order than they were raised and that the Tribunal requalifies objections relating to the scope of protection of shareholder-investors under the BIT, in accordance with its assessment of the requirements for jurisdiction and admissibility under Article 25 (1) of the ICSID Convention and the Argentina-Austria BIT" (*Casinos Austria International GmbH and Casinos Austria Aktiengesellschaft* v. *Argentina*, ICSID Case No. ARB/14/32, Decision on jurisdiction, 29 June 2018, para. 172).

247. *Gavazzi and Gavazzi* v. *Romania*, ICSID Case No. ARB/12/25, Award, 18 April 2017, para. 210; emphasis added.

As already alluded to, it bears emphasising how, next to the requirement to apply the law to the dispute as legally defined by the application and the reply, investment tribunals and annulment committees find that they may only go beyond the parties' legal reasoning so long as doing so respects the procedural right of the parties to be heard on such reasoning [248]. Moreover, the power of the tribunal to consider legal arguments other than those submitted by the parties is also considered to be limited by the contours of its jurisdiction, as construed on the basis of the jurisdictional clauses. Several example may be made to that effect.

3. *Human rights adjudication*

As already alluded to, the formidably extensive approach to *jura novit curia* taken by human rights courts has given effect to the *Kompetenz-Kompetenz* principle by often legally recharacterising the facts alleged in the complaints submitted to them. That has sometimes resulted in addressing alleged breaches of rights not invoked by the complainants, or disregarding rights invoked by them [249].

Such inherent power to recharacterise the claim submitted to human rights judicial bodies appears to flow from their "constitutional" task [250], namely that of enhancing the protection of human rights as they are enshrined in the relevant convention. This contention is supported by abundant case law. To that end, the reasoning of the ECtHR in *Loizidou* is particularly illustrative.

In that case, the respondent had raised preliminary objections based on reservations to the acceptance of the jurisdiction of the Court under

248. On the attention that a tribunal must pay to the right to be heard with a view to avoiding that uses of *jura novit curia* lead to annulment proceedings, see Tanzi, *op. cit.* See also, though with exclusive regard to commercial arbitration, J. D. M. Lew, Jura Novit Curia *and Due Process*, Queen Mary University of London Legal Studies Research Paper No. 72/2010.

249. Indeed, the ECHR routinely finds that it is unnecessary to adjudicate on specific allegations made by the applicant, especially when they relate to the same factual matrix which has been the object of a finding of non-violation. This practice may appear *prima facie* to contradict Article 32 of the Convention, but has not been regarded as an exercise of jurisdiction *infra petita*. See *Radomilja* v. *Croatia*, Application No. 37685/10, 20 March 2018, paras. 106-109. See also S. Forlati, *"Infra Petita"*, in *Max Planck Encyclopedia of International Procedural Law*. According to Palombino, this is a clear instance of "absorption" and an expression of judicial economy. See F. M. Palombino, "Judicial Economy and Limitation of the Scope of the Decision in International Adjudication", *Leiden Journal of International Law*, Vol. 23 (4), 2010, 909-932, 916 *et seq*.

250. See ECHR, Article 19, stating that the purpose of establishing the Court is "[t]o ensure the observance of the engagements undertaken by the High Contracting Parties in the Convention and the Protocols thereto".

Articles 25 and 46 of the Convention[251]. The Court upheld its jurisdiction, holding that a restrictive interpretation of jurisdictional clauses might "run counter to the aim, as expressed in the Preamble to the Convention, to achieve greater unity in the maintenance and further realisation of human rights"[252]. The Inter-American Court of Human Rights, too, has supported a restrictive approach to the interpretation of reservations to its optional jurisdiction clause in light of the object and purpose of the Inter-American Convention[253].

The above reasoning shows that human rights adjudicative bodies see the object and purpose of the treaties of which they are "guardians" as preventing limitations to their jurisdiction flowing from State consent. *A fortiori*, it appears that a limitation to the exercise of their function may not stem from a mere error of qualification of the human rights violation alleged by the applicant. When invoking inherent powers in relation to *jura novit curia*, the human rights case law emphasises how blurred the line, which divides the operation of *jura novit curia* at the preliminary jurisdictional phase from the merits is.

The point was well illustrated in its general terms by the ECtHR already in the 1980s, in *Foti* v. *Italy*. The Court stated as follows:

> "In the performance of their task, the Convention institutions [then Commission and Court] are, notably, free to attribute to the facts of the case . . . a characterisation in law different from that given by the applicant or, if need be, to view the facts in a different manner."[254]

---

251. *Loizidou* v. *Turkey*, Application No. 15318/89, Preliminary Objections, 23 March 1995, para. 73.

252. *Ibidem*, para. 77.

253. For example, in *Ivcher Bronstein*, the Court has maintained that "Interpreting the Convention in accordance with its object and purpose . . . the Court must act in a manner that preserves the integrity of the mechanism provided for in Article 62 (1) of the Convention. That mechanism cannot be subordinated to any restrictions that the respondent State might add to the terms of its recognition of the Court's binding jurisdiction, as that would adversely affect the efficacy of the mechanism and could obstruct its future development" (Inter-American Court of Human Rights, *Ivcher Bronstein* v. *Peru*, IACHR Series C No. 54, Judgment on Competence, 24 September 1999,. para. 35). For a review of the relevant case law, see A. Úbeda de Torres, "The Optional Contentious Jurisdiction of the Court", in L. Burgorgue-Larsen and A. Úbeda de Torres, *The Inter-American Court of Human Rights: Case Law and Commentary*, Oxford, Oxford University Press, 2011, p. 3 *et seq*.

254. European Court of Human Rights, *Case of Foti and others* v. *Italy*, Application Nos. 7604/76, 7719/76, 7781/77 and 7913/77, Judgment, 10 December 1982, para. 44.

The Court also addressed the time and procedure limitations to the exercise of the power of recharacterisation of the facts before it by observing that

> "[it] ha[s] to take account not only of the original application but also of the additional documents intended to complete the latter by eliminating initial omissions" [255].

In *König* v. *Germany*, the point was made in conjunction with the definition of the scope of *jura novit curia* in terms so extensive that they go far beyond what is recognised as applicable by inter-State and investor-State adjudicators, as we have just seen:

> "Once a case is duly referred to it, the Court may take cognisance of every question of law arising *in the course of the proceedings* and concerning facts submitted to its examination by a Contracting State or by the Commission. Master of the characterization to be given in law to the facts, the Court is empowered to examine them, if it deems it necessary and if need be *ex officio*, in the light of the Convention as a whole." [256]

The full statement of the Court's independent power to legally characterise the disputes submitted to it was later elaborated by the Court and regularly reiterated, as a refrain, to this day. Building on the landmark *Powell and Rayner* v. *United Kingdom* of 1990 [257], the leitmotif in question can be taken, among others, from the 1998 *Guerra* v. *Italy* Judgment. It reads as follows:

> "[S]ince the Court is master of the characterisation to be given in law to the facts of the case, it does not consider itself bound by the characterisation given by the applicant or the government. By virtue of the *jura novit curia* principle, it has, for example, considered of its own motion complaints under Articles or paragraphs not relied on by those appearing before it and even under a provision in respect of which the Commission had declared the complaint to be inadmissible while declaring it

255. *Ibidem.*

256. European Court of Human Rights, *Case of König* v. *Germany*, Application No. 6232/73, Judgment, 28 June 1978, para. 96

257. European Court of Human Rights, *Case of Powell and Rayner* v. *United Kingdom*, Application No. 9310/81, Judgment, 21 February 1990, para. 29 ("[t]he Court is the master of the characterisation to be given in law to the facts submitted to its examination").

admissible under a different one. A complaint is characterized by the facts alleged in it and not merely by the legal arguments relied on." [258]

This extensive jurisprudential attitude by the ECtHR has been corroborated all along by the Inter-American Court of Human Rights. It may suffice to recall the two Judgments of 1998 [259] and 2000 in *Cantoral-Benavides* [260]. Here, the Court asserted its power to assess *motu proprio* the lawfulness of the respondent's conduct under a provision of the Convention (Art. 2) not invoked by the Commission, arguing that "[t]he Respondent State cannot, by means of a preliminary objection, attempt to negate this authority which is inherent to the jurisdiction of the Court" [261].

In this sense, *jura novit curia* reasoning can be said to maintain a jurisdictional nature even when it is addressed at the merits stage. This flows from the self-evident conceptual preliminary dimension of the Court's legal recharacterisation of the facts complained of in the application. Furthermore, the power of an adjudicative body to recharacterise the claim impacts on a variety of procedural issues. Apart from the implication that the power in point has on the jurisdiction of the court – a matter already discussed at length – suffice it to recall that claims based on substantive rules different from those originally

258. European Court of Human Rights, *Case of Guerra and Others* v. *Italy*, Application No. 116/1996/735/932, Judgment, 19 February 1998, para. 44. See, *inter alia*, to the same effect, European Court of Human Rights (Grand Chamber), *Case of Scoppola* v. *Italy (No. 2)*, Application No. 10249/03, Judgment, 17 September 2009, para. 54; European Court of Human Rights, *Case of Tsezar* et al. v. *Ukraine*, Applications Nos. 73590/14, 73593/14, 73820/14, 4635/15, 5200/15, 5206/15 and 7289/15, Judgment, 13 February 2018, para. 41; European Court of Human Rights, *Case of Kurt* v. *Austria*, Application No. 62903/15, Judgment, 15 June 2021, para. 104; European Court of Human Rights, *Case of Shabelnik* v. *Ukraine (No. 3)*, Application No. 54806/18, Judgment, 4 November 2021, para. 31. For comments on the Court's practice of recharacterisation of claims, see D. Shelton, "*Jura Novit Curia* in International Human Rights Tribunals", *supra* n. 18, at pp. 194-199.

259. Inter-American Court of Human Rights, *Case of Cantoral Benavides* v. *Peru*, IACHR Series C No. 69, Preliminary Objections, 3 September 1998.

260. Inter-American Court of Human Rights, *Case of Cantoral Benavides* v. *Peru*, IACHR Series C No. 69, Merits, 18 August 2000.

261. *Cantoral Benavides* (Preliminary Objections), *cit.*, para. 46, also quoted in *Cantoral Benavides* (Merits), *cit.*, para. 175. It should, however, be noted, as aptly highlighted by Dinah Shelton, that "[w]ithout having the files and the pleadings, it is very difficult for the IACHR to challenge the characterization presented, except on matters of international law when obvious errors are spotted" (D. Shelton, "The Rules and the Reality of Petition Procedures in the Inter-American Human Rights System", *Notre Dame Journal of International & Comparative Law*, Vol. 5 (2015), p. 1 *et seq.*, at 25).

grounding the application are arguably subject to variations in the allocation of the burden of proof[262].

4. International criminal adjudication

Leaving aside the precedents of the Nuremberg and Tokyo Military Tribunals, one would rely on the Statutes, rules of procedure and case law of the *ad hoc* Tribunals established by the United Nations Security Council in the 1990s and on the ICC as a potential source for the principle under consideration. Yet no reference to *jura novit curia* is unfortunately made there either. Thus, the application of the principle at hand in international criminal adjudication must necessarily be looked for through the perspective of its nature as a general principle of international law.

In the field of international criminal law, the application of principles originating *in foro domestico* flows from domestic law notions whose application on the international level require particular caution with special regard to adjudicative proceedings, as indicated by the late Judge Antonio Cassese's separate and dissenting opinion in the *Erdemović* case in 1997[263]. Even though Judge Cassese's considerations were made at the beginning of the functioning of the ICTY, his admonition remains compelling today to the effect that "[r]eference to national law, if at all necessary, can only be made to take account, with all due caution, of the wealth of distinctions propounded by national courts"[264].

The observation was made at a time when a certain uneasiness surrounded questions concerning the powers of the international criminal judge precisely with respect to the legal characterisation of the facts provided by the prosecutor in the formulation of the charges. The basic reason for this can be found in the caution required by the fair

262. On such variations, see J. Mačkić, *Proving Discriminatory Violence at the European Court of Human Rights*, Leiden-Boston, Brill, 2018, p. 158 *et seq.*; Stirner, *op. cit.*, p. 149 *et seq.*

263. International Criminal Tribunal for the Former Yugoslavia, *Prosecutor* v. *Erdemović*, ICTY Case No. IT-96-22-T, Judgment of the Appeals Chamber, Separate and Dissenting Separate Opinion by Judge Cassese, 7 October 1997, para. 2 *et seq.*

264. *Ibidem*, para. 1. The paragraph goes on as follows: "[t]his reference to national law might cast some light on the possible implications and ramifications of the notion, but ultimately that notion must be autonomously construed on the basis of the international provisions of the Statute" *(ibidem)*.

trial guarantees which afford the accused the right to know in a timely fashion the charges against which to defend himself[265].

The 2000 Judgment of the ICTY Trial Chamber in *Kupreškić* provides a good illustration of the point at issue[266]. The Chamber first expressed its uncertainties, further explaining its concerns and, eventually, finding a solution which accommodated such concerns. In particular, the ICTY Trial Chamber conveyed its sense of uneasiness about the power of an international criminal judge to legally characterise the facts submitted to it, against the curious fact that neither the ICTY Statute established how the charges must be brought by the prosecutor. First, it found that:

> ". . . at least for the time being it is questionable that the *iura novit curia* principle . . . *fully* applies in international criminal proceedings"[267].

It then illustrated the horns of its dilemma, namely, the need to preserve the right of defence of the accused together with the requirement of objective administration of justice[268]. On the one hand, the Chamber considered that the accused would not be able to defend himself from a well-defined charge if – because of evidence emerging in the course of the trial – the Trial Chamber decided on crimes other than those contained in the charges formulated by the prosecutor. It observed as follows:

> "The task of the defence would become exceedingly onerous, given the aforementioned uncertainties which still exist in international criminal law. Hence, even though the *jura novit curia* principle is normally applied in international judicial proceedings, under present circumstances it would be inappropriate for this principle to be followed in proceedings before international criminal courts, where the rights of an individual accused are at stake."[269]

265. Such right is codified, *inter alia*, at Article 21 (4) *(a)* of the ICTY Statute, Article 20 (4) *(a)* of the ICTR Statute and Article 67 (1) *(i)* of the ICC Statute. On the matter in point, see W. A. Schabas, *The International Criminal Court: A Commentary on the Rome Statute*, 2nd ed., Oxford, Oxford University Press, 1028-1033.

266. International Criminal Tribunal for the Former Yugoslavia, *Prosecutor* v. *Kupreškić* et al., ICTY Case No. IT-95-16, Judgment, 14 January 2000. For a comment to the decision, see A. S. Galand, "Approaching Custom Identification as a Conflict Avoidance Technique: Tadic and Kupreškić Revisited", *Leiden Journal of International Law*, Vol. 31 (2018), p. 403 *et seq*.

267. *Prosecutor* v. *Kupreškić*, *cit.*, para. 723.

268. *Ibidem*, paras. 724-726.

269. *Ibidem*, para. 740.

The Chamber went on to stress that

> "It would also violate Article 21 (4) *(a)* of the Statute, which provides that an accused shall be informed 'promptly and in detail' of the 'nature and cause of the charge against him." [270]

On the other hand, the Chamber expressed its awareness of the possibility that the prosecution might incur errors in its formulation of the charges. Leaving such erroneous charges untouched would obviously amount to a serious impairment of the right to defence.

Based on these considerations, the Chamber came down to a balancing formula in three steps. The first step consists of the possibility to allow the prosecutor to amend the charges if, in the course of the trial, he or she realises that evidence is not sufficient to prove a given charge, or if the commission of crimes not included in the charges emerge from proven facts [271]. According to the second step, where the prosecutor cannot avail him or herself of the possibility to amend the charges accordingly, the Trial Chamber could consider itself vested with such a recharacterisation power [272]. Under either of the two circumstances just considered, the third step would require making sure that the accused be informed, promptly and in detail, of the new charges, thus, allowing for an effective defence [273].

As it was stressed by the Extraordinary Chambers in the Courts of Cambodia in a 2016 decision on a request for clarification concerning crimes against humanity and the nexus with armed conflict,

> "the *Kupreškić* Chamber criticised the application [of the *iura novit curia*] principle [only] when it had the effect of depriving the Defence of the opportunity to make submissions on a different

---

270. *Ibidem.*

271. The Chamber made reference to "the case where the Prosecutor realises that the charge of committing crimes against humanity in the form of deportation or imprisonment cannot be proved, while the charge of aiding and abetting in the execution of this crime can be substantiated by sufficient evidence" (*ibidem*, para. 742 (a)). The Chamber went on and acknowledged such power also in the case in which the prosecutor concludes during the proceedings that a more serious, or lesser, offence than that charged in the Indictment has been or may be proved (*ibidem*, paras. 742 *(b)* and *(c)*).

272. *Ibidem*, para. 742.

273. The Chamber expressed that "the accused must be put in a position to contest the charges and to this end he must be informed promptly and in detail of the 'nature and cause of the charge against him'" (*ibidem*, para. 742 *(b)*).

> or more serious legal characterisation of the crimes originally charged by the Prosecution" [274].

Subject to the procedural *caveat* in point, the *jura novit curia* principle was plainly applied by the Extraordinary Chambers and in very extensive terms [275].

As to the ICC, the freedom of the criminal judge to legally characterise the facts irrespective of the arguments advanced by the prosecutor and defendant has been firmly upheld as a requirement for the proper administration of justice. Here, the power of the judge to recharacterise the facts evidenced by the prosecutor has been codified at Regulation 55 [276]. In its jurisprudence, the ICC has consistently interpreted that rule as one prominently aimed at setting "several stringent safeguards for the protection of the rights of the accused" [277].

A decision adopted in 2014 by the Pre-Trial Chamber I dealing with the situation in the Republic of Côte d'Ivoire is particularly illustrative of the point at issue. The Chamber was asked to decide over a request of declaration of inadmissibility of the Amended Document Containing the Charges (ADCC). Based on its Statute, as well as on the Rules and the Regulations of the Court, the Chamber observed:

274. Extraordinary Chambers in the Courts of Cambodia, Case No. 003/07-09-2009-ECCC-OCIJ, Decision on Meas Muth's request for clarification concerning crimes against humanity and the Nexus with armed conflict, 5 April 2016, footnote 21.

275. *Ibid.*

276. For comments on this provision, see K. J. Heller, "'A Stick to Hit the Accused With': The Legal Recharacterization of Facts under Regulation 55", in C. Stahn *et al.* (eds.), *The Law and Practice of the International Criminal Court: A Critical Account of Challenges and Achievements*, Oxford, Oxford University Press, 2015, p. 981 *et seq.*; E. Fry, "Legal Recharacterization and the Materiality of Facts at the International Criminal Court: Which Changes Are Permissible?", *Leiden Journal of International Law*, Vol. 29 (106), p. 577 *et seq.*

277. International Criminal Court, *The Prosecutor* v. *Thomas Lubanga Dyilo*, ICC Case No. 01/04-01/06, Judgment on the appeals of Mr Lubanga Dyilo and the Prosecutor against the Decision of Trial Chamber I of 14 July 2009 entitled "Decision giving notice to the parties and participants that the legal characterization of the facts may be subject to change in accordance with Regulation 55 (2) of the Regulations of the Court", 8 December 2009, para. 85. See also the decision in the *Katanga* case of March 2013, whereby the Court, having reviewed ample human rights case law, excluded that a " notice of a legal re-characterisation at a late stage of the proceedings does not, in and of itself, violate the right to a fair trial" (*The Prosecutor* v. *Germain Katanga*, ICC Case No. 01/04-01/07, Judgment on the appeal of Mr Germain Katanga against the decision of Trial Chamber II of 21 November 2012 entitled "Decision on the implementation of regulation 55 of the Regulations of the Court and severing the charges against the accused persons", 27 March 2013, paras. 93-94).

"While the Prosecutor may indeed provide submissions as to the proposed interpretation of the applicable law for the purposes of the confirmation proceedings, any such submission does not constitute part of the charges of which the suspect is entitled to be informed in full. This is also consistent with the fundamental principle of *jura novit curia*, which places the responsibility to interpret the applicable law on the Judges rather than the parties." [278]

D. *Concluding remarks on* jura novit curia *and the assessment of the jurisdiction of international courts and tribunals*

This chapter covered some ground on the path which took us to the heart of *jura novit curia*. It drew from the case law of different international adjudicators important indications about its contents and boundaries. These indications contributed to the clarification of aspects such as the character of power and duty inherent in the principle at hand and illustrated the rationale of its application in two key phases of the proceedings – i.e. on jurisdiction and the merits – which are mutually entangled for the purposes of the operation of *jura novit curia* in terms which may impinge on the legal characterisation of the disputed facts by international adjudicators. They also allowed for the identification of markedly different forms and shapes of operation of *jura novit curia* throughout the three different areas of international adjudication under consideration – i.e. inter-State and investor-State, human rights and criminal litigation. Such differences will be further discussed at the end of this course, when pulling the strings of the various components of this analysis. Suffice at this stage to note that the differences in question are so marked that they impact on the operation of *jura novit curia* in each of the three adjudicative contexts at issue. And the extent of

278. International Criminal Court (Pre-Trial Chamber I), *Situation in the Republic of Côte d'Ivoire in the Case of the Prosecutor* v. *Laurent Gbabgo*, ICC Case No. 02/11-01/1514, Decision on Defence requests related to the continuation of the confirmation proceedings, February 2014, para. 14. See also Extraordinary Chambers in the Courts of Cambodia, Case No. 002/19-09-2007/ECCC/TC, Decision on Co-Prosecutors' request to exclude armed conflict nexus requirement from the definition of crimes against humanity, 26 October 2011, para. 5. This reasoning has also been adopted by other tribunals. See Special Court for Sierra Leone, *Prosecutor* v. *Taylor (Charles Ghankay)*, SCSL Case No. 03-01-A-1389, Appeal judgment, 26 September 2013, para. 439; Special Tribunal for Lebanon, Ayyash *et al.* case, *Prosecutor* v. *Ayyash (Salim Jamil)* et al., STL Case No. 11-01/I/AC/R176bis, Interlocutory decision on the applicable law: terrorism, conspiracy, homicide, perpetration, cumulative charging, 16 February 2011, para. 281.

the autonomous adjudicative powers that flow from *jura novit curia* is inversely proportional to the degree of autonomy of the parties, or consent factor, which grounds the mandate of the adjudicator in each of the three adjudicative areas under consideration.

So far, the inquiry has targeted an abstract and general understanding of *jura novit curia* in the jurisdictional and the merits phases, as mutually entangled in relation to the characterisation of the dispute. And it has provided cues for understanding the contents and boundaries of the powers and duties provided by *jura novit curia*, also in relation to the largely ancillary principles of *ne infra petita* and *ne ultra petita*. In particular, it has been noted how each of the latter two principles, respectively, either enhances, or constrains, the operation of *jura novit curia* in different modulations in each of the three adjudicative contexts under consideration.

The next chapter will complement such a discussion in relation to the application of the law in more concrete terms in deciding the case at the merits and reparation phases. In Chapter I, I anticipated that *jura novit curia* gives expression to just one of multiple forms of judicial discretion. I will now focus on some of the most problematic aspects which fall within a grey space of adjudicative discretion concerning the application of the law, where judicial decisions may be grounded on *jura novit curia*, or might be conflated with forms of *jura novit curia*, but should not. In the latter case, the adjudicator may either simply exercise its regular discretion in the interpretation and application of the law, or incur an excess of power through *ne ultra petita* or *ne infra petita*, which is not necessarily a matter of *jura novit curia*.

There is generally no judicial review of an appellate nature in international adjudication. Nonetheless, as already alluded to, international courts and tribunals do their utmost to stay within the boundaries of the legitimate exercise of their powers, both as a matter of fact and as a matter of considered judicial policy with a view to enhancing the judicial function and the confidence in it.

It is with that in mind that it appears all the more appropriate to elucidate the contours of the principles under consideration. It tentatively emerges from the analysis carried out so far that it is not problematic for international courts and tribunals to decide a dispute by applying the law according to interpretations of it other than those put forward by both parties. One may consider this as an exercise of *jura novit curia* powers, based on a restrictive scope of the principle at hand, i.e. a principle which provides only the power to decide a case based on interpretations – and not rules – other than those put forward by the parties.

Based on the analysis conducted so far, inter-State and investor-State litigation – differently from human rights and international criminal law adjudication – appears to operate under the strict command of *ne infra petita* and *ne ultra petita* as entangled with the consent-based jurisdiction and autonomy of the parties. Accordingly, within this cluster of adjudication, the *jura novit curia* judicial power of autonomous interpretation of the applicable law appears to be confined not only within the boundaries of the applicable law, but also of the opposite claims of the parties. Namely, within the boundaries of the rules and principles grounding the rights and obligations invoked by the parties, even if the scope of the applicable law would have allowed them to rely on more causes of action than those actually invoked.

It bears noting, by way of anticipation, that within such a framework, one would venture to say that, in inter-State adjudication, *jura novit curia* coincides with the general – and unquestionable – power inherent in the administration of justice to interpret and apply the rules invoked by the parties in terms other than those put forward by them. In Chapter IV, I am going to address some especially problematic aspects of, or even exemptions to, this statement.

CHAPTER IV

PROBLEMATIC ASPECTS CURTAILING *JURA NOVIT CURIA* IN THE MERITS PHASE

A. Introduction

The present chapter addresses circumstances where no specific rules are to be found within the scope of the applicable law that directly govern the entirety of the disputed facts. This is naturally connected with the principle expressing a prohibition of *non liquet* in international adjudication [279], as well as *ne infra petita*, insofar as the need to identify relevant rules where none are agreed or *prima facie* applicable to the dispute, or parts of it, will naturally test the latitude of discretion that can be exercised by an adjudicator. Such latitude allows an adjudicator to look for rules, or principles, within the realm of the system of international law, even where they do not appear strictly to belong to the law contained in the jurisdictional mandate of the adjudicator. This key aspect of international adjudication is not normally addressed through the lens of *jura novit curia*, however, the issue deserves analysis from a *jura novit curia* perspective insofar as it falls to the adjudicators, in the determination of the proper boundaries of their judicial function in general and the scope of their jurisdiction more specifically. The issue may arise for adjudicators as to the identification of those rules that may settle the dispute before them but which have not been pleaded by the parties, where there is disagreement as to the admissibility of such arguments or of the rules in question.

These problematic aspects are addressed in the present chapter in the following order. First, the prohibition of *non liquet* will be considered as a general principle operating in conjunction with the assumed completeness of the international legal order, thus *enabling*, rather than *requiring*, the adjudicator to resort to different gap-filling jurisdictional techniques revolving around problematic aspects of the interpretation and application of the law. Second, the chapter explores the distinction between the freedom that an adjudicator can exercise in the determination of the applicable law and the comparatively

279. On the connection between *non liquet* and *jura novit curia* see also *supra* Chapter III, Sec. C.1.

stricter constraints that ostensibly apply to the determination of facts. Third, it will address the elusive boundary between interpretation and application of the law as an aspect inviting the application of forms of *jura novit curia*. Finally, it will consider the relationship between *jura novit curia* and the time element, with special regard to the notion of intertemporal law and composite acts.

B. Jura novit curia *and the enabling role of the prohibition of* non liquet, *or the obligation to decide the dispute falling with the jurisdiction of the court or tribunal*

To frame our discussion of how the prohibition of *non liquet* in international adjudication may serve an enabling function with respect to the exercise of *jura novit curia* powers, we may refer to the wisdom of the Great Britain-US Arbitral Tribunal, which famously stated in 1923 that

> "International law . . . may not contain, and generally does not contain, express rules decisive of particular cases; but the function of jurisprudence is to resolve the conflict of opposing rights and interests by applying – in default of any specific provision of law – the corollaries of general principles." [280]

One could be forgiven for identifying an element of inconsistency in this passage: indeed, how can an international tribunal "resolve conflicts of opposing rights" in the absence of "any provision of law" from which to derive any such rights? However, the point rightly made by the arbitrators is precisely that, in the absence of legal rules specifically addressing the disputed facts, it would be for the international adjudicator to go all the way to draw from "general principles and their corollaries" rights and obligations which may be applicable to the case [281].

280. *Arbitral Tribunal (Great Britain-United States) constituted under the Special Agreement of 18 August 1910* (18 June 1913-22 January 1926), UNRIAA Vol. VI, pp. 17-190, at 114.

281. It may recalled that the problem of the completeness of the international legal system and the related challenge of having to fill lacunae was at the source of several controversial developments. These include the failure of the planned International Prize Court, which never came into being largely on account of parties' inability to come to an agreement as to the specific rules the new Court should have applied and on their uneasiness with regard to its ability to apply "principles of justice and equity" in the absence of a "generally recognized rule". See XII Hague Convention Relative to the Creation of an International Prize Court of 28 October 1907. On this topic, see also Skouteris, *op. cit.*; Fitzmaurice, *op. cit.*, 38; Y. Wang, "The Origins and Operation of the General Principles of Law as Gap fillers", *Journal of International Dispute Settlement*, Vol. 13 (4), 2022, 560-582.

Should the parties fail to argue such principles, however unlikely the circumstances, or should they invoke rules falling outside the applicable law, it is only by an outright exercise of *jura novit curia* by the adjudicator that the prohibition of *non liquet* can be respected [282]. Together with *ne infra petita* [283], this would be in accord with the general statement made by the ICJ in the Judgment on the merits in the *Continental Shelf case between Libya and Malta* whereby "[t]he Court must not exceed the jurisdiction conferred upon it by the Parties, but it must . . . exercise that jurisdiction to its full extent" [284].

Express prohibitions of *non liquet* in instruments governing the operation of international adjudicatory bodies are not common, but a good example is offered by Article 42 (2) of the ICSID Convention. The provision states that "[t]he Tribunal may not bring in a finding of *non liquet* on the ground of silence or obscurity of the law". That can be said to be in line with the aforementioned *dictum* of the ICJ supporting the view that an adjudicator is in any event required to apply the law "to its full extent" [285]. Indeed, when ICSID Tribunals do not do so, they incur a risk of annulment by reason of failure to apply the applicable law: this was the fate, for example, of the Tribunal in *Enron* v. *Argentina*, as asserted by the Annulment Committee in the same case [286]. I will return to this point when discussing *jura novit curia* in relation to the relevance of domestic law before international investment tribunals.

From a broader perspective, which also takes into account the principles of *non liquet* and *ne infra petita*, not only *jura novit curia* plays out as an element of judicial discretionary power, but also as a *duty* aimed at ensuring the proper administration of justice, especially when the disputing parties have given their consent to the procedure in question. To that end, one may recall the famous judicial statement

282. In this context, see D. Bodanski, *"Non Liquet"*, in *Max Planck Encyclopedia of Public International Law*.

283. See Tanzi, *op. cit.*; Tanzi, *op. cit.*

284. *Continental Shelf (Libyan Arab Jarnahiriya/Malta), Judgment*, *ICJ Reports 1985*, p. 13, at 23, para. 19.

285. See *supra* note 6.

286. The Committee argued that "Failure to deal with questions submitted to the tribunal has been considered in the case law of annulment committees to be a failure to state reasons for purposes of this provision. On the other hand, while a tribunal has a duty to deal with each of the questions . . . submitted to it, it is not required to comment on all arguments of the parties in relation to each of those questions" (*Enron Corporation and Ponderosa Assets, LP* v. *Argentine Republic*, ICSID Case No. ARB/01/3, Decision on the Application for Annulment of the Argentine Republic, 30 July 2010, para. 72).

by the PCIJ in the *Lotus* case back in 1927 [287]. The case concerned a navigation incident that occurred on the high seas. A French steamer named the *Lotus* collided with a Turkish vessel, causing significant damage. The case raised the question of which country's domestic courts had jurisdiction over the incident and the individuals involved. In its decision, the PCIJ ruled, *inter alia*, that, lacking an express prohibition, States had the freedom to exercise jurisdiction over acts committed on the high seas by their nationals or vessels [288]. The name *Lotus* subsequently became a shorthand for the principle whereby States are free to exercise their national jurisdiction in the absence of a prohibition, subject to the limitations of international law [289]. Accordingly, any such conduct would represent the exercise of a right flowing from such a general principle. The Court made the statement in question by way of *obiter dictum*, somewhat unnecessarily for the purpose of that particular case, since it could apply specific bilateral treaty rules, which had actually been invoked by Turkey to justify the exercise of its jurisdiction over the case [290].

This was long before specific international regulation on such matters was adopted under Article 11 of the 1958 Geneva High Seas Convention – as later confirmed by Articles 92 and 97 of UNCLOS – which afforded exclusive jurisdiction to the "flag state" – a rare example of a treaty effectively overruling – albeit narrowly – a decision of the World Court [291].

The permissive function of the *Lotus* principle has inspired the international case law for a while, especially in times when a voluntarist approach to international law was thought to prevail [292]. And resort to

287. *The Case of the S. S. "Lotus"*, PCIJ Series A, No. 70.

288. *Ibid.*, p. 30 ("The conclusion at which the Court has therefore arrived is that there is no rule of international law in regard to collision cases to the effect that criminal proceedings are exclusively within the jurisdiction of the State whose flag is flown").

289. *Ibid.*, p. 18 ("Restrictions upon the independence of States cannot therefore be presumed"). According to James Brierly, who commented that this holding rested on the "highly contentious metaphysical proposition of the extreme positivist school that the law emanates from the free will of sovereign independent States". See J. L. Brierly, "The Lotus Case", *LQ REV.*, Vol. 44, 1928, 154-156, 155.

290. See *Lotus*, *supra* note 10, at 5, referencing the Convention of Lausanne of 24 July 1923.

291. For this interpretation, see J. Crawford, *Chance, Order, Change: The Course of International Law, General Course on Public International Law*, Martinus Nijhoff Publishers/Brill Academic, 2014, 55.

292. For critical overviews of the impact of *Lotus* on the development of the law of jurisdiction, see A. Mills, "Rethinking Jurisdiction in International Law", *British Yearbook of International Law*, Vol. 84 (1), 2014, 187-239; C. Ryngaert, "Jurisdiction", *Concepts for International Law*, Edward Elgar Publishing, 2019, pp. 577-584.

general principles or systemic reasoning would simply be had in order to avoid inferring restrictions on State sovereignty where this had not been provided for by a specific rule. However, the approach was not devoid of problems. In this regard, an instructive example is offered by the *Legality of Nuclear Weapons* Advisory Opinion [293]. In that case, the Court was tasked to answer the question of whether the threat or use of nuclear weapons was in any circumstance permitted under international law [294]. In this regard, it would have been possible in principle for the Court to draw on the *Lotus* principle and conclude that, because no specific restriction existed, the use of nuclear weapons could not but be considered permissible [295]. However, the Court found that the use of nuclear weapons was subject to *some* law – the law applicable in armed conflict, including humanitarian law and the principle of neutrality [296]. Eventually, it found (by seven votes to seven, by the President's casting vote) that it could not definitively conclude whether the use or threat of nuclear weapons would be legal or illegal in a situation of extreme self-defence where the survival of a State is at stake [297]. This conclusion was referred to by a number of commentators as essentially amounting to a finding of *non liquet*, because, notwithstanding the successful identification of the law applicable to the matter at issue, the Court still found itself unable to make a definitive determination [298].

Whatever its merits, the Court's *dictum* in *Lotus* paved the way to the possibility or, rather, the duty for inter-State adjudicators to resort to such a systemic general principle – possibly, by way of *jura novit curia* – for want of specific rules that regulate the disputed facts. And this would prevent international judges and arbitrators to fail to decide the dispute, thus incurring a *non liquet* and *ne infra petita*. It bears repeating that, in investment arbitration, the prevention of *non liquet* is

293. *Legality of the Threat or Use of Nuclear Weapons*, Advisory Opinion, *ICJ Reports 1996*, p. 226.

294. *Ibid.*, at 5-7.

295. *Ibid.*, at 238-239 (citing *Lotus* as a byword for the argument that "[s]tates are free to threaten or use nuclear weapons unless it can be shown that they are bound not to do so by reference to a prohibition in either treaty law or customary international law").

296. It bears noting, however, that the States appearing before the Court "either accepted, or did not dispute, that their independence to act was indeed restricted by the principles and rules of international law, more particularly humanitarian law" (at 239, para. 22).

297. *Ibid.*, at 266-267, para. 105 ("However, in view of the current state of international law, and of the elements of fact at its disposal, the Court cannot conclude definitively whether the threat or use of nuclear weapons would be lawful or unlawful in an extreme circumstance of self-defence, in which the very survival of a State would be at stake").

298. McCormack, *op. cit.*; Weil, *op. cit.*

codified in Article 42(2) of the ICSID Convention, whereby, therefore, the arbitral tribunal is to find and apply the appropriate law for it to decide the dispute, irrespective of what the parties argue[299].

An additional question raised by the *Lotus* case is whether inter-State adjudicators, or investment arbitrators, may apply rules which, while pertinent to the dispute, fall outside the strict perimeter of the applicable law expressly consented to by the parties. Such concerns may be mitigated, if not eliminated entirely, where judicial resort to general principles and their corollaries is considered in the light of the blurred distinction, and ambiguous relationship, between interpretation and application of the law. This will be discussed in Section D below. Before doing so, however, it is necessary to address another blurred distinction relevant to the identification of the boundaries of *jura novit curia*: that between the facts and the law.

C. The fine line between facts and the law

The distinction between facts and the law is key for our purposes. In principle, the ascertainment of the facts would depend exclusively on the capacity of the parties to prove them, as distinct from the "knowledge" and application of the law, which would pertain exclusively to the adjudicator. The rigidity of this distinction is, thus, based on the division of roles and allocation of responsibilities in the proceedings according to the maxim that was evoked at the beginning of these lectures: *narra mihi factum, dabo tibi jus* ("tell me the facts, I will give you the law").

Such a rigid separation, if ever acceptable even in principle, evaporates entirely when it comes to practice[300]. In fact, the relevance of the disputed facts in any given case depends on whether such facts are contemplated by a given rule and on the interpretation of such rule in relation of such facts. Conversely, a given rule belonging to the applicable law is relevant to a given case only if it can be interpreted so as to apply to any given disputed fact, an operation which can be

---

299. See *supra* note 7 and accompanying text.

300. As a notable example, consider Jolowicz's treatment of the issue: "There is a presumption that the judge knows the law. There is no need, in theory, for the parties to provide him with the materials and information necessary for the decision of questions of law. No similar presumption is possible in relation to questions of fact. *Jura novit curia* may be plausible; *facta novit curia* is absurd. Nevertheless . . . at the end of the day, decisions of fact are as much for the judge as are decisions on the applicable law". See J. A. Jolowicz, *On Civil Procedure*, Cambridge University Press, 2000, 222.

described as a characterisation exercise not too far removed from the technique with the same name that is commonly employed in matters of private international law [301]. There, too, the facts will be controlling as to the identification of the law to be applied.

The crucial importance of the connection between the law and the facts was also raised by the International Court of Justice in the *Nicaragua* case [302], and in terms closely related to *jura novit curia.* After recalling that "[. . . f]or the purpose of deciding whether the claim is well founded in law, the principle *jura novit curia* signifies that the Court is not solely dependent on the argument of the parties before it with respect to the applicable law", the Court went on to observe that "[a]s to the facts of the case, in principle the Court is not bound to confine its consideration to the material formally submitted to it by the parties" [303]. Similar concerns were echoed in *Armed Activities on the Territory of the Congo*, where the Court observed that it would "first make its own determination of the facts and then apply the relevant rules of international law to the facts which it has found to have existed" [304].

In other words, the international adjudicator has the power to look for and appreciate the relevant facts *motu proprio*, as much as it is entitled under *jura novit curia* to look *sua sponte* for the legal arguments which are appropriate in order to decide the dispute, irrespective of what the parties submit. In fact, it is often not so easy – and, perhaps, neither necessary, nor appropriate – to distinguish between party-produced and court gathered evidence of the disputed facts, or between appreciations of facts and legal appreciations. As elegantly put by Professor

---

301. Z. Douglas, *The International Law of Investment Claims*, Cambridge, UK; New York, Cambridge University Press, 2009, 47.

302. *Military and Paramilitary Activities in and Against Nicaragua (Nicaragua v. United States of America),* Merits, Judgment. *ICJ Reports 1986*, p. 14.

303. *Ibid.* The Court had considered the matter elsewhere, for example in the *Lotus* case, where the Court stated that "having arrived at the conclusion that the arguments advanced by the French Government either are irrelevant to the issue or do not establish the existence of a principle of international law precluding Turkey from instituting the prosecution which was in fact brought against Lieutenant Demons, [it] observes that in the fulfilment of its task of itself ascertaining what the international law is, it has not confined itself to a consideration of the arguments put forward, but has included in its researches all precedents, teachings and facts to which it had access and which might possibly have revealed the existence of one of the principles of international law contemplated in the special agreement". See *The S. S. Lotus,* PCIJ Series A, No. 10, at 31. See also *Brazilian Loans*, PCIJ, Series A, No. 20/21, p. 124; Nuclear Tests, *ICJ Reports 1974*, pp. 263-264, paras. 31, 32.

304. *Armed Activities on the Territory of the Congo (Democratic Republic of the Congo* v. *Uganda)*, Judgment, *ICJ Reports 2005*, p. 168, at 200, para. 57.

Gourgourinis, "[c]laims of the parties to the dispute and relevant facts are closely related with the identification of any given applicable norm", in what is essentially considered as an exercise of "qualification juridique" [305].

1. Technical facts and domestic law

The problematic nature of the relationship between facts and law can be further elucidated by considering two specific areas, which place the operation of *jura novit curia* under a particular stress test. The first concerns the application of rules governing facts characterised by a highly scientific, or purely technical, relevance. The second concerns instead the evidence concerning domestic law, as well as its evaluation.

As to the first, in relation to the application of rules governing facts characterised by a highly scientific or purely technical relevance, the inevitability of the problem has been highlighted even outside of debates directly connected to international adjudication. As an illuminating example, it is worth mentioning that the issue was raised by the ILC Special Rapporteur on Protection of the Atmosphere, Professor Shinya Murase, who, referring to the ICJ, has argued that "*[j]ura novit curia* . . . can enable or even require the Court to consider *factual points* that have not been taken by the parties, by virtue of proper application of international law" [306].

In this domain, rules are characterised by a highly scientific or technical connotation. Over the last decades, rules of this kind have become more and more widespread, applying, *inter alia*, to matters relating to the protection of the environment, the allocation of natural resources and land or maritime delimitation. As I see it, the blurred distinction between the highly technological character of those rules, and of the facts governed by said rules, further blurs the boundary between two tenets of the process of international adjudication: the burden on the parties to prove the facts on the one hand, and the knowledge and application of the law by the judge on the other. In other words, in this domain, a more proactive and independent role should be envisaged for

305. See A. Gourgourinis, "The Distinction between Interpretation and Application of Norms in International Adjudication", *Journal of International Dispute Settlement*, Vol. 2 (1), 2011, 31–57, 44–45.

306. International Law Commission, Fifth report on the protection of the atmosphere, UN Doc. A/CN.4/711 (2018), at 45, para. 90. On these points, with reference to domestic civil procedure, see Jolowicz, *On Civil Procedure*, 222 ("at the end of the day, decisions of fact are as much for the judge as are decisions on the applicable law").

the judge in the ascertainment of scientific and technological facts, so as to apply *jura novit curia* in relation to such kinds of facts, as much as to the law [307].

The second circumstance in which the distinction between facts and law is particularly blurred – placing, again, the operation of *jura novit curia* under significant stress – relates to the evidence and evaluation of domestic law. This has to do with the fact that, where the domestic law of a State has relevance, it is normally because the conduct that is alleged to be wrongful under international law is also governed by the domestic law of the defendant State [308]. It is, of course, undisputed that what is lawful under a domestic law may not be so under international law. This is reflected in Article 3 of the Articles on Responsibility of States for Internationally Wrongful Acts, whereby

> "[t]he characterization of an act of a State as internationally wrongful is governed by international law. Such characterization is not affected by the characterization of the same act as lawful by internal law" [309].

The provision clarifies that the international judge will examine the State conduct complained of as a matter of disputed facts to which international law applies. This raises important questions concerning the role of domestic law in relation to the conduct in question [310]. In its 1926 Judgment in *Certain German Interests in Polish Upper Silesia*, the Permanent Court famously observed as follows:

---

307. For reasons of space, this question cannot be investigated fully. However, reference may be made to The Hague Lectures delivered in 2019 by Professor Makane Mbengue on "Science and International Courts and Tribunals", of imminent publication. See also M. M. Mbengue, "Scientific Fact-finding at the International Court of Justice: An Appraisal in the Aftermath of the Whaling Case", *Leiden Journal of International Law*, Vol. 29 (2), 2016, 529–50.

308. On the partially related question of the *validity* of domestic law, see M. Jarrett, "The International Validity of Domestic Law in Investment-treaty Arbitration", *Arbitration International*, Vol. 39 (1), 2023, 1-18.

309. *Articles on Responsibility of States for Internationally Wrongful Acts*, Article 3 ("ARSIWA").

310. These questions may also be investigated against the theoretical backdrop of the evolution of the dualist and monist tradition. See J. G. Starke, "Monism and Dualism in the Theory of International Law", *British Yearbook of International Law*, Vol. 17, 1936, 66-81; G. Sperduti, "Dualism and Monism: A Confrontation to Be Overcome", *Italian Yearbook of International Law*, Vol. 3, 1977, 31-49; G. Gaja, "Positivism and Dualism in Dionisio Anzilotti, The European Tradition in International Law: Dionisio Anzilotti", *European Journal of International Law*, Vol. 3 (1), 1992, 123–38; A. F. M. Maniruzzaman, "State Contracts in Contemporary International Law: Monist Versus Dualist Controversies", *European Journal of International Law*, Vol. 12 (2), 2001, 309-328.

> "From the standpoint of International Law and of the Court which is its organ, municipal laws are merely facts which express the will and constitute the activities of States, in the same manner as do legal decisions or administrative measures." [311]

Taking this reasoning to its extremes, it should naturally follow that *jura novit curia* should not apply to domestic law. Rather, the burden of proving relevant aspects of domestic law should rest on the parties. Yet the possibility that the parties would fail to do so exhaustively or correctly cannot be discounted. Here, again, in accord to the general considerations on the blurred distinction between facts and the law, it should be seen as appropriate for the international judge to take an attitude autonomous from the parties in obtaining and assessing factual information. This may be reminiscent of what domestic judges do when applying the law of foreign jurisdictions under the private international law rules of their legal order, save of course for the fact that the international judge is probably still presumed to *know*, though not expected to *apply*, domestic law [312].

It is, of course, possible for a particular domestic law – normally, but not necessarily, that of one of the parties to the dispute – to form part of the applicable law, displacing, or alongside to, international law. This is seldom the case in inter-State adjudication, but it may occur, as it did in the 1929 landmark case on *Brazilian Federal Loans Contracted in France*, between France and Brazil before the Permanent Court of International Justice. There, the Court observed that

> "Though bound to apply municipal law when circumstances so require, the Court, which is a tribunal of international law, and which, in this capacity, is deemed itself to know what this law is, is not obliged also to know the municipal law of the various countries. All that can be said in this respect is that [however] the

311. *Certain German Interests in Polish Upper Silesia*, PCIJ Series A, No. 7, p. 19. The Court was addressing the question of whether it could deal with a domestic statute, answering in the affirmative on the basis of the fact that it was ". . . certainly not called upon to interpret the Polish law *as such*; but there is nothing to prevent the Court's giving judgment on the question whether or not, in applying that law, Poland is acting in conformity with its obligations towards Germany under the Geneva Convention" (at 19, *emphasis added*).

312. See, for example, M. Cappelletti, Iura novit curia: *impossibilià di conoscere il diritto straniero richiamato dalle norme di diritto internazionale privato e metodo comparativo*, Giuffrè, 1967; I. Pretelli and S. Lalani, "Switzerland: The Principle *Iura Aliena Novit Curia* and the Role of Foreign Law Advisory Services in Swiss Judicial Practice", in Y. Nishitani (ed.), *Treatment of Foreign Law – Dynamics Towards Convergence?*, Cham: Springer International Publishing, 2017, pp. 375-393.

> Court may possibly be obliged to obtain knowledge regarding the municipal law which has to be applied. And this it must do, either by means of evidence furnished it by the Parties or by means of any research which the Court may think fit to undertake or to cause to be undertaken." [313]

By doing so, the Court enhanced the entanglement between facts and the law, by requiring the parties to provide "knowledge regarding the municipal law to be applied . . . by means of evidence" [314]. Second, it positioned itself in the matter as essentially carrying out its due diligence as an inter-State adjudicator, so as to take all appropriate measures "to obtain knowledge regarding the municipal law which has to be applied" [315]. One can clearly see how the comparison with domestic judges when applying foreign law based on their domestic conflict of law rules may not be as far-fetched.

One of the areas in which an international adjudicator is usually most likely to concern itself with domestic law is that of investment arbitration. Where this occurs, it is generally in ways which require some application of *jura novit curia*. The abundant practice on the point at issue in investment arbitration could provide useful cues for inter-State litigation, even though the ICJ has historically demonstrated a degree of caution or even mistrust towards investment arbitration case law [316].

At any rate, far from having a purely theoretical importance, the relevance of domestic law in investment arbitration has seriously occupied the minds of negotiators of international investment protection agreements. Suffice it to recall, for example, Article 8.31.2. of the *EU-Canada Comprehensive Economic and Trade Agreement* (CETA) [317].

313. PCIJ Series A, No. 21, at 124. See also Serbian Loans, PCIJ Ser A. No. 20, pp. 5, 16-19 ("From a general point of view, it must be admitted that the true function of the Court is to decide disputes between States or Members of the League of Nations on the basis of international law: Article 38 of the Statute contains a clear indication to this effect. But it would be scarcely accurate to say that only questions of international law may form the subject of a decision of the Court").

314. *Brazilian Loans*, *supra* note 36.

315. *Ibid.*

316. For the most prominent example, see *Obligation to Negotiate Access to the Pacific Ocean (Bolivia* v. *Chile)*, Judgment, *ICJ Reports 2018*, p. 507, at 559, para. 162. See, to the contrary, in favour of a mutually fruitful interaction between the ICJ and investment arbitration case law both ways, B. Simma and D. Pulkowski, "Two Worlds, but Not Apart: International Investment Law and General International Law", in M. Bungenberg, J. Griebel and S. Hobe (eds.), *International Investment Law (2015), 361;* Tanzi, *op. cit.*

317. Comprehensive Economic and Trade Agreement (CETA) between Canada, of the one part, and the European Union and its Member States, of the other part, OJ L 11, 14.1.2017, p. 23-1079.

The provision states that "the Tribunal may consider . . . the domestic law of the disputing Party as a matter of fact" [318]. For the avoidance of doubt, it adds that a CETA tribunal "shall not have jurisdiction to determine the *legality* of a measure . . . under the domestic law of the disputing Party" [319]. The same provision is to be found in the EU-Vietnam Agreement [320].

The rationale for these provisions may perhaps be found in the need to avoid the risk of a tribunal either considering domestic rules and court decisions as in any way binding upon them, or, on the opposite end of the spectrum, not paying the appropriate deference to domestic law *as such*, irrespective of the potential consequences that it may have on the rights of investors [321]. Thus, equating domestic law to facts simply purports to reiterate the separation between domestic law and international law, which leaves international adjudicators – not just investment arbitrators – charged with characterising the disputed conduct by the yardstick of international law. With that understanding and qualification in mind, the formula equating domestic law with facts before international courts and tribunals appears as fundamentally reasonable and appropriate, without prejudice to the more substantive qualifications below [322].

Another general qualification of the equation of domestic law with fact flows from the above recalled increasingly waning difference in the judicial treatment of facts and the law. This trend requires a more proactive role for the adjudicator in acquiring and evaluating disputed facts. Indeed, the specificity of any kinds of fact – be it scientific or legal – deserves specific attention and knowledge. This would dispel concerns about the appropriateness of dealing with domestic law as fact. And this, in fact, appears to be largely consistent with the rationale of the quoted passage from the PCIJ in *Brazilian Loans*.

As anticipated, this approach may turn particularly useful in relation to investment treaty arbitration where domestic law questions arise under

---

318. *Ibid.*

319. *Ibid.*, emphasis added.

320. EU-Vietnam Trade Agreement and Investment Protection Agreement (signed 30 June 2019; not yet entered into force), p. 3-1400, Article 3.43. para. 3.

321. On deference in general, see E. Shirlow, "Deference and Indirect Expropriation Analysis in International Investment Law Observations on Current Approaches and Frameworks for Future Analysis", *ICSID Review*, Vol. 29 (3), 2014, 595-626; J. H. Fahner, *Judicial Deference in International Adjudication: A Comparative Analysis*, Hart, 2020; E. Shirlow, *Judging at the Interface: Deference to State Decision-Making Authority in International Adjudication*, Cambridge University Press, 2021.

322. J. Hepburn, *Domestic Law in International Investment Arbitration*, Oxford, New York, Oxford University Press, 2017.

multiple circumstances, including when applying the relevant investment protection treaty. There, it appears particularly important for the proper administration of justice that the arbitrators adopt a proactive, *jura novit curia* approach to domestic law, if the parties' inaction renders it necessary. Consider, for example, the extremely common scenario where a tribunal must determine whether the claimant has a valid title to the disputed investment, or whether the investment was made in accordance with domestic law as a condition for the application of the treaty in question. Under such circumstances, the tribunal must make an appropriate appreciation of the domestic law *for the purposes* of the application of international law. Adopting this interpretation, it would make little difference for the arbitrator to represent domestic law as a factual precondition for the application of international rules, or as a piece of law incorporated, by reference, into the applicable international law [323].

Similarly, arbitrators may find themselves to have to seriously scrutinise domestic law where the claimant argues that, based on such law, it has developed certain expectations which were instrumental to making the investment. In order to assess under international law whether or not such expectations were legitimate and whether they had been frustrated by subsequent domestic legislation, administrative measures and/or judicial decisions, international arbitrators have to be very well informed and knowledgeable about the way in which the domestic jurisdiction in question works [324].

---

323. For several examples of the relevance of this point, see Douglas, *The International Law of Investment Claims*, 45 *et seq*.

324. For discussions of the notion of legitimate expectations, in particular insofar as it relates to the standard of protection known as "fair and equitable treatment", see M. Potestà, "Legitimate Expectations in Investment Treaty law: Understanding the Roots and the Limits of a Controversial Concept", *ICSID Review*, Vol. 28 (1), 2013, 88-122; P. Dumberry, "The Protection of Investors' Legitimate Expectations and the Fair and Equitable Treatment Standard Under NAFTA Article", *Journal of International Arbitration*, Vol. 31 (1), 2014; S. Hamamoto, "5 Protection of the Investor's Legitimate Expectations: Intersection of a Treaty Obligation and a General Principle of Law", *China and International Investment Law*, Brill Nijhoff, 2014, pp. 141-169; E. T. Laryea, "Legitimate Expectations in Investment Treaty Law: Concept and Scope of Application", *Handbook of International Investment Law and Policy*, 2020, 1-24; C. Henckels, "Legitimate Expectations and the Rule of Law in International Investment Law", *Investment Protection Standards and the Rule of Law (Oxford University Press, forthcoming), Monash University Faculty of Law Legal Studies Research Paper*, (3409086), 2020; G. M. Farnelli, "Recent Trends in Investment Arbitration Concerning Legitimate Expectations", *International Community Law Review*, Vol. 23 (1), 2021, 27.

Domestic law, however, can also play a different role where it is part of the agreed or default applicable law [325], and concerns may arise as to the role to be played by *jura novit curia*. Often, international investment protection agreements expressly indicate domestic law as the applicable law, together with the applicable treaty, and possibly general principles of international law. Domestic law may be more indirectly referred to by treaty provisions – the so-called "umbrella clauses" – which transform into an international treaty obligation any relevant commitment undertaken by the host State, including under domestic law. Under such circumstances, the validity of the commitment in question under domestic law is obviously crucial.

One sees no legally logical reason to exclude the relevance – and, specifically, the *legal* relevance – of domestic law, when it is actually included in the applicable law according to the applicable treaty or agreement. Aside from being the most logical option, recognising domestic law as law would also definitely provide more clarity for the purposes of the exercise of *jura novit curia* powers, or more simply for the application of the applicable law.

In fact, with few notable exceptions, where adjudicators have been given the option – rather than the duty – to apply domestic law that has not been argued by the parties, tribunals have overwhelmingly espoused the view that they could apply the law which would be essential in order to decide the case, irrespective of whether it was not argued by the parties. The point was made expressly in general by the Annulment Committee in *Enron* v. *Argentina* in 2010 [326], while in the 2013 *Methal-Tech* v. *Uzbekistan* Award it was corroborated with specific reference

325. On questions concerning applicable law and the relevance of domestic law, see Douglas, *The International Law of Investment Claims*, 39 *et seq.*; Y. Banifatemi, "The Law Applicable in Investment Treaty Arbitration", in K. Yannaca-Small (ed.), *Arbitration Under International Investment Agreements: A Guide to the Key Issues*, Oxford University Press, 2010; A. K. Bjorklund, *9 Applicable Law in International Investment Disputes*, Brill Nijhoff, 2014; M. V. Benedettelli, "Determining the Applicable Law in Commercial and Investment Arbitration: Two Intertwined Road Maps for Conflicts-Solving", *ICSID Review – Foreign Investment Law Journal*, 2022.

326. See *Enron Corporation* Decision on the Application for Annulment of the Argentine Republic, cit., para. 110. The *ad hoc* Commmittee made this point in the context of a discussion of the standard of review on annulment in relation to the alleged failure by the Tribunal to state reasons for its decision, stating that "the Tribunal was not required to comment on all arguments of the parties in relation to this issue". The Committee also made the point that "even in cases where a tribunal has failed to deal with a question submitted to it, the appropriate remedy may not be an application for annulment, but rather, an application to the tribunal for a supplementary decision, pursuant to Article 49 (2) of the ICSID Convention" (at para. 73).

also to domestic law, obviously, when applicable [327]. An opposite approach was ostensibly endorsed in *CME* v. *Czech Republic*, but in reality the case can be reconciled with the majority view because in that arbitration domestic law was not essential for the Tribunal to decide the case, whereas, as a matter of general principle, failure to apply the proper law is a ground for annulment [328].

It is worth pointing out that, while from a purely theoretical standpoint this line of reasoning is also consistent with the need to respect the prohibition of *non liquet* and the principle *ne infra petita*, the issues at hand have practical relevance. This can be demonstrated by considering the *Mobil Cerro Negro* case, which involved Venezuela as the host State [329]. The relevant BIT between the Netherlands and Venezuela contained an applicable law clause, which listed Venezuelan law, the provisions of the BIT itself, "special agreements relating to the investments" and "the general principles of international law" [330].

In 2014, a highly authoritative ICSID Tribunal [331] awarded 1.6 billion US dollars in favour of ExxonMobil as compensation for the expropriation of its Cerro Negro Project investments [332]. The Tribunal applied general international law in determining compensation [333]. In 2017, the Annulment Committee, also authoritatively composed, annulled part of the Tribunal's Award dealing with compensation [334]. The Committee annulled 1.4 billion out of the 1.6 billion US dollars in compensation ordered by the Tribunal. That meant leaving the claimant

327. *Metal-Tech Ltd.* v. *Republic of Uzbekistan*, ICSID Case No. ARB/10/3, Award, 4 October 2013, para. 121 ("The Tribunal's jurisdiction is governed by the ICSID Convention and by the BIT. Where these treaties are silent on an issue that is relevant to determine jurisdiction, e.g. the manner in which consent is given, such issue is subject to customary international law").

328. *CME Czech Republic BV* v. *The Czech Republic,* UNCITRAL, Final Award, 14 March 2003.

329. *Venezuela Holdings, BV* et al. v. *Bolivarian Republic of Venezuela*, ICSID Case No. ARB/07/27.

330. Agreement on encouragement and reciprocal protection of Investments between the Kingdom of the Netherlands and the Republic of Venezuela (signed 22 October 1991; entered into force 1 November 1993), Article 9.

331. Among the members of the Tribunal was Judge Gilbert Guillaume, a former President of the ICJ.

332. See *Venezuela Holdings, BV* et al. v. *Bolivarian Republic of Venezuela*, ICSID Case No. ARB/07/27, Award, 9 October 2014, para. 404. On the matter of such large monetary awards, see M. Paparinskis, 'A Case Against Crippling Compensation in International Law of State Responsibility', *The Modern Law Review*, Vol. 83 (6), 2020, 1246-1286.

333. *Ibid.*

334. *Venezuela Holdings, BV* et al. v. *Bolivarian Republic of Venezuela*, ICSID Case No. ARB/07/27, Decision on Annulment, 9 March 2017, para. 196.

with a mere 200 million US dollars by way of redress. The Committee reached its conclusion, arguing that the Mobil investment was created under Venezuelan law, which provided a limitation on liability [335]. The Committee found that, by applying general international law, the Tribunal had failed to apply the proper law, thus incurring manifest excess powers [336].

D. *Interpretation* v. *application of the law*

As it should be clear by now, the application of *jura novit curia* is replete with challenges arising from problematic distinctions. Another such distinction is that between the interpretation and the application of the law. The point can be elucidated by referencing its instructive formulation by Judge Shahabuddeen in his Separate Opinion in the 1988 ICJ Advisory Opinion on the *Applicability of the Obligation to Arbitrate under Section 21 of the United Nations Headquarters Agreement* of 26 June 1947 [337], which is worth quoting in full:

> "The phrase 'interpretation and application' has occurred in one version or another in a multitude of dispute settlement provisions extending over many decades into the past. In the Certain German Interests in Polish Upper Silesia case (PCIJ, Series A, No. 6, p. 14), it was held that it was not necessary to satisfy both elements of the phrase taken cumulatively, the word 'and' falling to be read disjunctively. The phrase in this case happens to be 'interpretation or application'. Satisfaction of either element will therefore suffice. But, further, since it is not possible to interpret a treaty save with reference to some factual field (even if taken hypothetically) and since it is not possible to apply a treaty except on the basis of some interpretation of it, there is a detectable view that there is little practical, or even theoretical, distinction between the two elements of the formula . . . t seems arguable that the two elements constitute a compendious term of art generally covering all disputes as to rights and duties having their source in the controlling treaty . . . It is, with much respect to the opposite view, not right to adopt an approach which

335. *Ibid.*, at para. 166 *et seq.*

336. *Ibid.*, at para. 188.

337. *Applicability of the Obligation to Arbitrate under Section 21 of the United Nations Headquarters Agreement of 26 June 1947*, p. 12, at 57 (Separate Opinion of Judge Shahabuddeen) (citations omitted).

> would seek to avoid this conclusion by dissecting the phrase in question, focusing separately on its individual elements, and then reading them as if they did not belong together in a single formula whose force indeed derives from its constituent parts but is not coextensive with their sum." [338]

Following the three-strand approach to international litigation adopted in the present analysis, the relevance of the distinction in point for the purposes of *jura novit curia* is particularly acute in relation to inter-State and investor-State litigation. That is so since, here, the scope of the consent-based jurisdictional powers is further curtailed by the claims of the parties under the commanding *ne ultra petita* principle [339], in terms which find no comparator in international human rights and criminal adjudication.

The power of the adjudicator to decide on the basis of autonomous interpretations of the rules invoked by the parties inherently flows from the very nature of its adjudicative function. In this regard, *jura novit curia* provides little added value. In matters of inter-State and investor-State litigation, *ne ultra petita* assumes a commanding role in determining the application of rules by international adjudicators. It is generally understood that the adjudicator is constrained by the rules that have been invoked by the parties in the case. However, there are instances where *ne infra petita*, in conjunction with the *non liquet*, may exceptionally trigger an extensive application of *jura novit curia*. Conversely, it is worth noting that in human rights and international criminal law adjudication, the proper administration of justice may necessitate the recharacterization of the facts of the case on the basis of rules other than those invoked by the parties. While this departure from the norm may seem exceptional, it is in fact not considered an extraordinary measure in that domain for the adjudicator to apply rules that were not initially invoked by the parties to ensure the proper administration of justice.

Against this background, three main scenarios deserve special attention in which the dividing line between interpretation and application of the law may present itself as particularly blurred. Namely, under the frameworks of Article 31 (3) *(c)* VCLT, Article 293 UNCLOS and of the application of equity in adjudication. These

338. *Ibid.*, at 59-60. See also S. F. Berman, "International Treaties and British Statutes", *Statute Law Review*, Vol. 26 (1), 2005, 1-12; *contra* Gourgourinis, *op. cit.*
339. See Tanzi, *op. cit.*

frameworks provide legal means for the international judge or arbitrator to rely upon international rules and principles apparently extraneous to those which stem directly from the applicable law. Therefore, in the admittedly unlikely scenario where counsel for either party fails to argue the case based on such legal frameworks, the question arises as to whether a judge or arbitrator doing so would be engaging in an autonomous exercise of mere interpretation, or outright application, of the law. Such uncertainties would reflect themselves on the definition of the dividing line between *jura novit curia* and judicial discretion.

1. Article 31 (3) (c) *VCLT*

As to Article 31 (3) *(c)* VCLT, it provides that, for the purposes of interpreting an international treaty, "[t]here shall be taken into account, together with the context: *(c)* any relevant rules of international law applicable in the relations between the parties" [340]. On the face of it, we are expressly within the domain of legal interpretation. Formally, interpreting "rule X" by taking into account "rule Y", which would fall outside the applicable law, should not mean to apply "rule Y".

Statements of principles aside [341], an examination of the practice of international adjudicators reveals that under the jurisdictional formula "interpretation and application", an interpretative exercise ("interpretation of the law") can hardly be disentangled from the "application of the law". In particular, if interpreting and applying "rule X" by taking into account "rule Y" were to result in recognising rights which would not exist otherwise, it would be difficult to argue that under Article 31 (3) *(c)* there would be no element of "application" or rules originating from outside of the confines of the agreed or default applicable law.

When "rule Y" is not argued by the parties and falls outside the ambit of the directly applicable law, this scenario may present a complex *jura novit curia* issue, either by exercising the power to "take into account" "rule Y" in question, or, conversely, failing to do so, from the perspective of a duty for the adjudicator to apply the law. Here, the problems of application of *jura novit curia* would coincide with

340. VCLT, Article 31 (3) *(c)*.

341. It is impossible to provide a comprehensive list of the literature on Article 31 (3) *(c)*. *Ex multis*, see C. McLachlan, "The Principle of Systemic Integration and Article 31 (3) *(C)* of the Vienna Convention", *The International and Comparative Law Quarterly*, Vol. 54 (2), 2005, 279-319.

problems of application of the secondary rule on treaty interpretation codified under Article 31 (3) *(c)*.

Sometimes, Article 31 (3) *(c)* is relied upon in the language of the judgment, or award, as a matter of principle, but with no material impact on the actual *ratio decidendi*. Multiple cases can be found in which a systemic interpretation and application of the law of the kind required under Article 31 (3) *(c)* is actually carried out, but with no express reference to it. Reference may be made to the 1993 ICJ Judgment between Denmark and Norway on *Maritime Delimitation in the Area between Greenland and Jan Mayen.* In that case, the Court was asked to delimit parts of the continental shelf and of fisheries zones between the two countries. In carrying out its task, it observed that

> "The fact that it is the 1958 Convention which applies to the continental shelf delimitation in this case does not mean that Article 6 thereof can be interpreted and applied . . . without reference to customary law on the subject." [342]

It is fair to say that reference to customary law, in the application of the treaty provision in point, was key for the Court in determining a line delimiting both maritime areas.

Similarly, a famous passage from the *Gabčíkovo-Nagymaros* Judgment may provide another example of the constraints imposed by Article 31 (3) *(c)*. In the context of the interpretation of the 1977 Treaty between Hungary and Slovakia, the ICJ observed that

> "new norms and standards have been developed, set forth in a great number of instruments during the last two decades. Such new norms have to be taken into consideration, and such new standards given proper weight, not only when States contemplate new activities but also when continuing with activities begun in the past" [343].

Another example is offered by the *Enrica Lexie* Award over the dispute between Italy and India concerning which of the two could exercise criminal jurisdiction over two Italian marines [344]. The dispute, which was brought under UNCLOS, saw the Tribunal apply Articles 58

342. *Maritime Delimitation in the Area Between Greenland and Jan Mayen (Denmark* v. *Norway)*, Judgment, *ICJ Reports 1993*, p. 38, at 58, para. 46.

343. *Gabčíkovo-Nagymaros Project (Hungary/Slovakia)*, Judgment, *ICJ Reports 1997*, p. 7.

344. *The "Enrica Lexie" Incident (Italy* v. *India)*, PCA Case 2015-28, Award, 21 May 2020. See A. M. Tanzi, "Adjudication at the Service of Diplomacy: The Enrica Lexie Case", *Journal of International Dispute Settlement*, Vol. 12 (3), 2021, 448-461.

(2) and 92 UNCLOS and take into account the international customary rule on the immunity from criminal jurisdiction of foreign officials for conduct performed in the course of official duties [345]. Based on the UNCLOS provisions in point, the Tribunal determined that the incident was subject to the concurrent jurisdiction of both States, but found that India was barred by immunity from exercising its criminal jurisdiction. To do so, however, the Tribunal did not mention either Article 31 (3) *(c)* VCLT or Article 293 UNCLOS. We will revert to this point in the next section.

In addition, it may be worth recalling that investor-State case law, too, has shown nuanced indications of tribunals taking into account human rights or environmental protection rules at a time when they were not incorporated into the new generation international investment agreements. One such instance may be found in the *Biwater* v. *Tanzania* case, which concerned water and sanitation services [346]. In a purely declaratory award, the Tribunal asserted multiple breaches of the investment treaty by the defendant State. Yet it awarded no compensation, a decision that has been explained by commentators by reference to Tanzania's obligation to afford its population the right to access to water and sanitation [347].

345. As the Tribunal put it: "The issue of entitlement to exercise jurisdiction encompasses, but is not conclusively answered by, the question as to whether the Marines enjoy immunity from jurisdiction in respect of acts that they undertook during the incident. In fact, both Italy and India have presented various other arguments, unrelated to the question of immunity, as to why each of them should or should not be entitled to exercise jurisdiction under different provisions of the Convention. Thus the question of the immunity of the Marines is one aspect out of several, albeit an important one, that requires examination in resolving the Parties' dispute". See *PCA, The "Enrica Lexie" Incident, Italy* v. *India, Award*, Case No 2015-28 (21 May 2020), para. 806. Note that the matter was the subject of disagreement. See, for example, the Concurring and Dissenting Opinion Dr. P. S. Rao, stating that "decision to assume jurisdiction over the issue of immunity, although it found that it is not as an issue covered by the Convention, but on the ground that it is an issue incidental to the dispute and necessary to discharge its mandate fully and completely is fundamentally wrong and based on untenable propositions" (at 12, para. 30).

346. *Biwater Gauff (Tanzania) Ltd.* v. *United Republic of Tanzania*, ICSID Case No. ARB/05/22, Award, 24 July 2008.

347. *Ibid.*, para. 814. See also para. 807 ("Given that none of the Republic's violations of the BIT caused the loss and damage for which BGT now claims compensation, it follows that each of BGT's claims for damages must be dismissed, and that the only appropriate remedies for the Republic's conduct can be declaratory in nature"). See E. De Brabandere, M. Fitzmaurice and P. Merkouris, "Human Rights Considerations in International Investment Arbitration", *The Interpretation and Application of the European Convention of Human Rights: Legal and Practical Implications*, Martinus Nijhoff Publishers, 2012, p. 183; U. Kriebaum, "Human Rights and International Investment Law", *Research Handbook on Human Rights and Investment*, Edward Elgar Publishing, 2018, pp. 13-40; On the potential relevance of the *amicus curiae*

2. Article 293 UNCLOS

Rules apparently falling outside the scope of the jurisdiction *ratione materiae* of the adjudicator concerned may also re-enter the picture by reason of a specific *renvoi* in the relevant applicable law clause. One illustrative example is provided by Article 293 (1) UNCLOS, which provides that "[a] court or tribunal having jurisdiction under this section shall apply this Convention *and other rules of international law not incompatible with this Convention*" [348]. Its clear wording, as compared to Article 31 (3) *(c)*, would suggest that the UNCLOS provision pertains to the *application* of rules outside those of the Convention, whereas Article 31 (1) *(c)* is confined to reference to external rules to be "taken into account" merely for purposes of interpretation.

Yet, as already mentioned, the distinction may be all but illusory. Its evanescence has been notably highlighted the 2015 *South China Sea* Award on jurisdiction and admissibility [349]. The Tribunal simply equated the two provisions in question for the stated purpose of interpreting Articles 192 and 194 UNCLOS in the light of the relevant provisions of the Convention on Biological Diversity [350].

Having regard to *jura novit curia* in the characterisation of the disputed facts for the purpose of assessing the tribunal's jurisdiction, as recently reiterated by the ITLOS in *Norstar*, Article 293 may not be relied on to extend the ITLOS jurisdiction, or that of an Annex VII Tribunal, over alleged breaches of rules other than those of the Convention [351]. However, so long as the external rules in question are incidental to the disputed facts which fall within the scope of the Convention, they may be applied to such facts.

We have already seen how the Annex VII Tribunal in *Enrica Lexie* – once satisfied that it had jurisdictional competence over the disputed

---

submission on the reasoning of the Tribunal, see H. Chen, "The Role of *Amicus Curiae* in Implementing the Human Right to Water in the Context of International Investment Law", *Review of European, Comparative & International Environmental Law*, Vol. 29 (3), 2020, 454-463.

348. UNCLOS, Article 293 (emphasis added).

349. *The South China Sea Arbitration (The Republic of Philippines* v. *The People's Republic of China)*, PCA Case 2013-19, Award on Jurisdiction and Admissibility, 29 October 2015.

350. Note that the Philippines had urged the Tribunal to do so, pushing for an endorsement of the "systemic" approach expoused in the *MOX Plant* case, on the ground that it "it respects the characterization of the dispute adopted by the party bringing the case, and because it better reflects the need for a coherent integration of different treaty regimes with each other". See Award, para. 280, citing Jurisdictional Hearing Tr. (Day 3), p. 47.

351. *M/V "Norstar" (Panama* v. *Italy)*, Judgment, *ITLOS Reports 2018-2019*, p. 10.

facts, which fell within the scope of the Convention – applied the customary rule on the jurisdictional immunity of foreign officials as incidental to the application of Articles 58 and 97 UNCLOS [352].

The *Saiga No. 2* case may also prove instructive. The case concerned an oil tanker which was operating as a bunkering vessel off the coast of West Africa, providing fuel to three fishing vessels that had licences from Guinea to fish within its 200-mile exclusive economic zone (EEZ) [353]. The *Saiga* was shot at and arrested by Guinean patrol boats, beyond the southern boundary of Guinea's EEZ, causing two people on board to suffer gunshot wounds. The *Saiga* was taken to Conakry, where the ship and crew were detained, its gas oil cargo was removed and its master prosecuted for violating customs regulations [354]. The International Tribunal for the Law of the Sea ruled that Guinea's actions violated UNCLOS and awarded damages to Saint Vincent and the Grenadines [355]. To do so, the Tribunal had to frame its application of the rules concerning the use of force, which fell outside of the scope of its jurisdiction *ratione materiae*. It did so by relying on Article 293 to argue that "[c]onsiderations of humanity must apply in the law of the sea, as they do in other areas of international law" [356]. Based on such an "interpretation and application" of UNCLOS, ITLOS reached the finding of wrongfulness of the forcible means adopted by Guinea in arresting the ship flying the flag of the Applicant and the crew. And, as stressed by the Tribunal, it did so "although the Convention does not contain express provisions on the use of force in the arrest of ships" [357]. It might be worth noting that the respondent in that case had not objected – or had not, at any rate, objected expressly – to the application of rules concerning the use of force [358].

Conversely, in *Guyana/Suriname*, another UNCLOS case involving similar circumstances, the respondent did object, and quite vigorously [359].

352. See *supra* note 66 and accompanying text.

353. *M/V "SAIGA" (No. 2) (Saint Vincent and the Grenadines* v. *Guinea)*, Judgment, *ITLOS Reports 1999*, p. 10

354. *Ibid.*, at 28, para. 33.

355. *Ibid.*, at 69, para. 181.

356. *Ibid.*, at 61-62, para. 155.

357. *Ibid.*

358. *Ibid.*, at 61, paras. 153-159.

359. *Guyana* v. *Suriname*, PCA Case 2004-04, Suriname's Rejoinder, at para. 4.7 ("Indeed, to the extent that the Tribunal is allowed to consider the UN Charter and customary international law, it is *only* as they relate to disputes concerning 'the interpretation or application' of the 1982 Convention. They can be secondary points of reference, but not the primary basis for bringing a claim. Indeed, where a tribunal's jurisdiction is predicated on the interpretation or application of a particular instrument, the tribunal must reject efforts by a party to rely upon other instruments or general

Nevertheless, the Annex VII Tribunal tasked with adjudicating the dispute did not find this to be a material difference, one which would prevent it from following the same line of reasoning. Thus, it cited with approval the decision of ITLOS in *Saiga No. 2* and proceeded to adjudicate the claims based on the use of force [360].

Similar issues arose in the *Arctic Sunrise* case [361]. Faced with arguments – if not outright claims – based on human rights instruments such as the ICCPR and the ECHR [362], the Arbitral Tribunal observed that, far from extending the jurisdiction of a tribunal, Article 293 (1) allowed it to "give full effect to the provisions of the Convention" [363]. Notably, the Tribunal observed that this may require, not only the application of "foundational or secondary rules of general international law such as the law of treaties or the rules of State responsibility" [364], but also of "primary rules of international law other than the Convention in order to interpret and apply particular provisions of the Convention" [365]. Eventually, the Arbitral Tribunal concluded that "if necessary, [it] may have regard to general international law in relation to human rights in order to determine whether law enforcement action such as the boarding, seizure, and detention of the Arctic Sunrise and the arrest and detention of those on board was reasonable and proportionate" [366], but it was at pains to point out that it did not have jurisdiction to apply directly provisions taken from human rights treaties [367].

---

international law that do not, by their own terms, confer jurisdiction upon the tribunal").

360. *Guyana* v. *Suriname*, PCA Case 2004-04, Award, 17 September 2007, paras. 405-406. It bears noting, however, that the Tribunal also found "that the conduct of Suriname in the disputed area constituted a breach of its obligations under Articles 74 (3) and 83 (3) of the Convention over which the Tribunal has jurisdiction by virtue of Article 293, paragraph 1, of the Convention". It is an open question whether or not the claims could have been "absorbed". See para. 406. For an analysis of the relationship between jurisdiction *ratione materiae* and the relevant applicable law clauses in these two cases, see Bartels, *op. cit.*

361. *The Arctic Sunrise Arbitration (Netherlands* v. *Russia)*, PCA Case 2014-02, Award on the Merits, 14 August 2015.

362. The difference was noted by the Tribunal. See Award on the Merits, paras. 193-196 ("at times, the Netherlands appears to invite the Tribunal directly to determine that there has been a breach by Russia of Articles 9 and 12 (2) of the ICCPR, to which both States are parties . . . By contrast, the Netherlands has not invited the Tribunal to determine whether Russia breached the ECHR").

363. *Ibid.*, at paras. 187-189.

364. *Ibid.*, para. 190.

365. *Ibid.*, para. 191.

366. *Ibid.*, para. 197.

367. *Ibid.*, para. 198.

In all the above cases, the external rules in point were argued by the parties, and, therefore, there was no need for the adjudicator to resort to *jura novit curia*. However, such systemic reference mechanisms, as those provided by Article 31 (3) *(c)* VCLT and Article 293 UNCLOS, considerably widen the potential margins for adjudicators to exercise their *jura novit curia* discretion. It should be stressed that, as we saw from the case law, such potential certainly works in relation to the application of the law to the merits, while there may be room for debate as to whether it extends to the *Kompetenz-Kompetenz* powers on the determination of the width of the jurisdictional competence of inter-State or investor-State courts or tribunals. Increasing case law on incidental, or ancillary, jurisdiction seems to corroborate an answer in the affirmative, to the effect that "[w]here a tribunal has jurisdiction in a particular matter, it is also competent with regard to all relevant incidental questions, subject to express provision to the contrary" [368].

3. *Equity*

(i) *Equity as a general principle of law*

In Chapter I, the translation of *jura novit curia* provided by Black's Law Dictionary as meaning "the court knows the law; the court recognizes rights" was addressed as problematic. This was so, *inter alia*, because the expression "the court recognizes rights" juxtaposed to "the court knows the law" appeared to imply a basis for adjudicators to award remedies in equity beyond those that are based in the law. This approach seems to hint at a *praeter legem*, if not *contra legem* configuration of equity [369].

It is possible to conceive of a general principle of law requiring that the application of rules of international law be carried out in an equitable and reasonable manner. This would be consistent with the constitutional

368. Bin Chen, *General Principles of Law as Applied by International Courts and Tribunals*, Bin Cheng, p. 266 of the 1987 (reprint). *Case Concerning Certain German Interests in Polish Upper Silesia (Germany* v. *Poland)*, Judgment of 25 August 1925, PCIJ Series A, No. 6, p. 18; Chagos, para. 220; Enrica Lexie, PCA Case No. 2015-28 (21 May 2020).

369. On equity *praeter legem*, see M. Akehurst, "Equity and General Principles of Law", *International & Comparative Law Quarterly*, Vol. 25 (4), 1976, 801-825, 801; C. Titi, *The Function of Equity in International Law*, Oxford, New York, Oxford University Press, 2021, 87.

principle of good faith [370]. By that logic, through provisions such as Article 31 (3) *(c)* VCLT and Article 293 UNCLOS, equity and equitable considerations would apply as a matter of interpretation or application of treaty law. Such an operation would remain squarely within the realm of an application of equity *infra legem*.

The same reasoning would apply to the interpretation and application of international customary law rules to the extent that one considers that also the latter are subject to interpretation. There is strong support in the literature for the view that international adjudicators, in applying a customary rule, embark on some kind of interpretative reasoning and inevitably engage in a process of identification and assessment of the rule in question. If this were correct, and on the basis of the assumption that the parties have to prove the facts, but not the law, which is to be known by the judge, the scope of *jura novit curia* would be substantially widened.

Be that as it may, equity need not be conceived as a force displacing legal rules. As put by Vaughan Lowe,

> "To the extent that broad principles which will do the work of equity can be found within the legal system, there is no need to apply equity *contra legem*: equity may motivate the decision, but the decision will be based on an interpretation and application of the law." [371]

In this regard, it is instructive to briefly consider the role of equity in municipal legal systems – or at least some of them. In these systems, corrective equity was applied as a form of justice separate from the law [372], and quite possibly in contrast with it. This is no longer the case even in those where equity was created in the late Middle Ages as an alternative to actions and remedies at common law [373]. This body of law was finally subsumed into the legal system of England and Wales

---

370. On the connection between equity and good faith, see S. K. Chattopadhyay, "Equity in International Law: Its Growth and Development", *Georgia Journal of International and Comparative Law*, Vol. 5 (2), 1975, 381-406, 387; V. Lowe, "The Role of Equity in International Law", *The Australian Yearbook of International Law Online*, Vol. 12 (1), 1992, 54-81, 72; R. Kolb, "Principles as Sources of International Law (with Special Reference to Good Faith)", *Netherlands International Law Review*, Vol. 53 (1), 2006, 1–36; Titi, *The Function of Equity in International Law*, 171.

371. Lowe, *op. cit.*, 67.

372. See, for example, Lowe, *op. cit.*, 54 ("A serviceable definition of equity is: general principles of justice as distinguished from any particular system of jurisprudence or the municipal law of any State").

373. B. Garner (ed.), Black's Law Dictionary, (10th ed.), 2014, p. 656.

after almost five centuries of increasingly consistent application of equitable principles by the Court of Chancery, which was eventually replaced at the end of the nineteenth century by the Chancery Division of the High Court of Justice [374]. In international law, equity was never conceived as separate from the law, except under the circumstance in which the parties decided to have a dispute settled *ex aequo et bono*, under Article 38 (2) of the Statute of the ICJ, and of its predecessor, the PCIJ [375]. Interestingly, this option does not seem ever to have been resorted to by disputing parties, who have always relied on the Court's application of the law for the settlement of their disputes [376]. From an empirical standpoint equity has been consistently addressed as part of the international law applicable by permanent international judicial bodies since their inception. The point was well illustrated in Judge Hudson's individual opinion in the *Diversion of Water from the Meuse* case, as follows:

> "The Court has not been expressly authorized by its Statute to apply equity as distinguished from law . . . The Court's recognition of equity as a part of international law is in no way restricted by the special power conferred upon it 'to decide a case *ex aequo et bono*, if the parties agree thereto' . . . It must be concluded, therefore, that under Article 38 of the Statute, if not independently of that Article, the Court has some freedom to consider principles of equity as part of the international law which it must apply." [377]

The normative dimension of equity, not just in its interpretive function, but also in substantive law terms, was clear from the beginning of international adjudication. This construction flows from the specific view of the constitutional structure of international law, as well as from the principle of good faith [378]. This approach requires that that rules of international law be interpreted and applied equitably and reasonably.

374. J. Baker, An Introduction to English Legal History (5th ed.), Oxford, 2019, p. 123.

375. See e.g. A.-G. Mérignhac, "Traité théorique et pratique de l'arbitrage international" (Larose 1895), cited in Titi, *The Function of Equity in International Law*, 105.

376. See Titi, *The Function of Equity in International Law*, 142 ("No international court is known to have exercised *ex aequo et bono* jurisdiction. Whenever the suspicion of an *ex aequo et bono* mandate reared its head, international courts – and states too – displayed maximal caution").

377. *Diversion of Water from the Meuse*, PCIJ Series A/B No 70, 28 June 1937, 76 (Individual Opinion of Judge Hudson).

378. On this point, see Kolb, *op. cit.*

It also calls for the production of rules allowing the settlement of conflicts in manners conducive to obtaining equitable and reasonable results.

While in principle all legal rules are characterised by a fair degree of generality and abstraction of their scope of application, the conceptual rationale of equity is that of ensuring the equitable result of the application of the law to the specific circumstances pertaining to a given case. In general, this rationale is given effect through equity as an interpretive general principle. Equity is expressed through customary principles and treaty rules that combine interpretive and substantive law, requiring consideration of specific circumstances. This occurs when those circumstances are clearly defined, even if only in the abstract. The equitable principle or rule in question will therefore require the examination of those particular circumstances.

As to customary law, reference may be had to such general rules as those of abuse of rights and unjust enrichment [379]. Such general principles of law can be considered to have been originally incorporated into international law as generally accepted principles *in foro domestico* of most, if not all, domestic legal systems, under Article 38 (1) *(c)* of the ICJ Statute. It is customary to rehash the traditional argument whereby the general principles *of law* in questions are simply those that international law "borrows" from domestic law – though not quite, as some would contend, "lock, stock and barrel" [380]. While the argument finds support in the proceedings of the Advisory Committee of Jurists, there is not much to be gained by the distinction. In fact, through widely repeated and consistent invocation and application in international diplomatic and adjudicative practice, these principles have arguably been converted into general principles *of international law* of a customary law nature [381]. Content-wise, they are characterised

379. J. Paulsson, *The Unruly Notion of Abuse of Rights*, Cambridge, Cambridge University Press, 2020.

380. See the Separate Opinion of Lord McNair in *Status of South-West Africa, ICJ Reports 1950*, at 148, "The way in which international law borrows from this source is not by means of importing private law institutions 'lock, stock and barrel' ready-made and fully equipped with a set of rules. It would be difficult to reconcile such a process with the application of 'the general principles of law'. In my opinion, [he said] the true view of the duty of international tribunals in this matter is to regard any features or terminology which are reminiscent of the rules and institution of private law as an indication of policy and principles rather than as directly importing these rules and institutions".

381. For similar views, see Titi, *The Function of Equity in International Law*, 105 ("General principles of law can metamorphose into customary international law, when courts and tribunals apply them and states invoke and recognise them. This process

by their direct applicability, which may complement and even displace the applicable law.

For the purposes of *jura novit curia*, it is unlikely that, where appropriate, such equitable customary principles will not be invoked by the defendant in any given case. However, particularly in case of *absentia*, the international judge would be under the duty to rely on such rules *sua sponte*. Having regard to treaty rules expressly giving effect to equity, I will make special reference to those governing the delimitation of terrestrial or maritime areas.

Both bodies of law are intrinsically permeated with equity. Interestingly, the conventional nature of the rules in question only buttresses and finesses in written form the corresponding customary law-making process. For the special purposes of *jura novit curia*, both also evoke the increasingly delicate issue, already discussed throughout this course, of the application of rules characterised by a highly scientific or technical contents and factual relevance. To repeat, in the judicial application of these rules, the distinction between facts and the law, as well as between the role of the parties and that of the adjudicator, over the production, gathering and legal appreciation of such facts, lose much of their importance. This may be seen as an application of *jura novit curia* to the specific kind of facts in question, so extremely entangled with the normative parameters of the rules in question and, at one and the same time, with equity, thus *infra legem* [382].

(ii) *Equity in maritime and land delimitation*

Perhaps one of the most visible areas in international case law in which equity plays a role is maritime and terrestrial delimitation. Articles 74 (1) and 83 (1) UNCLOS, respectively on the delimitation of the exclusive economic zone and the continental shelf, require the parties to reach "on the basis of international law, as referred to

---

also reflects the evolution of equity"); Tanzi, *A Concise Introduction to International Law*, 115 ("the expression 'general principles of international law' would therefore not be indicative of the municipal provenance of the principles in question, but of their content: namely, such expression would indicate a set of international customary rules having a content widely shared among states and, as such, one that would be instrumental in forging the systemic consistency of the international legal order. In that sense, like in any legal system, those are the building blocks and pillars of the rule of law in international law").

382. On the role of equity in maritime delimitation, see also M. Lando, *Maritime Delimitation as a Judicial Process*, Cambridge University Press, 2019.

in Article 38 of the Statute of the ICJ", an agreement aimed at an "equitable solution" [383].

Both sets of rules are meant to provide guidance for the parties to reach an agreement, but where this is not possible and the parties concerned go for adjudication, such rules will be applied judicially. An adjudicator will, in cases such as these, likely apply *jura novit curia* to the extent that its interpretation of the law – or even the identification of the law – might stray away from what the parties submit. In taking into account a technical factor, or circumstance, which has not been argued by the parties, the judge would be applying elements of equity *infra legem* in full autonomy from the parties.

An approach of this kind need not be seen as undesirable. As Vaughan Lowe put it,

> "[o]ne of the features of equity which makes its use appear desirable to judges and parties alike is obvious. Its invocation strengthens a decision made on other grounds, and particularly decisions taken on narrow technical grounds. Equity buttresses legal arguments. A decision based on technical legal rules may be shown to be consistent with principles of justice and fairness. This function is critical" [384].

Inter-State jurisprudence shows that when an international adjudicator is asked to decide a delimitation dispute, be it terrestrial or maritime [385], it almost always comes down to a line different from those claimed by each of the two disputing parties [386].

As stressed by Hersch Lauterpacht,

> "[i]f the business of the judge is to declare the existing frontier in regard to the disputed territory, then it is difficult to see why, in ascertaining the existing law, he should be bound by the assertions of the parties which may go beyond what they are legitimately entitled to claim. In fact, it may be assumed that they will tend to exaggerate their legal rights" [387].

383. UNCLOS, Articles 74 and 83.

384. See Lowe, *op. cit.*, 69.

385. P. Weil, "Délimitation maritime et délimitation terrestre", in S. Rosenne, Y. Dinstein and M. Tabory, *International Law at a Time of Perplexity: Essays in Honour of Shabtai Rosenne*, Dordrecht, The Netherlands, M. Nijhoff, 1989.

386. See for all G. Giraudeau, "Les différends territoriaux devant le juge international. Entre droit et transaction", Leiden-Boston, 2013, especially at Part I, Title I, Chapter II and p. 237.

387. H. Lauterpacht, *The Function of Law in the International Community*, 1st pbk. ed. Oxford; New York, Oxford University Press, 2011, 132.

This consideration would, in fact, apply to the generality of disputes where, inevitably, each disputing party tends to interpret the applicable law often by stretching its scope so as to serve its disputed interests. The role of the adjudicator is always that of deciding the case by applying the law according to its interpretation in relation to the disputed facts, provided it does so within the boundaries of the applicable law. If interpreting the applicable law in terms other than those pleaded by the parties is to be considered to be an exercise of *jura novit curia*, then the latter principle would permeate the judicial function in its entirety. As anticipated in Chapter I, this is not the view of the present writer.

Therefore, in order to assess the spectrum between the exercise of *jura novit curia*, the legitimate exercise of judicial discretion in the interpretation and application of the law, or even arbitrariness, one is inevitably confronted with the relation of equity to the law in any given case. And the issue is more acute with regard to certain categories of disputes than others. This is precisely the case with delimitation disputes, both maritime and terrestrial [388].

Lauterpacht captured the essence of the problem as follows:

> "It is the frontier as given by law, and not as arbitrarily defined by the litigants, that the arbitrator has to lay down. If he chooses an intermediate line, there is no reason for maintaining with any degree of cogency that the boundary chosen is a common denominator arrived at through a process of compromise and mediation, as distinguished from a strictly judicial procedure." [389]

In other words, when departing from the arguments submitted by both parties with specific regard to delimitation disputes, the adjudicator will necessarily engage in some kind of equitable assessment in *ex aequo et bono* terms, if not entirely *contra legem*.

Significant efforts are made in boundary disputes to make sure that the adjudicator's determination remains squarely within the scope of the application of the law. Suffice it to recall that in its 2006 Award in the arbitration between Barbados and the Republic of Trinidad and Tobago, relating to the delimitation of the Exclusive Economic Zone and Continental Shelf between them, the Tribunal felt the need to stress that "[t]here are no magic formulas for making such a determination

388. On the use of equity as the unifying factor between the two areas of international law, see P. Weil, *op. cit*.

389. See Lauterpacht, *The Function of Law in the International Community*, 140.

and it is here that the Tribunal's discretion must be exercised within the limits set out by the applicable law"[390].

Such concerns, having special regard to the delimitation of maritime boundaries, account for a troubled period of international lawmaking, where new rights of sovereignty were afforded over maritime zones. The latter were introduced since the second post-war period, without clear normative parameters over their delimitation between competing States – whose coasts are adjacent or opposite each other – that would objectively apply under all circumstances, such as the criterion of equidistance, without leading in some cases to inequitable results[391]. There is no denying that the international case law has, ever since, inspired the customary international lawmaking process in the field, including the elaboration and elucidation of UNCLOS, with special regard to Articles 74 and 83 on the EEZ and continental platform, respectively[392].

As it is generally recalled[393], such case law was started by the landmark 1969 Judgment in the *North Sea Continental Shelf Dispute Between Denmark and The Netherlands Against Germany*[394], and continued, among others, in *Fisheries Jurisdiction* cases[395], *Tunisia* v. *Libya Continental Shelf*[396], and *Libya* v. *Malta Continental Shelf*[397]. The ICJ more recent case law in maritime delimitation embedded in equity is also worth noting, with special regard to *Jan Mayen*[398], *Black Sea*[399], *Territorial and Maritime Dispute (Nicaragua* v. *Colombia)*[400] and *Maritime Dispute (Peru* v. *Chile)*[401].

390. *Barbados* v. *Trinidad and Tobago*, PCA Case 2004-02, Award, 11 April 2006.

391. *Ibid.,* at para. 373.

392. Interestingly, the ICJ itself referred to "customary law concerning the continental shelf as developed in the decided cases". See *Maritime Delimitation in the Area between Greenland and Jan Mayen (Denmark* v. *Norway)*, Judgment, *ICJ Reports 1993*, p. 38, at 61, para. 51.

393. See, for all, Titi, *The Function of Equity in International Law*, 39.

394. *North Sea Continental Shelf, (Germany/Denmark; Germany/Netherlands)*, Judgment, *ICJ Reports 1969*, p. 3.

395. *Fisheries Jurisdiction (Germany* v. *Iceland),* Judgment, *ICJ Reports 1974*, p. 175.

396. *Continental Shelf (Tunisia/Libyan Arab Jamahiriya)*, Judgment, *ICJ Reports 1982*, p. 18.

397. *Continental Shelf (Libya/Malta)*, Judgment, *ICJ Reports 1985*, p. 13.

398. See *Maritime Delimitation in the Area between Greenland and Jan Mayen (Denmark* v. *Norway),* Judgment, *ICJ Reports 1993*, p. 38.

399. *Maritime Delimitation in the Black Sea (Romania* v. *Ukraine)*, Judgment, *ICJ Reports 2009*, p. 61.

400. *Territorial and Maritime Dispute (Nicaragua* v. *Colombia)*, Judgment, *ICJ Reports 2012*, p. 624

401. *Maritime Dispute (Peru* v. *Chile)*, Judgment, *ICJ Reports 2014*, p. 3.

It is fair to say that in the *North Sea Continental Shelf* Judgment, and the following case law, at least until the completion of the formation process of a specific customary rule on the matter, the international adjudicator very much followed the reasoning of the Great Britain-United States Arbitral Tribunal expressed in the passage quoted at the beginning of Section B, i.e. "applying – in default of any specific provision of law – the corollaries of general principles" [402]. Equity was the general principle in point in the *North Sea Continental Shelf* Judgment [403]. And not as a corrective interpretive principle, but as a source of substantive international law. While the Court could not apply Article 6 (2) of the 1958 Geneva Convention on the Continental Shelf [404], as Germany was not a party to it, it found that delimitation was "to be effected by agreement in accordance with equitable principles, and taking account of all relevant circumstances" [405]. In fact, the Court could well be said to have applied the rationale of the conventional provision in point – in the sense that equidistance should be derogated from when special circumstances so require – crucially adding equity at its foundation. This was later incorporated into Article 83 (1) UNCLOS [406].

Indeed, amid some criticism [407] – including for applying a customary rule on continental platform delimitation that probably had not yet been formed at the time – the fact remains that the Court applied equity as a general principle of law requiring equitable factors to be taken into account in maritime delimitation when equidistance would lead to inequitable solutions. That means equity as a matter of law and not *praeter* or, let alone, *contra*, *legem*. Precisely to that end, the Court emphasised that

402. *Supra* note 2 and accompanying text.

403. *Convention on the Continental Shelf*, (Signed: Geneva, 29 April 1958; entered into force 10 June 1964), 499 UNTS 311.

404. *Ibid.* Article 6 (2) ("Where the same continental shelf is adjacent to the territories of two adjacent States, the boundary of the continental shelf shall be determined by agreement between them. In the absence of agreement, and unless another boundary line is justified by special circumstances, the boundary shall be determined by the application of the principle of equidistance from the nearest points of the baselines from which the breadth of the territorial sea of each State is measured").

405. *North Sea Continental Shelf, (Germany/Denmark; Germany/Netherlands)*, Judgment, *ICJ Reports 1969*, para. 101.

406. The provision reads as follows: "The delimitation of the continental shelf between States with opposite or adjacent coasts shall be effected by agreement on the basis of international law, as referred to in Article 38 of the Statute of the International Court of Justice, in order to achieve an equitable solution".

407. See Titi *cit.*, p. 41 and the authorities quoted therein, at fns 105 f.

> "[I]t is not a question of applying equity simply as a matter of abstract justice, but of applying a rule of law which requires the application of equitable principles, in accordance with the ideas which have always underlain the development of the legal regime of the continental shelf in [. . . the] field of its delimitation between States whose coasts are adjacent or opposite to each other." [408]

To that end, it is worth stressing how Article 83 (1) UNCLOS expressly provides that the delimitation to be effected by agreement "in order to achieve an equitable solution" is to be based on "international law, as referred to in Article 38 (1) of the Statute of the International Court of Justice". In other words, the factors to be considered by the negotiating parties in any specific case, or by the international judge if agreement cannot be reached, are enshrined in international law, be it a custom, a general principle of law or an inherent element of Article 83 (1). The latter does not lay down such factors, not even in non-exhaustive exemplary terms, but, interestingly, in *North Sea Continental Shelf*, the Court spelled out the following factors, the consideration of which may well be deemed to fall within the scope of the customary law of equity on continental platform delimitation:

> "(1) the general configuration of the coasts of the Parties, as well as the presence of any special or unusual features;
>
> (2) so far as known or readily ascertainable, the physical and geological structure, and natural resources, of the continental shelf areas involved;
>
> (3) the element of a reasonable degree of proportionality, which a delimitation carried out in accordance with equitable principles ought to bring about between the extent of the continental shelf areas appertaining to the coastal State and the length of its Coast measured in the general direction of the coastline, account being taken for this purpose of the effects, actual or prospective, of any other continental shelf delimitations between adjacent States in the same region." [409]

The point has been made above to the effect that, generally, the adjudicator who interprets an applicable rule differently from the

408. *ICJ Reports*, para. 101.

409. *North Sea Continental Shelf, (Germany/Denmark; Germany/Netherlands)*, Judgment, *ICJ Reports 1969*, para. 101.

interpretation propounded by either party, or both, exercises a normal degree of judicial discretion which does not amount to – or require by way of justification – resort to *jura novit curia*. Here, when one of the factors laid down in the just quoted passage is taken into consideration by the adjudicator without having been argued by the parties or having been argued differently, this would unquestionably constitute an exercise of adjudicative discretion, though a discretion falling short of an exercise of *jura novit curia*.

E. Jura novit curia *and the time element*

The relevance of *jura novit curia* can also be appreciated in those circumstances where the adjudicator is required to make a determination as to the relevance of a time element. This can involve a determination as to the applicability of a particularly relevant primary rule – for example, due to the application of the doctrine of intertemporal law, or because the scope of application of a given treaty is limited in scope – or due to the application of the relevant secondary rules to the disputed facts in the case – for example, with regard to a breach consisting of a composite act under the law of State responsibility, requiring the application of the relevant secondary rules. As already discussed, the distinction between these scenarios may be more elusive in practice than at the theoretical level.

1. Intertemporal law

As to the first scenario, it is important to list, first and foremost, the few certainties that we have concerning intertemporal law as operating in international law and international adjudication. First, the doctrine of intertemporal law essentially does not concern the validity in time of a particular legal rule, but only its temporal applicability. Accordingly, questions of applicable law arise where, assuming the validity of the law applying in different time slices, uncertainties exist as to which law would regulate the conduct or legal rights being adjudicated upon. Second, international law operates according to the principle *tempus regit actum*. As the Sole Arbitrator Max Huber put it in the *Island of Palmas* case,

> "[a] juridical fact must be appreciated in the light of the law contemporary with it, and not of the law in force

> at the time when a dispute in regard to it arises or falls to be settled"[410].

In many respects, certainties end here and other aspects of the doctrine of intertemporal law are far more controversial. In particular, a second prong of the doctrine essentially hinges on the distinction between the law supporting the creation of a right and the law allowing the continued existence of the same right. As Huber put it in the same landmark case,

> "The same principle which subjects the act creative of a right to the law in force at the time the right arises, demands that the existence of the right, in other words its continued manifestation, shall follow the conditions required by the evolution of law."[411]

This second prong of the argument is particularly testing. The difficulties in its application may be exemplified by the *Chagos* Advisory Opinion[412]. As is well known, the Opinion concerned the sovereignty of the Chagos Archipelago, a group of islands located in the Indian Ocean. In the 1960s, the UK had detached the Chagos Archipelago from Mauritius, which was then a British colony, and established a new colony called the British Indian Ocean Territory[413]. The UK also forced the Chagossians to make way for a joint military base with the United States on the island of Diego Garcia. The matter hinged on the existence of a right to self-determination at the time of the detachment of the archipelago. The UK argued that the detachment of the islands from Mauritius in 1965 was not unlawful as the right to self-determination did not exist at that time. However, the ICJ found that the right to self-determination was recognised in General Assembly Resolution 1514 (XV), meaning that the separation was unlawful[414]. As Steven Wheatley compellingly argues, there are three issues with the Court's decision: firstly, it would have been difficult to argue that a consensus existed among international lawyers as to whether Resolution 1514 (XV) represented customary international law at the time of its adoption; secondly, it is unlikely that the ICJ would have made the same ruling in the 1960s; and finally, the UK lawyers who advised on

---

410. *Island of Palmas (Netherlands* v. *USA),* (1928) 2 RIAA 829, 845.
411. *Ibid.*
412. *Legal Consequences of the Separation of the Chagos Archipelago from Mauritius in 1965*, Advisory Opinion, *ICJ Reports 2019*, p. 95.
413. *Ibid.*, at 108, para. 33.
414. *Ibid.*, at 132, para. 150 *et seq.*

the legality of the detachment *at its time* could not predict the future adoption of the Declaration on Friendly Relations [415].

It is easy to see how *jura novit curia* can play an important role in the context of disputes concerning intertemporal law. *Jura novit curia* allows for discretion in the application of the law and requires finesse in determining the applicable law through the characterisation of the acts. As Hugh Thirlway explains, "the intertemporal law principle is only adjective law – it is a technique for applying the appropriate law to the facts, not itself a rule of substantive law" [416]. This flexibility is but a function of the inevitable elusiveness of the doctrine. The difficulties faced by a decision-maker in its application were elegantly captured by Judge Al-Khasawneh in *Land and Maritime Boundary Between Cameroon and Nigeria*:

> "At a general level, the [doctrine of intertemporal law] is sustainable, but when we come to enquire more closely into its operation, problems start to arise: is appreciation in the light of the law contemporary with the judicial act, for example, a treaty of protection, the same as interpretation of such a treaty in the light of contemporaneous law? Or does it merely mean that in interpreting a treaty of the past one should be mindful, in applying the time-honoured and established canons of treaty interpretation of the temporal context that may shed light on the presumed intention of the parties and thus help ascertain it?" [417]

It is thus clear that the application of the doctrine requires finesse and nuance, which cannot be constrained by the arguments set out by the parties. This is also so because, as Al-Khasawneh continues, the appreciation of the law contemporary with conduct or acts being adjudicated never fails to include a systemic dimension: thus, "ascertainment of the true meaning of intertemporal law requires us to enquire into the quality of the juridical act in the light not only of the alleged practice, but in the light of the totality of the law", with a

415. S. Wheatley, "Revisiting the Doctrine of Intertemporal Law", *Oxford Journal of Legal Studies*, Vol. 41 (2), 2021, 484-509, 485.
416. H. Thirlway, "Law and Procedure of the International Court of Justice 1960-1989: Part One" (1989) 60 BYIL 1, 130.
417. *Land and Maritime Boundary Between Cameroon and Nigeria (Cameroon* v. *Nigeria: Equatorial Guinea intervening)*, Judgment, *ICJ Reports 2002*, p. 303, At 500, para. 12 (Separate Opinion of Judge Al-Khasawneh).

relevant factor in this operation being the requirement that other rules of law should be taken cognizance of [418].

This operation too, it is submitted, cannot be constrained by the arguments of the parties, for the identification and interpretation of rules relevant to the application of the doctrine are incidental and necessary to the identification of the rules to be applied by the adjudicator. Again, the theoretical significance of the distinction between interpretation and application of the law largely loses any practical relevance – if it ever had any theoretical significance to begin with in this context [419]. One can see how the oft-cited *dictum* from *Fisheries Jurisdiction* according to which an adjudicator must "render a judgment on the basis of the law as it exists at the time of its decision" can be seen as a springboard, rather than a constraint [420].

There is at least one circumstance where the exercise of *jura novit curia* powers may take an essentially obligatory character for the adjudicator, and that is the scenario of the emergence of a rule of *jus cogens*. On the one hand, the idea that a conflict should be resolved in favour of the emerging norm of *jus cogens* may be taken as an extension of the principle, codified in Article 64 of the Vienna Convention on the Law of Treaties, whereby "[i]f a new peremptory norm of general international law emerges, any existing treaty which is in conflict with that norm becomes void and terminates" [421]. The question *of jus cogens* – either contemporary or *superveniens* – in relation to intertemporal law was not tackled by the majority in the *Chagos* Advisory Opinion [422]. However, there are indications that it might be a relevant consideration. Thus, for example, Judges Shi and Koroma cited with approval the writers of the 1992 edition of *Oppenheim's International Law* to the effect that "in some respects the interpretation of a treaty's provisions

418. *Ibid.*
419. It may be added that the distinction was discussed during the works of the ILC on the codification of the law of the treaties, in particular in connection to the question of intertemporal law, but the topic was revealed to be highly controversial and any attempt to make a clear-cut distinction was dismissed. See L. L. Giacco, "Eureka! On Courts' Discretion in 'Ascertaining' Rules of Customary International Law", in J. Kammerhofer, N. Arajärvi and P. Merkouris (eds.), *The Theory, Practice, and Interpretation of Customary International Law*, Cambridge: Cambridge University Press, 2022, pp. 256-276.
420. *Fisheries Jurisdiction (United Kingdom* v. *Iceland)*, Judgment, *ICJ Reports 1974*, 3, para. 40.
421. Vienna Convention on the Law of Treaties, Article 64.
422. It was, however, raised in several individual opinions, including the ones of Judges Robinson, Sebutinde and Cançado Trindade.

cannot be divorced from developments in the law subsequent to its adoption" [423].

Another situation where this might be required has to do with the less momentous, but still important, situation in which the application of the intertemporal law is necessary since the law of the time did not resolve every aspect of the dispute: the situation arose in the *Grisbadarna* case between Norway and Sweden regarding the maritime boundary line between their respective territories [424]. The tribunal, tasked with determining whether the 1661 boundary treaty had fixed the boundary, ultimately concluded that the boundary line had been fixed by the treaty, but only up to a certain point. Beyond that point, the boundary line was found to be uncertain. Thus, it was necessary to determine what the correct boundary should be in accordance with the principles of international law that would have been used at the time of the conclusion of the 1658 Treaty of Roskilde, with which the territory was ceded by Denmark. The Tribunal applied the "general direction of the coast" principle, which was found to be valid at the time, even if it presumably assumed that it was no longer valid in modern international law [425].

(i) *Composite acts in the law of State responsibility*

Another scenario in which the existence of a time-related element may call for the exercise of adjudicative discretion in the form of *jura novit curia* powers arises out of the need to ascertain whether a breach of a substantive standard of protection occurs, not as a result of an instantaneous violation, but rather as a result of a breach consisting of a composite act. This definition, whose intellectual origins may be traced back to the work of Special Rapporteur Roberto Ago in the context of the work of the International Law Commission on State responsibility, has been conclusively adopted in the Articles on Responsibility of States for Internationally Wrongful Acts, where Article 15 provides as follows:

---

423. *Application of the Convention on the Prevention and Punishment of the Crime of Genocide (Bosnia and Herzegovina* v. *Serbia and Montenegro),* Judgment, *ICJ Reports 2007*, p. 43, at 280, para. 2 (Joint Declaration of Judges Shi and Koroma).

424. *Grisbadarna*, 23 October 1909, UNRIAA Vol. XI, pp. 147-166.

425. *Ibidem*. For a general discussion of this issue in the context of a thorough examination of the doctrine of intertemporal law, see T. O. Elias, "The Doctrine of Intertemporal Law", *American Journal of International Law*, Vol. 74 (2), 1980, 285-307.

> "1. The breach of an international obligation by a State through a series of actions or omissions defined in aggregate as wrongful occurs when the action or omission occurs which, taken with the other actions or omissions, is sufficient to constitute the wrongful act.
>
> 2. In such a case, the breach extends over the entire period starting with the first of the actions or omissions of the series and lasts for as long as these actions or omissions are repeated and remain not in conformity with the international obligation." [426]

The notion of a composite breach is well accepted in international law and indeed it is undisputed that some of the most serious breaches of international legal obligations may ordinarily be consummated as a result of composite acts – consider, for example, the prohibition of genocide [427]. Yet several difficulties remain, many of which were already highlighted by Special Rapporteur James Crawford upon the publication of the Commentaries to the ARSIWA. The first difficulty has to do with the fact that a composite breach, by its very nature, necessitates a temporal interval between the first act in a series and the last one. The first cannot, by definition, amount alone to the composite wrongful act (though it may well amount to a *different* wrongful act), as the wrongfulness of the conduct will only result from the aggregate of the various acts as assessed after the last one in the series has been consummated [428]. The second difficulty, inextricably connected to the first, has to do with the fact that the timing of the breach (which is relevant for the consequences of the breach in terms of responsibility) is identified with the first action or omission, irrespective of its legality *qua* individual act [429]. This, in turn, may raise complex evidentiary issues, as well as questions of characterisation of the acts and omissions in accordance with the agreed or default applicable law.

The notion of composite act can be particularly thorny in the context of investment disputes. It has been convincingly argued that "each of the common investment protection obligations in an investment treaty is capable of being breached by composite acts" [430]. For an investment tribunal tasked with settling a dispute relating to an investment, this raises both jurisdictional and substantive questions. Irrespective of the

426. ARSIWA, Article 15.
427. ARSIWA, Commentaries, p. 62.
428. *Ibid.*, at 63.
429. *Ibid.*
430. Z. Douglas, *The International Law of Investment Claims*, para. 627-628.

qualification of the conduct as wrongful or otherwise, it is necessary to establish whether or not it is covered by the investment agreement under which the Tribunal is exercising its jurisdiction. From the perspective of the law of State responsibility, this essentially entails a determination of whether, at the time of the (alleged, for the moment) breach, the host State was bound by the obligation in question. The consequence is that no conduct predating the entry into force of an investment treaty imposing substantive obligations can be relevant as a component of the composite act in question. One can certainly see in this approach an expression of the doctrine of intertemporal law – *tempus regit actum*.

The notion of composite act provides a stress test for this construction. On the one hand, the notion of composite act is beneficial to the investor insofar as it allows for a more expedient – and in many cases, more accurate – approach to the quantification of damages encompassing the entire period over which the breach, or its constituent elements, extended. But what if, in an effort to go backwards, the composite act is found to have commenced before the entry into force of the treaty? Some commentators have, in keeping with the Commentaries to the ARSIWA, argued that "the intertemporal principle once again trumps all other considerations" in respect to treaty claims [431]. Other commentators, instead, have argued, on the basis of awards more sympathetic to claimants, that the possibility may exist for specific breaches of investment protection standards to commence before the entry into force of the investment treaty so long as the cumulative effect of the components or would-be components of the composite act can be seen "as a series of acts that, over time, 'converge' so as to constitute the expropriation", with expropriation and denial of justice being singled out as the breaches most likely to fit this paradigm [432].

Be that as it may, it should be noted that, from the perspective of the Tribunal, conduct taking place before the entry into force of the BIT is, again, far from irrelevant. For example, irrespective of whether it is relevant to dispose of treaty claims, it is certainly possible to conceive the possibility that a tribunal may be able to adjudicate on a contract claim based on conduct predating the entry into force of the treaty [433]. Moreover, as the Commentaries to the ARSIWA clarify, the fact that a composite act cannot commence before the entry into force of the

431. Z. Douglas, *The International Law of Investment Claims*, para. 629.

432. See S. D. Murphy, "Temporal Issues Relating to BIT Dispute Resolution", *ICSID Review – Foreign Investment Law Journal*, Vol. 37 (1-2), 2022, 51-84, 82.

433. Z. Douglas, *The International Law of Investment Claims*, para. 617.

relevant treaty does not mean that facts preceding that date cannot be taken into account "for other purposes (e.g. in order to establish a factual basis for the later breaches or to provide evidence of intent)" [434]. Undoubtedly, this operation requires the exercise of a significant degree of adjudicative discretion in the identification of the law applicable to the breach in question. Such discretion ranges from the characterisation of the breach, as one relating to a contract or treaty claim, to the qualification of the act in question, according to the application of the relevant secondary rules, as a component of the composite act or one providing its context.

(ii) *Non-retroactivity in international criminal law*

Another area in which time-related elements may invite the exercise of discretion has to do with international criminal adjudication. Consider the application of the Rome Statute: the problem has arisen before the International Criminal Court of whether the Statute should be seen as substantive and binding on individuals, rather than jurisdictional in nature and only binding on States. As Marko Milanović convincingly argued, accepting the second approach essentially entails accepting that individuals may only be seen as accountable for customary crimes, with substantive statutory provisions reflecting them. If the first is accepted instead, statutory crimes may go beyond customary international law, but may infringe on the principle of legality in those situations where the Statute could not have been binding on the individuals – in practice, where a particular situation has been referred to the Court by the UN Security Council or by a non-State party. For all intents and purposes, these scenarios require a retroactive application of international criminal law.

As Talita de Souza Dias points out [435], retroactivity is not entirely proscribed under international law so long as it is formal, rather than substantive: in other words, what matters is for the individual to have been "put on notice by some prior source of criminal law, that his/her conduct was criminal and punishable" [436]. This, however, does not resolve all problems because the relationship between customary and

434. ARSIWA, Commentaries, at 64.

435. See T. de Souza Dias, "The Retroactive Application of the Rome Statute in Cases of Security Council Referrals and *Ad hoc* Declarations: An Appraisal of the Existing Solutions to an Under-discussed Problem", *Journal of International Criminal Justice*, Vol. 16 (1), 2018, 65-89.

436. *Ibid.*, at 67.

statutory crimes remains uncertain, for there may be a number of statutory crimes which go far beyond what custom requires. Thus, a number of solutions have been advanced to ensure that the principle of legality is upheld in cases where the Rome Statute risks being substantively retroactive. Such solutions range from checking the compatibility between the statute and customary international law or domestic law, or interpreting the statute in accordance with the principle of non-retroactivity under general international law, or relying on custom to displace the provisions of the statute in their entirety where they go beyond pre-existing custom in cases of Security Council referrals and *ad hoc* declarations [437].

2. Concluding remarks

During the merits phase of a dispute, adjudicators may need to exercise *jura novit curia* powers to successfully dispose of a dispute before them. However, their discretion in point is also subject to constraints imposed by existing rules on applicable law, evidence and interpretation. At the same time, these rules operate as a springboard for the exercise of the adjudicative decision-making discretion flowing from the principle under consideration. This discretion is necessary to ensure that the legal process remains flexible enough to accommodate the unique circumstances of each dispute and that the outcome is ultimately fair and just.

The overview provided here is intended to give a broad understanding of the principles and issues involved in the application of *jura novit curia* to questions of fact and law in the merits phase. It will serve as a foundation for the further exploration of these issues in the next chapter, which will consider its impact to matters of reparation.

437. *Ibid.*, at 69 *et seq.*

CHAPTER V

JURA NOVIT CURIA AND REPARATION

A. Reparation and the assessment of compensation

The question of the relationship between *jura novit curia* and reparation may be introduced with an observation that almost amounts to a truism: the remedial competence of adjudicators is characterised by inherent judicial discretion [438]. The exercise of *jura novit curia* in this area may therefore amount to an exercise of *jura novit curia* where the adjudicator awards a form of reparation other than those pleaded by the parties. It is often the case that, after finding in favour of the applicant on the merits, the adjudicator goes a third way between awarding the "very much" requested by the applicant and the "nothing" requested by the defendant. Aside from the quantum of compensation, *jura novit curia* may come into play with regard to the application of the "secondary rules" on the law of State responsibility, with special regard to those concerning the consequence of a breach of international law [439]. In this area, too, guidance may be drawn from the balance between the operation of *jura novit curia* and that of *ne ultra petita*, as well as from the relationship between fact and the law. Suffice it for the moment to recall the entanglement between the facts and the law of the case in the assessment of the damage caused and of the causal connection between the latter and the wrongful conduct.

To this end, this chapter will proceed as follows: in the first two sections, it will examine inter-State and investor-State adjudication.

---

438. Although the literature dealing with remedies in international law is abundant, general treatises on the topic are rare, possibly because of the profound differences between the relevant institutional frameworks. See C. Gray, "Is There an International Law of Remedies?", *British Yearbook of International Law*, Vol. 56 (1), 1986, 25-47; Brown, *A Common Law of International Adjudication*, 185 *et seq*. For examples of book-length treatments, see C. D. Gray, *Judicial Remedies in International Law*, Oxford University Press, 1990; E. Stoppioni, *La réparation dans le contentieux international de l'investissement : contribution à l'étude de la restitutio in integrum*, Pedone, 2014; D. Shelton, *Remedies in International Human Rights Law*, Oxford University Press, USA, 2015.

439. See ARSIWA, Article 28 *et seq*. See, in particular, Article 31 ("The responsible State is under an obligation to make full reparation for the injury caused by the internationally wrongful act. 2. Injury includes any damage, whether material or moral, caused by the internationally wrongful act of a State").

First, it will consider the application of *jura novit curia* to the choice of the forms of reparation in inter-State and investor-State litigation. Second, it will consider its application in the context of the assessment of the amount of compensation. In the two sections that follow, it will move on to discuss the assessment of the forms of reparation and of compensation in human rights adjudication and in international criminal justice. Finally, it will offer some conclusions on *jura novit curia* and its different rationales with regard to awarding remedies in different areas of adjudication, as well as on its status as a unifying principle of adjudication.

B. The choice of the forms of reparation in inter-State and investor-State litigation

1. Inter-State adjudication

The award of any form of reparation – from the declaration of wrongfulness, or the obligation to cease the wrongful conduct, to restitution or compensation – is inextricably linked to the judicial assessment of primary, or substantive, law [440]. A difference may actually occur between the obligations for whose breach a form of reparation is awarded and those whose violation has been invoked [441].

---

440. Consider, for example, Article 36 (2) *(d)* of the ICJ Statute, stating with regard to compulsory jurisdiction under the optional clause, that "[t]he states parties to the present Statute may at any time declare that they recognize as compulsory *ipso facto* and without special agreement, in relation to any other state accepting the same obligation, the jurisdiction of the Court in all legal disputes concerning . . . the nature or extent of the reparation to be made for the breach of an international obligation". In this regard, see also C. Tomuschat, "Article 36", in A. Zimmermann, C. J. Tams, K. Oellers-Frahm and C. Tomuschat, *The Statute of the International Court of Justice: A Commentary*, at 741 ("By listing 'the nature or extent of the reparation to be made for the breach of an international obligation' as one of the possible items of a legal dispute, the Statute underlines the close connection which exists between the level of primary rules of conduct and the level of secondary rules which deal with the legal consequences of a breach of a primary rule. This conclusion stands in perfect harmony with the authority of the Court to apply the relevant rules of general international law, no matter how specifically the subject-matter of a dispute has been delineated"). Consider, further *Military and Paramilitary Activities in and Against Nicaragua (Nicaragua* v. *United States of America)*, Merits, Judgment, *ICJ Reports 1986*, p. 14, at 142, para. 283 ("In general, jurisdiction to determine the merits of a dispute entails jurisdiction to determine reparation"). On the relationship between damage and the determination of the existence of an internationally wrongful act, see A. Tanzi, "Is Damage a Distinct Condition for the Existence of an Internationally Wrongful Act?", in B. Simma and M. Spinedi (eds.), *United Nations of Codification of State Responsibility*, Dobbs Ferry-New York-Roma: Oceana Publications, 1987, pp. 1-33.

441. Again, this raises questions of judicial, or at the very least "decisional" economy. See Palombino, *op. cit.*

Such discrepancy would obviously occur with regard to those parts of the claim on which the judge does not find for the applicant on the merits. Also, and just as obviously, the judge cannot decide reparation for conduct alleged to be in breach of obligations over which it found that is has no jurisdiction [442]. Naturally, no *ne infra petita* issue would arise here: when the Court curtails the scope of the dispute at the preliminary objections stage, the claimant adjusts its prayer for relief in its final submissions accordingly.

Second of all, and most importantly, the specific *jura / jus* factor, i.e. the applicable law element for the purposes of *jura novit curia*, consists of the secondary rules on the law of international State responsibility [443]. In its well-known codification by the ILC, Articles 35, 36 and 37 of the ARSIWA provide for three main forms of reparation: restitution, compensation and satisfaction [444].

In this area, the discretion of the adjudicator is limited with regard to the choice of such forms of reparation. As a matter of principle, nobody questions the primacy of restitution, either in its fully-fledged material form, or understood as amounting to the annulment of a domestic measure or judgment [445]. However, in practice, *some* choice will have

442. See in this connection C. F. Amerasinghe, *Jurisdiction of Specific International Tribunals*, Leiden; Boston, Martinus Nijhoff Publishers, 2009, 164 ("A basic principle relevant to jurisdiction in relation to remedies is one that applies to international adjudication in general, namely that jurisdiction is consensual and depends basically on the agreement of the parties").

443. The possibility of derogation cannot be excluded, consistent with Article 55 of ARSIWA ("These articles do not apply where and to the extent that the conditions for the existence of an internationally wrongful act or the content or implementation of the international responsibility of a State are governed by special rules of international law"). See, for example, Amerasinghe, *Jurisdiction of Specific International Tribunals*, 164 ("A corollary to this principle is the proposition that the Court must enjoy the jurisdiction as inherent which its judicial character requires. But the latter proposition has two aspects. First, the agreement of the parties may alter, modify or derogate from jurisdictional authority which would otherwise flow as inherent from the judicial character of the Court").

444. See ARSIWA, Articles 34 to 39, on "Reparation for Injury", listing the possible forms of reparation such as restitution (Art. 35), compensation (Art. 36), satisfaction (Art. 37) and their limits.

445. See *Factory at Chorzów*, Jurisdiction, Judgment No. 8, 1927, PCIJ, Series A, No. 9, p. 47 ("The essential principle contained in the actual notion of an illegal act – a principle which seems to be established by international practice and in particular by the decisions of arbitral tribunals – is that reparation must, as far as possible, wipe out all the consequences of the illegal act and reestablish the situation which would, in all probability, have existed if that act had not been committed. *Restitution in kind*, or, if this is not possible, payment of a sum corresponding to the value which a restitution in kind would bear; the award, if need be, of damages for loss sustained which would not be covered by restitution in kind or payment in place of it – such are the principles which should serve to determine the amount of compensation due for an act contrary to international law") (emphasis added). The Commentaries to the ARSIWA confirm

to be made with regard to which form of reparation should be pursued, if only because full reparation may well require a combination of the possible remedies mentioned above. The choice of one of these options, or of their combination on a case-by-case basis, may involve elements of *jura novit curia*.

According to Article 35 ARSIWA, restitution may be found to be either materially impossible or disproportionately onerous [446]. Under both circumstances, restitution would not need to be pursued, leaving the award of compensation as the main available option [447]. This choice, hinging on whether, as recalled above, restitution is in fact materially impossible or disproportionately onerous, might appear, on the face of it, to fall squarely in the realm of the appreciation of pure fact. Yet this operation is in no way different from the typical application of any piece of law to a set of facts. In this context, the law to be applied is nothing other than the secondary rules on the law of State responsibility. Here, *jura novit curia* would operate only where neither party would request forms of reparation other than restitution, alternatively or subsidiarily. This scenario, it is readily admitted, would be highly unusual.

Another relevant element flows from Article 36 ARSIWA, according to which compensation may be due beyond restitution where the latter would not redress the loss or damage suffered in its entirety [448].

---

the primacy of restitution insofar as it "most closely conforms to the general principle that the responsible State is bound to wipe out the legal and material consequences of its wrongful act by re-establishing the situation that would exist if that act had not been committed" (at 96).

446. See ARSIWA, Article 35 ("A State responsible for an internationally wrongful act is under an obligation to make restitution, that is, to re-establish the situation which existed before the wrongful act was committed, provided and to the extent that restitution: *(a)* is not materially impossible; *(b)* does not involve a burden out of all proportion to the benefit deriving from restitution instead of compensation"). See *CMS Gas Transmission Company* v. *Republic of Argentina*, ICSID Case No. ARB/01/8, Award, 12 May 2005, para. 406 ("Restitution is by far the most reliable choice to make the injured party whole as it aims at the reestablishment of the situation existing prior to the wrongful act. In a situation such as that characterizing this dispute and the complex issues associated with the crisis in Argentina, it would be utterly unrealistic for the Tribunal to order the Respondent to turn back to the regulatory framework existing before the emergency measures were adopted, nor has this been requested"). See also Douglas, *The International law of Investment Claims*, 101. See also A. M. Tanzi, "Restitution", in *Max Planck Encyclopedia of Public International Law*, Oxford, 2011.

447. Note that one such rule can be further specified. Thus, Article 14.D.13 of the USMCA provides that a tribunal adjudicating disputes under it may award either monetary damages and any applicable interest and/or restitution of property "in which case the award shall provide that the respondent may pay monetary damages and any applicable interest in lieu of restitution".

448. Indeed, Article 34 ARSIWA states that "Full reparation for the injury caused by the internationally wrongful act shall take the form of restitution, compensation and satisfaction, *either singly or in combination*, in accordance with the provisions of

This additional qualification, too, might add margins for adjudicative appreciation. However, judicial discretion based on *jura novit curia* would be entirely constrained if the applicant availed itself of the right to choose under Article 43 (2) *(b)* ARSIWA, which allows the injured State to elect the preferred form of reparation. Taken at face value, this provision would give effect to both *ne infra petita* and *ne ultra petita* in an extensive fashion, thereby constraining *jura novit curia* to a significant degree. However, the ILC commentary reveals that Article 43 (2) *(b)* is not to be interpreted as barring an element of *jura novit curia* discretion in the matter. It does so by expressing the unqualified *caveat* whereby the provision in point "does not set forth the right of election in absolute terms" [449]. The Commission, however, did not shed further light on the point, and, overall, international inter-State jurisprudence has shown much dependence on the parties' attitude, with special regard to the applicant.

By way of example, in *Fisheries Jurisdiction* [450], *Rainbow Warrior* [451] and *LaGrand* [452] the ICJ and the arbitral tribunals concerned abstained from considering compensation since the applicant had not requested it. In particular, *Fisheries Jurisdiction* and in *Rainbow Warrior* the negative decision in point is based on factual evidence [453] and on the

---

this chapter" (emphasis added). The Commentary confirms that "that full reparation may only be achieved in particular cases by the combination of different forms of reparation" (at 95).

449. There may be other situations in which such an appreciation may be required, for example, with regard to the injured the exercise of the right to choose its preferred form of reparation, which is not entirely unfettered. See in this regard Article 43 ARSIWA and Commentary thereto (at 120).

450. *Fisheries Jurisdiction (Federal Republic of Germany* v. *Iceland)*, Merits, Judgment, *ICJ Reports 1974*, p. 175.

451. *Case Concerning the Difference Between New Zealand and France Concerning the Interpretation or Application of Two Agreements, Concluded on 9 July 1986 Between the Two States and Which Related to the Problems Arising from the Rainbow Warrior Affair*, 30 April 1990, UNRIAA Vol. XX pp. 215-284.

452. *LaGrand (Germany* v. *United States of America)*, Judgment, *ICJ Reports 2001*, p. 466. Consider, however, the ICJ's treatment of the way in which Germany instituted proceedings (at 487, para. 57), which the Court said it would have taken into account if Germany's third submission had included a claim for indemnification (at 508, para. 116).

453. See *Fisheries Jurisdiction*, *supra* note 15, at 204, para. 76 ("In order to award compensation the Court can only act with reference to a concrete submission as to the existence and the amount of each head of damage. Such an award must be based on precise grounds and detailed evidence concerning those acts which have been committed, taking into account all relevant facts of each incident and their consequences in the circumstances of the case. It is only after receiving evidence on these matters that the Court can satisfy itself that each concrete claim is well founded in fact and in law. It is possible to request a general declaration establishing the principle that compensation

procedural requirement for the defendant to be able to react to a request that was actually not made, i.e. the so-called right to be heard [454].

Another important exception has to do with inter-State litigation initiated with a view to vindicating breaches of obligations stemming from rules on the protection of general interests [455]. In such cases, the applicant would be acting in the interest and on behalf of all the States which hold a right corresponding to so-called *erga omnes* obligations set out in a multilateral convention – such as the Genocide Convention – or flowing from a peremptory rule [456]. In such cases one would assume that inter-State adjudication would align with human rights adjudication, affording ample *jura novit curia* discretion, including with respect to awarding reparation. In fact, also in such rare cases the applicant State usually refers in its submissions to the widest range of

---

is due, provided the claimant asks the Court to receive evidence and to determine, in a subsequent phase of the same proceedings, the amount of damage to be assessed").

454. See *Rainbow Warrior*, *supra* note 16, at para. 119 ("New Zealand has not however requested the award of monetary compensation – even as a last resort should the Tribunal not make the declarations and orders for the return of the agents. The Tribunal can understand that position in terms of an assessment made by a State of its dignity and its sovereign rights. The fact that New Zealand has not sought an order for compensation also means that France has not addressed this quite distinct remedy in its written pleadings and oral arguments, or even had the opportunity to do so. Further, the Tribunal itself has not had the advantage of the argument of the two Parties on the issues mentioned in paras. 117 and 118, or on other relevant matters, such as the amount of damages").

455. See G. Gaja, "The Protection of General Interests in the International Community. General Course on Public International Law (2011)", *Recueil des cours*, tome 364 (2012), 9-185; G. Gaja, "Is a State Specially Affected When its Nationals' Human Rights Are Infringed?", *Man's Inhumanity to Man*, Brill Nijhoff, 2003, pp. 373-382; S. Villalpando, "The Legal Dimension of the International Community: How Community Interests Are Protected in International Law", *European Journal of International Law*, Vol. 21 (2), 2010, 387-419; E. Benvenisti, G. Nolte and K. Yalin-Mor, *Community Interests Across International Law*, Oxford University Press, 2018; S. Besson, "Community Interests in International Law - Whose Interests Are They and How Does One Identify Them?", *Community Interests Across International Law*, Oxford University Press, 2018, pp. 50-69; M. Longobardo, "The Standing of indirectly Injured States in the Litigation of Community Interests before the ICJ: Lessons Learned and Future Implications in Light of *The Gambia* v. *Myanmar* and Beyond", *International Community Law Review*, Vol. 1 (aop), 2021, 1-31; X. Mao, "Public-Interest Litigation before the International Court of Justice: Comment on *The Gambia* v. *Myanmar* Case", *Chinese Journal of International Law*, Vol. 21 (3), 2022, 589-609; A. Tanzi, "Is Damage a Distinct Condition for the Existence of an Internationally Wrongful Act?", in B. Simma and M. Spinedi (eds.), *United Nations of Codification of State Responsibility*, Dobbs Ferry-New York-Roma: Oceana Publications, 1987, pp. 1-33.

456. On the question of remedies for breaches of *jus cogens* norms, see A. Orakhelashvili, *Peremptory Norms in International Law*, OUP, Oxford, 2008, 241 *et seq.* For a more general discussion of the consequences of the peremptory nature of norms of international law, see D. Costelloe, *Legal Consequences of Peremptory Norms in International Law*, Cambridge University Press, 2017.

options for redress of material and immaterial damage, for itself, or the material victims when they do not coincide with the claimant State [457].

An example of this all-encompassing prayer for relief, leaving the Court with little need for any creative exercise of *jura novit curia* concerning remedies, is to be found in The Gambia's Application against Myanmar filed with the ICJ in 2019 [458]. The relevant part of the application, which is worth quoting in full, reads as follows:

> "The Gambia respectfully requests the Court to adjudge and declare that Myanmar:
>
> – has breached and continues to breach its obligations under the Genocide Convention, in particular the obligations provided under Articles I, III *(a)*, III *(b)*, III *(c)*, III *(d)*, III *(e)*, IV, V and VI;
> – must cease forthwith any such ongoing internationally wrongful act and fully respect its obligations under the Genocide Convention, in particular the obligations provided under Articles I, III *(a)*, III *(b)*, III *(c)*, III *(d)*, III *(e)*,IV, V and VI;
> – must ensure that persons committing genocide are punished by a competent tribunal, including before an international penal tribunal, as required by Articles I and VI;
> – must perform the obligations of reparation in the interest of the victims of genocidal acts who are members of the Rohingya group, including but not limited to allowing the safe and dignified return of forcibly displaced Rohingya and respect for their full citizenship and human rights and protection against discrimination, persecution, and other related acts, consistent with the obligation to prevent genocide under Article I; and
> – must offer assurances and guarantees of non-repetition of violations of the Genocide Convention, in particular the obligations

457. It is, however, important to note that other consideration might factor in the assessment of the nature or extent of remedies granted. For a discussion of the problem in human rights adjudication, see V. Fikfak, "Changing State Behaviour: Damages before the European Court of Human Rights", *European Journal of International Law*, Vol. 29 (4), 2018, 1091-1125; V. Fikfak, "Non-pecuniary Damages before the European Court of Human Rights: Forget the Victim; It's All About the State", *Leiden Journal of International Law*, 2020, 1-35.

458. *Application of the Convention on the Prevention and Punishment of the Crime of Genocide (The Gambia* v. *Myanmar)*, Application instituting proceedings and Request for the indication of provisional measures, 11 November 2019.

provided under Articles I, III *(a)*, III *(b)*, III *(c)*, III *(d)*, III *(e)*, IV, V and VI." [459]

In cases of this kind, the most commonly requested and awarded form of relief is the declaration of wrongfulness [460], along with the request of cessation of the conduct complained of, when of a continuing nature. The passage quoted above, however, also showcases a second potential problematic aspect of *jura novit curia*, concerning the application of another rule codified in the ARSIWA. Namely, Article 48 (2) *(b)* which states as follows:

> "Any State [other than an injured State] may claim from the responsible State: . . . performance of the obligation of reparation, in accordance with the preceding articles, in the interest of the injured State or of the beneficiaries of the obligation breached." [461]

Claims for declaration of wrongfulness and for the cessation of the *erga omnes* wrongful conduct are not in themselves problematic. They ordinarily include a request for satisfaction for the immaterial damage and are absolute and objective in essence by definition [462]. An issue relating to *jura novit curia* may thus arise in connection with the judicial assessment of the concrete kind of assurances and guarantees of non-repetition of the wrongful act [463]. Else, it may be the case that the same issue will arise in relation to the question of the reparation for

459. *Ibid.*, at 56-57, para. 112.

460. There are generally no concerns relating to the admissibility of a declaratory judgment. See *Interpretation of Judgments Nos. 7 and 8*, PCIJ Series A, No. 13, p. 20; *Northern Cameroons (Cameroon* v. *United Kingdom),* Preliminary Objections, Judgment, *ICJ Reports 1963*, p. 15, at 37 ("That the Court may, in an appropriate case, make a declaratory judgment is indisputable. The Court has, however, already indicated that even if, when seised of an Application, the Court finds that it has jurisdiction, it is not obliged to exercise it in all cases"). See also Citerei anche un articolo di elena fasoli in inglese che avevo supervisionato, penso su lapict, risalente di poco più di una decina d'anni) On declaratory judgments in general, see Brown, *A Common Law of International Adjudication*, 190; J. J. Quintana, *Litigation at the International Court of Justice: Practice and Procedure*, Brill, 2015, 1128; J. Mcintyre, "The Declaratory Judgment in Recent Jurisprudence of the ICJ: Conflicting Approaches to State Responsibility?", *Leiden Journal of International Law*, Vol. 29 (1), 2016, 177-195.

461. ARSIWA, Article 48 (2) *(b)*.

462. Again, Gambia's Application in *Application of the Convention on the Prevention and Punishment of the Crime of Genocide (The Gambia* v. *Myanmar)*, already recalled above, is instructive.

463. Article 30 of the ARSIWA bears recalling. The provision states that "[t]he State responsible for the internationally wrongful act is under an obligation: *(a)* to cease that act, if it is continuing; *(b)* to offer appropriate assurances and guarantees of non-repetition, if circumstances so require".

the material damage suffered by the third State or non-State actor [464]. In other words, the relevance of *jura novit curia* in this scenario is twofold: first, it hinges on the question of whether the Court could decide on such measures independently from the claimant's prayer for relief – and, obviously, from the defendant's claims to the contrary. Second, and at the procedural level, it also relates to the question of whether the Court could take one such decision without hearing the third State or non-State actor directly involved.

The scant case law on the matter is of little assistance. As already mentioned, the cases brought before the ICJ by a State vindicating breaches of *erga omnes* obligations, which have attained a decision on the merits, as of the time of the present writing going to press, are only two: the *Questions Relating to the Obligation to Prosecute or Extradite* case between Belgium and Senegal [465] and the *Whaling in the Antarctic* case between Australia and Japan [466]. In neither of the two Judgments were forms of reparation other than those requested awarded by the Court [467]. In the *Gambia* v. *Myanmar*, as already indicated, the applicant

464. Naturally, the question may arise of whether the damage is material to begin with, especially in the case of States invoking the responsibility of another State in the scenario described by Article 42 ARSIWA (especially where obligation is owed to the international community as a whole) or Article 48 (relating to the scenario where the "obligation breached is owed to a group of States including that State, and is established for the protection of a collective interest of the group; or *(b)* the obligation breached is owed to the international community as a whole"). Admittedly, especially in the second case, the State invoking the responsibility of another State is only entitled to request "*(a)* cessation of the internationally wrongful act, and assurances and guarantees of non-repetition in accordance with article 30; and *(b)* performance of the obligation of reparation in accordance with the preceding articles, in the interest of the injured State or of the beneficiaries of the obligation breached". From the perspective of an adjudicator, this may well amount to satisfaction by way of a declaration of the wrongfulness of the act as satisfaction for a moral or non-material injury. See ARSIWA, Commentaries, at 106-107 (quoting *Corfu Channel*, Judgment, Merits, *ICJ Reports 1949*, p. 4, at 35, stating that "[t]o ensure respect for international law, of which it is the organ, the Court must declare that the action of the British Navy constituted a violation of Albanian sovereignty. This declaration is in accordance with the request made by Albania through her Counsel, and is in itself appropriate satisfaction"). Perhaps more complex is the problem of whether the remedial competence of an adjudicator could extend to the order of remedies going far beyond that: for a discussion, see Quintana, *Litigation at the International Court of Justice*, 1163-1164.

465. *Questions Relating to the Obligation to Prosecute or Extradite (Belgium* v. *Senegal),* Judgment, *ICJ Reports 2012*, p. 422.

466. *Whaling in the Antarctic (Australia* v. *Japan: New Zealand intervening),* Judgment, *ICJ Reports 2014*, p. 226.

467. For example, in *Obligation to Prosecute or Extradite* the applicant did not request satisfaction specifically, and the Judgment admittedly went beyond it, finding unanimously that "the Republic of Senegal must, without further delay, submit the case of Mr. Hissène Habré to its competent authorities for the purpose of prosecution, if it does not extradite him" (at 463, para. 122). In *Whaling in the Antarctic*, instead, the applicant did not go beyond the request of a declaratory judgment, but the Court

basically advanced all the submissions for reparation that it possibly could, in line with 48 (2) *(b)* ARSIWA. Still, the question remains as to which adjudicative scenery one is to expect if the applicant falls short of asking adequate reparation for the directly injured third State or non-State actor.

Against this uncertain background, the limitations of a bilateral, decentralised and consent-based structural system emerge. I am referring to the deep tension between the newly developed substantive rules for the protection of collective, global, indivisible interests and the traditional private law-like consent-based system of international adjudication. Useful cues may possibly be drawn from the jurisprudential practice of human rights courts as a way to enhance the adjudicator's autonomy in the unlikely event that counsel for the parties were to fail in their mission of presenting an adequately complete and thorough request for relief. However, this might need to be combined with a degree of procedural judicial activism in order to give effect to the parties' – and interested parties' – right to be heard. This would effectively require third party involvement in the proceedings, possibly including non-State actors, a prospect that would require significant procedural reform.

2. *Investment arbitration*

In international investment arbitration the overwhelmingly prevailing relief awarded is monetary compensation, again, mostly due to the choice made by the claimants [468]. From the perspective of the claimant – the investor – it is often the case that resort to arbitration will occur when they believe the relationship with the local authorities is already compromised beyond repair, thereby making restitution unappeal-

---

decided "that Japan shall revoke any extant authorization, permit or licence granted in relation to JARPA II, and refrain from granting any further permits in pursuance of that programme" (at 300, para. 247). On these problems arising from the uncertain boundaries of the institution of declaratory judgment, see Mcintyre, *op. cit.*

468. On this topic, see T. W. Wälde and B. Sabahi, "Compensation, Damages, and Valuation", in P. Muchlinski, F. Ortino and C. Schreuer (eds.), *The Oxford Handbook of International Investment Law*, Oxford University Press, 2008, p. 0; B. Sabahi, *Compensation and Restitution in Investor-State Arbitration: Principles and Practice*, OUP, Oxford, 2011; S. Hindelang, "Restitution and Compensation Reconstructing the Relationship in Investment Treaty Law", *International Investment Law and General International Law: From Clinical Isolation to Systemic Integration, Nomos*, 2011, 161; Paparinskis, *op. cit.*; D. Pulkowski, "Remedies for Wrongful Conduct: Lessons from Investment Arbitration", *International Investment Law and General International Law*, Edward Elgar Publishing, 2023, pp. 246-278.

ing [469]. Article 54 (3) ICSID Convention also militates against the award of anything other than compensation, since this provision only affords compulsory enforceability to the "pecuniary obligations" stemming from the award [470]. It should also be pointed out that there are other reasons why arbitrators might be hesitant to award restitution in investor-State cases especially where, by doing so, a greater interference would occur with the host State's policy and regulatory space – and, ultimately, its sovereignty [471].

While restitution is rare in investor-State arbitration, it is not unheard of. A relatively early case that clarifies its place and the potential relationship it has with *jura novit curia* is *Goetz* v. *Burundi* [472]. In that case, the claimant had demanded restitution by way of a request for specific performance consisting of the reinstatement of the tax and customs free zone [473]. The Tribunal departed from the right of election of the applicant, followed by the ILC approach, and gave the respondent the right to choose between the relief asked and monetary compensation. It relied on a *soi-disant* "sovereign discretion" doctrine [474].

True, under Article 35 ARSIWA, the respondent State can always invoke some form of impossibility of restitution in terms of the specific performance required by the applicant [475]. Accordingly, the *Goetz* Award can possibly be construed as an exceptional form of *jura novit*

469. It is generally undisputed that investment relationships are not among the ones to which limitations to the right of choice of remedy arising from Article 43 ARSIWA might apply – in other words, they are not cases where a party "may not, as it were, pocket compensation and walk away from an unresolved situation": see ARSIWA Commentaries, at 120.

470. See ICSID Convention, Article 54 ("Each Contracting State shall recognize an award rendered pursuant to this Convention as binding and enforce the pecuniary obligations imposed by").

471. It bears noting, however, that the award of a large sum by way of compensation can amount to no less significant an interference. See Paparinskis, *op. cit.* And indeed, there may be circumstances where restitution may qualify as far less onerous for the finances of the State: see ATA Construction, *Industrial and Trading Company* v. *Hashemite Kingdom of Jordan*, ICSID Case No. ARB/08/2, Award, 18 May 2010, para. 131 (discussing restitution by way of a restoration of claimant's right to arbitration).

472. *Antoine Goetz* et al. v. *Republic of Burundi (I)*, ICSID Case No. ARB/95/3, Award (Embodying the Parties' Settlement Agreement), 10 February 1999.

473. *Ibid.*, para. 59.

474. *Ibid.*, para. 135.

475. See ARSIWA, Article 35. Note that the Commentaries clarify that material impossibility of restitution is qualified by the phrase "provided and to the extent that", which "makes it clear that restitution may be only partially excluded, in which case the responsible State will be obliged to make restitution to the extent that this is neither impossible nor disproportionate" (at 98).

curia, in which the adjudicator's discretion is aimed at the application of the secondary rules of State responsibility.

At any rate, one may detect a recent trend among investment arbitration tribunals towards the encouragement of restitution in the form of specific performance of the obligations breached. This aims at rebuilding the damaged relationship between the investor and the State, thereby also giving effect to the broader reasons for the existence of the investment protection regime, which sees foreign direct investment as beneficial for the capital-importing State. The topic would deserve a book-length treatment, and for the present purposes it will suffice to observe that, in cases such as these, there would be no exercise of *jura novit curia*. Rather, by collaborating closely with the parties to propose a specific form of reparation, the arbitrators would be carrying out a task that is more akin to that of conciliation, or mediation.

C. Compensation

1. Inter-State litigation

The situation is more complex with regard to the adjudicators' power to determine the amount of compensation to be awarded independent from the claims of the parties in inter-State adjudication.

In the 1949 decision on compensation in the *Corfu Channel* case before the ICJ, the Court-appointed experts found the damage suffered by the UK as being more extensive than what the applicant had claimed, and their estimate yielded a figure for the compensation to be awarded much greater than the one requested [476]. Nonetheless, the Court decided that "[it could not] award more than the amount claimed in the submissions". Thus, the Court took the view that *ne ultra petita* was the commanding principle in this scenario [477].

On the other hand, the question may arise of whether the adjudicator would run counter the *ne ultra petita* principle by awarding *less* than what the applicant claimed, or *more* than what the *defendant* proposed – an approach which, practice shows, is a matter of course. The question ultimately concerns the boundaries of the judicial discretion in the assessment of the quantum of compensation and whether such

476. *Corfu Channel (United Kingdom of Great Britain and Northern Ireland* v. *Albania)*, *ICJ Reports 1949*, p. 244, at 249.
477. See also S. Wittich, "Compensation", in *Max Planck Encyclopedia of Public International Law*, at para. 47.

discretion is in any way governed by *jura novit curia*. A short answer to this question would inevitably be in the sense that, in the exercise of its decision-making function, the tribunal is tasked, *inter alia*, with establishing the existence and extent of the damage, as well as the link of causality between the damage caused and the wrongful conduct. Once the adjudicator has determined these factor to its satisfaction, then *ne infra petita* would in principle apply and the compensation should be awarded accordingly.

It would seem that the calculation of the amount of damage and the link of causality should be qualified as an issue of fact to be proven by the parties. However, the point has already been made in the previous chapters that the line dividing the judicial treatment of the disputed facts and the law to be applied to them is quite blurred, thus it may be argued that elements of *jura novit curia* would apply to the judicial assessment of these two factors insofar they relate to the compensation to be awarded. A related issue relevant for our purposes is whether, in the assessment in question, there may be a role for equity to be applied by the judge.

The issue may be framed in the following terms: what is the configuration of equity in its relation to law in general, and more specifically, in relation to the law applicable to matters of reparation? The previous chapters have offered a discussion of the lawmaking trend in the field of substantive law towards incorporation and delineation of equity *within* the law. However, the case law shows that no such trend has emerged concerning the adjudicative assessment of reparation in general, and compensation in particular. Evidence provided by the parties concerning the causation and extent of the damages remains the governing factor. However, the adjudicator may adjust its assessment resulting from factual evidence in order to avoid inequitable results, under the specific circumstances of the case. Arguably, such an approach may be seen as inherent with the pursuit of the sound and proper administration of justice.

Supports may be drawn from Bin Cheng's assumption that compensation is but a function of equity *infra legem* [478]. Following this approach, an inherent power to resort to equity would inevitably coincide with an outright exercise of *jura novit curia* or at least feature elements reconcilable with *jura novit curia*. This is not to say that no issues could possibly arise. To name one, it is certainly possible to foresee

478. Cheng, *General Principles of Law*, 299.

difficulties where the adjudicator equitably adjusts the assessment of compensation to the circumstances of a given case departing from clear rules on compensation enshrined in the applicable law.

The 1998 Award concerning the *Loan Agreement* between Italy and Costa Rica is a perfect case study on the issue in point [479]. The dispute essentially revolved around the validity of a financial agreement, which provided clear terms for the loan and repayment plan, including interest. The Tribunal found that the Agreement was valid [480]. But, while under its terms the global sum to be paid back, including default interest, would amount to 22 million US dollars, as confirmed by the Tribunal, the amount awarded by way of lump sum compensation was limited to 15 million US dollars [481]. The Tribunal went to a great length to argue that this decision was grounded in equity, but stressed that it was equity as a general principle of law, rather than in its *ex aequo et bono* configuration [482].

To that end, the Tribunal quoted Judge de Visscher, who, writing extrajudicially, observed that "[l]a juste application du droit, c'est une interprétation libérale de la règle où celle-ci s'imprègne d'équité" [483]. For the present purposes, the significance of the Award lies in the fact that the amount it awarded in compensation was significantly lower than that which would naturally follow from the specific performance of the Agreement, of which the Tribunal declared the full validity. In awarding such a lower sum, the Tribunal indicated the aim to avoid the payment of an "excessive" sum, which would run counter to what it defined as "pertinent principles and practice of international law" [484].

It bears noting how the Tribunal also emphasised that it reached its assessment of the amount of compensation considering "all relevant circumstances", including the development co-operation purpose of the disputed Agreement, as well as friendly and co-operative relationship between the parties [485]. Most importantly, the Tribunal used clear

---

479. Case concerning the Loan Agreement between Italy and Costa Rica (dispute arising under a financing agreement), 26 June 1998, UNRIAA, Vol. XXV pp. 21-82.

480. *Ibid.*, at 54.

481. *Ibid.*, at 76.

482. *Ibid.*, at 73 ("Il convient d'éviter ici une confusion entre ce rôle des considérations équitables relevant du système de droit applicable").

483. *Ibid.*, at 69.

484. *Ibid.*, at 75 ("contraire aux principes et à la pratique pertinents du droit international public").

485. See also A. Bufalini, "Remarks on the Role of Equity in Determining War Reparations before the International Court of Justice", *Questions of International Law* (2022), p. 36 *et seq.*

language indicating its aim to submit to the parties, by way of a solution, parameters that they could – if they so wished – integrate within the framework of their comprehensive relations [486]. This solution the parties welcomed, with the Award marking the revival of their bilateral friendly relations. The Award itself was complied with fifteen years later in 2013. This case corroborates the view, espoused throughout these chapters, that in inter-State adjudication the application of the law can be seen as subservient to the overarching goal of the settlement of the dispute. In this respect, *jura novit curia* gives way to judicial discretion beyond the strict boundaries laid out by any agreed or mandated applicable law. To put it differently, there is a lot more to judicial discretion than *jura novit curia*, unless equity were to be considered as having an all pervasive *infra legem* configuration

Going back to the *Loan Agreement* case between Italy and Costa Rica, it bears noting that the Tribunal submitted its assessment on compensation to the parties for possible further negotiation. An approach of this kind essentially neutralises any controversial aspect of *jura novit curia* by putting it to the parties. Indeed, this approach "sanctifies" the autonomy of the parties and the consensual basis of inter-State adjudication. This judicial practice is on the rise in inter-State adjudication: suffice it to recall cases such as *Gabcikovo-Nagymaros* [487], *Diallo* [488], *Certain Activities along the San Juan River* [489], and, lastly, *Enrica Lexie* [490]. In all such cases, the Court and the UNCLOS Annex VII Arbitral Tribunal required the parties to engage in negotiations with a view to reaching an agreement, including on the quantum of compensation. The ICJ in *Diallo* [491] and *Certain Activities over the San Juan* [492], and the Arbitral Tribunal in *Enrica Lexie* [493], also reserved the right to decide on the quantum of compensation would an agreement between the parties not be reached.

486. *Ibid.*
487. *Gabčíkovo-Nagymaros Project (Hungary/Slovakia)*, Judgment, *ICJ Reports 1997*, p. 7.
488. *Ahmadou Sadio Diallo (Republic of Guinea* v. *Democratic Republic of the Congo)*, Merits, Judgment, *ICJ Reports 2010*, p. 639.
489. *Certain Activities Carried Out by Nicaragua in the Border Area (Costa Rica* v. *Nicaragua)*, Compensation, Judgment, *ICJ Reports 2018*, p. 15.
490. *The "Enrica Lexie" Incident (Italy* v. *India)*, PCA Case 2015-28, Award, 21 May 2020.
491. *Diallo*, *supra* note 54, at 691, para. 163.
492. *Certain Activities*, *supra* note 55, at 717-718, para. 142.
493. *"Enrica Lexie"*, *supra* note 56, at 305, para. 1089.

Eventually, the ICJ had to do so based on the Special Agreement [494], whereas Italy and India have reached an agreement.

Another example may be found in the 2002 Judgment in the boundary delimitation case between Cameroon and Nigeria [495]. The ICJ held that the injury suffered by Cameroon as a result of the occupation of the Bakassi territory was sufficiently redressed by the declaratory part of the Judgment which assigned that territory to Cameroon [496]. It, thus, ignored any request for reparation for the material damage advanced by Cameroon [497]. The Court did not state the legal ground for the exercise of such discretion. It did, however, observe that the Judgment was meant to represent, *inter alia*, an opportunity for co-operation between the two countries to the benefit of the populations concerned. Commenting on the Judgment, Professor Enrico Milano observed that "the Court made its best efforts to facilitate the settlement of the dispute [. . . by] sacrificing the application of the law of State responsibility" [498]. Again, a solution of this kind supports the view whereby in inter-State adjudication, the application of the law appears to be regarded as subservient to the dispute settlement function [499].

2. Investment arbitration

Jura novit curia may also be exercised exercised in investment arbitration for the purposes of determining the amount of compensation. Its application for these purposes is to be seen as yet another example of application of rules which cannot be seen as directly part of the applicable law.

This has historically been the case – and still is the case to a large extent – where the applicable law flows from investment agreements which do not contain provisions for the protection of the defendant State's public interest as defined through international environmental

494. *Ahmadou Sadio Diallo (Republic of Guinea* v. *Democratic Republic of the Congo)*, Compensation, Judgment, *ICJ Reports 2012*, p. 324; *Certain Activities Carried Out by Nicaragua in the Border Area (Costa Rica* v. *Nicaragua)*, Compensation, Judgment, *ICJ Reports 2018*, p. 15.

495. *Land and Maritime Boundary Between Cameroon and Nigeria (Cameroon* v. *Nigeria: Equatorial Guinea intervening)*, Judgment, *ICJ Reports 2002*, p. 303.

496. *Ibid.*, at 452, para. 319.

497. *Ibid.*

498. E. Milano, "General Principles *Infra, Praeter, Contra Legem*? The Role of Equity in Determining Reparation", in M. Andenas, M. Fitzmaurice, A. M. Tanzi and J. Wouters (eds.), *General Principles and the Coherence of International Law*, Brill, 2019, 65, at 73.

499. See on this point Donoghue, *op. cit.*

or human rights law [500]. In the legal literature, the point has been made that consideration of rules belonging to such bodies of international law may have sometimes contributed to the dismissal of the claimant's request for compensation. Reference has been routinely made to the *Azurix* Award of 2006 [501], which dealt with the provision of water utilities, explaining the possible reasons why the Tribunal awarded compensation in the amount 165 million US dollars instead of the 570 million US dollars requested by the applicant [502]. The same would apply to the 2007 Award in *Compañiá de Aguas del Aconquija*, in which Argentina was ordered to pay 99 million US dollars instead of the claimed 380 million dollars [503].

Another water and sanitation investment law case may provide a particularly useful example. I am referring to the already mentioned 2008 Award in *Biwater* v. *Tanzania* [504]. In that case, the respondent was found in breach of all possible obligations under the relevant BIT, including breaches of standard of protections such as fair and equitable treatment and full protection and security, as well as the prohibition of indirect and creeping expropriation [505]. Yet the Tribunal dismissed the claimant request for compensation [506]. Irrespective of whether this solution was legally or morally justifiable, considerations pertaining to the defendant State's obligations in the field of international human rights law arguably contributed to that decision. One such construction

500. It is, of course, possible for the BIT concerned to include such provisions. See e.g. M. Chi, "The 'Greenization' of Chinese Bits: An Empirical Study of the Environmental Provisions in Chinese Bits and Its Implications for China's Future Bit-Making", *Journal of International Economic Law*, Vol. 18 (3), 2015, 511-542; A. Keene, "The Incorporation and Interpretation of WTO-Style Environmental Exceptions in International Investment Agreements", *The Journal of World Investment & Trade*, Vol. 18 (1), 2017, 62-99; L. Boisson de Chazournes, "Environmental Protection and Investment Arbitration: Yin and Yang", *ACDI – Anuario Colombiano de Derecho Internacional (Colombian Yearbook of International Law)*, Vol. 10, 2017, 371-400.

501. See J. Krommendijk and J. Morijn, " 'Proportional' by What Measure(s)? Balancing Investor Interests and Human Rights by Way of Applying the Proportionality Principle in Investor-State Arbitration", in P.-M. Dupuy, E.-U. Petersmann and F. Francioni (eds.), *Human Rights in International Investment Law and Arbitration*, Oxford University Press, 2009, pp. 422–451.

502. *Ibid.*, para. 415 *et seq.*

503. *Compañiá de Aguas del Aconquija SA and Vivendi Universal SA* v. *Argentine Republic*, ICSID Case No. ARB/97/3 (formerly Compañía de Aguas del Aconquija, SA and *Compagnie Générale des Eaux* v. *Argentine Republic*), Award, 20 August 2007, para. 8.11 *et seq.*

504. *Biwater Gauff (Tanzania) Ltd.* v. *United Republic of Tanzania*, ICSID Case No. ARB/05/22, Award, 24 July 2008.

505. *Ibid.*, para. 166 *et seq.*

506. *Ibid.*, para. 773 *et seq.*

of the Award is suggested by the following observation by the Tribunal, made *obiter*:

> "Water and sanitation services are vitally important, and the Republic [of Tanzania] has more than a right to protect such services in a case of a crisis: it has a moral and perhaps even a legal obligation to do so." [507]

This line of jurisprudence may suggest the development of a hybrid form of judicial discretion, a combination between the inherent discretion of an adjudicator in the interpretation and application of applicable law to the disputed facts on the one hand, and *jura novit curia* on the other.

It also bears noting that those arbitration investment disputes – much like those deciding inter-State ones – increasingly elicit the agreement of the parties on the assessment of compensation. This is particularly the case with regard to the choice of the accounting methods and the determination of quantum, which remains a highly controversial area, one falling squarely into the domain of party-appointed experts. Among such tensions between accounting methods, one may mention the so-called DCF (discounted cash flow) and WACC (weighted average cost of capital) which usually lead to mutually highly inconsistent solutions and are therefore, as a rule, incompatible with one another [508]. It must be added that, since the disputed factual background usually pertains to economic activity, the threshold and extent of the damage suffered, particularly in terms of loss of profit, ceases to be connected to the determination of compensation alone and ultimately amounts to a yardstick for the assessment of the very occurrence of an international wrongful act arising from the measures targeted by the complaint [509]. This is usually the case in relation to breaches of the fair and equitable treatment standard, which frequently hinge on an assessment not only of whether the claimant's legitimate expectations were in fact betrayed, but of whether its expectations were in fact legitimate to begin with [510].

---

507. *Ibid.*, para. 434.

508. See T. Senechal, "Dealing with Uncertainty: Discounted Cash Flow (DCF) Versus Adjusted Present Value (APV)", *Transnational Dispute Management (TDM)*, Vol. 4 (3), 2007; M. Kantor, "Valuation for Arbitration", *Valuation for Arbitration*, 2008, 1-430; K. F. Schumacher and H. Klönne, "Discounted Cash Flow Method", *Contemporary and Emerging Issues on the Law of Damages and Valuation in International Investment Arbitration*, Brill Nijhoff, 2018, pp. 205-230.

509. On this point, reference may be made to Tanzi, *op. cit.*

510. This can be particularly problematic in cases hinging on the notion of regulatory stability. See F. Ortino, "The Obligation of Regulatory Stability in the Fair and Equitable

As already alluded to, the adjudicative practice of requesting the parties' agreement on the accountancy methods for assessing damage "sanctifies" the autonomy of the parties and the consensual basis of inter-State adjudication and international investment arbitration.

D. Judicial assessment of the forms of reparation and of compensation by human rights courts

Article 41 of the European Convention on Human Rights (ECHR) provides that

> "If the Court finds that there has been a violation of the Convention or the Protocols thereto, and if the internal law of the High Contracting Party concerned allows only partial reparation to be made, the Court shall, *if necessary*, afford *just satisfaction* [*satisfaction équitable*] to the injured party." [511]

The circumstance in which domestic legislation may "allow only partial reparation to be made" indicates an impossibility of restitution under domestic law. That could be linked, for example, to the inexistence of domestic procedural law which allows for renewal of a trial when an international judgment so requires. Clearly, the expression "just satisfaction" refers to compensation. The provision in point is consistent with the customary law of State responsibility on the forms of reparation. In this scenario, too, its judicial application may involve elements of discretion in *jura novit curia* terms, which appear to have been abundantly exercised by the ECtHR, even way beyond the limits set by *ne infra petita* and *ne ultra petita*, just on a par with the application of substantive law [512].

In some cases, the Court has decided that the declaration of wrongfulness of the conduct complained of was sufficient a form of reparation in terms of satisfaction, despite the applicant having requested

Treatment Standard: How Far Have We Come?", *Journal of International Economic Law*, Vol. 21 (4), 2018, 845-865.

511. ECHR, Article 41.

512. An interesting perspective is provided by Veronika Fikfak, who observes that "the expectation is that the Court will adjust the amount of compensation 'to the concrete situation of each victim and to their personal circumstances. But the current practice of the Court provides no clear principles as to when damages should be awarded and how they should be measured. Although the ECHR uses the term 'just satisfaction' to refer to monetary damages, it is unclear how the Court determines what is 'just'". See Fikfak, *op. cit.*; The Court's choice of form of reparation is also influenced by the intended purpose of occasioning behavioural change in the respondent. On these themese, see also N. Ridi and V. Fikfak, "Sanctioning to Change State Behaviour", *Journal of International Dispute Settlement*, Vol. 13 (2), 2022, 210-232.

compensation. In others, it awarded compensation despite restitution being possible. An example may be found in *Dokić v Bosnia and Herzegovina*[513], where the Court decided to award the value of the disputed flat – the title to which the national authorities had refused to register and had essentially repossessed – instead of the re-establishment of the right to property[514].

It is important to note that, under either circumstance, the Court's discretion does not necessarily have to be grounded on *jura novit curia.* On the one hand, the Court may rely on the applicant's consent – as it did in the last mentioned case. On the other hand, the Court's decision not to award the requested compensation may flow from the fact that it did not find that it was *necessary,* thus, that it would not be *just* or *equitable*, under the circumstances of the case. In so doing, the Court would be simply interpreting and applying Article 41 ECHR to the disputed facts in terms different from the interpretation by one party, which had obviously pleaded the rule in point. This would represent an adjudicative prerogative in the administration of justice, which does not require to be grounded in *jura novit curia.*

Most important for our purposes is where the Court awards compensation, when not requested, in order to vindicate a right which it finds to be characterised as absolute in nature. In *Chember* v. *Russia*[515], the Court noted that the applicant had not submitted any claim for "just satisfaction", as required under Rule 60 of the Rules of Court[516]. It then stated as follows:

> "In such circumstances the Court would usually make no award. In the present case, however, the Court has found a violation of the applicant's right not to be subjected to inhuman punishment. Since this right is of absolute character, the Court finds it exceptionally possible to award the applicant 10,000 euros in respect of non-pecuniary damage . . . plus any tax that may be chargeable."[517]

513. *Dokić* v. *Bosnia and Herzegovina*, No. 6518/04, Judgment (Merits and Just Satisfaction), 27 May 2010.

514. *Ibid.*, para. 78.

515. *Chember* v. *Russia*, No. 7188/03, Judgment (Merits and Just Satisfaction), 3 July 2008.

516. *Ibid.*, para. 75.

517. *Ibid.*, para. 76. In the case of non-pecuniary damages in particular, the Court may make a discretionary determination. In a large-scale empirical study considering Article 3 cases, Fikfak found that "out of 64 torture victims who made no claim for

In the end, contrary to the ICJ approach followed in the *Corfu Channel* case [518], the ECtHR plainly sidestepped the *ne ultra petita* principle in determining the quantum of compensation in terms higher than in the request for relief.

Turning now to the Inter-American Court of Human Rights (IACtHR), Article 63 (1) of the Inter-American Convention on Human Rights provides that:

> "If the Court finds that there has been a violation of a right or freedom protected by this Convention, the Court shall rule that the injured party be ensured the enjoyment of his right or freedom that was violated. It shall also rule, if appropriate, that the consequences of the measure or situation that constituted the breach of such right or freedom be remedied and that *fair compensation* be paid to the injured party." [519]

The Inter-American Court of Human Rights (IACtHR) has taken a proactive and creative approach to the matter, which is to be appreciated in the light of the broad language of Article 63 IACHR and in combination with the overall rationale of the Convention, whose intended function is to promote the rule of law and domestic policies in compliance with basic human rights and freedoms [520].

Against this background, it is only natural that the IACtHR should exercise ample autonomy in deciding forms of reparation on a case-by-case basis. Accordingly, no obstacles arise to the framing of the exercise of such judicial attitude as a form of *jura novit curia* in the application of the secondary rules of State responsibility. However, although such *jura novit curia* power could in principle be exercised at the reparation stage of the proceedings by the Court – in combination with the Commission – in the same way as it does at the jurisdictional and merits stages, in practice, this hardly ever occurs. That is so because the Commission, once it has exhausted its quasi-jurisdictional function, usually drafts its request for remedy in the most extensive terms. Thus, in any case in which the Commission entrusts the Court with the widest margins of appreciation of the most appropriate forms of reparation,

---

non-pecuniary damages, 54 victims were not awarded any non-pecuniary damage". See Fikfak, *op. cit.*, 348.

518. *Corfu Channel (United Kingdom* v. *Albania)*, Judgment (Compensation), *ICJ Reports 1949*, p. 244.

519. IACHR, Article 63 (1).

520. See e.g. Article 41 IACH, concerning the Inter-American Commission on Human Rights.

very much in line with Article 63 IACHR, there is no need for the Court to rely on *jura novit curia* to justify its latitude in choosing whatever form of reparation it finds appropriate. Indeed, the Court has embraced a creative and innovative approach to reparation, going beyond what may be requested by representatives of the applicants or by the Commission, nor suggested in argument by the respondent State [521].

Two examples from the IACtHR case law will suffice. In *Aloeboetoe* v. *Suriname* [522], on a breach of the right of access to education, the Commission had asked for just compensation, next to the declaration of wrongfulness of the conduct complained of [523]. Apart from the requested measures of repararation, the Court took into consideration that the children of the victims lived where the school had been shut down, in the town of Gujaba [524]. Therefore, it ordered Suriname "to reopen the school at Gujaba and staff it with teaching and administrative personnel to enable it to function" [525].

In November 2020, the same Court – in *Almeida* v. *Argentina* [526] – awarded a significant amount of compensation, as a substitute for restitution, which neither representative for the applicant, nor the Commission, had requested, and which, therefore, the defendant State had not had the opportunity to discuss [527].

In case of doubt about whether the exercise of such ample discretion goes beyond the scope of the autonomy afforded to the human rights judge by Articles 41 ECHR and 63 ACHR, *jura novit curia* could, in principle, provide a residual legal ground for the exercise of the discretion in point. In practice, this would seem a useless logical exercise. In fact, *jura novit curia* could come into play only to the extent that principles of justice, equity and fairness are considered *infra legem*. This would be the case insofar as they are read into Article 41 ECHR and Article 63 ACHR. Given the ample discretion which stems from these provisions, one would see no point in arguing reliance on the same principles in relation to a non-conventional source.

---

521. V. Krsticevic, "Remedies of the Inter-American Human Rights System", *Proceedings of the ASIL Annual Meeting*, Vol. 111, 2017, 261-263.

522. *Case of Aloeboetoe* et al. v. *Suriname*, Judgment of 10 September 1993 (Reparations and Costs).

523. *Ibid.*, para. 8.

524. *Ibid.*, para. 96.

525. *Ibid.*

526. *Case of Almeida* v. *Argentina*, Judgment of 17 November 2020.

527. *Ibid.*, para. 72 *et seq.*

E. Reparation and compensation in international criminal justice

The Statute of the ICC, at Article 75 on *Reparations to victims* provides that

> "The Court shall establish principles relating to reparations to, or in respect of, victims, including restitution, compensation and rehabilitation. On this basis, in its decision the Court may, either upon request or on its own motion in exceptional circumstances, determine the scope and extent of any damage, loss and injury to, or in respect of, victims and will state the principles on which it is acting.
>
> The Court may make an order directly against a convicted person specifying appropriate reparations to, or in respect of, victims, including restitution, compensation and rehabilitation . . ." [528]

In principle, this provision is quite notable for our purposes, as it appears to enhance *jura novit curia* powers on two counts. First, by vesting the Court with the power to "establish principles" concerning the various forms of reparation applicable to the criminal adjudicative contexts, i.e. stemming from individual criminal responsibility. Second, by underlying the consequent power to apply such principles to any specific case before it, including *sua sponte*, even though "in exceptional circumstances".

In practice – also looking at Rule 97 of the ICC Rules of Procedure – it looks as if the powers in question boil down to a merely factual assessment of any damage, loss or injury suffered by the victims in order to decide the appropriate forms of reparation. The factual factor here is corroborated by Rule 97(2), which affords the Court with the power to appoint experts for assistance in the determination of the damage, loss and injury suffered, as well as of the forms of reparation.

F. Concluding remarks

This chapter has provided a detailed examination of the influence and application of *jura novit curia* in the context of various forms of adjudication. We have explored how *jura novit curia* plays a pivotal

528. ICC Statute, Article 75.

role in defining the remedial competence of adjudicators, particularly in the realm of reparation. When adjudicators exercise *jura novit curia*, they often find a middle ground between the extremes pleaded by both parties, demonstrating the inherent discretion embedded within *jura novit curia*.

Our examination of the application of *jura novit curia* in inter-State and investor-State litigation, considering its role in the determination of the form of reparation, as well as of the assessment of compensation, illustrates how the principle can significantly shape the outcome of a dispute and influence the reparation phase. This is just as true, the appropriate adjustments having been made, in the context of human rights adjudication and international criminal justice. These realms, too, are impacted by the influence of *jura novit curia* in shaping the course and result of adjudication.

The key thread running through all these domains is the fundamental role of *jura novit curia* as a unifying adjudicative principle. Irrespective of the specific area of adjudication, *jura novit curia* emerges as a common influence that guides the adjudicator's decision-making process, having a bearing on the choice of form and quantum of reparation just as much as it does on the application of the "secondary rules" concerning State responsibility.

As we draw closer to the end of our exploration of the influence of *jura novit curia* across various forms of international adjudication, we prepare to delve into the divergent rationales that underpin its application. In the next, final chapter, we will elucidate the intersection of *jura novit curia* with distinct adjudicative mandates and the pivotal role played by notions of legitimacy and authority in supporting or limiting its application.

CHAPTER VI

CONCLUSION

Different rationales of jura novit curia *for different adjudicative clusters and a unifying procedural principle*

It is time to offer some conclusions based on the observations made throughout this study. To this end, a reference point may be found in the same *Asylum* case mentioned in an earlier part of this analysis [529]. In that case, the ICJ provided a clear indication that – at the inter-State level – the adjudicator may not apply the applicable law to the dispute by addressing legal issues that do not fall within the reach of the parties' claims, however germane they may be to the factual background of the case.

In so doing, *ne ultra petita* gives effect to party autonomy, effectively making the parties' claims into an integral component of the adjudicator's mandate. The conclusion that follows is that, in inter-State adjudication, *jura novit curia* is reduced to the minimum.

In other words, the international judge in inter-State adjudication may employ interpretive legal reasoning independent from the parties so far as it relates to rules pleaded by them. Such restrictive statement requires some qualification, or exceptions.

The first exception operates in the hypothetical and unlikely circumstance in which the rules invoked by the parties are inadequate, or insufficient, to decide the dispute. Here, the prohibition of *non liquet* and/or *ne infra petita* principles would bring *jura novit curia* back into play.

Secondly, the adjudicator may refer to rules that have not been invoked, by way of Article 31 (3) *(c)* of the Vienna Convention, Article 293 (1) or equity *infra legem*. In any case, such rules have to be incidental to the subject matter of the dispute.

Inter-State and investor-State case law show that, when the judge, or arbitrator, exercises elements of *jura novit curia*, the procedural rights of the parties, with special regard to the right to be heard, should always be given due consideration.

---

529. See *supra* Chapter III, Section B.1. *Asylum (Colombia* v. *Peru), ICJ Reports 1950*, p. 266.

In human rights adjudication the calibration between *jura novit curia* and *ne ultra petita* is reversed. Here, *jura novit curia* operates to the fullest extent, thus reducing the operation of *ne ultra petita* to less than the minimum. This allows human rights courts to legally characterise, or recharacterise, the facts submitted to it without constraints other than the scope of the relevant human rights convention as a whole.

As to international criminal adjudication, we have seen that *jura novit curia* entitles the judge to reformulate the charges presented by the prosecutor. Here, again, *ne ultra petita* is reduced almost to nil. At the same time, we saw how such *jura novit curia* powers are subject to the requirement that the defendant is provided with prompt and detailed information of any new or reformulated charges, thus affording the accused the right to defend himself from such charges.

The rationale for such a three-tier differentiated operation of *jura novit curia* – in combination with its cognate principles – according to each of the three areas of international adjudication in point – flows from the different nature of the judicial mandate and function of each of the three adjudicative contexts under consideration.

First, in inter-State and investor-State litigation, the highly consensual nature of the jurisdictional mandate renders the application, declaration and elucidation of the law subservient to the dispute decision function.

Second, in human rights litigation, the opposite is true. Here, the primary function of human rights courts is to ensure compliance with the relevant conventional instrument and to ensure its consistent interpretation and application with regard to similar factual situations. It is in that respect that human rights courts have been compared to domestic supreme courts, which are the guardians of their constitution and of consistency in its application.

Accordingly, in human rights litigation, the dispute settlement function becomes subservient to the application and elucidation of the law. As we have seen, this is epitomised by the extreme circumstance in which a human rights case may be allowed to continue even after the applicant has passed away and no heir is available.

Third, as to international criminal adjudication, a consistently sharp difference has emerged from the analysis in the application of the principle under consideration between the circumstance in which individual criminal responsibility is to be assessed, on the one hand, and when an inter-State or investor-State dispute is to be decided, or breaches of human rights and the corresponding relief to the victims are to be ascertained and determined, on the other hand.

The principle of legality in a criminal law context works in two directions: on the one hand, it prevents creative interpretation and application of the law; on the other hand, it requires formulation of charges based on clear and consistent interpretation and application of the law to the proven facts by the criminal judge, independent from what the prosecutor and defendant say. Based on this consideration, it has been emphasised how, after initial concerns and some disorientation, particularly in the judicial practice of the ICTY, criminal justice relies on *jura novit curia* in order to allow the judge to reformulate the charges formulated by the prosecutor, or to formulate new ones, when during proceedings evidence emerges that so requires. Procedural fair trial guarantees also apply in peculiar terms for the purposes of alignment with the principle of criminal law legality. Such fair trial guarantees include full, detailed and timely information of the charges when formulated or re-formulated, prior to the judgment.

And this brings me to my next concluding remark. Namely, that the one red thread which runs through each of the three adjudicative areas under consideration in a unifying fashion is the general procedural principle providing for the right of the parties to be heard. The importance of this right explains the generally proactive attitude by international courts and tribunals in their engagement with the parties in the conduct of proceedings including in the formal post-hearing brief. Otherwise, increasing judicial care is taken – or should be taken, particularly in human rights litigation – so that the judicial recharacterisation of claims be carried out as early as possible in the proceedings, thus affording both parties the opportunity to submit their arguments of law and fact concerning the newly judicially prospected rights and corresponding obligations.

And now that the contents and contours of *jura novit curia* have been delineated by some degree of approximation, the quiet elephant in the room may put the hard question: "and so what?". To the concrete mind in concrete times the question may indeed arise as to which practical use is to be made of such normative parameters for international adjudicators if there is hardly any judicial review in the international legal system.

The short answer is "legitimacy" and "authority". The relevance of such values to adjudication is key to the rule of law in any legal system. In a domestic context, where adjudication is compulsory, while the legality of judicial decisions may be tested through judicial review, the social perception of the legitimacy remains key to the political dynamics governing the legal process. In the international society, where adjudication is consent-based, perception of legitimacy is all the more important [530]. For there is consent to adjudication where there is confidence, and there is confidence where there is legitimacy [531]. And the perception of the legitimacy of the decision-making enhances its authority [532].

More generally, the main determinant of social confidence in the law corresponds to the degree of reflection of generally shared social values in the substantive legal rules in force at any given point time. While it would be for another specialised or general course to address such substantive law aspects of the international legal process, for purposes of the present course, it is worth stressing that the next determinant of social confidence, as one sees it, lies in the perceived propriety and fairness in the adjudicative interpretation and application of substantive law.

In light of the above, it becomes apparent that actors in international adjudication have a vested interest in ensuring that the normative framework guiding the fair administration of justice is made clear and transparent, particularly in regard to the principles of conceptual decision-making and legal reasoning. Spontaneous adjudicative compliance with such standards will be facilitated, and express reference to them by international courts and tribunals would be possibly encouraged, thus contributing to enhancing confidence in international adjudication and law.

530. The notion of legitimacy is, of course, a central one in both international law in general and the study of international adjudication. Among the many important works on this topic, see T. M. Franck, "Legitimacy in the International System", *The American Journal of International Law*, Vol. 82 (4), 1988, 705-759; S. D. Franck, "The Legitimacy Crisis in Investment Treaty Arbitration: Privatizing Public International Law Through Inconsistent Decisions", *Fordham Law Review*, Vol. 73, 2004, 1521; N. Grossman, "Legitimacy and International Adjudicative Bodies", 2010; G. Ulfstein, "International Courts and Judges: Independence, Interaction, and Legitimacy", *NYU Journal of International Law and Politics (2014)*, 2014, 14-13; H. G. Cohen, A. Follesdal, N. Grossman and G. Ulfstein, "Legitimacy and International Courts – A Framework", in N. Grossman, H. G. Cohen, A. Follesdal and G. Ulfstein (eds.), *Legitimacy and International Courts*, Cambridge University Press, 2018, pp. 1-40.

531. Joseph Raz, *Between Authority and Interpretation: On the Theory of Law and Practical Reason*, (OUP, 2009), Chap. 5; L. Boisson de Chazournes, "Plurality in the Fabric of International Courts and Tribunals: The Threads of a Managerial Approach", in *European Journal of International Law*, Vol. 28 (2017), p. 13 *et seq*.

532. E. Benvenisti and G. W. Downs, "Prospects for the Increased Independence of International Tribunals", in A. von Bogdandy and I. Venzke (eds.), *International Judicial Lawmaking: On Public Authority and Democratic Legitimation in Global Governance*, Berlin, Heidelberg: Springer Berlin Heidelberg, 2012, pp. 99-129; K. J. Alter, L. R. Helfer and M. R. Madsen, "How Context Shapes the Authority of International Courts", *Law and Contemporary Problems*, Vol. 79 (1), 2016, 1-36; F. Zarbiyev, "Saying Credibly What the Law Is: On Marks of Authority in International Law", *Journal of International Dispute Settlement*, Vol. 9 (2), 2018, 291-314.

BIBLIOGRAPHY

Akehurst, M., "Equity and general principles of law", *International & Comparative Law Quarterly*, Vol. 25 (4), 1976, pp. 801-825.

Alter, K. J., "The Multiple Roles of International Courts and Tribunals: Enforcement, Dispute Settlement, Constitutional and Administrative Review", in J. L. Dunoff and M. A. Pollack (eds.), *Interdisciplinary Perspectives on International Law and International Relations: The State of the Art*, Cambridge University Press, 2013.

Alter, K. J., L. R. Helfer and M. R. Madsen, "How Context Shapes the Authority of International Courts", *Law and Contemporary Problems*, Vol. 79 (1), 2016, pp. 1-36.

Alvarez, J. E., *International Organizations as Law-makers*, Oxford University Press, 2006.

Amerasinghe, C. F., *Jurisdiction of specific international tribunals*, Leiden; Boston, Martinus Nijhoff Publishers, 2009.

Banifatemi, Y., "The Law Applicable in Investment Treaty Arbitration", in K. Yannaca-Small (ed.), *Arbitration Under International Investment Agreements: A Guide to the Key Issues*, Oxford University Press, 2010.

Bartels, L., "Jurisdiction and Applicable Law Clauses: Where does a Tribunal find the principal norms Applicable to the Case before it", *Multi-Sourced Equivalent Norms in International Law, Oxford: Hart*, 2011, pp. 115-141.

Benedettelli, M. V., "Determining the Applicable Law in Commercial and Investment Arbitration: Two Intertwined Road Maps for Conflicts-Solving", *ICSID Review – Foreign Investment Law Journal*, 2022.

Benvenisti, E., and G. W. Downs, "Prospects for the Increased Independence of International Tribunals", in A. von Bogdandy and I. Venzke (eds.), *International Judicial Lawmaking: On Public Authority and Democratic Legitimation in Global Governance*, Berlin, Heidelberg: Springer Berlin Heidelberg, 2012, pp. 99-129.

Benvenisti, E., G. Nolte and K. Yalin-Mor, *Community interests across international law*, Oxford University Press, 2018.

Berman, F., *Authority in International Law* (2018).

Berman, S. F., "International Treaties and British Statutes", *Statute Law Review*, Vol. 26 (1), 2005, pp. 1-12.

–, *The International Court of Justice as an 'Agent' of Legal Development?**, Oxford University Press, 2013.

Besson, S., "Community Interests in International Law-Whose Interests are They and How does One Identify Them?", *Community interests across international law*, Oxford University Press, 2018, pp. 50-69.

Bitti, G., "Article 21 of the Statute of the International Criminal Court and the Treatment of Sources of Law in the Jurisprudence of the ICC", *The Emerging Practice of the International Criminal Court*, 2008, pp. 281-304.

Bjorklund, A. K., *9 Applicable Law in International Investment Disputes*, Brill Nijhoff, 2014.

Boisson de Chazournes, L., "Environmental Protection and Investment Arbitration: Yin and Yang", *ACDI – Anuario Colombiano de Derecho Internacional (Colombian Yearbook of International Law)*, Vol. 10, 2017, pp. 371-400.

Brewster, R., "Pricing Compliance: When Formal Remedies Displace Reputational Sanctions", *Harvard International Law Journal*, Vol. 54 (2), 2013, pp. 259-314.

Brierly, J. L., "The Lotus Case", *LQ Rev.*, Vol. 44, 1928, pp. 154-156.

Broude, T., and Y. Shany, *Multi-sourced Equivalent Norms in International Law*, Hart Publishing, 2011.

Brown, C., *A Common Law of International Adjudication*, OUP, 2007.

Cappelletti, M., *Iura novit curia: impossibilià di conoscere il diritto straniero richiamato dalle norme di diritto internazionale privato e metodo comparativo*, Giuffrè, 1967.

Cazala, J., "Good administration of Justice", *Max Planck Encyclopedia of International Procedural Law*, Oxford University Press, 2020, *Max Planck Encyclopedia of International Procedural Law*, 2020.

Charney, J. I., "Is international law threatened by multiple international tribunals?", *Recueil des cours*, Vol. 271 *(1998)*, pp 101-382.

Chattopadhyay, S. K., "Equity in International Law: Its Growth and Development", *Georiga Journal of International and Comparative Law*, Vol. 5 (2), 1975, pp. 381-406.

Chen, H., "The role of amicus curiae in implementing the human right to water in the context of international investment law", *Review of European, Comparative & International Environmental Law*, Vol. 29 (3), 2020, pp. 454-463.

Cheng, B., *General Principles of Law: As Applied by International Courts and Tribunals*, Stevens, 1953.

Chi, M., "The 'Greenization' of Chinese Bits: An Empirical Study of the Environmental Provisions in Chinese Bits and its Implications for China's Future Bit-Making", *Journal of International Economic Law*, Vol. 18 (3), 2015, pp. 511-542.

Cohen, H. G., A. Follesdal, N. Grossman and G. Ulfstein, "Legitimacy and International Courts – A Framework", in N. Grossman, H. G. Cohen, A. Follesdal and G. Ulfstein (eds.), *Legitimacy and International Courts*, Cambridge University Press, 2018, pp. 1-40.

Costelloe, D., *Legal Consequences of Peremptory Norms in International Law*, Cambridge University Press, 2017.

Crawford, J., *Brownlie's Principles of Public International Law*, 8 ed., Oxford, United Kingdom, OUP, 2012.

–, *Chance, Order, Change: The Course of International Law, General Course on Public International Law*, Martinus Nijhoff Publishers, Brill Academic, 2014.

Crawford, J., A. Pellet and C. Redgwell, "Anglo-American and Continental Traditions in Advocacy before International Courts and Tribunals Legal Tradition in a Diverse World: Keynote Contributions", *Cambridge Journal of International and Comparative Law*, Vol. 2, 2013, pp. 715-737.

d'Aspremont, J., "The Idea of "Rules" in the Sources of International Law", *British Yearbook of International Law*, Vol. 84 (1), 2014, pp. 103-130.

Daugirdas, K., "International Organizations and the Creation of Customary International Law", *European Journal of International Law*, Vol. 31 (1), 2020, pp. 201-233.

De Brabandere, E., M. Fitzmaurice and P. Merkouris, "Human rights considerations in international investment arbitration", *The Interpretation and Application of the European Convention of Human Rights: Legal and Practical Implications*, Martinus Nijhoff Publishers, 2012, p. 183.

de Souza Dias, T., "The Retroactive Application of the Rome Statute in Cases of Security Council Referrals and *Ad hoc* Declarations: An Appraisal of the Existing Solutions to an Under-discussed Problem", *Journal of International Criminal Justice*, Vol. 16 (1), 2018, pp. 65-89.

Devaney, J. G., "Introduction to the Symposium on Incidental Jurisdiction", Vol. 116, 2022, pp. 160-163.

Donoghue, J. E., "International Adjudication: Peaks, Valleys, and Rolling Hills", *Proceedings of the ASIL Annual Meeting*, Vol. 112, 2018, pp. 15-22.

Douglas, Z., *The international law of investment claims*, Cambridge, UK, New York, Cambridge University Press, 2009.

Dumberry, P., "The protection of investors' legitimate expectations and the fair and equitable treatment standard under NAFTA article", *Journal of International Arbitration*, Vol. 31 (1), 2014.

Dzehtsiarou, K., *Can the European Court of Human Rights Shape European Public Order?*, Cambridge University Press, 2021.

Elias, T. O., "The doctrine of intertemporal law", *American Journal of International Law*, Vol. 74 (2), 1980, pp. 285-307.
Fahner, J. H., *Judicial Deference in International Adjudication: A Comparative Analysis*, Hart, 2020.
Farnelli, G. M., "Recent Trends in Investment Arbitration Concerning Legitimate Expectations", *International Community Law Review*, Vol. 23 (1), 2021, p. 27.
Fikfak, V., "Changing State Behaviour: Damages before the European Court of Human Rights", *European Journal of International Law*, Vol. 29(4), 2018, pp. 1091-1125.
Fikfak, V., "Non-pecuniary damages before the European Court of Human Rights: Forget the victim; it's all about the state", *Leiden Journal of International Law*, 2020, pp. 1-35.
Fitzmaurice, G. G., "Some problems regarding the formal sources of international law", *Symbolae Verzijl: Présentées au professeur J. H. W. Verzijl à l'occasion de son 70e anniversiare*, Nijhoff, 1958, pp. 58-79.
Fitzmaurice, M., "The History of Article 38 of the Statute of the International Court of Justice: The Journey from the Past to the Present", in S. Besson and J. d'Aspremont (eds.), *The Oxford Handbook of the Sources of International Law*, Oxford University Press, 2017, p. 0.
Franck, S. D., "Legitimacy Crisis in Investment Treaty Arbitration: Privatizing Publlic International Law through Inconsistent Decisions, The", *Fordham Law Review*, Vol. 73, 2004, p. 1521.
Franck, T. M., "Legitimacy in the International System", *The American Journal of International Law*, Vol. 82(4), 1988, pp. 705-759.
Gaja, G., "Is a State Specially Affected when its Nationals' Human Rights are Infringed?", *Man's Inhumanity to Man*, Brill Nijhoff, 2003, pp. 373-382.
–, "Positivism and Dualism in Dionisio Anzilotti The European Tradition in International Law: Dionisio Anzilotti", *European Journal of International Law*, Vol. 3 (1), 1992, pp. 123-138.
–, "The Protection of General interests in the International Community. General Course on Public International Law (2011)", *Recueil des cours*, Vol. 364 (2012), pp. 9-185.
Gasbarri, L., "The Notion of Institutional Practice in United Nations Law", *Max Planck Yearbook of United Nations Law Online*, Vol. 24 (1), 2021, pp. 1-35.
Giacco, L. L., "Eureka! On Courts' Discretion in 'Ascertaining' Rules of Customary International Law", in J. Kammerhofer, N. Arajärvi and P. Merkouris (eds.), *The Theory, Practice, and Interpretation of Customary International Law*, Cambridge: Cambridge University Press, 2022, pp. 256-276.
–, *Judicial Decisions in International Law Argumentation: Between Entrapment and Creativity*, Bloomsbury Academic, 2022.
Ginsburg, T., "Bounded discretion in international judicial lawmaking", *Va. J. Int'l L.*, Vol. 45, 2004, p. 631.
Gourgourinis, A., "The Distinction between Interpretation and Application of Norms in International Adjudication", *Journal of International Dispute Settlement*, Vol. 2 (1), 2011, pp. 31-57.
Gray, C. D., *Judicial remedies in international law*, Oxford University Press, 1990.
Gray, C., "Is There an International Law of Remedies?", *British Yearbook of International Law*, Vol. 56 (1), 1986, pp. 25-47.
Grossman, N., "Legitimacy and International Adjudicative Bodies", 2010.
Hamamoto, S., "5 Protection of the Investor's Legitimate Expectations: Intersection of a Treaty Obligation and a General Principle of Law", *China and international investment law*, Brill Nijhoff, 2014, pp. 141-169.
Helmersen, S. T., "Finding 'the Most Highly Qualified Publicists': Lessons from the International Court of Justice", *European Journal of International Law*, Vol. 30 (2), 2019, pp. 509-535.
Henckels, C., "Legitimate Expectations and the Rule of Law in International Investment Law", *Investment Protection Standards and the Rule of Law (Oxford*

University Press, forthcoming), Monash University Faculty of Law Legal Studies Research Paper (3409086), 2020.

J. Hepburn, *Domestic Law in International Investment Arbitration*, Oxford, New York, Oxford University Press, 2017.

Hindelang, S., "Restitution and Compensation Reconstructing the Relationship in Investment Treaty Law", *International Investment Law and General International Law: From Clinical Isolation to Systemic Integration, Nomos*, 2011, p. 161.

Jarrett, M., "The international validity of domestic law in investment-treaty arbitration", *Arbitration International*, Vol. 39 (1), 2023, pp. 1-18.

Jolowicz, J. A., *On Civil Procedure*, Cambridge University Press, 2000.

Kantor, M., "Valuation for Arbitration", *Valuation for Arbitration*, 2008, pp. 1-430.

Keene, A., "The Incorporation and Interpretation of WTO-Style Environmental Exceptions in International Investment Agreements", *The Journal of World Investment & Trade*, Vol. 18 (1), 2017, pp. 62-99.

Klabbers, J., "International Organizations in the Formation of Customary International Law", *Customary International Law on the Use of Force*, Brill Nijhoff, 2005, pp. 179-195.

Kolb, R., "Principles as Sources of International Law (with Special Reference to Good Faith)", *Netherlands International Law Review*, Vol. 53 (1), 2006, pp. 1-36.

Kriebaum, U., "Human rights and international investment law", *Research Handbook on Human Rights and Investment*, Edward Elgar Publishing, 2018, pp. 13-40.

Krsticevic, V., "Remedies of the Inter-American Human Rights System", *Proceedings of the ASIL Annual Meeting*, Vol. 111, 2017, pp. 261-263.

Lando, M., *Maritime Delimitation as a Judicial Process*, Cambridge University Press, 2019.

Laryea, E. T., "Legitimate expectations in investment treaty law: concept and scope of application", *Handbook of International Investment Law and Policy*, 2020, pp. 1-24.

Lauterpacht, H., "The So-Called Anglo-American and Continental Schools of Thought in International Law", *British Year Book of International Law*, Vol. 12, 1931, pp. 31-62.

–, *The function of law in the international community*, 1st ed, Oxford, New York, Oxford University Press, 2011.

Lauterpacht, S. H., *The Development of International Law by the International Court*, Praeger, 1958.

League of Nations. Advisory Committee of Jurists, *Procès-verbaux of the proceedings of the Committee, 16 June-24 July 1920, with Annexes*, The Hague, Van Langenhuysen, 1920.

Longobardo, M., "The standing of indirectly injured states in the litigation of community interests before the ICJ: Lessons learned and future implications in light of *The Gambia* v. *Myanmar* and beyond", *International Community Law Review*, Vol. 1 (aop), 2021, pp. 1-31.

Lowe, V., "The Role of Equity in International Law", *The Australian Year Book of International Law Online*, Vol. 12 (1), 1992, pp. 54-81.

Maniruzzaman, A. F. M., "State Contracts in Contemporary International Law: Monist versus Dualist Controversies", *European Journal of International Law*, Vol. 12 (2), 2001, pp. 309-328.

Mao, X., "Public-Interest Litigation before the International Court of Justice: Comment on *The Gambia* v. *Myanmar* Case", *Chinese Journal of International Law*, Vol. 21 (3), 2022, pp. 589-609.

Mbengue, M. M., "Scientific Fact-finding at the International Court of Justice: An Appraisal in the Aftermath of the Whaling Case", *Leiden Journal of International Law*, Vol. 29 (2), 2016, pp. 529-550.

McCormack, T. L. H., "A *non liquet* on nuclear weapons – The ICJ avoids the application of general principles of international humanitarian law", *International Review of the Red Cross (1961-1997)*, Vol. 37 (316), 1997, pp. 76-91.

McIntyre, J., "Put on notice: The role of the dispute requirement in assessing jurisdiction and admissibility before the international court", *Melbourne Journal of International Law*, Vol. 19 (2), 2018, pp. 546-585.
–, "The Declaratory Judgment in Recent Jurisprudence of the ICJ: Conflicting Approaches to State Responsibility?", *Leiden Journal of International Law*, Vol. 29 (1), 2016, pp. 177-195.
McLachlan, C., "*Lis Pendens* in International Litigation", Vol. 336, 2009.
–, "The Principle of Systemic Integration and Article 31 (3) *(C)* of the Vienna Convention", *The International and Comparative Law Quarterly*, Vol. 54 (2), 2005, pp. 279-319.
Merryman, J. H., "On the Convergence (and Divergence) of the Civil Law and the Common Law", *Stanford Journal of International Law*, Vol. 17 (2), 1981, pp. 357-388.
Mills, A., "Rethinking Jurisdiction in International Law", *British Yearbook of International Law*, Vol. 84 (1), 2014, pp. 187-239.
Murphy, S. D., "Temporal Issues Relating to BIT Dispute Resolution", *ICSID Review – Foreign Investment Law Journal*, Vol. 37 (1-2), 2022, pp. 51-84.
Orakhelashvili, A., "The International Court and 'Its Freedom to Select the Ground Upon Which it Will Base its Judgment'", *International & Comparative Law Quarterly*, Vol. 56 (1), 2007, pp. 171-184.
–, *Peremptory Norms in International Law*, OUP, Oxford, 2008.
Ortino, F., "The Obligation of Regulatory Stability in the Fair and Equitable Treatment Standard: How Far Have We Come?", *Journal of International Economic Law*, Vol. 21 (4), 2018, pp. 845-865.
Palombino, F. M., "Judicial Economy and Limitation of the Scope of the Decision in International Adjudication", *Leiden Journal of International Law*, Vol. 23 (4), 2010, pp. 909-932.
Paparinskis, M., "Inherent Powers of ICSID Tribunals: Broad and Rightly So", in T. J. Weiler and I. A. Laird, *Investment Treaty Arbitration and International Law*, Vol. 5, Huntington, JurisNet, 2012, pp. 11-42.
–, "Inherent Powers of ICSID Tribunals: Broad and Rightly So", in T. J. Weiler and I. A. Laird, *Investment Treaty Arbitration and International Law*, Vol. 5, Huntington, JurisNet, 2012, pp. 11-42.
–, "A Case Against Crippling Compensation in International Law of State Responsibility", *The Modern Law Review*, Vol. 83 (6), 2020, pp. 1246-1286.
Paulsson, J., "Jurisdiction and admissibility", *Global Reflections on International Law, Commerce and Dispute Resolution*, 2010, p. 601.
–, *The Unruly Notion of Abuse of Rights*, Cambridge, Cambridge University Press, 2020.
Pellet, A., "Revisiting the Sources of Applicable Law before the ICC", in M. M. deGuzman and D. M. Amann (eds.), *Arcs of Global Justice: Essays in Honour of William A. Schabas*, Oxford University Press, 2018, p. 0.
Potestà, M., "Legitimate expectations in investment treaty law: understanding the roots and the limits of a controversial concept", *ICSID review*, Vol. 28 (1), 2013, pp. 88-122.
Pretelli, I., and S. Lalani, "Switzerland: The Principle Iura Aliena Novit Curia and the Role of Foreign Law Advisory Services in Swiss Judicial Practice", in Y. Nishitani (ed.), *Treatment of Foreign Law – Dynamics towards Convergence?*, Cham: Springer International Publishing, 2017, pp. 375-393.
Pulkowski, D., "Remedies for wrongful conduct: Lessons from investment arbitration", *International Investment Law and General International Law*, Edward Elgar Publishing, 2023, pp. 246-278.
Quintana, J. J., *Litigation at the International Court of Justice: Practice and Procedure*, Brill, 2015.
Ridi, N., and V. Fikfak, "Sanctioning to Change State Behaviour", *Journal of International Dispute Settlement*, Vol. 13 (2), 2022, pp. 210-232.
Ridi, N., "Rule of Precedent and Rules on Precedent", in E. De Brabandere (ed.),

International Procedure in Interstate Litigation and Arbitration: A Comparative Approach, Cambridge: Cambridge University Press, 2021, pp. 354-400.
–, "The Shape and Structure of the 'Usable Past': An Empirical Analysis of the Use of Precedent in International Adjudication", *Journal of International Dispute Settlement*, Vol. 10 (2), 2019, pp. 200-247.
Rosenne, S., and M. N. Shaw, *Rosenne's Law and Practice of the International Court, 1920-2015*, Brill Nijhoff, 2016.
Rosenne, S., Y. Dinstein and M. Tabory, *International law at a time of perplexity: essays in honour of Shabtai Rosenne*, Dordrecht, The Netherlands, M. Nijhoff, 1989.
Rosenne, S., M. N. Shaw and S. Rosenne, *Rosenne's Law and practice of the international court, 1920-2015*, 5th ed., Leiden, Boston, Brill, 2016.
Ryngaert, C., "Jurisdiction", *Concepts for International Law*, Edward Elgar Publishing, 2019, pp. 577-584.
Sabahi, B., *Compensation and Restitution in Investor-State Arbitration: Principles and Practice*, OUP, Oxford, 2011.
Schumacher, K. F., and H. Klönne, "Discounted Cash Flow Method", *Contemporary and Emerging Issues on the Law of Damages and Valuation in International Investment Arbitration*, Brill Nijhoff, 2018, pp. 205-230.
Senechal, T., "Dealing with Uncertainty: Discounted Cash Flow (DCF) Versus Adjusted Present Value (APV)", *Transnational Dispute Management (TDM)*, Vol. 4 (3), 2007.
Sereni, A. P., *Principi generali di diritto e processo internazionale*, A. Giuffrè, 1955.
Shany, Y., "Jurisdiction and admissibility", 2013.
Shelton, D., *Remedies in international human rights law*, Oxford University Press, USA, 2015.
Shirlow, E., "Deference and Indirect Expropriation Analysis in International Investment Law Observations on Current Approaches and Frameworks for Future Analysis", *ICSID Review*, Vol. 29 (3), 2014, pp. 595-626.
–, *Judging at the Interface: Deference to State Decision-Making Authority in International Adjudication*, Cambridge University Press, 2021.
Skouteris, T., "The force of a doctrine Article 38 of the PCIJ Statute and the sources of international law", in F. Johns, R. Joyce and S. Pahuja (eds.), *Events: The Force of International Law*, Abingdon, Oxon; New York: Routledge-Cavendish, 2010, p. 69.
Sperduti, G., "Dualism and Monism: A Confrontation to Be Overcome", *Italian Yearbook of International Law*, Vol. 3, 1977, pp. 31-49.
Starke, J. G., "Monism and Dualism in the Theory of International Law", *British Year Book of International Law*, Vol. 17, 1936, pp. 66-81.
Stone, J., "*Non liquet* and the function of law in the international community", *Brit. YB Int'l l.*, Vol. 35, 1959, p. 124.
Stoppioni, E., *La réparation dans le contentieux international de l'investissement: contribution à l'étude de la restitutio in integrum*, Pedone, 2014.
Tams, C. J., and J. Sloan (eds.), *The Development of International Law by the International Court of Justice*, Also available as eBook, 2013.
Tanzi, A. M., "Adjudication at the Service of Diplomacy: *The Enrica Lexie* Case", *Journal of International Dispute Settlement*, Vol. 12 (3), 2021, pp. 448-461.
–, "Il principio ne ultra petita nel processo internazionale", *Liber amicorum Angelo Davì. La vita giuridica internazionale nell'età della globalizzazione. Editoriale Scientifica, Naples*, Vol. 3, 2019, pp. 2095-2127.
–, "On judicial autonomy and the autonomy of the parties in international adjudication, with special regard to investment arbitration and ICSID annulment proceedings", *Leiden Journal of International Law*, Vol. 33 (1), 2020, pp. 57-75.
–, *A Concise Introduction to International Law*, The Hague, Torino, Eleven – Giappichelli, 2022.
Tanzi, A., "Is Damage a Distinct Condition for the Existence of an Internationally

Wrongful Act?", in B. Simma and M. Spinedi (eds.), *United Nations of Codification of State Responsibilit*, Dobbs Ferry-New York-Roma: Oceana Publications, 1987, pp. 1-33.

Taruffo, M., "Il processo civile di 'civil law' e di 'common law': aspetti fondamentali", *Il Foro Italiano*, Vol. 124 (11), 2001, pp. 345/346-359/360.

Thirlway, H., *The Sources of International Law*, OUP, Oxford, 2014.

Titi, C., and C. Titi, *The Function of Equity in International Law*, Oxford, New York, Oxford University Press, 2021.

Tzeng, P., "The Implicated Issue Problem: Indispensable Issues and Incidental Jurisdiction", *New York University Journal of International Law and Politics*, Vol. 50 (2), 2017, pp. 447-508.

Ulfstein, G., "International Courts and Judges: Independence, Interaction, and Legitimacy", *NYU Journal of International Law and Politics (2014)*, 2014, pp. 14-13.

Villalpando, S., "The Legal Dimension of the International Community: How Community Interests Are Protected in International Law", *European Journal of International Law*, Vol. 21 (2), 2010, pp. 387-419.

Waibel, M., "Investment arbitration: jurisdiction and admissibility", *University of Cambridge Faculty of Law Research Paper* (9), 2014.

Wälde, T. W., and B. Sabahi, "Compensation, Damages, and Valuation", in P. Muchlinski, F. Ortino and C. Schreuer (eds.), *The Oxford Handbook of International Investment Law*, Oxford University Press, 2008, p. 0.

Wang, Y., "The Origins and Operation of the General Principles of Law as Gap fillers", *Journal of International Dispute Settlement*, Vol. 13 (4), 2022, pp. 560-582.

Webb, P., *International Judicial Integration and Fragmentation*, Int ed., Oxford, United Kingdom, OUP, 2013.

Weil, P., "The Court Cannot Conclude Definitively ... *Non Liquet* Revisited Chapter 1: Questions of Theory", *Columbia Journal of Transnational Law*, Vol. 36, 1998, pp. 109-119.

Wheatley, S., "Revisiting the Doctrine of Intertemporal Law", *Oxford Journal of Legal Studies*, Vol. 41 (2), 2021, pp. 484-509.

Williams, D. A. R., "Jurisdiction and Admissibility", in P. Muchlinski, F. Ortino and C. Schreuer (eds.), *The Oxford Handbook of International Investment Law*, Oxford University Press, 2008, p. 0.

Zarbiyev, F., "Saying Credibly What the Law Is: On Marks of Authority in International Law", *Journal of International Dispute Settlement*, Vol. 9 (2), 2018, pp. 291-314.

PUBLICATIONS DE L'ACADÉMIE
DE DROIT INTERNATIONAL
DE LA HAYE

PUBLICATIONS OF THE
HAGUE ACADEMY OF INTERNATIONAL
LAW

RECUEIL DES COURS

Depuis 1923, les plus grands noms du droit international ont professé à l'Académie de droit international de La Haye. Tous les tomes du *Recueil* qui ont été publiés depuis cette date sont disponibles, chaque tome étant, depuis les tout premiers, régulièrement réimprimé sous sa forme originale.

Depuis 2008, certains cours font l'objet d'une édition en livres de poche.

En outre, toute la collection existe en version électronique. Tous les ouvrages parus à ce jour ont été mis en ligne et peuvent être consultés moyennant un des abonnements proposés, qui offrent un éventail de tarifs et de possibilités.

INDEX

A ce jour, il a paru sept index généraux. Ils couvrent les tomes suivants:

1 à 101	(1923-1960)	379 pages	ISBN 978-90-218-9948-0
102 à 125	(1961-1968)	204 pages	ISBN 978-90-286-0643-2
126 à 151	(1969-1976)	280 pages	ISBN 978-90-286-0630-2
152 à 178	(1976-1982)	416 pages	ISBN 978-0-7923-2955-8
179 à 200	(1983-1986)	260 pages	ISBN 978-90-411-0110-5
201 à 250	(1987-1994)	448 pages	ISBN 978-90-04-13700-4
251 à 300	(1995-2002)	580 pages	ISBN 978-90-04-15387-7

A partir du tome 210 il a été décidé de publier un index complet qui couvrira chaque fois dix tomes du *Recueil des cours*. Le dernier index paru couvre les tomes suivants:

311 à 320 (2004-2006) 392 pages Tome 320A ISBN 978-90-04-19695-7

COLLOQUES

L'Académie organise également des colloques dont les débats sont publiés. Les derniers volumes parus de ces colloques portent les titres suivants: *Le règlement pacifique des différends internationaux en Europe: perspectives d'avenir* (1990); *Le développement du rôle du Conseil de sécurité* (1992); *La Convention sur l'interdiction et l'élimination des armes chimiques: une percée dans l'entreprise multilatérale du désarmement* (1994); *Actualité de la Conférence de La Haye de 1907, Deuxième Conférence de la Paix* (2007).

CENTRE D'ÉTUDE ET DE RECHERCHE

Les travaux scientifiques du Centre d'étude et de recherche de droit international et de relations internationales de l'Académie de droit international de La Haye, dont les sujets sont choisis par le Curatorium de l'Académie, faisaient l'objet, depuis la session de 1985, d'une publication dans laquelle les directeurs d'études dressaient le bilan des recherches du Centre qu'ils avaient dirigé. Cette série a été arrêtée et la dernière brochure parue porte le titre suivant: *Les règles et les institutions du droit international humanitaire à l'épreuve des conflits armés récents*. Néanmoins, lorsque les travaux du Centre se révèlent particulièrement intéressants et originaux, les rapports des directeurs et les articles rédigés par les chercheurs font l'objet d'un ouvrage collectif.

Les demandes de renseignements ou de catalogues et les commandes doivent être adressées à

MARTINUS NIJHOFF PUBLISHERS

B.P. 9000, 2300 PA Leyde Pays-Bas **http://www.brill.nl**

COLLECTED COURSES

Since 1923 the top names in international law have taught at The Hague Academy of International Law. All the volumes of the *Collected Courses* which have been published since 1923 are available, as, since the very first volume, they are reprinted regularly in their original format.

Since 2008, certain courses have been the subject of a pocketbook edition.

In addition, the total collection now exists in electronic form. All works already published have been put "on line" and can be consulted under one of the proposed subscription methods, which offer a range of tariffs and possibilities.

INDEXES

Up till now seven General Indexes have been published. They cover the following volumes:

1 to 101	(1923-1960)	379 pages	ISBN 978-90-218-9948-0
102 to 125	(1961-1968)	204 pages	ISBN 978-90-286-0643-2
126 to 151	(1969-1976)	280 pages	ISBN 978-90-286-0630-2
152 to 178	(1976-1982)	416 pages	ISBN 978-0-7923-2955-8
179 to 200	(1983-1986)	260 pages	ISBN 978-90-411-0110-5
201 to 250	(1987-1994)	448 pages	ISBN 978-90-04-13700-4
251 to 300	(1995-2002)	580 pages	ISBN 978-90-04-15387-7

From Volume 210 onwards it has been decided to publish a full index covering, each time, ten volumes of the *Collected Courses*. The latest Index published covers the following volumes:

311 to 320 (2004-2006) 392 pages Volume 320A ISBN 978-90-04-19695-7

WORKSHOPS

The Academy publishes the discussions from the Workshops which it organises. The latest titles of the Workshops already published are as follows: *The Peaceful Settlement of International Disputes in Europe: Future Prospects* (1990) ; *The Development of the Role of the Security Council* (1992); *The Convention on the Prohibition and Elimination of Chemical Weapons: A Breakthrough in Multilateral Disarmament* (1994); *Topicality of the 1907 Hague Conference, the Second Peace Conference* (2007).

CENTRE FOR STUDIES AND RESEARCH

The scientific works of the Centre for Studies and Research in International Law and International Relations of The Hague Academy of International Law, the subjects of which are chosen by the Curatorium of the Academy, have been published, since the Centre's 1985 session, in a publication in which the Directors of Studies reported on the state of research of the Centre under their direction. This series has been discontinued and the title of the latest booklet published is as follows: *Rules and Institutions of International Humanitarian Law Put to the Test of Recent Armed Conflicts.* Nevertheless, when the work of the Centre has been of particular interest and originality, the reports of the Directors of Studies together with the articles by the researchers form the subject of a collection published by the Academy.

Requests for information, catalogues and orders for publications must be addressed to

MARTINUS NIJHOFF PUBLISHERS

P.O. Box 9000, 2300 PA Leiden The Netherlands **http://www.brill.nl**

TABLE PAR TOME DES COURS PUBLIÉS CES DERNIÈRES ANNÉES

INDEX BY VOLUME OF THE COURSES PUBLISHED THESE LAST YEARS

Tome/Volume 334 (2008)

Verhoeven, J. : Considérations sur ce qui est commun. Cours général de droit international public (2002), 9-434.

(ISBN 978-90-04-17289-0)

Tome/Volume 335 (2008)

Beaumont, P. R.: The Jurisprudence of the European Court of Human Rights and the European Court of Justice on the Hague Convention on International Child Abduction, 9-104.

Moura Vicente, D.: La propriété intellectuelle en droit international privé, 105-504.

(ISBN 978-90-04-17290-6)

Tome/Volume 336 (2008)

Decaux, E.: Les formes contemporaines de l'esclavage, 9-198.

McLachlan, C.: *Lis Pendens* in International Litigation, 199-554.

(ISBN 978-90-04-17291-3)

Tome/Volume 337 (2008)

Mahiou, A.: Le droit international ou la dialectique de la rigueur et de la flexibilité. Cours général de droit international public, 9-516.

(ISBN 978-90-04-17292-0)

Tome/Volume 338 (2008)

Thürer, D.: International Humanitariam Law : Theory, Practice, Context, 9-370.

(ISBN 978-90-04-17293-7)

Tome/Volume 339 (2008)

Sicilianos, L.-A.: Entre multilatéralisme et unilatéralisme : l'autorisation par le Conseil de sécurité de recourir à la force, 9-436. (ISBN 978-90-04-17294-4)

Tome/Volume 340 (2009)

Beaumont, P. R.: Reflections on the Relevance of Public International Law to Private International Law Treaty Making (Opening Lecture, Private International Law Session, 2009), 9-62.

Carbone, S. M.: Conflits de lois en droit maritime, 63-270.

Boele-Woelki, K.: Unifying and Harmonizing Substantive Law and the Role of Conflict of Laws, 271-462. (ISBN 978-90-04-17295-1)

Tome/Volume 341 (2009)

Bucher, A.: La dimension sociale du droit international privé. Cours général, 9-526.

(ISBN 978-90-04-18509-8)

Tome/Volume 342 (2009)

Musin, V.: The Influence of the International Sale of Goods Convention on Domestic Law Including Conflict of Laws (with Specific Reference to Russian Law), 9-76.

Onuma, Y.: A Transcivilizational Perspective on International Law. Questioning Prevalent Cognitive Frameworks in the Emerging Multi-Polar and Multi-Civilizational World of the Twenty-First Century, 77-418.

(ISBN 978-90-04-18510-4)

Tome/Volume 343 (2009)

Abou-el-Wafa, A.: Les différends internationaux concernant les frontières terrestres dans la jurisprudence de la Cour internationale de Justice, 9-570.

(ISBN 978-90-04-18513-5)

Tome/Volume 344 (2009)

Villiger, M. E.: The 1969 Vienna Convention on the Law of Treaties – 40 Years After, 4-192.

Alvarez, J. E.: The Public International Law Regime Governing International Investment, 193-452. (ISBN 978-90-04-18512-8)

Tome/Volume 345 (2009)

Meziou, K.: Migrations et relations familiales, 9-386.

Lauterpacht, Sir Elihu: Principles of Procedure in International Litigation, 387-530. (ISBN 978-90-04-18514-2)

Tome/Volume 346 (2009)

Kawano, M.: The Role of Judicial Procedures in the Process of the Pacific Settlement of International Disputes, 9-474. (ISBN 978-90-04-18515-9)

Tome/Volume 347 (2010)

Salmon, J.: Quelle place pour l'Etat dans le droit international d'aujourd'hui? 9-78.

Boisson de Chazournes, L.: Les relations entre organisations régionales et organisations universelles, 79-406.

(ISBN 978-90-04-18516-6)

Tome/Volume 348 (2010)

Bogdan, M.: Private International Law as Component of the Law of the Forum. General Course, 9-252.

Baratta, R.: La reconnaissance internationale des situations juridiques personnelles et familiales, 253-500. (ISBN 978-90-04-18517-3)

Tome/Volume 349 (2010)

Malenovský, J.: L'indépendance des juges internationaux, 9-276.

Wang, G.: Radiating Impact of WTO on Its Members' Legal System: The Chinese Perspective, 277-536. (ISBN 978-90-04-18518-0)

Tome/Volume 350 (2010)

Van Gerven, W.: Plaidoirie pour une nouvelle branche du droit: le «droit des conflits d'ordres juridiques» dans le prolongement du «droit des conflits de règles» (conférence inaugurale), 9-70.

Bonomi, A.: Successions internationales: conflits de lois et de juridictions, 71-418.

Oxman, B. H.: Idealism and the Study of International Law (Inaugural Lecture), 419-440. (ISBN 978-90-04-18519-7)

Tome/Volume 351 (2010)

Reisman, W. M.: The Quest for World Order and Human Dignity in the Twenty-first Century: Constitutive Process and Individual Commitment. General Course on Public International Law, 9-382.

(ISBN 978-90-04-22725-5)

Tome/Volume 352 (2010)

Daví, A.: Le renvoi en droit international privé contemporain, 9-522.

(ISBN 978-90-04-22726-2)

Tome/Volume 353 (2011)

Meeusen, J.: Le droit international privé et le principe de non-discrimination, 9-184.

Gowlland-Debbas, V.: The Security Council and Issues of Responsibility under International Law, 185-444.

(ISBN 978-90-04-22727-9)

Tome/Volume 354 (2011)

Lamm, C. B.: Internationalization of the Practice of Law and Important Emerging Issues for Investor-State Arbitration (Opening Lecture), 9-64.

Briggs, A.: The Principle of Comity in Private International Law, 65-182.

Davey, W. J.: Non-discrimination in the World Trade Organization: The Rules and Exceptions, 183-440. (ISBN 978-90-04-22728-6)

Tome/Volume 355 (2011)

Chemillier-Gendreau, M.: A quelles conditions l'universalité du droit international est-elle possible? (conférence inaugurale), 9-40.

Xue Hanqin: Chinese Contemporary Perspectives on International Law – History, Culture and International Law, 41-234.

Arrighi, J. M.: L'Organisation des Etats américains et le droit international, 235-438.

(ISBN 978-90-04-22729-3)

Tome/Volume 356 (2011)

Talpis, J.: Succession Substitutes, 9-238.

Lagrange, E.: L'efficacité des normes internationales concernant la situation des personnes privées dans les ordres juridiques internes, 239-552.

(ISBN 978-90-04-22730-9)

Tome/Volume 357 (2011)

Dugard, J.: The Secession of States and Their Recognition in the Wake of Kosovo, 9-222.

Gannagé, L.: Les méthodes du droit international privé à l'épreuve des conflits de cultures, 223-490. (ISBN 978-90-04-22731-6)

Tome/Volume 358 (2011)

Brand, R. A.: Transaction Planning Using Rules on Jurisdiction and the Recognition and Enforcement of Judgments, 9-262.

Hafner, G.: The Emancipation of the Individual from the State under International Law, 263-454. (ISBN 978-90-04-22732-3)

Tome/Volume 359 (2012)

Opertti Badán, D.: Conflit de lois et droit uniforme dans le droit international privé contemporain: dilemme ou convergence? (conférence inaugurale), 9-86.
Chen Weizuo: La nouvelle codification du droit international privé chinois, 87-234.
Kohler, Ch.: L'autonomie de la volonté en droit international privé: un principe universel entre libéralisme et étatisme, 285-478. (ISBN 978-90-04-25541-8)

Tome/Volume 360 (2012)

Basedow, J.: The Law of Open Societies — Private Ordering and Public Regulation of International Relations. General Course on Private International Law, 9-516. (ISBN 978-90-04-25550-0)

Tome/Volume 361 (2012)

Pinto, M. C. W.: The Common Heritage of Mankind: Then and Now, 9-130.
Kreindler, R.: Competence-Competence in the Face of Illegality in Contracts and Arbitration Agreements, 131-482.
(ISBN 978-90-04-25552-4)

Tome/Volume 362 (2012)

Arsanjani, M. H.: The United Nations and International Law-Making (Opening Lecture), 9-40.
Alland, D.: L'interprétation du droit international public, 41-394.
(ISBN 978-90-04-25554-8)

Tome/Volume 363 (2012)

Sur, S.: La créativité du droit international. Cours général de droit international public, 9-332.
Turp, D.: La contribution du droit international au maintien de la diversité culturelle, 333-454. (ISBN 978-90-04-25556-2)

Tome/Volume 364 (2012)

Gaja, G.: The Protection of General Interests in the International Community. General Course on Public International Law (2011), 9-186.
Glenn, H. P.: La conciliation des lois. Cours général de droit international privé (2011), 187-470.
(ISBN 978-90-04-25557-9)

Tome/Volume 365 (2013)

Crawford, J.: Chance, Order, Change: The Course of International Law. General Course on Public International Law, 9-390.
(ISBN 978-90-04-25560-9)

Tome/Volume 366 (2013)

Hayton, D.: "Trusts" in Private International Law, 9-98.
Hobér, K.: *Res Judicata* and *Lis Pendens* in International Arbitration, 99-406.
(ISBN 978-90-04-26395-6)

Tome/Volume 367 (2013)

Kolb, R.: L'article 103 de la Charte des Nations Unies, 9-252.
Nascimbene, B.: Le droit de la nationalité et le droit des organisations d'intégration régionales. Vers de nouveaux statuts de résidents?, 253-454.
(ISBN 978-90-04-26793-0)

Tome/Volume 368 (2013)

Caflisch, L: Frontières nationales, limites et délimitations. – Quelle importance aujourd'hui? (conférence inaugurale), 9-46.
Benvenisti, E.: The International Law of Global Governance, 47-280.
Park, K. G.: La protection des personnes en cas de catastrophes, 281-456.
(ISBN 978-90-04-26795-4)

Tome/Volume 369 (2013)

Kronke, H.: Transnational Commercial Law and Conflict of Laws: Institutional Co-operation and Substantive Complementarity (Opening Lecture), 9-42.
Ortiz Ahlf, L.: The Human Rights of Undocumented Migrants, 43-160.
Kono, T.: Efficiency in Private International Law, 161-360.
Yusuf, A. A.: Pan-Africanism and International Law, 361-512.
(ISBN 978-90-04-26797-8)

Tome/Volume 370 (2013)

Dominicé, Ch.: La société internationale à la recherche de son équilibre. Cours général de droit international public, 9-392. (ISBN 978-90-04-26799-2)

Tome/Volume 371 (2014)

Lagarde, P.: La méthode de la reconnaissance est-elle l'avenir du droit international privé?, 9-42.
Charlesworth, H.: Democracy and International Law, 43-152.
de Vareilles-Sommières, P.: L'exception d'ordre public et la régularité substantielle internationale de la loi étrangère, 153-272.
Yanagihara, M.: Significance of the History of the Law of Nations in Europe and East Asia, 273-435. (ISBN 978-90-04-28936-9)

Tome/Volume 372 (2014)

Bucher, A.: La compétence universelle civile, 9-128.
Cordero-Moss, G.: Limitations on Party Autonomy in International Commercial Arbitration, 129-326.
Sinjela, M.: Intellectual Property: Cross-Border Recognition of Rights and National Development, 327-394.
Dolzer, R.: International Co-operation in Energy Affairs, 395-504.
(ISBN 978-90-04-28937-6)

Tome/Volume 373 (2014)

Cachard, O.: Le transport international aérien de passagers, 9-216.
Audit, M.: Bioéthique et droit international privé, 217-447.
(ISBN 978-90-04-28938-3)

Tome/Volume 374 (2014)

Struycken, A. V. M. : Arbitration and State Contract, 9-52.
Corten, O., La rébellion et le droit international : le principe de neutralité en tension, 53-312.
Parra, A. : The Convention and Centre for Settlement of Investment Disputes, 313-410. (ISBN 978-90-04-29764-7)

Tome/Volume 375 (2014)

Jayme, E. : Narrative Norms in Private International Law – The Example of Art Law, 9-52.
De Boer, Th. M. : Choice of Law in Arbitration Proceedings, 53-88.
Frigo, M. : Circulation des biens culturels, détermination de la loi applicable et méthodes de règlement des litiges, 89-474. (ISBN 978-90-04-29766-1)

Tome/Volume 376 (2014)

Cançado Trindade, A. A. : The Contribution of Latin American Legal Doctrine to the Progressive Development of International Law, 9-92.
Gray, C. : The Limits of Force, 93-198.
Najurieta, M. S. : L'adoption internationale des mineurs et les droits de l'enfant, 199-494. (ISBN 978-90-04-29768-5)

Tome/Volume 377 (2015)

Kassir, W. J. : Le renvoi en droit international privé – technique de dialogue entre les cultures juridiques, 9-120.
Noodt Taquela, M. B. : Applying the Most Favourable Treaty or Domestic Rules to Facilitate Private International Law Co-operation, 121-318.
Tuzmukhamedov, B. : Legal Dimensions of Arms Control Agreements, An Introductory Overview, 319-468.
(ISBN 978-90-04-29770-8)

Tome/Volume 378 (2015)

Iwasawa, Y. : Domestic Application of International Law, 9-262.
Carrascosa Gonzalez, J. : The Internet – Privacy and Rights relating to Personality, 263-486. (ISBN 978-90-04-32125-0)

Tome/Volume 379 (2015)

Lowe, V. : The Limits of the Law.
Boele-Woelki, K. : Party Autonomy in Litigation and Arbitration in View of The Hague Principles on Choice of Law in International Commercial Contracts.
Fresnedo de Aguirre, C. : Public Policy : Common Principles in the American States.
Ben Achour, R. : Changements anticonstitutionnels de gouvernement et droit international. (ISBN 978-90-04-32127-4)

Tome/Volume 380 (2015)

Van Loon, J. H. A. : The Global Horizon of Private International Law.
Pougoué, P.-G. : L'arbitrage dans l'espace OHADA.
Kruger, T. : The Quest for Legal Certainty in International Civil Cases.
(ISBN 978-90-04-32131-1)

Tome/Volume 381 (2015)

Jayme, E.: Les langues et le droit international privé, 11-39.
Bermann, G.: Arbitrage and Private International Law. General Course on Private International Law (2015), 41-484.
(ISBN 978-90-04-33828-9)

Tome/Volume 382 (2015)

Cooper, D., and C. Kuner: Data Protection Law and International Dispute Resolution, 9-174.
Jia, B. B.: International Case Law in the Development of International Law, 175-397.
(ISBN 978-90-04-33830-2)

Tome/Volume 383 (2016)

Bennouna, M.: Le droit international entre la lettre et l'esprit, 9-231.
Iovane, M.: L'influence de la multiplication des juridictions internationales sur l'application du droit international, 233-446. (ISBN 978-90-04-34648-2)

Tome/Volume 384 (2016)

Symeonides, S. C.: Private International Law Idealism, Pragmatism, Eclecticism, 9-385. (ISBN 978-90-04-35131-8)

Tome/Volume 385 (2016)

Berman, Sir F.: Why Do we Need a Law of Treaties?, 9-31.
Marrella, F.: Protection internationale des droits de l'homme et activités des sociétés transnationales, 33-435. (ISBN 978-90-04-35132-5)

Tome/Volume 386 (2016)

Murphy, S. D.: International Law relating to Islands, 9-266.
Cataldi, G.: La mise en œuvre des décisions des tribunaux internationaux dans l'ordre interne, 267-428.
(ISBN 978-90-04-35133-2)

Tome/Volume 387 (2016)

Lequette, Y.: Les mutations du droit international privé: vers un changement de paradigme?, 9-644. (ISBN 978-90-04-36118-8)

Tome/Volume 388 (2016)

Bonell, M. J.: The Law Governing International Commercial Contracts: Hard Law versus Soft Law, 9-48.
Hess, B.: The Private-Public Divide in International Dispute Resolution, 49-266.
(ISBN 978-90-04-36120-1)

Tome/Volume 389 (2017)

Muir Watt, H.: Discours sur les méthodes du droit international privé (des formes juridiques de l'inter-altérité). Cours général de droit international privé, 9-410.
(ISBN 978-90-04-36122-5)

Tome/Volume 390 (2017)

Rau, A. S.: The Allocation of Power between Arbitral Tribunals and State Courts, 9-396. (ISBN 978-90-04-36475-2)

Tome/Volume 391 (2017)

Cançado Trindade, A. A.: Les tribunaux internationaux et leur mission commune de réalisation de la justice : développements, état actuel et perspectives, Conférence spéciale (2017), 9-101.

Mariño Menéndez, F. M. : The Prohibition of Torture in Public International Law, 103-185.

Swinarski, C.: Effets pour l'individu des régimes de protection de droit international, 187-369.

Cot, J.-P.: L'éthique du procès international (leçon inaugurale), 371-384.

(ISBN 978-90-04-37781-3)

Tome/Volume 392 (2017)

Novak, F.: The System of Reparations in the Jurisprudence of the Inter-American Court of Human Rights, 9-203.

Nolte, G.: Treaties and their Practice – Symptoms of their Rise or Decline, 205-397. (ISBN 978-90-04-39273-1)

Tome/Volume 393 (2017)

Tiburcio, C.: The Current Practice of International Co-Operation in Civil Matters, 9-310.

Ruiz De Santiago, J.: Aspects juridiques des mouvements forcés de personnes, 311-468.

(ISBN 978-90-04-39274-8)

Tome/Volume 394 (2017)

Kostin, A. A.: International Commercial Arbitration, with Special Focus on Russia, 9-86.

Cuniberti, G.: Le fondement de l'effet des jugements étrangers, 87-283.

(ISBN 978-90-04-39275-5)

Tome/Volume 395 (2018)

Salerno, F.: The Identity and Continuity of Personal Status in Contemporary Private International Law, 9-198.

Chinkin, C. M.: United Nations Accountability for Violations of International Human Rights Law, 199-320. (ISBN 978-90-04-40710-7)

Tome/Volume 396 (2018)

Jacquet, J.-M.: Droit international privé et arbitrage commercial international, 9-36.

Brown Weiss, E.: Establishing Norms in a Kaleidoscopic World. General Course on Public International Law, 37-415. (ISBN 978-90-04-41002-2)

Tome/Volume 397 (2018)

D'Avout, L.: L'entreprise et les conflits internationaux de lois, 9-612.

(ISBN 978-90-04-41221-7)

Tome/Volume 398 (2018)

Treves, T.: The Expansion of International Law, General Course on Public International Law (2015), 9-398.

(ISBN 978-90-04-41224-8)

Tome/Volume 399 (2018)

Kanehara, A.: Reassessment of the Acts of the State in the Law of State Responsibility, 9-266.

Buxbaum, H. L.: Public Regulation and Private Enforcement in a Global Economy: Strategies for Managing Conflict, 267-442.

(ISBN 978-90-04-41670-3)

Tome/Volume 400 (2018)

Chedly, L.: L'efficacité de l'arbitrage commercial international, 9-624.

(ISBN 978-90-04-42388-6)

Tome/Volume 401 (2019)

Wood, P.: Extraterritorial Enforcement of Regulatory Laws, 9-126.

Nishitani, Yuko: Identité culturelle en droit international privé de la famille, 127-450.

(ISBN 978-90-04-42389-3)

Tome/Volume 402 (2019)

Kinsch, P.: Le rôle du politique en droit international privé. Cours général de droit international privé, 9-384.

Dasser, F.: "Soft Law" in International Commercial Arbitration, 385-596.

(ISBN 978-90-04-42392-3)

Tome/Volume 403 (2019)

Daudet, Y.: 1919-2019, le flux du multilatéralisme, 9-48.

Kessedjian, C.: Le tiers impartial et indépendant en droit international, juge, arbitre, médiateur, conciliateur, 49-643.

(ISBN 978-90-04-42468-5)

Tome/Volume 404 (2019)

Rajamani, L.: Innovation and Experimentation in the International Climate Change Regime, 9-234.

Sorel, J.-M.: Quelle normativité pour le droit des relations monétaires et financières internationales?, 235-403.

(ISBN 978-90-04-43142-3)

Tome/Volume 405 (2019)

Paulsson, J.: Issues arising from Findings of Denial of Justice, 9-74.

Brunée, J.: Procedure and Substance in International Environmental Law, 75-240.

(ISBN 978-90-04-43300-7)

Tome/Volume 406 (2019)

Bundy, R.: The Practice of International Law, Inaugural Lecture, 9-26.
Gama, L.: Les principes d'UNIDROIT et la loi régissant les contrats de commerce, 27-343. (ISBN 978-90-04-43611-4)

Tome/Volume 407 (2020)

Wouters, J.: Le statut juridique des standards publics et privés dans les relations économiques internationales, 9-122.
Maljean-Dubois, S.: Le droit international de la biodiversité, 123-538. (ISBN 978-90-04-43643-5)

Tome/Volume 408 (2020)

Cançado Trindade, A. A.: Reflections on the Realization of Justice in the Era of Contemporary International Tribunals, 9-88.
González, C.: Party Autonomy in International Family Law, 89-361. (ISBN 978-90-04-44504-8)

Tome/Volume 409 (2020)

Shany, Y: The Extraterritorial Application of International Human Rights Law, 9-152.
Besson, S.: La *due diligence* en droit international, 153-398. (ISBN 978-90-04-44505-5)

Tome/Volume 410 (2020)

Koh, H. H.: American Schools of International Law, 9-93.
Peters, A.: Animals in International Law, 95-544. (ISBN 978-90-04-44897-1)

Tome/Volume 411 (2020)

Cahin, G: Reconstrution et construction de l'Etat en droit international, 9-573. (ISBN 978-90-04-44898-8)

Tome/Volume 412 (2020)

Momtaz, D: La hiérarchisation de l'ordre juridique international, cours général de droit international public, 9-252.
Grammaticaki-Alexiou, A.: Best Interests of the Child in Private International Law, 253-434. (ISBN 978-90-04-44899-5)

Tome/Volume 413 (2021)

Ferrari, F.: Forum Shopping Despite Unification of Law, 9-290. (ISBN 978-90-04-46100-0)

Tome/Volume 414 (2021)

Pellet, A.: Le droit international à la lumière de la pratique: l'introuvable théorie de la réalité. Cours général de droit international public, 9-547. (ISBN 978-90-04-46547-3)

Tome/Volume 415 (2021)

Trooboff, P. D.: Globalization, Personal Jurisdiction and the Internet. Responding to the Challenge of adapting settled Principles and Precedents. General Course of Private International Law, 9-321. (ISBN 978-90-04-46730-9)

Tome/Volume 416 (2021)

Wolfrum, R: Solidarity and Community Interests: Driving Forces for the Interpretation and Development of International Law. General Course on Public International Law, 9-479. (ISBN 978-90-04-46827-6)

Tome/Volume 417 (2021)

d'Argent, P.: Les obligations internationales, 9-210.
Schabas, W. A.: Relationships Between International Criminal Law and Other Branches of International Law, 211-392. (ISBN 978-90-04-47239-6)

Tome/Volume 418 (2021)

Bollée, S.: Les pouvoirs inhérents des arbitres internationaux, 9-224.
Tladi, D.: The Extraterritorial Use of Force against Non-State Actors, 225-360. (ISBN 978-90-04-50380-9)

Tome/Volume 419 (2021)

Kolb, R.: Le droit international comme corps de «droit privé» et de «droit public». Cours général de droit international public, 9-668. (ISBN 978-90-04-50381-6)

Tome/Volume 420 (2021)

Perrakis, S.: La protection internationale au profit des personnes vulnérables en droit international des droits de l'homme, 9-497. (ISBN 978-90-04-50382-3)

Tome/Volume 421 (2021)

Estrella Faria, J. A.: La protection des biens culturels d'intérêt religieux en droit international public et en droit international privé, 9-333. (ISBN 978-90-04-50829-3)

Tome/Volume 422 (2021)

Karayanni, M.: The Private International Law of Class Actions: A Functional approach, 9-248.
Mahmoudi, S.: Self-Defence and "Unwilling or Unable" States, 249-399. (ISBN 978-90-04-50830-9)

Tome/Volume 423 (2022)

Kinnear, M.: The Growth, Challenges and Future Prospects for Investment Dispute Settlement, 9-36.
Weller, M.: "Mutual Trust": A Suitable Foundation for Private International Law in Regional Integration Communities and Beyond?, 37-378. (ISBN 978-90-04-51411-9)

Tome/Volume 424 (2022)

Asada, M.: International Law of Nuclear Non-proliferation and Disarmament, 9-726. (ISBN 978-90-04-51769-1)

Tome/Volume 425 (2022)

Metou, B. M.: Le contrôle international des dérogations aux droits de l'homme, 9-294.
Silva Romero, E.: Legal Fictions in the Language of International Arbitration, 295-423. (ISBN 978-90-04-51770-7)

Tome/Volume 426 (2022)

Kuijper, P. J.: Delegation and International Organizations, 9-240.
McCaffrey, S. C.: The Evolution of the Law of International Watercourses, 241-384.
(ISBN 978-90-04-51771-4)

Tome/Volume 427 (2022)

Kaufmann-Kohler, G.: Indépendance et impartialité du juge et de l'arbitre dans le règlement des différends entre investisseurs et Etats (leçon inaugurale), 9-50.
Boyle, A.: International Lawmaking in an Environmental Context, 51-108.
Weller, M.-P.: La méthode tripartite du droit international privé: désignation, reconnaissance, considération, 109-210.
Mourre, A.: La légitimité de l'arbitrage, 211-288. (ISBN 978-90-04-52770-6)

Tome/Volume 428 (2023)

Laghmani, S.: Islam et droit international, 9-128.
Oyarzábal, M. J. A.: The Influence of Public International Law upon Private International Law in History and Theory and in the Formation and Application of the Law, 129-525.
(ISBN 978-90-04-54440-6)

Tome/Volume 429 (2023)

Moreno Rodríguez, J. A.: Private (And Public) International Law In Investment Arbitration, 9-702.
(ISBN 978-90-04-54462-8)

Tome/Volume 430 (2023)

Casella, P. B.: Droit international, histoire et culture, 9-610.
(ISBN 978-90-04-54463-5)

Tome/Volume 431 (2023)

Yeo, T. M.: Common Law, Equity and Statute. The Effect of Juridical Sources on Choice-of-Law Methodology, 9-88.
Frigessi Di Rattalma, M.: New Trends in Private International Law of Insurance Contracts, 89-200.
Roosevelt III, K.: The Third Restatement of Conflict of Laws, 201-284.
Sands, P.: Colonialism: A Short History of International Law in Five Acts, 285-410.
(ISBN 978-90-04-54464-2)

Tome/Volume 432 (2023)

Ruiz Fabri, H. : La justice procédurale en droit international, 9-44.
Shaw, M. : A House of Many Rooms: The Rise, Fall and Rise Again of Territorial Sovereignty?, 45-78.
Kovács, P. : L'individu et sa position devant la Cour pénale internationale, 79-421.
(ISBN 978-90-04-54465-9)

Tome/Volume 433 (2023)

Eyffinger, A. : The Hague Academy at 100: Its Rationale, Role and Record, 9-97.
Thorn, K. : The Protection of Small and Medium-Sized Enterprises in Private International Law, 99-205.
Moollan, S. : Parallel Proceedings in International Arbitration. Theoretical Analysis and the Search for Practical Solutions, 207-303.
(ISBN 978-90-04-54469-7)

Tome/Volume 434 (2023)

Stephan, Paul B. : Applying Municipal Law in International Disputes, 9-214
Casado Raigón, R. : La contribution des juridictions internationales au développement du droit de la mer, 215-511.
(ISBN 978-90-04-69182-7)

Tome/Volume 435 (2023)

Salam, N. : Rethinking the United Nations : 75 and Beyond, 9-32.
Hascher, D. : Le rôle du droit international dans le contrôle des sentences arbitrales, 33-72.
Blokker, N. : Legal Facets of the Practice of International Organizations, 73-324.
(ISBN 978-90-04-69432-3)

Tome/Volume 436 (2023)

Corten, O. : Le champ juridique international. Cours général de droit international, 9-389.
(ISBN 978-90-04-69912-0)

437 - 24 (III)/04-24